PARTNERSHIPS

Families and Communities in Early Childhood

FOURTH EDITION

Lynn Wilson
George Brown College

NELSON / EDUCATION

NELSON / EDUCATION

Partnerships: Families and Communities in Early Childhood, Fourth Edition

by Lynn Wilson

Associate Vice President, Editorial Director:
Evelyn Veitch

Editor-in-Chief, Higher Education:
Anne Williams

Publisher:
Cara Yarzab

Senior Marketing Manager:
David Tonen

Developmental Editor:
Sandy Matos

Photo Researcher:
Sheila Hall

Permissions Coordinator:
Sheila Hall

Production Service:
Macmillan Publishing Solutions

Copy Editor:
Jessie Coffey

Proofreader:
Dianne Fowlie

Indexer:
Maura Brown

Manufacturing Manager:
Joanne McNeil

Design Director:
Ken Phipps

Managing Designer:
Franca Amore

Interior Design:
Nelson Gonzalez

Cover Design:
Johanna Liburd

Cover Images:
Top: Rosanne Olson / Photographer's Choice / Getty Images

Left to right: Andresr / Shutterstock, Igor Stepovik / Shutterstock, Monkey Business Images / Shutterstock

Compositor:
Macmillan Publishing Solutions

Printer:
Edwards Brothers Malloy

Library and Archives Canada Cataloguing in Publication Data

Wilson, Lynn, 1946 Aug. 31-
   Partnerships : families and communities in early childhood / Lynn Wilson. —4th ed.

Includes bibliographical references and index.
ISBN: 978-0-17-650019-1

   1. Early childhood education—Parent participation—Canada. 2. Parent-teacher relationships—Canada. I. Title.

LB1139.35.P37W56 2009
372.119'2   C2008-908020-3

ISBN-13: 978-0-17-650019-1
ISBN-10: 0-17-650019-7

I dedicate this book to my students both past and present in recognition of their enthusiasm, creativity and dedication to families. They will make a difference!

CONTENTS

EXHIBITS LIST

A NOTE ON THE TEXT

Partnerships was developed as a resource for students, faculty, and teachers to encourage the development of positive, respectful relationships with families. Over the past few years, a significant shift has taken place in the relationship between families and teachers in both child-care and school environments. Many family members have demanded a more active role in their children's education and have challenged the notion of "teacher-as-expert." Research supports the benefits to children, teachers, and families when a strong alliance between all parties is formed, and it is from this perspective that the text has been written.

The fourth edition of *Partnerships* differs in several ways from the previous versions. There are more Inside Looks from teachers, other professionals in the field, and many more from ECE students themselves. Students have played a greater role in this text by providing their insights into their experiences while in training and by giving examples of their documentation of children's learning. They have also allowed me to share samples of their written communications with families. Many experts from around the country have also shared their ideas, as well as examples of programs that have been successful in their own communities. There is no question that the impact of the Reggio Emilia approach has influenced educators around the world, and this edition reflects its respect for families. A new chapter (Chapter 11: "Working with Families: An International Perspective") has been added to the text and, for the first time, information from a global perspective gives us insight into the challenges facing families. Canadians working abroad in support of children and their families are also highlighted in this chapter. Furthermore, the chapter also provides information for those ECE graduates that might be interested in teaching in the international community. New photos also improve the text and provide useful examples; statistics have been updated based on the 2006 census for topics on which new information has been released. Where appropriate, books have been suggested for children and adults on relevant topics, and website URLs have been included throughout.

 The companion website (**www.ece.nelson.com**) includes various forms, checklists, and other useful tools directly from the text that can be downloaded for student and instructor use. Throughout the text, a www icon will appear to signify to the reader that these items are available on the website. Students and instructors can easily access the companion website and be instantly connected to the websites that are highlighted throughout the book.

Chapter 1 discusses the issues facing families today based on the most recent research. The increasing diversity of Canadian society is explored in greater depth, as well as the impact of the growing religious diversity in Canada. The section on the roles of men and women has been expanded to include changes in women's employment, part-time work, and its implications for the family, as well as the expansion in technology jobs. There is an update on work and family conflict and a section on the impact of the women's movement on the family is also included. A section on housing and the challenges this presents for today's families is new to this chapter. Poverty continues to be a focus and we look at Canada and how it measures up compared to OECD (Organization for Economic Co-operation and Development) countries. Finally the chapter explores the issues of families faced with elder care while raising young children.

There are significant changes to Chapter 2 with an update on why child care is a good choice for Canadian families. Fraser Mustard and Margaret McCain's research informs this chapter. The descriptions of many national programs designed to support children and their families are expanded to include High Scope, Seeds of Empathy, Best Start, The Parenting Partnership, and Early Learning For Every Child Today. The expanded information on family resource programs also includes a section on programs for military families. The discussion of rural child care is expanded, and new information on child care in the North is included.

In Chapter 3, The Rights of Parents and Rights of the Child are added. Epstein's Six Types of Parent Involvement give us further insight into the role of families in early childhood settings. This chapter also includes input from students on their perceptions and the challenges they face in their work with families in their field placements. The section on men in early childhood education has been expanded, as has the section on the role of the supervisor and the teacher in providing leadership and support to the varying challenges facing families. The chapter also focuses on the need for a collaborative, interprofessional approach to ensuring that families have the support they need to raise healthy children. Student experiences in their work with families is also highlighted in this chapter. Overall, there is more information on how culture and educational experiences of parents may impact on their relationship with teachers.

Chapter 4 now includes more extensive information on home visits and their importance in establishing positive relationships with families in the centre. The section on separation and transitions to new playrooms has been expanded. New to this chapter is information on the transition from child care to school environments. The challenges for "latch key" children are also highlighted.

Chapter 5 highlights a more detailed approach to male friendly environments in child care centres. More suggestions for organizing successful meetings with families are discussed with practical suggestions. Advocacy information is now included in this chapter and explores the opportunities for teachers and parents to work together in raising the bar for early childhood education.

Chapter 6 expands the content on verbal and non-verbal interactions between families and teachers. A section on gestures has been added. A new section has been added with practical ideas on what to say when challenging situations arise. Conflict resolution strategies are outlined.

Chapter 7 expands the benefits of family-teacher conferences and strategies for successful interactions. Strategies are discussed for dealing with challenging situations that may arise in a conference.

Chapter 8 provides more guidelines for written communication. Many more practical examples have been added to the chapter. The section on technology—email, websites, and videos/DVDs—has been expanded.

In Chapter 9, the discussion of family "types" has been expanded and updated. Information on Aboriginal families has been greatly enlarged as has the section on multiracial, older families, and grandparents raising their grandchildren. The most recent information on foster families and those who are adopting reflects experts in the field and the most recent statistics. The section on LGBTQ families is expanded as has the informa-

tion on teen families, divorce, and newcomer families. The role of the teacher is expanded in all areas of this chapter.

Chapter 10 highlights Galinsky's stages of parenting. New to this chapter is a focus on mental health and an expanded section on chronic illness and its impact on the family. A section on children and hospitalization is included. The role of the teacher when a child or parent dies is discussed as is information on the grieving process. The substance abuse section is expanded and homeless families are a new addition. The child abuse section is largely expanded with the most recent research. Stress is a mounting concern in the lives of young children and this is also discussed. The section on families with an incarcerated parent has been expanded to include a discussion of how the prison system is attempting to support parenting skills and to improve visitation opportunities for families.

Chapter 11 is a new and exciting addition to the text. It explores the family in a global context. Information includes The Convention on the Rights of the Child, UN Millennium Development Goals, and a global perspective on child survival. The underlying and structural causes of maternal and child mortality are explored. We discuss the impact of war and terrorism on families. A variety of Canadian aid organizations are highlighted. The final section of the text provides opportunities for ECE students to evaluate the international competencies required for working in the international community and explores options for volunteering or working abroad.

THE INSTRUCTOR'S MANUAL

The accompanying Instructor's Manual outlines strategies for in-class exercises on a chapter-by-chapter basis. The manual contains examples for classroom discussions, assignments, and additional, supplementary material. It is available in both a printed version (ISBN-10: 0-17-647392-0/ ISBN-13: 978-0-17-647392-1) and as a downloadable resource on the faculty companion website.

A NOTE ON TERMINOLOGY

Those who work in the field of early childhood education are referred to by many different titles. These titles differ from province to province. I have chosen to use the word "teacher" in this text in its broadest sense—with its implications of both care and education—and with the understanding that the teacher's role in the ECE context is no less important than that of the teacher in the school system. The terms "mother" and "father" are used in this text but may refer to any significant woman or man in a child's life.

ACKNOWLEDGMENTS

I would like to acknowledge the enormous support and generosity of my colleagues at George Brown College. It is a privilege to work with such dedicated professionals, committed to the well-being of young children and their families. I would also like to thank the children, teachers, students, and families of the Queen Street Child Care Centre, Scotia Plaza Child Care Centre, and the University of Toronto Child Care on Charles Street for their participation in our photo shoot. Many of the photographs appear in the pages of the book and I thank you. A special thank you is extended to the kindergarten children at the Queen Street Child Care Centre, Richmond Adelaide Child Care Centre, and Scotia Plaza Child Care Centre for their exceptional drawings, which are highlighted throughout the text.

I want to thank the many individuals who have contributed their time and expertise to this latest edition. Each contributor is credited in the body of the text, but I want to acknowledge them for their outstanding efforts. I know the students will benefit from their insightful passages.

To the staff at Nelson Education Ltd., I am deeply indebted to my Developmental Editor, Sandy Matos; Publisher, Cara Yarzab; Director of Content and Media Production, Susan Calvert; Copy Editor, Jessie Coffey; Proofreader, Dianne Fowlie; Permissions Editor, Sheila Hall; Indexer, Maura Brown; and Gunjan Chandola, Project Manager of Macmillan Publishing Solutions. Their professional approach and many kindnesses extended to me made this edition a positive writing experience.

On a more personal note, I would like to thank my family; Charlie Dougall and my four children whose love, patience, and support have been a gift to my life. I have learned much from my children, Kelsey, Alexander, Kristen, and Katherine. They enrich my life in ways that words cannot express and are at the core of my teaching.

In the more than 40 years that I have been working with families, I have met many brave and inspired parents. Some remain my friends and many of their experiences are highlighted in the text. I would also like to thank the many students who have contributed ideas to the book and made me rethink others.

Finally, the following quotation from Barbara Coloroso (1989) perhaps best conveys the spirit of the text:

> Power is like a candle with a huge flame. Our flame as teachers can light up every child/family we come into contact with and never be diminished itself. The beauty of empowering another human being is that we never lose our own power. Instead what we have is a greater light by which to see.

Lynn Wilson

ABOUT THE AUTHOR

Lynn Wilson has taught in a variety of teaching environments since her graduation in 1966 from teachers' college. She spent a number of years in the public school system in primary classrooms, helped to establish a parent co-operative, and taught in a full-day kindergarten program in a child-care environment. Lynn supervised a George Brown College lab school and in 1990 became a member of the faculty. She has travelled to many child-care centres in western Canada as the project director of a Child Care Initiatives Fund project of Health and Welfare Canada on extended-hour child care. In cooperation with Ryerson Polytechnic University's School of Early Childhood Education, she delivered training workshops with colleagues to front-line teachers in Bosnia during the summers of 1999 and 2000. She was the Technical Advisor on a five-year Partnership Project in Early Childhood Education in Jamaica with the Association of Canadian Community Colleges. In 2008, funding for a Scaling Up Project in Jamaica will allow her and her colleagues to continue their work in Jamaica. In 2006, Lynn won a National Teaching Excellence Award from the Association of Canadian Community Colleges.

CHAPTER 1

The Changing Face of Canadian Families

© szefei / Shutterstock

"Here is where one has the first experience of love, and of hate, of giving, and of denying; and of deep sadness. . . . Here the first hopes are raised and met—or disappointed. Here is where one learns whom to trust and whom to fear. Above all, family is where people get their start in life."

—*Amy Swerdlow, Renate Bridenthal, Joan Kelly, and Phyllis Vine*

LEARNING OUTCOMES

After studying this chapter, you will be able to

1. describe families in today's society

2. identify various factors affecting families in Canada today

3. explore the implications of brain research on the role of the teacher and the family in providing optimal learning opportunities for children

In this chapter we examine the complex nature of today's families and the many factors that influence it. Though every attempt has been made to provide the most recent information on Canadian families, the student is encouraged to conduct individual research in order to obtain the most meaningful statistics, which are those that best reflect their own community.

> "Demographics do not dictate destiny. Attitudes, leadership, and values do."
> —Marian Wright Edelman

DEFINING A FAMILY?

> "A family is people who love each other."
> —Kate, age five

The poet Robert Frost once said that home is the place where, when you go there, they have to let you in. He could have defined "family" in much the same way, but the term has legal, political, sociological, and personal definitions. It is critical to a deeper and more meaningful understanding of the family in a global society that we, as teachers, extend our understanding of "family" beyond the North American perspective. Baker (2001: 31) states, "The term 'family' now encompasses a number of overlapping though distinctly different types of relationships and conveys multiple meanings of kinship, co-residence, and emotional intimacy." Families are never static. Families are fluid, always in motion, constantly changing and realigning themselves; events such as marriages, births, deaths, and divorce will shift and alter the relationships and living arrangements among

Lev Dolgachov / Shutterstock

The birth of a child has a tremendous impact on the family unit.

family members. A definition of family needs to respond to these changing variations. A family may include blended family members; grandparents parenting their grandchildren; siblings assuming responsibility for each other; families with children who are adopted; families headed by gay and lesbian parents; and those living with grandparents, aunts, uncles, more distant relatives, recent immigrants, and perhaps even friends. What is lost in the attempt to categorize families is the inevitable inability to find one definition that fits all. Families are not homogeneous

---

EXHIBIT 1.1 FAMILIES IN CANADA: A QUIZ

1. What city has the most same-sex couples?

2. In 2006, _____ percent of the 4 million young adults from 20–29 lived in the parental home.

3. In 2003, women working full time had average earnings of $36,500 or _____ percent of what their male counterparts made.

4. _____ percent of the total female population are members of a visible minority.

5. _____ percent of lone parent families headed by men.

6. There are _____ gay couples across Canada and _____ are legally married.

7. True or False: There more families in Canada without children than with children.

8. The average age of women giving birth in Canada in 2004 was _____.

9. In 2006, _____ different ethnic origins were reported.

10. What city in Canada has the largest Aboriginal population? _____

---

groups. Each one will have different perspectives, attitudes, and values based on its cultural identity. Even within cultural groups, the family may "look" different from others who ascribe to similar cultural underpinnings. For example, children of second- or third-generation immigrants may have ideas about how they will construct their own families that are dissimilar from their parents. An individualistic approach versus a collectivist approach may alter family relationships and create harmony or conflict.

Family scholars Bubolz and Sontag (1993: 435) have developed the following definition which attempts to reflect the changing face of Canadian families: "We define families in an inclusive sense to be composed not only of persons related by blood, marriage, or adoption, but also sets of inter-dependent but independent persons who share some common goals, resources, and a commitment to each other over time."

According to Riedmann, Lamanna, and Nelson (2003: 4), "Throughout much of this century, the tra-ditional nuclear family (husband, wife, and children in one household) has been considered the modern family. The progressively increasing family diversity that we see now has led some scholars to refer to today's family as the postmodern family." One assumption about families is the universality of the nuclear family. Some societies organize their kinship relationships so that monogamy is the exception rather than the rule. Some of the world's cultures reflect polygamy, that is, one man with several wives. Families may also be organized with not just an emotional connection but as a unit of economic pro-duction whether it is based in an agricultural or industrial community. Some languages have no word for family but rather the social unit is identi-fied as a "house" that may include many people.

How Canadians View the Family: What the Research Tells Us

In his research, *The Future Families Project* (2004), Bibby found about 6 in 10 Canadians see the tradi-tional family as the ideal family arrangement, while most of the remaining 40 percent—led by younger adults—take the position that there is no one ideal form. Although many people find a variety of family forms that work for them, rela-tively few put forward any specific alternative as ideal beyond the traditional family. However, the results are nearly unanimous in emphasizing the

importance of the family. As can be seen on the Vanier Institute of the Family website at **www.vifamily.ca**:

- 97 percent of respondents say that the family is essential to personal well-being.
- 97 percent also agree that the family is essential to instill values that are needed for interpersonal life.
- 95 percent say the family is essential to healthy communities.
- 95 percent also think the family is essential to a healthy nation.
- 90 percent say their mothers provided them with a good model for family life generally. Just over 80 percent say the same thing about their fathers.
- 77 percent say their mother provided a good model for marriage. 72 percent say the same thing for their fathers. (This means that 1 in 4 Canadians do not think their parents provided good marriage role models.)

Despite its challenges, it is clear that social scientists will continue to redefine the family as it continues to evolve throughout our history.

THE ROLE OF THE FAMILY

We all have strong feelings about our families. We may have positive feelings of love and caring for people in our family but, for others, the family is a place of misery and neglect. The family does not exist in a vacuum, and children will adopt the cul-ture, social class, status, and the religious and moral teachings of their family.

This definition reinforces the concept that evo-lution of the family has not diminished the impor-tance of its role. In the words of Alvi (1994: 11):

The family constitutes the basic unit of society; it is appreciated for the important socio-economic func-tions that it performs. In spite of the many changes in society that have altered its role and functions, it continues to provide the natural framework for the emotional, financial and material support essential to the growth and development of its members, particularly infants and children, and for the care of other dependants, including the elderly, disabled and infirm. The family remains a vital means of preserving and transmitting cultural values. In the broader sense, it can, and often does, educate, train, motivate and support its individual members, thereby investing in their future growth and acting as vital resources for development.

TABLE 1.1	CENSUS FAMILIES IN PRIVATE HOUSEHOLDS BY FAMILY STRUCTURE AND PRESENCE OF CHILDREN, 2006 CENSUS	
CANADA		
All families	8,896,840	
Without children at home	3,420,850	
With children at home	5,475,990	
Families of married couples	6,105,910	
Without children at home	2,662,135	
With children at home	3,443,775	
Families of common-law couples	1,376,870	
Without children at home	758,715	
With children at home	618,150	
Lone-parent families	1,414,060	
Male parent	281,775	
Female parent	1,132,290	

Source: Statistics Canada 2006 Census of Population, last modified 2007-09-19. http://www40.statcan.ca/l01/cst01/famil54a.htm

The Western association of love and marriage is unique to our modern culture. Historically, marriages were often arranged in the marriage market as business deals. Many elements of the basic exchange (a man providing financial support in exchange for the woman's childbearing and child-rearing capabilities, domestic services, and sexual availability) remain. Few traditional societies allowed young people to choose partners without the approval of parents or other relatives. In contemporary arranged marriages, the child's preference is often considered but not always deferred to. Today, arranged marriages are still prevalent in parts of the world, although the practice is diminishing.

Social scientists produce extensive research every year on the family and kinship systems. It is beyond the scope of this text to include them all in this chapter so we will focus on the work of one researcher, psychologist Urie Bronfenbrenner.

Bronfenbrenner (1979) studied the family and he described what he called the human ecological system. He states that the individual is linked to the family and the community in a reciprocal, influential relationship and that "the family seems to be the most effective and economical system for fostering and sustaining the child's development. Without family involvement, intervention is likely to be unsuccessful and what few effects are achieved are likely to disappear once the intervention is discontinued" (1974: 279). Bronfenbrenner

states unequivocally that parents are more capable of providing for the physical and psychological needs of a child when they have a third party who admires and loves them for their caregiving and he described four systems that influence individuals:

1. **microsystem**—the immediate setting within which a child develops and the interactions that take place there,

2. **mesosystem**—the interrelationship between the family unit and the child-care centre and/or school,

3. **exosystem**—the system that influences the child but with which the child does not directly interact (parent's workplace, government agencies), and

4. **macrosystem**—outside institutions of the culture, religious beliefs, political and economic influences, including the mesosystem and exosystem. (Bronfenbrenner, 1990)

Enormous pressures are exerted on families today. As the building blocks of our society, families provide social benefits that extend beyond their own homes. They enrich all our lives in ways more complex than those that can simply be deducted from a census form. But in our rapidly changing society families need constant care and support in order to succeed. Ideally, who is responsible for children and families? The answer is both simple and complex. We all are. Families, professionals, residents of communities and neighbourhoods, and taxpayers are all responsible in different ways. "In a system of shared responsibility, government is responsible for providing incentives and vehicles with which to empower families in caring for themselves and their children" (Kagan and Neville, 1994: 8). Governments at all levels could be doing much more to support healthy family functioning.

HOW FAMILIES ARE CHANGING

It is worrisome that as the Canadian economy improved over the 1990s, disparities between family income levels grew. Cutbacks in government spending at all levels led to increased demand for families to pay more from their own pockets for public services such as health care, public education, housing, recreation, and cultural activities. Families were expected to shoulder more responsibility for their own well-being and to rely less on government assistance. Infant and maternal mortality rates have decreased, life expectancy has increased, and the population is aging. Technology has changed the way we live and work. New technology and educational advancements require increasingly higher levels of education yet society is slow to provide enriching learning environments for our youngest children. In search of employment, some families move many times, creating a sense of isolation and a loss of support from the extended family. Economic challenges, along with the push for equal treatment for women, have influenced the very core of the traditional family. Traditional religious and moral codes have changed. More couples are postponing marriage in order to establish themselves in their work-related roles.

Canada's marriage rate is declining. Cohabitation has become more common, as has the decision for couples to remain childless. Independent incomes allow women more control over how they choose to live. Large families are becoming rare. Families with children average 1.8 children at home and common-law relationships average 1.7 (Canadian Council on Social Development, 2006: 10). Smaller families allow parents' greater flexibility in the pursuit of their own personal growth and satisfaction. The push for personal autonomy is reflected in the divorce rate and there are more lone-parent families than ever before. The increasing acceptance of same-sex couples is redefining spousal roles.

Today's families are smaller than ever before.

Young adults are leaving their parents' home at a later age and returning home in greater numbers. In 2006, 43.5 percent of the four million young adults aged 20–29 lived in the parental home. There is also a changing perception of the child within the family unit. While it appears that our society embraces a child-centred approach, many children live in situations that put them at risk. All these factors have tremendous influences on the fabric of Canadian lives.

THE INCREASING DIVERSITY OF CANADIAN SOCIETY

According to Statistics Canada (2006a) over 200 ethnic origins were reported by the total population. One in five Canadians was born outside the country, surpassing the five million mark; this is the highest proportion in 75 years. More than half of the newcomers arrive from Asia (58.3 percent). Visible minorities now comprise more than 16 percent of the total population: their number skyrocketed by 27 percent between 2001 and 2006.

The sharp growth in the visible minority population is largely due to the fact that three-quarters of new immigrants to Canada since 2001 were visible minorities. South Asians now account for a quarter of all visible minorities in Canada, or 4 percent of the total population. Those from the Indian subcontinent account for 69 percent; Pakistani, 9.3 percent; Sri Lankan, 7.8 percent; Punjabi, 4.1 percent; Tamil, 2.7 percent; and Bangladeshi, 1.8 percent (Canadian Press, 2008). Those with roots in China comprise

about another quarter of the country's visible minority population, with some 1.2 million identifying themselves as Chinese (Cohen, 2008). In 2006, over one-half of the black visible minority group—52 percent—reported Caribbean origins; another 42.4 percent reported African origins, and 11.6 percent reported British Isles origins. Of those from Latin America, the most frequently reported origin was Spanish. And among Arab visible minorities Lebanese was the most commonly reported origin (Canadian Press, 2008).

Quebec is unique in its composition of immigrants. Blacks, mostly from Haiti, are the largest group at 188,000, followed by Arabs, mostly from the French-speaking Maghreb, at 109,000. The largest concentrations of Arabs in Canada are located in Quebec (Siddiqui, 2008).

Younger immigrants will supplement a country where there are not enough children to do the work of the future and to support the growing older population. Immigrants accounted for 70 percent of the total labour force growth during the last decade. This is critical to Canada's development because the country is facing a workforce shortage resulting from low birth rates and an increasing rate of baby boomer retirement over the next two decades. As Riedmann, Lamanna, and Nelson (2003: 18) observe, Canada's immigrant population growth culturally affects the family and family life. First-generation immigrant families maintain their ethnicity, customs, traditions, and language, which are often lost with later generations (Dhruvarajan, 1993). When settling in Canada and the United

TABLE 1.2	NUMBER OF VISIBLE MINORITIES IN SELECT CENSUS METROPOLITAN AREAS	
CENSUS METROPOLITAN AREAS	VISIBLE MINORITY POPULATION	% OF CANADA'S TOTAL VISIBLE MINORITY POPULATION
Canada	5,068,090	100%
Toronto	2,174,065	42.9%
Vancouver	875,300	17.3%
Montreal	590,375	11.6%
Calgary	237,890	4.7%
Ottawa Gatineau	179,295	3.5%
Edmonton	175,295	3.5%
Winnipeg	102,940	2.0%
London	50,300	1.0%
Quebec	16,355	0.3%

Source: Statistics Canada, Census of Population, 2006; extracted Sep 2008 from http://www12.statcan.ca/english/census06/analysis/ethnicorigin /tables/table2.htm

States, immigrants gravitate toward communities with others from the same or neighbouring countries (Kazemipur and Halli, 1997). Importantly, for the immigrants and their families "who have experienced oppression in their country of origin because of their 'race' or ethnicity, immigration to Canada may provide an opportunity to celebrate a status that was previously devalued by others" (Riedmann, Lamanna and Nelson, 2003: 18).

But the better life immigrants come to Canada in search of remains elusive to many visible minorities who face language barriers, discrimination, culture shock, and the rejection of foreign credentials. And that's despite the fact that visible minorities are more likely than non-visible minorities in Canada to have a post-secondary education. Of the foreign-born immigrants who were eligible to become citizens, 85.1 percent did. This is the highest uptake on citizenship in any country! (Siddiqui, 2008). Canada is clearly reinventing itself.

RELIGIOUS DIVERSITY

Religious diversity is also emerging. According to Statistics Canada (2003d), the 2001 census data showed that seven out of every ten Canadians identified themselves as either Roman Catholic or Protestant. The census showed a continuation in a long-term downward trend in the population who report Protestant denominations. At the same time, the number of Canadians who reported religions such as Islam, Hinduism, Sikhism, and Buddhism has increased substantially. In addition, far more Canadians reported that they had no religion. This group accounted for 16 percent of the population in 2001, compared with 12 percent a decade earlier.

With Canada's increasing cultural diversity, interreligious conjugal unions are on the rise. Of the 14.1 million Canadians in a relationship, nearly 2.7 million had a partner from a different religious group. Not surprisingly, over half of these unions were between Catholics and Protestants, the two largest broad religious groups in Canada. A study based on census data by Warren Clark (2006) found that the likelihood of an interreligious union was associated with where you lived, how homogenous the religious mix of your community was, how religious you were, how traditional the doctrine of your religion was, and how long you had been in Canada. People in communities which were religiously homogenous and people who were highly religious were less likely to be in interreligious unions, as were immigrants and older individuals.

Teachers often may not know the religious background of a family but it may be an important element in family dynamics. Some families will share information that impact on practices in the child-care centre, such as religious celebrations. Variations in religious beliefs must be respected in the way that all other elements of acceptance of family practices are embraced. The world's great religions traditions have also recognized values that bind people together (see Figure 1.1). Although the words are different, the wisdom contained within the words is universal:

- **Buddhism:** Hurt not others in ways that you yourself would find hurtful (Udana Virga, 5:8)
- **Christianity:** All things whatsoever ye would that men should do to you, do ye even so to them (Matthew, 7:12)
- **Confucianism:** Do not do unto others what you would not have them do unto you (Analect, 15:23)
- **Hinduism:** This is the sum of duty: do naught unto others which would cause you pain if done to you (Mahabharata, 5:1517)
- **Islam:** No one of you is a believer until he desires for his brother that which he desires for himself (Sunnah)
- **Jainism:** In happiness and suffering, in joy and grief, we should regard all creatures as we regard our own self (Lord Mahavira, 24th Tirthankara)
- **Judaism:** What is hateful to you; do not to your fellow man. That is the law: all the rest is commentary (Talmud, Shabbat, 31a)

In all of the important human characteristics, we are all very much alike. What is important to remember is the need to see the commonalities within a multicultural world (Samovar et al., 2007: 359).

BOOKS FOR ADULTS

How To Be A Perfect Stranger: The Essential Religious Etiquette Handbook, 4th ed., by S.M. Matlins and A.J. Magida

AN AGING POPULATION

According to Statistics Canada (2003a), both job growth and the aging of the working population are driving the demand for highly skilled workers. While baby boomers (aged 37–55) made up 47 percent of

FIGURE 1.1   THE GOLDEN RULE

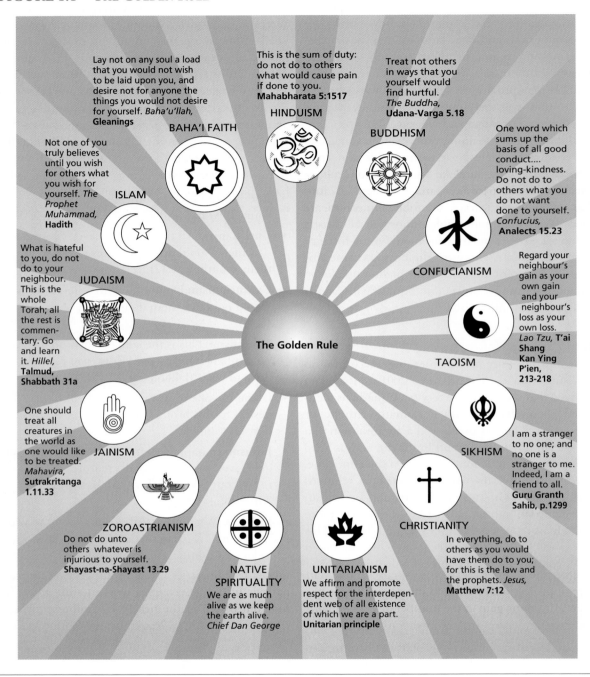

Lay not on any soul a load that you would not wish to be laid upon you, and desire not for anyone the things you would not desire for yourself. *Baha'u'llah,* **Gleanings**

BAHA'I FAITH

This is the sum of duty: do not do to others what would cause pain if done to you. **Mahabharata 5:1517**

HINDUISM

Treat not others in ways that you yourself would find hurtful. *The Buddha,* **Udana-Varga 5.18**

BUDDHISM

Not one of you truly believes until you wish for others what you wish for yourself. *The Prophet Muhammad,* **Hadith**

ISLAM

One word which sums up the basis of all good conduct.... loving-kindness. Do not do to others what you do not want done to yourself. *Confucius,* **Analects 15.23**

CONFUCIANISM

What is hateful to you, do not do to your neighbour. This is the whole Torah; all the rest is commentary. Go and learn it. *Hillel,* **Talmud, Shabbath 31a**

JUDAISM

The Golden Rule

Regard your neighbour's gain as your own gain and your neighbour's loss as your own loss. *Lao Tzu,* **T'ai Shang Kan Ying P'ien, 213-218**

TAOISM

One should treat all creatures in the world as one would like to be treated. *Mahavira,* **Sutrakritanga 1.11.33**

JAINISM

I am a stranger to no one; and no one is a stranger to me. Indeed, I am a friend to all. **Guru Granth Sahib, p.1299**

SIKHISM

Do not do unto others whatever is injurious to yourself. **Shayast-na-Shayast 13.29**

ZOROASTRIANISM

We are as much alive as we keep the earth alive. *Chief Dan George*

NATIVE SPIRITUALITY

We affirm and promote respect for the interdependent web of all existence of which we are a part. **Unitarian principle**

UNITARIANISM

In everything, do to others as you would have them do to you; for this is the law and the prophets. *Jesus,* **Matthew 7:12**

CHRISTIANITY

Reprinted with permission of Paul McKenna.

the labour force in 2001, it is estimated that by 2011 over half of them will be 55 or over and 18 percent will be over 60. Canada increasingly needs highly skilled workers but highly skilled immigrants have a hard time finding work. The unemployment rate of recent immigrants aged 24–54 was twice that of the Canadian population. The past two decades have shown no new job growth in the city of Toronto but the suburbs showed a 120 percent increase in jobs. This suburbanization of jobs has implications for low-income people, many of whom live in our city centres.

CHANGES IN THE LABOUR FORCE

Canada's workplace provides "employment for some 18 million people. Over 14 million earn their daily bread working for someone else: 3.3 million in the public sector, another 11 million in the private sector. About 2.5 million people are self-employed, earning their own income. Just over a million people are actively looking for work. According to some labour force statistics, 42 percent of all occupations and 35 percent of all industries are now experiencing skill or labour shortages" (Ford Kirk, 2007). What is clearly emerging is that employers are now realizing that they need to be more responsive to the needs and interests of their employees if they hope to keep them in their workplace. An Ipsos Reid survey conducted in July 2006 for Sympatico/ MSN asked more than 3,000 people to rank the following considerations when looking for work: salary, flexible hours, vacation time, a positive work environment, rewards and perks, and location. Two factors stand out, almost 4 in 10 respondents (39 percent) ranked money as the most important, while 41 percent were concerned about the difficulties they experienced balancing work and family time (Ford Kirk, 2007).

Two predominant themes emerge in this area: first, increased women's representation in the labour force and the dramatic shift in men's and women's roles over the past 50 years—a shift that has generated the need to redistribute homemaking and caregiving responsibilities—and second, workforce diversity. An aging workforce and the participation patterns of recent immigrants, visible minority populations, and people with disabilities imply that assumptions based on male breadwinner models and perceptions of workers as homogeneous in ethnic and linguistic background, family status, interests, and abilities simply no longer apply to the Canadian workforce.

Over the past decade, women's representation in several professional fields has improved. There has been a dramatic gain in the number of women with a university degree. In 1999, women accounted for 49 percent of business and financial professionals, 47 percent of doctors and dentists, and 35 percent of managerial positions. In spite of gains in selected areas, however, the majority of employed women continue to work in occupations with which women have traditionally been associated. In 1999, 70 percent of employed women worked in teaching, nursing, clerical, and sales and service occupations, down slightly from 74 percent in 1987. In contrast, only 29 percent of employed men work in one of these fields.

More children are living with parents who have post-secondary education—and this trend is increasing. Almost half of both mothers and fathers with children under the age of 12 have a post-secondary diploma, certificate, or degree (Canadian Council on Social Development, 2006: 13).

Blankenhorn et al. (1990: 10–12) state that "[t]he goals of women and of men, too, in the workplace are primarily individualistic: social recognition, wages, opportunities for advancement, and self-fulfillment. But the family is about collective goals . . . building life's most important bonds of affection, nurturance, mutual support, and long-term commitment." And so, many families attempt to restructure their work and private lives to reach some balance. Parents whose work falls outside of the standard workweek find it doubly difficult to coordinate child care and other family responsibilities. Spouses may work on different shifts—a strategy called "off-shifting"—to reduce child-care expenses, but these irregular hours may have a negative impact on relationships within the family. Carey (1999) states that for more and more families, shifts have become the norm. Quoting figures released by Statistics Canada, she says at least one partner in 634,000 couples worked shift work, or four out of ten of the nearly 1.7 million working couples in Canada in November 1995. One in four

---

INSIDE LOOK

I have to work and so does my husband. Without both incomes we wouldn't get by. But we have two little kids. So who is supposed to look after them? If I quit work, I could stay home with them, but we wouldn't be able to pay the bills. If we pay someone else to look after the kids, it takes almost all of my pay. Like it's almost impossible! I think maybe people won't be able to have families soon, unless something changes.

Source: Luxton, 2001: 318.

TABLE 1.3	AVERAGE TOTAL INCOME* BY ECONOMIC FAMILY TYPES		2001	2006
Economic families, two people or more			$70,814	$81,700
Two-parent families with children			79,983	93,500
	No earner		21,470	26,200
	One earner		56,364	66,300
	Two earners		81,179	93,300
	Three or more earners		99,542	117,800
Lone-parent families			36,837	45,800
Male lone-parent families			48,248	67,100
Female lone-parent families			34,357	40,900
	No earner		15,513	20,500
	One earner		33,880	40,800
	Two or more earners		53,819	55,300

Average total income refers to income from all sources, including government transfers and before deduction of federal and provincial income taxes.

Source: Statistics Canada CANSIM table 202-0403, Catalogue 75-202-XIE, last modified 2008-05-05. http://www40.statcan.ca/l01/cst01/famil05a.htm

husbands and one in five wives work shifts, and about 40,000 couples work at completely different times of the day. Younger husbands and wives and those with preschoolers are the most likely to be working shifts, which supports the theory that they're staggering their schedules in order to care for their children at home. Dr. Stanley Greenspan supports this juggling in his book, *The Four-Thirds Solution: Solving the Child-Care Crisis in America Today.* "Since quality child care can be expensive and hard to find, the book proposes that each parent work two-thirds of a full-time week. Then they devote the remaining time to their child" (Dunnewind, 2003: K6).

As de Wolff (1994: 1) observes, "One wage can no longer support a household. More people are working in conditions where the work has intensified and demands longer hours. Neither the government nor employers have moved in to provide adequate support to workers who are also caregivers. Worry about how to cope has become a daily part of workers', particularly women workers', lives."

Johnson, Lero, and Rooney (2001: 26–27) state that union membership is generally associated with higher wages but women traditionally have had a much lower rate of unionization than men. Over the past few decades this has changed. Between 1966 and 1992, the number of women who were

union members climbed from 320,000 to 1.6 million, a five-fold increase. By 1999, 31 percent of women were unionized as compared to 33 percent of men.

EMPLOYER ATTITUDES

Increased globalization, increasing competitiveness, and the integration of computer technologies have dramatically changed the work environment and put tremendous pressure on employers. This has necessitated "downsizing," contract work, and, for the employee, increased workloads and the need to acquire new skills in many areas in order to adapt. Employers are noticing the effect of the work–family conflict on their companies, particularly in terms of productivity and the bottom line, and "are looking for ways to support their employees in order to remain competitive and responsive to their own ever-changing operating environments" (Johnson, Lero, and Rooney, 2001: 1). In the public sphere, governments have also been examining the effect of the work–family conflict and "protracted stress in terms of the well-being of individuals and families, stress-related health problems, and productivity losses" (2001: 1). However, corporations have been slow to respond and this attention has translated into few progressive changes in the workplace.

The following strategies to reduce work–family conflict could be considered by employers:

- more flexible work schedules
- jobs that support young families, from 9 to 5, no shift work
- flextime for child care and school involvement
- a shorter workweek at full pay or a compressed workweek
- salary deferrals
- sabbaticals
- opportunities to work at home
- time-off to care for sick children (or elderly parents)
- job-sharing schemes
- voluntary part-time work
- telecommuting, mobile offices, and satellite offices
- counselling services
- workplace child care or extended-hour child care
- child-care resource and referral services
- supplementary unemployment benefits plan
- phased return from maternity leave
- voluntary summers off without pay
- respite care and other emergency referral services
- job training and retraining
- parenting courses
- prenatal and postnatal care for families and their babies
- a voucher system in which families choose from a range of company benefits those that best meet their needs, including reimbursement for child-care expenses for work responsibilities outside of regular hours

WORK–FAMILY CONFLICT

Duxbury, Higgins, and Coghill (2003: 75–76) outline the needs of Canadian workers to address work–life balance. Through their research, they have drawn the following general conclusions:

- Work–life balance is a complex phenomenon.
- Many factors contribute to high work–life conflict.
- Work and life are not separate domains.
- Many Canadians are having difficulties balancing work and family because organizations are not taking the issue seriously and are not treating it as a business issue.
- Some Canadians are having problems balancing work and family because of conditions at home.
- It would appear that for every Canadian whose personal or family circumstances are interfering with performance at work, there are five Canadians whose work and work circumstances are interfering with their family and life.
- Work–life conflict is impairing the health of many Canadians and creating problems within the family.
- The culture of the organization, which is set by the behaviour at the top, can sabotage the best attempts by organizations to help employees balance work and family.
- Achieving a successful work–life balance increases employees' sense of control.

Focusing on creating a more supportive work environment would assist Canadians in achieving a more harmonious work–life balance. See **www.worklifecanada.ca** for more information.

Since 2004, six weeks of EI Compassionate Care benefits are available for temporary absences from work to provide care for a critically ill child, parent, spouse, or common-law partner. Job protection for eight weeks is provided for federally-regulated employees under the *Canada Labour Code*.

According to a study done for Health Canada, 19.8 million workdays were lost in Canada in 1996 due to work–family conflicts. When this figure is multiplied by an average 1996 earning salary of $135 per day, employers ended up footing a $2.7-billion tab, not including indirect costs such as replacement of the employee during the absence, overtime costs, or reduced service or productivity (Lister, 1999). It has been suggested that such employer supports "may be rewarded through an increase in employee morale; reductions in employee stress, [reductions in] absenteeism, and turnover; and fewer promotion and transfer refusals" (Vanier Institute, 1994: 135). Statistics Canada (2003b) states, "Many employers have implemented employee assistance programs to address the human and financial costs associated with stress. The 1999 Workplace and Employee Survey found that 26 percent of employees had access to such programs."

Employers like Ontario Power Generation recognize the competing demands employees face in trying to balance their work and family responsibilities. The connection between organizational culture and employee performance, recruitment, and retention is clear. High-performing organizations—and those listed as Canada's Top 100 Employers—all have a spectrum of strategies and programs to attract new talent and enable employees to participate fully and effectively in all aspects of their lives. Workplaces that acknowledge and support the multiplicity of needs, interests, and responsibilities of employees tend to have an environment and culture that fosters engagement, commitment, and creativity.

At OPG, valuing diversity isn't just about respecting differences between the genders or different ethnic groups. Diversity is about acknowledging the different and changing life circumstances and situations of individual employees. An effective and supportive work culture views the employee not just as a worker, but as a "whole person." Employees cannot easily park their personal lives at the office or plant doors. Responsibilities, problems, and worries are baggage employees bring with them wherever they go. But we also know that what employees do outside of work can contribute in very real ways to their capabilities, creativity, and commitment to the job. So, regardless of the nature of work–life needs or interests, the company is committed to helping ensure that the different dimensions of employees' lives harmonize and complement each other—rather than conflict and collide. By reducing the potential for work–life conflict and minimizing the effects of role overload, we can help ease stress and increase engagement—resulting in healthier, happier employees in healthier, happier workplaces.

While achieving total work–life balance may be an elusive goal, employees of all ages and stages consider the management of work/life responsibilities and priorities as an important quality of life issue. It seems the roles and responsibilities of individual employees are increasing in number and complexity, especially with the significant numbers of workers today who are members of the "sandwich generation"—people who are attending to the needs of aging or ailing parents or other family members, while at the same time raising their own children. For these workers, the "struggle to juggle" may be particularly intense, especially if their family members do not live in the same city or country. But other workers feel the crunch too, in different ways. For new parents, the issue of finding and keeping quality child care is often a challenge. And across North America, younger employees without children are indicating they would prefer to work for employers that enable them to achieve balance in their lives. They are not adopting a "work-centric" style, preferring instead to find satisfaction on a number of different levels, such as getting more education, volunteering, travelling, or spending time with family and friends.

Clearly a "one size fits at all" approach is not the most effective way of finding solutions to the work–life challenges that confront us. Generally, the first step towards identifying a solution involves dialogue. Through dialogue and joint problem-solving, issues and ideas are explored. Usually what's called for is reciprocal flexibility—or some movement on both sides to find a mutually satisfactory solution. But what's the starting point for these discussions? Policies and programs, plus collective agreements, all serve as a vital springboard for work-life dialogue between employees, their managers and supervisors, and employee representatives or bargaining agents. While employers are not responsible for creating balance in the lives of its employees, OPG is proud of its long history helping employees find ways to effectively manage their work–life responsibilities. By providing an array of policies, programs, resources, and supports, we seek to enable our employees as they navigate the "every-day-a-thon" of modern life—contributing to individual and organizational well-being, and to the health of families, communities, and society.

Contributed by Kim Taylor, Manager, Recruitment Solutions and Diversity, Corporate Human Resources, Ontario Power Generation.

STRESS

There are enormous pressures on parents to be the best parents possible. One trip to a bookstore's Parenting Section or an Internet search will show you hundreds of experts who have written on every possible aspect of child rearing and parenting. Parents are sure to feel overwhelmed by the responsibility of their task when each expert has their own strategy for instructing parents on how to raise successful daughters and caring sons. For some, the information may be confusing, in conflict with cultural practices, too complicated, or too basic. Despite the availability of this literature, when parents are struggling, most turn to their families, other parents, or teachers.

In a 2008 survey on Canadian attitudes towards physical and mental health at work and at home, 74 percent of those surveyed think employees are overworked; 85 percent agree that employees work in a very stressful environment; 89 percent think, as the years go by, that more and more employees are suffering from burn-outs, major depression, anxiety, or other mental health problems; and 53 percent of workers are prepared to earn less money to work fewer hours per week (Desjardins Financial Security, 2008). A poll for Southam News and Global-TV found that two persons in every ten have as much stress in their life as they can manage and that any additional stress would push them over the edge. The poll also found that Quebeckers are more stressed than residents of other provinces. Canadian women between the ages of 18–54 are more stressed than their male counterparts; specialists say this finding coincides with the reality that women tend to be society's main planners, caregivers, and worriers. A recent Angus Reid poll showed that women with children at home suffer more stress than men in the same situation (see Figure 1.2). According to Lero (2003: 24), "High role overload and work–family interference are significantly related to employees' job stress, job satisfaction, organizational commitment, and absenteeism, and also are correlated with family outcomes. The latter include a higher incidence of work demands negatively affecting time with their spouse, perceived poor quality of couple and family relationships, lower levels of family satisfaction, and a great tendency to miss family activities due to work." According to Statistics Canada (2003c), occupation was a key determinant of stress. Managers and professionals were significantly more likely than workers in primary industries to report stress from too many demands or hours.

Changing family structures, economic pressures, eroding community support systems, and spending cutbacks at all levels of government contribute to stressors on the family that affect children's social, emotional, and intellectual development and can lead to clinical burnout. Ward (1998) notes that the effects of individual burnout have a direct effect on the family. Often emotional exhaustion goes hand-in-hand with physical exhaustion. Lero (2003: 24) states that "many families report cutting back on sleep as a primary strategy for dealing with time conflicts. As a result, the individual becomes susceptible to illness; stress is a direct factor in some

FIGURE 1.2   STRESSED OUT

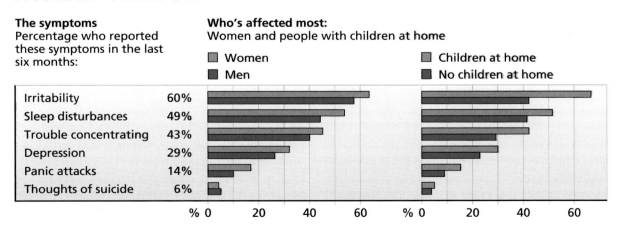

Reprinted with permission from The Globe and Mail and Angus Reid.

illnesses such as heart disease and ulcers. The stressed individual may also suffer psychologically. The reduced sense of accomplishment and self-esteem that accompanies burnout and the accompanying loss of zest for life are the central characteristics of depression" (2003: 302–3). Employees may consider quitting their job. They may turn down promotions that require travel, relocation, overtime, or extra responsibilities because accepting would jeopardize the already tenuous balance between work and family obligations. Stressed employees often leave their job to find new employment where family needs are more easily met.

Employees have voiced strong concern over the child-care difficulties they experience. Research shows consistently that employees with child-care responsibilities, when compared to employees without these responsibilities, experience higher stress levels, lower productivity, and higher absenteeism, all of which have a negative effect on their workplace performance. Organized labour and other concerned groups have proposed that child care be universally accessible and publicly funded. In taking this position, they support the view that child care is not only a women's issue or a parental responsibility but a societal issue that requires community involvement and support as well as family participation. It is interesting to note that today's 30-year-olds are the first generation of parents who may have been in child care themselves but they may be experiencing the frustration of not being able to find it for their own children.

Stress in the family can have an enormous impact on children. Children need a high level of care and involvement, combined with high but reasonable expectations to help them develop the confidence and social skills they need to maintain competence and the sense of perspective that shapes the way they react to stress. The interaction of these factors contributes to the child's achievement of resiliency (see more on this in Chapter 10).

One of the manifestations of the control that parents exercise over their children is found in the "hurried child syndrome" (Elkind, 1981). "At a time when wage-earning single parents and dual-earner families are the norm, there is an inevitable conflict between the pace of a child's life and the imposed pace of a parent's schedule. In this regard, time awareness in the family can be like a collective bargaining agreement whereby children gradually learn to ignore their own natural rhythms . . . and absorb the messages and attitudes about time sent

FIGURE 1.3 MULTITASKING IS A FACT OF LIFE FOR MANY PARENTS

by their busy parents" (Erkel, 1995: 36). When stress induces parents to put their own needs ahead of children's, then children are expected to adapt to adult schedules and timetables rather than adults adapting themselves to the pace of childhood.

POVERTY

"To be born poor is to face a greater likelihood of ill health—in infancy, in childhood, and throughout one's adult life. To be born poor is to face a lesser likelihood that you finish high school; lesser still that you attend university. To be born poor is to face a greater likelihood that you are judged a delinquent in adolescence and, *if* you are, a greater likelihood that you are sent to a correctional institution. To be born poor is to have the deck stacked against you at birth and to find life an uphill struggle ever after" (Standing Senate Committee, 1991: 74).

Poverty seems to have been with us forever but does it need to be? Many countries in Europe and many provinces right here at home have reduced poverty by drafting plans, setting goals, dedicating funds, and measuring progress. Tony Blair's initiatives in Britain cut child poverty by 23 percent in five years. Since 2005, Ireland has cut poverty from 15 percent to less than 5 percent. In Quebec, which has a law requiring governments to fight poverty, child poverty has plummeted to less than 10 percent in 2005, from 22 percent in 1996. A *Toronto*

Star editorial (2007: A14) stated that the child poverty rate in Canada is 11.7 percent, unchanged from 1989 when the House of Commons voted unanimously to eradicate child poverty by the year 2000. Despite a $13-billion federal surplus in the last fiscal year, Canada has made absolutely no progress in meeting that goal. The Senate noted that Canada ranks 22nd among 26 wealthy nations in terms of children living in relative poverty. Campaign 2000, an anti-poverty group, has proposed a strategy of joint federal–provincial action to reduce child poverty by at least 25 percent by 2012, and by at least 50 percent by 2017. The four cornerstones of their strategy are outlined below:

1. ***Make Work Pay:*** Any parent or adult working full-time, full-year, for 30 hours a week (1,500 hours a year) should not live below the poverty line. (In Ontario, this would require a minimum wage of $11.25 by 2012 a combined federal/provincial child benefit of $5,100 per year and an annual working tax credit of $2,400).

2. ***Dignity for the Disabled:*** A basic income system for people with disabilities equivalent to social security benefits available for seniors should be implemented.

3. ***Safety Net for the Unemployed:*** An income system for families with children who are unavailable for work due to temporary or extended difficulties that does not leave them destitute (i.e., welfare rates for families to be equivalent to 80 percent of minimum income

earned by families working full-time for a full year) is needed.

4. ***Public Supports for Families and Children:*** Employment Insurance coverage should be restored and basic drug and dental benefits should be provided for all workers, as well as more affordable housing and universal access to affordable child care. (Monsebraate and Whittington, 2007)

Regional variations and the different issues facing urban and rural populations make it difficult to measure precisely the depth of poverty in this country. However, we do know that a significant number of children in Canada live in circumstances that place them at social, physical, and emotional disadvantage.

An Organization of Economic Co-operation and Development (OECD) survey of 19 countries found social differences in educational participation a pervasive and constant characteristic of all educational structures. Poor children around the world are being pushed out of school. Mandell (1992: 27) states: "There is a persistent tendency for middle-class children to receive greater teacher attention, praise, and other rewards, while lower-class children receive criticism and punishment. Students perceive teacher encouragement to play a highly significant role in bolstering their self-esteem and keeping them in school." This documentation on school environments can most likely be transferred to the child-care community.

TABLE 1.4	CHILDREN LIVING IN POVERTY

In 2005, Ontario had 40.7 percent of Canada's children under 18, but 43.8 percent of children living in poverty.

PROVINCE	TOTAL NUMBER	PERCENTAGE OF TOTAL
Ontario	345,000	43.8%
Quebec	144,000	18.3%
British Columbia	126,000	16%
Alberta	64,000	8.1%
Manitoba	36,000	4.6%
Saskatchewan	27,000	3.4%
Nova Scotia	19,000	2.4%
Nfld & Labrador	11,000	1.4%
Prince Edward Island	N/A	0.1%
CANADA	788,000	100

Source: Statistics Canada

Money may not buy happiness, but it does afford a myriad of options, from sufficient and nutritious food, to eat to comfortable residences, to better health care, to education at prestigious universities, to vacations, household help, and family counselling. Consider that, among two-parent Canadian families with children aged four to eleven:

- Nearly 30 percent of poor children had changed school three times before they were 11 years of age, in contrast to about 10 percent of children in upper-income families. Children experiencing frequent transitions tend to have lower math scores, more grade failures, and more behaviour problems than children who remain in the same school.
- One-third of poor children four to five years of age display delayed vocabulary development, while less than 10 percent of children from high-income families are behind in vocabulary development.
- Organized and unorganized sports are less likely to be part of a poor child's activities than an advantaged child. About 25 percent of poor children participate in organized sports in contrast to 75 percent of children in high-income families.

Sources: Riedmann, Lamanna, and Nelson, 2003; Campaign 2000, 2001.

According to the Canadian Council on Social Development (2003), Canada now has the highest level of college and university graduates in the OECD and average earnings reflect this. In 2001, Canadian average earnings rose for the first time above $30,000 per year, to $31,757. Unfortunately, many Canadians are not sharing equitably in these increased earnings. The groups most likely to be earning less are younger Canadians, women, immigrants, and Aboriginals. While the number of earners making more than $80,000 a year soared in the 1990s, the proportion of Canadians making $20,000 or less has remained unchanged since 1981 at about 41 percent—and more of these low earners now have university degrees.

The Canadian Centre for Policy Alternatives (2007) reported that by 9:46 a.m. on January 2, 2007, the country's 100 highest paid business executives had earned, on average, an amount equal to what the average Canadian would earn in all of 2007—$38,010.

The relative earnings of immigrants have continued to decline: male immigrants aged 25–54 who came to Canada during the 1990s made almost 25 percent less than their Canadian-born counterparts, despite the fact that 40 percent of working-age immigrants have a university degree, compared to 23 percent of Canadian-born workers. Poverty among children from two-parent families of recent immigrants (arriving in Canada within the last ten years) grew to 39 percent; it is now more than double the national figure of 18 percent. In 2000, almost 321,000 children with at least one immigrant parent who arrived in Canada in the 1990s were living in low-income situations. Yet Statistics Canada reports that second-generation women earn more than women with similar education whose parents were born in Canada, while second-generation men earn considerably less than their male peers. It is suggested that delayed marriage and child rearing, as well as better access to high-paying jobs in urban areas may contribute to the comparative success of second-generation women (Grewal, 2007).

The poverty rate of lone-parent families with children has dropped below the 50 percent mark for the first time in 20 years, based on their before-tax income. The dramatic increase in incomes for lone-parent families has been due mainly to an increase in income from salaries and wages rather than from government programs and also to increasing government transfers. However, with low-income rates among lone-parent families still at 46 percent, this is not the time to think we have solved the poverty issue for lone-parent families.

There are also gender issues at work. If women were paid equitably, the poverty rate in Canada could be cut in half. The economic disadvantages to women are exacerbated for single mothers (Ambert, 2006, in Shimoni and Baxter, 2008: 159).

The Canadian Teachers' Federation characterizes the negative consequences of poverty in general:

> The physical symptoms displayed by hungry children include crying, throwing up water, pale skin, weakness, stomach cramping, headaches, dizziness and fatigue. Children may also appear disgruntled, antagonistic, irritable, restless, dizzy, unable to concentrate, and less inclined to learn. Many low-income children experience lower achievement, less participation in extra-curricular activities, less motivation to learn, delayed cognitive development, different types of teacher–student interactions, negative effects of streaming, lower career aspirations and expectations, interrupted school attendance, lower university attendance, increased risk of illiteracy, and higher drop-out rates. Poor children tend to experience difficulties in schools and have limited prospects for higher education.

Teachers may want to view the resources available from the National Anti-Poverty Organization at **http://www.napo-onap.ca/**.

Second Harvest

Given the pressing nature of poverty, many organizations have sprung up to provide community support to those in need. The number of people who use food banks in Canada is equivalent to the population of Quebec. In 1985, Ina Andre and Joan Clayton started Second Harvest by using their station wagon to pick-up fresh food, which would have otherwise gone to waste, and delivering it to local shelters and drop-in centres. In 2006–2007, Second Harvest in Toronto distributed 5.46 million pounds of food donated by grocery stores, food manufacturers, processors and distributors, hotels, restaurants, and caterers. Using a value of $2.00 per pound of food (based on consultation with The Canadian Association of Food Banks), this food was worth over 10.92 million dollars. This food went to 240 social service agencies and provided enough food for about 13,000 meals every day. Second Harvest relies on approximately 1,400 volunteers, in addition to financial donations and sponsorships. Many businesses support Second Harvest by donating products and services and in 2006–2007 this support was valued at over $900,000 and included truck insurance, courier costs, cell phone service, design and print work, event involvement, promotion, and prizing. What started as a two-person operation has grown to address the pressing needs of the poorest in this community

(Second Harvest, n.d.). You can read more about Second Harvest at **www.secondharvest.ca**.

Housing

According to Kirby (2007), "the average Canadian family has seen the value of their home jump more than 10 percent a year for three years in a row." But the more recent downturn in the economy suggests unsettling times ahead. House prices overall are up 60 percent in the last five years. But national averages never tell the full story. While prices in cities like Ottawa and Montreal have grown slowly, house prices in Toronto are up about 86 percent over the last decade to an average of $394,000, while the average home in Vancouver, at $570,000, has jumped 73 percent since 2003 alone. In Alberta, the average Calgary home has doubled in just four years to $432,000. To buy at those prices, Canadians have had to pile on mounds of new debt. Between 2000 and 2006 the total amount of outstanding residential mortgages ballooned by 62 percent to $694 billion, according to the Canada Mortgage and Housing Corporation, and many expect that figure will top $800 billion this year. Financial planners suggest a mortgage should never take up more than 32 percent of a household's gross income and many Canadians are pushing their limits. Low interest rates have proven to be beneficial for many, but there's no guarantee that rates will stay low (Kirby, 2007).

In almost every urban centre across Canada, conservative estimates indicate that there are 200,000 Canadians who are homeless. The fastest growing segments among the homeless are young people under age 18 and families with children (see Chapter 10 for a more in-depth look at homelessness).

Families on Welfare

Social assistance, or welfare, is the social safety net of last resort in Canada. It provides money to meet the basic needs of individuals and families who have exhausted all other means of financial support. There are 13 welfare systems in Canada—one in each province and territory. Determining eligibility for welfare is a multi-step process. First, applicants (between 18–65 years of age) must meet the administrative requirements. Then they undergo a needs test, which looks at their assets, income, and basic needs. Administrative rules vary throughout the country. According to the National Council of Welfare (2005), welfare incomes

EXHIBIT 1.2 A MOTHER'S MEMORIES OF POVERTY

How does poverty affect Canadian families? We can gain some understanding of this issue by considering Linda Marchotte's memories of mothering in poverty:

- the kids always having stained, patched, or out-of-fashion clothes;
- sending them to school with plain, unexciting lunches every day;
- no hot-dog or doughnut treats at school fundraising days;
- no cable TV, actually no TV for five years (I put it away so they wouldn't want what I couldn't buy them);
- no movies;
- arriving places tired from carrying stuff and worn out from waiting in the cold or wet or hot (depending on the weather), rumpled, dirtier from riding the bus than getting around by car;
- shame in inviting kids over: "Where's the couch?" "Where's your stereo?" "Where's your room?" were the kinds of questions from these young visitors;
- birthday parties, where kids asked, "Is this all there is?"
- saying no to Steven and Melanie all the time;
- worry and anxiety about money—"Will we make it to cheque day?"—and being scared anything will happen that costs anything, this fear taking energy away from living, having fun, and paying attention to the children;
- dragging the kids and two garbage bags full of dirty laundry on the bus every week to do laundry;
- always looking for money or returnable bottles on the ground;
- escaping by reading or watching TV;
- being constantly worried the kids weren't getting enough nutritious food to grow and be healthy;
- being homeless for four months and living with friends and at two different friends' houses while they were away, with our things stored on another friend's back porch;
- being aware of how outside of their peers' culture and experience my children were, and being powerless to do anything about it.

Source: S. Baxter, *A Child Is Not a Toy: Voices of Children in Poverty* (Vancouver: New Star Press, 1993), 169. Reprinted by permission.

declined in 2005, making life more difficult for the 1.7 million people—five percent of the population—forced to rely on welfare. In 2005, welfare incomes were at their lowest point since 1986. Nearly half a million of those on welfare were children. New Brunswick and Alberta had the lowest welfare incomes in 2005. In New Brunswick, a single person received $3,427 and a couple with two children received $17,567. In Alberta, the welfare income of a single person with a disability was $7,851 and a lone parent with one child received $12,326.

The majority of welfare incomes, when adjusted for inflation, peaked in 1994 or earlier. When the peak year welfare incomes were compared to 2005 welfare incomes, some of the losses were staggering: in Alberta, the income of a single person decreased by almost 50 percent; in Ontario, a lone parent's income decreased by almost $6,600 and a couple with two children lost just over $8,700. Across the provinces, one-third of households experienced losses of $3,000 or more. No welfare incomes were

remotely close to the poverty line, average incomes, or median incomes. Two provinces were consistently at the bottom of all three measures: New Brunswick for the single person, and Alberta for both the person with a disability and the lone parent with one child. By contrast, two provinces were the most generous across all three measures: Newfoundland and Labrador for the single person and lone parent with one child, and Prince Edward Island for the couple with two children. Although the federal government has increased spending on child benefits significantly since 1998, most welfare families with children have seen little, if any, improvement in their total income.

FEMINIST MOVEMENTS IN CANADA

The first wave of the women's movement was successful in gaining voting rights for women. The second wave, which occurred during the 1960s,

Feminist theorizing has contributed to political action regarding families in the following ways, among others:

1. Changes in policies that economically weaken households headed by women (for example, efforts to end gender and race discrimination in wages).
2. Changes in laws that reinforce the privileges of men and heterosexual nuclear families compared to other family types (for example, divorce laws that disadvantage women economically or laws that exclude nontraditional families from economic and legal supports offered to married people).
3. Efforts to stop sexual harassment and sexual and physical violence against women and children.
4. Advances in securing women's reproductive freedom (for example, through abortion rights).
5. New recognition and support for women's unpaid work, by involving men more fully in housework and child care and by efforts to fund good-quality daycare and paid parental leaves.
6. Transformations in family therapy so that counsellors recognize the reality of gender inequality in family life and treat women's concerns with respect.

Source: Goldner, 1993: 623–625.

In her groundbreaking book of the early 1960s, The *Feminine Mystique,* Betty Friedan chronicled women's struggle to break out of the confines of their domestic straightjacket. But Friedan also argued that the new role of women didn't mean they had to hate men or give up fulfilling romantic and sexual relationships with men. Much of the backlash against feminism in the past 30 years has centred on feminists as man-haters. Some believe being a feminist means women have to hate men or give up on marriage. Others say simply that the idea of romantic love is so entwined with traditional gender roles that it dies when those roles change and overlap. Still others say men react to the feminist challenge with a powerful backlash that includes violence. Friedan herself believed that feminism was not incompatible with romantic love and that the liberation of women would lead to the liberation of men.

Source: Angelini, 2007: 220.

included radical, liberal, and socialist feminist movements. Over time, the feminist movement has achieved many important victories "including federal legislation endorsing affirmative action for women and other disadvantaged groups; Manitoba legislation providing equal pay for work of equal value; Ontario legislation forbidding sexual harassment; and the decision to enshrine women's right to equality in the new Constitution" (Larson, Goltz, and Munro, 2000: 84). In the 1980s, funding was increased for women's shelters and child-care facilities, demonstrating further government response to women's needs. But the change in public attitudes may be the most significant outcome; it is no longer unthinkable that women with preschoolers might be employed outside the home, or that women are equal to men in business (Adamson et al., 1988).

With the increase of mothers in the workforce, child care continues to be a critical issue. Rosenberg (2001: 312) states, "Attempts to socialize child care outside the household—a project crucial to the redesign of motherwork and parenting—continue to meet with enormous resistance. In North America there is still much popular and official hostility to 'institutionalized' daycare." The intensity of the "fight for good daycare, defined as top-quality, universally accessible, twenty-four-hour-a-day and community controlled, illustrates that redesigning the job of parenting is deeply ideological, because it challenges the essentialist ideologies of 'the nuclear family' and 'motherhood', and the allocation of resources and funds" (Ross, 1979).

THE CHANGING ROLES OF WOMEN

Roles of men and women have changed over time, but living in our society remains a different experience for men and for women. Gendered messages and social organization influence people's behaviour, attitudes, and options. During this century, wives gradually changed their legal status from being their husbands' dependants to being their equal partners. This included, as milestones, the right to make contracts on their own behalf, the right to own and dispose of property, the right to keep their own name upon marriage, and the determination of domicile on an equal basis for both wife and husband. Legally, equality was supposed to be guaranteed with the implementation of section 15 of the Charter of Rights and Freedoms in 1985; however, socially, emotionally, and economically, this ideal has not yet been achieved (Eichler, 1997: 40).

Spousal roles continue to be blurred, and there are conflicting ideas about these roles in all sectors of society. The role of mothers varies from family to family, from culture to culture, and from province to province.

According to Lero (2003: 13–14), a number of factors have influenced women's employment and family roles. They include the following:

- A rapid rise in divorce rates, a lower marriage rate, and the tendency toward later marriages.

  These factors indicate that larger numbers of working-age women are spending longer periods unmarried, a condition that requires that they be self-supporting. When married or involved in a common-law relationship, women are less likely to relinquish their economic independence or risk the loss of their job or future career prospects.

- Low fertility rates, along with the tendency to delay marriage and childbearing.

  On average, women are deferring having children until their late 20s or 30s (with some having

children in their 40s). As well, women are having fewer children, apparently in part because of work demands and income security (Belanger and Ouellet, 2002). An extended period of time before childbearing allows women to establish themselves in the paid workforce, which promotes their ongoing involvement. In addition, the period of time when mothers have young children at home is compressed, since they are likely to have only one or two children.

- Greater access to post-secondary education.

  Greater access to post-secondary education and advanced professional training has enabled women to prepare themselves for a wider variety of occupations, including higher-paying professional and managerial positions. Today's women are the most highly educated of any generation; more women than men have university degrees. Both young men and women increasingly want work that enables them to use their education, skills, and talent and contribute in a meaningful way. "Nexus generation [the generation that represents a link between the Industrial Age and the Information Age]" and younger cohorts (both men and women) expect to have families and satisfying work.

- Changes in social attitudes toward women working outside the home, the influence of second-stage feminism, growing workplace diversity, and the demand for talent.

  General attitude change and government commitments to gender equality have led to increased acceptance, at least in principle, of women's rights to economic and social equality. To the extent to which this leads to increased opportunities for women and the removal of systemic barriers, it promotes men and women being involved as equal partners, both at home and in the paid workforce. Faced with an increasingly diverse workforce, a shrinking labour pool, and the need for new talent, employers are more likely to hire and promote women, providing additional opportunities and economic rewards for their participation.

- Additional opportunities in professions and in service-sector occupations traditionally occupied by women mainly.

  Women have been increasing as a proportion of managers and professionals, and making inroads even in traditional male-dominated occupations. However, there is also a continuing and strengthening demand for entrants into traditionally female-dominated occupations. These include education, health care, and services oriented to seniors, as well as other service occupations. Stronger labour market demands and more opportunities for women increase the likelihood of their participation.

Eichler (1997: 36) states: "In spite of the great influx into the labour force, wives continue to be economically disadvantaged compared to husbands. This is the result of being female and married and/or a mother. Women as a group continue to have lower incomes than men." Though more Canadian women are working than ever before, in 2003 women working on a full-time, full-year basis had average earning of $36,500—71 percent what their male counterparts made—and this has not changed substantially in the past decade (Statistics Canada, 2006b). Thirty-seven percent of lone mothers in the labour force earn less than $10 per hour; in contrast, 26.5 percent of *all* employees earn under $10 (which would yield an annual income of $18,000, based on a 35-hour week) (*Report Card on Child Poverty in Canada,* 1999).

Women are still underrepresented in corporate boardrooms and in political venues. In 2004, only 37 percent of all those employed in managerial positions were women, up from 30 percent in 1987. Women tend to be better represented in lower-level positions as opposed to those at more senior levels. Women also remain very much a minority among professionals employed in the natural sciences, engineering, and mathematics. The majority of employed women continue to work in occupations in which women have traditionally been concentrated. In 2004, two-thirds of all employed women were working in teaching, nursing, and related health occupations, clerical or other administrative positions, and sales and service occupations (Statistics Canada, 2006b). According to Perry (2003), women who work part-time are less likely than their full-time counterparts to win promotions or supervise other workers, despite high levels of education and long job tenure.

Women are much more likely than their male counterparts to work part time. In 2004, 27 percent of the total female work force was part-time employees, more than double the proportion of just 11 percent among employed men (Statistics Canada, 2006b). About 30 percent of women working part-time earned less than $9-per-hour. Hughes (1999) suggests that some women make the shift to self-employment in the hopes that this will give them more control over work hours and a better balance of work and family life. Marshall (2003) reports that "women had lower participation rates in flexible work arrangements than did men, and this held within occupation and industry. This finding suggests that even within occupations, women may perform tasks that are less amenable to flexible time or place." According to Lero (2003), in 1997, the last year for which information is readily accessible, wives earned more than their husbands in 14.3 percent of dual-earner couples and were the sole earner in 4.9 percent of all husband–wife families.

Women often take unpaid leave from paid employment in order to raise children; either by choice or necessity (affordable child care might be unavailable, for example). The implications of unpaid leave can be far-reaching and may include lost ground in their careers as technological advances outpace them, reduced contributions to pension plans, or the necessity of taking part-time employment that offers fewer benefits.

Women still do most of the housework and tend to feel more time-stressed than men do. But now more men are juggling household chores and paid work duties, while women are spending more time at the office according to a new time-use study. During the past two decades, the average total workday for people aged 25–54, including both paid and unpaid work, has increased steadily. In 2005, it amounted to 8.8 hours on average, up from 8.2 hours in 1986. For men this meant 0.6 hours, and 0.7 hours for women. Most of the increase for men came from unpaid work in the house on which they spent 2.5 hours per day on average in 2005, up from 2.1 hours in 1986. The gain for women came entirely from paid work. In 2005, they spent an average of 4.4 hours at the office, up from 3.3 in 1986. Canadian women have one of the highest labour force participation rates in the world, a rate that is converging with that of men (Statistics Canada, 2006c).

According to Lero (2003: 24) 62–65 percent of parents in dual-earner families and single parents (all employed full-time) reported high role overload; among women, those employed in professional and managerial positions were particularly likely to report high levels of work–life conflict and job stress. In 1989, Hochschild and Machung wrote

I feel as if I have already put in a full day's work by the time I get to the child-care centre. It takes incredible organization to have everything go smoothly so that I can get to work on time. All it takes is one broken shoelace or a stubborn daughter dawdling over her cereal to wreak havoc. At work I'm doing the work of two people as our organization has downsized—there is no relief at work. At the other end of the day my life is programmed around Girl Guides and swimming lessons, not to mention Saturdays at the hockey arena. After I finally get everyone into bed and do laundry, make lunches for the next day, I fall into bed completely exhausted.

what is now seen as a seminal work—*The Second Shift*—that states that working mothers have two jobs: one at their place of employment and another at home doing housework and child care. Since then, we do see a shift in many men assuming more responsibilities for homework and child care.

According to Daly (2000), "When compared with all other age groups, people who are in the prime child bearing and rearing years devote the highest proportion of time to paid and unpaid work activities. The 35–44 age group spent 38% of each day on productive activities (a combination of paid and unpaid work) compared to 30% for the Canadian average (aged 15 and over). Those in the 25–34 age category were close behind with 36% of their time devoted to productive activities."

Unless we value the work that women have traditionally done, few men will want to do it. The National Action Committee on the Status of Women reported that in 1995, the UN estimated that globally women perform $3 trillion worth of unpaid/unremunerated work. In Canada women's unremunerated work will inevitably increase. All research shows that it is women who take up the slack when social services are slashed. Even with the new emphasis on father nurturance, 56 percent of employed mothers wished that fathers would spend more time with the children, and 43 percent wished that fathers would help more with the chores (Hepworth Berger, 2000: 106).

Women continue to be held disproportionately responsible for the well-being of all members of the family. Indeed, many women with children in child care are faced also with caring for aging parents. The "superwoman" concept continues to drive women in all areas of their lives, as illustrated by Helen Schulman anecdote below:

I was guiding my father back to his wheelchair when I looked up and saw my son hanging precipitously off a climbing apparatus. Where was King Solomon when I needed him? If I let go of my father, who wavered like a feather in the air, he would have no choice but to fall. If I didn't run to my son, he would surely topple and hit the playground's cement hardtop. What would you have done?

Helen held onto her father, and watched her toddler drop to the ground. The child escaped with nothing worse than scraped palms. But that doesn't make the choice any less excruciating, the dilemma any less stark. Schulman's vignette, from her essay in *The Bitch In The House* (2003), illustrates a tug-of-war being lived out by a rising number of women everywhere, every day, mothers simultaneously tending growing children and aging parents—tiptoeing through a minefield of teenage rebellion at one end and seniors grasping their independence at the other, balancing the needs of kids on bicycles and elders on walkers. Statistics show that more than one in four Canadians is a caregiver and 70 percent of baby-boomers expect to care for an older family member in the near future. Overwhelmingly, they are women. Most are working full-time. The number of Canadians over 65—roughly 3.5 million today—will have doubled by 2020. The fastest growing segment of the population is 85 and older (Gordon, 2005). This is further complicated by the fact that many children are staying at home longer adding to the "burden."

One in seven women in Canada is a visible minority. More than two million women, or 14 percent of the total female population, are members of a visible minority and they are centred largely in Toronto and Vancouver. Twenty-one percent of visible minority women aged 15 or older had a university degree, compared with 14 percent of other women. But while visible minority women are better educated on average than other Canadian

Ottawa mother Maithreyi Ramanathan grew up in south India, where she says that typically, a mother goes to her own mother's house when she is eight months pregnant and doesn't return until the baby is three or four months old. When Ramanathan was pregnant in Canada with her son Sanjay, her grandmothers were genuinely worried. "How could you do this on your own? Who is going to help you? they asked. I told them my husband would," she says. "But what good is a man's help? they asked." Her grandmothers couldn't have appreciate that in today's North America, parenting takes place in more isolated nuclear families, often far removed from extended family members and without the support of once every-present neighbours who now head off to work each day. In that context, a father's effective early involvement is arguably a necessity.

Source: Hoffman, 2005.

women, they are somewhat less likely to be employed and earn less at their jobs than do other women (Statistics Canada, 2006b). Another factor to consider in the changing role of women is the number of women from immigrant and refugee families who have settled in Canada. Far from their families and far from support systems, many of these mothers parent in isolation in a country where their language and customs are not well understood. Their traditional values and ways of parenting may be very different from those they see around them.

According to Luxton (2001: 320), "Patterns of class, race, ethnicity, national origin, region, religion, and other cultural differences shaped the ways in which different populations both were located in the labour market and related to prevailing norms and the economic and social policies that presumed specific family forms and divisions of labour." According to Brand (1994) and Carty (1994), African-Canadian women have a history of higher than average labour-force participation rates. A woman described her mother's experience as an immigrant:

She came here in the fifties, as a domestic worker. She came because she had two daughters in Jamaica and she couldn't make enough to support us. The Canadian government wouldn't let her bring us so for years she sent money home and our grandmother raised us.

THE CHANGING ROLES OF MEN

There has been an increased emphasis on the changing role of fathers, and bookstores abound with titles that support fathers in their role in the birthing process, their parenting skills, and their role in the family. Fathers' interaction within the structure of the family is based on many variables—the attitude of partners toward traditional roles, the number of people living in the home, work responsibilities, income, number and ages of the children, health of family members, and so on. Historically, fathers have been the major providers for their family. In many cultures, fathers are the decision-makers in the family and in the community, and they are often supported in this role by religious beliefs. Because status in the family and community may depend on a father's ability to provide financially for his family, the shifting reality of our economic times is altering this position for fathers. Benoit LeBlond, a father, says:

The challenge is to develop a new definition of what a father is and does, now that the role of sole breadwinner is fading. This new generation often cannot look to its own fathers for role models. My father understands that I'm spending more time with my children. He misses having been able to do that himself. But from the point of view of his generation, he has mixed feelings about my decision to work on contract in order to spend more time with my family. (Mann, 1996)

Social services and educational programs focused on working with fathers and their families are also more readily available. As women enter the workforce, share in providing for their families, and expect to play a larger role in decision-making, the role of the father has become less clear. Certain sectors of society advocate a return to traditional roles, in which fathers are in control and mothers are responsible primarily for the home and the children. Violi (1997: 6) says, "At another level, there are the doubts that many people still express about

When Sanjay was a newborn, Ramanathan's modern-thinking, Canadian-born husband, David Stone, expected and wanted to be involved in baby care. "I knew right away that I would need his help and I welcomed it," she says. Even so, at first Ramanathan found it hard to leave David alone with Sanjay even or a few minutes. "I'd say, 'I'll be downstairs'," she recalls. "But I didn't really go downstairs. I stayed right there and kept an eye on them." Our blurring of gender roles notwithstanding, most new mothers still feel, on some level, that "This is my job and can this guy do it right?" The mother gains baby care skills quickly (she has no choice) and, as her skills increase, the father, whose skill level usually develops more slowly because he gets fewer cracks at taking care of the baby, falls farther and farther behind. It's hard to find his way in. He may withdraw to avoid feeling incompetent or because he thinks his efforts are unappreciated. Mom becomes more and more indispensable and starts to resent her partner's lack of involvement. None of this, of course, is good for father attachment. Some researchers have labeled this gatekeeping. The bottom line here is that mothers and fathers need to bend a bit. Fathers need to keep trying, and mothers need to give them some space.

Source: Hoffman, 2005.

fathers having the necessary sensitivity and skills to care for children. This level includes the barriers presented by mothers themselves, many of whom have difficulty accepting the perceived loss of power and influence. They seem to struggle with the ambivalence of overtly seeking paternal involvement but covertly experiencing an encroachment on their domain of perceived power and expertise."

The biggest roadblocks to active participation in child care by fathers are still sociocultural, with regard to how fathers see themselves. Another critical factor in the role fathers will play is the mother's attitude. Many women define their status within the family and community by their ability to care for and nurture their children. These women may in fact be resistant to allowing fathers greater involvement with the children, since it may undermine their position. If extended-family members live in the home, such as grandparents who aid in the caregiving of children, the father may play a more limited role.

The past two decades have seen a shift in fathers' involvement in their children's lives and in child-care settings. Mass media often depict fathers as intimately involved in their children's lives. Fathers are struggling to balance the sometimes conflicting roles of successful breadwinner and nurturing parent. Although extensive research exists on mothers and mothering, very little research focuses on fathers, fatherhood, or single fathers. One of the few studies to pay attention to this area was funded

by the Social Sciences and Humanities Research Council of Canada (SSHRC) and undertaken by Doucet and Arnup, who interviewed about 60 fathers and 12 couples in a "qualitative look at the different experiences of stay-at-home dads, single dads, and dads who share responsibility for primary care" (Doucet and Arnup, 2001).

Studies show that fathers are conspicuously absent when it comes to spending time with very young children. A cross-cultural study undertaken in 1995 examined the lives of four-year-olds in 11 countries and found that the four-year-olds studied spent, on average, at least five of their waking hours under their mothers' supervision and less than an hour under the supervision of fathers (Evans, 1999). Evans also reports that there are no data to identify the length of time fathers need to spend with their children in order to have a positive impact.

The quality of the marital relationship is significantly associated with the nature of both the father–child and mother–child interaction. The more positive the relationship, the more involved the father is likely to be in child care and vice versa. This idea is supported by Engle and Breaux (1994) in their review of the literature. They note that the more the father cares for the child, the more he becomes involved with the child (1994: 21). Fathers who have, at times, exclusive responsibility for the child develop caregiving skills and gain confidence. It is also important to note that fathers may play different roles at different stages of their children's development.

There are many ways in which the concept of "good fathers" is interpreted, particularly across cultures. According to Pleck and Stueve (2001) the available comparisons of majority and minority racial/ethnic father-present families reveal more similarities than differences in the average level of father involvement with children. The critical variable is the father's place of residence. When minority racial/ethnic fathers reside with their children, they are just as likely to be involved in their children's lives as are Caucasian European American fathers (Fagan and Palm, 2004: 25). Religious affiliation may also play a role, a study by Wilcox (1999) revealed that religious fathers are more likely than non-religious fathers to be involved with their children in one-on-one and group activities and to praise and hug their children; they are less likely to yell at them (Fagan and Palm, 2004: 26).

Clearly, more analysis needs to be done on father involvement, cross-cultural differences, the impact of religious beliefs, and the impact of father involvement in the lives of their children.

In some work environments, fathers may take advantage of parental leave when their child is born. "It depends on who your manager is, not where you work," says Linda Duxbury, an associate professor of business at Carleton University in Ottawa (pers. comm., 1997). If the manager doesn't approve, men aren't likely to take advantage of policies intended to help them parent. Men, more than women, are seen as less good corporate citizens if they take time off for family-related events or demands. And since many top people in companies are older, traditionally-minded men—with wives at home—they may have little sympathy for a man who asks to leave work at noon because his eight-year-old has taken sick at school. Many companies talk a better game than they play. In the jargon of the day, they don't walk the talk (*Today's Parent*, 1993).

After the federal government's extension of parental benefits, fathers' participation in the program rose from 38 percent in 2001 to 55 percent in 2008 (Statistics Canada, 2008). This claim rate for fathers moves Canada ahead of many other countries, but still leaves us considerably behind those that offer fathers non-transferable leave. In Norway, for example, almost 80 percent of fathers take parental leave (Marshall, 2003). Women who return to work after maternity leave undergo far more stress than men who take similar time off. In

Many fathers play an active role in their children's lives.

fact, 62 percent of mothers reported that the transition between leave and work was stressful and 20 percent described it as very stressful. Sixty-five percent of fathers rated the transition as not too stressful or not stressful at all. The data shows that nearly half of the parents cited balancing job and family responsibilities as the main source of stress associated with their return to work (Statistics Canada, 2008).

Duxbury also says, "They used to say that as women entered the workforce and there were more dual-earner families, women would become more like men." However, Glossop and Theilheimer (1999) observe that the opposite has occurred: "Men are becoming more like women: stressed out, suffering the same kind of overload, the same kind of interference patterns between work and family as women traditionally have."

With the high incidence of divorce, many fathers are estranged from their children. York University sociologist Anne-Marie Ambert blames the absentee-father syndrome on continuing conflict between the parents; fathers who can't or won't pay support; and children who, as they get older, don't want to give up their social lives to be with dad on the weekend. Starting a second family or becoming attached to their new wife's children may result in less affection for the children from

Anne Gauthier, from the University of Calgary, has conducted a study that analyzed the 24-hour diaries of parents from eight different countries. The study found that preschoolers in Canada can count on an extra hour of undivided attention from their parents each day, compared with what their mums and dads received from their own parents 30 years ago. In fact, Canadian dads are leading the Western world in story-book readings, bedtime duty, and general playtime ahead of fathers in the United States, Norway, Sweden, Germany, Australia, Finland, and Italy. To squeeze in the extra hour with their children, Canadian parents are giving up on sleep, TV viewing, and tidy homes. For mothers, the extra time with children was financed almost entirely by a decline in housework. Fathers partly compensated by doing 36 more minutes of household chores a day than they did in the past. Fathers and mothers are almost tied when it comes to reading and playing. But mothers remain the main providers of infant care and of children's personal care.

Source: Anderssen and McIlroy, 2004: A1.

the original family, and they resent having to support two families. Half of all fathers don't pay any court-ordered child support, and another one-quarter pay only part of it. Poorer fathers are the least likely to pay and also the most likely not to see their kids. (Carey, 1999)

On the other hand, some fathers may in fact see more of their children and take on more child-related responsibilities than they did when they were living with their partner.

Concerns about absent fathers through divorce, separation, never-married, or incarcerated fathers continue to rise. Seventy-nine percent of the American public agreed with the statement "the most significant family problem in America is the physical absence of the father from the home." In a U.S. study, 41 percent of nonresident fathers talk to their children several times a year or less, 20 percent talk to their children several times per week, and more than two-thirds of fathers never have their children stay overnight with them (Stewart, 1999). Never-married fathers are even less likely than divorced or separated fathers to spend time with their children (Marsiglio et al., 2000). Scholars involved in the study of fathers have suggested that the connections between men and children have become very complicated. On one hand there is growing pressure on fathers residing with their children to be actively involved in the care and rearing of offspring. On the other hand, fathers are increasingly less likely to live with their biological children, and they are more likely to live with other children (i.e., children of their current partner). It is perhaps the very fact that the connection between

Healthy Images / Public Health Agency of Canada

Some fathers decide to work at home in order to spend more time with their children.

men and children has become so complicated that has resulted in growing interest in fathers (Fagan and Palm, 2004: 5–6).

Fathers Helping Fathers

Herman Goodden writes in the *London Free Press* (London, Ontario) about a group called Fathers Helping Fathers. With about 200 members, this group meets twice a month. There is no agenda—whatever issues turn up on a given night are the issues that get discussed. The group offers a chance for ex-husbands (who too often find themselves cast in the role of ex-dads as well) an opportunity to "unload," as they call it, to share experiences and suggest strategies that might improve their situations. A family lawyer offers free legal advice on questions and issues that the group brings forward. Routinely hashed out at each meeting are the heartbreaking plights of men struggling under the double whammy of daunting custody payments and limited or no access to their kids. This group also assists grandparents, aunts and uncles, and cousins who suddenly find themselves cut out of children's lives.

Dads Can

Dr. Neil Campbell, assistant professor in the Departments of Family Medicine and Psychiatry at the University of Western Ontario, is an expert on fatherhood, prenatal dads, expectant fathers, and first-time fathers. He is also executive director of Dads Can (**www.dadscan.ca**), an organization that promotes responsible and involved fathering. He explains that the role of fathers has changed a great deal over the past several decades. The father is no longer seen only as the provider. A more responsible, involved fathering model is emerging along with an awareness of the importance of "fatherneed" and "fathercare." This new fatherhood means a man must come to understand his sense of intimacy, identity, and integrity and embrace these qualities.

BOOKS FOR ADULTS

Dads Under Construction, by Neil Campbell
(See Chapter 5 for more resources for fathers)

MATERNITY AND PARENTAL LEAVE

Amendments to the Employment Insurance Act in December 2000 increased parental leave benefits from 10 weeks to 35 weeks, effectively increasing the total maternity and parental paid leave time from six months to one year. In addition, the threshold for eligibility was lowered from 700 to 600 hours of insurable employment. The 35 weeks of benefits can be taken by one qualifying parent, or split between both qualifying parents, with only one waiting period required between them. The benefit entitlement remains at 55 percent of average insured earnings, up to a maximum of $413 per week. The proportion of all new mothers receiving maternity or parental benefits increased from 54 percent in 2000 to 61 percent in 2001. Science now provides us with valuable information about the healthy development of young children. International research demonstrates the critical impact of the early years on every facet of later life. This development is dramatically influenced by the supports,

challenges, and risks connected to family, school, and community life. The impact of pregnancy, birth, and the early years will have a long term impact on the life of a child. How can we support families in their efforts to raise children who will realize their potential?

BRAIN RESEARCH AND THE EARLY YEARS STUDY: IMPLICATIONS FOR PARENTS

The release of the *Early Years Study* in April 1999, co-chaired by the Honourable Margaret Norrie McCain and J. Fraser Mustard, provided options and recommendations with respect to the best ways to prepare young children—including those at risk or with special needs—for scholastic, career, and social success. Research on brain development has affected families and teachers in their effort to understand its implications on their day-to-day lives with children. Fraser Mustard states that "it is now understood not only that the environment affects how the brain cells are wired, but that these effects are long-lasting and that stress on early brain development has a measurable negative impact" (McCain and Mustard, 1999: 17).

Marie Goulet, a faculty member in the School of Early Childhood at George Brown College, contributes the following information about the importance of brain development and the role of parents and educators:

> The brain is the master control of our health and well-being, competencies and coping skills. It directs all aspects of bodily functions through established biological pathways. We have long accepted the involvement of the brain in intellectual pursuits. We now know that there is a clear physiological basis that links stressful circumstances and increased vulnerability to disease. (Bertrand: 2001)

Brains are central to health, learning, and coping, and families are central to the environments that support brain growth.

Parents' genes make a major contribution to who we become. Most researchers estimate that genetic inheritance accounts for about 50 percent of that outcome, leaving 50 percent to be influenced by life's experience. The brain integrates genetic and environmental influences. We now know that genes are not blueprints that create destiny. Genes have chemical switches that control how, when, and if that gene is expressed. A variety of environmental factors influence these switches. Parents play a significant role in passing on genes and in the expression of genes, beginning in the womb. The womb can be a child's most powerful environment. The mother's health, nutrition, exposure to toxins, and emotional well-being are important to brain development. The womb is naturally stimulating, providing the fetus with the sensory stimulation it requires. The fetus's brain is protected when maternal stress is low. This keeps cortisol, the stress hormone, at safe levels that will not interfere with brain development in utero.

The unborn child's brain development is also protected when the mother's environment is free of contaminates like lead. "Between about four months in utero and two years after birth, babies' brains are exquisitely sensitive to the quantity and quality of nutrients consumed" (Eliot, 1999: 445). "The World Health Organization and the Canadian Pediatric Society recommend breast-feeding into the second year of life" (Canadian Child Care Federation, 2001). A diet made for brain development during those years consists of breast milk, protein, dairy products, grains, and fresh vegetables and fruits.

Touching also plays an essential role in brain growth. Physical affection produces oxytocin, which is an antidote to cortisol. In infancy, touching and physical affection not only protect the child from stress, they are the means by which infants orient to and learn from visual and auditory stimulation. Parental warmth and affection continue to contribute to intellectual and emotional well-being throughout the early years and into adolescence.

Responsiveness is also important from birth. Responsiveness means responding to the child's physical needs, and his or her needs for stimulation and for social interaction. Responsiveness requires parents to recognize that each child is unique. This means that they determine their child's individual needs. Uniqueness includes a child's preference for stimulation. Individuals have preferences for the type and amount of stimulation they experience. Young children require adults who help manage stimulation so that children do not become over-whelmed. Responsive parents protect their children from over-stimulation and they aid in recovery when children are overwhelmed. This protection and responsiveness strengthen brain structures involved in self-regulation and coping. When parents are sensitive to their child's signals and respond predictably, they support the child's

Children deserve the best start in life.

competence and security. Security produces the brain's chemical balance that supports learning and coping. Secure children are free to explore and their repeated explorations strengthen brain connections.

When parents and children are involved in one-on-one play where the parent and child focus attention on the same activity and have fun, the conditions are right for learning, concentrating, and coping. Joint attention and fun experienced in the child's most important relationship ensure that learning will persist and that the brain chemicals required to turn short-term memories into long-term learning are present. In the warmth of the relationship, parents provide appropriate challenges that a brain requires for learning. Parents do not provide the answers. They help the child figure out what to do to reach the challenge. This ensures that the child's brain is active. The more the child thinks then the better he or she becomes at thinking.

Parents' genetic gifts, the provision of a healthy environment (from conception), and their responsive relationships with their children play important roles in their children's brain development. These positive family factors produce brains that are ready for life—brains that are central to good health, learning, emotional well-being, competence, and coping.

WHAT DO WE NEED?

Families are constantly changing and realigning themselves. An event, whether it is happy or devastating, will shift and alter the relationships among family members. It is critical for Early Childhood Education (ECE) students to recognize that they will not be able to use their own family experience as the "norm" for other families. The ability to suspend judgment and to be open to learning about how other families care and plan for their children is critical to positive teacher–family relationships. Teachers in child care have much to learn from the families they meet. Each family has its own history and, if teachers build trusting relationships, they may be fortunate enough to have the family share that history with them.

Paul Steinhauer (1998: 14–16) says:

> [A]ll the services in the world by themselves are not what this nation needs. We need changes in six main areas of society if we are going to bring up a healthier, more productive, competent generation of children. We need changes in our families, businesses, communities and mainstream services, such as child-care centres and schools. We also need changes in our specialized services; we need to get more of the highly specialized professionals out of their own clinics and hospitals and into areas in the community where children are actually present. We also need changes in government. When it comes to families, we need to get more fathers involved in parenting when their children of either sex are young. . . . Every study we have seen shows that when both parents are working, as in most families today, the bulk of the housework and the bulk of parenting fall on the mothers. Never have parents spent as little time with their children as they do today. So if we are going to increase parenting time, we are not going to do so by putting more stress on mothers. We need to get fathers more involved with their children. We have to do something about the workplace. We need more family-oriented workplaces. . . . Somehow we have to get across to our friends, colleagues, relatives and neighbours in the business community that there is more than just the bottom line. . . . Now governments notice children and even talk about them. We have to get to the point where governments do not just talk about doing what is right for children, but will give it the highest priority. We must get informed and stand up in community meetings at all levels and make contact with elected politicians on a regular basis—to let them know that there is a community of people out there who care just as much about what is happening to the nation's children as what is happening to the nation's economy. They are both important, but our children should be our nation's most important interest.

ANSWERS TO EXHIBIT 1.1 FAMILIES IN CANADA: A QUIZ

1. Toronto
2. 43.5 percent
3. 71 percent
4. 14 percent
5. 19.9 percent
6. 45,345 (7,465 are legally married)
7. True
8. 29.7 years
9. 200
10. Winnipeg

REFERENCES

Adamson, N., L. Briskin, and M. McPhail. 1988. *Feminist Organizing for Change: The Contemporary Women's Movement in Canada*. Toronto: Oxford University Press.

Alvi, S. 1994. *The Work and Family Challenge: Issues and Options*. Ottawa: Canada Committee for the International Year of the Family, the Conference Board of Canada.

Anderssen, E., and A. McIlroy. 2007. "Canada's Dads Are the Best." *Globe and Mail*. April 3. A1.

Angelini, P.U. 2007. *Our Society. Human Diversity in Canada*, 3rd ed. Toronto: Thomson Nelson.

Baker, M. 2001. *Families: Changing Trends in Canada*, 4th ed. Toronto: McGraw-Hill Ryerson.

Baxter, S. 1993. *A Child Is Not a Toy: Voices of Children in Poverty*. Vancouver: New Star Press.

Belanger, A., and G. Ouellet. 2002. "A Comparative Study of Recent Trends in Canadian and American Fertility, 1980–1999." In A. Belanger, ed., *Report on the Demographic Situation in Canada 2001: Current Demographic Analysis*. Catalogue no. 91-209-XPE. Ottawa: Ministry of Industry, Statistics Canada.

Bertrand, J. 2001. *Children's Developmental Health: Nourish, Nurture and Neurodevelopment*. Ottawa: Canadian Child Care Federation.

Bibby, R. 2004. "The Future Families Project: A Survey of Canadian Hopes and Dreams." Ottawa: Vanier Institute of the Family. Available at http://www.vifamily.ca.

Blakenhorn, D., S. Bayme, and J. Bethke Elshtain, eds. 1990. *Rebuilding the Nest: A New Commitment to the American Family*. New York: Institute of American Values.

Brand, D. 1994. "'We Weren't Allowed To Go Into Factory Work Until Hitler Started the War': The 1920s to the 1940s." In P. Bristow et al., eds., *We're Rooted Here and They Can't Pull Us Up: Essays in African Canadian Women's History*. Toronto: University of Toronto Press.

Bronfenbrenner, U. 1974. "Is Early Intervention Effective?" *Teachers College Record* 76 (2): 279–303.

———. 1979. *The Ecology of Human Development*. Cambridge, MA: Harvard University Press.

———. 1990. *The Ecology of Human Development: Experiments by Nature and Design*. Cambridge, MA: Harvard University Press.

Brooks, J.B. 1998. *Parenting*, 2nd ed. Toronto: Mayfield Publishing.

Bubolz, M.M., and S. Sontag. 1993. "Human Ecology Theory." In P.G. Boss, W.J. Doherty, R. LaRossa, W.R. Schumm, and S.K. Steinmetz, eds., *Sourcebook of Family Theories and Methods: A Contextual Approach*. New York: Plenum Press.

Campaign 2000. 2001. *Child Poverty in Canada: Report Card 2000*. Toronto: Campaign 2000.

———. 2003. "Higher Child Benefits Needed to Counter Persistent Poverty." Available at http://action.web.ca/home/c2000.

Canadian Centre for Policy Alternatives. 2007. "No New Year's Hangover For Top CEO's." January 2. Available at http://www.policyalternatives.ca/index.cfm?act=news&call=1523&pa=BB736455&do=Article.

Canadian Child Care Federation. 2001. Supporting Breastfeeding in Child Care. Resource Sheet, Spring #57.

Canadian Council on Social Development. 1999. *The Progress of Canada's Children into the Millennium*. Ottawa: Health Canada.

———. 2003. "March 10 Census Release Summary: Education in Canada and the Earning of Canadians, 2003." Ottawa: Canadian Council on Social Development.

———. 2006. "The Progress of Canada's Children and Youth." *Family Life*. Ottawa: Health Canada.

Canadian Press. 2008. "Minorities Top 5 Million." *24 Hours*. April 3. 10.

Carey, E. 1998. "Good Kids Have Caring Parents, Study Says." *Toronto Star*. 29 October: A2.

———. 1999. "The Damage Done When Father Quits the Family." *The Toronto Star*. 29 June: E1.

Carty, L. 1994. "African Canadian Women and the State: Labour Only, Please." In P. Bristow et al., eds., *We're Rooted Here and They Can't Pull Us Up: Essays in African Canadian Women's History*. Toronto: University of Toronto Press.

Clark, Warren. 2006. "Interreligious Unions in Canada." *Canadian Social Trends*. Catalogue no. 82 (11-008-XWE). Available at http://www.statcan.ca/english/freepub/11-008-XIE/ 2006003/main_interreligious.htm#study.

Cohen, T. 2008. "Visible Minorities Hit 5 Million." *The Toronto Star*. April 2.

Daly, K. 2000. "It Keeps Getting Faster: Changing Patterns of Time in Families." Ottawa: Vanier Institute of the Family. Available at http://www.vifamily.ca/library/cft/faster.html.

DeMara, B. 1998. "Births up among Homeless Women." *The Toronto Star*. 28 July. B3.

Desjardins Financial Security Survey on Canadian Attitudes towards Physical and Mental Health at Work and Home. 2008. "Researcher SOM." *Macleans*. May 26.

de Wolff, A. 1994. *Strategies for Working Families*. Toronto: Ontario Coalition for Better Child Care.

Dhruvarajan, V. 1993. "Ethnic Cultural Retention and Transmission among First Generation Hindu Asian Native Canadians in a Canadian Prairie City." *Journal of Comparative Family Studies* 224 (1): 63–80.

Doucet, A., and K. Arnup. 2001. "Research Works at Carleton University." Available at http://www.carleton.ca/cu/research/spring2001/article4.html.

Dunnewind, S. 2003. "Tag-team Parenting Involves Tricky Moves." *The Toronto Star*. 8 February.

Duxbury, L., C. Higgins, and D. Coghill. 2003. *Voices of Canadians: Seeking Work–Life Balance*. Ottawa: Human Resources Development Canada.

Eichler, M. 1997. *Family Shifts: Families, Policies, and Gender Equality*. Toronto: Oxford University Press.

Eliot, L. 1999. *What's Going on in There? How the Brain and Mind Develop in the First Five Years of Life*. New York: Bantam Books.

Elkind, D. 1981. *The Hurried Child: Growing Up Too Fast Too Soon*. Reading, MA: Addison-Wesley Publishing Company.

Engle, P.L., and C. Breaux. 1994. "Is There a Father Instinct? Fathers' Responsibility for Children." Paper prepared as part of the project Family Structure, Female Headship and Maintenance of Families and Poverty. Population Council and the International Centre for Research on Women, Ottawa.

Erkel, R.T. 1995. "Time Shifting." *Family Therapy Networker* 19, 33–39.

Evans, J.L. 1999. "Men in the Lives of Children." Available at http:///www.ecdgroup.com/cn/cn16lead.html.

Fagan, J., and G. Palm. 2004. *Fathers and Early Childhood Programs*. New York: Thomson Delmar Learning.

Ford Kirk, J. 2007. "Immigrant Trends." *Toronto Star*. September 8. B9.

Galinsky, E. 1987. *The Six Stages of Parenthood*. Reading, MA: Addison-Wesley.

Globe and Mail. 1999. "Family Matters." September 11. A7.

Glossop, R., and I. Theilheimer. 1999. "Does Society Support Involved Fathering?" Available at http://www.cfc-efc.ca/docs/00000003.htm.

Goldner, V. 1993. "Feminist Theories." In P.G. Boss and J. William, eds., *Sourcebook of Family Theories and Methods: A Contextual Approach*. New York: Plenum Press.

Goodden, H. 2001. "Fathers' Group Takes Family Approach." *London Free Press*. 1 March.

Gordon, A. 2005. "Raising Expectations. Phases of Motherhood, Part 3." *The Toronto Star*. March 26. L4.

Grewal, S. 2007. "The Stronger Sex." *The Toronto Star*. November 3.

Hepworth Berger, E. 2000. *Parents as Partners in Education*. Columbus, Ohio: Merrill.

Hoffman, J. 2005. "When Dads And Babies Build A Strong Relationship, Everybody Wins." *Today's Parent*. April.

Hughes, K. 1999. *Gender and Self-employment in Canada: Assessing Trends and Policy Implications*. Ottawa: Canadian Policy Research Networks.

Johnson, K.L., D.S. Lero, and J.A. Rooney. 2001. *Work–Life Compendium 2001*. Centre for Families, Work and Well-Being. Guelph, ON: University of Guelph, Human Resources Development Canada.

Kagan, S.L., and P.R. Neville. 1994. "Parent Choice in Early Care and Education: Myth or Reality?" *Research and Clinical Issues, Zero to Three* 14 (4). February–March.

Kazemipur, A., and S.S. Halli. 1997. "Plight of Immigrants: The Spatial Concentration of Poverty in Canada." *Canadian Journal of Regional Science* 20 (1/2): 29–48.

Kirby, J. 2007. "Is It A Bubble? Is It About To Burst?" *Macleans*. December 19.

Larson, L.E., W.J. Goltz, and B.E. Munro. 2000. *Families in Canada: Social Contexts, Continuities, and Changes*, 2nd ed. Toronto: Prentice Hall Allyn and Bacon Canada.

Lero, D.S. 2003. "Dual-Earner Families." In M. Lynn, ed., *Voices: Essays on Canadian Families*, 2nd ed. Toronto: Thomson Nelson Learning.

Lister, T. 1999. "Businesses Save Money by Promoting Work–Family Balance." Available at http://www.pwcglobal.com/extweb/manissue.nsf.

Luxton, M. 2001. "Family Coping Strategies: Balancing Paid Employment and Domestic Labour." In B. Fox, ed., *Family Patterns: Gender Relations*, 2nd ed. New York: Oxford Press.

Mandell, N. 1992. "Children, Poverty and Schooling." *Canadian Woman Studies* 12 (3): 26–27.

Mann, B. 1996. "New Times, New Fathers." Available at http://www.ottawamenscentre.com/news/19960807_new_fathers.htm.

Marshall, K. 2003. "Benefiting from Extended Parental Leave." *The Daily*. 21 March. Available at http://www.statcan.ca/Daily/English/030321/d030321b.htm.

Marsiglio, W., P. Amato, R.D. Day, and M.E. Lamb. 2000. "Scholarship on Fatherhood in the 1990s and Beyond." *Journal of Marriage and the Family* 62: 1173–1191.

McCain, M.N., and J. F. Mustard. 1999. *Early Years Study: Final Report*. April. Toronto: Children's Secretariat. Available at http://www.childsec.gov.on.ca.

Monsebraaten, L., and L. Whittington. 2007. "Politicians Challenged to Combat Child Poverty." *The Toronto Star*. September 12: A1.

National Council of Welfare. 2003. "Welfare Incomes 2002." Spring. Available at http://www.childcarecanada.org/policy/polstudies/can/NCW_welfare02.html.

Perry, A. 2003. "Long-term Effects of Part-Time Hours: Study Finds Women Bear Costs in Job Quality—Fewer Promotion, Supervisory Roles and Lower Wages." *The Toronto Star*. 5 July.

Philip, M. 2003. "Tallying the Homeless in Canada." *The Globe and Mail*. 6 November.

Report Card on Child Poverty in Canada 1989–1999. 1999. Toronto: Campaign 2000.

Riedman, A., M.A. Lamanna, and A. Nelson. 2003. *Marriages and Families*. Toronto: Thomson Nelson.

Rosenberg, H. 2001. "Motherwork, Stress, and Depression: The Costs of Privatized Social Reproduction." In B. Fox, ed., *Family Patterns: Gender Relations*, 2nd ed. New York: Oxford Press.

Ross, K.G. 1979. *Good Day Care: Fighting for It, Getting It, Keeping It*. Toronto: The Women's Press.

Samovar, L.A., R.E. Porter, and E.R. McDaniel. 2007. *Communication Between Cultures*, 6th ed. New York: Thomson Wadsworth.

Sarick, L. 1999. "Hardship, Uncertainty Mark Life in Shelters." *The Globe and Mail*. 16 October.

Schulman, H. 2003. "My Mother's Ring: Caught Between Two Families." In C. Hanauer, ed., *The Bitch in the House: 26 Women Tell the Truth about Sex, Solitude, Work, Motherhood, and Marriage*. New York: HarperCollins.

Second Harvest. N.d. Available at http://www.secondharvest.ca.

Siddiqui, H. 2008. "The Latest Canadian Portrait." *The Toronto Star*. April 3.

Stewart, S.D. 1999. "Nonresident mothers' and fathers' social contact with children." *Journal of Marriage and the Family* 61: 894–907.

Statistics Canada. 1999. *Characteristics of Dual-earner Families, 1997*. Catalogue no. 13-213. Ottawa: Minister of Industry.

———. 2001. "Census Families in Private Households by Family Structure, Presence of Children and Labour Force Activity of Husband/Male Common-law Partner, Showing Labour Force Activity of Wife/Female Common-law Partner or Lone Parent, for Canada, Provinces and Territories, 1996 Census." Available at http://www.statcan.ca/english/census96/june9/econ2.htm

———. 2003a. "February 11 Census Release Labour Market Data Show Critical Skills Shortage and Skills Going Unused." Ottawa: Canadian Council on Social Development.

———. 2003b. "Part-time Work and Family-Friendly Practices." *The Daily*. June 26. Available at http://www.statcan.ca/Daily/English/030626/d030626g.htm.

———. 2003c. "Sources of Workplace Stress." *The Daily*. June 25. Available at http://www.statcan.ca/Daily/English/030625/d030625c.htm.

———. 2003d. "Overview: Canada Still Predominantly Roman Catholic and Protestant." Available at http://www.12statcan.ca/english/census01/Products/Analytic/companion/rel/canada.cfm.

———. 2006a. "Minority Distribution: Count, percentage, distribution and relative ratio of visible minority population by census metropolitan areas, 2006." Available at http://www12.statcan.ca/English/census06/analysis/ethnicorigin/tables/table2.htm.

———. 2006b. "Women in Canada." *The Daily*. March 7. Available at http://www.statcan.ca/Daily/English/060307/d060307a.htm.

———. 2006c. "General Social Survey: Paid and Unpaid Work." *The Daily*. July 19. Available at http://www.statcan.ca/Daily/English/060719/d060719b.htm.

———. 2007. Census Families in Private Households by Family Structure and Presence of Children, by Province and Territory, 2006 Census." Available at http://www40.statcan.ca/l01/cst01/famil54a.htm.

———. 2008. "Labour Productivity, Hourly Compensation and Unit Labour Cost." *The Daily*. June 13. Available at http://www.statcan.ca/Daily/English/080613/d080613b.htm.

Steinhauer, P. 1998. "How a Child's Early Experiences Affect Development." Paper presented at Linking Research to Practice: A Canadian Forum, Banff, Alberta, 25–27 October.

Swerdlow, A., R. Bridenthal, J. Kelly, and P. Vine. 1989. *Families in Flux*. New York: Feminist Press.

The Toronto Star. 2007. "Editorial." May 7. A14.

Today's Parent. 1993. "From Boardroom to Playgroup." June.

Vanier Institute of the Family. 1994. *Profiling Canada's Families*. Ottawa: Vanier Institute of the Family.

Violi, D. 1997. "Fathering Futures: Fathers, Fathering and the Way Ahead." Available at http://members.ozemail.com.au/~dviolo/fathers.htm.

Ward, M. 1998. *The Family Dynamic: A Canadian Perspective*, 2nd ed. Toronto: ITP Nelson.

Wilcox, W.B. 1999. "Emerging Attitudes About Gender Roles and Fatherhood." In D. Eberly, ed., *The Faith Factor in American Fatherhood: What America's Faith Communities Can Do To Restore Fatherhood*. Lanham, MD: Lexington Books.

Wood, O. 2002. "Counting an Invisible Population: Why Coming up with Statistics on the Homeless Is So Difficult." *CBC News*. 10 November. Available at http://www.cbc.ca/news/indepth/background/homeless.html.

Courtesy of Lynn Wilson

CHAPTER 2

Supports to Children and Families

"*I implore you to see with a child's eyes, to hear with a child's ears, and to feel with a child's heart.*"

—*Antonio Novello*

LEARNING OUTCOMES

After studying this chapter, you will be able to

1. analyze the effects of the changing family on the child-care community

2. evaluate the benefits of universal quality child care for children and their families

3. discuss ways in which employers and governments can support families

4. discuss the role of teachers in a wide range of services to families

5. evaluate the range of services from which families can choose and the ways in which children, family members, and teachers can benefit from them

It is not possible in the context of this book to capture all the inventive, responsive programs that have been put in place to support children and their families. The following information provides an overview of child care in Canada and highlights a variety of different programs and initiatives.

THE FIELD OF EARLY CHILDHOOD EDUCATION IN CANADA

Child care in Canada consists of a patchwork of services, established in an ad hoc manner by non-profit organizations, parent groups, commercial operators, employers, and, to a limited degree, local municipalities. Provincial and territorial governments have jurisdictional authority for child care; they are responsible for setting licensing standards and operational regulations for group-care facilities for children and for controlling the supply of and funding to these programs. Regulated child-care programs include full- and part-day programs in child-care centres and nursery schools, supervised home-based programs, and before- and after-school programs for school-age children; there is no central organization at any level of government. There is no significant support for families who struggle to pay high fees for child care or for those families who make the decision to have a parent stay at home with their children. More than 30 years after women started to enter the workforce in increasing numbers, we still do not have a comprehensive child-care program in place. The research is in place, it is time to act!

IS CHILD CARE A GOOD CHOICE FOR CHILDREN, FAMILIES, AND CANADA?

Perhaps the first question we should be asking is "What policies need to be in place to support families in Canada?" As Taylor (2006) states,

> What we don't have in 2006 is a clear commitment to young children in the form of a comprehensive family policy. At the federal level, there is the extended maternity and parental leave, the $5,000 Child Tax Benefit for all families with children, a maximum $7,000 per child tax deduction for those paying child-care expenses and additional benefits targeted at the poorest families—all of which critics say must be increased significantly. There is

some funding for child care, but it doesn't nearly approach the need. There is no baby bonus, no way to give parents who choose to stay home a significant financial acknowledgement for their sacrifice.

Canadians are often subject to the whims of elected governments. The Conservative government gave families $1,200 for each child under the age of six and initiated incentives for businesses to create work place child-care spaces; however, this does little to address the pressing issues facing the child-care sector. From 1992 and 2006, the number of child-care spaces in Quebec rose by more than 280,000 while in the rest of the country only 78,000 new spaces were created. Only part of this is because of the creation of entirely new child-care spaces; the population of children under 12 is shrinking, thus freeing up more spots. The number of children under the age of five with mothers in the labour force declined from 1.4 million in 1992 to 1.2 million in 2005. During the same period, the number of 6-to-12-year-olds with working mothers rose from 1.5 million to 1.8 million (Hoffman, 2008).

The research evidence is clear: the foundations for good adult physical health, social competence, communication skills, adaptability, literacy, and numeracy are laid down before entry into kindergarten (McCain, Mustard, and Shanker, 2007). Children who experience high-quality early learning and care develop better social skills, have fewer behavioural problems, and score higher on achievement and language tests than children who experience low- or mediocre-quality care. High-quality early learning and care is particularly important for children living in poverty, children with special needs, new Canadians, and children in minority communities: it gives them opportunities to develop the foundational knowledge and skills, resilience, and emotional maturity they need to succeed in school and society. High-quality care is equally important for children from stable, advantaged families who experience negative effects if the programs do not provide responsive, stimulating environments. The quality of early learning and care services depends on four key factors:

- effective policies, funding, and infrastructure;
- knowledgeable, committed practitioners with post-secondary education in early childhood development who are appropriately compensated for their work;

- well designed programs with the capacity to meet the needs of all children; and
- strong partnerships with parents. (Report of the Expert Panel on Quality and Human Resources, 2007).

Cleveland and Krashinsky (1998), in their economic study of child care, conclude that for every dollar invested in high-quality child care, there is a two-dollar benefit to children, parents, and society. This traditional economic cost–benefits analysis concludes that:

- public spending for high-quality child care is a good investment for Canada;
- high-quality early childhood care and education has long-lasting effects on all children's social, intellectual, and emotional development, regardless of socioeconomic background or mother's workforce participation;
- high-quality child care provides not only private benefits for children and parents but public benefits for society at large;
- the public benefit comes from the future effects of enhanced child development (higher school performance, high-school completion and income) and mothers' work-force participation;
- development is enhanced only if child care is good quality; and
- high-quality child care is not likely to be produced through the free-market approach to child care currently employed in Canada. (Cleveland and Krashinsky, 1998).

Cleveland and Krashinsky (2003) further state that research using the National Longitudinal Study of Children and Youth in Canada (Willms, 2002) finds that parents are far and away the biggest influence in their child's development. Studies associated with the National Institute of Child Health and Human Development (NICHD) have also found that parents matter more than anything else. The review sponsored by the National Research Council and the Institute of Medicine (Shankoff and Phillips, 2000: 235) surveys the evidence that non-parental care does not undermine a child's primary relationships. Healthy, well-functioning families are the key to healthy, well-functioning, happy children. Good child care is a necessary support to parents which allows them to work or go to school, and which allows families to function well at the same time (Cleveland and Krashinsky, 2003:

51–52). Clearly, this information presents a strong case for a government agenda that addresses the child-care needs of families in Canada.

In 2003, David Dodge, as governor of the Bank of Canada, advocated for early childhood development. The biggest "bang for the buck," he concludes, is early childhood development. Dodge is not the first, though, to recognize the importance of investing in early childhood development. James Heckman, the University of Chicago economist who shared the Nobel Prize in economics in 2000, is another. Likewise, both The World Bank and the Inter-American Development Bank also recognize the critical role of early childhood development. But Dodge's support for such initiatives is important, given his economic expertise and experience and the high regard in which he is held by Canadians (Crane, 2003).

Surveys conducted over the years demonstrate Canadians' concern for a comprehensive approach to child care. One such study shows the increasingly growing support: 90 percent of Canadians say they strongly agree (51 percent) or agree (39 percent) with the statement "Canada should have a nationally coordinated child-care plan." And 86 percent strongly agree (32 percent) or agree (54 percent) that "there can be a publicly funded child-care system that makes quality child care available to all Canadian children" (Child Care Advocacy Association of Canada, 2003).

Children who are in child care and other early childhood programs have a head start in school compared to those who stay at home with a parent, according to the National Longitudinal Study of Children and Youth (NLSCY), a ground-breaking Statistics Canada study that is tracking nearly 20,000 Canadian children from birth to 13 years. By the time they get to kindergarten, the children who were in early childhood programs have better communication, learning, and math skills, regardless of family income or their mother's education level, according to Statistics Canada. Thirty-nine percent of Canadian children between the ages of two and three—about 192,000 youngsters—attended some form of early childhood care and education in 1994–95, when the study began. Programs included daycare, nursery school, and playgroups. About 40 percent of the children, once they began kindergarten two years later, were judged by their teachers to be at the top of their class in communication and learning skills, compared with just one-quarter, who did not take part in the earlier programs.

Children benefit from a quality child-care setting with responsive teachers.

Kerry McCuaig, executive coordinator of the Child Care Education Foundation, states in the NLSCY that the federal study is the fourth since 1986 to show that early childhood care and development are a wise investment. The Statistics Canada study found mothers who have completed high school or higher are more likely to enroll their children in early childhood programs. Children whose mothers hold a post-secondary diploma or degree are nearly twice as likely to have their children in such programs, compared with those whose mothers did not finish high school. Moreover, children from households whose total income is $40,000 or more are three times more likely to attend early childhood programs than those from households with incomes under $20,000 (Carey, 1999: A1, A30).

Keating (2000) states that, in a truly integrated system, at-risk children will have earlier intervention. We know that, currently, one in four to one in five children has an identifiable learning, behavioural, or emotional disorder. Getting to those early-intervention services in a timely fashion will dramatically reduce later negative effects across the board—substandard

performance in school, behavioural disorders, and emotional disorders.

In the Early Years Study (1999), conducted in Ontario under Fraser Mustard and McCain, the authors found that child care and other early child development opportunities are important in the development of a child's brain. They made two key recommendations: (1) that learning in the early years are based on high-quality and developmentally attuned interactions with primary caregivers, and (2) that children are given opportunities for play-based problem-solving with other children. They also recommend that parents be a key part of early child development programs (1999: 48). Mustard and his Founders' Network compared children's readiness for kindergarten and standardized test results in Grades 3 and 6. They have concluded that children who lag behind early on will generally remain behind, even years later. Mustard says the study helps explain why overall results on standardized tests in reading, writing, and math have stalled, despite the millions of dollars invested into remedial programs. That investment should be made earlier, he argues, in programs aimed at early childhood development: "If the evidence is

The NLSCY (National Longitudinal Survey of Children and Youth, a joint project of Human Resources Development Canada and Statistics Canada) data tells us most kids are doing okay. That's good news, but we could make it much easier for families. During the Early Years Study we were confronted by the array of services—child care, drop-in play groups, nursery schools, kindergarten, head start, family resource and parenting centres, among others. It may sound as if the field is covered but, in fact, we were witnessing the fallout of inadequate public policy—a scattering of disconnected, poorly resourced programs. Few parents know what services exist or what they do. The quality of parenting is paramount for children but parents are under a great deal of pressure. We add to their stress and guilt by loading them with information and then abandoning them to the hunt for quality child care. What parent of a young child doesn't need help? It is difficult for an individual parent to replicate the stimulation provided by a good-quality child-development program. For example, how many would consider that mucking around in goop is a great sensory experience for a toddler? Or who is prepared to cover their floor in paper every day so a child doesn't have to focus on "being careful" as she develops her fine motor skills with paint and markers? Mothers are in the work force—over 60 percent will return to work by the time their child is three—and there are plenty of economic, social, and political reasons to support their participation. There is also ample brain research indicating we should be very concerned about the nonparental care their children receive. Now we have to wait for governments to catch up.

Source: Bertrand, 2008: 4.

that trajectories are set early in life, the possibility of substantially changing a child's academic performance is limited no matter what investments are made in the school system" (Mustard, in Rushowy, 2004).

Fraser Mustard's latest report, *Early Years Study 2: Putting Science Into Action* (Mustard, McCain, and Shanker, 2007), shows Canada ranked dead last among developed nations (OECD countries, such as Europe, the United States, Australia, New Zealand, Japan, and Mexico) in its spending on early childhood education despite overwhelming evidence of how crucial the first six years of life are. Canada spends 0.1 percent of its GDP on early childhood education, an amount which is almost half of the average spent by other OECD countries. One problem is the country-wide "chaotic mess" of programs and assistance that exists. To replace it, Mustard proposes a system of community hubs—ideally located in schools—that would offer play-based preschool activities, help for parents, social service referrals, and child care. In Ontario alone, Mustard estimates the cost of behavioural and mental health problems triggered by problems in early childhood to be $30 billion. With the right programs in place that number could decrease to less than $15 billion a year, and probably even lower

than that. If Ottawa spent at least one percent of its GDP, that would more than cover the cost of child/parenting centres (Rushowy, 2007). Though largely ignored in Canada, Mustard's expertise has been welcomed by the policy makers of Australia.

Figures released by the Paris-based OECD show that while Canada is the fourth wealthiest (per capita) of the 20 nations surveyed, we rank:

- 20th (last) in access to regulated child care for three to six year olds,
- 17th in public spending on benefits and services for families with young children, and
- 14th in spending on early childhood education programs. (Hoffman, 2008)

www.childcarecanada.org

FINDING HIGH-QUALITY CHILD CARE

The challenge of locating high-quality care is an issue for families across the country, regardless of income level. Many families are looking for a community support system to strengthen their family unit. While there are many different kinds of programs across Canada, both formal and informal,

EXHIBIT 2.1 IMPROVING CHILD-CARE SERVICES IN CANADA

GOVERNMENT INITIATIVES

In March 2003, federal, provincial, and territorial ministers responsible for social services reached an agreement on a framework for improving access to affordable, quality, provincially- and territorially-regulated early learning and child-care programs and services. This initiative builds on the September 2000 First Ministers' commitment to improve and expand early childhood development programs and services. A total of $900 million over five years will be made available by the federal government to support provincial and territorial government investments in early learning and child care. Of this, $100 million will be available in the first two years, $150 million in year three, $300 million in year four, and $350 million in year five. The federal budget also provides an additional $35 million over five years for early learning and child-care programs for First Nations children, primarily those living on reserves. Quebec did not participate in developing these initiatives but will receive its share of federal funding.

Child-care advocates were hopeful that this would signal an improved approach to promoting early childhood development and increased accessibility to families.

---

some parents are unsure how to choose the program that best suits their family; sometimes they lack access to the program they've identified as the one they need. A family's needs depend, at least in part, on whether parents are working or going to school. Some will need full-time care, others only part-time or seasonal care.

Child-care choices are made based on factors such as the age of the child (it is especially difficult to find infant group care and school-age care), family income, and parental understanding of the available options. Most parents rely on an informal network of friends and relatives for information— information that may or may not be comprehensive or accurate. The more knowledgeable the family is, the more likely it will find the type of care that works for it. Families are encouraged to become good consumers by accessing information within their community, visiting programs, and talking with the professionals in each location. Other factors that affect choice are the distance from the child-care centre to home and work, the centre's hours of operation, and the cost of the service.

According to Donna Lero, a co-director of the 1988 National Child Care Survey, "47% of children younger than 6 and 45% of school-age children have child-care needs that do not conform to the 'standard' work week" (Lero, 1994: 13). This clearly has an impact on the families searching for child-care arrangements that provide extended hours. Not all provinces have special licensing regulations, guidelines, or standards with respect to extended-hour care.

The search for child care is especially problematic for disadvantaged groups. Already burdened by subtle, overt biases against parents as a whole, subgroups of disadvantaged and minority parents may experience additional disenfranchisement and choice limitation. Victimized by stereotypes regarding both their effectiveness as parents and their abilities as citizens in comparison with mainstream groups, low-income parents are in double jeopardy; they lack real options and are often encumbered by the unfounded opinions and low expectations of others (Kagan and Neville, 1994: 14).

Research has shown that children in home environments that expose them to environmental risk are more likely to be placed in poorer-quality child care. Parents who are less stressed, better educated, or feel in better control of their children are likely to use better-quality child care. Further research has shown that parents, as consumers, may be inattentive to the basic elements of care and to overrate its quality (Childcare Resource and Research Unit, n.d.).

QUEBEC LEADS THE WAY

Child-care centres in Quebec are known as Centres de la petite enfance, or CPEs; there are 1,000 CPEs in the province. In 1997, after the Social and Economic Summit of 1996, the Quebec government announced a family policy to create a Quebec child-care system where parents could pay $5-a-day per child; this figure was raised to $7 in 2004. In 2007 the system had approximately 200,000 spaces.

EXHIBIT 2.2 IMPROVING CHILD-CARE SERVICES IN CANADA

OUR CHILD CARE WORKFORCE

The steering committee of the *Our Child Care Workforce* report, co-chaired by Gyda Chud and Jenna MacKay-Alie, is representative of some of the most respected early childhood advocates in our country. To improve child-care services in Canada, they recommend the following:

PUBLIC POLICY, LEGISLATION, AND FUNDING

- A commitment to affordable, accessible quality care and to the value of a well-paid, competent, and stable work force
- A commitment to child care that meets the changing needs of today's labour market

INFRASTRUCTURE

- A commitment to a stable infrastructure for child care and related early childhood services

WAGES, BENEFITS, AND WORKING CONDITIONS

- A commitment to equitable wages, benefit levels, and working conditions

TRAINING AND EDUCATION

- A commitment to a trained and competent workforce
- A commitment to make training and education more accessible
- A commitment to opportunities for career mobility

RESEARCH

- A commitment to build and sustain a coordinated, comprehensive body of research on child care in Canada

Source: *Our Child Care Workforce: From Recognition to Remuneration: More Than a Labour of Love*, Executive Summary (Ottawa: Child Care Human Resources Steering Committee, 1998). Additional information available by e-mail from ccf@sympatico.ca. Reprinted by permission.

Children of parents on social assistance are entitled to free enrollment for 22.5 hours a week (Bertrand, 2008: 49). Quebec has the highest percentage of children in organized child care, at 29 percent. New spaces have been promised by all political parties because lack of space is chronic in the Greater Montreal region. The Quebec government has favoured the nonprofit model for child care. All CPEs are nonprofit social enterprises chartered by the Quebec government. They receive $16–21-a-day per child from the province, along with the parental fee. (pers. correspondence).

In recognition of the direct link between specialized training and quality child care, the Quebec government has imposed stricter regulations regarding training in early childhood care and education. The government provides financial support to child-care providers who are already actively working in the sector and enroll in college-level courses, making it easier for them to access professional development.

WHERE ARE THE CHILDREN?

According to Campaign 2000, "Even though more than 70% of young children have mothers in the paid labour force, only 12% of children 0–12 have access to a regulated child-care space. The supply of high-quality spaces is woefully short in every province and territory. High costs prevent many moderate- to low-income families from enrolling their children in ECEC [Early Childhood Education and Care in Canada] services; of those children who are in regulated child care, only 22% have a fee subsidy" (Campaign 2000, 2002). Every province in Canada has a subsidy program to help low-income families pay for child care but a number of eligibility criteria must be met, including level of income.

According to Early Childhood Education and Care in Canada (2007), there were 837,923 regulated child-care spaces in Canada in 2007. This represents an increase of 26,661 spaces since 2006,

In 1997 the Quebec government adopted a complete reform of its politics on family and daycare centres, which included, amongst many other aspects (a $5-a-day fee for parents, a tremendous increase of daycare places, a substantial raise of wages for daycare workers, etc.), the adoption of a common educational program for all daycare centres. This program was entitled "Programme éducatif des centres de la petite enfance" and was partly adapted from High Scope.

The program was revised in 2007 and entitled *Accueillir la petite enfance* (Ministère de la Famille et des Aînés, 2007). It carries on the fundamental assumption that working with families is a major issue for daycare workers to ensure the global development of children. The program insists on the importance of the staff knowing and understanding the family reality of each child, together with his or her social and cultural habits and values, and, for the family, to know and understand what is going on with their child in the daycare centre: the kind of services their child might receive, the kind of interventions used by the educators, and the values which are implied. All through the province, the daycare centres are still working on these goals.

In the mean time, the "Association québécoise des CPE" created the Odyssey initiative, aiming to stimulate social innovation and thus improve the quality of child care by focusing on the sharing of expertises and linking scientific research to practice. At the end of 2008, the Odyssey initiative will publish an important and long-awaited for report which will contain an important chapter on greeting and supporting parents in daycare centres.

Source: Contributed by Edith Joyal, Cégep de Saint-Jérôme

the smallest increase in regulated child care in some years. In 2007, 83 percent of total regulated child-care spaces for children aged 0–12 were centre-based; of 837,923 spaces, 697,242 were in centres with the remaining 141,581 in regulated family child care. Fifty-seven percent of centre-based spaces were for children 0–5 years of age while 43 percent were for school-aged children. In 2007, 80 percent of centre-based child-care spaces were not-for-profit, a slight increase from 79 percent in 2006 (Childcare Resource and Research Unit, 2007).

WORKPLACE CHILD CARE

According to Lero, Johnson, and Rooney (2001: 46), the number of work-related child-care centres is growing. Although they still account for a minority of centre-based spaces, the number of child-care facilities sponsored by an employer, union, or employee group has nearly doubled in the last decade. In 2000, there were 338 work-related child-care centres in Canada, up from 176 in 1991. Workplace child care may take many forms. It may be an on-site centre run by an independent operator or it may be managed by the employer. It may be a centre organized off-site,

perhaps for reasons of safety or lack of space. A consortium may be an option for some employers, joining with other companies to provide child care for all their employees and to share the cost of operation. Employers may offer other options such as a subsidy to a worker who has found a child-care space in the community. Referral services offered by the employer might provide information and guidance for employees searching for child care, or they may connect employees with family daycare providers or private-home daycare agencies. Other systems, such as a cafeteria approach, allow employees to choose from a number of benefits offered by the company; for example, some may choose a fitness membership while others choose a child-care subsidy.

Many benefits accrue to companies that offer child care. They may be better able to market their company, thus attracting more suitable candidates and raising their employee-retention rate; they may reduce absenteeism and lateness; and they are more likely to benefit from increased morale and productivity. The employer is also seen in a more positive light in the community. Employees are less stressed and conflict is reduced when they're able to stay close to their children. This is especially

This mother is able to visit her child during her breaks and on her lunch hour.

apparent when their children become ill. The family enjoys cost savings, and the child-care centre may provide flexible hours to accommodate their work schedule.

CHILD-CARE CO-OPERATIVES

"As parent co-operatives spread, develop, and extend their influences further, they will develop world kinship at the very roots of being in the growth of children, their families and their teachers."

—K. Whiteside Taylor

Community members, including parents, have been operating co-operative child-care services in Canada for over 65 years. The country's oldest co-op nursery, Manor Road Co-operative, celebrated its 70th Anniversary in Toronto in 2007. Approximately 1,000 child-care co-operatives are in operation in Canada; 80 percent are pre-school co-ops and 20 percent are full-day child-care co-ops. Ontario, Saskatchewan, and Manitoba have the largest concentration of child-care co-operatives. Many of these co-operatives arose through a period of development in the 1970s and 1980s. Today, they form an important part of the early childhood education sector, providing child care for almost 40,000 families.

Co-ops are democratic organizations owned and controlled by their members. All child-care co-ops are nonprofit and use any surplus funds to increase or improve their services. Most co-ops are incorporated provincially under a provincial co-operative statute. Child-care co-ops are developed by parents, early childhood educators, and community members.

INSIDE LOOK

The following newspaper report outlines the importance unions place on family-oriented policies:

The generous child care and university tuition subsidies won by the Canadian Auto Workers union in its deal with Ford has set a benchmark for other workers and companies. Under the three-year contract reached on September 21 [1999], workers at Ford Motor Co. of Canada Ltd. will get up to $2,000 a year for every child age 5 and under using a licensed, non-profit daycare centre or licensed in-home care. Workers with older children will get an $800 a year subsidy for university or community college tuition. Historically in Canada, employer involvement has been limited to creating a day care centre on site or nearby, and providing information referral services, but not actually assisting in paying for child care. The union also won up to $150,000 from Ford that will go toward working with existing centres to make them more accessible to people doing shift work. In 1989, the union, with seed money from the auto companies, established the CAW Childcare Centre in Windsor. The centre, which cares for kids from age 3 months to 12 years, is open from 5:30 a.m. until 1 a.m., which helps to accommodate parents on both day and afternoon shifts. A similar centre that opened in Oshawa in 1996 services workers at GM.

Source: *Toronto Star*, "Auto Union Makes Child Care Job One." October 2, 1999. L3. Reprinted with permission.

The Copper House, a workplace child-care centre at Husky Injection Molding Systems Ltd., in Bolton, Ontario, reflects an outstanding commitment to the families it serves. Their approach is rooted firmly in the commitment to continually ask oneself if the expectations for a child's well-being and development are ever high enough. In light of this question, you will agree that what we are achieving at the Copper House should be the norm. The magic of the Copper House does not lie in the aesthetics of the building but rather in the sustained commitment of its team. At the root of our approach lies a passion for nurturing the child and family. If we can provide the opportunity for child and family to spend quality time together with minimal outside interference, then we are meeting our primary objective. Ours is a passionate vision, and we strive to do what has not been done before. By sharing the following we will perhaps motivate others to meet child and family needs beyond the too-established and structured manner of child care today. A more effective partnership between families and community must be encouraged. We need to support our working parents more effectively, by taking an active role in decreasing the stress that they and their children experience daily. If we achieve this, we give the parent and child a gift that lasts a lifetime—saved time and energy to nurture one another. What an excellent contribution to give to young children!

The Copper House's initiatives are many. The following are done with minimal cost, if any, to the parent, team, or centre:

- Team members attend school activities—parent–teacher interviews; classroom visits; holiday concerts; field trips; communions, and so on—in an effort to unite child, school, home, and child care and provide opportunity for parental support.
- Team members may work privately for parents on evenings or weekends in another effort to encourage parents to plan for quality time together.
- We pick-up or drop-off a child to help out when the parent is away on business.
- Light suppers are served to children who are busy with extracurricular activities so that parents won't have to scramble to fit this in before the lesson.
- Child-care pyjama parties are provided for the children to encourage parents to have quality time together—uninterrupted time together that allows them to nurture their own relationship.
- Piano or music lessons are provided at the Copper House, and practice time is supported at any time during the child's day.
- Team members will drive a child to hockey, swimming, or gymnastic lessons when possible to help decrease parent stress.
- Haircuts are given during Copper House time to remove one item from the parents' weekend errands list.
- The centre provides the opportunity for parents to purchase supplies, equipment, and food items through the centre itself.

Source: Contributed by Valerie Nease, Director of The Copper House

Parents are active on the Board of Directors, work on committees, and assist with various other tasks. They also have a chance to attend evening discussion groups, workshops, and lectures.

Co-ops get their revenues from fees charged to parents, minimal direct operating grants from municipal or provincial governments, and fund-raising. Co-operatives recognize the importance of people and communities defining their own needs and working together to meet those needs. They are a powerful and democratic way to put decision-making into the hands of those who need and use the services.

Co-operative child care provides parents with an alternate choice which can be very satisfying for the participating families because the programs:

- foster collaborative and co-operative practices that support healthy childhood development;
- support early learning;

The CIBC Children's Centre is designed to provide a back-up child-care service when full- or part-time staff members regular child-care arrangements are not available. A comprehensive child-care service for infants through school-age children up to 13 years of age includes special play areas for infants, toddlers, preschoolers, and school-age children, with activities designed specifically for each age group. Lunch is to be provided by the employee, and the centre will provide two snacks per day. CIBC employees may use the centre up to 20 days a year, but may not use it for more than five consecutive days without special authorization. The centre is open from 8:00 a.m. to 6:00 p.m. Monday to Friday. Staff may call as far ahead as 30 days in advance or as late as the morning of the day that care is needed. Reservations are taken on a first-come first served basis. CIBC pays for the operation of the CIBC Children's Centre; there is no direct charge to employees. Employer-provided child care is a taxable benefit in Canada, and that after-tax cost to most employees is about $20.00 per day of use. There is a one-time cost of $20.00 to reflect a first-time administration fee. Trained early childhood teachers provide developmentally appropriate care and education.

Source: Contributed by the Canadian Imperial Bank of Commerce

- provide opportunities to meet other parents and their children;
- support the whole family;
- provide access to experts on child development;
- provide opportunities to attend parent education workshops and meetings;
- give parents opportunities to contribute their skills and existing abilities to benefit their child and the organization, including fund-raising;
- provide practical ideas for helping the child at home and in other non-school settings; and
- enable parents to make decisions and vote on policies for the child-care co-op.

Children benefit in a co-operative/parent participation program because they:

- participate in age appropriate early learning activities;
- experience having their parent mutually share and participate in their activities at school;
- have opportunities to experiment physically, socially, emotionally, and intellectually in a place specifically designed and equipped for their age group;
- can be curious and creative in a positive safe atmosphere;
- can participate both as individuals and as a member of a group; and

- experience a warm, accepting environment that supports and respects diversity.

The results of a recent study by John Anderson, Carol Brown, Lynne Markell, and Mary Stuart on the benefits and advantages of co-operative child-care is available on the Canadian Co-operative Association website at **http://www.coopscanada .coop**.

For those family members who are able to actively participate, duty days are eagerly anticipated by children, who benefit enormously from the co-operative's rich, play-based environment—an environment in which curiosity and creativity are actively promoted. Co-ops provide a friendly, natural source of support and advice to parents. Included in the mandate of most co-ops is a commitment to parent education, which may come in the form of workshops, meetings, and the active support of the playroom teacher. Families are encouraged to share their knowledge, expertise, and ideas with others. Through direct involvement with the program, parents can have their concerns answered and feel more confident in their child-raising ability. The centre provides an opportunity for children and adults to learn together. As the above account illustrates, families too have much to gain from the co-operative experience.

Co-operatives are also active in the inclusion of children with special needs, so the child, his or her

Co-operative child care has a long and successful record in Canada and is often described as the nation's best kept secret. It is where parents, teachers, and children learn together. Across the co-op child-care sector, many options are available, including playschools, nursery schools, kindergarten enrichment, full-time daycare, part-day programs, before- and after-school activities for school-age children, and flexible hours and after-hours care. The trend for a majority of nonprofit centres, whether they are preschools or child care, is building on parent partnerships, which is one of the cornerstones of the PCPC [Parent Co-operative Preschool Council] philosophy. The Mustard/McCain report reiterated what all educators know, that the earlier a parent is involved in their child's education and social well-being and the continuation thereof, the better the child will be in the public school system. With a limited number of spaces in traditional daycares and a growing group of parents determined to be actively involved in raising and educating their children, the co-operative approach is an effective model for many families.

When families with diverse backgrounds share their expertise and talents with teachers, other families, and the children, a rich and stimulating environment for learning is created. Family involvement has a direct impact on the quality of care their child receives and allows the parent to ensure continuity of care. Because of family involvement, staff costs and overhead are reduced through the provision of services on a voluntary basis. Since these costs amount to 80 percent of operational expenditures, budgets are smaller than in non-co-operative centres.

Co-operatives are run by a board of directors and provide a wonderful opportunity for parents to gain administrative skills as well as political savvy. Staff do not sit on the board but they are invited to be part of the organizational structure that works together to run the centre. Boards have insurance that protects them while they are making decisions as volunteers at the centre. In general, parents who belong to a co-op are expected to work on scheduled duty days, attend or organize parent meetings that deal with school administration or family life education, serve on parent committees, and assist with fundraising projects. Working parents who are unable to commit to regular participation during the day may contribute by serving on committees, on the board of directors, or in other tasks outlined by the co-op. In some co-operatives, other family members or nannies may fill in for parents on their duty days—that is, days on which they serve as members of the playschool teaching team. With more women working and with growing demands on families, co-operatives have adapted and changed based on the needs of the community they serve. In some centres, more staff have been hired in place of family volunteers; in others, hours have been extended to include after-school programs.

Source: Contributed by Nancy Auer, award-winning executive director of the Toronto and District PCPC (Parent Co-operative Preschool Council) and Mary Stuart, Manager, Early Childhood Services, PCPC.

The playschool was my first opportunity to see a large number of children the same age as my son Ryan. I had always felt that Ryan was a very demanding and challenging child, and when I saw other children interacting in such a positive way with their parents, I realized that something was not working in our relationship. Over the two years that we were in the playschool, the teacher worked closely with us to help us set reasonable limits for Ryan and then most importantly to follow through with them. I realized that Ryan was desperate for us to put some boundaries on his behaviour. I'll be forever grateful to that teacher and to the families who supported us.

parents, and the families can learn and help with the special need. Relationships developed in a co-op may become a springboard for lifelong friendships. Some parents are so inspired by their experiences in the playschool that they go on to train for employment in co-operative and teaching environments.

Teaching in a co-operative setting is a rewarding and challenging experience—one that requires excellent communication skills, confidence in one's teaching abilities, the ability to support and encourage families from a wide range of backgrounds, strong interpersonal skills, and unfailing enthusiasm.

CO-OPERATIVES ACROSS CANADA

VICPA, Vancouver

This association, in operation since 1949, supports 15 parent-participation preschools on Vancouver Island and the Gulf Islands. It has been an advocate for high-quality early childhood education for children and professional standards for adults who work with them. VICPA is affiliated with Parent

Co-operative Preschools International (PCPI). The mainland council can be reached at **office@ cpppreschools.bc.ca** and the website for the Vancouver Island Co-operative Preschool Association can be found at **www.vicpa.org**.

Parent Co-operative Preschools International (PCPI)

PCPI is a nonprofit international council dedicated to the family and the community. PCPI represents more than 50,000 families and teachers, providing ongoing support to families, educators, and social agencies who recognize the value of parents as teachers of their children and the necessity of educating parents to meet the developmental needs of their children. Membership is open to schools, councils, libraries, and individuals who uphold its purposes. The organization was founded in 1960 on the initiative of Katharine Whiteside Taylor, who was inducted into the Co-operative Hall of Fame in 1996 in recognition of her work on behalf of co-operative child care. Its website is **www.preschools.coop/**.

My first team-teaching experience was as a teacher and director of a co-operative nursery, where the parents were both my employees and my bosses! Having come from an individual classroom model, I was initially unprepared for the setting. I had three pairs of parent eyes watching me throughout the teaching day, I had to direct their work with explanations that made sense of them, and we needed to collaborate in planning for and carrying out the curriculum each day. One of the most important things I learned from that experience was that we must have a professionally valid reason for every plan, every disciplinary action, and every direction to team members.

Source: Bergen, 1994: 243.

MULTIAGE GROUPINGS

This section was contributed by Judith Bernhard, Professor, School of Early Childhood Education, Ryerson Polytechnic University

Within the child-care sector, other options are being developed in response to new research. In the last 15 years, changes in cultural and ethnic diversity of the population, along with a move toward increased economic efficiency, have resulted in re-opening questions of quality of care and optimal grouping models for young children. Advocates for effective education with diverse populations have become involved in promoting multiage settings because they are thought to promote both a family atmosphere and the preservation of language and culture. The issues have also arisen in relation to children with disabilities.

In a summary of the Ryerson Multiage Early Childhood Education Project (2000), researchers state that many people in the field of early childhood education have begun to question whether identified patterns in development apply to everyone regardless of context. In searching for alternative and better ways of conceptualizing children's development, many educators have turned to approaches derived from the work of Lev Vygotsky. He focused on measuring the difference between the potential and actual development, labelled the Zone of Proximal Development (ZPD). Apprenticeship and collaboration with adults or more competent peers who bring different perspectives to bear upon a problem are central to aiding children's social, emotional, and cognitive development. Multiage groupings may particularly facilitate such learning processes in children.

Perhaps one of the real advantages to families in multiage groupings is that the children stay with the same teachers from infancy until they enter public school. This continuity allows for strong relationships to form between teachers and families, with none of the difficulties associated with transitioning from one age group to the next.

Several researchers have pointed out the artificiality of age segregation, and the amount of literature on the effects of multiage groupings in North America and Europe has grown in recent years. Many of the findings have been positive: an increase in prosocial behaviours, leadership ability, and enhanced communicative skills. Studies have also found benefits in academic achievement, particularly for students learning a new language while at the same time preserving their native language and culture and for children with special needs.

The findings of the Ryerson study indicate that the multiage model is often a response to family and community values. In all centres, older children were taught to be careful with babies and were effective in protecting them. There was the belief that every caregiver was each child's caregiver and that parents could relate to all the caregivers. Parents mentioned feelings of belonging and openness, and of feeling welcome to drop by and participate. Despite this, the hoped-for legislative changes that would provide ratios that allow for these mixed ages have not been forthcoming.

The following discussion outlines some of the ways in which the multiage model supported families.

Grouping Siblings Together

All the parents expressed satisfaction with their children being in the same group. They believed the siblings benefited by being together. This was particularly significant for children who spoke languages other than English or French or were new to the centre. We found home-language subgroups within some multiage programs that seem to provide support for the children and families. During a site visit in Ontario, a Polish mother said: "I think that kind of grouping is great, especially for my younger child. She was very shy, and she had a hard time communicating with people. Family grouping is indispensable for my children; it helps my children to communicate in their second language."

A number of people commented that multiage grouping was particularly important for "only children," who benefit from being with children a bit older or younger than they are. Multiage groupings allow "only children" to take on the older or younger role and to have the opportunity to experience sibling-like conflicts—an important part of growing up.

Children with Special Needs

An important finding of the site visits is that multiage programming can facilitate the full inclusion into the program of children with special needs. Teachers at a Quebec site told us that moving to multiage programming enabled many teachers to see beyond the "labels" and "categories" of developmental stages. We observed that children quickly became aware of different forms of expression and responded to them when communicating with children with special needs. In the case of an Ontario child with limited expressive speech and multiple handicaps, teachers said the children quickly learned which of this child's sounds were happy ones.

A parent of a child with special needs described the multiage setting as beneficial to her son:

> Because of the variety of kids he stands out less; there isn't the placement issue about where he fits in with his developmental needs. In a multiage environment he's just another kid. It's interesting to watch children's reaction to him. Little ones come and stroke his chair and there is a natural interaction with the older ones.

It seems that multiage programs work well for children with special needs because problems of stigmatization are eliminated and teachers are less likely to compare children with peers. Though much research remains to be done on how multiage programs can work well, the findings indicate that such groupings do support families whose children are in child-care centres.

Healthy Images / Public Health Agency of Canada

Multiage groupings allow for greater interaction between siblings.

REGULATED FAMILY CHILD CARE

Family child care is a term used to describe the care of young children in the home of a caregiver. Unlike informal, unlicensed home care, under regulated family child care, an agency is licensed to contract with own-home caregivers and operates according to existing regulations, which vary from province to province and address such issues as the number of children who may be in care, qualifications of the caregivers, registration, and so on. Caregivers who work for a licensed agency work with a team of professionals to ensure the best possible care for the children and families they serve. Although agencies across the country differ from one another, many consider their mandate to provide trained staff to:

• support the caregiver and the family of the children in care;

- train caregivers in child development and appropriate programming, nutrition, and first aid;
- monitor the child-care home for safety, cleanliness, and the number and ages of children in care in each home; and
- ensure that prospective caregivers and their families are in good health and have completed a criminal reference check.

For some families, regulated family care is the best possible fit. Some children may be more comfortable in a smaller, more intimate group of children in a home setting. With a smaller group, the caregiver is able to get to know the child intimately and has more flexibility throughout the day than he or she would in many child-care centres. Families who find licensed care near their home may significantly reduce travel time. The caregiver may also be able to support the family's varying work schedule. Other families may like the idea of their child being cared for in a multiage setting.

Through the agency, families will be able to visit a number of homes that may be available to them. Suggestions from Family Day Care Services of what to look for appear in Exhibit 2.4.

UNREGULATED FAMILY CHILD CARE

According to Gestwicki and Bertrand (1999: 20), "Unregulated family child care is the most common type of remunerated child-care arrangement in Canada; it is also the least visible and the most varied model of child care." Dunster, Maxwell, and Mosher (1998) point out the lack of information on unregulated child-care providers, a lack they find astonishing because these providers make up nearly 95 percent of the family child-care providers in Canada.

NANNIES AND OTHER IN-HOME CARE ARRANGEMENTS

Many families prefer the flexibility of having their children cared for in their own home, where the child will be secure in his or her own environment with a consistent caregiver. This arrangement may also provide parents with more flexibility with regard to their work and travelling schedules and may meet their need for evening, weekend, or extended-hour care. These caregivers—often referred to as nannies—live in the home with

the family. Many live-in nannies immigrate to Canada through the Live-in Care Program (LCP), a federal immigration program designed to allow "future employers to sponsor immigrants who wish to enter Canada to provide in-home child care" (Gestwicki and Bertrand, 1999: 22). This program is not ideal, however, despite some improvements on freedom of movement and criteria for landed immigrant status. According to Arat-Koç (2001: 336):

> The LCP continues in the tradition of immigration policies regarding domestic workers by imposing the kind of status and conditions on workers that lead to abuse and the unfavourable working environment. Under the LCP, the temporary work permit system and the mandatory live-in requirement still prevail, while women have to prove higher qualifications to work as domestic workers. The new program enables Canadian employers to obtain higher qualified labour for less pay while doing little to help domestic workers to improve their conditions.

Nannies may allow parents greater flexibility in their child-care arrangements.

EXHIBIT 2.3 LIVE-IN CAREGIVERS

Foreign live-in caregivers must meet certain Citizenship and Immigration Canada criteria before being admitted to Canada. These criteria reflect the education, language, and skill level necessary for the foreign worker's successful integration into the Canadian labour market:

1. successful completion of the equivalent of a Canadian high school education;

2. six months of full-time training or 12 months of experience in a field or occupation related to the job you are pursuing; and the

3. ability to speak, read, and understand either English or French. The caregiver must be able to function independently in a home setting.

Successful applicants receive an Employment Authorization allowing them to work in Canada as live in caregivers. After two years of employment, which must be completed within three years of the caregiver's arrival in Canada, program participants can apply to become permanent Canadian residents.

Source: Human Resources and Social Development Canada, 2008.

EXHIBIT 2.4 HOW DO I FIND A GOOD HOME CHILD-CARE ARRANGEMENT?

Start by making some lists:

- A list of your child-care requirements including hours of care, days of care, ideal locations (e.g., near home, school, or work), and special needs of your children (e.g., food requirements, allergies)
- A list of the child-care arrangements your friends, neighbours, or co-workers have made or researched
- A list of the child-care agencies working in your neighbourhood
- A list of the phone numbers of the agencies you want to call
- A list of the questions you want to ask about the offered child care, including questions about
  - the length of time in operation
  - experience of caregivers
  - training and support offered to caregivers
  - insurance coverage
  - vacation and sick policies
  - fee schedule and availability of fee assistance
  - average length of stay of children in homes
  - availability of care that meets your particular needs
  - support given to the family by the agency
- Learn about the caregiver by asking:
  - What formal or informal training and education has she completed?
  - What other jobs has she done?
  - Why has she chosen home child care as her work?
  - How many children are in the home? Are her own children in care?
  - What are her thoughts on child development and parenting?
  - How does she handle discipline when it is required?
  - What is her policy on television and videos? Is it similar to your own?
  - Will the caregiver be driving the children? Is the car safe and equipped with seatbelts and car seats?
  - What equipment will you need to supply to the caregiver?
  - What meals and snacks are available to your child? Will a variety of foods be available?
  - What are the daily routines for activities and outdoor play?
  - What are the learning and reading opportunities?
  - Are there quiet-time activities?
  - What about sleep schedules and meal times?

Source: Courtesy of Family Day Care Services.

FAMILY RESOURCE PROGRAMS

The Canadian Association of Toy Libraries (CATL) was established in 1975. Thirteen years later CATL merged with a network of parent–child resource centres to form the Canadian Association of Toy Libraries and Parent Resource Centres (TLRC Canada). In 1994 the name of this organization was changed to the Canadian Association of Family Resource Programs. Health Canada (1998) reported that "according to Statistics Canada, in 2001 there were 2,128,850 children under the age of six in Canada." Assuming that this number represents about 1,600,000 families with one or more children under six years of age, and based on an estimate that 2,000 family resource programs exist in Canada (with an average reach of approximately 300 families per program/centre), we can estimate that family support programs are reaching almost 40 percent of Canadian families with children under six. The mission of the Association is to promote the well-being of families by providing national leadership, consultation, and resources to those who care for children and support families. Parent or caregiver education and support stand out as one of the most important and common types of services offered by family resource programs (FRPs). The association is dedicated to strengthening families through community-based prevention-oriented programs and services. The association also has links with other national and international groups that support families and children and produces a quarterly newsletter called *Play and Parenting Connections* to its 600 members across the country as well as a number of other informative publications. FRP Canada holds a biennial national conference.

The growth of alternative family structures over the past two decades has resulted in a need for more diverse family support services. Many FRPs take a community development approach to service provision and stress the involvement of parents, volunteers, and community members in the design and day-to-day delivery of programs. As a result, programs are as diverse as the communities they serve. Some programs are mobile services; others have their own facilities. Still others share facilities with community centres, churches, schools, libraries, hospitals, or military bases (Kellerman, 1994: 12).

Resources available through FRPs may include

- parent–child drop-in centres
- play groups or nursery schools
- seasonal daycares
- toy-lending libraries
- child-care registries
- mobile resource units for parents and caregivers
- parent discussion groups or support groups
- warm line (telephone service offering noncrisis support and information for parents)
- KidsTALK (warm line for children)
- food banks or community kitchens
- breakfast clubs or nutrition programs
- programs for teen mothers
- counselling (peer, professional, etc.)
- programs for families with children who have special needs (crisis intervention, infant stimulation programs, toy libraries with adapted toys, etc.)
- respite care
- emergency care for sick children
- summer camps
- training courses or workshops (e.g., volunteer and board training)
- conferences or symposiums
- information services (prenatal or childbirth education)
- referral services
- consultation with child-care and other community groups
- student placements
- hub model
- outreach (home visits, play groups in parents' or caregivers' homes)
- literacy, ESL, and life-skills programs
- health care and information
- participating in or sponsoring community planning
- advocacy on behalf of resource programs, parents, and children
- *Play and Parenting Connections* (quarterly newsletter)
- Canadian directory

No individual program offers all of the above services; each community attempts to target the resources that are most relevant and meaningful to the families it serves.

An estimated 2,000 FRPs serve tens of thousands of families every year. The following statistics illustrate the wide reach of these programs:

- 40 percent of FRPs serve children with special needs, the majority integrating these children into existing programs.
- 65 percent serve single parents.
- 64 percent serve fathers as well as mothers.
- 35 percent serve teenage mothers.
- 18 percent serve teenage fathers.
- 29 percent serve the unemployed and students.
- 27 percent of FRPs in large urban areas have ethnocultural minorities as a major user group.
- 21 percent of Aboriginal people located off-reserve are major users of FRPs.

To encourage working parents to participate, many FRPs extend their hours of operation by scheduling events on weekends or on Friday evenings from 6 p.m. to 8 p.m. and by offering parent–child programs from 4:30 p.m. to 7 p.m., with supper served. These programs are connecting with the workplace too, by holding brown-bag lunch sessions and workshops. Even specialized segments of society, such as the Canadian military, have adopted the FRPs idea:

> The Department of National Defense has recognized that military families often have issues that are different from civilian families and thus require different types of supports. A variety of programs are offered to families through the 43 Military Family Resource Centres (MFRCs) at all Canadian bases, wings and stations including some foreign locations in the U.S. and Europe. MFRCs employ over 700 people and have more than 1,500 volunteers. Programs are designed to provide needed information, promote health and social well-being; assist in preventing individual, family and community breakdown and help individuals or families in distress. Like other family resource centres, MFRCs are guided by community-based elected Board of Directors (of which at least 51% must be civilian spouses of Canadian Forces members). (Reeves, 2002: 12)

Though evidence shows that these preventive, less costly services are critically important, their real and potential contributions are often ignored. For the most part, FRPs in Canada have developed in the absence of a clear legislative and funding framework. Because many of them cut across categorical approaches to service delivery by combining health, recreation, educational, and social services (including social support, child welfare, and child care), they do not easily fit into traditionally structured government departments and funding categories and thus often fail to obtain recognition and funding.

The Westcoast Child Care Resource Centre, Vancouver, BC

The Westcoast Child Care Resource Centre is an example of a successful FRP. A three-year grant from the Child Care Initiatives Fund enabled this centre to grow from three employees to 30 and to develop programs that provide a variety of child-care-related resources and services to the community. An advisory committee supports each program, which may be co-sponsored by other agencies or organizations. Programs and services include the Westcoast Resource Library, Child Care Resource and Information Services, Early Childhood Multicultural Services, Information Daycare, Vancouver Child Care Support Program, Child Care INFORM, and Child Care Financial and Administrative Services of Vancouver. Member organizations include the Early Childhood Educators of BC, the Children's Services Employees' Union, the BC Daycare Action Coalition, the School Age Child Care Association, and the Western Canada Family Day Care Association (Skulski, 1995: 26–30). This organization responds to enquiries about child-care policy and practice, program administration, child-care training and professional development, child-care facility and playground design, multilingual child-care resources, and current child-care issues. Their library includes a collection of books, magazines, videotapes, and posters that can be borrowed free of charge. Their website, **www.westcoast.org**, offers more information on their programs and services.

KINDERGARTENS

In almost all jurisdictions, Ministries of Education have responsibility for kindergarten. Kindergarten is publicly funded with no parent fees and is an entitlement in most provinces. Approximately 335,000 five-year-old children and another 128,000 children under the age of five attend public kindergarten programs in Canada (Bertrand, 2008: 51).

Kindergarten is part-time (usually 2.5 hours a day) in most jurisdictions but in three provinces—New Brunswick, Quebec, and Nova Scotia—kindergarten is a full school day; in some cases, children attend on alternative days.

Many early childhood centres provide full-day programs for four- and five-year-old children, following the same guidelines as set out by the Ministry of Education of each province. Parents may choose this option because it provides quality care and education throughout the whole day—a seamless day—and does not necessitate a mid-day transition from one environment to another environment for their child.

In Ontario, Junior Kindergarten is available in almost all school boards and more than 90 percent of all four-year-olds attend. In Quebec, kindergarten for four-year-olds is offered in inner-city neighbourhoods as an extension of the school system. As part of a pilot project, Nova Scotia is currently offering pre-kindergarten to four-year-olds within public schools. There is limited kindergarten for four-year-olds through the public education system available in Winnipeg. Saskatchewan has introduced more than 100 pre-kindergarten classes for three- and four-year-old children living in designated community schools located in high need areas (Bertrand, 2008: 51).

PRIVATE SCHOOLS

Private schools may offer care for children of all ages and may offer special training in music, computers, religion, art, and so on; the costs for these programs vary from community to community. Each private school may have its own specific philosophy, according to which it develops its own unique programs. Three examples of these philosophies and programs are introduced below.

Montessori Schools

Early in the 20th century, Dr. Maria Montessori who trained in a degree in engineering and, later, medicine—an unusual choice for women at that time—created an approach to education that challenged the methods in place at the time. As a result of her work with children who were classified as mentally retarded during her medical training, she went on to further her studies in education. She began her work in a housing project in Rome and would develop a radically different approach to education; this approach further developed to

become the Montessori approach. Dr. Montessori designed equipment specifically for young children and developed materials to teach a specific concept. Her system of teaching was developed over her lifetime, and her goal to find a better way to educate children became grander with each passing year. Her ultimate aim was to help humanity be its best self: "Our principal concern must be to educate humanity—the human beings of all nations—in order to guide it toward seeking common goals. We must turn back and make the child our principal concern. The efforts of science must be concentrated on the child, because he is the source of and the key to the riddles of humanity…He needs much broader opportunities than he has been offered thus far. Might not this goal be reached by changing the entire structure of education?" (Montessori, 1972, in Lillard, 2007: 31).

Specifically,

[t]he Montessori philosophy includes introducing children to varieties of practical life skills, such as washing dishes, sweeping floors, and watering plants. The curriculum also includes sensorial components, which involve providing materials to help children broaden and refine their sensory perceptions, and conceptual components, which means using concrete academic materials to introduce children to reading, writing, mathematics, and social studies. . . . One abiding distinction of the Montessori philosophy is the respect for children and their abilities and accomplishments. (Gestwicki and Bertrand, 1999: 44–45)

During the later years of her life, Montessori devoted her time and energy to developing schools throughout Europe and North America, and she trained thousands of teachers in the Montessori method. Note that the name Montessori is in the public domain, so anyone can use it. The Canadian Council of Montessori Administrators (CCMA) urges parents to learn what constitutes a legitimate Montessori education and which Montessori schools are accredited.

Waldorf Education

First developed by Rudolf Steiner in 1919, the Waldorf philosophy emerged with an emphasis on a child's learning experiences and the development of the whole child. Today, the Waldorf philosophy is an international movement that develops a long-term relationship between teacher and child. The teacher moves with the class from Grades 1–8 and

Teachers in Waldorf Schools are aware of the impact of the environment on children's behaviour.

their role is that of a mentor. The children are coached, rather than instructed, on how to understand the how and why of learning—inquiry and emergent curriculum through experimentation and action. Waldorf classrooms use natural fabrics and natural lighting to instill a sense of tranquility and peace. Children are given materials that allow them to engage in practical tasks such as bread-making, table-setting, dish-washing, knitting, sewing, and cleaning-up at the end of the day. The children are fully involved in the planning and organization of their play environment:

> "Children in Waldorf schools gain knowledge through their daily experiences of life. Rudolf Steiner states 'teaching could never be boring if it was related directly to life. Our highest endeavour must be to develop free human beings who are able of themselves to impart purpose and direction to their lives'." (Leighton, 2005).

Family involvement is integral to the Waldorf philosophy. Celebrations are common place in a Waldorf school in order to involve families:

> Central to Waldorf education is the belief that the deepest and most universal human values can only arise when education brings into healthy balance the faculties of thinking, feeling and willing that live in each child. Learning at the Waldorf School is a vital and dynamic process, permeated with the power of imagination and working with the spiritual, emotional, and physical development of the individual within the social context. Reverence and awe for the wonders of nature, gratitude and respect for the efforts and accomplishments of others, and the responsibilities of dutiful self-discipline are guiding principles of Waldorf Education. (Andre and Neave, 1992: 148)

High/Scope

The section was contributed by Moya Fewson, Senior Trainer, Sheridan High/Scope Teacher Education Centre

High/Scope is based on longitudinal research, and it is not only research-based, it is research-validated. High/Scope has goals and objectives and uses Key Developmental Indicators as the basis of their curriculum. Key Developmental Indicators are learning objectives which cover all domains of child development. The cornerstone of the High/Scope curriculum is Active Learning. Research has shown that children learn best when they are actively involved with people and things.

By providing materials that children can manipulate, by embedding choice in what children do, by promoting language, and by giving ongoing adult support and scaffolding children develop initiative, autonomy and self confidence. Children learn to manage their day through the plan–do–review process: they make plans, carry them out, and reflect on their actions. Plan–do–review increases cognitive ability and allows children to feel in control of their actions. The Daily Routine in a High/Scope classroom includes child-initiated times such as Work Time and adult initiated times such as Group Time. The routine is consistent so that children can feel secure. The Learning Environment in a High/Scope program is carefully planned to allow children to make choices and to use interesting and stimulating materials.

Adult–Child Interactions are very important in a High/Scope program. Adults and children share control: children are in control of "child-sized" decisions while adults take care of adult responsibilities. Adults develop genuine, respectful relationships with children. Furthermore, High/Scope programs use a problem solving approach to social conflict. Children are taught how to negotiate, communicate, and compromise. Adults use encouragement techniques with children, including making specific comments about the children's efforts, noticing children's efforts, and putting children in control of judging their own work.

High/Scope has a strong focus on developing and supporting early literacy. Adult-initiated times are based on early speaking, listening, reading, and writing experiences. Math and science are also a focus of adult-initiated times with activities based on Classification, Seriation, Numbers, Space, and Time. Parents are an important part of High/Scope and their input is highly valued. Classrooms reflect the positive aspects of children's families and communities. Parents and educators see themselves as partners in learning. Parents are given feedback on their child's interests and progress on a regular basis both through the sharing of anecdotal notes taken on an ongoing basis by teachers and through parent/teacher interviews held to discuss findings on the Child Observation Record (COR).

Other programs have been developed, too, such as the Froebel Schools, which are based on the philosophy of Freidrich Froebel, the German educator who coined the term "kindergarten," or "garden of children." Throughout the country many communities have organized programs and initiatives that support families. They are as varied as the communities that they serve.

THE COMMUNITY ACTION PROGRAM FOR CHILDREN (CAPC)

WHAT IS CAPC?

At the 1990 United Nations World Summit for Children, the leaders of 71 countries made a commitment to invest in the well-being of vulnerable children. The Government of Canada responded with the Child Development Initiative (CDI). CAPC is the largest programme of this initiative.

CAPC provides long-term funding to community coalitions to deliver programs that address the health and development of children (0–6 years) who are living in conditions of risk. It recognizes that communities have the ability to identify and respond to the needs of children and places a strong emphasis on partnerships and community capacity building.

CAPC targets children living in low-income families; children living in teenage-parent families; children experiencing developmental delays, social, emotional or behavioural problems; and abused and neglected children. Special consideration is given to Métis, Inuit, and off-reserve First Nations children, and to the children of recent immigrants and refugees, children in lone-parent families, and children who live in remote and isolated communities.

There are 464 CAPC projects across Canada, which deliver 1,790 programs in more than 3,035 communities. In a typical month, 53,872 children and 48,721 parents/caregivers participate in CAPC programs. The common threads for all the CAPC projects are the Guiding Principles:

- Children First
- Equity and Accessibility
- Community Based
- Strengthening and Supporting Families
- Flexibility
- Partnerships

Kids R First, Summerside, PEI

Kids R First, which operates in Summerside, PEI, offers a wide range of family and child-oriented programs and supports aimed at parents and children. The Coalition of Community Action Programs for Children (CAPC) in Prince Edward Island was formed to work collaboratively to develop projects that could serve a diverse range of needs and populations and address the seven provincial priority areas for CAPC:

- child abuse and neglect,
- lack of economic resources,
- mental and physical disabilities,
- poor health and nutrition,
- substance abuse and its negative impact on the child,
- unplanned pregnancies, and
- youth and inexperienced parents.

A Family Resource Centre model was the solution agreed to by all members of the coalition. It is a unique model on the island, capable of providing a wide range of services and activities to people around Summerside. Activities like play groups, clothing exchanges, community kitchens, and toy-lending libraries are available at the main Kids R First location and at its three outreach sites in Kensington, Borden, and Wellington (a francophone site). All services at Kids R First are free in order to make them more accessible to low-income families. Transportation to and from the centre is also included. The sites offer prenatal support and emergency respite for postnatal mothers whose babies are over six months old but still need help, and they also offer a very popular cooking program. Various parenting programs like Nobody's Perfect and Magic 1-2-3 (an effective discipline for children two- to twelve-years-old developed by Thomas W. Phelan) are run by the centre to support young or inexperienced parents.

Wolseley Family Place, Winnipeg, MB

Located in Winnipeg's West Broadway neighbourhood, Wolseley Family Place provides a wide range of support for families. Child development activities include child care for children up to six years of age and a drop-in playtime each day. There are classes in Mother Goose (a literacy program), storytelling times, infant massage, and other educational parenting classes. Participants can also get information on and support for dealing with shaken baby syndrome, FAS and FAE (fetal alcohol syndrome

and fetal alcohol effect), breastfeeding, addiction, nutrition and healthy eating, children's health and safety, first aid, and CPR training. A doctor works at the centre once a month to provide check-ups and to answer questions. The centre has an outreach worker who goes out into the community to make contact with extremely isolated women and their children and provides some early childhood support for them. Prenatal and postnatal classes for expectant and new mothers, as well as a popular mother's group, help ease tension and stress. Cultural awareness is an important component of the activities at Wolseley Family Place because a large percentage of the participants are Aboriginal.

BEST START

Best Start: Ontario's Maternal Newborn and Early Child Development Resource Centre supports service providers who are working on health promotion projects to improve the health of expectant parents and their young children from birth to age six who live in conditions of risk. The program is based on the principle that communities are best positioned to recognize the needs of their children and have the capacity to draw together the resources to address these needs. The Centre provides workshops and conferences, resources, consultations, and subject-specific information.

Babies Best Start trains and supports parents from a variety of ethno-cultural backgrounds to act as Home Visitors to parents and their children living in low-income neighbourhoods. The home visiting program—designed to help give infants the 'best start' in life by promoting the importance of health and the development of young children in vulnerable families through early intervention and education—is the backbone of the Babies Best Start program. Home Visitors, who are paid an hourly wage, attend 70 hours of in-depth training over a three-week period, and additional, continuous education is mandatory for all Home Visitors. Team meetings are held regularly and opportunities to attend community workshops on relevant topics (such as family planning, nutrition, parent-child bonding, child development, behaviour management, community resources, child abuse, and conflict resolution) are provided. Additionally, Home Visitors—in teams of six—attend a supervisor-facilitated peer support group meeting every two weeks. Many home visits are spent discussing stages of growth, nutrition, baby food preparation, and appropriate toys; home visits last approximately one hour. The Home Visitors are also able to connect families to other programs offered in the community such as Nobody's Perfect, Mother Goose, etc. A variety of fitness programs, sewing circles, First Nations 'sweat houses', cooking groups, picnics, seasonal celebrations, and country outings all have been initiated or supported by Babies Best Start.

THE CANADIAN PRENATAL NUTRITION PROGRAM (CPNP)

Similar to CAPC, the Canadian Prenatal Nutrition Program (CPNP) provides funding to community groups that aid vulnerable pregnant women. There are currently 274 ongoing projects in 227 communities. These projects reach pregnant adolescents; youth at risk of becoming pregnant; pregnant women who abuse alcohol or other substances; pregnant women living in violent situations; pregnant women living in isolation or without access to services; refugee and immigrant women; and Métis, Inuit, and First Nations women. CPNP provides support to services that offer nutrition, health, and lifestyle education and counselling with the goal of improving the health of mothers and babies. Additional services include one-on-one and group prenatal nutrition counselling, food supplements, collective kitchens, peer counselling, resource mothers, breastfeeding education and support, and post-partum support. Projects are delivered in partnership with community organizations such as Rotary clubs, food banks, high schools, school boards, liquor control boards, physicians, public health units, religious groups, and professional organizations such as the Canadian Dietetic Association. Both CAPC and CPNP are administered through the regional Health Canada offices that support community projects and groups.

THE PARENTING PARTNERSHIP (TPP)

The Parenting Partnership is a prenatal and parenting educator program that Invest in Kids has developed and is testing. This free, one-and-a-half year education program is developed for first-time expectant couples, and provides information on pregnancy, childbirth, couple relationships, baby care, parenting, and child development. The program includes both online sessions and face-to-face classes that are facilitated by two parent educators, one who is a health practitioner and one who is a counsellor.

To watch a family grow from pregnancy to the baby's first birthday is an amazing thing. A couple goes through so many changes with the preparation of the baby's arrival and that whole first year. It's been valuable that these parents have had each other to turn to for specific questions or just moral support. It's been even more advantageous for these parents to have parent educators to go to for any other issue, problem, and moral support too. (Parent Educator, Health Practitioner).

The newly designed program provides excellent medical evidence-based information about the prenatal needs of both mothers and fathers-to-be as well as providing couple information which is very important to ensuring that new parents are able to keep the channels of communication (open) in order to be proactive when it comes to issues that may arise within the couple relationship. In addition, the course is offered prenatally right through to the early post natal period (up to 12–18 months old) which are the two most critical periods for new parents and when the most challenging of parental issues arise. (Parent Educator, Counselor)

ONTARIO EARLY YEARS CENTRES

Funding for Ontario's new Early Years initiatives is part of the National Children's Agenda, through which the federal government is transferring funds to provinces to enhance Early Years programs and services. Early Years Centres are to provide a central location where parents and caregivers can get information about the programs and services that are available for their children. The centres will also give caregivers the chance to speak to early year's professionals as well as other families in their community. Programs will focus on the important role a parent has as primary teacher to their child, and all centres will provide literacy and interactive learning activities involving parents and children, as well as parenting programs covering all aspects of early child development, prenatal and postnatal resources, training, referrals to link families with external services, and outreach to encourage parent participation across the province. A total of 103 centres are to be in place when the program is fully implemented.

TORONTO FIRST DUTY PROJECT

Toronto First Duty (TFD) was a pilot program based on the Mustard/McCain report for the Ontario Government, *The Early Years Study*, in 1999, and the follow-up report *Early Years Study 2: Putting Science into Action*. This project brought together the three streams of kindergarten, child care, and parenting supports into a single program with a seamless structure designed to meet the learning needs of children at the same time as it met the care needs of parents. Through the five initial Toronto First Duty sites, parents were able to access the full range of child and family supports available in their community. The three-year project (2002–2005) supported each site's ability to

- create a high-quality learning environment that combines learning expectations, activities, and routines from existing kindergarten, early childhood education, child-care, and parenting programs.
- develop an early childhood team that works together to deliver and achieve program goals.
- form a local governance structure to determine the allocation of resources, service planning, monitoring, and program policies.
- provide seamless access to an expanded and comprehensive early learning and care program providing a continuum of supports and services to all families and children.
- increase parent participation in their children's early learning and development through direct involvement in programs, planning, and decision-making.

The *Toronto First Duty Phase 1 Summary Report* concluded that integrated professional supports improve the quality of early childhood programs and reduce risks for parents and children. By engaging parents in the school and their child's early learning, the child's social, emotional, and academic readiness for school was enhanced. Integrated program delivery was also cost-effective, serving more families, more flexibly, for the same costs. For more information, visit **www.toronto.ca/firstduty**.

Toronto First Duty to Toronto Best Start

The project's findings influenced the Ontario government and are reflected in its "Best Start" strategy. The core elements, goals, objectives,

training, and tools of the TFD model are incorporated into the Toronto Vision for Children: Best Start Plan. Toronto First Duty has fulfilled its goals of making integrated service provision public policy (Bertrand, 2008: 38).

EARLY LEARNING FOR EVERY CHILD TODAY (ELECT)

Early Learning for Every Child Today: A Framework for Ontario's Early Childhood Settings (*ELECT*) is a province of Ontario Best Start initiative that describes how young children learn and develop. *ELECT* provides a curriculum guide for early childhood settings with a statement of six principles that review current research and practice, a continuum of development, guidelines for practice, statements on assessment and monitoring, and an international curriculum framework review.

One of the six principles in ELECT states "Partnerships with families and communities strengthen the ability of early childhood settings to meet the needs of young children." This principle begins:

> The web of family and community is the child's anchor for early development. Families are the first and most powerful influence on children's early learning and development. Families live in, and belong to, multiple communities that may support or thwart their ability to support young children's optimal development. Relationships between early childhood settings and families and their communities benefit children when those relationships are respectful of family structure, culture, values, language and knowledge. (Weiss, Caspe, and Lopez, 2006)

This important principle invites early childhood educators to expand their practice to include parents in decision making and planning curriculum; to expand their knowledge and presence in centre and family communities; to connect families with each other; to provide families with information and links to resources that support them meeting the diverse needs of their children and to exchange observations and information on each child's learning, development, and daily experiences. Family and community involvement is a focus for educational change and improvement that promotes children's learning and development, health, and well-being.

Early Learning for Every Child Today: A Framework for Ontario's Early Childhood Settings

(ELECT) is available at **www.children.gov.on.ca/CS/en/programs/BestStart/early.htm**.

ARTISTS AT THE CENTRE PROJECT

This section was contributed by Paul Fralick, a former member of the faculty of the ECE program at Mohawk College.

An exciting journey continues in Hamilton, Ontario. Inspired by the Reggio Emilia approach, local artists are in turn inspiring young children to draw, to paint, to mould, to design. The Artists at the Centre Project, begun by Karyn Callaghan and Paul Fralick in March 2001, is made possible by generous funding from the Ontario Trillium Foundation and the Hamilton Community Foundation. McMaster Children's Centre is the lead organization for the project; the other locations include a variety of child-care and family resource centres in Hamilton. The artists at the centre are both the children and the adult artists who work with them. And always, as part of the circle of the children learning and thinking, there are their early childhood educators. Metaphorically, this project also places art and creative expression in all its forms at the centre. The artists' knowledge about art media has helped the children to translate their thinking and understanding into the language of paint or markers or casting material. With this support, the children have many opportunities to explore the so-called 100 languages of the Reggio approach. The educators and artists involved are leaders; interest in the approach is growing in the Hamilton area because of their work. There is an annual exhibit of the children's artwork and thinking. Locations so far have included the Art Gallery of Hamilton and the Hamilton Children's Museum. Each exhibit has given hundreds of visitors the opportunity to glimpse the complexity and depth of children's interests.

HOME INSTRUCTION PROGRAM FOR PRESCHOOL YOUNGSTERS (HIPPY)

Developed in 1969 at the Hebrew University of Jerusalem in Israel, the HA'ETGAR (HIPPY in English) Program is now used in 12 countries and serves over 22,000 families who want to provide stimulating experiences for their children in their home. HIPPY programs are currently operating in Australia, Canada, El Salvador, Germany, New Zealand, South Africa, and the United States, to name a few. Discussions are underway regarding new programs in China, Portugal, Singapore, and Zimbabwe (Hepworth Berger, 2004: 332). HIPPY Canada is a nonprofit organization that receives its revenue from the federal government, donations, and its own fundraising. In 2005–2006, 385 low-income families were served for an expenditure of $206,299 through six sites in British Columbia, one site in Montreal, and one site in Toronto. Five of the HIPPY sites in British Columbia serve Aboriginal families (Doherty, 2008). The skill areas included are tactile, visual, auditory, and conceptual discrimination, in addition to language development, verbal expression, eye-hand coordination, pre-math concepts, logical thinking, self-concept, and creativity.

A professional coordinates the program, but paraprofessionals are selected from parents who were in the program. Their website states that the HIPPY program builds on the basic bond between parents and children. Supported by easy-to-use activity packets, home visits, and group meetings, HIPPY parents learn how to prepare their children for success in school and beyond. Children enter the program at the age of three and families are required to make a two-year commitment to participate in the program for 30 weeks during the school year. The family is visited at home every second week to review materials with the parent using role playing and parents are then expected to spend a minimum of 15 minutes a day doing activities with their child. The HIPPY program is very structured and is implemented across sites in the same way using a standard curriculum and standard materials. Parents receive a progressive series of 60 weekly packets of daily activities. All of the parent instructional materials are prepared at a grade three level and are available in a number of languages; in the Aboriginal communities the materials have been rewritten to be more culturally sensitive. Every other week they attend group meetings with other parents and HIPPY staff.

Learning and play mingle throughout HIPPY's structured curriculum as parents encourage their children to recognize shapes and colours, tell stories, follow directions, solve logical problems, and acquire other school readiness skills. Canada has also contracted with Let's Talk Science, a national organization that develops learning programs to improve science literacy (Doherty, 2008). More information is available at **www.hippy.org.il/html/aboutus.html**.

THE PARENT–CHILD MOTHER GOOSE PROGRAM

The Mother Goose Program (Programme la Mere l'Oie pour parents et enfants) is a nonprofit organization that operates in eight provinces and the Yukon. It receives funding through provincial and municipal government grants, agency-paid fees for staff training and for the use of the program materials, and overall approach and donations. The program provides a one-hour group experience for parents/caregivers and their children for 30 consecutive weeks. They receive demonstrations and education on how to use interactive rhymes, stories, and songs with their children to enhance the child's language and communication skills. Printed versions of the rhymes and songs are supplied to participants for use at home but there is no requirement that parents work with their child between sessions. Nationally, the agencies delivering the program have reported serving a total of 1,649 adults (Doherty, 2008).

BETTER BEGINNINGS, BETTER FUTURES PROGRAM

Better Beginnings, Better Futures, which began operation in 1994, is a 25-year longitudinal demonstration project based in Ontario. Compensatory programs are established to support families whose children may be disadvantaged or delayed. There are eight sites, each in a different Ontario community:

- Five sites follow the Infant/Preschool Model and focus on children from birth to age four:
  - Guelph's Willow Road neighbourhood: 625 children
  - North Kingston neighbourhood: 1,095 children
  - Southeast Ottawa's Albion-Heatherington-Fairlea-Ledbury neighbourhood: 690 children
  - Toronto's Moss Park-Regent Park neighbourhood: 1,125 children
  - Walpole Island First Nation: 250 children.
- Three sites follow the Preschool/Primary School Model and focus on children aged four to eight:
  - Cornwall's four francophone primary schools: 530 children
  - Highfield's Highfield Junior School neighbourhood: 517 children
  - Sudbury's Flour Mill/le Moulin à Fleur and Donovan neighbourhoods: 503 children

This project is the first early childhood intervention project of its kind in Canada. The communities themselves have defined what services they need to promote their children's development and to alleviate the impact of economic disadvantage. Each project is unique, but most now offer early childhood intervention services, such as home visits, family support programs, and school and child-care centre enrichment, which are coordinated with other early childhood development services in each community. Better Beginnings has an exciting research component in which the impact on children, families, and communities will be monitored and a group of children and families will be followed for 20 years to measure the long-term effects of the program (Gestwicki and Bertrand, 2003: 19).

One of the most ambitious research projects on the long-term impacts of early childhood prevention programming for disadvantaged children in Canada, this project has received wide national and international attention, interest, and support. Better Beginnings is a unique opportunity to apply knowledge about Canadian community-driven solutions that are countering the negative effects for at risk children living in poverty through early childhood intervention. The diversity of the participating communities (Francophone, Aboriginal, recent immigrants, and multicultural) increases the likelihood that findings will be applicable to children across Canada. Findings will provide specific direction to the development of prevention and intervention programs and will enable more informed decision-making about social policy. For more information, visit **http://bbbf.queensu.ca/ research.html**.

NOBODY'S PERFECT PROGRAM

Nobody's Perfect is a positive and empowering parent-support and education program that informs parents about the "whens," "whats," and "whys" of the first five years of childhood. It offers up-to-date information to parents on their children's health, safety, development, and behaviour, and it helps them to develop effective parenting and coping skills. The program was developed by the Regional Health Promotion Committee, a coalition of representatives from the Atlantic Region Health Promotion and Social Development Office of Health Canada and the departments of health of the four Atlantic Provinces. The coalition worked to create a health promotion program that would meet the needs of parents who possess one or more of the following characteristics: young, single,

Courtesy of Lynn Wilson

The Better Beginnings bus provides transportation to and from the centre.

culturally or geographically isolated, low-income, and limited formal education. Participation is voluntary and free of charge. The program is not intended for families in crisis and is coordinated through a national office by the Canadian Association of Family Resource Programs and the Canadian Institute of Child Health. Introduced nationally in 1987, Nobody's Perfect parent materials were extensively revised and updated in 1997 and are published in both French and English.

Nobody's Perfect is offered as a series of six to eight weekly group sessions. The program is built around five easy-to-read books which are given to parents free of charge. During the meetings, trained facilitators support participants as they work together to discover positive ways of parenting. The program begins with the parents' personal experiences and interests and actively involves participants in the learning process. It builds networks among parents and encourages them to see one another as sources of advice and support. Across Canada, over 5,000 community workers, parents, and public health nurses have been trained as Nobody's Perfect facilitators. Networks in every province and territory provide ongoing support for facilitators and trainers. Several major evaluation and impact studies have found Nobody's Perfect to

be successful at reducing isolation and increasing parenting skills and confidence.

SUCCESS BY 6

This program was begun by the United Way in the Minneapolis area in 1988, and is one of the largest networks of early childhood coalitions. Today more than 350 initiatives across the United States and Canada are in operation. Operating under the local United Way organizations, Success By 6 is a community partnership dedicated to increasing awareness of and investment in early child development. Success By 6 coalitions galvanize businesses and governments around early learning by raising awareness of the importance of early childhood development, increasing access to services, advocating for public policies and improving systems—budgets, laws and supports—to improve young children's lives.

The goal of Success By 6 is to offer all children a good start in life so that by the time they begin Grade 1 they are physically, socially, and emotionally healthy and ready to learn. The focus is on supporting parents, promoting healthy births, promoting early learning programs, protecting children from abuse and neglect, and supporting neighbourhoods. In the last five years, more than 500,000 children have benefited from Success By 6 early learning, child care, parent education, health, literacy, and family resource centre programs. To learn more about Success By 6 in Stormont, Dundas, and Glengarry go to http://www.unitedwaycornwall.com/bysix.htm.

HIGHLIGHTING PROGRAMS ACROSS CANADA

Early Learning and Child Care/Early Childhood Development in Saskatchewan

Saskatchewan parents have the primary responsibility for the care and learning opportunities for their own children, but everyone in Saskatchewan shares an interest in their physical, intellectual, social, and emotional development. Children's well-being is a measure of our development as a community. Early childhood educators play a key role in supporting parents to fulfill that important responsibility by providing quality care and education opportunities that serve the dual roles of nurturing children to reach their fullest potential, and supporting parents to work or go to school. In Saskatchewan, early childhood educators work with families in a range of settings and programs. The largest number of educators works with preschoolers, infants, toddlers, and school-age children in licensed child-care centres. Children who are identified as having special needs, either at birth or soon after, may be eligible for the Early Childhood Intervention Program (ECIP). Early childhood educators employed through this home visiting program work with children and their families, both at home and at child care if applicable, to ensure that the children benefit from stimulating activities to enhance their development prior to entering school. The relationships between early childhood educators and families are the key component of the ECIP program. Early childhood educators are also employed as family support workers in other family services organizations that provide children's programs as part of their supports to families. These include women's shelters and parenting centres, as well as programs sponsored by the Government of Canada such as Community Action Program for Children (CAPC) and Aboriginal Headstart (AHS). In many Saskatchewan schools, particularly in areas with large numbers of families living in circumstances of risk, pre-kindergarten programs are offered to three- and four-year-old children.

Some pre-kindergartens offer the children's program four half-days per week, with the remaining half-day reserved for family activities. Early childhood educators are hired as assistants in pre-kindergarten, kindergarten, and elementary classrooms.

KidsFirst

This section was contributed by Gail Russell, Director, Early Childhood Development Unit, Early Learning and Child Care Branch, Saskatchewan

As part of Saskatchewan's early childhood development strategy, with funding provided through the Early Childhood Development Agreement (September 2000), the province implemented the KidsFirst program. KidsFirst is an integrated program that is targeted to vulnerable families in nine communities across the province deemed to have the greatest concentration of at-risk families. The program consists of a home visiting program—home visitors being paraprofessionals working with the family to develop strengths and the capacity to nurture their children—dedicated early learning and child-care opportunities, and mental health and addictions support, as well as parent support programs that vary in each KidsFirst community. This program highlights the demands that early childhood educators are faced with, as they become part of a team that serves diverse family needs through the early learning and child-care setting.

Fort McMurray, AB, in the Regional Municipality of Wood Buffalo

This section was contributed by Hope Moffatt, Instructor, Keyano College, Fort McMurray, Alberta

Three preschool programs in Fort McMurray recognized the importance of family involvement and designed their programs to include parent components. The Children's Centre, which was founded in 1993, directs its attention to families in the high-risk category and offers preschool, parent-toddler drop-in, prenatal, and new mother programs as well as focusing on children on the FAS spectrum. Educare Early Intervention program was launched in 1997 by the determined work of one woman, Kim Farrell, who wanted to address the language, academic, and social readiness needs of the children who came into her kindergarten classes. Since then

Educare has expanded and relocated. It now includes Early Childhood Development (preschool) with Speech-Language and Family Literacy components, a Rock-A-Tots Music Program, and a Sensory Integration Program.

The newest program is The HUB Family Resource Centre, which opened its doors on September 12, 2003, and just recently won the Fort McMurray Chamber of Commerce "Not For Profit Flame Of Excellence Award for 2007." In the first year of operations The HUB Family Resource Centre partnered with approximately 26 agencies, business, and organizations to provide programs and services to the public. Partnerships with Keyano College Childhood Studies Programs, Fort McMurray Housing, FCSS Family & Community Support Services, Alberta Alcohol and Drug Abuse Commission (AADAC), Educare Preschool Program, and the RCMP allowed them to deliver multi-level services free of charge. Attendances at The HUB Family Resource Centre exceeded 10,100 visits in the first year alone, with individuals accessing services, programs, or information on a wide variety of community programs and resources.

In response to the community growth and needs, and in recognition of The HUB's success, Alberta Children's Services named The HUB as an Alberta Parent Link Centre. This initiative brought new opportunities with the creation of "The HUB on Wheels" program which allowed The HUB to take its programs out to various areas of the community and to outlying areas in Anzac, Janvier, and Conklin. The HUB on Wheels addresses a major barrier for families who do not always have access to transportation to attend programs in another part of the city or region. As a result of this innovative program, attendance at HUB programs jumped to over 15,000 visits in 2004, the second year of operations.

Since becoming an Alberta Parent Link Centre, The HUB Family Resource Centre now employs eight full-time staff and six casual/part-time staff. In 2006 the attendance at programs offered by The HUB Family Resource Centre had grown to over 20,000 visits. In March 2008, The HUB opened a second site to accommodate the huge influx of new families. The HUB Family Resource Centre has remained true to their vision of *"Honouring Children, Engaging Parents, and Connecting Community."* The residents of the Wood Buffalo region are fortunate in having an organization such as The HUB, which is so dedicated to understanding and meeting the unique needs of families in this fast-paced, diverse region, and which, through the compassion and caring of its staff, helps bring a sense of welcome to newcomers and a sense of belonging to those of us who choose this beautiful region in which to live, work and raise our children.

Manitoba's Families First Program

Families First, part of the provincial Healthy Child Manitoba initiative, has the capacity to provide home visits to 1,581 families using a 2005–2006 budget of $9,486,000. This includes not only the province's universal screening of every family with a newborn in Manitoba, but also an in-depth assessment of families identified as possibly vulnerable to determine whether they should be referred to Families First. The home-visiting program visits every week for 9–12 months, or as needed, and delivers a specific parenting and child development curriculum that addresses basic care, health and safety, and strategies to enhance family functioning. Home visitors create an individual binder of activities and information that is left with the family and they discuss with parents ways to incorporate their new learning into their daily routine (Doherty, 2008).

Quebec's Services integers en perinatalite et pour la petite enfance a l'intention des familles vivant en contexte de vulnerabilite (SIPPE)

SIPPE, a program that targets women who are pregnant, under age 20, and/or living in extreme poverty, and/or are recent immigrants, is provided across the province. The mother and father may continue to participate in the program until the child is five years of age. Participants are referred by hospitals, or by other health and social services. In 2006–2007, SIPPE served 5,240 women—an estimated 56 percent of the eligible population—and had an annual budget of $48 billion. Participants are provided with a variety of support including home visits lasting 60 to 90 minutes every second week beginning in the twelfth week of pregnancy, information about good nutrition and health practices, food coupons, and prenatal vitamins. After the birth, there are weekly home visits until the child is six-weeks-old, every second week until he or she is 12-months-old, and then monthly until the age of five. The home visitors' activities are tailored to meet the needs of families which may include child development information, effective parenting strategies, educational activities to do with the child, budgeting and other life skill counseling, assistance in accessing other services such as child care and job training, and accompanying a parent to an appointment. Generally, the home visitor is a nurse who has access to other many specialists such as speech and language therapists, medical doctors, nutritionists, social workers, etc. Home visits are supplemented by group activities for parents and their children and parents are encouraged to enroll their preschool-aged child in regulated child care as a means of providing a group educational experience (Doherty, 2008).

PROGRAMS SUPPORTING LITERACY

Parents, as their child's first teachers, have enormous influence on their child's literacy levels. In order to set the stage for lifelong learning, it is critical that families incorporate a love of language, storytelling, and reading into their everyday life. Educators can support this development in a variety of ways. One such example is Family Literacy Day, which occurs every year on January 27. It is a positive way to encourage reading and storytelling. More information about Family Literacy Day and other issues related to literacy can be found on ABC Canada's website at **www.abc-canada.org**. All the programs described in this chapter focus on literacy to one degree or another, but some unique programs have been established in Canada.

Dlunkat Hit, Teslin, Yukon

Contributed by Patty Wiseman, director of Dlunkat Hit; Ann Gedrose, Child Care Services, Yukon

Dlunkat Hit, a child-care program in the Yukon, hosts a program that involves the larger community in the daily daycare program: students from Grades 3 through 9 are hired to read to the younger children at the daycare. Each student provides a letter from their parents indicating their approval. Next, the student has an interview with the daycare director and then they sign a contract binding them to make the commitment, and to follow through on it. The students select the books they will read to the daycare children. While the daycare children have the fun of hearing stories, the students are improving their reading, and gaining some work experience, and gaining an appreciation of the work of caring for and educating the younger ones. This program, which began as a volunteer program, is now funded by a grant from the Literacy Action Committee Department of Education, Yukon.

Parenting and Family Literacy Centres

"In 1981 the Toronto Board of Education initiated Parenting and Family Literacy centres in its inner-city schools. The goal of the program was to improve educational outcomes for children by involving the family with the school early-on and by offering support and information to parents in their role of child rearing" (Gordon, 1992: 2). These groundbreaking programs were the first and largest programs of their kind in Canada.

Parenting and Family Literacy centres give parents a positive introduction to the school system and deliver a range of play-based, problem-solving activities to parents and children ranging in age from newborn to the age of six. Each Parenting and Family Literacy centre is unique, as it reflects its immediate neighbourhood, so programs are delivered in a culturally sensitive environment. Respect for the values of the parents is paramount—staff work with parents to establish the needs that the parents themselves identify. Parenting staff (parent workers) are trained in the identification of early disabling conditions and routinely refer children to appropriate medical services.

In addition to being highly multicultural, Parenting and Family Literacy centres tend to be multigenerational. At one centre, three Chinese grandfathers socialize as they care for their grandchildren, while at the opposite end of the city teenage mothers meet with their infants and often bring along their own mothers or sisters. Most centres have three generations represented at every session.

Joanne Davis, acting program manager of Parenting and Family Literacy Centres, Toronto District School Board, contributes the following:

The centres tend to be located in our most inner-city schools and reflect the typical issues facing the community. Subsequently staff (parent workers) need to familiarize themselves with local resources in the community so that they can make referrals

This display highlights the family literacy work of the parenting centres of the Toronto District School Board.

around issues such as housing, legal advice, food banks, ESL classes, and family shelters.

The parent is seen as the first and most important teacher and is supported in this role. In keeping with the special focus of literacy and numeracy learning, parents and their children are read to many times a day. Each centre has a range of inexpensive "in-house" learning materials which offer parents opportunities to teach their young children literacy and numeracy concepts in a non-threatening play environment. Parents are exposed to age-appropriate activities and develop realistic expectations for their children.

We are constantly explaining child development to the parents so they can recognize the milestones and enjoy them. The common denominator here is fun. If a child feels loved and connected to one parent, their classroom learning will improve.

Today the Toronto District School Board [TDSB] has 54 Parenting and Family Literacy centres in public schools supporting 10,000 families. The Ministry of Education is now transferring funds directly to TDSB to maintain the centres and to open an additional four centres. In addition, the province has allocated funds to open 40 more Parenting and Family Literacy Centres (PFLCs) in eight other school boards throughout the province. The unique location of these centres facilitates a familiarity with the school setting and a successful transition to kindergarten. Each centre includes

- a multilingual book-lending library;
- low-literacy books for adults;
- textless books;
- story tapes and tape recorders;
- a family literacy and numeracy program;
- a book library; and
- child-centred activities (with sand, water, blocks, house centre, paint, crayons, construction toys, puzzles, Play-Doh, music, story time, picture books, riding toys, slides, tunnels, balls) (Gordon, 1992: 2–3).

The notion that ESL parents who read to their children in their first language are inhibiting the development of English-language skills is strongly rejected by parenting centres. Programs are premised on the belief that the intimacy of the parent–child relationship drives literacy learning and that if the first language is subtracted from this relationship the learning is diluted. In the words of one parent worker:

Working from the Parenting Centres with families in a respectful, inclusive way raises the parents'

Reading is an integral part of the parenting centre philosophy.

self-esteem and empowers them to be advocates for their children's education. The informal visits from teachers and principals to the parenting centres go a long way to even the power imbalance that many low-literacy parents feel in our schools. We find that [when we demystify] the school system [for] parents, they are far more likely to become involved with their children's education. Parents will show up for interviews and help in the classroom when they understand jargon such as 'literature-based reading programs' or 'invented spelling' and when they feel welcomed by teachers.

The number one thing the parents are told is that they are their child's first teacher. When parents realize they have this power, Mary Gordon says, they can help their children learn (*The Toronto Star,* 1998). The centre's work is supported by the National Longitudinal Study, which found that children whose mothers read to them more than once a day scored about six percent higher than children whose mothers seldom read to them. Regularly reading to a preschool child not only improves vocabulary skills but has a stronger effect on behaviour than any other factor (Carey, 1999).

"This parenting/literacy program is an integrated early childhood development program that makes use of the profession of early childhood educators and the skills of parents. This program creates a very positive social environment in early childhood development that, at the same time, builds the skills of parents. It is a low-cost, highly effective program when done in partnership with the school system" (Mustard, 1998). Mary Gordon states that society has lost the fabric of the community. Parenting centres knit community members together once again!

A PROGRAM LIKE NO OTHER: ROOTS OF EMPATHY

The early years are critical in the development of social and moral knowledge. It is during this time that their ideas and beliefs about equality or inequality, differences in gender, race, and disability manifest themselves. Paley (1992: 3) notes: "by kindergarten . . . a structure begins to be revealed and will soon be carved in stone. Certain children will have the right to limit the social experiences of their classmates. Henceforth, a ruling class will notify others of their acceptability and the outsiders learn to anticipate the sting of rejection. Long after hitting and name-calling have been outlawed by the teachers, a more damaging phenomenon is allowed to take root, spreading like a weed from grade to grade."

Fortunately, an innovative and powerful program, Roots of Empathy, has been developed by Mary Gordon. A kindergarten teacher by training and the former administrator for the Parenting and Family Literacy centres at TDSB, Mary is now the founder and president of, and inspiration behind, Roots of Empathy (ROE). Gordon brings tremendous passion and energy to her work, which has been celebrated by numerous awards and honours. When she speaks, she recounts one success story after another, and those who have heard her will not be surprised to learn that the Clinton administration, the Manitoba government, the United Nations, Nelson Mandela Children's Fund, and the Organization for Economic Co-operation and Development are among the organizations that have studied her techniques for dealing with inner-city kids.

According to the organization's website, **www.rootsofempathy.org**, Roots of Empathy's mission is to build caring, civil, and peaceful societies through the development of empathy in children and adults. The long-term focus of ROE is to build the parenting capacity of the next generation of parents. More immediately, ROE focuses on raising levels of empathy, which results in more respectful and caring relationships and the reduction of bullying and aggression. The innovative classroom program is offered to more than 10,000 students, aged 3–14 years, in 400 classrooms across Canada. The Roots of Empathy program uses the loving relationship between a parent and infant as a concrete, hands-on, interactive approach to demonstrate empathy. Throughout the school year, a volunteer family with a new-born baby and a trained instructor visit a classroom. The instructor coaches the students to observe how the baby forms an attachment to the parents. The infant's development is chronicled and children learn to recognize the baby's cues and unique temperament, while celebrating developmental milestones. Knowledge of infant development and safety issues (shaken baby syndrome, fetal alcohol spectrum disorder, SIDS) prevents future child abuse and builds parenting skills for the next generation.

Inclusion, respect, and good citizenship are core values in Roots of Empathy instruction. The instructor conducts additional sessions before and after each family visit, for a total of 27 sessions over the course of a year. The University of British Columbia has taken a leadership role in conducting research to evaluate the efficacy of the Roots of Empathy program. In the 2001–02 evaluation of the ROE program, 670 participating children demonstrated increased emotional understanding; increased prosocial behaviours as rated by their peers, including sharing, cooperativeness, fairness, trustworthiness, and kindness; decreased teacher-rated proactive bullying and aggression; and decreased teacher-rated relationship social aggression.

Seeds of Empathy

In 2005, Mary Gordon created Seeds of Empathy (**http://www.seedsofempathy.org/AboutOrg.html**) as a program to bring the messages of Roots of Empathy to preschoolers. Seeds of Empathy is designed for Early Childhood settings to foster social and emotional competence and early literacy skills and attitudes in children three to five years of age, while providing professional development for their educators.

Books for Adults

Roots of Empathy: Changing the World Child by Child, by M. Gordon

Child Care in Rural Communities

It can be hard to find and access services in rural Canada, whether for children, families, youth, adults, or seniors. Even if social services are available, they are often not available in all communities, during the hours families need them, or in a way that responds to individual needs. Governments and social service agencies across Canada struggle to successfully respond to the specific challenges of rural, remote, and northern communities. These challenges include large geographic distances, low population base, cultural diversity, seasonal employment patterns, and rural demographics. The Integrated Hub Model (IHM) is examining ways to make services more available and accessible to citizens living in these rural, remote, and northern communities.

As a farm child growing up in the farm workplace, my safety was often compromised due to lack of child-care options. I can remember having heat stroke from long hours in the hayfield sitting on my mom's knee on the tractor mowing or raking. Almost every farmyard has a dugout. I remember my brother and I playing a game of Russian Roulette with ours—using an old car hood as a raft to see if we could make across before it would sink. Neither one of us could swim. As children, we had no fear; after all, we were invincible then.

Now as a parent of farm children, I have a lot of fear. I fear for my children's safety, that they might not be as lucky as my brother and I were to escape unhurt. When my husband and I were first married, we both inherited a basic assumption from our farm parents—that it was possible to be both farmers and parents at the same time. If we survived being farm children, so would our children. The children would be safe with us while we worked. There was no daycare in our town for our two boys to attend. My parents were running their own farm and my husband's parents were willing but not able to care for two active children. Regular baby-sitters were not available and the ones that were, sometimes were not reliable. We were clever at devising ways to keep our children safe while we worked. During calving time, the boys rode in a wooden box attached to the rear of our three-wheeler Honda, much like a miniature set of stock racks. We could drive from calf to calf, tagging, castrating, doctoring, while they played inside this box. We also had a child's car seat mounted inside our cab tractor for seeding and haying time.

Of course, there were problems with these ideas. The Manitoba climate is not always kind to young children, being very cold in the winter and hot in the summer. Mosquitoes were bad and conditions were dusty and noisy. It seemed like we were working twice as hard and getting half as much done, trying to keep the boys safe and happy. Our third child was three weeks old when we finally admitted to ourselves that the situation was not good. We were loading cattle. Our two older boys were inside the truck and our baby was sleeping in the baby carriage. I had parked the carriage in front of the truck for shelter, not realizing my husband could not see it over the hood of the truck. Just minutes before my husband drove over the carriage, my baby cried and I picked him up to comfort him. If he had not awakened, he would have been in the carriage when it was crushed by our farm truck.

This incident shook both myself and my husband and opened our eyes to the dangers our children were facing in the farm workplace. Dangerous equipment, chemical use, noise levels, extremes in weather—we may do our best to protect them from these. But under stress, we can all make mistakes. Stress from heavy workloads is the unseen danger that threatens every child attending the farm workplace with their parents. Without alternative child-care options, I decided to stay home with the children. We would not place our children's lives at risk again.

My husband worked longer hours, seven day a week, to get all the work done on his own. This was very difficult on our family life. Then an option never before considered possible in a small town like ours became a reality; or should I say a miracle. Lakeview Children's Centre opened its doors. It began as a pilot project with federal grants to see if rural day care was needed and if it was viable. That year I enrolled our three boys and started helping my husband farm full-time. We got our work done faster, more efficiently, and with less stress. We discovered more leisure time to spend with our children, as my husband could now take weekends off work.

The child-care centre provided for our children all the things that family, baby-sitter, and the car seat in our tractor could not:

- Flexible hours, open from 6:00 a.m. to 10:30 p.m. if needed.
- Affordable, through subsidy programs, for low-income families.
- Quality, with experienced, educated caregivers.
- Structure, in the lives of our children. They knew what to expect on a day-to-day basis.
- And, as a bonus, it was 'guilt-free'—our children loved it!

We could see them growing and blossoming in the positive atmosphere of our rural child-care centre. Our children and our family life benefited from daily interaction at Lakeview Children's Centre. Daycare funding cuts have forced us to face an important question "Could we go back now, to the way things were before?' NO. We have discovered a child-care system that is truly viable—that cares for the lives of our children and keeps them safe and happy while we are at work. My greatest wish is that all farm kids will someday have equal access to the same care that my kids have right now.

As farm parents who want the best for our children, we must unite on this issue and fight for a universal child-care policy that includes the needs of the farm child. We must do this for the sake of our children's safety, physical and mental well being, and for the overall health of the farm community. I am not talking about a temporary measure, but in fact a permanent, structured, quality system where we can entrust our most precious resource, our children to grow, flourish, and remain safe while we are at work.

Source: JoAnn Egilson. The article first appeared in *Child Care Focus*, Fall 1993, Manitoba Child Care Association.

A VISION FOR RURAL CHILD CARE

"Rural Child Care is the creative development and operation of stable, quality, flexible, safe and affordable child-care choices within a process of local community building that includes parents, community members, organizations, agencies, businesses and adequate responsive government supports"

—Ontario Rural Child Care Committee, 1995

Statistics Canada defines a rural area as one that has attained a population concentration of fewer than 1,000 people and has a population density of fewer than 400 people per square kilometre. Doherty (1994) states that rural characteristics and their implications for child care include:

- seasonal variation as a predominant work pattern,
- fluctuations in the need for child care from year-to-year,

- a scattered population with relatively few users for any one type of service,
- long travel distances and lack of public transportation,
- the presence of commuters who live in rural areas but work in a town or city and drive long distances to work each day, and
- the presence of stay-at-home parents who may be without a car all day.

In many rural locations, there are few licensed child-care options. Centre-based care is expensive to provide in these communities. As Doherty notes, child-care centres cannot afford to hire the number of staff required to operate age-segregated groups (1994: 19). The needs of rural families are varied and include seasonal care, extended hours, emergency care, and full-time or part-time care. Finding teachers who are willing to engage in seasonal care is a particular challenge for centres in such regions.

INSIDE LOOK

I had an opportunity to work with diverse rural families and in different environments. An Ontario Early Years Centre provided drop-in centres, programs, and farm care for families in need. I worked on an "on call" basis which meant that I would be scheduled and booked for a different farm family daily. My shifts would differ from 7:30 a.m.–3:30 p.m., 8:00 a.m.–4:00 p.m., 9:00 a.m.–5:00 p.m., 10:00 a.m.–6:00 p.m.; flexibility was the order of the day. My responsibilities included preparing meals for the children as well as supervising and implementing activities. I also communicated with families to find out the types of experiences or activities they would like their children to engage in. Working in the family's homes made the interactions more personal and this strong relationship made it easier to provide quality care since, in most cases, I watched the children grow.

Source: Stefani Chiapponi, ECE graduate

Rural Voices

Rural Voices is a national support network which provides a way for communities across Canada to connect with, and learn from each other. Initially operating as a virtual network, Rural Voices has become a means for rural, remote, and northern communities to benefit from knowledge, learning, and best practices in early childhood education and care locally, provincially, and nationally. Their mission is to help build quality child care in rural remote and northern Canada, one community at a time. Participation in the Rural Voices network is voluntary and free. The network is maintained in a variety of ways, including through email and their website, a toll-free telephone line, and distribution of public education materials.

Although the realities and changes in rural life continue to lessen the gap between urban and rural child-care needs, the challenges of population base, geography, and irregular employment patterns means rural input into public policy development is critical if future public policy development is to respond to rural families. It is important to note that in Canada approximately 30 percent of the population lives in non-urban areas and 80 percent of our land mass is non-urban; the people who live in these areas are guaranteed access to social programs under Social Union Framework Agreement. Provincial and territorial governments all acknowledge there are needs for rural child care in rural, remote, and northern communities. The current issue focuses on whether or not new service models need to be developed and put in place to effectively meet the diverse needs of individual communities.

Communities Achieving Responsive Services (CARS)

To help rural, remote, and northern communities access the services they need, Rural Voices has developed a process called Communities Achieving Responsive Services. CARS is a value-based and consumer-focused process that improves how well services respond to the needs of community people. It is an opportunity for community people to influence how services are made available to community children and parents. It also is an opportunity for the community to help decide what services will ultimately look like in their community. Through a three-year project funded by the Lawson Foundation in Ontario, this process is being shared with other communities across Canada. Community members will be trained throughout Canada to be facilitators in the CARS process. There are a series of 10 steps in this process, which are divided into three areas of activity: Dare to Dream, Making It Happen, and Working for Change. More information can be found at http://ruralvoices.cimnet.ca.

Canadian Rural Partnerships

Contributed by Elliot Hewitt, Senior Policy Advisor, AB, NWT, NU, Rural Secretariat

The Rural Secretariat's Canadian Rural Partnerships (CRP) program was developed to provide funding for rural community development. Over the past year, the CRP has contributed to several innovative projects in the Nunavut territory, including the following three examples.

There are 26 communities in Nunavut, all dispersed over thousands of miles, three time zones, and accessible only by air. In each community there are democratically elected 'District Education Authorities' (DEAs) who have vaguely defined powers in overseeing local school matters; however, there has been no existing association to represent the collective voice of DEAs. The Coalition of Nunavut District Education Authorities was loosely organized in August 2006 to help parents across Nunavut gain a voice in public education through networking, exchanging information, conducting research, establishing partnerships, and fostering capacity building. The objective of the project funded in partnership with the CRP is to achieve a greater impact for the voice for parents on education policies, laws, and practices by establishing a Nunavut wide partnership between the 26 DEAs.

The community of Kugluktuk has faced rapid changes which have forced the abandonment of core traditional values and ways of living, thereby impacting on all cultural, economic, social, and physical aspects of the community. These impacts, while resulting in some increased economic opportunities for the community, have also created significant social issues (alcohol and drug abuse, gambling, child neglect, violence, suicides). The Tahiuqtiit model proposes the development of a stable community based infrastructure that facilitates an appropriate assessment of needs and provides support for continuous skills/learning development opportunities in order to strengthen

The Energetic City, Fort St John, BC

Fort St John (FSJ), the largest city in British Columbia north of Prince George, is a remote community situated in the Peace River region in north-eastern corner of the province, where the long days of summer are limited and warm and the short days of winter are long and cold. The economy is primarily based on raw resource extraction—oil and gas exploration, forestry, agriculture (grain farming and ranching), and hydroelectric power.

On June 29, 2007 there were only five houses and three suites advertised for rent in the local paper. The average cost of purchasing a home at the end of 2006 was $220,000 (*Alaska Highway News*, 2007a). The population of the city of FSJ, which has a median age of 29, has been expanding at a rate of 1.7 percent per year over the past decade, mainly due to the robust oil and gas economy (BC Stats, 2004). The high demand for low skilled labour has triggered an influx of transient workers from across the nation. Approximately 17,280 people or 54 percent of the Peace region population live within the city boundaries. The cumulative FSJ and area population of 60,000 people includes the District of Taylor, the community of Charlie Lake, the Doig River First Nations Reserve, the Blueberry First Nations Reserve, and the Halfway River First Nation reserve (BC Stats, 2004). In 2001 less than 64 percent of 18-year-olds had graduated from high school. The teenage pregnancy rate was the highest in the province at 35.8 per 1,000 girls aged 15–17 years of age (BC Stats, 2000; 2002).

Fort St John is a difficult place for women and children:

Fort St John is a 'man's world', we cope the best we can living in a community with the highest rate of spousal and sexual assault in Canada. Basically everything falls on the women's shoulders . . . everything from finances, to running the household to caring for the children. A lot of these men are gone from 3 weeks to 2 months and they come home and it creates tremendous stress and tension in the home because you're really used to doing everything yourself." (Reid, 2007)

"The city of Fort St John doesn't have any available buildings at the moment, and the high rent rate makes commercial spaces less of an option for daycares, which turn a marginal profit" (Eglinksi, in *Alaska Highway News*, 2007b). "The large number of families in FSJ with young children strains local social services and child-care facilities. This is due in part to how difficult it is to attract and retrain qualified workers because of low pay, lack of amenities, the remote location and the inclement weather" (Reid, 2007). Finding quality affordable child care, especially for children under three years of age is a major community issue. At the current time (2008) there is only one licensed group child-care program for children under three: it has eight spaces and has a wait list of over two years.

Source: Locher, 2007.

community capacity building for Kugluktuk community stakeholders and residents namely, young adults.

The Tahuiqtiit model implementation has been organized according to four phases of development which constitute the project objectives:

- Phase I: To document how the Tahiuqtiit model engages the community in participating and taking action for its well-being and to improve its quality of life. This will include determining key determinants of success, pitfalls avoided, and lessons learned.

- Phase II: Test the model by strengthening and initiating a community lifelong learning environment, including community capacity building activities. For example, learning activities could include proposal writing, project planning, and project evaluation.

Tulita is an isolated Native community of approximately 500 people in the Northwest Territories. It is situated where the Great Bear River meets the Deh Cho (Mackenzie) River. The symbolic Bear Rock overlooks the community. The Sister Celeste Child Development Centre was established in 1981. It has half-day programs for three- and four-year-olds that promote the continuity of learning between the highly valued family and three-hours-a-day in an early childhood environment.

Community involvement is one of the primary strengths of the program. The centre is staffed by Native women and men from Tulita, coordinated by Sister Celeste, and is governed by a committee of community members. Another strength of the program is its continuously developing blend of Native culture and early childhood practices. Play is the form of curriculum that includes cultural values and customs as well as opportunities for exploration and the practice of developing skills. The centre includes a Slavey language program and local stories from elders and others in the community have been translated into preschool books written in both Slavey and English for use in the centre and in homes. In response to the concerns of elders, the children receive instruction from a local Native drummer on how to dance, how to listen to the drum, and how to play hand games. Children snowshoe in the long winter months and snare rabbits in the nearby bush. The game is then prepared and shared first with elders at the feast.

Source: Contributed by Sister Celeste, Director of the Sister Celeste Child Development Centre, Tulita, Northwest Territories. Sister Celeste Goulet was awarded the Prime Minster's Award for Excellence in Early Childhood Education in 2008.

- Phase III: Develop and implement the evaluation framework of the Tahuiqtiit Model, inclusive to the community and relying on the participatory approach.
- Phase IV: Promote the model within the community and with other northern communities and interested parties.

The Northern Community Partnership Initiative is a multi-government horizontal coordination and collaborative approach that allows governments to work together at streamlining programs and service delivery for northern communities. This approach is being tested with federal and territorial government partners in Nunavut. The approach will be tested with one northern community—Pangnirtung, Nunavut—in their development and implementation of the Nunavut Partnership Pilot Project, focused on crime prevention through social development of children, youth, and their families. The project will evaluate the effectiveness of participatory approaches in building community capacity and fostering change through the management and delivery of the model.

EXHIBIT 2.5 LESSONS LEARNED, ROADS TRAVELLED—MOBILIZING COMMUNITIES FOR RURAL CHILD CARE

The federal government funded a project called Strong Families . . . Strong Communities: Developing Community Responsive Rural Child Care Services and Supports in Your Community. The products of the project include a workbook and four information videos. All materials were developed with the assistance of rural community partners from Newfoundland, Ontario, Nova Scotia, Manitoba, and Alberta, as well as the active participation of participants at a national symposium. The project strives to do three things: It encourages rural community members to develop responsive, community-driven childcare services; it challenges community groups to claim their share of resources from government through advocacy and awareness; and it reinforces the right of communities to get on with finding alternative ways of meeting their needs in the spirit of self-reliance and self-direction.

Source: C. Gott, *Lessons Learned . . . Roads Travelled: Mobilizing Communities for Rural Child Care* (Human Resources Development Canada and Bruce Grey United Way, 1999). Reprinted by permission of the author.

REFERENCES

Alaska Highway News. 2007a. June 29.

———. 2007b. July 11.

Andre, T., and C. Neave. 1992. *The Complete Canadian Day Care Guide*. Toronto: McGraw-Hill Ryerson.

Arat-Koç, S. 2001. "The Politics of Family and Immigration in the Subordination of Domestic Workers in Canada." In B. Fox, ed., *Family Patterns: Gender Relations*, 2nd ed. New York: Oxford University Press.

BC Stats. 2000–2002. *Community Facts*. Victoria, BC: Province of British Columbia.

———. 2004. *Community Facts*. Victoria, BC: Province of British Columbia.

———. 2006. *Community Facts*. Victoria, BC: Province of British Columbia.

Bergen, D. 1994. "Developing the Art and Science of Team Teaching." *Childhood Education*. Summer.

Bertrand, J. 2008. *Understanding, Managing and Leading Early Childhood Programs in Canada*. Toronto: Nelson.

Campaign 2000. 2002. *Poverty amidst Prosperity. 2002 Report Card on Child and Family Poverty*. Available at http://campaign2000.ca/rc/rc02/intro.html.

Canadian Association of Family Resource Programs. 1993. *Play and Parenting Connections*. Fall.

Canadian Federation of Agriculture, et al. 1995. *Take the Challenge*. Ottawa: Canada Safety Council. Media package.

Carey, E. 1999. "Where Do Day-Care Kids End Up? Top of the Class, Study Shows." *The Toronto Star*. 15 October.

Child Care Advocacy Association of Canada/Canadian Child Care Federation. 2003. "90% of Canadians Support National Child Care Plan, 86% Want Publicly Funded System." 27 January. Available at http://www.childcareadvocacy.ca.

Childcare Resource and Research Unit. 2001. Executive Summary: Starting Strong—Early Education and Care Report on an OECD Thematic Review. August.

———. 2007. *Space Statistics 2007*. Available at http://www.childcarecanada.org.

———. n.d. *What Does Research Tell Us about Quality in Child Care?* Toronto: University of Toronto.

Cleveland, G., and M. Krashinsky. 1998. *The Benefits and Costs of Good Child Care: The Economic Rationale for Public Investment in Young Children*. Toronto: Childcare Resource and Research Unit, Centre for Urban and Community Studies, University of Toronto.

———. 2003. Fact and Fantasy. *Eight Myths about Early Childhood Education and Care*. Toronto: Childcare Resource and Research Unit, University of Toronto.

Crane, D. 2003. "Investing in the Very Young Pays Dividends to All." *The Toronto Star*. 24 May.

Doherty, G. 1994. "Rural Child Care in Ontario." *Occasional Paper No. 4*. Childcare Resource and Research Unit and the Centre for Urban and Community Studies, University of Toronto.

Dunster, L., A. Maxwell, and P. Mosher. 1998. "The Family Child Care Workforce: Linking Research to Practice." *A Canadian Forum*. 25–27 October.

Early Years Study. 1999. "Final Report." Co-chairs Honourable Margaret Norrie McCain and J. Fraser Mustard. April. Toronto: Children's Secretariat. Available at http://www.childsec.gov.on.ca.

Family Day Care Services. n.d. Available at http://www.familydaycare.com.

Gestwicki, C., and J. Bertrand. 1999. *The Essentials of Early Education*. Toronto: Thomson Nelson Learning.

———. 2003. *The Essentials of Early Education*, 2nd ed. Toronto: Thomson Nelson Learning.

Gordon, M. 1992. "Family Literacy: Centres Involve Parents Early." *Literacy Works* 3 (3): 2–3.

Gott, C. 1999. *Lessons Learned … Roads Travelled: Mobilizing Communities for Rural Child Care*. Ottawa: Human Resources Development Canada; Owen Sound: Bruce–Grey United Way.

Health Canada. 1998. *Strong Families, Healthy Children: Canada's Community Action Program for Children (CAPC)*. Ottawa: Minister of Public Works and Government Services Canada.

Hepworth Berger, E. 2004. *Parents as Partners in Education: Families and Schools Working Together*, 6th ed. Columbus: Pearson Merrill Prentice Hall.

Hoffman, J. 2008. "Report Card." *Today's Parent*: 67–70.

Human Resources Development Canada. 2008. "Live-In Caregivers." Available at http://www.hrsdc.gc.ca/en/workplaceskills/foreign_workers/ei_tfw/lic_tfw.shtml.

Kagan, S.L., and P.R. Neville. 1994. "Parent Choice in Early Care and Education: Myth or Reality?" *Research and Clinical Issues, Zero to Three* 14 (4). February–March.

Keating, D. 2000. "A Head Start for All of Society." *The Toronto Star*. 15 January. L4.

Kellerman, M. 1994. "Connecting Family Resource Programs." *Focus on Child Care Initiatives Fund Projects*. July.

Kenna, K. 2003. "Taking Peace to the World." *The Toronto Star*. 2 August.

Leighton, D. 2005. "The Waldorf Experience: A Parents' Perspective." *Canadian Children: Journal of the Canadian Association for Young Children* 30 (1): 40.

Lero, D. 1994. "In Transition: Changing Patterns of Work, Family Life, and Child Care." *Ideas* 1 (3).

Lero, D., K. Johnson, and J. Rooney. 2001. *150 Canadian Statistics on Work, Family and Well-Being*. Ottawa: Human Resources Development Canada; Guelph, ON: Women's Bureau and Centre for Families, Work and Well-Being, University of Guelph.

Lilliard, A.S. 2007. *Montessori: The Science Behind the Genius*. New York: Oxford University Press.

Locher, L. 2005. "Parent Survey: Workshop Package." *Success By 6*.

Luxton, M. 2001. "Family Coping Strategies: Balancing Paid Employment and Domestic Labour." In B. Fox, ed., *Family Patterns: Gender Relations*, 2nd ed. New York: Oxford University Press.

McCain, M.N., and F.J. Mustard. 2002. *The Early Years Study Three Years Later: From Early Child Development to Human Development Enabling Communities*. Toronto: Founders' Network of the Canadian Institute for Advanced Research (CIAR).

McCain, M.N., F.J. Mustard, and S. Shanker. 2007. *The Early Years Study 2: Putting Science into Action*. Toronto: Council for Early Child Development.

Ministère de la Famille et des Aînés, 2007. *Accueillir la petite enfance. Le programme éducatif des services de garde au Québec. Montréal: Ministère de la Famille et des Aînés.* Available at http://www.mfa.gouv.qc.ca/publications/pdf/programme_educatif.pdf.

Montessori, M. 1972. *Education and Peace* (H.R. Lane, Trans.). Washington, DC: Henry Regnery.

Mustard, F. 1998. Personal communication, 10 March.

Ontario Rural Childcare Committee. 1995. *Rural Child Care Now . . . We're Worth It.* County of Grey–Bruce: Ontario Rural Childcare Committee.

Our Child Care Workforce: From Recognition to Remuneration: More Than a Labour of Love. 1998. Executive Summary. Ottawa: Child Care Human Resources Steering Committee.

Paley, V.G. 1992. *You Can't Say You Can't Play.* Cambridge, MA: Harvard University Press.

Phipps, S.A. 2001. "Lessons from Europe: Policy Options to Enhance the Economic Security of Canadian Families." In B. Fox, ed., *Family Patterns: Gender Relations*, 2nd ed. New York: Oxford University Press.

Reeves, K. 2002. *2002 Status Report on Canadian Family Resource Programs.* Ottawa: FRP Canada.

Reid, C. 2007. *Women's Employability and Health Research Project: Coalition for Women's Economic Advancement.* Fort St John, British Columbia. Available at http://www3.telus.net/public/wnn/RESEARCH_PUBLICATIONS/FSJ_Report.pdf.

Reid, R. 1994. "Stronger Children, Stronger Families." Address to the International Conference on Children's Rights, Victoria, BC. June.

Report Card on Child Poverty in Canada. 1999. Toronto: Campaign 2000.

Report of the Expert Panel on Quality and Human Resources. 2007. *Investing in Quality: Policies, Practitioners, Programs and Parents.* March. Available at http://www.childcareontario.org/action/07election/qhr_report_march07.pdf.

Rushowy, K. 2004. "Pre-school Crucial." *The Toronto Star.* 27 March. A1.

———. 2007. "Canada 'Dead Last' In Spending." *The Toronto Star.* 26 March. A1.

Shonkoff, J.P., and D.A. Phillips, eds. 2000. *From Neurons to Neighborhoods: The Science of Early Childhood Development.* Washington, DC: National Research Council and Institute of Medicine, National Academy Press.

Skulski, J. 1995. "The Westcoast Story." *Focus on Child Care Initiatives Fund Projects.* March.

Statistics Canada. 1999. "National Longitudinal Survey of Children and Youth, 1996–97." Ottawa: Statistics Canada. Available at http://www.statcan.ca/Daily/English/991213/d991213c.htm.

Taylor, L. 2006. *The Ottawa Citizen.* June 4. Available at http://www.canada.com/ottawacitizen/news/citizensweekly/story.html?id=1ed75588-68b2-4.

The Toronto Star. 1998. "Praised Parenting Centres Feel Future Slipping Away." 22 April. B1.

———. 1999. "Auto Union Makes Child Care Job One." 2 October. L3.

Vanier Institute of the Family. 1994. *Profiling Canada's Families.* Ottawa: Vanier Institute of the Family.

Weiss, H., M. Caspe, and M. Lopez. 2006. "Family Involvement in Early Childhood Education." *Family Involvement Makes a Difference.* Harvard Research Project Series, No. 1. Cambridge, MA: Harvard University.

Whiteside Taylor, K. 1970. *Parent Cooperative Preschools International Journal.* Fall.

Willms, J.D., ed. 2002. *Vulnerable Children.* Edmonton, AB: University of Alberta Press.

You Bet I Care! Survey. 1998. Ottawa: Human Resources Development. Available at http://www.cfc-efc.ca/docs/00001269.htm.

Yukon Department of Health and Social Services. n.d. Available at http://www.hss.gov.yk/prog/fcs/index.html.

Courtesy of Lynn Wilson

CHAPTER 3

Building Effective Partnerships

"Transformative education is defined as two people or groups coming together and interacting in such a way that both parties learn something and are changed for the better by the interaction"

—*Janet Gonzalez-Mena (2007)*

LEARNING OUTCOMES

After studying this chapter, you will be able to

1. identify the key features of successful relationships with families
2. discuss the particular benefits of partnerships for family members, children, and teachers
3. describe the barriers to effective partnerships
4. identify the strategies that supervisors and teachers can use to build effective partnerships with families

When you heal a child you heal a family.

When you heal a family you heal a community.

When you heal a community you heal a nation.

The same can be said for the love and care of a child:

When you provide love, support and care to a child, you provide care and support to a family.

When you provide care and support to a family, you provide care and support to a community.

When you provide care and support to a community, you provide care and support to a country.

—Ovide Mercredi, 1992.

WHY WE NEED PARTNERSHIPS WITH FAMILIES

Developing partnerships with families is an integral part of the role of an early childhood teacher. To work effectively with children, teachers must work effectively with their families. But how do we define this partnership? Since different child-care centres have different perspectives and serve different communities, it is not surprising that family–teacher partnerships may take many forms. The child-care centre is a microsystem—it operates within a community, never in isolation, influenced by a larger macrosystem of political, economic, and social issues. All the elements of the microsystem and macrosystem influence relationships between families and teachers (see Figure 3.1).

Declining achievement scores, rising educational costs, and a growing distrust of bureaucratic institutions have focused attention on parents' rights and responsibilities with respect to their child's education. Family involvement is critical to children's development and achievement and in preventing or remedying educational and developmental problems.

WHAT THE EXPERTS SAY

Countless experts tell us of the benefits of family involvement, including higher achievement rates, higher attendance rates, lower delinquency and dropout rates, and higher high school completion and college or university admission rates. Importantly, most of this research is based on families whose children are at high risk for school failure. Many leading early childhood organizations support the critical need for collaborative partnerships with families. Several examples of this support are listed below.

The Canadian Child Day Care Federation's document on quality child care (1991) underscores the importance of parent partnerships when it states:

> Quality child care maintains an open, friendly and informative relationship with each child's family and encourages their involvement. The interaction among all persons in a child care setting reflects mutual respect, trust and co-operation. The family and the child care providers become partners who communicate openly for the mutual benefit of the children and themselves.

The National Statement on Quality Early Learning and Child Care (2007) describes a collaborative partnership as one that honours the family's role as the child's primary caregivers, respects its child-rearing beliefs and values, and provides meaningful opportunities for families to determine their children's early learning and care experiences. This is supported by The Occupational Standards for Child Care Practitioners (2003) which states that the ability to establish and maintain an open, cooperative relationship with each child's family is a key

FIGURE 3.1 LINKS

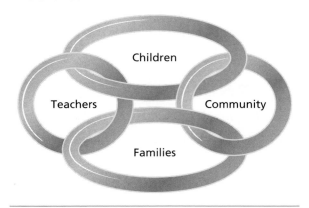

Teachers play a powerful role in the lives of children.

competency of practitioners. The Occupational Standards for Child Care Administrators (2007) states that administrators need to have the ability to create a family-friendly environment, and those administrators play an important role in providing a positive experience for the family and the child, and they also support families with their child-rearing responsibilities.

The National Association for the Education of Young Children (NAEYC) (1996: 5) advocates that "for the optimal development and learning of all children, educators must accept the legitimacy of children's home language, respect (hold in high regard) and value (esteem, appreciate) the home culture, and promote and encourage the active involvement and support of all families including extended and non-traditional family units."

UNICEF's priority is that family and community capacities are strengthened to promote caring, supportive, and protective environments in which children can reach their fullest potential.

It is clear that we have a great deal of direction from prestigious organizations and individuals and many principles upon which to build. The real test is how this theory will be translated into practice!

Partners in Quality Study

Gillian Doherty shares results of the Canadian Child Care Federation (CCCF) study *Partners in Quality,* a mail-out survey conducted in the fall of 1997, in which 42 percent of the respondents identified parent involvement as one of the most important elements of quality care. Among people working directly with children (family- and centre-based care providers and centre directors), 54 percent identified the need for two-way communication between parent and care provider. Among the people identifying this as an important mechanism, 84 percent felt that such communication should be daily.

Twenty-seven percent of respondents working directly with children said that parent involvement in boards of directors in parent advisory groups was desirable. Other forms of involvement identified as desirable were parent assistance on field trips (28 percent of respondents working with children) and parent involvement in fundraising (13 percent of respondents).

The CCCF survey also asked people how, apart from face-to-face communication, their settings communicate with parents. Thirty-three percent identified written notes or journals, 32 percent reported that their setting has an open-door policy, and 19 percent reported encouraging parents to be involved in program activities. The most frequently cited desirable way of reaching out to parents was through a program or social event (43 percent of people working directly with children). When asked how child-care settings can support parents, respondents suggested the following:

- frequent two-way communication (59 percent)
- providing resources such as information on child development or information on other community services (56 percent)
- providing a caring and nurturing environment for the child (52.3 percent)
- offering parent workshops or other forms of parent education (16 percent)

Respondents were asked how they handle situations in which they and the family have different approaches to parenting. Seventy-six percent of people who work directly with children said they would discuss the situation with the family. Respondents noted the need "to be respectful of family and cultural values," to "talk openly about differences," to "foster open discussion about values and philosophy," and to "exchange ideas." The second most frequent response was to provide the family with information on child development (38 percent).

Seventy-one percent of the field respondents identified parents as the main barrier to family involvement in the child-care setting. Sixty-nine percent of these respondents suggested that the main difficulty was parental time constraints. Only 21 percent of respondents identified staff as a barrier. Time pressures (95 percent) and defensiveness (6 percent) were the most frequently cited staff issues related to parent or family involvement.

This survey provides valuable insight into the attitudes of staff toward family involvement. It shows that teachers and parents are not equal partners in the child-care setting. Instead, the power rests with the teachers, who remain the perceived experts in the child-care context. Clearly, much work remains to be done to establish a true partnership among equals.

The Rights of Parents

Loris Malaguzzi (n.d.) outlines the Reggio Emilia approach's "A Charter of Rights for Parents" below:

> It is the right of parents to participate actively and with voluntary adherence to the basic principles in the growth, care, and development of their children who are entrusted to the public institution. This means no delegating and no alienation. Instead, it confirms the importance of the presence and the role of parents, who have always been highly valued in our institutional tradition. Parent participation enables a communication network that leads to fuller and more reciprocal knowledge, as well as to a more effective shared search for the best educational methods, content, and values. Then we have parents who are mainly young, of different trades and professionals, different backgrounds and experiences, and often of different ethnic origins. But all these parents have to struggle against the lack of available time, the cost of living, the difficulty of their responsibilities as parents, and the desire to identify, discuss, and reflect on their problems, especially those concerning the growth and education of their children. When school and parents are able to converge toward a cooperative experience, an interactive experience that is the rational and advantageous choice of everyone concerned, then it is easy to see how hostile and mistaken is the pedagogy of self-sufficiency and prescription, and how friendly and fertile is the strategy of participation and shared research.

New families may be confused by the hundreds of "experts" who offer conflicting opinions on raising children. Parenting is a demanding role that requires ongoing support systems within the extended family as well as within the community. Some parents may feel ill-prepared because of a lack of effective parental modelling during their own childhood and an insecure sense of their personal efficacy to manage in a role as educator (Bandura, 1997). However, when parents believe they have an important role in their child's development, they act on that belief in ways that encourage the child's potential

(Hoover-Dempsey and Sandler, 1997). When families and teachers set goals and objectives together, the chances for the child's success increase significantly. Involved parents are more likely to communicate the value of the program to their children and to reinforce the program's goals within both the child-care setting and the home. According to Bronfenbrenner (1974), parents' self-esteem increases as they become more effective parents; once they see they can do something about their child's education, they see also that they can do something about housing, their community, and their jobs. Establishing teacher training that emphasizes the family's primary caregiving role and is responsive to different parenting practices is critical to the work of early childhood teachers.

The Rights of the Child

Although there is a more detailed discussion about the rights of the child in Chapter 11, children have the right to families that support and protect them. The United Nations Convention on the Rights of the Child emphasizes how important families are in a child's socialization. Governments are expected to make every effort to keep families intact, and to provide support and assistance to parents so they can fulfill their

responsibilities. Even young children are entitled to know about their human rights. Families can engage in activities that help children learn about their rights and that help them put their rights and responsibilities into practice as they prepare to be responsible citizens.

REACHING OUT TO FAMILIES

For families to expect teachers to care for their children without the needed supports and alliances is irresponsible. Likewise, for teachers to see their teaching role as limited to the children in their classroom is foolish. Only as teachers and families develop a vision of themselves as highly important and positive partners in children's lives can these strategies carry meaning (Swick, 1991: 34).

Gonzalez-Mena and Widmeyer (1989: 23) describe three distinct stages in teachers' perceptions of parents:

[F]irst, they may see themselves as saviours, rescuing the children from their parents. Second, they move toward a perception of parents as clients, whom they work toward reeducating, and last they come to see parents as partners, whose needs are listened to and integrated with the teacher's professional expertise to provide what is best for the children without a sense of imposing ideas.

EXHIBIT 3.1 WHAT MAKES RELATIONSHIPS WORK?

SIX BASIC QUALITIES

1. **A relationship needs to balance reason and emotion.** Many aspects of a relationship are not rational. We often react emotionally, not logically, in pursuit of some purpose. Emotions such as fear, anger, and frustration may disrupt otherwise thoughtful actions. Emotions are normal, necessary, and often essential to problem-solving. They can convey important information, help us marshal our resources, and inspire us to action. Wisdom is seldom found without them. Nonetheless, the ability of two people to deal well with their differences will be greater to the extent that reason and emotion are in some kind of balance.

2. **Understanding helps.** If we are going to achieve an outcome that will satisfy the interests of both and leave each of us feeling fairly treated, we will need to understand each other's interests, perceptions, and notions of fairness. Whether we agree or not, the better we understand each other, the better our chance of creating a solution we can both accept.

3. **Good communication helps.** The more effectively we communicate about our differences, the better we understand each other's concerns and the better our chances for reaching a mutually acceptable agreement. The more openly we communicate, the less basis there is for suspicion.

4. **Being reliable helps.** Well-founded trust, based on honest and reliable conduct over a period of time, greatly enhances our ability to cope with conflict. The more honest and reliable we are with respect to each other, the better our chance of producing good outcomes.

5. **Persuasion is more helpful than coercion.** Each of us will try to affect the other's decisions, and the way in which we do so will have a profound effect on the quality of the relationship. At one extreme, I can try to inspire your voluntary cooperation through education, logical argument, moral persuasion, and my own example. At the other extreme, I can try to coerce you by worsening your alternatives and by warnings, threats, extortion, and physical force. The more coercive the means of influence, the less likely it is that the outcome will reflect both our concerns, and the less legitimate it is likely to be in the eyes of at least one of us. The less coercive the modes of influence, the better our ability to work with each other.

6. **Mutual acceptance helps.** If we are to deal well with our differences, we need to accept each other as someone worth dealing with. Feeling accepted, worthy, and valued is a basic human psychological need. Unless you listen to my views, accept my right to have views that differ from yours, and take my interests into account, I am unlikely to want to deal with you. And if we do not deal with each other, we will not even begin to resolve our differences.

Based on these six concepts, here is a checklist that will help teachers assess their relationships with families:

1. **Goal:** Am I trying to win the relationship or improve it? How well do we resolve differences? How often do I think about improving the process for working together over the long term?

2. **General Strategy:** Do serious issues disrupt our ability to work together? Do I tend to retaliate by doing things that weaken our ability to deal with each other in the future? Do I ignore problems or sweep them under the rug rather than deal with them?

3. **Balance of Emotion and Rationality:** *Awareness*: What emotions, mine and yours, are affecting our interactions? *Effect*: How are emotions helping and hurting our decision-making?

4. **Degree of Understanding:** How well do I empathetically understand your perceptions, interests, values, and motivation? How well can I state them to your satisfaction? How well do you understand mine? Can you state them to my satisfaction?

5. **Effectiveness of Our Two-Way Communication:** How regularly do I consult you before making decisions? What important subjects don't we discuss? Why? How extensively and frequently do we communicate? Do I listen?

6. **Reliability, or Your Degree of Confidence in My Future Conduct:** Might I be more reliable? How? How could I be more worthy of trust? Do your perceptions suggest some changes I might make? What risks do I see in relying on you? Are those risks well-founded?

7. **Persuasion or Coercion:** Do I try to persuade you on the merits? Could I be more open to persuasion? How? How well do I avoid threats, warnings, and commitment tactics?

8. **Degree of Mutual Acceptance:** Do I fully accept you as someone with whom to deal? Do you matter in my scheme of things? Am I giving serious attention to your interests and views? Do I recognize the potential long-term quality of this relationship?

Source: Adapted from *Getting Together: Building a Relationship That Gets to Yes* (Boston: Houghton Mifflin), by Roger Fisher and Scott Brown. Copyright © 1998 by Roger Fisher and Scott Brown. Reprinted by permission of Houghton Mifflin Company. All rights reserved.

FIGURE 3.2 CULTURAL IDENTITY CIRCLE

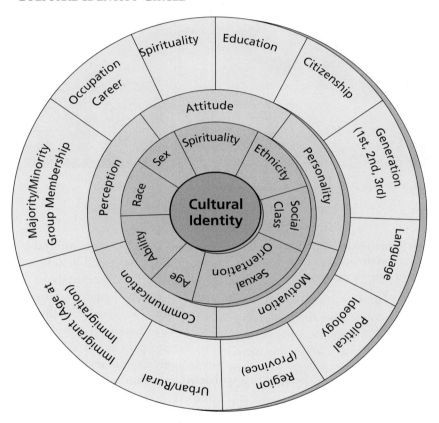

Source: Carl E. James (1999). *Seeing Ourselves: Exploring Race, Ethnicity and Culture,* 2nd edition. Toronto, Thompson Education Publishing.

FAMILIES, TEACHERS, AND CULTURAL INFLUENCES

The strategies for effective partnerships will vary from community to community and from family to family. Families are not a homogeneous group and each will have different perspectives, attitudes, and values that need to be reflected on and openly discussed. As illustrated in Figure 3.2, each family develops its own cultural identity based on (starting from the inner circle) individual factors, personal factors, and psychological and social factors. Vygotsky's contextual theory supports the fundamental ideology that knowledge comes from culture.

Gonzalez-Mena (1998: 224) states:

Culture is invisible. It has been said that one moves in one's culture the way a fish moves through water. The water is so much a part of the fish's experience that the only time it becomes aware of the water is when it suddenly finds itself surrounded by air. We are immersed in our culture

Children thrive when their identity, culture, and home language are recognized and supported.

the way the fish is immersed in water. We may be unaware of how much our culture influences our actions, our thoughts, our very perceptions.

When we discuss families and their cultural identity we must always remember the great diversity within cultures and avoid stereotyping because it ignores the great individuality of group members. "Learning to embrace diversity is not intended to threaten anyone's way of living and being; nor is it about cultures being right or wrong. It is about understanding and accepting difference and extending equal human rights to all. Each of us is entitled to the way of living and being that is best for us. However, as early childhood educators, when we enter the workplace, we are in a public arena, one that must be accepting of all children and their families. If we are not, we devalue children and families in our care" (Dever and Falconer, 2008: 277). Families will bring different beliefs and expectations to their child care experience. Some will come from cultures where involvement in the child-care centre is not encouraged and others may openly challenge policies and procedures in the centre. Some parents may be reluctant to engage because they are uncomfortable with their language skills. Early childhood programs must adapt and respond to the needs of families. It is an exciting yet challenging approach, and one that is completely congruent with the principles and practices of honouring diversity. It is exciting, too, in that it opens doors to reconceptualizing work with families, and challenging in that it places the onus on child-care programs and staff to elicit, respect, and respond to families' needs, wants, and desires.

Underlying the concept of family-centred, culturally sensitive child care are the following core beliefs (Chud and Fahlman, 1995: 146–47):

- The family is central to the child's life.
- Each family has its own particular strengths, competencies, resources, and ways of coping.
- Each family must be accepted and respected on its own terms, with no judgments or preconceptions.
- The racial, cultural, ethnic, religious, and socioeconomic diversity of families must be honoured.

- Services and programs for families are effective only insofar as they support the family in meeting its own identified needs and concerns.
- Policies or practices that limit access or exclude families from service because of their diversity must be eliminated.

Our capacity to respond thoughtfully and sensitively to family diversity depends on the following:

- our respect for the role and importance of family in the lives of children;
- our understanding of the challenges which are common to all parents and those that may be shared particularly by parents in minority positions;
- our commitment to the concept of family-centred, culturally sensitive child care; and
- our personal willingness to open our hearts and minds to family viewpoints and perspectives that might be different from our own.

LaGrange, Clark, and Munroe (1994: 30) describe three important tenets of family-centred, culturally-sensitive child care:

> First, all children living in a multicultural society need attitudes, knowledge, and skills that help them to positively and comfortably respond to diversity. Second, children from minority backgrounds thrive when their identity, culture, and home language are recognized and supported. Third, all children need guidance to understand and resist unfairness, prejudice, and discrimination.

Switsun (1994) stresses the importance of developing an environment in which children and parents feel free to ask questions about disabilities, culture, or race. Gonzalez-Mena and Widmeyer (1989: 73) caution teachers not to predict a child's behaviour solely on the basis of his or her culture: "Individuals are guided by their individual values, inclinations, behavior styles, and cultural background. Knowing a person's culture tells you something about the probability that he or she will behave in a certain way; it doesn't tell you that he or she will behave in a certain way."

EPSTEIN'S SIX TYPES OF PARENT INVOLVEMENT

Epstein (1995) identified six types of parent involvement and suggested strategies that teachers could employ to develop a working partnership with parents. While some of her focus is based on school-aged children, much can be adapted to early learning environments.

1. **Parenting:** Help all families establish home environments to support children as students.
   a. Parent education and other courses or training for parents
   b. Family support programs to assist families with health, nutrition and other services
   c. Home visits at transition points to preschool, elementary, middle and high school

2. **Communication:** Design effective forms of school-to-home and home-to-school communications about school programs and children's progress.
   a. Conferences with every parent at least once a year
   b. Language translators to assist families as needed
   c. Regular schedule of useful notices, memos, phone calls, newsletters, and other communications

3. **Volunteering:** Recruit and organize parent help and support.
   a. School and classroom volunteer programs to help teachers, administrators, students, and other parents
   b. Parent room or family centre for volunteer work, meetings, and resource for families
   c. Annual postcard survey to identify all available talents, time, and locations of volunteers

4. **Learning at Home:** Provide information and ideas to families about how to help students at home with homework and other curriculum-related activities, decisions, and planning.
   a. Information for families on skills required for students in all subjects at each grade
   b. Information on homework policies and how to monitor and discuss schoolwork at home
   c. Family participation in setting student goals each year and in planning for college or work

5. **Decision Making:** Include parents in school decisions, developing parent leaders and representatives.
   a. Active PTA/PTO or other parent organizations, advisory councils, or committees for parent leadership and participation
   b. Independent advocacy groups to lobby and work for school reform and improvements

c. Networks to link all families with parent representatives

6. **Collaborating with Community:** Identify and integrate resources and services from the community to strengthen school programs, family practices and student learning and development.

   a. Information for students and families on community health; cultural, recreational, and social support, and other programs/services

   b. Information on community activities that link to learning skills and talents, including summer programs for students. (Epstein, 2002)

STUDENT PERCEPTIONS

Gestwicki (2000) notes that ECE students, when surveyed, are aware that they may have an ideal image of the family and an understanding of how societal influences helped produce it. Nevertheless, "they may be unaware of how insidiously this subliminal image can influence their encounters with real families. If an ideal, lurking unknowingly in the teacher's value system, is considered the 'good,' a negative evaluation can be made of any family that does not measure up to this standard" (2000: 8).

Year after year, ECE students experience the same concerns about their field placements.

Being able to identify these potential "triggers" allows us to discuss these concerns in a frank and open manner. Some of the most worrisome issues are:

- What if I disappoint them? What if I don't know as much as they think I should or perform as well as they would like?

- How can I effectively communicate with families who home language is not English?

- What if I am culturally insensitive without being aware of it?

- How can I hope to know everything I should about so many diverse families?

- How will I address controversial issues such as spanking when we have conflicting ideas about what is best for the child?

- What happens when families do not respect or agree with my teaching methods?

- I know that I lack confidence. I'm worried because I am shy and stepping up into the role of the teacher will be hard for me.

- As a new graduate in my early 20s I'm worried how older parents will respond to me. Will they think I am mature enough to work with their children?

- What if we don't connect? How will I deal with criticism and conflict?

INSIDE LOOK

A Map for Early Childhood Educators

Swick (2000) speaks to five starting points for early childhood professionals to use in their crafting of their "map" for being truly high-quality family helpers:

1. The human development and learning process is the result of everyone's effort, that is, it is an interactive and renewing process that is influenced by all parts of the human community.
2. An empowering approach to working with the diverse and ever-changing needs and contexts of children and families must replace a deficit-oriented way of related to children and families.
3. The power of parents and families to nurture healthy and proactive ways of living in children can occur within various forms and structures—the key is for families to have strong and nurturing relationships with each other and their supportive helpers.
4. Early childhood educators must create diverse and adaptive ways to support families in a world of constant change and stress.
5. Early childhood educators must lead the way for "community transformation" to create family embracing ways of functioning.

Source: Couchenour and Chrisman, 2000: xi.

EXHIBIT 3.2 PARENTS' COMMON BOND

Regardless of their cultural or socioeconomic backgrounds, parents the world over exhibit many of the same characteristics.

1. **Parents love their children.** The vast majority of parents experience the bond with their children as a love relationship. Children's innocence, dependence, freshness, and beauty evoke feelings of protectiveness, nurturing, caring, and connectedness. Although parents may demonstrate love for their children in myriad ways or may lack the physical or emotional resources to express their love in ways that others consider to be appropriate, the love relationship between parents and children stands strong as a force that unites parents the world over.

2. **Parents want the best for their children.** At the heart of the parent–child relationship is the parents' desire for the child to experience a good and happy life and to reach full potential—in ways the parents themselves may have failed. Whether "the best" means meeting basic needs for food, shelter, or clothing or, for parents of greater means, providing opportunities for education and other life-enhancing experiences, most parents want for their children the things they value in their own lives and in their own dreams. Wanting the best for their children often motivates parents to make sacrifices on their children's behalf.

3. **Parents learn to parent from their own parents.** The primary and most powerful teachers of parenting attitudes and skills are our own parents. Parenting styles fall into patterns that find expression in the small details of everyday life as well as in fundamental beliefs and approaches to child-rearing. Whether our experiences in being parented were characterized by warmth or coldness, nurturance or neglect, permissiveness or authoritarianism, the likelihood that we will later display those characteristics ourselves, as parents, is great. However, change too is a part of the human condition, and parenting is no exception to the rule.

4. **Parents can learn new ways of parenting.** Despite the power of the past, parents can and do make the choice to unlearn old ways of behaving and learn new ways of relating to children. A belief in the capacity of parents to discard unsuccessful child-rearing practices in favour of new practices is at the core of all parent-education endeavours. Through a growing number of books, videos, self-help materials, education campaigns, group sessions, and support groups, or through individual counselling, parents are encouraged to learn about their role in "people making." Parent education is a growth industry for the future of healthy families and the most hopeful avenue we have for promoting positive change.

Source: Chud and Falman, 1995: 144.

FAMILY TYPES

At the beginning of each semester, I survey my students (in an urban community college) to determine the "family types" with which they are most familiar and comfortable. Based on their responses, I modify my course to ensure we broaden their perspective by addressing the family types with which they are least familiar and comfortable. Over the last several years, we have discussed the following family types (listed here from the ones with which my students were least familiar/comfortable to those with which they were most familiar/comfortable). The list below ranks the family types from "least comfort/exposure/experience" to "most comfort/exposure/experience":

- Native Families
- Refugee Families
- Foster Families
- Same-sex Families
- Grandparents Raising Their Grandchildren
- Adoptive Families
- Teen Families
- Older Parents
- Multiracial Families
- Blended Families
- Lone Parents
- Divorced Families
- Immigrant Families

A key feature of the family–centre collaboration is that it is a constantly evolving relationship. As Braun (1992: 186) observes, "Working with parents . . . provides workers with sources of help, of friendship and of support—but also of challenge and a constant need to review and rethink approaches. It ensures that no one and no place becomes static and complacent, but that things change to meet changing people, circumstances, and needs." Different types of families are discussed in greater detail in Chapter 9.

THE BENEFICIARIES OF EFFECTIVE PARTNERSHIPS

Families are the first and most important teachers in the child's life. When families and teachers work effectively in an atmosphere of mutual trust and respect that honours diversity, exchanging ideas, and exploring goals for the child, much can be accomplished. Partnerships mean equity and shared power. Family-centred care and education in a partnership that includes the community is the focus of this text.

BENEFITS FOR FAMILIES

- With trained teachers working in partnership, families have access to information and resources that may assist them in building on their knowledge of their child in all areas of development—social, emotional, physical, creative, and cognitive.

- In a caring environment, families may add to their own repertoire of parenting strategies, such as expanding on effective pro-social techniques.

- Through examples seen in the playroom, families may be able to create activities and experiences for their child in the home environment.

- Involving families in meaningful learning experiences with their children can increase parents' self-esteem. Parents who have a positive self-image tend to have a deeper understanding of their children, to spend more time with them in learning activities, and to have a more positive attitude toward teachers and the educational process (Swick, 1991: 34).

- Families who observe their child's interaction with other children and with adults, are better able to set realistic goals for their child.

- Parenting can be a daunting task but when families and teachers develop a reciprocal relationship, it allows for partners to problem-solve and openly and safely share their frustrations and concerns.

- Effective partnerships provide an opportunity for parents to share exciting moments with other adults who know and care about their child.

- A strong relationship with the child-care team may help to lessen the isolation some parents may feel.

- In situations where strong bonds exist between families and teachers, it can be theorized that teachers play a significant role in the "extended family."

- Some families may develop a supportive network with other families as well as with the teachers in the child-care centre.

- As volunteers in the program, parents may acquire new skills or expand on existing skills that can augment their résumés.

- The more involved parents are in the program, the more they may come to appreciate and value the efforts and dedication of the teachers, further enhancing the relationship.

- Family members may also be able to make meaningful suggestions for improvement and to contribute actively to curriculum development.

BENEFITS FOR CHILDREN

- The climate of mutual respect engendered by an effective partnership enables teachers and families to create a consistent, nurturing, and emotionally stable environment for the child through trust, security, and attachment.

- As the parenting skills of the family members improve through direct observations, sharing of resources, and so on, the child is guided by confident parents who display increased self-esteem.

- Extensive research suggests that children achieve more when families are actively involved in their child care and school experiences. Larsen and Haupt (1997) say, "Family participation has been linked to greater awareness and responsiveness in children, more complex language skills, greater problem-solving abilities in children, increased academic performance and significant gains in cognitive as well as physical skill development."

- When families, as the primary caregivers, share information about their child, the teacher is better able to support the child in all areas of his or her development. Conversely, when teachers share information about the child, families are better able to establish for their child realistic goals that will maximize his or her growth and therefore improve the family–child bond.

- When children see their families validated by teachers they trust and respect, their own self-esteem is enhanced.

- Resources available at the centre can be shared with children and their families. Items such as travelling suitcases with story books, art supplies, science experiments, etc., can enrich the home environment.

- As family members become more involved, benefits accrue also to younger siblings, who will reap the rewards of strong ties to the centre.

- A child is constantly absorbing cues about how one is to behave from those people in their lives who are important to them. An effective teacher has the opportunity to model moral and ethical behaviours in everyday interactions with

the children, other teachers and the community at large.

- Through watching interactions between their parents and teacher, children can learn about communication skills and how issues can be resolved in a respectful and caring manner.

BENEFITS FOR TEACHERS

- Having their work valued and respected by families is important to teachers' self-confidence and professionalism.

- When the partnership goes well, teachers have the satisfaction of knowing that they have made an important contribution to the lives of the families they work with.

- When challenges arise and are successfully resolved, teachers and families strengthen their partnership and become more confident in their interactions.

- The more experience teachers have with families, the more they develop effective interpersonal strategies for dealing with all types of situations. The teacher experiences ongoing learning as each new family joins the centre.

Children in diverse settings have much to learn from one another.

"When I chose to work with young children, I did it because children inspired me" says Amanda Hestbak, who has been working since November at the Wetaskiwin Head Start Society in Wetaskiwin, Alberta. "I've quickly discovered that children come with families and that being with children involves being with parents, too." Penny Pelton has watched many students come to this realization in her years of teaching in the Early Childhood Care and Education Program at Heritage College in Gatineau, Quebec. Penny compares the relationship between a family and their child-care practitioner to paddling a canoe together on the river. "When we pay attention to our partner and coordinate our strokes, the canoe moves smoothly through the water. We glide along and everyone can relax and enjoy the ride. Then if we do happen to hit rough water, we know we can get through it because we have practiced working together. There is trust that we can cooperate and keep the canoe upright and moving forward."

Source: Mann, 2008: 27.

- Learning about the child from the family enables the teacher to use that information to plan successful and relevant learning experiences.

- Many teachers feel positively toward families whose members actively participate in the program, since participation underscores the value that families place on the teachers.

- When families share their expertise, experiences, and resources, they enrich the program and the lives of everyone who works in the centre.

- When families volunteer in the playroom, teachers are able to engage in more one-on-one time with the children.

- Some families may involve themselves in decision-making at the centre or volunteer on committees and thus share the workload with supervisors and teachers.

- When strong relationships exist between families and teachers, a positive work environment is established, teachers' morale improves, and they experience less stress and anxiety.

- Detached from the intensity of family relationships, the teacher is often in the best position to observe the interaction between family members and their children and is thus able to contribute valuable information to the partnership.

- Evaluations of the program completed by families provide opportunities for improved teacher performance.

BENEFITS FOR EVERYONE: COMMUNITY INVOLVEMENT

Families cannot function in a vacuum. The support or lack of support within the community will have a dramatic impact on the family unit. Strong communities can lessen the stressors facing families and when it works, provide support services for children, parents, and families. As we have moved from an agricultural to a more industrialized culture, the feeling of connectedness has not always been maintained. Every neighbourhood has a stake in early childhood education. Each and every individual has a responsibility for making the community a safe and productive place for all families. As teachers we have specialized education that can help and support families but most importantly we must provide leadership in our communities. The opportunity to connect families and professionals from diverse backgrounds such as health, social work, and education allows for a family-centred interprofessional association. This collaboration allows for partners to work together in support of healthy families. Teachers should make available information on all resources in the community that support families in their raising of their children, counseling services, job training, social services, housing referrals, addiction services, respite care, etc.

- Promoting community involvement requires the establishment of networks and connections evidenced by policies, procedures, and actions which extend and support all adult's and children's engagement with the wider community.

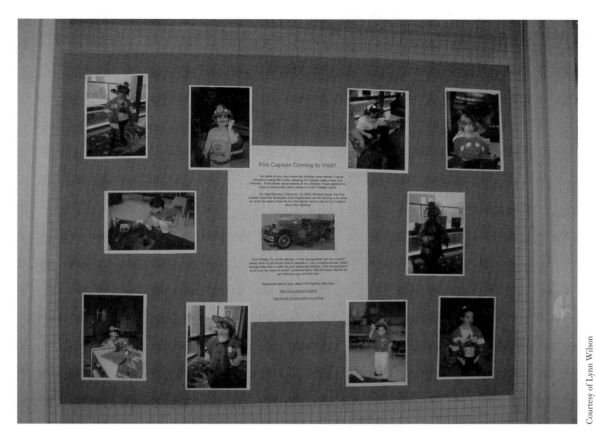

Look to the community: a visit from the local fire captain was a highlight for these children.

- Child-care centres are well placed in most communities to foster the community connections that create some of the knowledge, confidence, relationships, and sense of connectedness that families need for effective child-rearing.

- Professionals in the community may be more than willing to come and speak to teachers and families on a variety of issues facing families.

- Linking with health services, local food banks, employment agencies, and social services may also benefit families.

- Centres must have a professional, collegial relationship with other services and with local schools to ensure smooth transitions and to benefit from shared best practices.

- Family members who establish strong, supportive working relationships with teachers in child-care centres tend to anticipate continuing their active participation when their child enters the elementary-school system.

- Family involvement provides children with a positive role model of active participation in the community.

- Highly involved families are more likely to support program policies, offer financial assistance, participate in fundraising efforts, and rally community efforts in support of the centre.

- Community businesses may be more than ready to support projects initiated at the child-care centre (for example, construction, fund raising, donating materials etc.). These connections may provide great financial relief to the centre!

- Advocacy should extend beyond our local communities. We need to gain a commitment from all levels of government to implement a stable, high quality, universally accessible child-care system in Canada. Teachers, families, and all concerned citizens should lobby and help to educate members of all political parties.

- Family members who are involved in child care may well become effective long-term advocates for families, children, and teachers. We have an opportunity in our child-care centres to create the foundation for life long advocacy for children and their families.

Leaders from the ECEC sector, faith communities, housing providers, employers, labour unions, the education, public health, social planning and development organizations, academic community, chambers of commerce, policy "think tanks," the justice system, and government are collaborating in the About the Community Indicators Project, which is underway to raise public awareness about early childhood education and care in participating provinces and across Canada and to foster and strengthen the links between the early childhood education and care sector and the broader community. Four provinces—Newfoundland, Ontario, Saskatchewan, and British Columbia—will pilot this project. The project participants include a project advisory committee comprised of representatives from the following national partners:

- Campaign 2000
- Canadian Association of Family Resource Programs
- Canadian Child Care Federation
- Child Care Advocacy Association of Canada
- Childcare Resource and Research Unit
- Citizens for Public Justice
- Family Services Association of Toronto

More information about this project is available at **http://www.campaign2000.ca/ci/**.

CHALLENGES TO EFFECTIVE PARTNERSHIPS

In this section we will examine the potential barriers to meaningful partnerships with families.

HAVING REALISTIC EXPECTATIONS

Parents and teachers participated in an informal survey about their expectations of each other, and the results of this survey follows below. As you review these survey responses, you will see that it is apparent that both teachers and families expect the other to "walk on water."

What Makes A Good Teacher: Parents Talk!

- They take their job seriously
- Knowledgeable with a firm pedagogical background
- Professional, positive role model
- Respectful of families and their value systems
- Strong communication skills
- Motivated, value what they are doing
- Confident, positive self image
- Friendly, patient, warm, trusting, sincere
- See themselves as nurturers
- Genuine interest in each and every child

- Empathetic, kind, and openly affectionate with children
- Displays of happiness, joy of life, sense of humour
- Will work with parents when a difficult issue comes up
- Ability to identify a child's strengths and nurture them
- Has first aid training
- Facilitates play
- Enthusiastic, high energy, and the ability to engender the same in others
- Ability to listen
- Flexible, approachable, sensitive
- Non-judgmental
- Don't use parents/children to meet their own needs
- Accept that parents' lives are complicated and may not be able to contribute as much as they would like
- Accepting of parents' need to work and don't hold it against them when there are issues with their child
- Uses positive guidance techniques establishing clear developmentally appropriate limits and boundaries through consistency

- Calm, gentle, encouraging, ability to view situations from the child's point of view
- Effective programming and curriculum development is evident
- Imaginative, creative, resourceful, inquisitive

What Makes A Good Parent: Teachers Talk!

- Keeps lines of communication open
- Sensitive to the feelings and attitudes of others
- Open-minded, able to see both sides of an issue
- Will suspend judgment and avoid open censure
- Tries to do his/her best to recognize their child's needs and tries to meet their needs
- Interested in the child's day
- Concerned, loving, understanding
- Relaxed when dealing with child-care issues
- Understand the advantages/disadvantages of group care
- Understands that the teachers are trying to meet the needs of all the children
- Repects staff and willing to discuss any problem or concern
- Respectful and appreciates teachers as professionals
- Willing to work as a team with teachers
- Appreciative of the teacher's skills and efforts
- Will discuss problems with staff first before going over their heads
- Open to feedback and takes suggestions graciously
- Friendly and flexible
- Reads messages and responds promptly with money, forms, etc.
- Calm, patient, and even-tempered
- Keeps diapers and change of clothing stocked
- Puts their child's name on their clothing
- Asks questions when unsure

When we consider the diversity that exists among families—the myriad of beliefs, values, feelings, and concerns that each parent brings to the child-care centre—and the diversity of staff attitudes and behaviours, effective family involvement may seem an overwhelming task. The mix of older and younger families and staff, experienced and inexperienced families, and teachers presents many roadblocks to forming positive relationships. When families and teachers work together, it is only natural that there will be occasions, as in any relationship, when difficulties arise. Both parents and teachers experience job stress. For parents, the number of hours they work, the amount of job autonomy and job demands, and relationships with supervisors affect their other relationships. For teachers, the job stress also is affected by the number of hours worked, schedules, amount of autonomy, role ambiguity, physical demands of the job, and clarity of the program (Galinsky, 1988). Teaching is physically and emotionally exhausting, and reaching out to parents is sometimes viewed as one more burdensome task. So, in fact, both parties to the relationship are buffeted by strains and tensions in their worlds.

TEACHERS' CONFLICTING ATTITUDES ABOUT PARTNERSHIPS

While the concept of families as partners in their child's child-care centre experience is gaining in popularity, it is not always supported in practice. Family roles and responsibilities may not be entrenched in the centre's philosophy. Even if they are so entrenched, they may be poorly communicated to families. Teachers may be convinced that parents are unwilling or unable to participate, so they make no effort to involve them. Some centres fail to encourage participation; they never take the time to explain to families how they might become involved. It is not uncommon for families to be unsure of the rules and boundaries that are in place, and as a result conflict and tension are created. A philosophy statement that sets forth strong ideals about family partnership is worthless if these ideals never translate into action.

Kagan and Neville (1994) note that many teachers see themselves as the experts in the parent–teacher relationship. Such partnerships tend to be based on the communication of knowledge from teacher to parent. Parents are left out of the decision-making process and are thereby rendered powerless. Worse still, they may come to internalize teachers' negative assessments of their abilities to make good decisions and choices (1994: 15).

Much of what happens in the family–teacher relationship is based on power and control. In many centres, when families are invited to participate it is on the teachers' terms and they may limit that participation to tedious tasks. There is no point in stating that the centre has an open-door policy if the teachers have closed minds! Some teachers who are less confident in their teaching abilities try to keep families at arm's length, because they fear criticism of their work.

Some teachers worry that involving families will place an additional burden on their limited time and energy, because some families may be too forward and others may need considerable direction and support. Teachers may worry about confidentiality as well, when parents witness incidents in the room that they might inappropriately share with other families. Other teachers worry that parents, lacking formal training, will deal with the children inappropriately. An unwillingness to respond to family suggestions—even when the ideas are appropriate and innovative—undermines the partnership.

"The tendency to treat parents as inferior in some way, and in need of advice, has obscured the fact that most parents are well able to contribute to, as well as receive, services. Parents can be effective partners only if educators take notice of what they say and treat their contributions as intrinsically important" (Kastings, 1992: 9). When teachers focus on the family's problems or deficits rather than on their strengths, a collaborative relationship is unlikely.

Teachers may be resentful of families who do not actively participate in the centre or who fail to demonstrate qualities they feel are important to effective parenting. They focus on the family's faults rather than their strengths. A parent who tries to micromanage the teacher's interactions with their child may really be feeling like the "gate keeper" of their child's well being because of the guilt they may feel about leaving their child in the care of others. Not understanding the complexities of a parent's life, some teachers become resentful when parents arrive late, don't keep diapers in their child's bin, or fail to comply with what the teacher perceives to be a simple request. Many teachers become discouraged when their attempts to build relationships with

families are not appreciated and, in some cases, are rebuffed. When a parent is angry, it is hard for teachers to remember that it is important for families to be advocates for their own child; all children need an advocate who will be on their side.

In other situations, teachers may see families as placing unreasonable demands on them. Teachers may also be resentful of parents who earn more money than they do and have higher-status jobs, critical though the work of caring for and nurturing children is. Teachers have also commented that some families do not value or respect the importance of the work they do with children— that they don't see them as professionals, many think that they just "play all day." This lack of societal acknowledgment is reflected in the low pay generally afforded teachers who work in early childhood environments. Many teachers, knowing how hard they work, often comment on how unappreciated they often feel. Some families simply do not understand the challenges of working with young children or the implications of working in group care. In Galinsky's (1988) survey of five well-respected child-care programs, 62 percent of the staff reported that the hard work they did was not appreciated by the parents. Teachers want families to appreciate that the work they do is vital to the development of future generations. However, many families never really acknowledge how talented, caring, resourceful, and committed most teachers really are.

Some ECE students report that they are often shocked by the negative way in which children and families are discussed in staff rooms. This leads to a concern that impressionable students are being influenced by seasoned teachers and may adopt this negative approach to working with families. Other teachers may also be influenced by their colleagues' comments and carry these biases into their interactions with the families.

INSIDE LOOK

If you feel concerned about parent empowerment, it is important to remember that people who feel powerless are more likely to be critical and demanding, needing to have everything go their way. They are less likely to see others' perspectives. On the other hand, parents and teachers who feel genuinely competent and resourceful are much better at "sharing the care," listening to others' ideas, and becoming mutual advocates for children.

Source: Keyser, 2006: 18.

FAMILIES' CONFLICTING ATTITUDES ABOUT PARTNERSHIPS

While family members and teachers share an equal responsibility to make the relationship work, parents filter their perceptions of teachers through their own experiences, stereotypes, and ideas about educational settings. Family members who have had negative experiences with school settings in the past may bring feelings of discomfort and apprehension into the child-care environment—feelings so strong, in some cases, that a parent will refrain from any form of involvement in the centre. Other family members may see the teacher as another part of the "system," which they do not trust.

Some families don't know what to expect from the centre and lack an understanding of their rights and their ability to voice concerns. Some families may not understand the importance of early intervention and the benefits for their child; they may feel that asking for support from the centre undermines their role. Many parents feel vulnerable about their role as a parent and indicate that they lack the skills that the teachers demonstrate in the centre. They feel that teachers are always watching them, assessing their parenting skills, and as a result parents can end up feeling too intimidated to ask for help or to offer help or assistance in the centre. Many families feel that they have nothing to contribute and lack the self-esteem to participate. Some families may be reluctant to share personal information because they do not trust the teacher to respect confidentiality. In some families, a situation such as domestic violence may be occurring and this family "secret" may not be revealed. When families have not developed a trusting relationship with the teachers, they may feel that a teacher's questions and interest in their family is invasive. Other families may defer to the teacher as the authority figure because they feel that the teacher is the one who knows best and any criticism would be unthinkable.

Some families say that teachers demonstrate little appreciation or understanding of their cultures or values. Some parents may be uncomfortable because they dropped out of school and did not complete their education. Other families may feel that by paying their fees they fulfill their responsibility to the centre. Even families who are motivated to work with the centre may come to resent the fact that child-care decisions are made by teachers and administrators without their input. Nothing is more demoralizing for families than to realize that the centre's idea of involvement is the rubber-stamping of decisions made by staff in the absence of parental input. Some families complain that centres are slow to respond to concerns and provide families with no opportunity for evaluation or feedback.

DEMANDS ON FAMILIES

The extent to which families choose to be involved in a child-care centre's activities is determined by many of factors, including the demands of their work, family responsibilities, relationships with the staff, language proficiency, and general interest in participating. Each family has its own set of values, challenges, and needs. Often it is not a lack of interest that keeps families from becoming involved in the centre. Many families, overwhelmed by the stresses and responsibilities of their day-to-day life (see Figure 3.3), are unable to do more than engage in minimal interactions with teachers during drop-off and pick-up. On a more basic level, A.N. Maslow has created a hierarchy of human needs. Basic needs must be met before higher-level needs are addressed. These needs are the following:

- Biological—food, rest, water, shelter, clothing
- Safety—protection from physical danger, absence of abuse or neglect
- Love and belongingness—friendship, affection, acceptance
- Self-esteem—self-esteem, respect, independence
- Intellectual—social and academic endeavours, internally motivated
- Aesthetic—to produce art, philosophy, creativity
- Self-actualization—realizing one's own potential

It is not hard to understand, after reviewing this model, that a family may not be interested in volunteering in the playroom because its members are concerned with where their next meal will come from or how to pay the gas bill. Their energies are taken up by providing basic needs for their family. Placing additional demands on this family would be unacceptable.

Galinsky (1988: 5) suggests that parental involvement in large measure reflects the characteristics of a parent's work life. "[J]obs differ a great deal and . . . certain characteristics of jobs such as autonomy (whether one has control over the tasks and timing of the job) and job demands (whether the job is demanding and hectic) affect parents' stress, health, marriages, and feelings of satisfaction and effectiveness as parents."

FIGURE 3.3 Parent Responsibilities

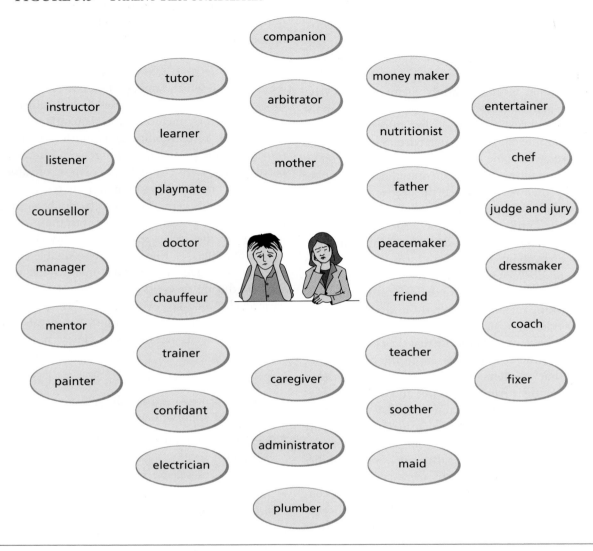

Demands on Teachers

The changing nature of today's families has had a tremendous impact on family–teacher relationships. As a result of shifts in roles and responsibilities, the diverse, mobile group of families teachers may now serve may be very different from the intimate small community that teachers may have served in the past. The support, income, and resources made available to teachers have not kept pace with the increasing workload placed on them. The commitment to integrating children with special needs into child-care programs, for example, has not always resulted in the provision of training and ongoing support for playroom teachers.

Canada's changing demographic composition has challenged teachers to learn more about different cultures and values. Additionally, some teachers suffer from low self-esteem. Others may be working with an age group that does not suit their preferences or abilities; still others may not share the philosophical approach of other staff members or have not participated in workshops or upgrading to enhance their skills or knowledge. New research requires that teachers integrate new knowledge into their programs therefore making time for professional development is critical. Low wages may also put pressure on teachers who struggle to make ends meet.

Government legislation and changes in government policy can place more demands on teachers, who—recognizing the importance of advocacy work in the field of early childhood education—often stretch themselves too thin as they lobby and meet with other advocates. Such teachers may view family involvement as too time-consuming. Finally, many teachers are parents themselves, with the same demands on their time and energy as the families with whom they are working. All these factors tend to raise a teacher's stress level.

LACK OF COMMUNICATION

Lack of communication is a key barrier to an effective partnership. It is sometimes difficult for families and teachers to know where the boundaries lie in their interactions: families may wonder how much information they should share with teachers, while teachers may worry that families will regard their requests for information as intrusive. But when teachers don't know the "family story" they can't understand why a simple request is met with resistance. Teachers may also be unsure of the extent to which families should be involved in programming for the children. Parents may feel that they have nothing to contribute to the centre if teachers make no effort to communicate exactly how families can participate. Many parents do not understand how the centre is run and, as a result, they just don't know how to be involved.

When issues arise, teachers may not always respond appropriately. Avoiding parents who the teacher believes are challenging does nothing to resolve the underlying issues. Because our culture encourages avoiding conflict in the workplace, teachers are often reluctant to speak directly about their concerns with families over such things as sleep routines, feeding, toilet learning, guiding behaviour, educational philosophy, and roles and responsibilities. In other situations, teachers may offer advice that is unwanted or, in a misguided effort to console a family member, make statements such as "I know just how you feel."

When teachers and families fail to communicate clearly with one another, children are put in an unenviable position. As York (1991: 188) observes, "A teacher may expect children to behave one way and the parents expect their child to behave in an opposite way. [Thus] a child is caught in the middle when a teacher wants him to ask for the toy that he wants to play with and his Native culture teaches him that it is selfish to ask for what he wants."

GUILT

Uttal (2002), in her study of mothers who had children in child-care arrangements, found that the responsibility for choosing care and education programs for their children was left up to mothers, even if fathers or other family members were involved. With responsibility comes the potential

Ryan McVay / Photodisc Green / Getty Images

Parents wanting to be involved with their children are not always able to participate in the child-care centre due to family and work pressures.

for error. The mothers wanted very much to believe that their children were getting high-quality care but they were worried that perhaps they had made a bad choice and their children were not in the best situation. Gestwicki (2004: 200) reports that 50 percent of all parents and 59 percent of minority parents report that they are never sure how well their children will be treated when they leave them in a centre.

Worries about safety, programming, and staffing were high on the list of concerns for mothers in Uttal's (2002) study. Every article printed in the paper or broadcast on television about suspected child abuse only adds to a parent's worry. This is particularly evident in families where their children are in unregulated private homecare where other adults are not present to monitor the each other's behaviour. Uttal's study confirmed that the mother's comfort level with the child-care professionals made a difference. Relationships matter!

OPPOSING VALUES AND ATTITUDES

Conflict is bound to arise when teachers and families—each with their own values and attitudes—interact. Teachers and families will have divergent styles, cultural backgrounds, approaches, and interpersonal skills. People often have different perspectives on the same issues. Many teachers grew up in middle-class families where education was valued and where emotional and economic support was available to them. Not all family members have had the same experience; for some, their interactions with schools and authority figures have been negative experiences. Some may be embarrassed by their lack of education and their memories of schools may be ones of humiliation and the resulting anger. It is difficult not to look through our own "lens" when interacting with families. Some teachers have acquired biases and prejudices towards others, for example, teachers' reactions to families who are more educated or economically advantaged may differ from their reactions to families with lower education and economic status, and these reactions affect the family–teacher relationship.

Preconceived ideas on the role of the parent will also affect teacher–family attitudes. Issues such as independence versus dependence and autonomy versus compliance may affect the family–teacher relationship, and so too may cultural influences such as individualistic versus collectivist approaches.

As Lieberman (1998: 15) states:

In individualistic cultures, people who sacrifice important personal goals for the sake of others may be considered masochistic, immature or overly dependent. In a collective culture, a person who fails to sacrifice personal goals for the welfare of others is often rebuked as selfish, disloyal and untrustworthy.

Another area of conflicting values and attitudes in the guiding of behaviour is the one in which an authoritarian outlook meets a more democratic approach. Issues related to the development of morality, spoiling, self-help skills, and gender may all be contentious areas. Each teacher will have issues that they react to with great passion. One teacher may be resentful of families who send their ill child to the centre while another teacher may have the preconceived idea that children raised in a lone-parent family are disadvantaged. Issues that arise may relate more to the fact that parents do not always demonstrate their caring for their child in a way that meets the teacher's expectations!

Families too will feel more strongly about some issues than others. They may be shocked to learn that their child, who is used to sleeping with them, is required to sleep in a dark room, away from other adults and children during naptime. Other parents may rely on nontraditional health interventions and use rituals or practices that are foreign to the teachers in the room. Though teachers see themselves as professionals, family members may see teachers as their employees and consider them babysitters.

DIFFERING EDUCATIONAL PHILOSOPHIES

Families may not fully understand the educational goals that teachers have established for the children with whom they are working. Conversely, teachers may give little time or thought to the goals the families would like their children to achieve. Some parents, concerned about their child's ability to achieve, exert pressure on teachers to focus on a more academic curriculum. Murphy Kilbride (1997: 72) states:

[A]s early childhood educators, we are sometimes guilty of preaching pompously to parents. We tell them that they just don't understand the developmental needs of young children. We say that all children benefit most from an unstructured, open-ended, play-based program. This says two things to some parents: the highly structured, very strict programs they went through as children were all wrong; they have no idea what is best for their

Communication with some families and their children may include more than verbal interactions. Delia Avarell, a deaf ECE graduate student and currently an educational assistant and ASL and Early Literacy Consultant for the Ontario Cultural Society of the Deaf, contributes the following:

Some children were curious and asked questions about why I had an interpreter and others asked why I couldn't hear. Some of the preschoolers picked up some basic signs quickly during lunch, snacks, play activities, and outdoors. One preschooler liked reading books with me because I believe she enjoyed seeing the signs. One of the preschoolers thought the interpreter was my mother. She was a little confused and was wondering why I was always with interpreters. I found it very challenging since our methods of communication were different. However, I felt they were lucky to have exposure to a deaf student teacher. Since interpreter support was not always available during the day, communicating with families was difficult. It emphasizes the importance of having a full-time interpreter available for ECE deaf students doing their placements in hearing environments. Many parents were anxious for me to sign with their children. Deaf students can use text messaging, TTYs/BRS [Tele-typewriter and Bell Relay Service] to communicate with hearing parents and also writing on paper if necessary. Hearing parents and deaf students need to show patience with each other and respect differences.

The book *Baby Signs* by Acredolo and Goodwyn indicates that signing babies scored higher in intelligence tests, understood more words, had larger vocabularies, and engaged in more sophisticated play. At a deaf field placement, I had gained a lot of experience teaching deaf children since it was a sign language environment and was fully accessible. I felt I had a positive relationship with those deaf students. I looked up to the deaf teacher as a role model and she taught me so many things. It has been a real investment in my future career and it has enriched my life. I have strong interpersonal communication skills, and my positive approach enabled me to work effectively with a number of teachers and staff at the school. I have a passion about the accessibility of child-care centres for the deaf community. American Sign Language and Deaf culture are critical to effective communication and its effect on children's health, safety, and well-being in both the deaf and hearing communities. I am a Deaf advocate in early childhood education and I support the delivery of high-quality care and education for children and their families. My interest is to protect the rights of Deaf children by working with their families for the best life possible by helping them become effective advocates who are knowledgeable about their child's rights and their rights as parents.

BOOKS FOR ADULTS

Simple Signing With Young Children: A Guide for Infant, Toddler, and Preschool Teachers, by C. Garboden Murray

own child. These messages are not only confusing and insulting, they are untrue.

Gonzalez-Mena (2008: 28) draws attention to another pressure faced by many families: "parents are targets for marketers who want to sell them goods and services. Virtually all parents want the best for their children. They want their children to be smart, competent, and successful and marketers prey on parents' hopes and dreams." Many families pressure teachers to create programs that focus primarily on academic skills.

Lowell Krough (1994: 327–28) provides an account of the conflicting educational philosophies that arose at a Montessori school that functioned as a parent co-operative:

[O]ne year, a couple of the fathers decided that the teachers should be more accountable for the progress of their pupils. They put forth the idea that charts should be made showing how many children in each class had "mastered" each of the pieces of Montessori equipment. Teachers with the highest score would get the biggest raises. The teachers were horrified at this total misinterpretation of Montessori's views of individualized, self-paced learning. Banding together, they realized that they hadn't been doing a sufficient job of parent education. The result was a monthly newsletter containing articles about Montessori's philosophies, and guest-teacher visits at the parent meetings in which the teachers answered questions about what was happening in the classrooms. The fathers eventually agreed to retreat from their plan until they received more information on the Montessori philosophy. While they later tried to reintroduce the plan, other families had become sufficiently knowledgeable that it was voted down.

It is critical for teachers to understand how education is delivered around the world. Many families come to us from an educational system that is very formal and teacher directed, very different from the play-based, child-centred emergent curriculum approach that is utilized in early childhood environments today. It is our role as ECE teachers to help parents understand the benefits of this play-based, child-centred method. A family's approach to an individualistic or collectivist viewpoint will also influence their interactions with teachers. Parents with a strong individualistic approach will see the importance of children learning that they are unique and special individuals while those with a collectivist perspective are more likely to support group needs over the individual and want teachers to reflect a sense of social responsibility within the centre.

EXCLUSIONARY OR OFFENSIVE TERMINOLOGY AND PRACTICE

It would be an interesting exercise for students to brainstorm about the many rules that are in place in child-care centres that present barriers to families' full participation. Flexibility is essential to stay focused on our goals. No matter how well planned our efforts, there are always details to work out, new information to absorb, and new ways to incorporate change that supports our families.

Often the practices and language teachers' use offend or exclude families. Here are some examples:

- Centres where hours of morning entry are rigidly reinforced, for example, "All children must be in the centre by 9:30 a.m." does not respect the fact that many families may work non-traditional hours and the early morning hours may be the one time that the family can be with each other.

- Teachers use the terms "they" or "those parents" rather than referring to family members as individuals. The use of these terms creates a feeling of exclusion while creating an "us" versus "them" mindset among the teachers.

- Teachers who describe parents and other family members as noncompliant, uncooperative, or difficult convey the message that only teachers

should dictate the conditions of the partnership. Similarly, labelling families as dysfunctional, in denial, overprotective, uninvolved, or uncaring may imply a judgment that fails to incorporate a full understanding of a family's circumstances (Hughson, 1994–95: 56).

- The terms "atypical" and "at risk" should be avoided. They imply that there is something wrong with the child or the family and that somehow they are to blame for their problems.

- To refer to children as coming from "broken homes" is to ignore the fact that many children live in lone-parent homes where they are well cared for, stimulated, nurtured, and loved.

- The term "one-parent family" is misleading, since many children continue to have contact with both parents as well as other relatives. To use the term "single-parent family" denotes marital status that may not reflect the family's situation.

- Terms such as "reconstituted," "blended," and "step" are used to describe some families. It is important for teachers to know which term each family prefers.

- Some families may object to siblings who are not related by blood being called "stepsister" or "stepbrother" or "half-sister" or "half-brother" and may prefer the term "sister" or "brother."

- For gay and lesbian families, forms that request information about fathers and mothers instead of parent or co-parent set them apart.

- For parents who are illiterate, complicated written communications make informing parents of centre practices, policies, and events nearly impossible.

- Centres that do not consider the importance of communicating in the parents' first language exclude those families.

- The celebration of Father's Day and Mother's Day may be stressful for children who have only one parent, who come from gay or lesbian families, who are adopted, or who are in foster care.

- Some teachers are unaware of how their use of language may offend adoptive parents—when, for example, a teacher refers to the birth parent as the "real" parent or "natural" parent rather than the biological parent (see Chapter 9).

- Some educators, when using the term "primary caregiver," seem to forget that families are the primary caregivers. Educators must not forget that families are the primary caregivers and families have the long-term relationship with the child. Educators need to see themselves as supplements and supports to the family, and not assume parental responsibilities.

- What's in a name? Some parents may feel that their child is accepted into the child-care program more easily if the child has an English-sounding name. We must reassure parents that all children are welcomed with their given names and that teachers will pronounce these names correctly.

- Favouritism is another behaviour which leads to exclusion. Few things are more destructive to the family–teacher relationship than the thought that the teacher prefers some families and children over others.

RACISM

"Once social change begins, it cannot be reversed. You cannot under educate the person who has learned to read. You cannot humiliate the person who feels pride. You cannot oppress the people who are not afraid anymore."

—Cesar Chavez

Painful as it is to admit, when we reflect on why socioeconomic minority families come to school less than we think they should, we need to remind ourselves of realities such as those Carol Phillips has written about:

> We must examine institutional racism and how it operates. Many of us have been taught to understand racism only as an individual attitude, and therefore we believe that individual "bigots" are responsible for all the racist damage.... We must explore the stereotypes we have learned that are racist and ethnocentric and develop strategies for changing what we believe about ourselves and others. Too many of us still unconsciously treat light-skinned children better than dark-skinned ones, and the working mother better than the one on welfare. (Phillips, in Greenberg, 1989: 70)

Another parent says:

> As I see it, the "multiculturalists" fail to exhibit any sign of awareness of cultural diversity within a race (i.e., they don't distinguish between Northern Chinese, Cantonese, Fukienese, Shanghai people, etc., let alone Japanese, Vietnamese, Malays, Lao, etc.); they tend to lump us all into one group, implying "they're all the same, you can treat them all this way." And they have nothing to offer as solutions to conflicts within a race, e.g., the long-standing tension between Chinese and Japanese. They don't even acknowledge that such intra-racial conflicts exist. I say if they don't know about this, the cultural differences or conflicts, it's hard for me to believe they care. (Lindsay, 1999)

Teachers may be reluctant to examine their own biases and attitudes about diversity in families.

INSIDE LOOK

A classroom teacher's experience highlights the influence of background and the challenges to re-creating a bridge. Participating in a teacher group discussion of intercultural communication, a teacher wrote (as if realizing it for the first time):

> Culture means more than holidays and food; it includes all of the subtle patterns of communication, verbal and nonverbal, that people use every day. I noticed how easily I valued cultural diversity in the abstract or in the form of occasional holidays yet how readily I rejected cultural differences when they appeared in the form of parents' different approaches to child rearing.

She went on to write about the group's reflection:

> We realized that unexamined values, beliefs, and patterns of interaction learned when we were children exert a powerful influence on our communication and care giving routines. Our sincere intentions didn't prevent us from rejecting parents' diverse values when they challenged our own cherished beliefs. We were often unable to set aside our own cultural values long enough to listen to parents.

Source: Sturm, 1997: 34–35.

It is my conviction that, although we are not born with racial and prejudicial concerns, through experience, observation, learning and interactions with society as a whole, we soon develop these characteristics and they become ingrained into our personalities whether we realize it or not. . . . Through an intelligent examination of our belief and value systems, we can perhaps begin to focus on where our biases have come from and help to change where they may be heading. (James, 1989: 68)

Janmohamed (2005) has suggested that in an effort to be inclusive and to encourage a pluralistic approach to education we have lost the opportunity to challenge the dominant culture and seem unable to equip students for putting anti-racism education principles into practice. Racism, sexism, and class bias are economically, politically, educationally and institutionally produced. Teachers can help ECE students overcome these social barriers by engaging them in explorations of different ways to resist oppression. When ECE students are asked how they integrate anti-bias approaches in field placement, countless numbers have discussed the Spanish music they shared, or how they made fruit salad with "exotic" fruit.

Clearly a more strategic process needs to be developed within the discourse of anti-racism education so that students with early childhood diplomas do not limit their experience to simulated or mock celebrations of Diwali and Hannukah. Instead of focusing on festivals there needs to be a greater emphasis on diverse child rearing practices beyond the dominant Western understanding. The shift from an anti-bias perspective to an anti-racist education perspective is a difficult one that questions the implications of how ECE training programs are delivered. However, if there is a desire to ensure that real change happens, changes do not happen without teachers, and teachers do not institute changes unless they understand them and believe in them (Gaine, 2000).

Unfortunately, as James and Muhammad (n.d.: 1) argue, "The culture of minorities tends to be seen as 'foreign' or 'add-on' rather than an integral part of our Canadian culture." According to Brown (1979: 19), "[W]e nurture racism in children until by the time they are adults they fit into the structures of racism that is our society. Society should intervene at the earliest possible time in a child's life with positive initiatives in the area of racial attitudes. Daycare, nursery school, and kindergarten are opportunities to develop a positive response to different cultures."

Howard Clifford, child-care advocate, has said, "A daycare program that results in a child's feeling ashamed of his family or shaken in his confidence and pride in his ethnic or cultural heritage is a failure." The need to create a better atmosphere has even been touched on and lobbied for by those outside the child-care education sector. Maya Angelou has been quoted as saying:

We must re-create an attractive and caring attitude in our homes and in our worlds. If our children are to approve of themselves, they must see that we approve of ourselves. If we persist in self-disrespect and then ask our children to respect themselves, it is as if we break all their bones and then insist that they win Olympic gold medals for the hundred-yard dash.

Bernhard et al. (1995: xi) state that in their study,

46 percent of teachers at diverse centres with an average of seven years of experience in the ECE field reported they had never, during their careers, seen what they would describe as a racial incident between children. On the other hand, a majority (54 percent) of all teachers interviewed reported having seen such problems. Because of this, and the frequency of parent reports, we are inclined to believe that there continue to be problems of systematic racism, irrespective of the good-will of centre staff.

Despite efforts to reduce barriers, the needs of immigrant children and youth for health, education, and social services are not being met, according to a 1999 survey of service providers in major urban areas. Of the 88 agencies across Canada that were involved in the survey, more than three-quarters found that immigrant children and families face barriers in accessing their services. The most common barriers were language, insufficient access to interpreters, and too few written materials in the various languages. Almost all the organizations surveyed have tried to reduce the barriers, but they reported that they lack the resources to adequately service new immigrants, and recent financial cutbacks have made the situation worse (Canadian Council on Social Development, 1999: 29). It is necessary for us as teachers to examine our own attitudes, experiences, and impressions in regards to oppression, marginalization, and racism in order to create a community that is inclusive of all.

RIVALRY

A parent comes into a centre one morning and enthusiastically says, "I have to tell you, Lily took her first step yesterday!" The teacher smiles and replies, "Oh, she walked here last week." The teacher's remark wasn't meant to hurt, but it made the parent feel unimportant—and, what's more, it created competitive feelings (Weissbourd, 1992). It is important that as a teacher we never take these moments away from families. Firsts—whether they are a first step, a first tooth or a first word—should be left for families to discover.

Some families may secretly resent the ease with which their child has made the transition from homecare to child care, and their underlying fear is that the teacher will replace them in their child's affection. When rivalry exists between a parent and a teacher, the child is placed in the untenable position of having to decide where his or her loyalty lies; this can be a devastating experience for the child. "When caregivers and teachers seem to know more, have better skills, and can handle their children better than the family can, the feelings of competition can be devastating" (Gonzalez Mena, 2008: 37).

When the most personal aspects of a child's care are taken over by another, it is understandable that parents may feel uncertain. Teachers may also become strongly attached to children in their care. At times they may cross the boundary between the appropriate practice of caring for and supporting the child to inappropriate thoughts of "rescuing" the child. This may be a reflection of the teacher's need to be wanted and loved, as well as the feeling that the teacher would be a better parent. This feeling is an occupational hazard for those who work with children—the feeling that we would be better parents and that we somehow have to make up for the parent's real or imagined failings. Teachers need to monitor their emotional dependence. Rivalry may also occur when teachers feel resentful of the income disparity between themselves and some of the parents in the centre or be envious of a particular family and their lifestyle or relationship.

FEELINGS OF VULNERABILITY AND FEAR

When families have contact with teachers, they, like the teachers themselves, feel vulnerable to criticism. After all, their child, who is an extension of themselves, is on view. First-time parents particularly can be quite frightened of the teacher's opinion, and all families yearn to know that the teacher likes their child and that the child is doing well. The relationship can be doubly sensitive when a parent, usually the mother, seeks validation of her own worth as a person by ascertaining that the teacher approves of her offspring. She is all too ready to believe the teacher (and to feel threatened and angry) if blame is implied (Hendrick and Chandler, 1996: 162).

Fear of reprisal against their children silences many parents. They fear that if they speak up about a concern or an issue, the teacher may be upset and take his or her anger out on the child. Teachers, too, may withhold information that parents should have because they fear reprisal from the parents.

Some parents would be surprised if they knew how vulnerable some teachers really are, especially inexperienced ones. Both families and teachers may feel anxious about one another. Both may be eager to

---

please, hold the other in awe, feel respect or fear, feel hostile or submissive—a full range of emotions may be clearly evident. For Gestwicki (1992: 122–25), a barrier to effective parent–teacher relationships is fear: **fear of criticism** (both families and teachers can be concerned about being judged by the other); **fear hidden behind a professional mask** (an insecure teacher may use his or her status as a professional to intimidate families or keep them at arm's length); **fear of failure** (teachers need to understand that it takes work, time, and energy to build effective partnerships); and **fear of differences** (many teachers have difficulty relating to or accepting cultures, values, or customs that differ from their own).

Some teachers may have negative feelings about working with children with special needs. These feelings may be grounded in their fear of not knowing how best to support the child and family in this situation. They may be afraid of doing something that harms the child, or they may be reluctant to learn about the equipment or medical intervention that the child requires.

Some teachers are fearful to admit that they do not have the skills to support a family in their time of need. It is important for teachers to recognize the limitations of their ECE training and not be afraid to suggest more appropriate resources in the community, such as counselors, parent support groups, pediatricians, and psychologists.

LACK OF TEACHER TRAINING AND PROFESSIONAL DEVELOPMENT

Many teachers enter the field of ECE because they want to work with children, but they underestimate the importance of family involvement and the amount of time that teachers spend interacting with other adults. The very qualities that enable teachers to work effectively with young children may make them uncomfortable in their dealings with adults. Galinsky (1988: 8) reports on a study that found that "professionals with the most positive perceptions of parents were more likely to have more education and to be more experienced."

Bernhard et al. (1995: xi), in the study *Paths to Equity*, state that 33 percent of ECE students felt, upon graduation, unprepared for working with children of diverse backgrounds; faculty members agreed that many of the new graduates were unprepared. Teachers reported rewarding experiences in encountering differences but had difficulty relating to parents and questioned their parenting practices and their desire for involvement. Parents generally respected the teachers' professionalism but felt teachers were often too busy and were uninterested in discussing the child or comprehending the parents' culture and values. Teachers perceived language barriers to be the largest challenge in working with diverse populations.

Not surprisingly, teachers who have been in the field for a number of years may be susceptible to burnout. Hepworth Berger (2004: 411) states that "[b]oth teachers and parents experience burnout. It is felt most when what you are trying to do seems unproductive, or you may think you have few alternatives that would change or improve the course of events. This frustration can lead to a feeling of being trapped. It can happen to any teacher and any parent.... Those who set high standards and aim for perfection are sometimes more likely to experience burnout, as are those who feel a need to be in control. Feelings of anger, guilt, depression, self-doubt, and irritability are symptoms of burnout."

Unfortunately, this condition is rarely addressed in the context of family–teacher interactions. Support for teachers who are tired and overworked should be an ongoing part of professional development. Too often professional development is not supported by the administration of the centre. Many administrators lack a clear understanding of how their support would ensure a healthy and revitalized staff. Like any professional, keeping up with new research should be an integral part of a teacher's and centre's responsibility. In addition, community college and university training programs need to reflect the needs of families as partners in education. Students' field experiences seldom provide enough emphasis or time to develop meaningful relationships with families. Students have difficulty practising the skills they learn in their courses because most family members want to speak to the teacher to discuss issues or concerns rather than to the student.

NEGATIVE ATTITUDES ABOUT MEN IN ECE

Beach, Bertrand, and Cleveland (1998) estimate that men make up three percent of all early childhood educators. A study by Robinson (1988) revealed that men working in child care were motivated by "their love and enjoyment of working with children, appeal of the content of the child-care program and desire to contribute something of value to the young children for whom they cared" (1988: 55).

Male teachers have much to offer early childhood environments.

Essa and Young (1994: 445) report that "men leave the field of early childhood education at an even greater rate than women do. Some male teachers who changed careers reported that they were subject to subtle prejudicial attitudes from parents, female coworkers, and administrators. They were considered not as good as women because they had never been mothers." Becker (2005) a member of a men's networking/support group offered through the Manitoba Child Care Association states "the biggest factor for leaving reported was low pay. It was unrealistic to try and support a family on a child-care worker's salary, and so a few returned to higher paying vocations even though they expressed a wish to stay in the field." Research supports this sentiment. The main reason men do not work in child care is not that they are not capable or suited for the work but because the rewards of salary and status do not meet their expectations. Robinson (1988) states that the majority of men working in the field are married with at least one child. It is not difficult to understand how raising a family on the salary of an ECE teacher would be arduous. In his study of men still working in the field,

Robinson (1988: 57) reports on attitudes to men in the field:

> [Sixty percent] of the men were discontent about subtle unspoken assumptions from parents, the women they worked with or their administrators simply because they were men. Many said they were treated with mistrust and suspicion by parents and their co-workers. Several men said that their colleagues believed that they, as women, were better equipped by nature to work with young children. Others reported beliefs that because they had never been mothers, their co-workers felt they could not make accurate judgments concerning discipline, the health of the children and approaches to teaching and supervising children.

Hinsliff (2003) says, "But just as women breaking into male-dominated professions may fall victim to an old boys' network, research found that some male child-care providers complained of being patronized by female colleagues . . . . One complained of being 'cut off' by a female colleague who would interrupt him when he talked to parents, while another two men reported that women colleagues would jump in before a possible problem could occur or would assume they couldn't do some things with the children properly."

Becker (2005) writes that "knowing the barriers to male participation in the ECE field is the first step towards changing the future. But real change starts with the individual. As Neugebauer wrote: 'we all like to see ourselves as open minded and accepting. But if you, the director, or front-line worker believe that men aren't by nature nurturing, or that men are more likely to be abusers, your efforts to employ men or accept them as peers will be half-hearted. When staff recognize their own attitudes towards men as caregivers, they can work together to create a healthy and positive, gender-inclusive environment.'"

Daycare Trust Study, England

A recent study from England for the charity Daycare Trust showed that 84 percent of parents would let a man look after their child, while seven in ten wanted more male caregivers. Male nannies are becoming increasingly popular, particularly with single mothers who want male role models for their children. The study also found that 27 percent of men would consider working in a

The field of early childhood education has always strived to recognize and celebrate diversity, to accept individuals for who they are, what strengths they possess and what they contribute to the child-care program. The male early childhood education student is a part of the diversity of a "predominantly female" field. At this time, the focus and diversity of the male student is placed on gender rather than competence or contributions to the child-care community. As is the case for women who have forged into some non-traditional areas, there are often biases, myths, and barriers for men in child care to overcome. There are usually few men in child-care classes, and therefore, men can be singled out solely because of gender. Since gender difference is obvious and easily observable, it may become a focus of discussion by female students and even faculty. Because men in a child-care centre are a rarity, male students are welcomed and valued as part of the training program. However, many female students have at times believed that male students are "students of privilege."

Many have perceived that male students are so unique and welcomed by faculty, that expectations are differed and that they will always be successful, and never fail. The reality is that learners must demonstrate the skills, knowledge, and abilities to successfully meet the outcomes of the early childhood program and this is not assessed and evaluated through one's gender. Studies by Skeen et al., (1986) have shown that women are often suspicious of men working in child-care centres. What eventually changes these suspicions is the experience of actually working alongside male colleagues. Female students are therefore encouraged to examine their own biases and be open to the experience of being in a coeducational environment even though it has been a traditionally female dominated area.

Men too must bear responsibility for their own attitudes and behaviours while enrolled in an early childhood education program. Men need to be aware that there will be suspicions and stereotypes about their interest and motivation for being in the child-care field. Such stereotypes and suspicions encompass areas which can range from sexual orientation to parent/staff concerns over male caregivers working so closely with very young children. To address these issues, men working in child care must be accountable at all times. Men must be aware that it is, in the majority of cases, other men who have taken advantage and abused the trust of women and children.

Accountability and maintaining professional behaviour—in the classroom and field practicum environments—are critical steps to take to earn the trust and respect that many male students deserve. Male students may feel isolated in class and in their field practicum settings. Isolation is the number one stressor for men working in the child-care field (Bloom, 1989). Again, because of their obvious gender differences, men are often excluded from conversations or plans by staff for social functions (weddings, showers). Isolation may be a reality, so it is important for the male student to seek out support from other men in the program or in the field. Support groups for men in child care are few but are now in existence as numbers and interest increase. Men are often expected to do the "traditional male" tasks such as supervise the woodworking area, lift heavy objects, work with school-age groups, etc. Men have even perceived themselves as being singled out unintentionally by faculty in child development classes regarding birthing and breast feeding. Even though men are not able to experience firsthand these wondrous events, they still must be knowledgeable and sensitive to these critical experiences in the development of young children.

Building solid and trusting relationships with female colleagues is critical. Avoiding nuances, sexist remarks or overtones are critical when communicating with the women in the program. Romantic relationships between classmates have been known to create changes in class dynamics. If and when such relationships flounder, the impact is felt not only by the two individuals involved in the relationship, but also by other classmates. It can create tense situations for all. Maintaining professional and friendly relationships is the way to go for the male student in child care. Many of the above issues, such as isolation and communication, also pertain to female students; however, it is the intent of this Inside Look to examine such issues as they relate to the male perspective.

Source: Michael Pimento, former faculty at Centennial College

nursery or out-of-school club, rising to 38 percent of men who were fathers themselves. "We are seeing some kind of beginning of a cultural shift," said Stephen Burke, director of the Daycare Trust. "Now what we need to do is support men who want to go into this career." However, 57 percent of those asked identified fears of pedophiles targeting children as the main barrier to male childcare providers—even though only one man has ever been convicted of sexual abuse in a British nursery. Burke said fears could be tackled by proper vetting of nursery staff; when parents trusted the management, they were inclined to believe their children would be safe around the staff (Hinsliff, 2003).

In England and Scotland, targeted marketing to men includes television, newspaper, and poster campaigns featuring male workers, handing out brochures (including one with the provocative title "Are You Man Enough for Childcare?") at venues where men are likely to be found, and providing men-only orientation sessions at secondary schools and career fairs. Several Nordic countries also use targeted marketing (Bertrand, 2008: 173).

INSIDE LOOK

My decision to pursue a career in early childhood education came about quite haphazardly. It was during a pediatric rotation as a student nurse that I realized that my true calling lay not with treating the symptoms associated with illness and disease. Instead, I was lured by the prospect of promoting holistic health and wellness through education and, thus, preventing many of the illnesses and injuries that currently plague young children in this country. As I began my studies at George Brown College in Toronto, I was well aware of many of the stereotypes that follow men into female-dominated vocations. The brief time I spent in nursing ensured encounters with such discrimination—both subtle and overt. Would my interest in working with children be misconstrued as pathological? Would families, faculty, and colleagues judge my competence as a nurturing presence in the lives of children based solely on my skill as an early educator or simply on the basis of my gender? Would my decision to enter a profession with so few males as front-line workers yield assumptions about my sexual orientation and promote further discrimination? These questions were initially the source of much hesitation and self-doubt.

Fortunately, two years and four placements later, the fears that gave me pause in the beginning have not yet materialized. First of all, my college faculty epitomized what one frequently seeks in a mentor. Their encouragement and support served as the foundation from which I've been able to grow as a competent, integrative, and comfortable member of the early childhood community. Second, centre staff and supervisors have welcomed my involvement in their centres and bestowed upon me a definitive sense of belonging. In fact, my second placement with school-age children led to full-time summer employment. Of particular importance, however, is the way in which children and families have embraced my presence in their lives. I frequently receive positive feedback from parents who are excited by the reports they receive from their children about our daily interactions. In their eyes, I am seen as both an educator and a role model. The rapport I've established with the children in my care is most evident in their sense of trust in my abilities, driven by consistent response to their individual needs and manifested through the frequent interactions and displays of affection that one would expect in a nurturing relationship.

The experiences I have garnered thus far have put to rest my earlier fears about being a male early childhood practitioner. As time passes, the notion that males and nurturing are somehow incompatible is no longer at the forefront of my thinking, nor has it affected the partnerships I have established with children and families. Instead, I hope to focus some of my efforts on encouraging continued recruitment of men into this profession. Clearly, the potential benefits for society as a whole are numerous.

Source: Ryan Campbell, ECE graduate

Greater male involvement in the field of early childhood education is long overdue.

STRATEGIES FOR ACHIEVING EFFECTIVE PARTNERSHIPS

In this section we explore these questions and look at what supervisors and individual teachers can do to promote meaningful relationships with families.

WHAT CAN THE SUPERVISOR DO?

"The early childhood program director/supervisor is the keystone to carrying the program's vision (purpose and philosophy) forward. He or she can bring clarity or confusion, calm or chaos, stability or fragility to the daily lives of children, their families and the staff team" (Bertrand, 2008: 215).

Supervisors should be aware of research that will help to support the teachers in the program. For example, according to research, several characteristics appear to positively influence parent–teacher partnerships. The relationships are enhanced when teachers' personal attributes include warmth, openness, sensitivity, flexibility, reliability, and accessibility (Comer and Haynes, 1991; Swick, 1992). The partnerships are positively influenced when parents' personal attributes include warmth, sensitivity, nurturance, the ability to listen, consistency, a positive self-image, personal confidence, and effective interpersonal skills (Swick, 1992). While neither teachers nor parents may have all these positive personal attributes, supervisors, who have this information, may be more adept at forming partnerships with families.

Be a Leader

The supervisor's leadership is strongly influenced by the policies and procedures established by the administration of the centre, such as a board of directors. The board should ensure that the philosophy of the centre entrenches active family involvement and is reviewed on a regular basis. Sullivan (2003: 7) states "leaders are any individuals who influence others in a way that encourages them to higher or better performance and personal development. Effective leaders may or may not have authority, position, or status. They do, however, have integrity, dignity and respect for others. Leaders empower, encourage and support others in a shared effort to achieve goals or create change…They take action where action is needed and they enable others to take action when another person's strengths and ability are needed."

Hire Outstanding Staff

Supervisors are often in the position of hiring new staff and this often involves members of the Board of Directors. One way in which it is possible to create a strong team is to hire outstanding teachers that reflect the community served and to make every effort to hire male teachers. We know that our ECE workforce is not stable—many teachers leave the profession because of poor working conditions, low pay and the lack of career opportunities. While many of these issues are out of the supervisor's control, it is the supervisor's responsibility to create a work climate that is rewarding and supportive while also knowing how to keep knowledgeable, committed teachers who understand the importance of partnerships with families. Successful hiring also applies to those who also work in the centre to support families, including cooks, caretakers, and others who may volunteer who have enormous opportunities to contribute.

Be an Effective Communicator

The role of the supervisor begins with the first contact with the family. He or she will often determine whether a family will become involved in the centre. The supervisor's role in a child-care centre is a multidimensional one, rooted in an understanding of the importance of effective interpersonal communication. Her positive attitude toward families provides a role model for teachers. She is responsible for ensuring that orientation information and all other forms of written communication are relevant, up-to-date, and inclusive of all types of families. Having material translated into the first language of the families in the centre and providing interpreters for deaf parents are critical to effective communication. As the supervisor becomes more familiar with the families in the centre, she can catalogue their various skills, talents, and resources and encourage them to share them with the centre.

Be Accessible

Accessibility is an important issue. Supervisors with busy schedules should set aside periods when they will be available to families, since in many small centres the supervisor is also a playroom teacher. The supervisor who is on the floor during drop-off and pick-up times can free up teachers so that they can discuss important issues with families. Floor time also provides supervisors with opportunities to speak with families themselves and to observe the family–teacher interactions.

It is important that the supervisor has a strong visible presence in the centre.

Develop a Team Approach

All hires must be able to demonstrate a commitment to working with families. A clear and concise job description should exist for each position in the centre. Supervisors are responsible for establishing a sense of common purpose among a group of teachers who may come from diverse backgrounds and who may have different philosophical approaches to their work and conflicting attitudes toward family involvement. Establishing a sense of group identity is an enormous undertaking but necessary for creating an effective team.

Jorde Bloom (1995) describes the culture of a centre as encompassing the basic assumptions and shared beliefs that unite the staff. These assumptions and beliefs include standards of appropriate everyday behaviour and a shared code of ethics guiding professional practice. The supervisor's role is to mesh the home cultures of the families in the centre with the early childhood culture.

Staff meetings are also a good forum for providing psychological support and time for reflection. Rather than focus on curriculum, timetables, or other business items, reflective practice allows staff members to share their feelings, their successes, and their concerns about their work with families and with one another. They may reflect on how they might like to do things differently the next time. In a trusting environment, these reflective practice meetings are real opportunities for change. Journal writing, on a regular basis, may provide insight and topics for discussion at these meetings.

There is a great deal of research on this topic: Haigh (2004: 81–82) reviews the literature on reflective practice and co-inquiry. Abramson and Atwal (2004: 87) describe the Reggio Approach as "based on relationships" among teachers, children, parents, and the community (Malaguzzi, 1993).

These relationships are enhanced and sustained by working together to achieve a common goal, an effort referred to as "collaboration." The Italians [involved in child care] see collaboration as vital for improving the quality of early care and education, as well as the quality of life for everyone involved. The value of collaboration extends beyond achieving consensus. Even greater benefits are derived when a "learning group" comes together to investigate problems and search for meaningful solutions (Krechevsky and Mardell, 2001: 285). By engaging in "collaborative inquiry" (co-inquiry), a process that "consists of repeated episodes of reflection and action" (Bray, Lee, Smith, and York, 2000), the interests and concerns of individual participants coalesce into a group question that can be studied over a period of time. During co-inquiry, participants learn to bridge differences in life experiences and interpretations, recognize the humanity of one another, share meaning, and find solutions.

In the Reggio Approach, two critical tools for co-inquiry are "listening" and "dialogue." According to Rinaldi (2002: 2), collaboration requires a commitment to "listening" in a way that is "open and sensitive to the need to listen and be listened to." Although an individual may have a particular take or perspective on a situation, true collaboration means "letting go of the outcome" in the collaborative search for meaning and a willingness on the part of individuals in the group to contemplate new ideas and never-before-thought-of directions.

Support Families and Teachers

Supporting both families and teachers requires tact and sensitivity on the part of supervisors. The supervisor has the difficult task of supporting teachers while at the same time giving due consideration to parental concerns and complaints. Being an effective listener is crucial to the supervisor in

---

INSIDE LOOK

One of the things that was most reassuring to me as a parent was that Pam was always there. She would be busy with one parent or another, helping out in a room or making coffee for parents who wanted to stay behind and talk. Pam was quick to assess situations where her helpful support would be welcome. She had the uncanny knack of being able to talk my four-year-old into getting on his snow pants long after I had given up in exasperation. I appreciated the encouragement and support she gave to our family.

her role as a mediator in family–teacher disputes. Supervisors need to let teachers know that they expect to be informed when conflicts with families arise; they can then follow up with a phone call or a discussion at the end of the day to reassure the family. As an objective observer, she may be able to suggest strategies for improving the relationship. She may also note times when teachers show an unconscious preference for a child or a family; she can bring this favouritism to the attention of teachers and redirect them into fair and more consistent practice.

The supervisor is also able to monitor the degree to which the families who are active in the centre reflect the centre's family population as a whole. It is not uncommon for a group of active and influential parents to form a clique and, whether intentionally or unintentionally, exclude other families that wish to participate. The supervisor is in a position to advocate for all families to be involved in decision-making by identifying groups not represented and target them for involvement.

The supervisor must also be able to appraise the skills of centre staff and determine where further support is needed. The work of teachers in early childhood environments is demanding, and it is incumbent on supervisors to help create support systems that encourage and motivate staff. In addition to providing regular feedback to teachers about their role in the playroom, their interpersonal skills, and their ability to work effectively with colleagues and families, the supervisor can help those teachers who require additional training to access the necessary resources or workshops. Supervisors also should advocate at the board level for paid time for staff during family–teacher conferences, home visits or staffing at the end of the day so teachers have real time to communicate with families.

Support Families Experiencing Poverty and Financial Difficulties

The administration of the centre in conjunction with the supervisor can provide assistance to families experiencing financial difficulty. Supervisors should know which support agencies are available in the community so that they can quickly help families gain the resources they need. The addresses of local food banks should be prominently displayed on the bulletin board so that families can access this information without having to ask. Centres should consider providing breakfast programs and hearty snacks for their school-age children. Centres that receive discounted rates for buying in bulk could allow families to purchase staple items at a reduced rate. Centres in which the cook prepares nutritionally sound "one-pot meals" could allow families to purchase these meals to take home.

Centres may need to spread child-care payments over a longer period of time to help families experiencing financial difficulty. Centres should also be aware of the impact of asking families for extra funds to cover special events, etc. Children of unemployed parents will need extra attention and reassurance; these parents may be invited to the playroom to volunteer or to share a special skill, which might provide a needed boost to a worried or concerned child. Families could be encouraged to participate in exchanges (clothing, shoes, skates, and so on) as their children outgrow their belongings. Families with a garden and surplus produce can establish a help-yourself table at the centre. Centres—where space allows—could create a neighbourhood garden in order to further strengthen their ties with the community. This also provides a vehicle for compassion and empathy for those in our communities who need support—a valuable lesson for young children. Centres can approach local companies that may be generous with goods if they know the cause is genuine and children are involved. Supervisors and teachers should work closely with antipoverty groups in pressing governments at all levels for a comprehensive plan to eliminate poverty. On this note, using food in art or sensory experiences should be discouraged. Families that have lived subsistence lives or that find it difficult to make ends meet may find such activities particularly offensive.

Supervise the Development of Appropriate Emergent Curriculum

The supervisor has a role to play in helping staff develop an emergent curriculum that is relevant, inclusive, and reflective of all the families in the centre—and who better to provide this insight than the families themselves! Staff meetings and individual room meetings provide opportunities for the supervisor and teachers to evaluate the curriculum and to develop strategies for remedying those aspects of the curriculum that serve as barriers to effective family–teacher partnerships. Creating a curriculum that reflects caring—caring for self, for others, for the environment will help to create a positive and empowering "culture" within the centre. Input from families should be an integral part of this process. In conjunction with teachers

Students, too, have much to contribute and bring many strengths to the program.

and families, supervisors may wish to organize special celebrations for the Week of the Child and National Family Week in October.

Acknowledge Teachers' Strengths

Supervisors need to carry out performance evaluations on a regular basis. Acknowledging the efforts and strengths of teachers in the centre is an important part of a supervisor's job. Too often the contributions of teachers go unnoticed; too often others take credit for their ideas. When teachers feel that they have no ability to suggest or make changes in their work environment, they become discouraged. The supervisor needs to empower teachers so they feel an improved sense of self.

The supervisor can do much to enhance the self-esteem of teachers by celebrating their accomplishments. Articles in local community newspapers, radio interviews, and public meetings are some of the means by which the supervisor can share the important work that is going on in the centre. She should look for opportunities to nominate teachers for special community awards. Jorde Bloom (1995) recommends giving business cards to teachers and

encouraging them to use them. They help teachers feel more professional, and they also publicize the centre. Displaying photos of the teachers and a biographical sketch in the centre for families to read also enhances the role of the teacher. With the teachers' permission, the supervisor can profile teachers in newsletters, letting families know about professional and personal milestones reached. The supervisor can also make teacher recommendations to local community colleges when they are in need of part-time or sessional ECE appointments, and she can encourage staff to supervise student placements.

Supervisors can also organize workshops in the community for teachers to lead. One supervisor approached a local bookstore and staff conducted story times for children in the community. Supervisors can encourage teachers to create a portfolio that reflects their academic achievements and an ongoing record of events and milestones they deem memorable and worth celebrating. It is also important that the supervisor model continuing professional development. As she attends workshops and seminars or returns to school to upgrade her own academic credentials, she may well inspire staff to do the same.

Being aware of the newest research is part of a supervisor's responsibilities and an opportunity to demonstrate leadership in its implementation. Karen Haigh (2004: 83–84), as Director of Programs at the Chicago Commons Association, has been working with staff to explore and experiment with various ideas and influences from Reggio Emilia. This collaborative approach is demonstrated in the following examples.

Some Ways Staff Have Worked Together at Chicago Commons to Practice Results

1. Learning to share, revisit, and reflect together at weekly meetings, in-services, out-of-town conferences, and seminars by allowing time for dialogue among staff.
2. Viewing videotapes of children together to see and discuss strengths and abilities of children, which has grown into searching for children's interests or areas to pursue.
3. Talking and thinking together about why photos are taken.
4. Reviewing and interpreting children's work (actual words, drawing, videotapes, slides, etc.).
5. Developing environment plans that consider the entire building, such as classrooms, bathrooms, hallways, and entrance ways.
6. Viewing slides together as a means of looking at the environment or the languages of children.
7. Allowing teams to have their own exploration. Each site developed research questions to explore as they were asked, "What do you wonder about children?"
8. Experiencing staff explorations of materials such as watercolors, wire, charcoal, clay, and paper.
9. Learning to think about how and why portfolios are used to collect children's work.
10. Talking and thinking together about how to ask questions.
11. Sharing and discussing documentation among sites.
12. Doing presentations for each other within the agency.
13. Viewing each other's environments.
14. Sharing, documenting, and revisiting our ideas, especially when we go to seminars and conferences.
15. Having an introduction to the Reggio Approach for new staff.
16. Focusing on specific research for each year.
17. Focusing on questions to think about and discuss together during the year.
18. Thinking about the purpose and meanings of journals.
19. Thinking and talking about "What is society's image of the child and what is the public schools' image of the child?"
20. Choosing, designing, executing, and evaluating documentation panels together.
21. Using quality circles to make decisions, policies, and procedures about specific aspects of our program (e.g., choosing agency-wide topics for research).
22. Planning, executing, and evaluating two-day Learning Tours together.

Haigh states, "I believe staff at the Commons have had the most dramatic change in terms of relationships, as they have had to reconstruct their relationships with children, with parents, with the community, and with each other."

While families are often surveyed for their opinions, teachers are often overlooked. Conducting an in-house survey about new strategies for creating an effective team environment will give the supervisor important feedback for change.

Connect with the Community

Perhaps one of the best models of community involvement in early childhood is the town of Reggio Emilia in Italy. Adults and children work collaboratively with teachers in creating positive learning environments. Families are actively involved in critical decision-making and the strong sense of community is evident in the connectedness amongst all participants. While supervisors cannot exactly replicate the Reggio model, the connection to the community is critical. Developing a team approach involves the community. The supervisor should be responsible for educating the community about education, social, and family needs that exist in the community and participate in problem solving strategies. "The supervisor can develop multiple outreach mechanisms to inform families, businesses, and the community about family involvement policies and programs through newsletter, slide shows, videotapes and local newspapers" (Whitaker and Fiore, 2001: 161). Classes and programs take place in libraries, museums, zoos, and other community facilities and supervisors can support teachers in their efforts to move beyond the playroom. Public spaces that support young families are critical. Betrand (2008: 252) states that "[r]aising the social capital of communities raises social cohesion—the level of trust and sharing, a recognition that we are all responsible in some sense for each other, and that we all share a responsibility for the next generation. Socially cohesive neighbourhoods are better places to live, characterized by less crime and isolation, more public and community spaces, and greater volunteerism and intergenerational reciprocity."

Supervisors can initiate relationships with community leaders from a wide range of cultures, seeking their advice and support. Supervisors can also use the child-care facility to serve community needs and to facilitate learning for the wider community. Because child-care centre supervisors are in a position to form networks they can connect with other centre supervisors, agencies in the community that support families, businesses that may lend their assistance, media connections, and so on. According to Jorde Bloom (1995), "Directors who have ... buil[t] strong community connections report a lower incidence of vandalism at their centres, fewer problems in recruiting volunteers and prospective staff, and longer waiting lists" (1995: 49).

The You Bet I Care! study (1998) asked supervisors about their satisfaction with the availability of support from 11 different community sources. Their responses indicate that their greatest support comes from their health unit or nurses (56 percent),

Courtesy of Lynn Wilson

This child-care centre, Studio 123, is housed in a building where many artists have their studios. One contributed this spectacular whimsical sculpture for the children's playground.

from other centre directors (54 percent), and from resource teachers (41 percent). This interdisciplinary approach has much to offer.

Supervisors can also reach out to elementary schools in their community to help ease the transitions for families and their children, and they can encourage teachers in early childhood environments to hold meetings with families and children in their new school environments with new teachers to share goals for each child.

It is also important to stay connected to post-secondary institutions that offer early childhood education where new research may be of benefit to teachers and families. Looking for opportunities to take students from ECE programs in order for them to complete their field practicum provides an opportunity for mentoring and staying afresh of new ideas and techniques.

Finally, the Child Care Human Resource Sector Council has prepared an occupational standard (2006) for early childhood program supervisors that articulates the roles and responsibilities of pedagogical leaders.

What Can Teachers Do?

Commit to Family Involvement

Programs that fail tend to do so not because teachers lack the skills but because they lack sufficient commitment to family involvement. Before teachers work on building and refining the skills they need to create effective partnerships, they must first ask themselves if they truly want to involve families in the first place. Pelletier and Brent (2002: 45) state that "the teacher has been identified as the key to facilitating parental involvement in early childhood education programs." This implies that teachers possess certain skills, attitudes, and behaviours that translate into strategies to encourage parent participation. Swick and McKnight (1989) found that teachers who were educated with regard to the value of parent education and involvement, who were encouraged to remain active through professional organizations, and who were given the essential supports such as small class size, administrative help and appropriate working conditions, were the most supportive of parent involvement and education. There has been concern regarding an overemphasis on "large group" parent involvement; research suggests that a more successful approach entails increased individual contact among parents and teachers, conferences, small group discussions, and the use of parents' talents and skills (Swick and

---

INSIDE LOOK

Expanding Horizons—Reaching Out to the Community

The bustling, busy nature of early learning and care centres often draw the attention of supervisors inwards. The many competing demands of parents, children, staff and licensing requirements may make it difficult to find either the time or the energy to reach out to the broader community.

Early learning and care centres are just one, albeit a very important, component of a continuum of programs and services for young children and their families. Centre directors and staff, in recognition of the benefits of a truly integrated service delivery system, must seek every opportunity to develop a more comprehensive understanding of the range of supports available within their community.

Equally important is participation at local planning tables or children's services networks. Child care centre directors may not be invited to these tables. In some communities, licensed child care is viewed as separate and apart from the range of agencies providing children's mental health, public health and parent support programs. However, this is not the case, and while participation at these tables does take time and energy, it is critical that the child-care community be well represented.

There are many reasons why both increased knowledge about what is available and active participation at planning tables are so important some of which are identified below:

- Increased capacity to provide "one-stop shopping"[1] for parents seeking additional programs and services for their children.
- The ability to provide parents with current and accurate information about a wide range of support services in response to specific requests or needs.
- Enhanced opportunities for shared, multi-sectoral professional development, which strengthen the capacity of all sectors to provide comprehensive, quality programs and services.
- Increased knowledge about the important role played by licensed child care in a continuum of supports and services that support healthy children and families.

[1] Parents who require additional supports and services for themselves or their children endure additional stresses over and above the day-to-day challenges faced by all working parents. The capacity to get informed information from one place reduces the number of times that a parent has to share what may be a difficult story and increases the likelihood that the services sought will best fit family needs.

Source: Contributed by Sue Hunter, Principal, Hunter Consultants

---

Child Care and Much More!

With a small, one-time grant from the York Board of Education in 1978, The Learning Enrichment Foundation has grown to become a model of community economic development through the integration of services that meets local needs. LEF's 34 child-care programs lay a solid foundation for approximately 1,500 children every day. The magic of LEFs centres is in the wide breadth of support offered: sensitivity to family cultural needs, integration of children with special needs, professional development, strong evaluations, nutritious meals and snacks, and parent workshops. LEF ensures that language and settlement needs of the newcomer community are addressed in a comprehensive and caring way. LEF offers Language Instruction for Newcomers to Canada (LINC) to eligible adult newcomers who are assessed for language proficiency and enter one of LINC's 8 levels of English instruction. In addition to language training, participants are offered child care, transportation assistance, a computer lab, field trips, and volunteer opportunities. They also have the opportunity to use other LEF services for job search skills, employment, financial management, resource centre access, and additional skills training. Skills training may include cooks training, industrial skills, forklift certification, early childhood assistant, project management, construction, and a variety of workshops to meet the needs of the participants. LEF has more than 200 partners in the community that assist in a variety of ways to help them meet their goals of providing community responsive programs and services which enable individuals to become valued contributors to their community's social and economic development.

McKnight, 1989). Teacher strategies that incorporate this approach encourage parent involvement and overcome barriers to communication often perceived by teachers and parents in a culturally diverse context. When parents learn how to talk and interact with teachers, they feel capable of making changes themselves, and realize their own possibilities for involvement; teachers, in turn, come to recognize these parents as "effective" participants in their children's education (Bernhard, Lefebvre, Kilbride, Chud, and Lange, 1998). Family-centred care must find the strengths in every family and include not just parents but all of the people that are significant in the child's life. Create a sense of belonging!

Lay the Foundation

When families first arrive at the child-care centre, the concept of family involvement is articulated, expectations are discussed, roles are established, and the partnership begins. Successful encounters early on in the family–teacher relationship are critical to its long-term success and have a ripple effect. Teachers should envision the child inside the circle of his or her own family and understand the intricate tapestry that each family weaves. Simple strategies such as knowing how each family member wants to be addressed—for some

a formal approach is best and for others being on a first name basis would be expected—help to get the relationship off on the right foot. The home visit is also an integral part of this connection because it is crucial that teachers become well acquainted with families. This visit allows families to discuss their hopes for their child and for the teacher to begin the partnership. Teachers should plan for and encourage the involvement of fathers as well as mothers and other significant family members. Teachers need to focus on the whole family unit: "Teachers and parents who are able to relate to each other as real people with strengths and vulnerabilities can validate each other, share responsibilities, and focus on the common goal of providing the best growing ground for the child. In this way, teachers and parents develop authentic relationships as partners, collaborators, co-educators, and co-decision makers in the life of the child" (Coleman, 1997). The closer we move to establishing trusting relationships with the families we work with, the more realistic our expectations will be. Act with humility.

Maintain Confidentiality

Teachers often establish such trusting relationships with families that they are often privy to very

An open door policy should be in place—everyone should feel welcomed.

personal information. Greenman and Stonehouse (1996: 263) state:

> It is tempting to justify knowing the details of a family's private life because it may help us "understand" or "teach" a child. But we have no right to know the ins and outs of family life any more than parents have a right to know about *our* private lives in order to monitor program quality or to better understand the centre . . . . Respect for parents demands that unless the situation is one of abuse or neglect, the parents control what information they wish to share. If we come to know something about the family, as professionals we should ask the parent if they mind our sharing the information with colleagues or supervisors.

Develop Strong Interpersonal Skills

By the time that students graduate from their ECE programs, they have gained valuable insight into the strengths and challenges in their communication style. Field placement experiences, feedback from faculty and co-operating teachers, and opportunities to interact with families will help the student teacher formulate a personal action plan for building stronger interpersonal skills. Teachers who are successful at involving parents tend to possess the same skills that make for good teachers. Their ability to be

caring, to individualize and personalize their interactions, and to be self-reflective and evaluate their interactions with families makes for good teachers. They must also be able to integrate their theoretical knowledge of effective communication into their interpersonal style. Effective communicators have a strong sense of self, an awareness of their strengths and weaknesses, and a desire to improve their skills.

Gestwicki (2000: 166) underscores the importance of humility: "Teachers with humility are able to step outside normal frames of reference and find creative, novel ways to work with parents, because they are not limited by believing only the traditional methods will work."

Communicate on a Regular Basis

Despite the fact that much of the information we exchange with parents happens at drop-off and pick-up, when both teachers and families are tired or rushed, these daily interactions are critical to successful relationships. Teachers can get the relationship off on the right foot by communicating with families on a regular basis and by sharing with them information and positive stories about their child. *"Samir has been really supportive to the new child in our room. He spent most of the morning with her explaining the different activities and showed her*

Community Program, San Romanoway Revitalization Association

The Jane and Finch area is known to be one of Toronto's toughest neighbourhoods. Three apartment buildings—No. 5, No. 10, and No. 25 San Romanoway—are among the most populated buildings in the area; these buildings contain 892 units and are home to approximately 4,400 residents of whom 2,800 are children and youth. The crime rate within the San Romanoway neighbourhood was a staggering 128 percent above the national average per 1,000 households in 2002, according to the Neighbourhood Quality of Life Survey, which was conducted by Dr. George S. Rigakos, Professor of Law and Criminology at Carleton University in Ottawa, Ontario.

Stephnie Payne, a nurse who emigrated from England almost 40 years ago has lived, she says, "in the shadow of these buildings." Seeing children, youth and families in crisis, Stephnie saw an immediate need for safe and supportive programs for the residents. Her desire to increase community capacity for all people, and the promise of dedicated resources and support from all levels of government, public and private agencies, and local involvement of residents formed the basis for the creation of the San Romanoway Revitalization Association (SRA). The SRA is a charitable, nonprofit organization serving approximately 4,400 people living in this Jane and Finch community. Today, the SRA works collaboratively with all stakeholders and oversees culturally sensitive programs for children, youth, seniors, and families. They offer a breakfast club, an afterschool program, a homework club, and a literacy program. There is a children's summer camp, music school, a parenting program (offered in partnership with the Children's Aid Society of Toronto), a senior's drop-in, teen violence prevention training, a domestic violence program with support and counseling, among others programs. Some comments from the participants of the programs and community members are:

- "Three of my five children attend the SRA's breakfast and afterschool program. I have fewer worries on my mind now. I am certain my kids are taken care of; they arrive in the morning to a full breakfast and return to a home-cooked, culturally-sensitive dinner. Their academics have improved since they have qualified tutors and volunteers who sit with them one-on-one to assist them with homework. I am also fortunate to have leftover food sent home for my younger two children and myself."
- "My son has attended the SRA summer camp for the past three years and had made new friends and enjoyed visits to Ontario Place, the Metro Zoo, and a baseball game."
- "Since the inception of the SRA, crime in the three buildings has significantly dropped. Life for me before the inception of the Association was a lot harder."

Their motto, "Making it Happen Together" is based on an innovative, collaborative community–private sector approach to revitalization. Their mandate is to provide community development and safety, to find proactive solutions to solve the problems of youth violence in the neighbourhood, and to provide cultural/social enrichment programs for children, youth, seniors, and families.

In 2004, Dr. George Rigakos re-administered the Neighbourhood Quality of Life Survey and reported that there was an overall decrease of 22.8 percent in violent crime and a decrease of 23.7 percent in property crime. In addition, overall satisfaction rates with community programming were very high. "There is no doubt that there is still work to be done in San Romanoway and by no means have we met our objectives. Nevertheless, the survey shows that our support for and efforts on behalf of the neigbourhood families, children, at-risk youth and seniors is creating a safer and healthier environment," says Stephnie Payne, Executive Director of San Romanoway Revitalization Association.

 For more information about this unique collaborative community initiative, visit the website at **www.srassociation.ca**.

Source: Contributed by Trudy Ruf, Early Childhood Consultant, Humber College Institute of Technology and Advanced Learning, and Lisa Teskey, Program Coordinator, Early Childhood Education Department, Humber College Institute of Technology and Advanced Learning

Sensitive, caring teachers understand the importance of strong partnerships with families.

how we help ourselves at lunch. He was a great help." Teachers must also listen attentively and act accordingly when families share pertinent information about their child—his health, mood, whether he has had breakfast or not, events happening in the family, etc. Teachers must also consider the multitude of ways in which they can connect with families. There are many verbal, written, and visual means of communicating, all of which should be implemented to strengthen the centre–family bond (see Chapters 5, 7, and 8).

When teachers share something of themselves, families are more likely to see a "human" side to the teacher. We are all more than our "presentation self." It is important for teachers to be insightful observers because much of what we communicate is done non-verbally. When we see parents having difficulty separating from their children, we can encourage their participation in a variety of ways in order to help them deal with the stress and for some, the guilt of leaving their child in care. Teachers can support these parents by making them feel that they are an integral part of the child-care community. When family members are involved, it provides an opportunity to exchange information about the child and a chance for the

teacher to encourage parents in their critical role. This partnerships allows the teacher to plan in a more sensitive and responsive manner for the child.

Be Responsive and Accommodating

Teachers should try to organize their time so that they are available to talk to families at both the beginning and the end of the day. The supervisor can certain play a supportive role here. Home visits, family–teacher conferences, and social and educational events should be organized with a view to accommodating family schedules; child care should be provided when needed. This flexibility is critical. It is important that teachers acknowledge parental concerns and then act on them immediately. A teacher who promises information or specific support should always follow through. This allows a climate of trust to develop between teacher and family.

Many teachers encounter families who are in crisis or who have great difficulty meeting the most basic of their children's needs. Teachers need to be able to respond to these situations in an appropriate manner. Warren (1979) suggests that teachers recall difficult moments with their own children or the children they have worked with in

Supervisors need to organize time for teachers to discuss issues with family members.

order to find common ground with parents "whose good moments are rare and whose self-image as parents may be so tarnished and torn that they present an outward appearance of not caring, or self-righteousness, or abdication of parenthood" (1979: 9).

If teachers hope to develop a partnership with parents and families that encourages the holistic development of children, they must learn to recognize the strengths inherent in every family. When parents are discouraged, teachers can help families feel hopeful. In many situations, families are supported by the simplest of gestures. An offer to make coffee, a moment to talk, being a responsive listener—these can make all the difference. Teachers may want to consider what professional behaviour is: Does it mean keeping families at arm's length or does it mean reaching out, crossing traditional boundaries? A teacher who stays past her shift to care for a sick child because she knows it will be hard for this parent to leave work early is demonstrating a very different approach from the teacher who works according to the theory that "this child is sick and must go home!" Teachers must be aware of all families, especially the ones who appear to be withdrawn or uncomfortable in

INSIDE LOOK

Boundaries! I taught for a very long time in early childhood environments and the word "boundaries" always troubled me. I cared deeply about the children and their families and the word suggests that there must be some "box" I was suppose to put around my interactions and connections with them. I have stayed in touch with so many of the families that I have worked with, some of the children are now getting married and having children of their own. I have been privileged to share in important moments in their lives—graduations, baby showers, difficult times, and sometimes just someone dropping by my office for a chat. Over the years I have received awards and accolades for my teaching but the rewards have been all mine. Boundaries just didn't work for me.

the centre. They need to take the time to find out about the family's interests and concerns and to look for opportunities to include them.

For example, teachers should try to figure out why a parent drops his or her child off without a word or calls for the child to leave at the end of the day without entering the room. Rather than labelling the parent as "uninterested" or "difficult," teachers should avoid making judgments and be curious about why this is happening. They need to look to themselves first before laying blame on the parent. Remembering that the centre is the teacher's "home" environment, how can she create a more welcoming situation for this parent? When teachers put time and effort into doing this, they are rarely disappointed in their efforts.

Tell the Truth and Be Patient

A teacher's credibility depends on their ability to be truthful. We need to be honest with the families we serve and they will expect this of us. Truth telling is often most challenging for teachers when they know that sharing difficult information will be painful for parents. Despite this, teachers have the professional responsibility to share information in a kind and respectful manner. The way in which the information is given is critical; it is most likely to be received in a positive manner when the parents and teachers have mutually respectful relationships. There may be times when parents do not believe what the teacher has to say because they are shocked, hurt, or embarrassed. It is important for teachers to be patient and to continue to provide support and encouragement to

these parents. Change is difficult for many of us and so the ability to take time to be patient and tolerant as parents struggle with difficult issues is critical.

Demonstrate Empathy

Empathy is perhaps a teacher's greatest quality. Our interactions with families provide us with insight into many of the stressors that make parenting challenging. Empathy has been recognized as important to both general communication competence and as a central characteristic of competent and effective intercultural communication. It is the bedrock of intercultural communication (Samovar et al., 2007).

Bell (1987) states that "cognitively, the empathic person takes the perspective of another person, and in so doing strives to see the world from the other's point of view. Affectively, the empathic person experiences the emotions of another; he or she feels the other's experiences. Communicatively, the empathic individual signals understanding and concern through verbal and nonverbal cues." We must also be aware of how our own cultural orientation will impact on our interactions with others. For some "saving face" will sometimes elicit comments when they really mean something else. Learning to suspend judgment about issues that reflect your own experiences and knowing that others will have a different frame of reference will help you to be more open to others words and actions.

The ability to respond to a family in crisis may make all the difference, as the following Inside Look demonstrates.

INSIDE LOOK

When Barinder's mother, Sarah, became critically ill after the birth of her second child, we knew that the family was under considerable stress. At a staff meeting we discussed ways in which we might support the family through this trying time. We knew that Barinder's dad wanted to spend as much time at the hospital with Sarah as he could, so doing the drop-off and pick-up at daycare was very difficult for him. One staff member suggested that he could pick up Barinder on his way to work and drop him off at his grandmother's house on his way home. Two other staff members who lived close to the family offered to look after Barinder in the evening when his grandmother was unable to provide child care. Several other staff members dropped off food for the family. Fortunately, Sarah fully recovered and the family was very appreciative of our support. We were all invited to a wonderful home-cooked meal where we celebrated her return to good health. This simple gesture, which in the end was so easy for us to organize, made a significant difference to this family and in the process we became part of their extended family.

In one of my placements, one of the toddler's parents was pregnant but there were problems with the baby. The mother had to have an early delivery in order to save the child's life. It was hard on the parents and I offered my help. I would stay a few hours at the end of the day and spend time with their child and I also volunteered on the weekends to help out. During the days that I was in placement, I brought in materials to help distract the toddlers and if they wanted to take them home they could. Going that extra mile made me feel good and my efforts were appreciated by the family.

Source: Ashley Dias, ECE graduate

In other situations empathy may be displayed by planning workshops in the centre that support family needs. At a parent's request, a lawyer in the community gave a free seminar on preparing wills. In another centre, teachers hold a sleep-over pyjama party on Valentine's Day. The children look forward to the event and it allows parents to have time alone with each other, strengthening their relationship. This is especially helpful for families who cannot afford a babysitter. Parents have been very receptive and appreciative of staff efforts. At times an observant teacher can smooth the way for more active participation in the centre. One teacher organized a car pool for a group of families when she realized that many were not attending meetings because they lacked transportation. She also helped parents who lived near one another organize a walking pool so that when they left meetings at night they had someone to walk home with.

Greenman and Stonehouse (1996: 286) suggest that

> nothing communicates caring and goodwill so much as unexpected acts of kindness and generosity, such as a card on the parent's birthday, an unexpected appreciative note, an offer of tea, coffee, or a breakfast roll, perhaps a photograph of their child, or marking the anniversary of the family's time in the center. Offer a needed ride to the repair shop or home on a rainy day. If the program seeks out ways to make families happy, the resulting parent–staff relationships should weather nearly any storm.

Respect Diversity in Families

Successful teachers are those who truly value and respect children, and who accept that children have their own world-views, life experiences, and likes and dislikes. Successful teachers are concerned with broadening and expanding children's experiences, not discounting or trivializing them. Successful teachers are able to enter into a child's world rather than simply demanding that the child enter into *their* world. Successful teachers do not give children double messages or resort to such phrases as "Do as I say, not as I do."

An integral part of respecting children is accepting and celebrating their diversities. In nurturing diversity, teachers need to assess their own values and attitudes when developing and implementing a bias-free approach to their work. This approach must include not just cultural sensitivity but totally inclusive practice incorporating ability, age, appearance, beliefs, family composition, gender, race, socioeconomic status, and sexuality. Teachers need to be able to critically evaluate such materials as books, kits, teaching aids, and DVDs and to replace those that promote stereotypes with more sensitive materials. Gonzalez-Mena and Bernhard (1998: 15) state:

> [C]aregivers must become aware that there is nothing in a young child's day that comes separate from its cultural context. Culture is not directly taught, but grows out of the interactions between caregivers and children. Babies are born with the need to attach to and become involved with other people and their surroundings; they naturally observe and attend. Sensitive adults respond by constantly adjusting their behaviours and structuring the environment in ways that provide support for development and learning. Culture is the medium in which all this occurs and in child care, whether that medium matches or is in conflict with the home culture is very important. Steps should be taken to create an optimum match for infants and toddlers, especially those at risk of losing or rejecting their home culture.

The curriculum must be developed in a manner that combats sexism, ageism, racism—all of the "isms." The teacher in the playroom must demonstrate inclusive strategies that develop respect and tolerance for each child and family. The teacher will demonstrate zero tolerance for racist or exclusionary behaviour. This approach has the additional advantage of modelling for the children how to stand up for themselves and for others when dealing with bias of any kind. There may be times when teachers are called on to correct misinformation or to challenge racist or ethnic jokes made by colleagues or parents.

INSIDE LOOK

Racial identity can result in social adjustment issues for individuals belonging to ethnic minority groups in the United States and Canada. Studies on minority mental health have identified numerous ways in which negative racial identity can affect psychological well being through self esteem, anxiety and feelings of inferiority (Phinney, 1990; Akbar Chambers & Thompson, 2001).

The development of identity is associated with an individual's physical features and social stereotypes. The persistence of colour stereotyping and colour bias can influence the identity formation process for both monoracial and biracial children (Dutro, Kazami, Galvan et al., 2005). The development of racial attitudes among black children is an area that has been studied by social researchers for many years. One early study by Clark and Clark (1940) indicated a strong racial preference among young black children towards identifying with the white majority racial group. Several subsequent studies have facilitated similar findings which indicate that young black children attribute more positive characteristics towards individuals with a white skin tone than towards individuals with a darker skin tone (Landreth and Johnson, 1953). These studies seem to suggest that black children, who have learned to attach lesser positive characteristics to their own race and attach higher positive characteristics to the white majority racial group, could possibly reject the cultural norms of their own race in favour of the values and norms of the white majority racial group. Yet, the social changes that have occurred within the local, provincial, national, and the international environment will have an influence on their racial identity formation.

The inhabitant within one's social environment also plays a role in the identity process. The racial composition in North America has changed significantly due to the increased levels of immigration and the resulting population growth. Canada has become a country inhabited by a multitude of races from all over the world. In Toronto alone, blacks, who represented a very small population group as recently as the 1950s, now represent the third largest minority and racial group (Christiansen, 1980; Statistics Canada, 2001).

Parents are influential in many areas of their children's lives (Kelly, 1998; Rong and Brown, 2002). Children learn about their own race through parental relationships. Ogbu (1981) comments that parents socialize their children in preparation for the skills they will need to participate competently as an adult according to the cultural group or population in which they live. Parents can work in partnership with child-care providers to inform their children about his/her racial group, culture, history, and heritage in an effort to contribute to positive racial identity in children. Parents in partnership with child-care providers can attempt to prepare children for racial barriers as well as equipping them with the competencies needed to negotiate negative race-related experiences that contribute to the process of racial identity formation (Marshall, 1995; Hughes and Chen, 1997).

In Cross's model (1978), the premise is that before people experience identity, they are first unaware of their race and the race of others; however, children aged three to five have a basic understanding of race (Adler, 2001). Due to the early recognition of race with young children, there is a need to address racial identity with children and caregivers need to reflect this knowledge in their curriculum and in partnership with families.

Source: Contributed by Cameile Henry, faculty

Children need to see themselves and their families in the child-care environment.

Derman-Sparks (1989) suggests that teachers deal with parental biases in the following manner:

> Invest time and energy with individual parents by engaging them in a series of conversations. Find out what underlies the parent's racist (or sexist or handicappist) stance. Remember that none of us is free from bias. Each of us needs other people to help us sort through our experiences and identify contradictory attitudes and areas we want to change. (1989: 107)

Cultural differences and conflicts will be overlooked, transgressions forgiven, and children will thrive as long as teachers care and value their students. Children treated with respect, dealt with honestly, and lavished with kindness succeed (Cardinal, 1994: 23–24). When the same generosity is applied to relationships with parents and the child's extended family, the groundwork is established for effective partnerships.

INSIDE LOOK

Ten Keys to Culturally Sensitive Care

1. Provide cultural consistency in harmony with what goes on at home.
2. Work toward representative staffing.
3. Create small groups.
4. Use the home language verbally and in writing.
5. Make environments relevant, reflecting the culture of the families served.
6. Uncover your cultural beliefs.
7. Be open to the perspectives of others.
8. Seek out cultural and family information.
9. Clarify values.
10. Negotiate cultural conflicts.

Lieberman (1998: 17) states that our own strong personal feelings about families may put us in a position where

> we can fall prey to [our feelings] when working with people from another culture. It is easy to experience their values and beliefs as hurdles that we need to surmount if we are to help the child. We need instead to search for an understanding of how their values fit into the very fabric of who parents are and how they see their children, themselves, their families, their lives, us, and the world at large. This enhances our empathy for parents and cuts down to size our preconceptions of what we can accomplish in "improving" each family's life.

Practice in the child-care centre needs to reflect an understanding that there is more than one way to raise a child.

At the Little River Child Care Centre, the older children invited parents and planned their own celebration for the holidays, with staff playing a supporting role. Whereas festivities in the past had always emphasized Christmas, this year things are different. Small groups of children speak and sing in honour of Chanukah, the Hindu festival of Diwali, and the African-American celebration, Kwanza. One parent speaks with great passion about her hopes for a future in which celebrations such as these are commonplace in child-care centres across Canada.

Judith Bernhard, PhD, Ryerson University–Early Authors Program (EAP)

I have had the fortunate opportunity to work with Alma Flor Ada and Isabel Campoy in implementing and assessing a literacy program entitled the Early Authors Program (EAP). Originally developed in California, the program was implemented in 32 child-care centers in Miami-Dade County, Florida. The evaluation of the project was completed by a team consisting of Dr. Charles Bleiker (Florida International University), Dr. A. Winsler (George Mason University), and myself.

Working with Dr. Jim Cummins of the Ontario Institute Studies for Education–University of Toronto and the SSHRC-funded project entitled Multiliteracies Project, we are working to implement EAP in schools in the Greater Toronto Area. The Early Authors Program is unique. It involves the production of several books for each participating child. The books are self-published within each program site. Parent involvement includes, among other things, authoring books that have their children as the protagonists, taking photographs to illustrate the stories, and reading the books to their children. Each EAP site has a computer, colour printer, digital camera, and laminating machine to support the publication of the books. The books are written in the home languages of the participating preschoolers.

The Early Authors Program builds the children's self-esteem, involves the parents in their children's education, and increases reading at home. The children become familiar with books and enter school with more of the foundation skills required for success. The Early Authors Program represents an innovative, effective means of supporting young children's literacy. Its value has been demonstrated in the American studies. Piloted and proven successful with children whose families speak languages other than English, it offers an attractive alternative to deficit-based family literacy programs. Having documented the effectiveness of the EAP in Florida, I would very much like to see it adapted for use in Ontario. It has the potential to increase the school readiness and preparation for literacy instruction of all preschoolers, including preschoolers whose families are in the process of learning the language of instruction in their local schools. (Bernhard, 2004)

Expect Conflict and Be Open-Minded

Conflict is an inevitable aspect of any working relationship; it can even be a catalyst for positive change. Teachers should learn to expect conflict and to value it as an opportunity to improve their communication skills. It is also important for teachers to examine their own feelings and biases when a conflict arises. Both teachers and parents will filter their perceptions about a conflict through their own experiences in both their personal and professional lives. Teachers are faced with many types of families. Some may be reluctant to be involved in the centre, while others may be overinvolved in a manner that is not supportive. Some will have blind trust in teachers; others will challenge them at every turn.

Teachers need to feel confident that they have the ability to resolve problems. Remaining professional in any conflict, staying calm when a parent's anger escalates, and working towards common ground is critical when tempers are high. Teachers should strive to avoid being defensive, arguing, or becoming aggressive with the parent. They need to be respectful and remember that for many family members it takes great courage to bring forth a concern. There is also a strong possibility that if one parent is concerned, others are too. When listening to criticism, teachers should keep an open mind and try to see things from the parent's perspective. They should also solicit the parent for ideas about possible solutions. Rather than give up on parents or react angrily or defensively, teachers should concentrate on searching for common ground (see Chapter 6 for more strategies for resolving conflict).

Further, as Elkind (1988) points out, teachers need to be flexible enough to adapt to a wide variety of families. One should go about involving parents who see teachers as hired help differently than one goes about involving parents who see teachers as in a class above themselves. To involve parents who see teachers as employees means that we have to take away parents' feeling of superiority. We do this best by communicating that we are professionals. We convey this impression when we refer to our training as well as to theory and research in our discussions with these parents. With parents who are intimidated by the school and by us, our task is the opposite. We need to take away their feeling of inferiority and give these parents a sense of being competent and involved in their child's education. We do this best by "giving away" early childhood education.

Ask for Help

Too often, teachers feel that they have to shoulder the burden of so many tasks in the centre and often forget that many parents are anxious to help. In many situations, just asking is all that is necessary. This allows families to enjoy the feeling of accomplishment that comes with partnering with the teacher.

INSIDE LOOK

The other day I was trying to put together a camping curriculum, and I just mentioned in passing to a parent that I was looking for small tents. She said she had a couple I could use, and then she got so excited about the curriculum that she offered to bring in some camping pictures and equipment we could use. She even called another parent to ask if they had some old flashlights to donate. I keep forgetting what incredible resources families are to our program. Somehow, I always think I have to do everything myself.

Source: Keyser, 2006: 7–8.

INSIDE LOOK

I worked in a centre that believed kids should get dirty and be little scientists—it had a wonderful adventure playground. Parents...would say: "We don't want our kids going outside. We spend an hour and a half on their hair. Two minutes later they are covered with sand. We can't get that stuff out and we spend our whole evening cleaning it up. So we don't want our kids going outside." For a while our earnest and empathetic response was "Gee, that's too bad. But this really is good for the children." Of course, our knowing response implied, "You poor, ignorant person, valuing appearance over good child development." Conflict continued and we learned.

Now the response to this sort of issue is "Okay, let's figure this out. Obviously it's important to you how your child looks. And you know it's very good for children to have these sorts of experiences. Let's come up with a solution." The assumption is two legitimate points of view—let's work it out together. In this instance, the answer was shower caps for the kids (Greenman, 1989: 11).

Source: Reprinted with permission from *Child Care Information Exchange*, P.O. Box 3249, Redmond, WA 98073. (800) 221-2864.

Engage in Reflective Practice

Mayfield (2001) offers the following about reflective practice:

> Reflection is characteristic of effective early childhood educators. It helps educators gain better perspective, insight, and understanding. It is critical to developing self-confidence and professional judgment. Reflection can be an individual or group process. Some educators keep journals; others participate in peer discussion groups. Some questions for self-evaluation and reflection include the following:
>
> Why am I doing this?
>
> How did it go?
>
> What does it mean?
>
> What did I do well?
>
> How could I have done it differently, better, more effectively, or more efficiently?
>
> Where do I need to improve? How can I do this?
>
> How can I better meet the children's needs?

Part of being a reflective professional is to continually examine our profession, its practices, and standards and to question the status quo. Especially as a student, you need to ask yourself—and others—why our profession values this, believes that, or does the other. Being reflective means not accepting current assumptions and practices without question.

Be Involved in Professional Development

Most people who enter the child-care field are caring and compassionate people. But the treadmill of activity that consumes their time and energy on the job often keeps them from establishing close relationships with one another. The physical layout of space, time pressures, and conflicting schedules are just some of the barriers that prevent staff from exchanging information, sharing ideas, and lending and receiving support (Jorde Bloom, 1995: 47). Other barriers include the cost of conferences and professional development opportunities; the lack of wage-related recognition for any advance training; the lack of paid professional development time, and the cost to the centre of providing replacement teachers. Teachers need time to meet with their peers and exchange concerns and ideas. Receiving positive, constructive feedback helps a teacher to build both self-confidence and the energy to deal with everyday situations that arise in the centre. An environment of empathy and support is especially important for new teachers, who may be enthusiastic about relationships with families but who lack the expertise of their more seasoned colleagues. New graduates are most likely to succeed and stay in the field when they have been mentored by gifted teachers who are committed to the field. A mentoring approach is a much needed strategy to help create a stable and strong early childhood community.

No teacher should feel that the responsibility for strong family–centre relationships rests entirely on his or her shoulders alone. Each teacher brings his or her own strengths and by sharing these with other teachers in the centre, a more cohesive and effective approach can be forged. For example, one teacher may be a gifted writer, another a budding artist; each can utilize his or her individual strengths and apply them to projects and events at the centre. There is strength in individual talents and expertise that is combined for the greater good. It is also important for teachers to link with other teachers in a variety of different programs in their community. These collaborative ventures allow teachers to share new ideas.

Personal development and growth are also fundamental to teachers. According to Swick (1990: 40), "Teachers who are in a process of continuing personal growth are more receptive to parent involvement and actually take more initiative to pursue the partnership process." Teachers secure in their personal development are more likely to be responsive to both children and parents in terms of their cultural and individual needs. Swick also observes that teachers trained in early childhood education programs (where parent–teacher involvement course are often mandatory), instead of elementary or middle-school programs, more fully support parent involvement and education (1991: 19–30). This information is further supported by the National Institute for Early Education at Rutgers University, which reports that "[n]ew research finds that young children's learning and development clearly depends on the educational qualifications of their teachers. The most effective preschool teachers have at least a four-year college degree and specialized training in early childhood" (Barnett, 2003).

INSIDE LOOK

When I look back on my first few years of teaching, I realize how important my relationship with the more experienced staff and the supervisor in my centre was. I often worried about whether parents would accept me in my role as a teacher, and I worried about whether I handled situations appropriately. One teacher in particular was always willing to help me sort through the range of emotions I felt as I tried to improve on my skills and learn the ropes. Now, years later, I try to provide the same kind of support to new teachers as they are hired on in our centre as well as to the ECE students I am supervising. I still remember how vulnerable I felt.

INSIDE LOOK

According to Campaign 2000, in 1998, 71 percent of all early childhood education and care teaching staff held one-, two-, or three-year ECEC credentials or post-diploma credentials. ECEC staff members, regardless of their poor remuneration, also continue to pursue professional development opportunities throughout their careers. They tend to be a dedicated professional group often supported by their employers in their quest to develop skills and knowledge beyond what they learned in basic training. For example, in a three-year period in Ontario, 74 percent of the ECEC centres supported their staff to take courses, workshops, or in-service training on how to respond to challenging behaviours. In British Columbia 43 percent focused on how to develop their programs to accommodate children with developmental delays. In Saskatchewan staff in 33 percent of the centres pursued anti-bias and cultural diversity topics.

REFERENCES

Abramson, S., and K. Atwal. 2004. "Teachers as Co-Inquirers: Fostering Positive Relationships in a Multicultural Community." In J. Hendrick, ed., *Next Steps toward Teaching the Reggio Way: Accepting the Challenge to Change.* Columbus, OH: Pearson Merrill Prentice Hall.

Adler, S. 2001. "Racial and Ethnic Identity Formation of Midwestern Asian-American Children." *Contemporary Issues in Early Childhood* 2: 265–294.

Akbar, M., J. Chambers, and V. Thompson. 2001. "Racial Identity, Africentric Values and Self-esteem in Jamaican Children." *Journal of Black Psychology* 27: 341–358.

Bandura, A. 1997. *Self-efficacy: The Exercise of Control.* New York: W.H. Freeman.

Barnett, S.W. 2003. "Better Teachers, Better Preschools: Student Achievement Linked to Teacher Qualifications." *Preschool Policy Matters* 2. March. Available at http://www.childcarecanada.org/research/complete/Uspsteach_traning.html.

Beach, J., J. Bertrand, and G. Cleveland. 1998. *Our Child Care Workforce: From Recognition to Remuneration.* Ottawa: Child Care Human Resources Steering Committee.

Becker, S. 2005. "The Good, The Bad And The Few: Men In Child Care." Available at http://www.cccf-fcsge.ca/practice/policy/men_en.html.

Bell, R. 1987. "Social Involvement." In J. McCroskey and J. Daly, eds., *Personality and Interpersonal Communication.* Newbury Park, CA: Sage Publications.

Bernard, J.K. 2004. "Early Authors Program." Available at http://www.ryerson.ca/~bernhard/early.html.

Bernhard, J.K., M.L. Lefebvre, G. Chud, and R. Lange. 1995. *Paths to Equity: Cultural, Linguistic and Racial Diversity in Canadian Early Childhood Education.* North York, ON: York Lanes Press.

Bernhard, J., M.L. Lefebvre, K.M. Kilbride, G. Chud, and R. Lange. 1998. "Troubled Relations in Early Childhood Education: Parent–Teacher Interactions in Ethnoculturally Diverse Child Care Settings." *Early Education and Development* 9 (1): 5–28.

Bertrand, J. 2008. *Understanding, Managing and Leading Early Childhood Programs in Canada.* Toronto: Thomson Nelson.

Braun, D. 1992. Quoted in G. Pugh, ed., *Contemporary Issues in the Early Years: Working Collaboratively for Children.* London, UK: Paul Chapman Publishing in association with the National Children's Bureau.

Bray, J.N., J. Lee, L.L. Smith, and L. York. 2000. *Collaborative Inquiry in Practice: Action, Reflection and Making Meaning.* Thousand Oaks, CA: Sage Publications.

Bronfenbrenner, U. 1974. *A Report on Longitudinal Evaluations of Preschool Programs, vol. 2: Is Early Intervention Effective?* Washington, DC: DHEW Publishing.

Brown, R. 1979. "Children and Racism." Paper presented at the Fourth Canadian Conference on Children, Ottawa. June.

Campaign 2000. 2002. "Diversity or Disparity? Early Childhood Education and Care in Canada (ECEC)." October.

Canadian Child Day Care Federation. 1991. *National Statement on Quality Child Care*. Ottawa: Health and Welfare Canada.

Canadian Council on Social Development. 1999. *The Progress of Canada's Children into the Millennium*. Ottawa: Health Canada.

Cardinal, E. 1994. "Effective Programming: A Native Perspective." *Early Childhood Education* 27 (1): (Spring–Summer).

Christiansen, J. 1980. *West Indians in Toronto*. Toronto: Family Services Association.

Chud, G., and R. Fahlman. 1995. *Honouring Diversity within Child Care and Early Education: An Instructor's Guide, vol. 11*. Vancouver: British Columbia Ministry of Skills, Training and Labour and the Centre for Curriculum and Professional Development.

Clark, K., and M. Clark. 1940. "Skin Color as a Factor in Racial Identification of Negro Preschool Children." *Journal of Social Psychology* 11: 159–169. Available at http://psychclassics.yorku.ca/Clark?Skin-color/ (accessed January 18, 2007).

Comer, J. P., and N.M. Haynes. 1991. "Parent Involvement in Schools: An Ecological Approach." *Elementary School Journal* 91 (3): 271–277.

Couchenour, D., and K. Chrisman. 2000. *Families, Schools, and Communities: Together for Young Children*. New York: Delmar Thomson Learning.

Cross, W.E. 1978. "The Thomas and Cross Models of Psychological Nigrescence: A Literature Review." *Journal of Black Psychology* 5: 13–31.

Derman-Sparks, L., and the ABC Task Force. 1989. *Anti-Bias Curriculum: Tools for Empowering Young Children*. Washington, DC: National Association for the Education of Young Children.

Dever, M.T., and R.C. Falconer. 2008. *Foundations and Change in Early Childhood Education*. Toronto: John Wiley and Sons, Inc.

Dutro, E., E. Kazemi, R. Balf, R. Galvan, and R. Meyer. 2005. "The Aftermath of "You're only half": Multiracial Identities in the Literacy Classroom." *Language Arts* 83: 96–107.

Elkind, D. 1998. "From Our President, David Elkind." *Young Children*. January.

Epstein, J.L. 2002. *What Research Says about Parent Involvement in Children's Education In Relation To Academic Achievement*. Lansing, MI: Michigan Department of Education.

Essa, E., and R. Young. 1994. *Introduction to Early Childhood Education*. Toronto: Nelson Canada.

Fisher, R., and S. Brown. 1988. *Getting Together: Building a Relationship That Gets to Yes*. Boston: Houghton Mifflin.

Gaine, C. 2000. "Anti-racist Education in 'White' Areas: The Limits and Possibilities of Change." *Race, Ethnicity and Education* 3 (1): 65–79.

Galinsky, E. 1988. "Parents and Teacher–Caregivers: Sources of Tension, Sources of Support." *Young Children*. March.

Gestwicki, C. 1992. *Home, School and Community Relations: A Guide to Working with Parents*, 2nd ed. New York: Delmar.

———. 2000. *Home, School and Community Relations: A Guide to Working with Parents*, 4th ed. New York: Delmar.

———. 2004. *Home, School and Community Relations*, 5th ed. New York: Thomson Delmar Learning.

Gonzalez-Mena, J. 1998. *Foundations: Early Childhood Education in a Diverse Society*. Toronto: Mayfield Publishing.

———. 2008. *50 Early Childhood Strategies for Working and Communicating with Diverse Families*. Columbus, OH: Pearson, Merrill Prentice Hall.

———, and E.D. Widmeyer. 1989. *Infants, Toddlers, and Caregivers*. Mountain View, CA: Mayfield.

———, and J.K. Bernhard. 1998. "Out-of-Home Care of Infants and Toddlers: A Call for Cultural Linguistic Continuity." *Interaction* 12 (2).

Greenberg, P. 1989. "Parents as Partners in Young Children's Development and Education: A New American Fad?" *Young Children*. May.

Greenman, J. 1989. "Living in the Real World: Diversity and Conflict." *Exchange* 69 (October).

———, and A. Stonehouse. 1996. *Prime Time. A Handbook for Excellence in Infant and Toddler Programs*. St. Paul, MN: Redleaf Press.

Haigh, K. 2004. "Creating, Encouraging, and Supporting Relationships at Chicago Commons Child Development Program." In J. Hendrick, ed., *Next Steps toward Teaching the Reggio Way: Accepting the Challenge to Change*. Columbus, OH: Pearson Merrill Prentice Hall.

Hartzell, M., and B. Zlotoff. 2004. "Parents as Partners." In J. Hendrick, ed., *Next Steps Toward Teaching the Reggio Way: Accepting the Challenge to Change*. Columbus, OH: Pearson Merrill Prentice Hall.

Hendrick, J., and K. Chandler. 1996. *The Whole Child: Developmental Education for the Early Years*, 6th ed. Toronto: Prentice Hall Canada.

Hepworth Berger, E. 2004. *Parents as Partners in Education. Families and Schools Working Together*, 6th ed. Columbus, OH: Pearson Merrill Prentice Hall.

Hinsliff, G. 2003. "Men Battle Prejudice in Childcare." *The Guardian*. 7 June. Available at http://www.childcarecanada.org/ccin/2003/ccin6_7_03.html.

Hoover-Dempsey, K.V., and H.M. Sandler. 1997. "Why Do Some Parents Become Involved In Their Children's Education?" *Review of Educational Research* 67: 3–42.

Hughes, D., and L. Chen. 1997. "When and What Parents Tell Children about Race: An Examination of Race-related Socialization among African American Families." *Applied Developmental Science* 1: 198–212.

Hughson, P. 1994–1995. "Learning Together: A Parent's Perspective." *Research and Clinical Issues, Zero to Three* 15 (3). December–January.

James, C.E. 1989. *Seeing Ourselves: Exploring Race, Ethnicity and Culture*. Instructional and Human Resource Development. Oakville, ON: Sheridan College.

———, and H.H. Muhammad. N.d. *A Study of Children in Childcare Programs: Perceptions of Race and Race-Related Issues*. Toronto: Municipality of Metropolitan Toronto Children Services and Multicultural and Race Relationships Divisions.

Janmohamed, Z. 2005. "Rethinking Anti-bias Approaches in Early Childhood Education: A Shift Toward Anti-racism Education." In George Dei and Gurpreet Singh Johal, eds., *Critical Issues in Anti-racist Research Methodologies*. New York: Peter Lang.

Jorde Bloom, P. 1995. "Building a Sense of Community: A Broader View." *Child Care Information Exchange* 101. January–February.

Kagan, S.L., and P.R. Neville. 1994. "Parent Choice in Early Care and Education: Myth or Reality?" *Research and Clinical Issues, Zero to Three*. February–March.

Kastings, A. 1992. "Partnerships with Parents: What Centres Say." *The Early Childhood Educator: The Journal of Early Childhood Educators of British Columbia*. April.

Kelly, J. 1998. *Under the Gaze: Learning to be Black in White Society*. Halifax, NS: Fernwood Publishing.

Keyser, J. 2006. *From Parents to Partners: Building a Family-Centered Early Childhood Program*. St. Paul, MN: Redleaf Press.

Krechevsky, M., and B. Mardell. 2001. "Form, Function and Understanding in Learning Groups: Propositions from Reggio Classrooms." In Project Zero/Reggio Children, eds., *Making Learning Visible*. Reggio Emilia, Italy: Reggio Children.

LaGrange, A., D. Clark, and E. Munroe. 1994. "Culturally Sensitive Programming: An Alberta Study." *Early Childhood Education* 27 (1). Spring–Summer.

Landreth, C., and B.C. Johnson. 1953. "Young Children's Responses to a Picture and Inset Test Designed to Reveal Reactions to Persons of Different Skin Color." *Child Development*, 24: 63–80.

Larsen, J. M., and J.H. Haupt. 1997. "Integrating Home and School: Building a Partnership." In C.H. Hart, R. Charlesworth, and D.C. Burts, eds., *Integrated Curriculum and Developmentally Appropriate Practice Birth to Age Eight*. Albany, NY: SUNY.

Lieberman, A.F. 1998. "Culturally Sensitive Intervention with Children and Families." *Newsletter of the Infant Mental Health Promotion Project* 22. Fall.

Lindsay, J. 1999. "Views of a Concerned Parent." Available at http://www.jefflindsay.com/Education.shtml.

Lowell Krough, S. 1994. *Educating Young Children: Infancy to Grade Three*. Toronto: McGraw-Hill.

Malaguzzi, L. 1993. "For an Education Based on Relationships." *Young Children* 49 (1): 9–12.

———. n.d. "A Charter of Rights for Parents."

Mann, B. 2008. "Welcoming Families As Partners In Child Care." *Interaction*. Spring.

Marshall, S. 1995. "Ethnic Socialization of African American Children: Implications for Parenting, Identity Development, and Academic Achievement." *Journal of Youth and Adolescence* 24: 377–396.

Mayfield, M.I. 2001. *Early Childhood Education and Care in Canada: Contexts, Dimensions, and Issues*. Toronto: Prentice Hall.

Mercredi, O. 1992. "Our Traditions, Our Children, Our Future: Native/Aboriginal Early Childcare." Fredericton, New Brunswick. 6–7 November.

Murphy Kilbride, K. 1997. *Include Me Too! Human Diversity in Early Childhood*. Toronto: Harcourt Brace Canada.

National Association for the Education of Young Children, Division of Early Childhood/Council for Exceptional Children, and National Board of Professional Teaching Standards. 1996. *Guidelines for Preparation of Early Childhood Professionals*. Washington, DC: National Association for the Education of Young Children.

Neugebauer, R. 1994. "Recruiting and Retaining Men In Your Center." *Child Care Information Exchange*. May/June: 5–11.

Ogbu, J. 1981. "Origins of Human Competence: A Cultural-ecological Perspective." *Child Development* 51: 413–429.

Pawl, J.H. 1993. "Impact of Day Care on Parents and Family." *Pediatrics* 91 (1). January.

Pelletier, J., and J.M. Brent. 2002. "Parent Participation in Children's School Readiness: The Effects of Parental Self-Efficacy, Cultural Diversity and Teacher Strategies." *International Journal of Early Childhood*, 34: 45–61.

Phinney, J. 1990. "Ethnic Identity in Adolescents and Adults: Review of Research." *Psychological Bulletin* 3: 499–514.

Rinaldi, C. 2002. "The Pedagogy of Listening: The Listening Perspective from Reggio Emilia. Innovation in Early Education: The International Reggio." *Exchange* 8 (4): 1–4.

Robinson, E.C. 1988. "Vanishing Breed: Men in Child Care Programs." *Young Children* 43 (6).

Rong, X., and F. Brown. 2002. "Socialization, Culture and Identities of Black Immigrant Children: What Educators Need to Know and Do." *Education and Urban Society* 34: 242–273.

Statistics Canada. 2001. "Community Highlights for Toronto." Available at http://www.12.statcan.ca/english/profil01/CP01/Details/Page.cfm?Lang=E&Geo1=CSD&Code1=3520005&Geo2=PR&Code2=35&Data=Count&SearchText=Toronto&SearchType=Begins&SearchPR=35&B1=All&Custom=.

Sturm, C. 1997. "Creating Parent–Teacher Dialogue: Intercultural Communication in Child Care." *Young Children* 52 (5): 34–38.

Sullivan, D. 2003. *Learning To Lead*. St. Paul, MN: Redleaf Press.

Swick, K. 1991. *Teacher–Parent Partnerships to Enhance School Success in Early Childhood Education*. NEA Early Childhood Education series. Washington, DC: National Education Association and Southern Association on Children under Six.

———. 1992. *Teacher–Parent Partnerships*. ERIC Digest. Champaign, IL: ERIC Clearinghouse on Elementary and Early Childhood Education. (ERIC Document No. ED351149).

Swick, K., and S. McKnight. 1989. "Characteristics of Kindergarten Teachers Who Promote Parent Involvement." *Early Childhood Research Quarterly* 4: 19–29.

Switsun, D. 1994. "Do You Know Your Anti-Bias Curriculum?" *Child Care Focus* 29. Spring.

Uttal, L. 2002. *Making Care Work: Employed Mothers in the New Childcare Market*. New Brunswick, NJ: Rutgers University Press.

Warren, R.M. 1979. *Accepting Parents*. Washington, DC: National Association for the Education of Young Children.

Weissbourd, B. 1992. "Building Parent Partnerships." *Scholastic Pre-K Today*. August–September.

Whitaker, T., and D.J. Fiore. 2001. *Dealing with Difficult Parents and With Parents in Difficult Situations*. Larchmont, NY: Eye on Education.

York, S. 1991. *Roots and Wings*. St. Paul, MN: Redleaf Press.

You Bet I Care! Survey. 1998. Ottawa: Human Resources Development. Available at http://www.cfc-efc.ca/docs/00001269.htm.

daddy

momy

declam

Hamish

CHAPTER 4

First Impressions

"It is well to give when asked, but it is better to give unasked, through understanding."

—*Kahlil Gibran*

LEARNING OUTCOMES

After studying this chapter, you will be able to

1. identify effective communication practices teachers can use in their initial contact with families

2. describe the process of orienting a new family to a child-care centre

3. outline the elements of a successful home visit and identify some of the barriers to home visits

4. discuss the separation process and how teachers can facilitate children's transition to the centre, to new playrooms and to school environments

INITIAL CONTACT WITH A CHILD-CARE CENTRE

Many families who are searching for child care for the first time are unsure of how to make the right choice. Different families require different types of care and there is no one-size-fits-all approach. Most families are introduced to a centre when they phone to ask about a space for their child. This call is usually followed by a visit to the centre and a meeting with the supervisor and teachers. If their first impressions are favourable and a position is available for their child, the family may make a commitment to enroll. Then, once the child is registered, the family begins what may be a long-term relationship with the centre.

The first few months in this new environment often set the stage for the type of interaction that will characterize the family–centre relationship—hence the importance of a systematic orientation process. The following information illustrates the process most families follow when they enter a child-care centre for the first time.

THE FIRST TELEPHONE CALL

The phone rings. A harried staff member, dealing with a sick child in her arms, picks up the phone and curtly names the centre. She informs the parent that she is too busy to deal with her questions and tells her to call back when the supervisor can speak to her. The parent, listening to the crying child in the background and the teacher's agitated voice, consults her list and decides to call another centre.

You never get a second chance to make a first impression. Working in a child-care centre can be frantic. Not only must teachers deal with sick children on a regular basis, but because most centres cannot afford the luxury of full-time secretarial support, most of the day-to-day administrative responsibilities fall to the supervisor and teachers. Given that the first impression of the centre is usually based on a phone call, then, the development of telephone skills is essential.

Information given over the telephone should be communicated in a positive, caring manner. Families are listening not only for details about the centre but also for a tone of warmth and genuine interest in their participation. Though teachers may repeat this information many times over the course of a year, it is important to remember that families will be hearing it for the first time. Personalizing the call and asking questions about what the family is looking for will help the centre begin the process of building a positive relationship. A good strategy is to record all the information from the call on a standard form. If the family decides to visit the centre, this form can be used by the supervisor to prepare for the visit.

WRITTEN COMMUNICATION

Once families have expressed interest, the next step is to send them written information about the centre. Because families continue to evaluate the centre on the basis of this written material, it should be professional in appearance and error-free; it should also effectively convey the philosophy of the centre. (Detailed guidelines for written communication with families are provided in Chapter 8.) The written communication should also include a checklist advising families on what to look for in any child-care centre. Families will become better, more discriminating consumers who are more informed about issues that are critical to the development of quality care. The Canadian Child Care Federation, provincial ministries, or municipal agencies are good sources for this information. When necessary, this information should be translated into the family's first language.

VISITING THE CENTRE

For families whose children will be starting around the same time, a group orientation may be set up to facilitate introductions. Not all new families are able to visit during the day; staff will need to make arrangements to meet with these families at the end of their workday or on weekends. Visits that are set up outside of business or school hours may allow other family members to come to this first, most important visit. Visits are best timed when staff members are available to talk to families.

When setting up the first visit, it may be appropriate for families whose first language is not English to bring along another family member or trusted friend to help them feel more comfortable. If this is not possible, a centre staff member who comes from the same cultural and language background may be able to assist in the orientation, or a professional interpreter may be hired. From the moment families enter the centre they are gathering information about the culture of this environment. Creating a positive impression is based on many factors.

CREATING A WELCOMING ENVIRONMENT

The importance of a welcoming physical environment cannot be underestimated; it plays a crucial role in our ability to adapt and adjust. As Greenman (1988: 44) notes, "Children reared in fortresses barricaded against the world outside, or in dingy

This poster represents many languages that may be spoken at the centre.

basements, or in worlds of fluorescently-lit plastic and tile will have different aesthetic sensibilities than those raised in light, airy, open places with plants and easy access to the outside."

The physical design of a centre can affect the relationships among those who work there and those who visit. The family's impression of the centre begins before they meet anyone who works there: parking should be accessible and there should be a safe drop-off and pick-up location for children who arrive by bus or in a car pool. The centre should also be accessible for people with disabilities. Staff should routinely check for such things as peeling paint, unweeded flower beds, and cluttered walkways. The means of entry should be clearly explained at the entrance. (For example, a security code is required in many centres to ensure the safety of the children.) Positive, welcoming, legible signs should be posted inside the centre to provide guidance to families; these signs should be in the languages that reflect the families in the centre.

A welcoming foyer provides a gradual transition to the playrooms and a comfortable gathering place for families. Too often child-care centres are designed only with children in mind. There should be designated spaces just for adults—places to hang up their coats, safe places to store their bags and

Environments send powerful messages.

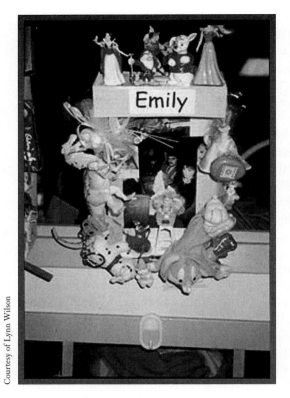

Emily's shadow box helps her identify her space as well as reminding her of home.

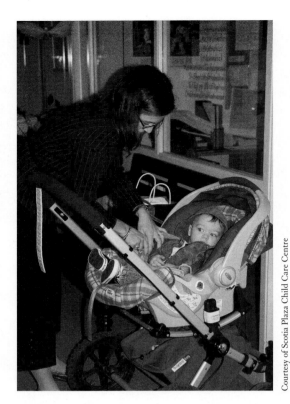

Convenient storage space for strollers is appreciated by families.

briefcases, and a location for reading family resource materials.

A home-like atmosphere will have more appeal to families than an institutional look. Function and comfort should go together. To accommodate those families who walk to and from the centre with strollers, adequate storage space should be provided. Cubby areas should be designed so that families can easily assist their children in their dressing routine. It is also an opportunity for families to personalize this space with family artifacts or pictures to make the connection from home to centre.

Maintain a bulletin board near the main entrance to keep families informed about relevant news and events. The bulletin board might include photographs of families who are involved in centre activities; photographs, names and brief biographies of permanent staff, regular supply teachers, students who are doing field placements, and volunteers; information about upcoming centre events; and copies of recent newsletters.

Playrooms should be labelled by age group, with the names and photos of the teachers prominently displayed. Bulletin boards placed directly outside

Biographies of the teachers, which include their educational qualifications, will help to reassure families that their children are being cared for by professionals.

Imagine a room where there are bright splashes of colour, often attached to moving bodies, and warm, muted hues on the carpet and walls. Sunshine catches the light of a prism in one corner and on the floor is a patch of sunlight so bright it makes you squint. There are soft, indirect lights, as well as shadows and cool, dark corners. There are hanging baskets of trailing green plants, flowers, pussy willows and cattails, angel hair, and dried grasses. The beauty of life is captured in artwork by Monet and Wyeth and assorted four-year-olds. There are the smells of fresh earth, lilacs and eucalyptus, garlic, and baking bread. One hears laughter and singing, animated conversation, soft classical music, and the backbeat of reggae from somewhere in the corridor. There is a ticking of clocks, a chirping of birds, and the squeaking and rustling of a guinea pig. There is a breeze from an open window as one walks around feeling heavy, dark wood and silky fabric; hard, cold metal and warm fur; complex textures and watery, slippery, gooey things.

Source: Greenman, 1988: 63.

the playrooms can be used to keep families up to date about happenings in specific rooms—for example, by posting the name, photo, and background of a supply teacher.

In the playroom there should be open spaces, cozy spaces, bright spaces, peaceful spaces, gathering places, working places, loft spaces, climbing spaces, resting spaces, and outdoor spaces. Variety is essential! The environment must be functional, too, in the sense that it accommodates the specific needs of the children and adults in the room. Particular attention should be given to "soft" spaces to create an inviting and comforting feel.

Organizing bulletin boards, displaying artwork, and storing children's equipment should be done in a manner that avoids visual clutter. Are there area rugs on the floor? Are there pictures and posters on the wall? Is music being softly played? Are there display tables showing off the children's work? Is the centre's "story" evident?

Courtesy of Scotia Plaza Child Care Centre

A simple gesture, such as having a comfortable place to sit and read, can make a difference to a weary parent.

We were nervous when we arrived at the centre. Mario is our first child. We were undecided about whether to look for someone in our neighbourhood to look after him once I went back to work or to bring him to the Janeway Child Care Centre. We had heard a lot of positive things about the centre, so we wanted to take a look. Theresa, the supervisor, was very friendly, and it wasn't long before we felt comfortable enough to ask the thousand and one questions we had about group care. She was very patient with us. It was clear that she was very proud of the centre and the teachers who worked there. She took us on a tour of the centre, and when we got to the infant room we were very impressed with what we saw. The teachers were warm and caring, and despite the constant activity they handled everything in a calm manner. All the information about the centre was reviewed with us, and we especially enjoyed the video of the infant room that showed us what a typical day for Mario might be like. This first visit really made a difference for us. Now we know that this centre is where we want him to be.

EXHIBIT 4.1 TWO DIFFERENT FIRST IMPRESSIONS

CENTRE VISIT A

Maria and Jeremy Palmer are looking for a daycare space for their three-month-old daughter, Amanda. Unaware that they needed to plan so far in advance, both parents are worried they will not find a suitable centre before Maria has to return to work in four weeks.

They arrive at the Janeway Child Care Centre. The supervisor of the centre, Theresa Sanchez, had provided clear directions in an earlier—and very positive—telephone exchange. Some of the windows at the front of the centre are decorated with children's artwork. A large and colourful sign out front provides directions to the daycare. Instructions for entering the centre are located above the intercom system on the outside door. A pleasant-sounding voice responds to their request for entry and they are buzzed in.

Inside, they are greeted by a large bulletin board that features photographs and short but informative biographies of the teachers and supervisor. Maria and Jeremy are very impressed with the educational credentials of the staff; they are especially interested to see that one of the teachers was raised in El Salvador, Maria's home country.

Samples of children's artwork line the hallway. At the end of it is a large sign with the word "welcome" written in a number of languages. Maria and Jeremy are encouraged by the bright and warm feeling exuded by the centre.

As they reach the entrance to the playrooms, the supervisor approaches them, her hand extended in a gesture of welcome. She shows them an area designated for families where they can hang up their coats and leave their bags and briefcases. She then invites them into her office for a cup of coffee and freshly made fruit bread. The orientation process and the partnership between the centre and the family have begun.

CENTRE VISIT B

Sandra is a single parent who is new to this neighbourhood. As the mother of two children—a school-age child and a preschooler—she is pleased to discover that the local school has a daycare centre attached to it. She hopes to be able to place her two children in one location.

Sandra calls the centre for information about the availability of spaces. She is told that the teacher is too busy to talk to her and she should call again later and speak to the supervisor. Sandra leaves a message for the supervisor to call her back. Two days later she has still not heard from her. Knowing she has only a few days left before she must return to work, Sandra decides that she will pay the centre a visit in the hope of meeting with the supervisor.

At the school's front entrance there is no sign to indicate the location of the daycare. Sandra tries to get directions from the main office, but the secretary is busy with a student and the principal is in a meeting with a parent. Finally, Sandra is given directions.

Feeling like an intruder, Sandra is debating whether to leave when finally the supervisor appears in the hallway. After Sandra explains her situation, the supervisor tells her she is on her way to a meeting but will call her as soon as she can. As she talks, the supervisor escorts Sandra outside the building. She seems reluctant to allow Sandra to observe the centre without her being present. The supervisor does not apologize for failing to return Sandra's phone call. Sandra leaves the centre with no information but with very strong reservations about placing her children in such an inhospitable environment.

The two very different experiences, outlined in Exhibit 4.1, demonstrate the importance of the human connection. When we welcome families into the centre in the way that we would welcome friends into our home, we understand the impact of the role of the staff.

THE ROLE OF THE SUPERVISOR

Introducing new families to the centre is one of the supervisor's most important roles, and one that requires a great deal of thought and effort. When the supervisor's office is near the entrance to the centre, it is well situated not only to welcome visitors but as a place where families can touch base as they come and go. One centre supervisor has framed all the teachers' ECE diplomas, other educational diplomas, and professional development certificates on the wall above her desk. Several families have informed her that they were reassured to see these.

The supervisor should be waiting when the family arrives. An enthusiastic, friendly greeting gets the visit off to a good start. An assortment of toys, books, papers, and markers should be kept on-hand for children who are accompanying their families on the visit. This is a big day for the child, so the visit should be as pleasant and stress-free as possible. Families are alert to how the supervisor interacts with their child; this interaction sets the tone for the visit as a whole.

Courtesy of Lynn Wilson

Seeing children actively engaged sends positive messages to new families.

An offer of refreshments as everyone gets acquainted is a good way to begin the orientation and demonstrates that the centre has planned for the visit. While refreshments are being organized, the supervisor might show families a photo album featuring parents, children, and teachers in a variety of centre-related activities. Supervisors should be wary of sitting behind their desk and creating barriers between themselves and the parents. In the ensuing discussion, supervisors should provide families with a clear understanding of the licensing requirements (and how the centre meets them) and the philosophy of the centre. The supervisor should ask questions about what the family is looking for, what special interests they have, and so on. Families will want to know what makes this centre unique and if it will be a good match for them.

It is important for the supervisor to listen as much as she talks. Families will have an in-depth understanding of their child; for example, they will know if their child is very physical and active. In such a case the family may be looking for a centre with an emphasis on outdoor play and a good outdoor space with equipment and materials to support this area of their child's development. Families will want to know how you will respond to their child's individual temperament.

A checklist of quality indicators can be a helpful tool for parents. Some centres have developed a DVD that takes families through a typical day at the centre; families may also be provided with a take-home DVD in which the information given during the visit is summarized. The take-home DVD is particularly helpful if some family members are not able to attend the orientation. There may be resistance to the concept of group care from family members who did not grow up with this option, and the DVD may support the parents' choice. This information can also be conveyed in brochures or family handbooks. Previous issues of the centre's newsletter provide additional insight into the centre and highlight milestones and achievements. All of this information can be organized ahead of time and presented to families as they leave.

Supervisors can prepare themselves for parents' questions by keeping a record of commonly asked questions. It is important for supervisors to strike a balance between overwhelming families with material and conveying too little information. What they should emphasize is the importance of the family–teacher relationship to the centre experience and the centre's professional approach.

TOURING THE CENTRE

A tour of the centre early in the visit helps consolidate the information provided during the discussion. During the tour the supervisor can point out ways in which the centre's philosophy translates into action. The supervisor should also point out contributions families have made in order to reinforce the active role families play in the centre. A parent of a child already attending the child-care centre may also be asked to join the orientation at this point, to contribute a different perspective.

Teachers in each of the rooms should be prepared for the visit and greet the visitors with enthusiasm. Family members should be encouraged to call the teachers and the supervisor by their first names. The supervisor should give the family some basic information about the teacher's education and work experience. It is reassuring for families to know about the people who will be working with their child. The supervisor should point out the important areas of the room and the materials that are available to the children. If learning outcomes are posted in each of the interest centres, families will see the possibilities for active child participation and growth. The daily schedule and the program plan can also be discussed.

Families often worry that group care will make it impossible for their child to receive the individual attention he or she needs. The supervisor should review with families the ratios in the room and the size of the group. Staff willingness to celebrate the uniqueness of each family should be evident in their interactions and be imbedded in the environment. Family members should be invited to stay and observe in the playroom. Opportunities will arise to demonstrate the centre's philosophy with respect to guiding children's behaviour, exploration of materials, and problem-solving. Talking about children in the group who may share interests with the visitors' child can help instill in new families a sense of belonging. ("You mentioned that your child is very interested in dinosaurs. Sarah, our resident dinosaur expert, is the same age as your daughter. She will look forward to having someone to share her dinosaurs with.")

In their discussion of the role of the supervisor in talking to prospective parents, Kaiser and Rasminsky (1994) offer this insight:

Small events tell families a great deal about the atmosphere at your centre. If a child asks you to tie his shoe or an educator wants you to stay

Materials available to children should reflect a wide range of cultures.

with her group while she takes someone to the bathroom, parents will notice that the children all know you and the staff is relaxed when you are around. Seeing this level of comfort is very reassuring.

Families should also visit the kitchen and meet the cook, with whom menus and food issues can be discussed. Not unlike a home environment, the kitchen is the heart of the centre. Parents often come to seek advice and problem solve. The cook, like each member of the child-care team, plays an integral role reflecting commitment and constant attention to the children and their families.

The tour can conclude with an examination of the outdoor environment. The outdoor environment must reflect places for active play, solitude, groups, art, interactions with nature, gardens, sand, water, etc. Here the supervisor can talk about the measures taken to ensure the safe use of equipment and, more generally, about the importance of an exciting outdoor play-based environment.

ENSURING QUALITY: HELPING PARENTS KNOW WHAT TO LOOK FOR

Some centres may create an observation sheet that draws the visiting family's attention to important aspects of the program.

The kitchen is often the heart of the child-care centre.

New families should be able to see how the centre's outdoor play space provides meaningful learning opportunities for children.

Courtesy of Lynn Wilson

It should be evident during all stages of the tour that the centre is one that celebrates diversity. Figure 4.1 and Figure 4.2 list some of the items and objects through which a centre can express its commitment to diversity.

When it is time for the family to leave, a thoughtful gesture may be to take a photo of the child in the room and print it for the child to take home. The child can share this picture with others in the family, and it may ease some of the tension related to the forthcoming, official first day. After the tour, the family may return to the supervisor's office for a discussion of any issues that arose from their observation. If the supervisor, parents, and teachers have planned carefully for this visit, the family should begin to feel a sense of belonging and connection to the centre.

If a space is not currently available, the supervisor may outline the waiting-list procedures and advise families that they will be kept informed about their status. Supervisors can stay in touch with those families on the list by sending invitations to centre events and copies of newsletters. Some families may also request the names of families in the centre who may be willing to speak to them about their experience at the centre. While they are waiting, families should also be encouraged to visit as many programs in their community as possible in order to determine the best possible fit for them.

INSIDE LOOK

Haigh (2004: 79) recounts an innovative strategy developed by the Chicago Commons Child Development Program for demonstrating the importance of children and their families. "We saw that photos of children or families displayed within a center can become documentation of the history and life of the center itself. We asked each child who attends the center to make a simple self-portrait with black marker on a beige tile. . . In this way, we have created a way to respect the children and support the center's history as we portray work from all who have attended the program."

EXHIBIT 4.2 SAMPLE ITEM FROM OBSERVATION SHEET

In our preschool room, you can observe the following ways in which we encourage self-help skills:

- At meal time, children serve themselves from small serving bowls and pour their own milk and juice.
- Snack is set up during the morning, and the children decide when they will come and eat, after washing their hands.
- After eating, children return their plates and utensils to labelled bins on the serving cart.
- The washroom is located in the room and has child-sized toilets and sinks for easy access. Children use it independently during the day.
- Children are encouraged to brush their teeth after lunch, using brushes and toothpaste stored near the washroom sinks.
- Paper cups are stored in the washroom so that when the children are thirsty they can help themselves.
- Cubbies are set up for easy access to assist the child in retrieving clothes when dressing.
- The equipment in the room is scaled to children's height to allow for independent use.
- Equipment is stored in small bins that are easily lifted out and returned by the children.
- Playroom carts are labelled pictorially so that children can return their bins to the correct space.

FIGURE 4.1 EXPRESSING DIVERSITY I

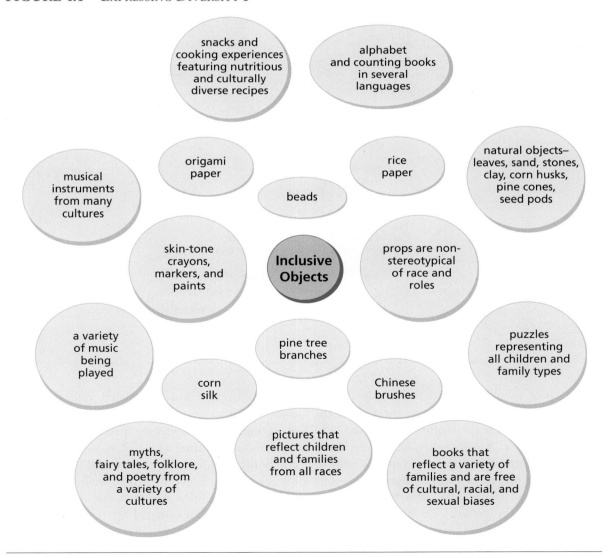

FIGURE 4.2   EXPRESSING DIVERSITY II

If a space is available and the family decides that they would like to come to the centre, the family should review the required forms and policies of the centre. A comprehensive family handbook (see Chapter 8) will provide families with an overview of important centre information. The issue of fees should be clearly addressed. Supervisors may assist English-as-a-second-language parents if forms are not available in their first language. Forms translated into the most common languages in the community will greatly assist non-English-speaking parents. The supervisor should outline who will have access to the child's file; families will be reassured to know that all information is confidential. Finally, the expectations of the families should be discussed and parents should be encouraged to provide relevant information about their child, including possible separation issues, experiences in previous child-care settings, and so on.

HOME VISITS

I want you to come to my house,

and yet I don't.

You're so important,

but our screen door has a hole in it,

and my mother has no fancy cake to serve.

I want you to come to my house, teacher,

and yet I don't.

My brother chews with his mouth wide open,

and sometimes my dad burps.

I wish I could trust you enough, teacher,

to invite you to my house. (Cullum, 1971: 50)

The home visit is one of the most effective ways of creating a sense of partnership with families. According to Brooks (1994: 17), the home visit enables the teacher "to establish a personal and authentic relationship with individual children who are able to see the teacher as someone their parents invite into their homes. This parental approval is reassuring for children."

Home visits provide teachers with insights into family–child interactions, the care strategies that work best for parents, and the values and priorities that families wish to instill in their child. "The information we gather in the home in just one hour would perhaps take us several months to collect in a more alien environment of the classroom with other children demanding our attention" (Brooks, 1994: 17). When teachers have an opportunity to see what families are trying to accomplish at home with their children, they can look for ways to support these efforts in the child-care environment. Parents too may feel more comfortable discussing a difficult issue in their home than at the child-care centre. Through the home visit, a teacher can learn about a child's

- relationship with family members and siblings
- position in the family (effects of being the youngest, oldest, etc.)
- living environment (blended family, lone-parent, joint-custody situation, two-parent, parent who is ill, elderly parents living with the family, etc.)
- developmental level of play
- parent attitude to play
- social skills
- communication skills
- exposure to books and materials for manipulation and exploration

Home visits are much anticipated events.

- level of independence
- general knowledge and interests
- favourite playthings
- access to available neighbourhood resources (library, community centre, etc.)

Haigh (2004: 78) reports that in the Head Start preschool program in United States, home visits are now required at the beginning of the year for participating families. The staff began to rethink their approach in establishing new relationships:

Instead of giving parents a barrage of information, we began to ask them about their ideas. This was done by asking them their hopes and dreams for their children. Interesting enough, parents did not say that they hoped their children would learn their ABCs and 1, 2, 3s. Some examples of their hopes are:

"I hope he grows up to be a professional person."

"I hope he has a sense of humour."

"I hope my child finishes school before having children."

"I hope my child will do for others."

We have now added other questions to encourage parents to share their ideas. Some of them are:

"What kind of adult would you wish your child to be?"

"What was your favourite family activity as a child and what is your family's favourite activity now?"

"What was your first day of school like and do you have a picture of yourself as a young child?"

The ideas that parents have shared are then displayed within the centre or the classroom, so in some way the voice of the parent is included and visible within the program.

The home visit provides families with an opportunity to ask more questions about the centre and its philosophy, and to learn more about the person who will be working closely with their child. The main benefit of home visits for children is that they begin their relationship with the teacher on familiar territory and will not be encountering a stranger when they come to the centre for the first time. With this information the teacher can plan a more meaningful entry for the child by incorporating activities and experiences that are sure to be of interest.

Some centres continue to use home visits throughout a child's placement at the centre. Additional home visits can be especially beneficial for those children who have had difficulty adapting to life in the centre. Visits might also be scheduled when an important event has occurred in the home (the birth of a baby, for example). A child-centred home visit affords older children an opportunity to show initiative. As host, the child can help organize the event. Home visits are also warranted when

INSIDE LOOK

Personally, our home visits changed our lives. We came away from our children's home with respect and admiration for families doing the best they could, some under dire circumstances. We realized that all parents want a good education for their children . . . . In the past it was easy to blame parents for a child's lack of school success by saying, "I wish someone at home cared about this child." We discovered instead that of course parents do care! When teachers make an effort to meet parents a little more than halfway, they find many ways to help children. After our home visits we found ourselves relating more often, verbally and emotionally, with the children. The children were delighted to tell their classmates that last night the teacher came to visit. After talking to parents in such a personal way, we began to view all of the children in our classes more compassionately and with greater understanding. Now we know that each child has a unique and special life. Our goal is to nourish the skills children do have and to appreciate parents and encourage them to be an integral part of their child's education.

Source: Excerpt from M.S. Gorter-Reu and J.M. Anderson, "Home Kits, Home Visits, and More!" *Young Children* (1998), p. 73. Reprinted by permission from the National Association for the Education for Young Children.

families are unable or reluctant to meet with the teacher at the centre.

ELEMENTS OF A SUCCESSFUL HOME VISIT

Home visits should be discussed with the family in the initial meetings with the supervisor as part of the orientation process. Families should be clear about the purpose of the visit—it's an opportunity to lay the foundation for a strong partnership between the home and the centre. They should also be reassured that any special planning or preparation for the visit is not necessary. A telephone or written reminder to families just before the date of the visit is a good idea. Teachers should be thoughtful about how they dress for this occasion in order to create a comfortable but professional impression. Parents should know the expected length of the visit in advance. It is important for the teacher to arrive on time. While home visits usually last from 30 minutes to an hour, teachers should be sensitive to indications that they are overstaying their welcome.

The teacher may wish to bring a small gift or book for the child. Some resourceful teachers create a box of goodies that they take on all their home visits. These colourful boxes might include age-appropriate puzzles, puppets, or books, and they serve as a nice icebreaker. If the teacher brings markers and paper, the child might create a picture that the teacher can take to the centre. When the child arrives at the centre, he or she will see her picture proudly displayed. The teacher might also consider bringing a small photo album with photographs of children playing in the room at the various interest centres. The teacher and child can talk about the fun things that will happen when the child arrives at the centre. Taking a photo of the child and their family and placing it on a bulletin board will provide both a way to introduce the family to existing parents and a fun reminder of the home visit for the child. If there are other children in the family, the teacher should be prepared for this and should include them in the visit in order to avoid feelings of exclusion. For the families, teachers might bring a brochure about centre involvement or a booklet that provides information about all the community resources that they might want to access—libraries, community centres, swimming pools, clinics, special attractions, and so forth.

Perhaps the most essential element for a successful home visit is an ability to accept family behaviours and conditions that differ from those the teacher has experienced. An open and accepting attitude on the part of the teacher is essential to the success of a home visit. Respect for individual family styles and cultural preferences are a critical part of providing support to families and of building a trusting relationship. An effective home visitor will be sensitive to the expressed and unexpressed needs of the child and other family members, will demonstrate versatility and flexibility during the visit, and will avoid alienating families by coming across as an "expert." It's important to be informal and approachable, but not too casual.

The home visit is a good chance for the teacher to underscore the importance that he or she places on the parents' input and to learn more about the uniqueness of each family. Asking families to provide reading material that reflects their values and cultural beliefs may also be an important learning

INSIDE LOOK

When I arrived, the first place Jeremy took me was to his room. It was filled with models and books about dinosaurs. He even had dinosaur wallpaper. When I asked him to show me his favourite book, he brought me *Patrick's Dinosaur*. On Jeremy's first morning at the centre I set up the sand table with dinosaurs and rocks and created a tropical feel by adding trees and small bushes that I made out of construction paper and tubing. In the library area I brought out books about dinosaurs and on the table I stood *Patrick's Dinosaur*. When Jeremy entered the room, he was very hesitant and stuck close to his father. They slowly walked around the room and eventually they wandered over to the sand table. Jeremy noticed the dinosaurs right away. He turned to look at me and a huge smile spread across his face. He let go of his father's hand and from that moment on he was actively involved.

opportunity for a teacher. Reinforcing the importance of the role of the family in the centre is critical to building lasting partnerships.

Teachers and families might address some, or all, of the following topics during the home visit:

- previous experiences in child care
- life in other cities or countries
- important events in the child's life
- activities the child likes to do at home
- favourite toys, snuggle blankets, and so on
- outdoor activities the child enjoys
- responsibilities in the home
- schedules and routines
- comforting strategies
- fears or concerns the child has
- relationship with siblings
- food restrictions, and nutrition generally
- eating habits (favourite and least favourite foods)
- child's attitude toward the centre
- upcoming separation
- ways of incorporating religious or family customs into centre life
- family expectations for the child
- family interests and skills (create a skills bank for later use)
- nature and degree of family involvement in the centre
- family activities and community supports

It is also possible to find out during a home visit how family members might be interested in participating in the centre. The teacher should be careful not to pressure families but suggest a variety of ways in which the centre might utilize their skills and talents; for example, by asking about how families might be willing to participate; if they would be interested in attending parenting meetings, collecting "trashables" for art experiences, helping with gardening activities, building equipment or doing repairs in the centre; driving or supporting field trips; working on a newsletter or participating on the board of directors; volunteering in the play room; arranging a visit to their workplace; contributing children's books or dramatic play items; or carrying out an activity based on their interests, skills, community activism.

Teachers can also use the home visit to find out more about special family arrangements. In the case of divorced families, for example, teachers will want to know if visitation restrictions apply to the other parent and if that parent should receive centre mailings and invitations to family–teacher conferences. If foster families are involved, what role would they like to play? In a more relaxed environment, one that is familiar territory for the parent, this opportunity for one-on-one interaction allows for more direct communication. Feedback is immediate and various family members may participate in the conversation.

It is not uncommon for families to offer refreshments. It is important for teachers to take part in the sharing of this food. Many families will have gone to a great deal of trouble. Teachers may also bring food that reflects their family favourites.

You might, based on your observations, like to extend an invitation to a family member or an older sibling who has a particular talent or skill. One teacher was admiring the necklace the child was wearing and the child mentioned that her mother had made it. The mother showed the teacher her work and the teacher was so impressed that she invited the mother to the centre to demonstrate her

---

INSIDE LOOK

As we drove up to the house we could see Jill watching out the window for our arrival. By the time we had walked up the path, she was already hopping up and down in the doorway. Mom, with Jill's baby brother on her hip, was just behind her. "Do you like banana muffins?" [asked Jill], searching our faces anxiously and reaching for her mom's hand. . . . When we assured her that they were indeed our very favourite kind, her face broke into a wide grin of relief. "Good, we made some for you!" (Brooks, 1994: 14)

jewellery-making to the children. Finally, it is critical that the teacher maintain confidentiality, respecting the family and their lifestyle.

FOLLOW-UP TO THE HOME VISIT

Following the home visit, the teacher should send the families a note expressing enthusiasm about the visit and thanking them for their hospitality. The teacher should also add to the child's file any information that might assist other teachers in supporting both the child and the family. In assessing the success of the home visit, teachers can use the checklist in Exhibit 4.3 to rate their own performance.

WHY HOME VISITS AREN'T DONE MORE OFTEN

There are a number of reasons why home visits, despite their benefit to all concerned, are not a more regular part of a centre's interaction with families.

Time

Many ECE teachers say their work is too demanding and time-consuming to allow for home visits. It is up to all centre staff to look for creative ways to accommodate these visits. For example, constructing a visiting schedule by grouping children according to their neighbourhoods will minimize travelling time. It may not be possible to begin by visiting all existing families, but the process can be put in place as new families arrive. Teachers must weigh the demands on their own time against the benefits that ensue from these visits. Home visits may feel labour intensive up front, but the benefits are enormous.

Money

Some teachers may insist on being paid for conducting visits on their own time. Many centres lack overtime budgets and they can't afford to hire extra staff to replace teachers who are away on home visits during regular work hours. One solution is to have volunteers or the supervisor take over while teachers visit families. Centres should also consider paying staff for mileage.

Reluctant Families

For any of several reasons, families may be reluctant to have the teacher visit them in their home. Those who have not developed a trusting relationship with teachers may view the visit as an invasion of their privacy, as a form of harassment, or as an opportunity for the teacher to make value judgments about their family life. Some families worry that the teacher wants to visit because their child is not doing well and the teacher plans to instruct them on how to be a better parent. Other families may be so overwhelmed by problems resulting from such situations as poverty or illness that they cannot deal with a visitor to their home. Teachers should respect the wishes of such families and perhaps arrange for meetings to take place in the centre.

Reluctant Centres

In some situations, teachers may see the real benefits of home visits but receive little or no support from their supervisor. When, for some reason, a home visit is not feasible, the teacher can invite families to

---

INSIDE LOOK

I was having great difficulty with the mother of one of the children who had just transitioned to our preschool room. She was openly hostile to me and it was evident that she had little confidence in my ability to deal with her son. She would criticize me in front of him and she just seemed angry all the time. The more I tried to discuss issues, the more antagonistic she became. Things came to a head when her son began to act out in class and say things like "My mum says that I don't have to listen to you!"

Just when I was at my wit's end, the supervisor suggested that I set up a home visit. The idea was that the mother might feel more comfortable and less threatened in her own home. The mother reluctantly agreed. I was really worried about this visit, but in fact it had a positive effect on our relationship. The mother confided that she had built up such a strong relationship with the toddler teacher that she was having a great deal of difficulty separating from her. Over tea and cookies, we began the process of making a fresh start. I left feeling much relieved—and confident that we would be able to work things out.

In China, my home country, our teacher was much revered in our village. She was an honoured guest at our birthday gatherings and would often share a meal with us. We took great pride in her visits, which were often discussed long after they were over. We considered her a part of our extended family.

Source: Grace Liu, ECE student

the centre for a special lunch or even to her own home. For some families a neutral place in the community may make them feel more comfortable. Families who are unwilling to meet under any circumstances can be contacted by letter or telephone.

Reluctant Teachers

Some teachers are discouraged by the time and effort required to plan and carry out a home visit. Others are unsure of what to expect or how to conduct themselves outside the confines of the teaching environment. Some teachers feel that a home visit might be too intrusive, while others worry about offending families from other cultures because of their lack of understanding. However, there may be well-respected community members able to provide support and guidance on these issues.

In some rural communities great distances must be travelled to meet with families. In other situations, some teachers feel that they are putting themselves at risk by visiting families with histories of drug or alcohol abuse. "High-crime neighbourhoods or . . . isolated rural areas can be dangerous. Visitors in problem areas often carry cellular phones in case of emergencies" (Rockwell, Andre, and Hawley, 1996: 185). In such cases, teachers may decide to visit in pairs or the teacher and supervisor may visit together or arrange to meet in the centre.

EXHIBIT 4.3 THE HOME VISIT: TEACHER SELF-REVIEW

DID I:

- contact families well in advance?
- let families know ahead of time the purpose of the visit?
- arrange the meeting at the parents' convenience?
- call or send home a note confirming the date and time of the visit?
- arrive on time?
- bring something special to share with the child?
- interact with all family members?
- allow the child to lead the play, show me his or her room, favourite toys, pets, and so on?
- concentrate on paying attention to the family rather than scrutinizing their home?
- listen more than I talked?
- remember my role as a "support person" as opposed to an "expert"?
- act in a respectful and mannerly fashion?
- find out more about the family's philosophy of child-rearing?
- encourage family participation in the centre?
- help ease any anxieties that the child or family members may have had?
- send a thank-you note?

DO I:

- feel that the home visit made a positive difference in my partnership with this family? If not, why?
- feel the child and I have become closer as a result of the visit?
- feel more informed and more able to support this family?

As a teen parent, I could tell that the teachers in the infant room felt that I was less than capable in my parenting role. This was never openly discussed but I could tell by the looks they exchanged with each other and their voice tone when they spoke to me. They played the role of "expert," as if I didn't really understand the importance of nutrition, responsive caregiving, and so on. So I decided to invite the teachers to my apartment for a home visit. We spent a long time talking. I shared my dreams for my daughter and talked about my role as a mother. There was a marked change in their attitude toward me. It was more respectful and they were more willing to work with me instead of against me. Several years later when we were leaving the centre, one of the teachers in the infant room confided to me that I had helped her become a better teacher. She explained that the home visit had not only changed her attitude about me as a teen parent but more importantly made her examine her own bias about teen parents.

Source: Jennifer Wells, ECE student

A Different Type of Home Visit—A Block Walk

Try a block walk while the weather is warm and sunny. Map the location of all your student's homes and divide the area into blocks. Schedule a series of block walks, and escort the children living in each block area to their homes on a selected day. Let families know that you will be coming. On the appointed day, walk or ride the bus to the chosen block. Meet the parents outside and chat with them about school. You may also accumulate some curriculum materials such as leaves, sidewalk rubbings, or bits of neighborhood history to be used later by the children in the classroom. This initial contact with parents will be positive and possibly make a second meeting even more productive.

Source: Hepworth Berger, 2008: 151.

GETTING STARTED

For centres who would like to begin this process, they might begin with all new incoming families and for the other families, the supervisor might send home a letter to families, explaining the purpose of the home visit and asking them to respond back if they are interested in participating.

THE SEPARATION PROCESS

Leaving a child at the centre for the first time is a difficult transition for families. Much of the literature on separation focuses on the child, very little of it considers the parents. It is critical for teachers to recognize that powerful emotions are at work. How well parents separate affects how well their children adjust to the centre and has an enormous impact on the teacher–family relationship. Some families may be so distressed by, and so filled with guilt at, their child's anguished response to separation that they find it difficult to leave the centre each day. Other parents may be so desperate for the new arrangement to succeed that they unconsciously place untenable pressures on the child or the teachers. Helplessness, denial, guilt, sadness, anger, relief, jealousy, resentment—all are emotions that may be felt by parents at one time or another. No matter what the parent's response, it is critical for teachers who work with families to understand the seriousness and complexity of this transition. Discussing these responses ahead of time with families may help them acknowledge their own feelings in an atmosphere that is empathetic and understanding of the process of separation.

Preparing written information—magazine or journal articles on the subject of separation, for example—ahead of time for families to read may

This skillful teacher eases the transition for this parent and child by focusing on the child's interest in dinosaurs.

be useful. Teachers might ask families who are well established in the centre to describe their first few months in a centre and provide some guidance and support. In some family situations, siblings may now be separated for the first time, and that should also be taken into account.

INSIDE LOOK

Jason was a wonderful participant in the three-year-old nursery. He painted with flourishing strokes at the easel and built bridges and roads in the block corner. His only difficulty seemed to be separating from his mother each morning. He happily appeared each morning at the door with mother in tow. The teacher encouraged him to hang up his coat and to say good-bye, which he did. The mother stood at the door with some last-minute reminders: "Mommy will be back in three hours, Jason!" "Don't be upset when Mommy leaves, Jason." "Mommy loves you, Jason." With each comment, Jason became a little less certain of his willingness to move into the room. The teachers who watched this display were somewhat annoyed at this over-protective mother. After a few weeks, a parent conference was scheduled. The teacher shared that she wanted to help Jason separate more easily each morning and so asked his mother for her perspective. During the conversation, Jason's mother shared that Jason was her only child and that she and her husband had waited years to adopt a baby. Their first attempt at adoption had resulted with the child being given back to the birthmother, who had changed her mind about the adoption. It was a heart-breaking story, but the teacher understood a great deal more about the separation dilemma. During the next few weeks, the mother and the teacher worked together to transition Jason into school and to alleviate the mother's fears.

Source: Springate and Stegelin, 1999: 197.

Family members are not the only people a child becomes attached to. Although a child is likely to become strongly attached to one or two particular persons and prefer them to all others, the child may also form deep attachments to other people, such as daycare providers, in secondary or subsidiary relationships (Bowlby, cited in Barker, 1993: 4).

It is natural for babies to feel anxious when their mother or father leaves them. This anxiety usually first appears at six months, when infants gain an awareness of their parents, and themselves, as separate beings. Afraid of being abandoned, they become wary and anxious around strangers. Separation anxiety can continue to occur in children of all ages and may be aggravated by divorce, illness, hospitalization, or a parent's sudden return to work.

The length of time it takes a child to adjust to centre life varies. Most children take two to three weeks to settle in, but the range is great. Gregarious children may take off without a backward look, leaving their families feeling a bit downcast. Some children seem fine for a week or so—or even six months—and *then* fuss, as though testing to see whether you are serious about this new routine. A few can take as long as three months to settle in. Children who find it hard to adapt to new things may have the occasional tearful episode when they abruptly remember where they are—or, rather, where they are not.

The manner in which infants are nurtured varies within each subculture as well as across cultures. The well-being of the child is affected by the quality of care as well as the resiliency of the child. One child may thrive while another deteriorates, in environments that seem identical. The child, the caregiver, and the environment intertwine in the child-rearing process, making every child's experience unique. The essential bond between child and caregiver emphasizes the significance of the parents' role (Bowlby, cited in Barker, 1993: 1).

According to one observer:

The more familiar and sensitive the caregiver, the more familiar the environment, and, ultimately, the fewer changes in caregivers, the less intense the distress. Although the separation and attachment process is a natural part of the human cycle, the anxiety that accompanies separation will not disappear overnight. The effects of separation issues are long lasting; children learn to better cope with them as they become increasingly autonomous. (Bowlby, cited in Barker, 1993: 5)

ROLE OF THE TEACHER IN THE SEPARATION PROCESS

Teachers may have strong feelings associated with separations, and these events can remind them of painful or difficult experiences in their own lives. Teachers need to be aware that this may affect their ability to respond appropriately to families and children. To instill a sense of empathy in the child, Weissbourd (1992) suggests that teachers draw on memories of their own experiences with separation, "whether it was losing a best friend when he or she moved, losing a pet, or even tougher situations such as being a child of divorce or losing a parent" (68).

Teachers need to be patient with the separation process. They need to realize that families respond to separation in different ways, and that having a tearful child is generally not a reflection on their skill as a teacher. The teacher needs to be in tune with each child's abilities and rhythms and respond in those terms. This means the teacher sets aside her rhythms to accommodate the child—challenging work when a child is distressed and there are several needs to meet.

Bell and Ainsworth (1972) identify promptness as the single most important factor in stopping crying: the notion that responding immediately to crying spoils the child is clearly dead. Bell and Ainsworth's research demonstrates that among infants 6–12 months old, those whose mothers respond immediately cry less. Conversely, ignoring a baby's cries may increase crying. Teachers should comfort a distressed child in a manner that is consistent with the child's preferences. For example, though some children like to be held, others prefer to be engaged by a stimulating toy or object.

INSIDE   LOOK

It was like having my heart ripped out. I know that sounds melodramatic, but hearing Samantha screaming for me as I left the centre on that first morning was absolutely overwhelming. I was in tears, and if the teacher hadn't phoned to say that Samantha was happily playing with her new friends, I'm not sure I would have made it through the day.

This supervisor calls to reassure a worried parent.

More recently, Gunnar has shown that "by the end of the first year, children who have received consistent, warm, and responsive care produce less of the stress hormone cortisol, and when they do become upset, they turn off their stress reaction more quickly. This suggests that they are better equipped to respond to life's challenges" (Gunnar, n.d.).

Having one teacher who consistently cares for the new infant has a positive effect on the child's ability to separate successfully. It is also important to consider that the relationship between other parents and other children is a factor in separating. If an older child looks forward to seeing a playmate in the room in the morning, this enhances the morning routine. Families with similar experiences have opportunities to discuss the issues that are of concern to both parties.

While continuity is desirable, its complexities make it far from easy to achieve. Children in groups may be

> happy, resilient, and alert or depressed and lethargic; tall or short; self-actualized or dependent on direction; secure and outgoing, or reticent and shy. Children encounter a wide variety of teachers—creative or structured; open or closed; authoritarian, laissez-faire, or authoritative; self-actualized or discouraged—and each of these may

vary day by day. Families are just as varied—disorganized or stable, extended or nuclear, enriching or restrictive, verbal or nonverbal, nurturing or punishing—with many of the characteristics changing with conditions. (Hepworth Berger, 1991: 4)

Teachers can help families cope by developing a checklist of reactions and behaviours that they might expect and ways to support the child. For example, the parents and the child might discuss what the day will be like for both of them, or they might participate in such rituals such as packing a lunch. Teachers can suggest to families that they engage in an activity with their child at the centre before saying goodbye. For example, a parent might say, "I will read one book and we'll paint one picture together and then I must go." If the child is crying, parents should acknowledge that he or she is upset but remain calm themselves, reassuring the child that they will return as they give their parting kisses and hugs and letting the child know that they will miss them too. Leaving the child with a positive thought about the end of the day is always helpful ("When I pick you up we will go to Grandma's house for supper").

Gestwicki (2004: 261) provides a handout for parents that suggests things they can do in the

As you and your child get used to life in our classroom, feel free to stay if you can. Some things you could do:

- Help your child develop a morning routine of putting things in the cubby.
- Find the child's name tag and move it to our "We're Here" board.
- Wash hands in the bathroom.
- Look around at each interest centre to notice new materials.
- Go say good morning to our fish Henry.
- Choose a book and read to your child and any other child who wants to join you.
- Say goodbye and leave without lingering when you are ready—teachers will help you say goodbye.
- Feel free to call or stop back and see us later in the day.

classroom during the first few days of school: Teachers and families can facilitate the separation process in the following ways:

- Be set up and ready to receive the children and their parents.
- Greet children warmly as they arrive (commenting on a new haircut or a big smile will go a long way to easing a child's anxieties). Observe the child's emotional and physical state.
- Plan activities that will instantly captivate children as they enter the room.
- Create lotto games or memory games using photos of the children and their families.
- Involve the children in each other's play.
- Give older children a job when they arrive (let them check themselves in on a giant attendance sheet, for example, or help with the setup).
- Have a fishbowl filled with folded slips of paper, each with the name of one of the various centres in the room. Invite the children to pick one slip and start their day off there.

Courtesy of Scotia Plaza Child Care Centre

When families can spend a few minutes helping their child settle into the program it can be time well spent for everyone.

- Invite family members to stay for tea or coffee, if they have the time.
- Have the child's mother leave a "lipstick kiss" on the child's hand.
- Spray the mother's perfume on a sleep blanket.
- Take a picture of the child at the centre and give it to family members to keep in their workplace.
- Take a picture of the child at the centre and give it to the child to share with other family members.
- If they are interested and would like more photos, have families leave a disposable camera with the teachers.
- Keep a collection of comfort toys in the room so that the children can help themselves.
- Play calming music. (In one centre the parent taped herself singing her child's favourite sleep song and it was played during naptime.)
- Have a photo of the family scanned onto a pillowcase or blanket for nap time.
- Leave welcoming messages or family photos in the children's cubbies.
- Give families a small photo album and ask them to fill it with family photos and return it to the centre. These can be stored in the book centre or in the child's cubby.
- Give parents a disposable camera to take to their work. Have a co-worker take photos and create a bulletin board or placemat for the child, or put the photo under the Plexiglas at the lunch table.
- Videotape positive "happenings" for families to view.
- Ensure that there are sheltered spaces where children can retreat.
- Make use of the indoor and outdoor environments to engage children in dramatic play.
- Encourage children to create drawings for their parents, expressing, if appropriate, their feelings about the separation.
- Phone families who were especially anxious about the separation to reassure them that their child is all right.
- Invite the parent to extend an invitation to a grandparent or older sibling for the child to take on a tour of the room. If people they trust are in this space, then it must be a good place!
- Avoid high energy activities at the end of the day, and help the children wind down in anticipation of the arrival of their parents.
- Set up a craft activity at the end of the day to engage both parents and children, in order to

Many children are reassured by a familiar photo.

help them reunite with each other in a positive way, and to make the transition from centre to home go more smoothly.
- Create a cross-over activity in which children and families complete a simple project at home to be brought to the centre.

THE FIRST DAY AT THE CENTRE: STRATEGIES FOR A SUCCESSFUL TRANSITION

A child's first day at the centre is a major event for all family members. It is important for families to understand that they set the tone for what will happen. A positive, cheerful approach with the child is critical to a successful transition. Children are quick to notice any tension in the parent's touch, voice, and mannerisms. The age of the child is another factor; a school-aged child who has been in care for most of his or her life will probably make an easier transition than an 18-month-old toddler who is coming into care for the first time.

To make the transition as smooth as possible for the child, teachers should encourage families to:

- ensure that the child gets a good night's sleep before the big day
- have positive conversations with the child about their previous visit to the centre
- invite the child to participate in labelling with his or her name the items that will be coming to daycare (blanket, pillow, stuffed toy, and so forth)
- have the child select the family photo that will go into his or her cubby

- make use of the centre-supplied "What to Bring on First Day" list
- write down key words in the child's language if it is a language other than that spoken by the teachers
- complete all the necessary paperwork (medical documentation, for example) and bring it to the centre
- arrive after the morning rush, when things are not quite so hectic at the centre

For their own part, teachers should:

- ensure that interpreters are available for families who need them
- be on hand to greet the family as they arrive and have bright and colourful name tags ready for them
- ensure that the child's cubby and any other storage areas are labelled and cleaned in advance
- introduce families to staff members and other parents who might be in the centre at the time of arrival
- create a bulletin board message with photo and a description of the family as a welcoming gesture
- have a parent, as part of a welcoming committee, meet with them in the playroom for a brief period to reassure the new family and discuss some of the strategies that helped them over the first few weeks

- look for common interests or needs between parents—those who use the same bus line, live in the same area, or have jobs, hobbies, or languages in common
- ensure that all staff members (cooks, caretakers, security people, and so on) understand their important role in supporting and welcoming new families
- give parents specific instructions about how they might be involved during the orientation period, since many family members are unsure of what to do in the room
- refer to planning sheets to give family members an idea about emergent curriculum
- fill out any necessary paperwork, and assist the parents in understanding their role in completing them
- show family members where the centre keeps its medication sheets, permission forms, and other paperwork
- show the families the message area so they know where to pick up communiqués
- confirm with parents how staff should contact them if an emergency occurs
- share positive stories about the child when parents return at the end of the day
- be available to meet with parents to discuss how the transition is proceeding

Children in a new environment are reassured by a familiar face.

Courtesy of Scotia Plaza Child Care Centre

Ideally, the transition should be a gradual one, occurring over the course of a week. However, teachers need to be flexible in supporting parents who may not be able to take long periods of time off work. Creative planning might involve having the mother available on the first day, the father on the second, and a grandparent the next. Older children might be paired with a preschool or school-aged child who is familiar with the centre and can help the newcomer through the routines for the first week or so. Parents might also appreciate a written overview of their child's adjustment to daycare. Teachers can record their observations of the child's progress in a journal for the first month or so and then share it with parents.

EXHIBIT 4.4 SAMPLE ORIENTATION WEEK FOR YOUNGER CHILDREN IN CARE SITUATIONS

MONDAY

- Parent and child arrive after 9 a.m., when much of the hustle and bustle of early arrivals is winding down.
- Parent and child are greeted by supervisor and directed to the playroom.
- Teacher greets child and invites parent and child into the room.
- Parent and child are introduced to parents, children, and teachers.
- Teacher shows child the cubby in which his or her special items will be stored.
- Parent and child stay for the morning program and the child is gently encouraged to participate.
- Parent discusses with staff the child's likes and dislikes, medications, schedules, sleep-time rituals, feelings about separation, and so forth.
- Parent is given a detailed tour of the room.
- Parent and teacher ensure that paperwork (for example, completing charts, permission to give medications) is in order.
- Teachers should encourage parents to participate as much as they feel comfortable.
- Supervisor is available throughout the day to answer parent's questions or to cover for teacher while she spends time with parent.

TUESDAY

- Parent and child arrive at regular drop-off time.
- Child and parent are invited to participate.
- As child's comfort level increases, parent assumes a more passive role, observing and encouraging child to interact with other children and teachers.
- Toward the end of the morning, parent leaves the room for a cup of coffee or a chat with the supervisor.
- After lunch, parent and child observe beginning of nap-time procedure and leave shortly thereafter.

WEDNESDAY

- Parent continues to support the child through the program but spends increasingly longer periods away.
- Parent and child stay through the lunch program and naptime.
- Parent and child leave about 3 p.m., following a short play at wake-up.

THURSDAY

- Parent and child stay for a full day.
- Throughout the day, the parent's time away from child is lengthened.

FRIDAY

- Similar to the Thursday schedule but with longer periods of separation between parent and child.

Leaving my grandson when I drop him off at daycare is hard for me. I know my daughter depends on me to do this task. At first, I was disappointed with my daughter and son-in-law for not staying home and looking after my grandson as my wife had done. I know financially my daughter has to work in order for her to support her family but at the same time it is hard to let old ideas go. The staff at the centre encouraged me to stay longer and longer and now I feel they really appreciate the time I spend with the children and my grandson certainly enjoys my "position" in the child-care centre. Surprisingly, I am enjoying my time at the centre, and my latest project is showing the school-age children how to build a bird house. I was a cabinet maker before I retired, and I'm having fun sharing my skills with the children. My wife kids me about the amount of time I'm spending at the centre.

END OF THE DAY

Greenman (1988) suggests awarding the family a congratulatory certificate from the teachers and the supervisor at the end of the first day that the family and child spend apart. The certificate reinforces the partnership while acknowledging that the first day is always the hardest. Children may also respond at the end of the day in ways parents don't always anticipate. The child who does not rush into his or her parents' arms may upset the parent; however, the child may be so engrossed in the activity he or she is doing that they don't want to leave. In other situations, the child may be resisting another transition, or the child may be so secure in his or her attachment that he or she sees no need to jump up and go home. Some children may act out to test the limits.

After the family has been in the centre a few months, it might be helpful and informative for the staff to carry out another home visit, organize a conference at a convenient time for all parties, or arrange for the parents and supervisor to meet to review the orientation process. Parents who are unable to meet centre staff in person might be provided with a written questionnaire or agree to take part in a telephone discussion or respond by email.

THE ORIENTATION PROCESS: FAMILY QUESTIONNAIRE

- How well did the orientation support your and your child's entry into the centre?

- What were your first impressions of the centre?

- Was there anything about your initial contact with the centre that you think we might have handled better?

- Do you have any questions that were not addressed during the orientation process?

- What aspects of the orientation process could the centre improve on?

- How helpful was the written information you were provided with in advance of the first day?

- Did the video help solidify the information you received on your first visit?

- Did you feel the staff members were warm and welcoming?

TRANSITIONS TO NEW PLAYROOMS: SUPPORTING FAMILIES

A new transition will be required as the child moves to the next age group. As teachers, we tend to focus on the needs of the child during this time, forgetting how difficult the new transition can be for parents, especially those who have built strong relationships with the infant staff and have come to rely on them for support and advice. Such parents may be anxious and reluctant to begin a relationship with the toddler staff. Teachers can remind parents that it took time to build their relationship and this will no doubt happen again in the toddler room. Infant teachers need to encourage parents to build a partnership with the toddler staff while at the same time letting parents know they can stay in touch with them, and that they, too, will assist in the child's transition. Remember that all of the teachers are responsible for all of the children in the centre; it is not the case that infant teachers interact only with infants. Some families may be reassured to learn of this inclusive approach.

Continuity of care is a critical factor in the life of a young child. Some centres use a system that allows the same caregiver to remain with the child throughout the infant and toddler years. The teacher moves up with the child until the transition to the preschool room, when the teacher returns to the infant room. A multiage grouping, as outlined in Chapter 2, is another model that supports continuity of care.

Families and teachers should discuss the possibility of the upcoming transition well in advance, so that both parties can begin to think through the implications of such a move. If several children are to be transitioned at the same time, a meeting might be arranged with families to discuss the procedure, to outline the room's approach, to tour the various centres in the room, and to review such topics as developmental norms for this age group and changes in routines. A video depicting daily life in the room can be an excellent educational resource for parents. Along with this meeting, a room handbook prepared by staff and based on the information that is specific for this age group is very reassuring to parents and is a useful tool that they can refer to again and again. A home visit at this time may also support this transition. Above all, teachers should be available to discuss any concerns that family members have.

INSIDE LOOK

At the Janeway Centre when we have a group of infants moving up to the Toddler Room, we host an orientation meeting. We begin the session with a presentation of what a day might be like in the toddler room. Parents can then see the emphasis we place on a play-based environment and the encouragement we give to a hands-on, sensory approach. We then discuss the similarities and differences between the infant room and the toddler room. We always include information about toddler behaviour—and how we deal with biting, since this is one issue that almost always comes up. We leave lots of time for parents to ask questions. We are also very interested in feedback from parents. It is only through ongoing communication that our program can change to better reflect the needs and interests of the children and the parents. We find that having the parents meet together is reassuring for them. We also encourage parents to visit and to feel free to contribute when and where they are able. Theresa always attends these meetings and is available to answer questions.

EXHIBIT 4.5 TRANSITIONING CHILDREN TO NEW PLAYROOMS

Nadia Hall, Margaret McLellan, and Linda Silver developed the following model for transitioning infants to the toddler room.

SUGGESTED STRATEGIES AND IMPLICATIONS

1. PLANNING THE TRANSITION

Understanding the child is the primary goal of this stage. It is vital that both those who are letting go and those who are taking on the care of this child have a sensitive understanding of who the child is and how she behaves. In order for the child to make a secure transition, she must trust that her signals will be read accurately and responded to empathetically. She must feel known, and therefore safe.

When the decision to move the child has been agreed upon by supervisor, staff, and parents, the following procedure can be put into place:

- **Visits to the infant room.** The assigned prospective caregiver visits daily for half an hour with the baby in the infant room. In this way the baby can be observed in her natural context of relating. The infant caregiver in the secure environment can support the infant in this period of acquaintanceship with the new caregiver. This process optimally occurs over a two-week period prior to the transition.

- **Transition conference.** A transition conference brings together a variety of individuals who have or require intimate knowledge of the child—the infant caregiver, toddler caregiver, and parents. Such a meeting offers the opportunity to share information in an organized manner. The meeting occurs after several visits, so that all participants come with some level of understanding of the child. This information will be incorporated into an individualized plan of transition. This also provides a formal opportunity for the infant caregiver to begin to separate from the child and for parents to begin to separate from the infant caregiver.

2. IMPLEMENTING THE TRANSITION

Supporting the child's entry into, and growing comfort level with, the new physical and social environment is the primary goal of this stage. Through a patient and thoughtful process, the child's disruption and sense of loss are minimized. This process ultimately promotes the establishment of new supportive relationships.

- **Two-week adjustment process.** During the minimum two-week transition process, the infant caregiver accompanies the child to the toddler room in order to provide a secure base from which the child can explore and familiarize herself with the physical environment, the people, and the new routines. In week one, time spent in the new room is gradually increased for both the child and caregivers. In week two, the infant caregiver gradually decreases her time in order to allow a relationship to develop between the new caregiver and the child. This should enable the closure of one period and the passage into another. This process must, of course, take into account the child's individual needs and may look different for different children.
- **Transitional objects.** Such objects as blankets, pacifiers, and cuddle toys provide comfort and familiarity, and may be particularly supportive to the child during this period of transition. These objects should be identified during the conference and should be available to the child whenever wanted. Many children have special objects that are important to them and sharing them with their teachers and peers is exciting. It is also an opportunity for everyone to learn about a new object, how to share and take care of them.
- **A transitional book.** This book is a collection of photographs of familiar people and objects (mommy, daddy, room at home, favourite toy, previous caregiver, previous peers, and so on). This book enables the child to refer to familiar and comforting images that reassure and support the child. The book could be kept in the child's own cubby and be available to the child whenever she wants it.

3. INFANT SUPPORT WORKER

Transition times make additional emotional demands both on staff who are losing children with whom they have formed strong bonds and on those who must establish new connections. The realities of group care may not always provide the support required to assist staff and children through this process. To optimize and support all relationships affected by the transition, an infant support worker could facilitate the process. This role is filled, ideally, by someone from the staff (the supervisor, for example) who has an in-depth understanding of attachment, separation, and loss and can therefore support and guide those involved.

In conclusion, this extremely sensitive period in a child's life must be managed with empathetic understanding of the child's experience. Child care can support children and families. Optimally, however, all those involved must work in partnership to bridge and ensure safe passage from infancy to toddlerhood. This careful attention to the child's transition experience builds on the foundation of positive early relationships and can enhance future relationships.

Source: N. Hall, M. McLellan, and L. Silver, "Moving from Infancy to Toddlerhood in Child Care," *Ideas: The Journal of Emotional Well-Being in Child Care* 1, no. 1 (May 1993). Reprinted by permission.

TRANSITIONS FROM CHILD CARE TO SCHOOL ENVIRONMENTS

The Harvard Research Project comments on the transition from child care to school environments. Because of the importance of linkages across settings over time, policymakers, practitioners, and researchers recently have begun to focus their attention on the period of transition from preschool to formal schooling. Although research in this area has not focused on which transitions practices relate to specific child outcomes, there is growing consensus that both early childhood settings and elementary schools have a responsibility to support families and help them to sustain their family involvement trajectories. Unfortunately as children transition to public school, teacher and family contact decreases and there is a shift away from parent-initiated communication. Logistical barriers (e.g., no summer salary for teachers, little teacher training in this area, etc.) hinder ideal transition practices (Pianta, Taylor, and Cox, 2001). However, schools that provide more opportunities for family involvement and occasions for nontraditional contact—such as home visits, parent discussion groups, parent resource rooms, and home lending libraries—enjoy increased levels of family participation (Ramey et al., 2000). The best transition practices will increase the family's sense of connectedness to the elementary school, ensure a collaborative relationship and together become more focused on providing the best resources to create better child outcomes.

Barnard (2001) states that compared to non-preschool parents, parents of children who participated in preschool activities had higher occupational aspirations for their children, more satisfaction with their children's school performance, and greater parent involvement in elementary years at home and in school. Teachers in early childhood environments can encourage networking amongst families whose children will be attending the same school and if some of the parents have already transitioned with an older child, they may be a valuable resource. The early childhood teacher can also walk the children to the new school as part of a community walk, post pictures of the new school in the playroom, and read children's books that support this transition. We also need to recognize that for many parents this transition may bring some sadness as the child enters a new phase of childhood. Teachers will also experience a sense of loss as the child and family move on to a new environment.

INSIDE LOOK

Invest In Kids

Comfort, Play and Teach: A Positive Approach to Parenting

Whether it's your child's first time away from you or he's making the transition from child care to school, here are some things you can do to help make the move easier.

1. Talk about the new routine.
2. Talk about what won't change.
3. Visit the school in advance.
4. Find out the name of your child's teacher.
5. Ease your child into class.
6. Reassure your child that you will be back.
7. Be enthusiastic about school.
8. Help your child find friends from school.
9. Share your own stories.
10. Get ready together.

Source: www.investinkids.ca

LATCHKEY KIDS

There are times when children have to leave child care; parents may no longer be able to afford the fees or no programs may be available for the child's age group. While many children successfully make the transition from group care to self-care, others report being bored or lonely, concerned about their personal safety, deprived of opportunities to socialize, or burdened with excessive family responsibilities such as caring for younger siblings. Latchkey children are a growing phenomenon. Jo-Anne Kilpatrick, Executive Director of Sundowners Day Care and Resource Centre in Windsor, Ontario, operates a "Warm Line" designed for children 10–12 years of age who are left at home. As her poignant account of a seven-year-old boy illustrates, children well below the age of 10 are being left at home to care for themselves:

> This little seven-year-old boy…spent all his after school hours alone in his home under his bed, locked in until as late as 6 p.m. each school day evening. The house had to be kept darkened with no light, TV, or radio playing so "people wouldn't know he was home alone." He wasn't allowed to answer the door or use the phone until after his mom got home—well after dark each school winter night. The little guy found out about the Warm Line from a discarded flyer an older child had left on his school playground. Hidden in his lunch bag from his mom, he brought it home and kept our number under his bed. He used it to call when the empty house got too scary or when other older kids from the neighbourhood, knowing he was home alone, taunted him by ringing the door-bell and banging on the door. I'll never forget our last conversation. It was a particularly horrible night for him and he was calling, crying, from the closet of his room. Mom still wasn't home and the "Warm Line" was shutting down for the evening. Out of desperation, I started asking personal questions of him, trying to identify where he lived in case intervention became necessary. This line of questioning is only used when a child is thought to be at risk. In our experience, most children normally have to be discouraged from sharing this type of information to our phone-line staff, because of the inherent trust they have in adults. The child hung up and never called again. I lost him because he had been trained well in how to survive as a latchkey kid . . . "Don't let anyone know you are alone…keep our family secret and you will be safe." The child's parent, for a lot of good reasons, insulated her son from the dangers of the outside world, but also isolated him from getting help to save himself. I can only guess what scars the chronic isolation, loneliness, and fear have left him with. The lessons we can learn from this one child's nightmare aren't so much about age, as they are about responsibility. We have children who are home alone legally at age 10 who are every bit as isolated and terrified as this young child. The reasons they are home alone, regardless of age, are varied and complex involving societal attitudes, and policies from three levels of government. I know changes are coming in child care…but I also know, at least for one little seven-year-old boy, by the time these changes come to Windsor it is going to be much too late. (Kilpatrick, 1993: 13)

In light of this reality, teachers and families can prepare school-age children to take care of themselves by alerting them to potential dangers in their own neighbourhoods and communities. For example, children need to know when play areas are off-limits due to spring run-off. Children should also be provided with a set of house rules relating to cooking and emergency procedures. Teachers can provide emergency training and first-aid courses and teach children how to use the telephone.

BOOKS FOR CHILDREN

On My Very First School Day I Met…, by N. Stiles

I Am Too Absolutely Small For School, by L. Child

First Day Jitters, by J. Danneberg

When You Go To Kindergarten, by J. Howe

Welcome To Kindergarten, by A. Rockwell

Do I Have To Go To School, by P. Thomas and L. Haker

Starting School, by K. Petty, L. Kopper, and J. Pipe

Franklin Goes To School, by P. Bourgeois

BOOKS FOR ADULTS

Everyday Goodbyes: Starting School and Early Care: A Guide To The Separation Process, by N. Balaban

Children Starting School: A Guide to Successful Transitions and Transfers for Teachers and Assistants, by H. Fabian

REFERENCES

Barker, K. 1993. "Infancy: New Perspective for Caregiving." *Ideas: The Journal of Emotional Well-Being in Child Care* 1 (1). May.

Barnard, W.M. 2001. *Early Intervention, Parent Involvement in Early Schooling and Long-Term School Success.* Unpublished doctoral dissertation, University of Wisconsin, Madison.

Bell, S.M., and M.D. Ainsworth. 1972. "Infant Crying and Maternal Responsiveness." *Child Development* 43.

Brooks, M. 1994. "Home Visits." *Early Childhood Education* 27 (1). Spring–Summer.

Cullum, A. 1971. *The Geranium on the Window Sill Just Died but Teacher You Went Right On.* Holland: Harlin Quist.

Gestwicki, C. 2004. *Home, School, and Community Relations. A Guide to Working with Families*, 5th ed. New York: Thomson Delmar Learning.

Gorter-Reu, M.S., and J.M. Anderson. 1998. "Home Kits, Home Visits, and More!" *Young Children* 53: 71–74.

Greenman, J. 1988. *Caring Spaces, Learning Places: Children's Environments that Work.* Redmond, WA: Child Care Information Exchange.

Gunnar, M. N.d. *Caregiving and the Stress Response. The First Years Last Forever: I Am Your Child. The New Brain Research and Your Child's Health Development.* Toronto: Canadian Institute of Child Health.

Haigh, K. 2004. "Creating, Encouraging, and Supporting Relationships at Chicago Commons Child Development Program." In Joanne Hendrick, ed., *Next Steps Toward Teaching the Reggio Way: Accepting the Challenge to Change.* Columbus, OH: Pearson Merrill Prentice Hall.

Hall, N., M. McLellan, and L. Silver. 1993. "Moving from Infancy to Toddlerhood in Child Care." *Ideas: The Journal of Emotional Well-Being in Child Care* 1 (1). May.

Hepworth Berger, E. 1991. *Parents as Partners in Education: The School and Home Working Together*, 3rd ed. Toronto: Collier Macmillan Canada.

———. 2008. *Parents as Partners in Education: Families and Schools Working Together.* Columbus, OH: Pearson Merrill Prentice Hall.

Kaiser, B., and J.S. Rasminsky. 1994. "Encouraging Parent Participation." *Interaction.* Canadian Child Care Federation. Summer.

Kilpatrick, J. 1993. "Latchkey Children A National Shame." *Exploring Environment.*

Rockwell, R.E., L.C. Andre, and M.K. Hawley. 1996. *Parents and Teachers as Partners: Issues and Challenges.* Toronto: Harcourt Brace & Company.

Springate, K.W., and D.A. Stegelin. 1999. *Building School and Community Partnerships through Parent Involvement.* Columbus, OH: Pearson Merrill Prentice Hall.

Weissbourd, B. 1992. "Building Parent Partnerships." *Scholastic Pre-K Today.* August–September.

Courtesy of Lynn Wilson

CHAPTER 5

Ways to Involve Families

"It's not only children who grow. Parents do too. As much as we watch to see what our children do with their lives, they are watching us to see what we do with ours. I can't tell my children to reach for the sun. All I can do is reach for it, myself."

—*Joyce Maynard*

"One looks back with appreciation to the brilliant teachers, but with gratitude to those who touched our human feelings. The curriculum is so much necessary raw material, but warmth is the vital element for the growing plant and for the soul of the child."

—*Carl Jung*

LEARNING OUTCOMES

After studying this chapter, you will be able to

1. identify and evaluate various strategies for involving families in centre activities with an emphasis on creating Male-Friendly environment

2. discuss strategies for developing effective formal and informal family gatherings

3. discuss strategies for recruiting, training, and evaluating volunteers

4. plan and evaluate a fundraising project

5. describe strategies for involving families in child-care celebrations

6. describe the roles and responsibilities of family members who serve on the board of directors

7. discuss ways to involve families in the evaluation of the staff and the centre program

STRATEGIES FOR INVOLVING FAMILIES

Family involvement begins when the family first visits the centre. By the time they actually enroll their child in the centre, family members should be aware of the opportunities for them to become meaningful participants in the program. Centres should create a welcoming atmosphere. They should also find innovative ways to maximize the input of busy parents while at the same time setting realistic goals with regard to what can be expected from both teachers and family members. These goals need to be re-evaluated on an ongoing basis to determine their relevance to the needs of the families and teachers.

MALE-FRIENDLY ENVIRONMENTS

The involvement of fathers or significant males in the raising of our families is an issue that affects all of us. All of us have once been the child of a father. This carries its own unique personal experiences and often has a life-long impact. Our society is the mirror of the quality of relationships between parents and their children. It takes a village to raise a child; it also takes a village to support fathers in bringing out the best in their children. Society has a collective responsibility to support and promote positive father involvement. The degree to which we contribute collectively to this goal is a reflection of our commitment to being truly a caring society.

Courtesy of Scotia Plaza Child Care Centre

This father and son enjoy time together at the child-care centre.

There are many benefits of greater father involvement for the child.

According to Levine, Murphy, and Wilson (1993: 9), "Children benefit from warm and nurturing relationships with men, and men are most likely to develop those sorts of relationships in environments which value, support, and encourage them. As a kind of shorthand, we call such settings 'Male-Friendly environments'." Fathers and other significant males in children's lives—whether grandfathers, uncles, or stepfathers—need to be included in the parent–centre partnership. But these significant males face many stereotypes. Some see fathers as either invisible or incompetent second-class parents. Many programs for families have traditionally served women and children and have excluded active involvement of men, at times because that was their choice and at other times because mothers did not want them to be involved.

Many think that mothers are best suited to be the primary and most influential parent. Until recently very little research has been available regarding the role of fathers in their parenting and the impact on their children. There is a communication challenge: while mothers may talk about mothering on a regular basis with each other, fathers are more likely to talk about other topics and so there is little opportunity for an exchange of information about their fathering role. Men will speak about their own relationships with their fathers which were often distant as their fathers were absorbed in work and interests outside the family or weren't present at all. Unlike what mothers learned from their own mothers, many men are on their own in figuring out the best way to parent. They are creating new ways of parenting!

The centre must make fathers feel welcome, give them opportunities to interact with their child,

Men need to feel that they are welcomed and encouraged to actively participate in the centre.

and allow them to participate in staff planning and programming. Evans (1999) states that changes in families and living situations happen rapidly and we cannot predict how these changes will affect families and the care they provide for young children. She states that it is crucial to identify the following within each context:

- the presence of fathers and other men in young children's lives
- men's expectations of themselves in relation to their children and the children's mothers
- mothers' expectations of men
- the community's expectations of men
- the ways men are responding to these expectations, both productively and destructively
- the supports for and impediments to men's involvement in the lives of their children

BARRIERS TO GREATER FATHER INVOLVEMENT

Negative myths, stereotypes, and lack of information too often characterize our attitudes as a society towards fathers.

- There are not enough positive, male parenting role models. Examples of negative stereotypes:
- By nature, women are more capable as nurturers of children than men
- Women support the family through their relationships, men support the family by being the traditional breadwinner
- Until recently, there have been few positive images of fathers in the media

In the past, the role model of today's fathers may have been:

- Preoccupied with work
- Mainly the disciplinarian
- Emotionally unavailable, for a variety of reasons

While traditional roles are changing, men in active parenting roles at times may feel criticized and:

- May be thought less of at work or by their peer group if overtly involved in "softer" areas of parenting
- May get negative or mixed feedback from their own parents
- Some women may feel threatened by fathers who want to take a more active role

Strong father involvement strengthens the relationship between the parents and increases the mother's success as a parent:

- Mothers feel more secure, more patient, and more flexible, more available and affectionate
- Single strongest predictor of a mother's ability to successfully breastfeed is support from her partner (City of Toronto, 2002)
- Initiatives to involve more men are more likely to succeed when men take the lead in the organization.

The physical environment of the child-care centre should reflect the fact that fathers are welcome; photographs from magazines or posters that show fathers in nurturing roles will send positive messages.

Mary Gallagher, a teacher in a family resource program in Ottawa, observes that "men [in family resource programs] rarely join the women chatting on the sidelines as their children explore the play area. Men come to me to ask for information or referrals rather than connecting with the network of other parents and caregivers. They're down there on the floor, involved with their kids the whole time. Or they bring in their newspaper and

Fathers must be included in the picture if the...[global goals for children] are to be most effectively met in sustainable ways. For almost every goal [e.g., immunization, health, children's rights, nutrition, education] the father's role makes a difference. . . . Men in families may influence child survival, growth and development through the decisions they make about resource allocations, through supporting women in decision-making, through economic contributions to the family which make the seeking of care more possible and through their caring for children.

Source: United Nations, 2001.

read." Three thousand miles away, at Burnaby Family Place, BC, Val Mayne sees the same thing: men come looking for a well-equipped place to play with their children or for a break; their needs for adult contact are filled elsewhere (Mann, 1999).

In Fagan and Palm's (2004) research, several fathers suggested that programs would be successful in getting fathers involved if they organized a trip to a sports event. Other father stated, "If it's sports oriented, we'll be there" (2004: 128). He stated this event would give men a chance to network. There are men who are looking to do positive things in the community and by bringing fathers together, the men could talk among themselves and devise some way to contribute more to the early childhood program.

Levine and Pitt (1997: 38) state that preschools usually say that they are welcoming to both mothers and fathers, but one school in Great Britain that prided itself on its nonsexist approach decided to demonstrate just how equally it treated all parents. Using videotapes, the director of the Pen Green Centre of Corby recorded the comings and goings of mothers and fathers on the playground, dropping

Healthy Images / Public Health Agency of Canada

These fathers enjoy an early-morning breakfast at the centre.

The Macaulay Child Development Centre and the United Way established *More Than A Haircut* as a one-day pilot project in 2006, in the aftermath of unprecedented youth violence in Toronto and amid growing angst over absentee fathers, particularly in the Caribbean community. According to Statistics Canada, 46 percent of black children lived in single-parent homes in 2001. The pilot drew so many men that the United Way agreed to fund regular sessions in 2007 and 2008.

Conversations about fathering are being held in local barbershops, a frequent "hangout" for Caribbean men. These conversations, led by African-Canadian men who are fathers themselves, are a chance to find out what others are thinking about being a father, about handling the responsibilities, and about enjoying their children right from the beginning. They talk about how they could better support their wives, girlfriends, fiancées, and former partners in raising their children, and they talk about guns, gangs, and fatherless kids being at higher risk of going astray. They talk about dad's involvement as a crucial ingredient to children's sense of security and self-esteem. "It was a refreshing surprise" recalls Robinson, 43-years-of-age with seven children. "I was sitting there listening to all this wisdom. I didn't have to go to a program in a centre. But they were structuring and formalizing a discussion that would impact the wider community." As workshop facilitator, Dalton Higgins says "black-male and black-father bashing seems to be in vogue. In the face of misconceptions and stereotypes, Afro-Canadian fathers need encouragement and camaraderie and a place to address the issues—including poverty, racism, and teen parenthood—that affect them and their children. We're not there to paint a pretty picture. We're there to have frank, blunt discussions."

Source: Gordon, 2008.

off and picking up their children, talking with staff. To their surprise, the tape revealed two totally different types of interaction. Staff greeted mothers more frequently, both verbally and with waving or handshaking. Staff initiated conversations more frequently with mothers and held longer conversations with mothers than fathers.

Fagan (1997) explored the types of activities that fathers and mothers engage in when they drop-off, pick-up, or visit the child-care centre. On the average, mothers talked with teachers almost every day that they visited the centre. By contrast, fathers talked with teachers slightly more than half the time that they visited the program. Mothers and fathers participated in many of the same activities in the centre. In the order of their occurrence, the most frequent activities were talking with the care-giver, playing with the child, holding the child, talking with other parents, observing the child, and talking with the child director. Aside from mothers talking significantly more often to caregivers, the only other activity in which mothers demonstrated greater participation than fathers was talking with the child-care director. There were no significant differences between mothers and fathers in the

frequency of their communications about the child's activities, health, mood, and peer relationships (Fagan and Palm, 2004: 95–96).

GETTING FATHERS INVOLVED WITH THEIR CHILDREN

The Canadian Association of Family Resource Programs, the umbrella organization for family resource programs, with funding from Health Canada developed a handbook to assist staff of these programs to help fathers become more involved in their children's development. Research conducted by McCrae Consulting Associates for the handbook included focus groups held across Canada with fathers and program staff from family resource centres. Some of the findings suggest the following:

- Few supports exist for men.
- Fathers seem to view their role as different from that of their own father.
- Men want to tell their stories.
- An effective way to start supporting fathers is to hold a focus group and ask fathers what they want in the way of support.

- Many program staff said, "We need to be where they [fathers] are, not where we [staff] want them to be."

- Men generally don't seek support unless they are in crisis. Society expects them to be self-reliant and independent.

- Wives, children, and loved ones tend to be the catalyst for men to seek support, so work through them.

- Centres should provide supports without using labels that stigmatize. For example, avoid "anger management," and "deadbeat dad." "Live-away" or "live-with" language is more appropriate than "non-custodial parent"—custodial language promotes the notion of children as property to be battled over.

The focus on having fathers actively involved in the centre is not meant to minimize the role of mothers or other family members but to develop effective strategies for all those who are actively involved in the child's life.

Father Involvement Initiative

The Father Involvement Initiative's roots go back to 1997 when Health Canada commissioned a literature review aimed at developing an action plan to promote Father Involvement in Ontario. It had

A child-care centre in a workplace environment allows family members to share meals.

EXHIBIT 5.1 HOW EFFECTIVELY ARE MEN INVOLVED IN YOUR PROGRAM?

The following checklist—which refers to men—is intended to include not only fathers but grandfathers, family friends, and other significant males who may aid teachers in their efforts to provide inclusive male environments. Assign a value of 1, 2, or 3 to each of the statements below, where

1. means we're doing a great job

2. means we're not doing badly

3. means this needs work

   1. The philosophy statement of the centre specifically targets the involvement of men in the life of our centre. _____

   2. We have male staff members in our centre. _____

   3. Staff have identified who the significant males are in the lives of the children in our centre. _____

   4. We do home visits and they are scheduled to include men. _____

   5. Staff actively encourage and expect male participation. _____

   6. When fathers are at the centre, we plan activities that are reflective of male socialization, such as physical activities, nature experiences, woodworking, etc. We make an effort to get them through the doorway, in both indoor and outdoor environments. _____

   7. We speak directly to men rather than through their female partners. _____

   8. When men volunteer we give them a variety of tasks, not just maintenance and repair. _____

9. Men participate on our board of directors and work on committees. _____

10. Men volunteer in our program, in the playroom, and on field trips, and take us to their place of business. _____

11. Specific activities are carried out that target men. We encourage the formation of groups and help to organize classes on parenting or other issues that are of interest and are relevant to the community. _____

12. We support play based events, such as Dads and Tots, and opportunities for gatherings at the centre that reflect the interests of fathers and their children. _____

13. With both parents' agreement, we communicate verbally and in a written format and encourage fathers to be involved in events at the centre when they are not living with their children. _____

14. We are flexible when we organize family–teacher conferences so that all members of the family can attend. _____

15. Men participating in our centre are encouraged to recruit other men as well as "mentor" new families. _____

16. We videotape children in our program including significant males interacting with the children. This video is distributed to new families so they know that fathers are welcome. _____

17. We know we are responding to male participants' needs and interests because we ask them. We survey men and let them know we value their opinions. _____

18. We understand that differences in male and female experiences are universal and we make every effort to understand how this will impact on our relationships with the men in our program. _____

19. Posters, magazine pictures, photos of fathers, and books in our program reflect men from a variety of racial and ethnic backgrounds in nurturing roles, involved in child care and working in non-traditional jobs. _____

INSIDE	LOOK

Too many early childhood workers, engaging fathers in services seems a daunting task, but the reality is that with strategic planning, commitment at all levels of the organization, and hard work to proactively engage fathers, services can do this very successfully. There are numerous examples of projects that have developed services that successfully engage with fathers and provide resources and support to them as parents.

Fathers Direct in the U.K. has a website specifically for practitioners that contains numerous case studies and principles for best practice in this area (**www.fathersdirect.com/fatherwork**). Successful Male-Friendly services tend to have a strong value base (i.e., they know why they are engaging fathers); understand the research on fatherhood and working with fathers; and have staff who are reflective, positive, reliable, and enabling and with whom fathers can identify. The environment communicates that fathers are welcome, and that the service is committed and proactive in its efforts to recruit fathers into the service. These services support positive relationships between fathers and children in all their services (including work with mothers), offer a range of support to fathers with differentiated needs, and support their staff in this work.

Source: Contributed by Tom Beardshaw, Project Management, former head of research at Care For The Family, U.K., editor of Dad Magazine. Pierce Bronson (James Bond), a father of five, is on the cover of the U.K.'s first magazine for fathers, DAD.

become clear at that time that fatherlessness presented a challenge in relation to healthy child development and resiliency. With this first report entitled *Father Involvement: A Supportive Condition to Healthy Child Development*, Health Canada developed a working partnership with the Peterborough Family Resource Centre in order to begin the process of implementing some of the recommendations that came from the report. From these modest beginnings has evolved a long-term vision and strong commitment which, over time, has led to some significant collective achievements involving over 25 communities and several provincial and national partnerships. Their website (**http://www.cfii.ca/fiion/**) offers students a list of a variety of organizations across the country that support fathers in their parenting role.

BOOKS FOR CHILDREN

My Dad, by A. Browne

David's Father, by R. Munsch

Dad Goes To School, by M. McNamara and M. Gordon

Just Me and My Dad, by M. Mayer

My Dad Is Awesome, by N. Butterworth

BOOKS FOR ADULTS

The Collected Wisdom of Fathers, by W. Glennon

Fathering Right from the Start: Straight Talk about Pregnancy, Birth and Beyond, by J. Heinowitz and W.F. Horn

Fathering Your Child from the Crib to the Classroom: A Dad's Guide to Year 2–9, by A. Brott

Becoming Dad: Black Men and the Journey to Fatherhood, by L. Pitts Jr.

Crawling: A Father's First Year, by E. Cooper

FAMILY–CENTRE GET-TOGETHERS

Get-togethers can be held for a variety of purposes. Family members may wish to discuss a particular issue as outlined in the bylaws, to share general information, or simply to enjoy one another's company. Families may be surveyed formally and informally to find out what types of gatherings they would like to participate in and what topics interest them. Families are more likely to attend these events if they are involved from the beginning in their organization.

FAMILY GATHERINGS: FORMAL SESSIONS TO SUPPORT PARENTING SKILLS

But what makes parents parent the way they do? Parenting is the family involvement process that includes the attitudes, values, and practices of parents in raising young children.

Factors That Influence Parenting

Knowledge of child development, personal beliefs and expectations, their own experiences, and the socioeconomic environment are just some influencing factors. Jay Belsky (2005), from the Institute for the Study of Children, Families and Social Issues at Birkbeck, University of London, U.K., highlights a number of forces that shape parenting. These include the attributes of the children, the developmental history of the parents and their own psychological makeup, and the broader social context in which parents and this relationship are embedded (Krakow, 2007: 2). Nurturing, responsive parent–child relationships and parental participation in child-centred activities relate to positive learning outcomes in early childhood. Nurturing relationships provide an emotional refuge for children, fostering the development of a healthy sense of belonging, self-esteem, and well-being. When parents are sensitive and responsive to children's emotions, children are more likely to become socially competent and show better communication skills. Lamb-Parker et al. (1999) state that "warm, reciprocal parent–child interactions and fewer life stresses in the home facilitate children's prosocial behaviour and ability to concentrate." Children who play at home and whose parents understand the importance of play in development are likely to demonstrate prosocial and independent behaviour in the classroom (Fantuzzo and McWayne, 2002). However, parenting is embedded in social and cultural contexts that influence parenting styles. Poverty is related to access to fewer social parenting supports, which in turn is associated with maternal depression and less nurturing parenting behaviour (Marshall et al., 2001). Belsky (2005) also states that children who were negative, irritable, or aggressive were found to have received less supportive, if not problematic, parenting. Inconsistent, rigid, or irritable explosive discipline, as well as low supervision and involvement, have been closely associated with the development of child conduct problems.

HOW THE CHILD-CARE CENTRE CAN SUPPORT PARENTING

The relationship between an early childhood environment and the families it serves may provide many opportunities for families to connect with one another, share their issues and concerns, and find support and encouragement in their parenting. Parental knowledge about child development, the use of effective parenting strategies, etc., can affect their child's outcomes. But those of us who are parents also know that these skills do not come naturally. Very little preparation for parenthood takes place to help families develop their parenting skills. Research informs us that when qualified staff deliver family-centred, sustainable support programs that respond to parent needs, parents' confidence and competence is enhanced and the impact on their relationships with their children supports their optimal development. It is also important to acknowledge that many parents will have expertise and, with encouragement, may be willing to share with teachers and other families. A collaborative approach is always more successful than a deficit approach!

According to Schorr (1997: 17–18) successful programs share certain attributes. Successful programs:

- are comprehensive, flexible, responsive, and persevering;
- see children in the context of their families;
- deal with families as parts of neighbourhoods and communities;
- have a long-term preventive orientation, a clear mission, and continue to evolve over time;
- are well managed by competent and committed individuals with clearly identifiable skills;
- operate in settings that encourage practitioners to build strong relationships based on mutual trust and respect; and
- train and support staff to provide high-quality, responsive services.

When parents request such support, there are many programs that the centre can make available to assist them in their parenting, and teachers may also benefit. The involvement of teachers as learners is critical to avoid the "teacher as expert" model. Our role is to empower parents and empower ourselves at the same time! Several programs which strive to achieve these goals are discussed below.

The Hanen Language Program

You Make the Difference is a program in which parents learn special ways help their child communicate and learn. Language is the single most important predictor of a child's ability to learn. Children learn by engaging in the world around them, and their parents are the most important part of that world. The aims of this program are to help parents recognize that they have the power and ability to foster their child's communication skills; to give parents specific ways to use everyday activities and play time as opportunities to help their child learn; to help parents become more confident by giving them information and support; and to provide a forum for early identification and referral of children who show signs of language delay. Parents and children attend nine weekly sessions for approximately three hours of parental group learning; their children are cared for by qualified child-care staff during the sessions. Time is also provided for each parent to practise what they have learned. The program is supported by the parent guidebook *You Make the Difference in Helping Your Child Learn* (Manolson, Ward, and Dodington, 1995) and a teaching videotape. More information is available at **www.iser.com/hanen-ON.html**.

Triple P—Positive Parenting Program

On March 21, 2005, the Healthy Child Committee of Cabinet announced support of $1.4 million to implement the *Triple P—Positive Parenting Program* in Manitoba. Over the following year, Healthy Child Manitoba sought out community agencies, regional health authorities, child-care centres, family resource centres, school divisions, pediatricians, and others to partner on this new approach to supporting Manitoba's parents.

Triple P is a world-renowned parenting program which promotes positive, caring relationships between parents and their children and helps parents learn effective management strategies for dealing with a variety of childhood developmental and behavioural issues. The program suggests simple routines and small changes that can make a big difference for families. It helps parents understand the way their family works and uses what they already say, think, feel and do in new ways. Positive parenting includes:

- ensuring a safe and engaging environment,
- encouraging positive behaviour,

- creating a positive learning environment,
- having realistic expectations, and
- taking care of yourself as a parent.

Research shows that positive parenting is the single most important factor in building a strong foundation for a child's life. The *Triple P* approach both strengthens the knowledge, skills, and confidence of parents to better meet the needs of their children and increases parents' sense of competence in their own parenting ability while reduces parenting stress. *Triple P* is a population level prevention strategy, which means that the program is for all parents. Twenty-five years of research and evaluation have demonstrated that *Triple P* is very effective in supporting families. The program has been implemented in a dozen countries around the world. Find out more at **http://www.triplep.net/**.

Canadian Parenting Workshops: Preparing Children for School Success

Canadian Parenting Workshops are a set of ten research-based workshops that have been developed, field tested, and evaluated by Ryerson University's School of Early Childhood. These workshops have been created specifically for parents with young children. The workshops include topics of particular interest to parents of preschoolers and elementary aged children, including teaching and learning activities that empower parents; ten workshop modules, fully scripted and ready for use by experienced or novice facilitators; a facilitator's guide; and learning evaluation instruments. The workshops have been written by Judith Bernhard, Melinda Freire, Vickie Mulligan, and published by Chestnut Publishing Group. There is a website **www.ryerson.ca/~bernhard/canadian.html**.

BOOKS FOR ADULTS

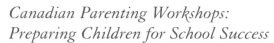

The Essential Parent Workshop Resource, by Michelle Graves

Pathways to Competence for Young Children: A Parenting Program

Written by Canadians Sarah Landy and Elizabeth Thompson, "*Pathways to Competence for Young Children: A Parenting Program* is designed to help professionals support parents in understanding and managing of their child's behaviour while encouraging an active role in guiding social-emotional

development. Developed from Sarah Landy's book, *Pathways to Competence*, this manual-and-CD set shows how to set-up, lead, and evaluate a parenting program for parents of children from birth to age seven. There are more than 140 parent handouts, instructions on structuring and leading sessions, problem-solving tips, and evaluation guidelines. Field tested for 10 years with hundreds of parents, this program has proved highly successful in improving child behaviour and enhancing parenting skills. Materials can be used for a 10-, 15-, or 20-week parenting group, and professionals can tailor the program to suit the needs of the families. The program is appropriate for a wide range of audiences, including parents with depression, teen mothers, and parents of children with behaviour problems. **www.brookespublishing.com/store/books/landy**.

Systematic Training for Effective Parenting

A program developed by Don Dinkmeyer, Gary D. McKay, and Joyce McKay more than 20 years ago, *S.T.E.P.* discusses how to improve relationships and establish a democratic atmosphere in the home. The kit contains videos, a comprehensive leader's resource guide, and a parent's handbook, which includes material about single parents, stepfamilies, schoolwork, homework, drugs, violence, and gangs. Kits are available for early childhood and teenaged children. A *S.T.E.P.* kit is also available in Spanish. **www.lifematters.com/step.asp**.

Parent Effectiveness Training

The *P.E.T.* program is based on the work of Thomas Gordon, a licensed psychologist who began the program almost 40 years ago as the first national parent-training program in the United States, to teach parents how to communicate more effectively with kids and offer step-by-step advice to resolving family conflicts so everybody wins. Gordon developed the concept of "*I*" language and encouraged active listening and win–win problem-solving solutions. His book on this topic was updated most recently in 2000 and more information can be found at **www.gordontraining.com**.

Active Parenting Now

Active Parenting Now, written by Michael H. Popkin, is based on the theories of Alfred Adler and Rudolf Dreikurs. The basis for this program—designed for parents of children aged

5–12 years—encourages an examination of the goals of misbehaviour, logical consequences, active communication, and family meetings. Parents will acquire skills that help them develop cooperation, responsibility, and self-esteem in their children. They'll also learn positive, non-violent discipline techniques so they can avoid power struggles. The program kit outlines six sessions and includes a video. Visit the *Active Parenting Now* website at **http://www.activeparenting.com/xapn.htm**.

Barbara Coloroso's Winning at Parenting

Barbara Coloroso has written extensively on supporting parents with successful and relevant strategies for improving family relationships, and she speaks throughout the world on these important issues. Her cassettes, manuals, and videos provide positive strategies for dealing with the challenges of parenting young children. Her work can be explored further in her books: *Winning At Parenting Without Beating Your Kids* (audiocassette), *Kids Are Worth It: Giving Your Child The Gift Of Inner Discipline*, *The Bully, the Bullied and the Bystander: From Pre-School to High School—How Parents and Teachers Help Break the Cycle of Violence*, and *Extraordinary Evil: A Short Walk To Genocide*; Coloroso's books are also available in Spanish.

The Incredible Years Program

Carolyn Webster-Stratton's *The Incredible Years Program* is designed to strengthen young children's social competence and problem solving abilities while reducing aggression at home and school. It is presented in four formats: parenting group sessions that focus on basic parenting skills, parental communication, anger management, and promoting children's academic skills; a teacher classroom management series; two-hour weekly, small therapy sessions for children; and lesson plans that can be delivered one to three times a week for teachers. *Incredible Years* has been tested with three- to eight-year-old children with conduct problems as well as with children two to six years of age who are at high risk due to poverty. More details about the program can be found at **www.incredibleyears.com**.

The Parent Kit

Developed by an international advisory board including Penelope Leach, William Sears, Martha Sears, Otto Weininger, and Penny Shore, this parent kit provides essential information and advice for parents. It includes a 30-minute video entitled *An Introduction to Joyful and Confident Parenting* and a series of five guide books: *Joyful and Confident Parenting*, *Growth and Development*,

---

INSIDE LOOK

A Professional Development Opportunity

Invest in Kids offers a one-day session which familiarizes participants with strategies to enhance the numerous parenting capacities called upon to nurture a child's development. This training maximizes the effectiveness of the child's development, and the planning and recording tools in the accompanying Activity-Based Guide are a vehicle to support parenting capacities, knowledge, and skills. The Activity Guide, which was prepared by experienced Canadian experts in early childhood education, early intervention, child development, home visiting, and family support, features:

- a section on making an effective telephone contact and a framework for the initial home visit;
- a section on sharing the planning process with families;
- 50 activities that strengthen such parenting capacities as confidence, self-esteem, resourcefulness, sensitivity, problem solving, communication and motivation; and
- a section of corresponding handouts that can be reproduced and shared with families.

The "Comfort, Play, and Teach" section of the guide contains more than 150 parent–child focused activities in the areas of cognitive, social-emotional, and language development for children from infancy to age five. Additionally, a Frequently Asked Questions (FAQs) section addresses concerns relating to common parenting issues in the early years of development. More detailed information can be found on the *Invest in Kids* website at **www.investinkids.ca**.

Emotional and Social Development, *How Your Baby and Child Learns*, and *Positive Discipline*. Also included is a parent medical emergency guide and a health record journal. Information about the kits is available by request at **info@theparentkit.com**.

Film Night

Many films have been developed for the express purpose of parent education. A film, or two videos with opposing viewpoints, might be shown and followed up with a discussion. An excellent video that both informs and involves family members is Stanley Greenspan's *Floor Time*. Another series of videos has been produced by Catholic Family Services in conjunction with Cable Regina, which has produced over 40 videos on various family life issues, some of which have won national awards for content and production. Many Canadian experts have contributed to the development of these videos. Some video topics include toddlers and temper tantrums, the importance of play, attention deficit disorder, children of separation and divorce. Consult their website at **http://em.ca/rcfamily/products.php3**.

Book Night

With respect to books, family members could be asked to read a relevant book a month in advance. They could then meet to assess the book and discuss controversial issues. Family members might also be interested in learning more about bias-free children's literature. Another example might be reading *How to Talk So Kids Will Listen and Listen So Kids Will Talk* by Faber and Mazlish.

Brown-Bag Lunches

Brown-bag lunch sessions may be most appropriate for family members whose child-care centre is in a workplace environment. One centre held biweekly sessions on issues that parents had identified in a survey. Each week either a centre teacher or a parent introduced a different topic about which family members and staff entered into lively discussion. Family members were free to attend all sessions or only the ones that were of particular interest to them. The lunch provided for the parents encouraged attendance, particularly when the children had a hand in its preparation.

Alumni Night

Some families might benefit from advice from "old" parents who have moved on to the school system. They may be able to answer questions about the child-care centre to primary school transition, and suggest ways to make the situation less stressful. Alumni can form networks with families to discuss issues relevant to the group. Alumni are often more than willing to help with fundraising at the centre given the strong connection they may feel with their "old" centre.

Family–Teacher Panel Discussions

Another way for family members to share their expertise is to hold panel discussions. A topic can be chosen or a series of questions organized and given to the panel in advance. A panel might consist of one teacher and one family member from each of the age groups in the centre.

The Open House

An open house provides an opportunity for teachers to showcase their playrooms as organized and inviting spaces and to deal with broad programming issues. These events may also be opportunities to meet with families who are transitioning to a new age group in the centre to meet their "new" teachers and talk about the changes that will occur.

INSIDE LOOK

In order to encourage an interest in books, our centre holds an "I Love Books" event for parents and their children. We begin with a potluck dinner, at which a local storyteller tells some interesting tales. The teachers then give families a short overview of what to look for when buying books for children of different ages, and our local librarian talks about some of the children's favourite books. Families can purchase books at a display set up by a local bookstore and discuss their purchases with the teachers. This event has been so successful that we are thinking about organizing a Make-a-Book Night, at which parents and their children could make and illustrate a book that is then laminated and placed in the family resource area for families to share.

FIGURE 5.1   MEETING TOPICS

Meeting Topics

sibling rivalry	gender stereotyping
superheroes	infant attachment
balancing work and family	computers and education
sexuality	community resources for parents
biting	childproofing the home
art experiences in the home	sleep issues
divorce/separation	hospitalization
effective parenting	self-esteem
street proofing	toilet learning
physical fitness	nutrition issues
challenging behaviour	fostering a love of books
child development	separation issues
violence and young children	antibiotics and young children
media and children	death
communication issues	children's fears
language development	stress in children and adults
curriculum development	travelling with children
influence of TV	first aid/CPR

INSIDE LOOK

When action figures were very popular with the preschool children, the teachers in our centre sent families a package containing articles about the relationship between violence, children, and television as well as a list of books on the subject. The teachers invited the family members to contact them if they were interested in participating in a panel discussion on television violence. The response rate was high, so a meeting was scheduled. Families came to the meeting loaded with information, and a serious and heated discussion ensued. Teachers and families struggled with the possible consequences of children's exposure to action figures. The discussion inspired some parents to find out about organizations concerned with television violence. These families invited a guest speaker from the Alliance for Children and Television to address the next panel discussion.

Each spring we have an open house for family members whose children will be transitioning over the summer months to a new playroom. We have found that families have so many questions about this transition that it is helpful to have everyone together at the same time. We explain to families what they might expect from this age group with respect to their emotional, social, physical, language, and cognitive development. We show a video of the children at "work." Making videos is an integral part of our program and videos are made of special events and of some everyday occurrences. The children are eager to sign them out and take them home, and they allow parents to get to know other families and children in the room. We set up the room so that activities are available at each of the learning centres. We give parents a map with all of the centres located on it and pertinent information recorded. Each centre presents a different challenge. The activities give families a chance to try out the equipment and see firsthand the learning that takes place there. Families receive a handbook that is specific to our room and that reviews the material covered during the open house. Finally, we create a bulletin board featuring the work that parents do during the evening. The children are always very excited to see their parents' work the next day!

The week before my planned visit to the daycare, my daughter talked of nothing else. She told me how they were decorating the room and how they were preparing a special lunch. When the morning arrived, Tangy was awake long before she needed to be and urged me out of bed so we could have an early start.

At the centre the teacher took us through a typical morning and the children led us through a variety of activities. We all sat in the circle and sang songs, did art activities, made towers in the block area, and made a boat in the woodworking centre. I had an opportunity to get to know the children that Tangy talks about at home and to meet some of the other family members. I was a bit uncomfortable in the beginning, but everyone's enthusiasm for the event was overwhelming. Tangy is already planning next year's event.

Participation Days

To increase family participation in the program, centres may set aside a Saturday for child-care events. Such an arrangement allows for the involvement of families who are unable to take time off work to attend during the week. Since Saturday may be a religious day for some members of the centre, an evening event might be warranted.

PREPARING FOR EFFECTIVE MEETINGS

The meetings should convey the sense that families have a great deal to contribute to the success of the home-to-centre collaboration. Combining meetings for both parties suggests to families that teachers are interested in lifelong learning. If meetings are not properly organized, family members may attend one or two and never return. Their lives are far too busy for them to set aside time for meetings that don't meet their needs. To ensure success, family members should be surveyed (an organizing committee of parents and teachers can be established to carry out this function) to find out what types of meetings they might be interested in attending. In the spirit of "the buck stops here," one person should be designated as the facilitator of the event; depending on the type of meeting, this person could be a family member, a supervisor, or staff person.

Although in many cases the child-care centre will serve as an appropriate venue, some meetings may require a larger gathering space. Family members can be good sources of information about locations within the community that can be booked at a nominal cost. It may also be possible to find community businesses that might be willing to underwrite the cost of the event or donate materials. In the survey mentioned above, family members should also be asked to state their preferences with respect to meeting times. For example, meetings might be best held at the end of the daycare day with a potluck dinner served. Meetings should also be planned so that family members are able to get their children home in time for their bedtime routines. Conversely, a breakfast meeting may be especially convenient for parents in workplace centres. Families that would struggle to afford a babysitter to attend a meeting will benefit from those held during the day while the children are at the centre. Meetings should always begin promptly at their scheduled time; this will encourage punctuality at future meetings. If guest speakers are to be included, they should come highly recommended and be dynamic and upbeat.

Much thought should go into the preparation of the invitations that are sent home to families; children might assist in the design and, if required, translation should be provided. An invitation from the family members involved in the planning of the meeting may be more effective than one from the centre. A variety of media should be used to advertise the upcoming event, and all advertising should be done well in advance.

When adult-only events are planned, it is important for the centre to offer child care. Planning special events for the children is one way to encourage families to attend. One centre arranged for the children to be entertained by a magician during a pizza dinner while the parents attended the annual general meeting. Volunteers or students doing their field placements in the centre can be recruited to assist with the child care while teachers attend the meeting. Incentives offered for attending, such as a door prize, are often well received. Transportation may be a concern for some families; a car-pool sign-up sheet can assist those parents in need of transportation to or from the meeting. A personal phone call from an "old" parent to new families with an offer to pick them up may ensure a greater turnout. Having fathers call may encourage other men to attend.

Refreshment breaks provide an opportunity for social interaction. A meeting's focus is best maintained if refreshments are served at the beginning or end of the meeting. At some events a potluck dinner may be held before the meeting begins. It is always very special for families when their children have taken part in the preparations (by creating

FIGURE 5.2 INVITATION

Join us for a potluck
BREAKFAST
on Tuesday, March 8th
and meet
Sarah Blevens

Sarah is the president of the organization
Parents Against Media Violence.
She will discuss the role families and teachers
can play in advocating for violence-free television.

Tuesday, March 8th
8 a.m. – 9 a.m.
Gross Motor Room

table centrepieces, for example, or making punch). Family members might join teachers in volunteering their services as guest chefs. Plan something unique, such as a pizza night, where each family brings a pizza with their favourite toppings for sharing and the centre provides the drinks, plates, napkins, dessert, and so on. Another idea might be to include an ice-cream meeting, where families bring ice cream, toppings, cones, and cookies. Letting families know that photos will be taken is another way to encourage participation, as everyone looks forward to seeing the photos. Having special displays set up by the children is also a fun incentive to attend.

The furniture in the meeting room should be comfortable and arranged to facilitate communication among all participants. If visuals are used, care should be taken to ensure that everyone has an unobstructed view.

Copies of the agenda should be circulated before the meeting begins. Families should be informed of the agenda in advance of the meeting so that they

---

INSIDE LOOK

ORGANIZING EFFECTIVE MEETINGS: A CHECKLIST

1. ❑ Solicit information from family members on their preferred type of meeting and topic.
2. ❑ Nominate an organizing committee, including teachers and family members, and designate a facilitator.
3. ❑ Coordinate and delegate responsibilities.
4. ❑ Community is canvassed for donations to host the event and donators are invited.
5. ❑ How much time is needed? Is it a breakfast event or one that last over several weeks?
6. ❑ Determine the purpose of the meeting and establish goals.
7. ❑ Invite visitors or guest speakers.
8. ❑ Plan for interpreters, if necessary.
9. ❑ Plan and book an accessible location and an appropriate meeting date and time.
10. ❑ Sign-up for car pooling is posted in advance and parking is available.
11. ❑ Send families a variety of communiqués—and well in advance.
12. ❑ Set up the family bulletin board to increase interest in the meeting.
13. ❑ Prepare publicity inside and outside the centre.
14. ❑ Arrange for child care.
15. ❑ Order all necessary materials.
16. ❑ Prepare a meeting agenda.
17. ❑ Arrange for refreshments that are culturally appropriate (be careful about asking those families who would find it financially difficult to bring in food).
18. ❑ Select, organize, and arrange topic-related displays.
19. ❑ Prepare handouts for families.
20. ❑ View videos ahead of time.
21. ❑ Arrange the furniture to support the format of the meeting.
22. ❑ Secure all necessary equipment (slide projectors, overheads, extension cords, and so forth) and test everything before the meeting begins.
23. ❑ Adjust the heat or air conditioning.
24. ❑ Remind teachers about personally inviting families to attend.
25. ❑ Telephone all families the night before as a final reminder.
26. ❑ Display large signs at entrances and exits on the meeting day.
27. ❑ Have name tags ready.
28. ❑ Make sure the videographer is ready to videotape the event for those who cannot attend.
29. ❑ Assume that everything will go wrong and have back-up plans ready (a flashlight might be useful in an emergency).

Analyze this photo. Does this meeting environment reflect what you have learned in this chapter?

can prepare materials. Additional copies of the agenda should be available at the time of the meeting. Articles or pamphlets relevant to the agenda should be placed in a conspicuous location so families can pick them up as they enter or leave the meeting. These materials can also be provided to parents who were unable to attend the meeting, along with a summary of the meeting. A handwritten note indicating that they were missed is a personal touch many families appreciate. This written summary of meeting highlights can serve as a valuable post-meeting review for families as well as teachers.

HOW TO RUN EFFECTIVE MEETINGS

The facilitator's role is a critical one. Before the meeting begins, the facilitator needs to ensure that the number of attendees is sufficient to reach a quorum, if the meeting is the type that requires one. Unless the bylaws specify a procedure for conducting the meeting, *Robert's Rules of Order* is generally used. The facilitator may wish to begin by taking a few moments to introduce herself or else to be introduced by a member of the organizing committee.

The facilitator should welcome families in a warm and friendly manner. She can also use this time to acknowledge guests, to convey the regrets of those unable to attend, to thank those family members and staff who contributed to the organization of the meeting, and to make announcements that are of interest to the group. The location of washrooms and designated smoking areas should be given when the meeting facility is unfamiliar to families. Suggestions for icebreakers are provided below in order to encourage families to socialize with one another.

- **Mixer Bingo for Families of Younger Children.** In this icebreaker, parents determine which family members fit each of the descriptions shown in Figure 5.3 and write the name of that person on the line provided.

- **Envelopes.** As family members arrive, they are given an envelope containing six photocopied pages from an ECE supplier's catalogue, each page depicting a different children's toy. Parents are asked to rank the toys from most expensive to least expensive and share their answers with each other before the facilitator announces the correct responses.

- **Name Tags.** Family members are given a piece of tag board from a plastic name tag. They are then asked to decorate the border of the tag (coloured markers are supplied for this purpose). Finished tags are placed in the middle of the floor. Parents are asked to choose a tag for themselves and put their name on it. The person who decorated a particular name tag then identifies himself or herself to the person wearing it.

- **Photo Name Tags.** Since most parents are identified as "Renata's mom" or "Connor's dad" by the children and other parents, name tags could be made for each family member that include a wallet-size photo of their child and a space for the parent's name. (When official school photos are taken, colour reproductions can be made and stored at the centre for records, individual classroom use, and occasions such as this.)

- **List-Making.** Family members are asked to record on a chart point-form details about their child (for example, favourite daycare lunch, favourite toy or piece of equipment in the playroom, and favourite learning centre).

- **Sharing Stories.** Each parent is asked to name one of the most challenging things about raising an infant (or toddler, etc.); a group discussion ensues. Family members in small-group meetings could share one funny (or embarrassing, or touching) story about their child.

- **Roots.** Family members write their names on small adhesive notes and, on the world map positioned at the front of the room, place their stickers on their country of origin. Discussion can follow on how their roots have influenced their parenting style. Families might also bring in an item that is important to their family and explain its significance.

- **Treasure Hunt.** "One of the ways to help parents explore the children's learning environment is to set up a treasure hunt through the classroom looking for designated objects. Cards can be given to small groups of parents instructing them to look for an activity that promotes children's creativity, an activity that helps children learn to read, an activity that helps children develop eye-hand co-ordination, and an activity that helps children learn language" (Keyser, 2006: 99).

- **Quilt Making.** At the beginning of an Open House, the kindergarten teachers at our lab school have each family create a square to contribute to a quilt that is made every year and hung in the room.

- **The Eyes Have It.** Photos are taken of the children and only their eyes are exposed on the photo. Parents are to find their own child and match the eyes with the child's name.

Meetings should be conducted in an atmosphere in which family members feel free to ask questions and discuss issues that are important to them. Some parents may feel vulnerable discussing their parenting role; others may not even attend certain meetings for fear they will be labelled as ineffective parents; still others may feel that some issues are too personal to be discussed in a public forum. As a matter of pure practicality, many second-language parents may decline to attend meetings if interpreters are not provided. Therefore, a skillful facilitator will be needed to alleviate any fears or concerns by helping families to understand that they will be safe and their opinions respected.

Another of the facilitator's responsibilities is to find common ground among the diverse participants. As Chastain (1980: 34) observes, "Each participant at a meeting brings a different perspective conditioned by age, sex, work experience, family background, education, religion, professional training, and other factors." In many meetings one or two parents dominate the discussion. The facilitator must be skillful at directing the conversation in such a way that all family members are involved. At the same time, the facilitator must respect the wishes of those parents who would rather listen than actively participate. Timing, pace, and a sense of order are crucial factors in a meeting. The facilitator must be able to read the audience and know when to move on. As a general rule, meetings that involve active participation rather than a lecture format will be more successful. When difficult topics are being discussed, the facilitator must be able to respond to open hostility and be able to ensure that every participant's ideas will be respected. Open debate is a positive strategy for change but bullying or aggressive tactics must be addressed. Creating a "parking lot" for ideas that are "off topic" is a strategy for acknowledging the speakers ideas with a promise to address the issues later in the meeting or at another time.

The following criteria for group communication may encourage attendance by giving parents a clearer understanding of the role they might play in meetings:

1. Come to the meeting ready to ask questions and share your ideas.

2. Once your ideas and thoughts are given to the group, do not feel compelled to defend them. Once shared, they become the group's property to discuss and consider. Clarify meaning

FIGURE 5.3   MIXER BINGO

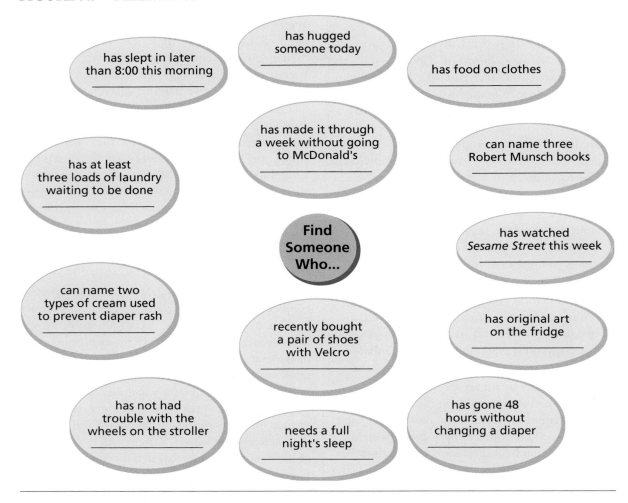

if it helps the group proceed, but don't feel responsible for the idea just because you suggested it.

3. Speak freely and communicate feelings. Listen to others with consideration and understanding for their feelings.

4. Accept others in the interchange of ideas. Allow them to have opinions that differ from yours. Do not ignore or reject members of the group.

5. Engage in friendly disagreements. Listen critically and carefully to suggestions others have to offer. Differences of opinion bring forth a variety of ideas.

6. Be sincere. Reveal your true self. Communicate in an atmosphere of mutual trust.

7. Allow and promote individual freedom. Do not manipulate, suppress, or ridicule other group members. Encourage their creativity and individuality.

8. Work hard, acknowledge the contributions of others, and focus on the group objectives. (Hepworth Berger, 2000: 243)

The facilitator should use the final minutes of the meeting to summarize what has been discussed and perhaps set a new agenda for tasks that are to be set or events that are to be planned as a result of the meeting. If smaller groups have been organized, bring everyone back to the larger group to share the information gathered; this provides an effective means of closure. The end of the meeting might also be a good time to give out special awards or recognize a contribution of a volunteer, family member, or teacher. The meeting might conclude with a call to parents to bring one other family in the centre to the next meeting.

When I first began my field placement, I was exceptionally nervous about working so intimately with such a diverse variety of parents and caregivers. I decided that it was time to challenge myself so I offered to do a workshop on a topic that families were most interested in knowing more about. I did my workshop for about 20 parents, some of whom I was meeting for the first time, on Toilet Learning. I don't ever remember being so nervous! But my hard work and interactions with these families paid off. At the end of the workshop they approached me and told me how wonderful it was to get together and talk about their concerns. Families thought they were the only ones going through these issues. One parent said, "It gave me relief to know other parents were going through it too! I don't feel so alone." That was important to me, helping parents make connections!

Source: Christine Mota Cabral, ECE graduate

FOLLOW-UP

Having family members evaluate the meeting can provide teachers and organizers with the information they need to improve future meetings. Families can be asked to complete evaluation forms on which the following questions might appear:

1. Was the timing of this meeting convenient for your family?

2. Was enough time allowed for discussion?

3. Did you like the format of this meeting?

4. How well did the speaker cover the topic?

5. How useful was this information to you?

6. What topics would you like to see addressed at future meetings?

Sending a personal note home to families thanking them for attending and participating in the meeting is always a welcome gesture. Any information about upcoming events or future meetings should be included in the note. A record should be kept of those who attended the meetings so that teachers can make a point of encouraging those who did not attend. The meetings might also be videotaped for them. Minutes should be taken during the meeting and sent out to families and posted in a public place.

When attendance at meetings is lower than expected, the organizing committee might reflect on the following questions:

- Did the meeting arise out of interest indicated by a family member survey or was it purely a centre initiative?

- Were families involved in the planning and organizational stages?

- Did the meeting time conflict with family schedules, religious celebrations, or other events in the community?

- Was adequate advance notice given to families?

- Was child care offered so that all families could participate?

- Did teachers in the playrooms actively encourage families to attend?

- Did the organizing committee do a telephone reminder?

- Were signs posted on the day of the event?

- Were interpreters provided, if needed?

INFORMAL FAMILY GATHERINGS

Informal gatherings may provide the greatest opportunities for families and teachers to build on their relationships; many families develop friendships at daycare that last long past their association with the centre. An informal gathering may consist of small numbers of parents meeting to discuss issues relevant to the specific age group of their children, to share information and expertise, and to socialize. Other opportunities for gatherings may be more playful, for example, a Pet Day on which families bring in their pets. The following overview provides suggestion for such gatherings.

While we hope that all families will want to be included, it is important for teachers to encourage newcomer families to participate in informal gatherings. As Murphy Kilbride (1990: 36) observes: "As [immigrant] families learn from each other,

FIGURE 5.4 ACTIVITIES FOR INFORMAL GATHERINGS

FIGURE 5.4 ACTIVITIES FOR INFORMAL GATHERINGS

INSIDE LOOK

Once a year at our centre we rented a Girl Guide campsite for the weekend. All the parents and their children were invited to attend, usually 10 to 15 families participated in this event. The tents were already set up for us, and each family brought its own food. Teachers organized activities during the day, and the families organized the bonfire in the evening. The children absolutely loved being in the woods, participating in scavenger hunts and enjoying simple tasks such as bringing water from the pump. The sense of camaraderie established during this weekend extended well into the year. The children talked about their experience for weeks afterward, and I got to know families in a way that would not have been possible without this event.

they share tips on how to interact with systems and to gain what is needed. This provides a very important message to families. As we know, families may represent all levels of adaptation and integration into the new culture. They have each had different experiences and successes (and frustrations) with the system. These [they can share] with each other."

One centre organized a lone-parent support group for parents in the school and in the child-care centre. This group meets on a regular basis and discusses a range of topics, including wills, financial planning, children's feelings about separation and divorce, and community resources. Other centres organized short courses on topics of particular interest to parents (for example, accounting and sewing). Another centre created a Parent Salon, where the families meet in one another's home on a rotating basis once a month and invite guest speakers to share their expertise. The last half of the meeting is devoted to lively discussion by individual family members about the topic.

Evans (1999) states that as roles are changing for everyone, both men and women are left with uncertainties about what constitutes appropriate behaviour in relation to children: "It can be very threatening to address some of these fears in cross-sex groups. One way for men to explore their feelings, fears, and concerns about parenting is to create men-only discussion groups. These groups provide men with the psychological and physical space they need to talk about their role as fathers."

Fathers also indicate that some among them may be intimidated by women because of the widespread assumption that on account of their gender alone women know more about parenting. McBride and McBride (1993: 5–8) describe one program, titled Daddy and Me, that was developed specifically for fathers and their preschool children. Once a week for ten consecutive weeks a two-hour meeting was held that involved group discussion and father–child playtime. Common discussion topics included the changing nature of fatherhood, balancing work and family roles, overcoming stereotypes of fatherhood, shared parenting responsibilities of mothers and fathers, parent burnout and coping mechanisms, and the father's role in influencing child development. Findings from this project suggest that fathers increased their belief in their own competence in parenting—and also increased their active involvement in child-rearing

Tobogganing is a great family–centre outing.

responsibilities. Fathers spent more time with their children on non-work days and experienced fewer feelings of isolation and parental stress.

A program in Weyburn, Saskatchewan, reserves two hours every second or third Saturday morning for a program called "Just Me and My Dad." Coordinator Diane Farney has found that the men come to play with their kids: "They use the gross motor skills equipment for some rough and tumble play. Many researchers have noticed that men play more physically than women, right from the time their children are infants. When they are in a group of fathers, men are more comfortable letting that preference come out" (Mann, 1999).

Carter and Harvery (1996: 5) found that

[g]roup norms of reciprocity and shared power create opportunities for parents to claim their strengths and view themselves as teachers as well as students. The parent who lives alone may become a resource to the parent whose partner is rarely home. The parent who has successfully negotiated with a community resource may become an inspiration and mentor for a less

The most meaningful meeting I ever attended at the centre was when all the families of toddlers got together to discuss what it was like living with a two-year-old. I can't tell you how relieved I was to know that other parents were struggling with the same issues that I was, and that I wasn't alone in my feelings. With the support of the teacher, we were able to discuss the issue of biting in the playroom and I made some new friends in the process. This meeting turned into a monthly event at our centre, and we all looked forward to hearing one another's stories. I think I am a better parent because of this connection.

assertive parent. And the parent who describes a challenging situation may elicit responses from participants that broaden everyone's ability to imagine more creative options and possibilities.

Celebrations for children's birthdays are common in child-care centres. When family members are involved, it becomes a special event. This may mean hosting the event at the end of the day when it is most convenient for the parents but not necessarily the best timing for the children. The challenge for some families is when each birthday party celebration "ups the ante" for the next family—a magician, a juggler, or enormous party loot bags to take home may make it impossible for some families to participate in this way. Therefore many centres have adopted more

modest celebrations that focus on the child in a more developmentally appropriate manner.

FAMILY GATHERINGS AND CHILD-CARE CELEBRATIONS

"Early childhood programs should be involved in celebrations that are meaningful to our children: celebrations that are magical, bigger than life, fantastical, full of hope and power and love, and that make each child feel they belong; festivals that show the brighter side of humanity; music, dance, togetherness, the importance of children, and the power of community to care for children" (Wardle, 1994: 43).

Celebrations in a child-care centre can be joyous events that promote camaraderie among children, parents, and staff. Encouraging families to share their

Gatherings such as this annual picnic allow families to get together and celebrate the arrival of summer.

celebration practices with the centre is critical to the success of the home–centre partnership. A number of questions must be addressed by families, teachers, and the board of directors when planning celebrations:

- Will the celebrations reflect the philosophy of the centre?

- What role will the families and children play in organizing the celebrations?

- Will celebrations teach positive values and broaden the children's awareness of others?

- How can the centre ensure that the celebrations are age-appropriate for the children?

- How much time will the centre devote to celebrations?

- How will the centre respond to families who express concerns that holidays are too commercialized?

- If there is little diversity in the centre, should a more comprehensive approach to celebrations be implemented?

- If there is a great deal of diversity in the centre, should every event be celebrated?

- Will everyone feel welcome at the celebrations?

- Is there a procedure in place if a family member objects to a specific celebration?

- How will teachers' time be organized to allow for preparation for these events?

- How can we coordinate celebrations with the school for our school-age children?

Bonnie Neugebauer (1994) suggests the following alternatives to traditional celebrations: milestones (the first tooth, learning to whistle, printing one's name, moving from one age group to another, tying shoelaces, telling a story, making a

This father has just won the tricycle race at this centre's annual barbecue.

One mother has written, "When my son was in junior kindergarten, I suggested to his teacher that she consider [celebrating] festivals reflecting the background of the non-Christian children in the class as well as Easter, Halloween, and Christmas. She showed surprise because the thought had not occurred to her. After some reluctance, she agreed to consider the suggestion if I and other non-Christian parents organized the festivals. This was progress, but she missed the point. For the little children in her class, she was the authority figure, the one with knowledge and power, the one who legitimized learning activities. In terms of legitimacy of what went on in her classroom, they saw the difference between what she planned and initiated and what she allowed to happen."

friend); points of learning (the number three, worms, the colour red, a favourite story, Thursday); children and families (the birth of a sibling, a grandparent's visit, moving to a new house); a great meal by the cook; a winter picnic; an ice sculpture; inventors; natural and man-made events (a shuttle launch, the first snowflake, puddles, a thunderstorm).

If celebrations are to be meaningful, developmentally appropriate, and healthy, the focus must always be on what is in the best interests of the children. When this focus is absent, the results can be disastrous. Recounts Wardle (1994: 43): "I have experienced early childhood graduations where children cried, staff got mad, and parents literally walked over some children to videotape their own child in cap and gown. The atmosphere was tense; the children were bored. And the entire activity

was adult dominated and only for the benefit of adults."

In some centres, teachers have decided to do away with all celebrations in an effort to not offend anyone but in doing so they miss wonderful opportunities to celebrate events that are meaningful in the lives of young children and their families.

BOOKS FOR ADULTS

An Anti-Bias Guide To Holidays in Early Childhood Programs, by Julie Bisson

VOLUNTEERS

Volunteers are generally motivated by a desire to help others and to feel needed and useful. Some people engage in volunteer work to reduce the

---

EXHIBIT 5.2   CELEBRATIONS: A QUESTIONNAIRE FOR FAMILIES

1. What special days do you celebrate in your family?

2. How would you like our program to be involved in your celebrations?

3. How do you think we could celebrate everyone's special days in a centre as diverse as ours?

4. What are some of the myths or stereotypes about your culture that you would like us to understand so as not to perpetuate them?

5. How do you feel about celebrations at the centre that are not part of your family's tradition?

6. What can we do to celebrate our centre as an inclusive "human" community?

7. Would you have time to

    - read a favourite story in your first language?
    - share a favourite family recipe?
    - donate articles of clothing that you no longer use for our dress-up corner?

Source: B. Neugebauer, "Beginnings Workshop: Going One Step Further—No Traditional Holidays," *Child Care Information Exchange* 100 (November–December 1994). Reprinted with permission from Child Care Information Exchange, P.O. Box 3249, Redmond, WA, 98073. (800) 221-2864.

One Day at School: Sae Hae Bok Man Hee Ba Du Se Yo

My adopted son's preschool class vigorously planned a celebration of the Lunar New Year. No one seemed to know anything about Korean New Year customs. A bit reluctant because of my limited knowledge, I nonetheless took the plunge and volunteered to lead a Korean New Year activity for the class. The one Korean woman with a child in the class shied away from any involvement, so I went ahead on my own. The morning of our special day, we arrived at school with Eric's han-bok, which he was refusing to wear at all, 30 purses made from cotton for the children to decorate, and thread with satiny cord, a few pictures, and lots of pennies. I saw my Korean friend there and self-consciously hoped I wouldn't butcher the language I was attempting to teach. To my surprise, when she saw Eric's han-bok, she asked if I'd mind if she ran home to get her daughter's. She did, and as a result Eric decided it would be all right to wear his too. What followed was a wonderful morning. The children drew on and threaded their purses. I transported the children via pretend plane to Korea and told them a story about two children anticipating the holiday. Eric and Alice proudly showed off their han-boks to a very admiring audience of their peers. Then I explained the bowing and the words while Myong Ja, Alice's mother, demonstrated and corrected my pronunciation! I was surprised that every child in the class wanted to try bowing. (Of course, the pennies helped.) They loved it; and days later children were still coming up to me and saying, "Sae Hae Bok Man Hee Ba Du Se Yo." We repeated our performance for the other class, and the greatest rewards were the pride in Eric's and Alice's faces, the new friendship with a Korean woman, and the delight with which all the children learned about a culture different from their own.

Source: Sheehan and Wood, 1993: 60.

loneliness and isolation they feel; others volunteer in order to enhance their job skills; still others have specific skills they wish to share with others. According to a study by Volunteer Canada in conjunction with the Canadian Centre for Philanthropy, people who give their time to a volunteer activity are happier and healthier in their later years. A lot of benefit comes from being in touch with others and having an impact on their lives according to Dr. Neena Campbell, director of the Centre for Aging at the University of Victoria (Fox, 2002).

As a supervisor, I sometimes found it challenging when we had social gatherings with families when all of the children and siblings as well as teachers were all in the centre at the same time. When the children acted out, which was to be expected on these types of special events, no one really knew who should deal with the children when a problem arose. Teachers in the centre were resentful when some adults sat back and chatted to each other while the children engaged in less than desirable interactions and in other situations the teachers were afraid of embarrassing the parent if they stepped in. From the parent's perspective, I also could tell that they felt as if they were on "our territory" and so seemed reluctant to get engaged with directing their child or others. They worried about creating a situation that would offend us. So in preparation for the event, I explained in the newsletter that we were happy to be hosting the event and this would mean that the teachers would be busy helping to set up and organize so we would appreciate it if the family assumed responsibility for "crowd" control. At the same time, we also wanted families to have time to interact with each other so the teachers organized an activity where the children could be involved and teachers volunteered to supervise these experiences. This has made a huge difference in our informal gatherings. We could all relax and just have a good time enjoying each others company!

FAMILY MEMBERS AS VOLUNTEERS

As part of the orientation process, families can be encouraged to volunteer in ways that suit their lifestyles, work commitments, and interests. Based on information gathered in the home visit, the supervisor of the centre should keep a logbook of family members who are willing to serve as volunteers; their areas of expertise and interests could also be recorded. The type of program offered in the centre to some extent determines the kind of volunteers it attracts; in co-operatives and workplace child-care centres, for example, family members may assist during lunch hours or after work.

When family members volunteer, they send positive messages to their children. Volunteering in meaningful ways gives parents insight into the day-to-day running of the centre and an opportunity to observe firsthand the interactions between the teachers and their child. Family members are more likely to participate when they see that their involvement benefits their child and that their efforts are valued by the centre. Teachers benefit by having an extra adult in the room, and they gain an opportunity to more closely observe the parent–child interaction and obtain greater insight into their relationship.

Some fathers want to play an active role in the centre. Once fathers begin to participate, they develop enthusiasm. Some noncustodial fathers may play a more active role than custodial fathers or those in intact family units. It's a way of being part of a child's routine without interfering with the mother.

ELDERS AS VOLUNTEERS

A growing body of evidence today suggests that interaction between young children and older adults in structured environments is beneficial to both groups, that it has a positive impact on the growth and learning of young children and on the quality of life of older persons (Lyons, 1986: 21).

Stereotypes about aging are challenged when children and adults work together. Valuing the attributes and diverse lifestyles of the elderly is a positive experience for children, families, and teachers. As Smith and Newman (1993: 33) observe: "Beyond their benefits to children, older adults make important contributions to the children's families and other program staff. The power of generational roles, for example, can be seen in the way young parents, especially mothers, gravitate to the older adult, the 'grandparent,' in the

Courtesy of University of Toronto, Child Care "on Charles Street"

This mother volunteers once a week in this child-care centre.

Elders bring their expertise and knowledge to the child-care centre.

classroom." Booth Church (1994: 40) states that "elders—grandparents and great grandparents—are our greatest resources for connecting children with the customs and observances of the past." A study by Newman and Riess (1992) reveals the beneficial effects of intergenerational child-care programs. Older workers who took part in the study reported increases in feelings of self-worth; teachers reported positive changes in the classroom environment resulting from the presence of older workers.

COMMUNITY MEMBERS AS VOLUNTEERS

Volunteers may include high school, college, or university students who need fieldwork or community hours; Girl Guides or Boy Scouts; and members of groups and organizations with special interests such as gardening or boating. Busy families will be grateful to centres that are able to organize out-of-centre events that might not otherwise be available to their children. Centres may want to seek out volunteers who are physically challenged or who come from different cultural backgrounds. In centres where staff is predominantly female, male volunteers might be actively recruited; it is important for children to see men in nurturing roles. In centres where the languages spoken by the teachers are not congruent with the families at the centre, contacting community agencies for volunteers who would be willing to provide translation/interpreting skills would be of great benefit to the centre. This volunteer might also be willing to hold language classes to help teachers become more proficient in the home language of the families.

In some communities, volunteers can be solicited through a volunteer registry where appropriate criminal reference checks are carried out. Other recruitment methods include posting notices on boards, advertising in local newspapers, or appearing on local cable television or radio shows. Photographs of the children (with family permission) are a wonderful asset, and it may be possible to set up displays in such places as the local community centre, community colleges, and seniors residences. Staff and families could speak to friends and acquaintances about doing volunteer work. A formal tour and open house might also generate interest in the community. By establishing direct contact with the community via volunteer efforts, teachers are able to disseminate information about the important work being done in child-care centres.

EXHIBIT 5.3 INTERGENERATIONAL PROGRAMMING: DAY CARE CONNECTION

In April 1991, Day Care Connection in Toronto received funding from the federal government's Child Care Initiatives Fund to hire a coordinator for the development of an intergenerational daycare program. The centre is located in a seniors' complex. After surveying 12 intergenerational programs involving preschool children in southern Ontario, Day Care Connection established the following objectives for their centre:

- to provide an opportunity for social interaction between seniors and children;
- to foster positive attitudes between generations;
- to improve the quality of life for older citizens by providing an opportunity for them to grow and develop, gain a sense of worth, and be stimulated;
- to improve the quality of child care for young children by providing them with enriched programming;
- to break down stereotypes by increasing knowledge of, and sensitivity toward, the elderly;
- to help children develop relationships with seniors that add to their sense of extended family;
- to promote in children an understanding of the process of aging; and
- to make children aware of the knowledge, skills, abilities, and talents of older adults.

An open house was held at which staff described the program to resident seniors and took them on a tour of the centre; the tour included the screening of a video on a day in the life of a child at the daycare. Later a survey was sent to the residents of the complex to determine their level of interest. Personal contact was made whenever possible. An orientation for volunteers covered such issues as health, safety, and behaviour management.

Activities have included crafts, movies, storytelling, games, cooking, magic tricks; trips in the community; seasonal events such as barbecues, Halloween tea, and pancake breakfasts; volunteer appreciation night; swimming instruction; computer instruction for seniors and children; visits to seniors' apartments; assisting in the program (serving lunch, dressing, one-to-one time).

This intergenerational program is the subject of a video titled *Here We Are Together*.

Source: Adapted from C. Ryerse (1993, October). "Day Care Connection Intergenerational Program," *Focus*. Canadian Child Care Federation, pp. 37–42.

INSIDE	LOOK

The Volunteer Grandparents Society of British Columbia

This organization was founded in 1973. Its objective is to match grandparents (aged 40 and over) with families who lack the presence of grandparents in their lives and whose children are between the ages of 3 and 12. There is no contract and no committed hours; the level of commitment is mutually agreed on. After an application is made, an in-person interview is held, and a police check and references (including one from a physician) are requested. A counsellor comes to the grandparent's home to discuss his or her expectations for a relationship with a family. The counsellor then reviews the families in the area and looks for a likely match.

The first meeting usually takes place in the family's home, with the counsellor present. "The greater the number of loving adults the child has in his/her life," says the founder of Volunteer Grandparents, "the wider the definition of 'normal'.... This fosters acceptance of self and tolerance of diversity in others."

Source: Walters Anderson, 1993: 3.

These children are learning how to paddle a canoe, thanks to a volunteer from a local boating organization who offered to train them in the fundamentals.

Centres may wish to recruit specific types of resource people. A centre that needs help in the design of its handbook or brochure might contact a local community college and try to enlist the services of students in the graphic arts department. Often community organizations contribute to the child-care centre with fundraising efforts, donating supplies, hosting child-care events, or sharing their expertise. Children can give something back to the community by participating in environmental projects (planting, cleanups); by providing local businesses with original artwork; or by helping seniors with yard work, shopping, and other tasks.

WAYS TO VOLUNTEER

There are many ways in which volunteers can play meaningful roles in the operation of the daycare.

Administrative Duties

- Serving on the board of directors
- Participating on committees organized by the families or board of directors
- Working on hiring committees
- Typing, filing, and assisting with clerical duties (e.g., photocopying)
- Providing bookkeeping services
- Fundraising
- Helping with public-relations activities

- Organizing a clothing or sports equipment swap, a pizza day, a book fair, or co-op food purchases for families

Communication Tasks

- Maintaining bulletin boards
- Participating in the production of a regular newsletter
- Being part of a new family welcoming group
- Organizing translation services for families
- Organizing social events (retirement parties, goodbye events, yearly family reunions, and so on)
- Organizing family discussion groups
- Serving as a playroom representative
- Establishing a Block Parent group

Maintenance Tasks

- Assisting with centre repairs, painting, cleaning, and so forth
- Helping children set up a garden in the indoor or outdoor environment
- Creating a butterfly garden
- Building new equipment
- Assisting teachers with outdoor cleanup

Program Development

- Designing project boxes that reflect children's interests
- Designing, organizing, and running a family resource area
- Teaching children the safe use of construction tools while completing woodworking projects
- Serving as the guest "chef" or assisting with cooking projects
- Helping over lunch hour or naptime
- Accompanying the children on trips
- Providing one-on-one support for exceptional children
- Videotaping or taking photographs of children during their daily routine or on special occasions
- Sharing expertise with the children (in woodworking, for example, or jewellery-making, pottery skills, or playing musical instruments)
- Collecting resources and setting up a learning centre

- Helping children learn a new language
- Showing slides or movies about life in other countries or from trips they have taken
- Sharing their expertise about a family celebration
- Sharing information about local history
- Typing up children's stories
- Playing games with the children
- Coaching in school-age programs (baseball, cricket, basketball, hockey, and so on)
- Creating or collecting dramatic play clothing
- Working with teachers to develop emergent curriculum

A community volunteer project developed in Vancouver might easily be initiated in any child-care centre: "We're all familiar with some of the challenges faced by immigrants to Canada as they learn to adapt to life here—coping with different customs, perhaps learning a new language. Many newcomers also have a hard time finding familiar foods, fresh vegetables in particular. Daikons and yard-long beans and black soybeans are as important to us at festivals as turkey is to Canadians at Christmas," says Hisako Masaki, a member of Vancouver's Japanese community. This Vancouver program—funded by the United Way and the BC government and named "Roots and Shoots"—is helping immigrants grow food from their homeland. Ethiopian, Pakistani, Filipino, Somalian, Cambodian, and Aboriginal families have all shown interest (*Canadian Gardening*, 1999: 18).

TRAINING OF VOLUNTEERS

Clear goals and objectives should be established so that all participants are aware of their roles and responsibilities. Training should involve not only the supervisor but also the teachers who will work with the volunteers. A parent volunteer may participate by talking about his or her experiences; including pictures or a video of volunteers working with the children is often a positive way to begin and may relieve anxious participants. A video series from the National Association for the Education of Young Children (NAEYC) titled *The Caring for Our Children* consists of a set of six 30-minute tapes that show volunteers how to keep young children healthy and safe. In-house videos can also be

New trees are planted outside the child-care centre by a parent volunteer.

created to emphasize positive interactions between volunteers and the children.

Family volunteers should be provided with a handbook outlining regulations, fire drills, and emergency procedures. The handbook, advises Lowell Krough (2006), who worked on the video series, should "be clear about what is and isn't permitted on the site: rules for personal use of the telephone, length and flexibility of time for breaks, customs regarding personal use of the refrigerator, and so on. It is embarrassing for people to learn after the fact that they have broken rules they didn't know existed."

The importance of confidentiality must be impressed upon volunteers. Issues that come up in the playroom must not be discussed outside the centre. Volunteers should approach their work in a professional manner. They must be reliable and flexible enough to adapt to the busy nature of a child-care centre. The supervisor should monitor the interactions between the teachers and volunteers on an ongoing basis, supporting when necessary and encouraging a positive and nurturing environment.

PREPARING FOR VOLUNTEERS

To prepare children for the arrival of the volunteer, teachers can ask them to think of ways to make the person feel welcome. Children should also be prepared for whatever special circumstances may apply (coping with the presence of a wheelchair, for example, or a cane). It is a good idea to have the volunteer simply observe on the first day. The teacher can make use of "teachable moments" to inform and orient the new volunteer as well as to reinforce the routines and strategies that were learned during training. The teacher should be available to answer the many questions that most volunteers have at this stage. A volunteer who appears difficult or defensive might feel at a loss. Given a specific task in which they have an interest, may make them the teacher's greatest asset. The volunteer should be introduced to the families as well as the children and made to feel comfortable. A rocking chair on a carpet with lots of big cushions for the children to lie on is a wonderful gathering place. Family volunteers should be made aware of the possible reaction of their own child to their presence. The child may resent the time and attention other children receive from his or her parent. The teacher can support this transition by explaining to the children that the volunteer has come to help all of them while at the same time setting aside time for the family member and child to spend with each other.

VOLUNTEER RESPONSIBILITIES: A CHECKLIST

1. Be honest and open with the supervisor and staff, beginning with the interview, regarding intent, goals, needs, and skills so that a good placement is possible.

2. Understand the requirements of time and duties of assignments before accepting them, and, once you do accept them, fulfill the commitment to the best of your ability.

3. Work to deserve being treated as a recognized and respected member of the team. There is no room for temperamental prima donnas, off-and-on-again types, and "no shows."

4. Take the commitment seriously enough to participate in planning and evaluating the volunteer program and in whatever training or learning opportunities are available.

5. Share ideas with staff. Volunteers frequently have a fresh perspective that is valuable. However, do not be hurt or resentful if your ideas are not always implemented, for the staff's ideas aren't always carried out either.

6. View staff as allies and mentors, for much can be learned from them.

7. Respect the confidentiality of the agency and its clients.

8. Seek and accept honest feedback on performance. Remember, negative feedback is valuable too, when viewed as an opportunity for growth.

9. Serve as goodwill ambassadors and interpreters for the centre and its services in the community at large.

10. Be informed and therefore more effective advocates of change when change is needed.

EVALUATION OF THE VOLUNTEER PROGRAM

Volunteers should regularly receive constructive feedback on their role and interactions in the centre. An evaluation process involving all participants should be in place to identify what has worked well and what areas need improvement. If it is conveyed in a positive manner, most volunteers appreciate the feedback. At the same time, volunteers should also have an opportunity to present their own evaluation of the program and their participation in it.

It is important that teachers acknowledge volunteers' contributions (see Figure 5.5 for some ideas) and that they share the administration's enthusiasm for volunteers. Unless teachers are prepared to treat volunteers as co-workers, the chances of successful and meaningful interactions are severely limited. If staff are involved in the initial planning, training, and evaluation process, they are likely to feel a greater commitment to the volunteer program.

When assessing the success of the volunteer program with regard to number of recruits, it is important for teachers to remember that family members may have a good reason for not volunteering. They may lack child care for their own children, they may be ill, or they may already have too many demands on their time. The decision not to volunteer should therefore not be interpreted as lack of enthusiasm for the centre or its teachers. Families with demanding work schedules can still participate. One busy mother who is a doctor organized an in-depth tour of her workplace for her child's group. Teachers need to understand also that many ESL family members will not participate unless teachers are particularly encouraging in

EXHIBIT 5.4   IF YOU WANT MY LOYALTY, INTEREST, AND BEST EFFORT, REMEMBER THAT...

1. I need a sense of belonging, a feeling that I am honestly needed for my total self, not just for my hands or because I take orders well.
2. I need to have a sense of sharing in planning our objectives. My need will be satisfied only when I feel that my ideas have had a fair hearing.
3. I need to feel that the goals and objectives arrived at are within reach and that they make sense for me.
4. I need to feel that what I'm doing has real purpose and contributes to human welfare—that its value extends even beyond my personal gain, beyond my working hours.
5. I need to share in making the rules by which, together, we shall live and work toward our goals.
6. I need to know in some clear detail just what is expected of me—not only my detailed tasks but where I have an opportunity to make personal and final decisions.
7. I need to have some responsibilities that challenge, that are within range of my abilities and interest, that contribute toward my reaching my assigned goals, and that cover all goals.
8. I need to see that progress is being made toward the goals that we have set.
9. I need to be kept informed. What I'm not up on, I may be down on. (Keeping me informed is one way to give me status as an individual.)
10. I need to have confidence in my superiors—confidence based on assurance of consistent fair treatment, or recognition when it is due, and trust that loyalty will bring increased security. In brief, it really doesn't matter how much sense my part in this organization makes to you—I must feel that the whole deal makes sense to me.

Source: M. Wilson, *The Effective Management of Volunteer Programs* (Boulder, CO: Volunteer Management Association, 1976), p. 55.

FIGURE 5.5   RECOGNIZING VOLUNTEERS

The children had great fun celebrating the efforts of their favourite volunteer.

Courtesy of Lynn Wilson

their recruitment efforts. Students may wish to further review information on volunteers at **www.worldvolunteerweb.org/interact/contribute**.

FUNDRAISING

It is an unfortunate reality that the economic survival of many programs depends on the fundraising efforts of families and teachers. Fundraising gives those who participate in it an opportunity not only to publicize the centre but to have fun and build on their relationships with one another. There may also be times when dollars are respectfully diverted into a special fund to help pay for trips or in-centre events that some families may not be able to afford. Before any fundraising begins, the following questions should be asked:

1. Is the activity appropriate for the community?

2. How much money do we have to spend on our fundraising efforts and where will it come from?

3. Will the initial investment in the project be recovered at the end of the event?

4. Will the gains be large enough to warrant undertaking the fundraiser?

5. Who will be responsible for the money and keep appropriate records? Will we need to open a bank account?

6. Do we have the time necessary to carry out the fundraising activity?

7. Will we have enough participation from beginning to end to carry out the project?

8. What materials will we require?

9. How will we handle publicity?

10. Should we hire an outside company to organize the event? Can we afford it? If not, who will coordinate the event?

11. Instead of paying for outside assistance, can we call on families and/or teachers whose services we could use?

HOW TO PLAN A SUCCESSFUL FUNDRAISING EVENT

When organizing a fundraising event, it is important to canvas everyone involved—families, teachers, and older children—for their ideas. An organizing committee should be established to oversee the event. It is important at the outset to determine what the community can contribute to the fundraising drive. Are corporate sponsorships available? It is also important to establish a specific goal (to raise $1,500 for a new piece of play equipment, for example) rather than simply to raise money to be allocated at another time.

Whether to hold one large fundraiser each year or several small ones is another decision that has to be made based on the amount of time available. The date or dates should not conflict with religious celebrations or national holidays. Some families prefer not to get involved with fundraising because of their time schedule, and some simply feel too awkward asking friends and neighbours to buy things on a regular basis. Therefore, some families have responded positively by making a contribution whenever a fundraising event is organized.

It is important to publicize the event in both the centre and the community. Posters, fliers, newspapers, cable television, and radio are among the vehicles that can be used to publicize the event. A local celebrity may be willing to act as a spokesperson for the centre. Personal invitations to the event can be sent to dignitaries, members of government, and community leaders. Centres may also want to enlist the support of families that have "graduated" from the centre; they may be pleased to come back and see old friends. This is also a good time to have the telephone committee spread the word!

Accurate and up-to-date records of the fundraising event should be kept. Once the event is over, a summary of the efforts should be distributed to families. Records should be kept so that they can be referred to the following year if the event is repeated; this will save a great deal of time. Not all fundraisers are outright successes. When an event fails to meet expectations, it is important to determine what went wrong and how it can be avoided next time. A survey could be distributed to families to elicit their feelings about the project. Everyone who participated in the event should be thanked through personal letters, bulletin-board displays, acknowledgment in the local newspaper, or centre newsletters. As teachers we must not forget the value of involving parents and older children in projects that contribute to their communities. Not all fundraising needs to be self-serving.

FUNDRAISING IDEAS

Many books are available on the subject of fundraising, so the library is a good place to begin your search for ideas. The following list outlines several innovative ways of fundraising, as reported by various centres.

- Sell plants started by the children, calendars decorated with the children's art, or T-shirts or tote bags that school-age children have designed.
- Sell herb vinegars and garlic oil, potpourri, jellies, and jams.
- Take on a newspaper route with proceeds going to supplies for the centre.
- Hold auctions featuring items donated by families and the community,ell raffle tickets (one centre raffled tickets on a monthly basis with a family member donating a different service).
- Hold a fashion show.
- Show a movie, or a series of them, and charge admission.
- Arrange (possibly in collaboration with other centres) a visit by a popular children's singer or theatre group (the performance could take place in a local high school auditorium) or invite a popular guest speaker or storyteller and charge admission.
- Organize bake sales or craft sales (selling parent- and child-made items).
- Buy food or ECE resources in bulk from suppliers and sell to families.
- Organize a bingo or casino night, or organize a car wash.
- Produce and sell cookbooks featuring favourite family recipes.
- Hold a wine-tasting event.
- Organize a tour of historical houses.
- Sell fertilizer.
- Organize a community fish fry.
- Hold a walkathon, bikeathon, jumpathon, or readathon.
- Arrange errand services for elderly or bedridden members of the community.
- Sell various services (window washing, lawn mowing, snow shovelling, etc.).
- Hold garage sales.

It started as a way to comfort a child while her father was away in Bosnia as part of the Canadian contingent of the UN peacekeepers stationed there. Jodie Boone and Julie Speichts at Burnside Children's Centre in Dartmouth, Nova Scotia, were telling the children that Caitlin George's dad, First Class Petty Officer William George, was coming home. The children wanted to know why Caitlin's daddy was away. The teachers responded by saying that the people in Bosnia were having an argument about who owns the land, and Caitlin's dad was there to help. Together, they found where Bosnia was on the globe. Caitlin told the children that, in his letters, her dad told her that he was there to help children who didn't have a house to live in or toys to play with. The teachers' and the children's compassion was the foundation for much classroom discussion.

When First Class Petty Officer George returned home, Jodie and Julie approached him with an idea that would extend sharing beyond the walls of their classroom. Why not have a toy and clothing drive in their centre for the children in Bosnia? Caitlin's dad was able to make arrangements through the Canadian navy for the transport of the toys and clothes to Bosnia. Even the littlest people can make the world a better place!

Carl Jung said that collective change is brought about by individual change. Julie and Jodie's curriculum has included compassion and sharing beyond their classroom, and they have empowered the children in their class by showing them that each one of them can have an effect on the world in some way. Children who realize that they have this power will have more potential to grow into socially responsible adults.

Source: *Child Care Connection*–N.S., 1995: 4.

- Sell magazine subscriptions.
- Have a local pizza shop donate money to the centre on the basis of the number of pizzas sold by families.

Not only do children enjoy face-painting events, but such events can raise money for their centre.

FAMILIES AS MEMBERS OF A BOARD OF DIRECTORS

In this section, Pat Campbell contributes her expertise on the role of parents on a board of directors.

Many child-care centres and parent co-operatives in this country are run by volunteers who serve on a governing board. This board is responsible for the overall operation of the centre and is elected by the "members" (parents) of the centre at an annual general meeting. Some centres have only parents and the supervisors on the board, while others have a few representatives from the larger community. There could be a school principal, a church member, a community centre director, a public health nurse, or others. Most governing boards meet on a monthly basis. The board hires the supervisor and evaluates his or her performance; the supervisor reports to the board on a regular basis. As with any other volunteer organization, there are some years when a strong bond exists and everything seems to work fairly well. In other years, when the board members are new to community work and do not understand what their responsibilities are, more guidance and support are required from an experienced supervisor or outside consultant.

Some child-care centres exist within a larger organization and may serve a function there, such as a lab school in a community college. These centres often have a parent advisory board. This kind of board has invited board members who may meet several times per year to consult with the management of the centres. The members are expected to offer advice and resources and also to raise concerns about current and future issues that affect the quality of care their children are receiving. They have no actual responsibilities to the centre, and their advice and concerns are for consideration only.

The following are specific responsibilities of the most common type. The governing board

- **develops all long-range and strategic plans affecting the organization**
- **ensures that the centre meets the needs of the people it serves through the design, development, and monitoring of appropriate programs**
- **develops, reexamines, and revises the mission statement, bylaws, and policies that govern the overall operation of the centre**
- **plans for and carefully monitors the financial solvency of the organization**
- **ensures that the organization meets all legal standards and government requirements**
- **maintains complete and accurate records of board meetings and operations**
- **approves all major contracts involving the organization**
- **selects the supervisor and delegates to her or him the authority to carry out the policies and deliver the programs**
- **provides a complete job description for the supervisor and regular performance-based reviews**
- **ensures that fair hiring and personnel policies are established and maintained**
- **determines staff responsibilities in job descriptions and sets out working conditions**
- **negotiates staff salaries and benefits each year**
- **assists the supervisor to market services, advocate, and fundraise**
- **works cooperatively at all times with the supervisor and the staff to accomplish objectives**

- **designs and administers family and staff questionnaires to monitor client satisfaction and program quality**
- **establishes standing committees that are required to report regularly to the board**
- **holds annual general meetings as outlined in the bylaws**
- **ensures regular communication with the general membership**
- **monitors and responds to government policies**
- **evaluates their own performance, as a board, in relation to established mission statement and goals**
- **ensures continuance of the organization through effective board succession**

In general most supervisors have a close relationship with the governing board of a child-care centre. Many arrange meeting times, meeting places, refreshments, copies of reports and minutes, and even run the meeting itself. For example, the supervisor might divide meeting agendas into three categories: items for information, items for decision, and items for discussion in order to help the meeting run efficiently. Other boards that are more independent will welcome the supervisor, hear his or her report, and carry on board business without help. Some staff members and supervisors are expected to attend board meetings but do not have a vote. The supervisor's most important role in supporting board governance is to help board members to understand what they can and cannot do. Some inexperienced board members in their enthusiasm will try to intervene in the day-to-day operations of the centre. These responsibilities lie with the supervisor, acting within board policies.

Some centres have instituted a system whereby one or two parents in each playroom are designated parent representatives. Their primary role is to keep families abreast of new developments in the centre and to be available to respond to parents' questions and concerns. The names and telephone numbers of parent representatives may be posted on a centre bulletin board. Some centres invite family representatives to monthly staff meetings. Any family member should be welcome to any board meeting, on the understanding that he or she will not have a vote. Confidentiality may become challenging when so many families know each other but personal information about individual

Supervisors working with a volunteer parent daycare centre board can expect to see a high turnover among the key players. Therefore, a supervisor must always be prepared to deal with changes among the board membership, sometimes at short notice. While there are many advantages to having the diverse experience and knowledge that a volunteer board brings to a centre, numerous difficulties may arise as well. Some family members join the board of directors solely to attend to their own agenda; they have great difficulty viewing the broader needs of the organization. It is vitally important, however, that the board take all children, parents, and staff into consideration when making a decision. Some family members feel that a position on the board of directors entitles them to make autonomous decisions in regard to the operations of the centre. Others may join the board and contribute little, either to discussions or assuming a portion of the workload. Some family members have a wealth of wonderful ideas but fail to follow through. Others have little understanding of the importance of legislation that affects the overall running of the centre. Supervisors need to be flexible, supportive, and involved in family education when working with a board of directors.

Source: Val Seibert, Supervisor, Kew Beach Child Care Centre

families should never be shared with others. Minutes of board meetings, omitting sensitive financial or personnel information, should be posted. This helps families to be informed about, and feel involved in, the centre's operations.

In addition to the board of directors, committees may be established to encourage family participation. Committees enable families or staff with specialized knowledge to apply their expertise and skills to the centre's advantage. They also provide a means of empowering family members who are unwilling or unable to take on the more demanding task of serving on the board of directors. Small working groups ensure an equitable distribution of responsibilities within the centre. Some examples of committees are Publicity Committee, Social Committee, Newsletter Committee, and committees organized for specific purposes such as redesigning and equipping the outdoor play space.

Many centres hold annual general meetings to review the previous year's work. Reports are made by the president of the board, an audited financial statement is presented, information by various committees and board members and a report by the supervisor or staff of the centre. This is an opportunity to vote on business items or changes to the bylaws of the organization. Individual family members may bring up situations or events that they have been particularly pleased with. Families

may use the annual general meeting to voice concerns and debate issues relevant to the program and operation of the centre. Additional general meetings can also be called by the board as needed or when a sensitive issue must be voted on. Members themselves may call meetings to discuss an issue, to pass a resolution or replace directors (Bertrand, 2008: 119). Minutes of board meetings are official records of the centre and should be stored as an historical record and posted for families to see.

THE FAMILY'S ROLE IN EVALUATION

Teachers have a responsibility to continually assess their performance and their interactions with the children, the parents, and their colleagues. Evaluations of the teachers by the supervisor and a member of the board of directors should be carried out on a regular basis. Teachers should also provide self-evaluations in which they detail their accomplishments, the areas they would like to target for further improvement, and their goals along with an action plan for achieving them.

The supervisor should also be part of a process that requires ongoing evaluation and goal-setting exercises. Teachers and families should both be represented in these evaluations of the supervisor, since these parties are affected by the supervisor's ability to provide leadership.

TABLE 5.1	COMMUNICATION WITH FAMILIES						
		ALWAYS	FREQUENTLY	OCCASIONALLY	SELDOM	NEVER	N/A
FAMILIES ARE VIEWED AS THE PRIMARY SOURCE OF LOVE AND CARE.							
A. ECEs recognize differences in family cultures							
• We consult with you about belief systems and preferred practices.							
• Pertinent information is available in different languages.							
• Efforts are made to learn significant words and phrases in families' home language.							
B. Consistent communication is the cornerstone to building confidence and partnership							
• The orientation process provided you with important information about your transition to the centre.							
• We are available (and approachable) at the beginning and end of the day.							
• Your views are acknowledged and responded to in a timely fashion.							
• Written communication occurs daily.							
• You are always informed if there is a concern during the day.							
• We ensure that you receive pertinent information on a timely basis.							
• We respond to your requests for formal or informal discussions.							
• The centre supervisor is available for formal or informal discussions.							
• Policies and procedures are outlined in the Family Handbook.							
• Program plans are posted to keep you informed of day-to-day activities.							
• The monthly newsletter is informative and gives relevant information about our centre.							
C. ECEs act as resources for families							
• We respond to concerns thoughtfully with resources appropriate to the situation.							
• A resource area (e.g., books, videos, cassettes) is available for your use.							
• Family bulletin boards reflect topics of interest to you.							
D. Families are encouraged to involve themselves in the centre							
• You and your children are greeted warmly.							
• Meetings are organized with family input and support your parenting role.							
• You are welcome in the centre at any time.							
• You are encouraged to participate in events such as field trips, committee work, special events, and volunteering in the playroom or for the advisory board. Your input regarding curriculum is encouraged.							
• You are informed of who the Family Representatives are.							
• Staff are responsive to your concerns and you are able to influence change in the centre in cooperation with staff.							
E. There is clear and ongoing communication whenever there is a change in your child's life							
• You receive information about the practices via print material and/or discussions with us.							
• Transitions are gradual and your child's progress is monitored and shared.							
• You receive enough information to feel comfortable when your child enters the centre.							
• You receive enough information to feel comfortable when your child moves from room to room.							
Comments							

Source: Courtesy George Brown College

Teachers and supervisors receive informal feedback from families through their daily exchanges. If families are to be true partners in the operation of the centre, their ideas and criticisms should be of vital importance to the staff and administration. While it may not always be feasible to implement parents' suggestions, families must have their ideas taken seriously and implemented whenever possible. A suggestion box located at the centre allows families to anonymously express their observations, ideas, and comments. The contents of the box must be read and responded to on a regular basis. A centre might acknowledge in its newsletter suggestion-box ideas that have been integrated into the program.

Janeway

Child Care Centre

EXIT SURVEY

We hope that the time you have spent with us at Janeway Child Care Centre has been a positive experience for your child and your family. We would appreciate it if you took a few minutes to give us some feedback about what pleased you and areas in which you feel we could improve our performance. Our focus is always to provide the best possible environment for the children in our care, and your comments will give us insight into areas where we could enrich our program.

1. How old was your child when you first enrolled in the centre?
2. How old is your child now?
3. As a new parent, how satisfied were you with the orientation you received?
4. Did you find the home visit a helpful part of the orientation process?
5. Have you been satisfied with the care your child has received at the centre as well as our ability to provide a healthy and safe environment:

    in the infant room _____ in the preschool room _____
    in the toddler room _____ in the school-age room _____

6. Did you feel the program met your child's needs emotionally, socially, intellectually, physically, and creatively?
7. Did you feel that staff were friendly, respectful, and professional in their communications with you?
8. Was there a welcoming atmosphere in the centre and did you feel that you and your extended family were able to make spontaneous visits?
9. Did you feel that you were adequately informed about events, parent meetings, and information related to the centre through newsletters, bulletin boards, telephone calls, and so on?
10. Did you feel that the supervisor and board of directors were responsive to any concerns or issues that were important to you?
11. Did you feel that you had ample opportunity and encouragement to participate in the centre if you wanted to?
12. Did you feel that the family–teacher conferences were positive opportunities to share information? Was there anything about the conferences that you would like to change?
13. Did you feel the physical environment (indoors and outdoors) was suitable and that adequate toys and materials were available?
14. Would you recommend our centre to another parent?
15. Please feel free to add any other comments.

Other centres distribute parent questionnaires biannually or annually. These more formal assessments can be used to find out

- the types of meetings families might be interested in,
- family members' thoughts about the orientation they received when they joined the centre,
- the topics families would like to have addressed at meetings and in newsletters,
- family ideas about fundraising,
- the talents and interests families have that could be shared with the children or be used to improve the centre,
- family ideas for field trips,
- which committees family members would be willing to serve on,
- family ideas about food and ideas for recipes that reflect cultural backgrounds, and
- how family–teacher conferences could be improved.

Family questionnaires should be clear about the purpose of questionnaire, well-designed, and concise (families may not respond to a survey that is unduly time-consuming). The results of the questionnaires should be communicated to families as soon as possible and acted on when necessary. Another valuable assessment tool is the exit survey. A sample of part of a family questionnaire and exit survey are provided in Table 5.1.

Exit surveys are perhaps the most honest feedback we will ever receive. Families are leaving the centre and they have nothing to lose in giving us their true opinions. Despite asking for feedback, some families will hold back afraid that their input may jeopardize their relationships with the teachers and in some instances that their comments if negative would be "taken out" on their child.

Putting surveys on the centre's website will also give families an opportunity to respond when they are most able and can be sent back electronically.

INVOLVE FAMILIES IN ADVOCACY

There is no question that families and teachers should be aware of public policy and how it affects families in our country. Municipal, provincial, and federal governments make decisions that affect the quality of life that families can provide for their children. But many teachers and families are hesitant to become involved because they feel powerless and lack the confidence to effect change: they often do not feel they have the time to become involved; they state that they don't know enough about how government legislation affects child care; and, for some families, any involvement with government officials may bring back difficult memories and they may be afraid to get involved. Informed supervisors and teachers can keep families abreast of changes in legislation and impending decisions that will have consequences for their children.

INSIDE LOOK

In order to draw attention to the government's pending child-care cuts, the Burnaby Association for Community Inclusion (BACI) in British Columbia began the "Diaper Campaign" in 2002. BACI parents began sending one diaper per child to the minister responsible for the child-care budget with a note asking for cuts to be reconsidered. This action received attention in the press, prompting a letter to the editor from the minister. At the same time, BC Parent Voices, a project sponsored by the Child Care Advocacy Association of Canada and funded by the Social Development Partnerships Program of Human Resources Development Canada, launched the BC-wide diaper campaign at the Coalition of Child Care Advocates' annual general meeting. Parents from across British Columbia participated in the campaign, sending diapers to MLAs, the finance minister, and the premier.

This supportive action greatly magnified the power and impact of the original diaper message.

Source: www.childcareadvocacy.ca/parent_voices.

But reporting on research and data is not enough. We need to involve all of the stakeholders and decision makers and engage them in moving from theory to practice. The health and well-being of our children should be of concern to all Canadians, they are our future! With support and encouragement, families can become important allies in this process. Strong bonds are established when staff and families join forces to advocate on behalf of children and there is safety in numbers. Governments at all levels should be pressured to guarantee that early childhood teachers are well paid and trained so that they have the ability and time to invite family participation and the knowledge to provide parents with clear strategies for rich relationships with their children. Many family members who become involved in child-care-related issues are inspired to write to community newspapers or government officials, to gather petitions, to appear as interviewees on radio and TV shows, and to attend relevant workshops and conferences.

The importance of parents to lobbying efforts on behalf of children is well expressed by Pat Wege, past chairperson of the Manitoba Child Care Association:

> It is critical that parents who rely on child care to "keep Canada working" be at the forefront of lobby issues. When our association meets with government, we are often reminded that the majority of parent users are silent on child-care issues. What we say to government is then viewed as self-serving. The future growth and stability of child care in Canada will rest in the hands of parents who must be educated as lobbyists, along with the parents of tomorrow, grandparents, aunts, uncles, employers. Everyone has a stake in child care.

At the 2008 Leighton G. McCarthy Memorial Panel Discussion, "Acting On A Vision For Universal Child Care: Integrating Early Childhood Education and Support Services for Families,"—hosted by the Institute of Child Study 2008—panel members Professor Carl Corter, Janet Davis, the Honourable Ken Dryden, Paul Tough, Justin Trudeau, and the Honourable Margaret Norrie McCain spoke eloquently about the need for family involvement in advocating for the support systems that they need to raise healthy families. The public needs to be engaged to understand that early experiences get under the skin. We need to help parents understand that they have power and as advocates for these families, we all need to support their efforts to organize to speak up on behalf of their families. Every parent should understand how far behind we are; reports from the OECD make it clear that we are lagging behind world efforts for young children and their families in industrialized countries. In our own communities, how many people know about the work being done in early childhood? Funding will not come without public engagement.

INSIDE LOOK

Hats off to Jody Dallaire and the other hard-working parents of Parents for Quality Care in Moncton, New Brunswick. They have worked cooperatively and collaboratively to share information, experiences, and challenges; discuss successful campaigns, activities, and strategies; highlight child-care issues; and bring parents' perspectives to the child-care advocacy movement at the provincial, territorial, and pan-Canadian level. Over the last year Jody has represented Parents for Quality Care (Moncton) and has participated with other committed parents in the Parent Voices Network and in the Child Care Advocacy Association's Council of Child Care Advocates. Parent Voices: Making the Case for Child Care is a project sponsored by CCAAC, and funded through the Social Development Partnerships Program of Human Resources Development Canada. Parent Voices is all about working with parents from coast to coast to coast to make the case for quality, affordable, and accessible child care. The funding allows us to provide a range of supports to parent advocacy. It has also provided excellent opportunities and encouragement for parent representatives and groups, including New Brunswick's Parents for Quality Care, to participate with others in child-care advocacy efforts. See their website at **www.parentvoices.ca**.

Source: Dianne Goldberg, Project Consultant, Parent Voices Network

ORGANIZATIONS THAT SUPPORT ADVOCACY EFFORTS

Collaborative Centre of Knowledge for Child and Youth Well-Being in Ontario

The Offord Centre for Child Studies and Voices for Children are calling for a Collaborative Centre of Knowledge for Child and Youth Well-Being in Ontario. This independent Collaborative Centre would bring together multiple partners representing a diversity of sectors and perspectives including government, universities, health, education, social services, private foundations, independent agencies and community-based groups, and individuals including parents and youth. The goal of the Centre is to be a catalyst for transforming the knowledge landscape by bringing together partners to build on promising approaches and create practical and lasting solutions to gathering and sharing knowledge about the healthy development of children and youth in their communities across Canada. Once the centre is established, it would link up with or help to create other such provincial centres across Canada to form a national network that would connect, expand and improve data, research, reporting and knowledge mobilization efforts across the country (Gardner and Vine, 2007).

The Vanier Institute of the Family

The Vanier Institute of the Family is another organization dedicated to advocating for child care and the Canadian family. Their website provides the following description of the organization:

> The vision of the Vanier Institute is to make families as important to the life of Canadian society as they are to the lives of individual Canadians. Their mission statement is to create awareness of, and to provide leadership on, the importance and strengths of families in Canada and the challenges they face in their structural, demographic, economic, cultural, and social diversity. Information from the Institute's research, consultation, and policy development is conveyed through advocacy, education, and communications vehicles to elected officials, policy makers, educators and researchers, the business community, the media, social service professionals, the public, and Canadian families themselves.
>
> The Vanier Institute of the Family, established in 1965 under the patronage of Their Excellencies Governor-General Georges P. Vanier and Madame Pauline Vanier, is a national, charitable organization

dedicated to promoting the well-being of Canadian families. It is governed by a volunteer board with regional representation from across Canada. (http://www.vifamily.ca/about/vision.html)

Family Involvement Network of Educators

Another important advocacy website is the Family Involvement Network of Educators (FINE)—http://www.finenetwork.org—sponsored by the Harvard Family Research Project. It provides an opportunity to exchange ideas, resources, and tools to strengthen the capacity of families, schools, and communities for effective partnership. In the resource section there is a rich and diverse offering of research materials and tools.

Harvard Family Research Project

Harvard Family Research Project (HFRP) believes that for children and youth to be successful from birth through adolescence, there must be an array of learning supports around them. These learning supports include families, early childhood programs, schools, out-of-school time programs and activities, higher education, health and social service agencies, businesses, libraries, museums and other community based institutions. HFRP calls this network of supports complementary learning. Complementary learning is characterized by discrete linkages that work together to encourage consistent learning and developmental outcomes for children (Weiss, Caspe, and Lopez, 2006). More information is available online at **www.gse. harvard.edu/hfrp/projects/fine/resources/research/ earlychildhood.html**.

Canadian Child Care Federation

Contributed by Karen Chandler, founding member of the CCCF

The Canadian Child Care Federation (CCCF) is a national organization that plays a leadership role in research and policy development, providing information services and publications for members and the general public aimed at improving services for young Canadian children and families. CCCF facilitates networks among families, government policy makers, and other relevant organizations. It has many projects and services helpful to practitioners, families, and those working with families, including an award-winning magazine **Interaction**, which has many articles focused on

First Call

As a child-care advocate, my involvement with First Call has been a deepening and broadening experience in a multitude of ways. First Call is a coalition of over 40 organizations in British Columbia that advocate on behalf of children, youth, and families. While each organization has its own particular focus and mandate, First Call brings us together in a powerful collective voice regarding issues and activities of shared concern.

To this table I have brought information and advocacy initiatives to advance high-quality, affordable, accessible child care. At this table I have found important new allies to help take the child-care message forward. Through this table I have learned from others and have become informed and engaged in a myriad of other concerns—child poverty, child labour, the plight of sexually exploited youth, the desperate need for preventative services to families, and the lack of coherent social policies and programs to meet community needs.

Within First Call I have developed personal and working relationships with many knowledgeable, passionate activists, who are tireless in their effort to promote social justice, equity of outcomes, meaningful community development, and citizen empowerment. From them I have learned how interconnected our issues really are, and how child care is indeed a cornerstone in the building of healthy families. Thanks to First Call I have sharpened my own skills in effective advocacy strategies and have in turn been able to share those skills with students, colleagues, and the many child-care organizations in which I volunteer. Having taken part in brief writing, postcard campaigns, media connections, public rallies, and networking in the family services community, I say hats off to First Call for the energy, mutual support, organizational strength, and collaborative approach they model!

Source: Gyda Chud, Vancouver Community College. Reprinted by permission.

work with families. Over 80 resource sheets for families; sample topics include respecting children's rights at home, travelling with infants, and sun safety. This information can be accessed through the Federation's website at **www.qualitychildcare-canada.ca**.

Centre of Excellence for Early Childhood Development

The Centre of Excellence for Early Childhood Development operates under the administrative leadership of the University of Montreal, in partnership with the following organizations:

- Canadian Childcare Federation, Ottawa, Ontario
- Canadian Institute of Child Health, Ottawa, Ontario
- IWK Grace Health Centre, Halifax, Nova Scotia

- University of British Columbia, Vancouver, British Columbia
- Conseil de la Nation Atikamekw, Wemotaci, Quebec
- Queen's University, Kingston, Ontario
- L'Hopital St-Justine, Montreal, Quebec
- Institut de la santé publique du Québec, Quebec City, Quebec
- Canadian Paediatric Society, Ottawa, Ontario
- Centre de Psycho-Education du Québec, Montreal, Quebec

These organizations make up the core group that provides direction to the work of the centre, as it support parents and families to raise children with happy and healthy lifestyles by providing useful, readable information on the early years. Using traditional communication methods such as articles, newsletters, and workshops, as well as state-of-the-art multi-media, including videos and CD-ROMs, the centre consolidates expert knowledge on early childhood development and disseminates it to parents and service providers.

The Childcare Resource and Research Unit

The CRRU focuses on research and policy resources in the context of a high quality system of early childhood education and child care in Canada. The Childcare Resource and Research Unit was established to provide public education, resources, and consultation on ECEC policy and research; foster and support research in various fields focusing on ECEC; carry out relevant research projects and publish the results; and support, promote, and provide communication on ECEC policy and research.

CRRU plays an integral role in the policy development process by:

- anticipating the need for information resources on particular ECEC issues;
- collecting, organizing, packaging and disseminating ECEC information resources;
- keeping up-to-date on new information and developments related to programs, research and policy in the ECEC field;
- facilitating communication among people involved in ECEC;
  providing interpretations of research and policy materials in a form useful for people with an interest in ECEC in Canada; and
- undertaking research and evaluation as well as supporting and consulting with others involved in these activities.

CRRU produces a number of publications including an Occasional Paper series, *BRIEFing NOTES*, other publications and videotapes. Part of CRRU's mandate is to collect, organize, and synthesize ECEC information resources and to make them widely available; CRRU's website supports this mandate. The website collects and provides links to noteworthy ECEC research and resources, policy developments, news clippings, links, and events. The website (**www.childcarecanada.org**) is also updated with new materials on a weekly basis and a weekly email notification provides links to new resources.

REFERENCES

Belsky, J. 2005. "Social-Contextual Determinants of Parenting." In R.J. Tremblay, R.E. Barr, and R. Peters, eds., *Encyclopedia of Child Development*. Montreal, QC.

Booth Church, E. 1994. "Learning from Our Elders." *Scholastic Early Childhood Today*. November–December.

Canadian Gardening. 1999. "Putting Down Roots." October–November.

Carter, N., and C. Harvey. 1996. "Gaining Perspective on Parenting Groups." *Zero to Three* 16 (6).

Chastain, D. 1980. "Qualities of a Successful Trainer." *Voluntary Action Leadership*. Spring.

Child Care Connection–N.S. 1995. "Sharing beyond Our Classroom Borders: Our World of Caring—Toys and Clothes to Bosnian Children." Fall: 4.

City of Toronto. 2002. "MOH Keynote Address." Toronto Father Involvement Forum. April. Available at http://www.toronto.ca/health/moh/fif_index.htm.

Evans, J. 1999. "Men in the Lives of Children." Available at http://www.ecdgroup.com/cn//cn16lead.html.

Fagan, J. 1997. "Patterns of Mother and Father Involvement in Child Care." *Child and Youth Care Forum* 26: 113–126.

Fagan, J., and G. Palm. 2004. *Fathers and Early Childhood Programs*. New York: Thomson Delmar Learning.

Fantuzzo, J., and C. McWayne. 2002. "The Relationship Between Peer-Play Interactions in the Family Context and Dimensions of School Readiness For Low-Income Preschool Children." *Journal of Educational Psychology* 94 (1): 79–87.

Fox, L.A. 2002. "The Gift That Gives Twice." *The Toronto Star*. October 26. R5

Gardner, S., and C. Vine. 2007. "What Do We Know About Ontario's Children and Youth? The Critical Case for a Collaborative Centre of Knowledge Innovation for Child and Youth Well-Being in Ontario." Final Report, April.

Gordon, A. 2008. "They Cut Problems Down To Size." *The Toronto Star*. May 17. L7.

Hepworth Berger, E. 2000. *Parents as Partners in Education*. Columbus, Ohio: Merrill.

Hoffman, J. 2005. "When Dads And Babies Build a Strong Relationship, Everybody Wins." *Today's Parent*. April. Available at http://www.cfii.ca/fiion.

Keyser, J. 2006. *From Parents to Partners: Building A Family-Centered Early Childhood Program*. St. Paul, MN: Redleaf Press.

Krakow, E. 2007. "Parenting Matters." *Bulletin of the Centre of Excellence for Early Childhood Development* 6 (1). March.

Lamb-Parker, F., A.Y. Boak, K.W. Griffin, C. Ripple, and L. Peay. 1999. "Parent–Child Relationship, Home Learning Environment, and School Readiness." *School Psychology Review* 28 (3): 413–425.

Levine, J., and E.W. Pitt. 1997. "Community Strategies for Responsible Fatherhood: On-Ramps to Connection." *Zero to Three* 18 (1). August–September.

Levine, J.A., D.T. Murphy, and S. Wilson. 1993. *Getting Men Involved: Strategies for Early Childhood Programs*. New York: Scholastic.

Lyons, C.W. 1986. "Interagency Alliances Link Young and Old." *Children Today*. September–October.

Mann, B. 1999. "New Times, New Fathers." Available at http://www.cfc-efc.ca/docs/00000112.htm.

Marshall, N.L., A.E. Noonan, K. McCartney, F. Marx, and N. Keefe. 2001. "It Takes An Urban Village: Parenting Networks of Urban Families." *Journal of Family Issues* 22 (2): 163–182.

McBride, B., and R. McBride. 1993. "Parent Education and Support Programs for Fathers." *Childhood Education.* Fall.

Meyerhoff, J.K. 1994. "Of Baseball and Babies: Are You Unconsciously Discouraging Father Involvement in Infant Care?" *Young Children.* May.

Murphy Kilbride, K., and J. Pollard. 1990. "Differences in Interactions of Teachers with Visible Minority Children." Available at http://ceris.metropolis.net/Virtual%20Library/education/kilbride1.

Neugebauer, B. 1994. "Beginnings Workshop: Going One Step Further: No Traditional Holidays." *Child Care Information Exchange* 100. November–December.

Newman, S., and J. Riess. 1992. "Older Workers in Intergenerational Child Care." *Journal of Gerontological Social Work* 19 (2): 45–66.

Ryerse, C. 1993. "Day Care Connection Intergenerational Program." *Focus.* Canadian Child Care Federation. October.

Schorr, L. 1997. *Common Purpose: Strengthening Families and Neighborhoods to Rebuild America.* New York: Anchor Books Doubleday.

Sheehan, N., and L. Wood. 1993. *Adoption and the Schools Project: A Guide for Educators*, vol. 2. Children's Bureau, Administration for Children, Youth and Families, Office of Human Development Services, U.S. Department of Health and Human Services.

Smith, T.B., and S. Newman. 1993. "Older Adults in Early Childhood Programs: Why and How." *Young Children.* March.

United Nations. 2001. *The State of the World's Children 2001.* New York: The United Nations Children's Fund (UNICEF).

Walters Anderson, M. 1993. "The Formative Years." *Volunteer Grandparents Society of British Columbia.* Commemorative Issue (Fall).

Wardle, F. 1994. "Beginnings Workshop: Celebrations, Festivals, Holidays: What Should We Be Doing?" *Child Care Information Exchange* 100. November–December.

Weiss, H., M. Caspe, and M.E. Lopez. 2006. "Harvard Research Project, Family Involvement in Early Childhood Education." *Family Involvement in Early Childhood Education* 1 (Spring).

Wilson, M. 1976. *The Effective Management of Volunteer Programs.* Boulder, CO: Volunteer Management Association.

Courtesy of Lynn Wilson

CHAPTER 6

Verbal Communication with Families

Courtesy of University of Toronto, Child Care "on Charles Street"

"Your beliefs become your thoughts. Your thoughts become your words. Your words become your actions. Your actions become your habits. Your habits become your values. Your values become your destiny."

—*Mahatma Gandhi*

LEARNING OUTCOMES

After studying this chapter, you will be able to

1. discuss and analyze the strategies for achieving effective communication among family members and teachers

2. identify the sources of family–teacher conflict and outline a strategy for conflict resolution

3. summarize the research on day-to-day interactions with families and suggest strategies for making these interactions more meaningful

Principles of Effective Verbal Communication

In the field of early childhood education, a teacher's ability to communicate with family members in an effective and responsive manner is the basis on which meaningful relationships are developed. In order to establish a positive climate for communication, teachers must acknowledge the critical role that family members should play in the operation and day-to-day functioning of the centre. Teachers' interactions with family members must reflect a belief that they are valued members of the child-care team and have a right to be represented when decisions are made that will affect their children. When family members feel valued and believe that their ideas are listened to and acted on, they become more responsive. When this climate of mutual respect is established, the parent, teacher, and child all benefit enormously. When teachers look for opportunities to support family members, they eliminate the adversarial approach so detrimental to effective and meaningful communication. Since each partnership with each family will be unique, teachers need to be effective and skillful in their interactions.

Powell (1989) identifies three types of parents who use child-care centres. The **first type** views the centre and the family as independent systems; these parents rarely communicate with staff and avoid discussing family matters or child-rearing values. The **second type** sees themselves as dependent on the centre for child-rearing information but communicate little about their families or their expectations for the program. The **third type** exhibits an interdependent pattern of communication; they receive information from the centre and openly share information and family values with the centre. The teacher will need to use different interpersonal communication strategies for each of these groups.

There is no question that the building of meaningful relationships between family members and teachers requires a time commitment from all parties, particularly from the teacher. Good teachers will embrace this concept and accept that they will not always be financially compensated for the time they commit to establishing a significant alliance with families. The reward for their efforts comes in the form of an effective partnership with families and a better working environment.

What Makes an Effective Communicator?

According to Adler and Towne (1993), effective communicators are people who are able to get what they are seeking from another person while maintaining the relationship on terms that are acceptable to all parties. Competent communicators, they suggest, are able to take others' points of view into consideration and to analyze a situation in a variety of ways. Chud and Fahlman (1995: 109) suggest the following guidelines for developing effective communication skills:

1. Listen without making assumptions.
2. Check personal perceptions.
3. Seek feedback.
4. Resist making judgments.
5. Practice self-awareness.
6. Take risks and be willing to make mistakes.
7. Extend patience, good will, and caring.

In order to establish strong working relationships with families, teachers must be able to establish a basic foundation of trust. This process must begin the first moment families enter the centre. Teachers who express acceptance, support, and enthusiasm in their initial dealings with families are establishing the groundwork for an effective partnership. In the sections that follow, various communication strategies that teachers can employ in building this partnership are examined.

Language Use

Words can reflect attitudes of respect or disrespect, inclusion or exclusion, judgment or acceptance. The words you choose can facilitate or impede communication. Taking care with language enables professionals to examine their own thoughts and attitudes and helps them build collegial, open, and respectful relationships with families (Hughson, 1994–95: 56). One of the first steps is to be able to call each family member by their correct name and use the proper pronunciation.

Effective verbal communication is critical to the success of the family–teacher relationship. Initiating, developing, and maintaining positive working relationships with families take considerable skill and effort. Teachers must be able to adjust their language interactions based on the individual family members in their room. They must also avoid the use of accusatory language. "Alex is

A trusting relationship is the foundation of positive interactions.

acting out in the centre. Is something going on at home?" implies that the teacher suspects the problem lies with the parent. The use of more inclusive language to describe the behaviour is more likely to encourage cooperation: "We've noticed that Alex has been very weepy at daycare the last few days. Have you noticed this at home?" "Preaching, judging, interrupting, laughing and ridicule, commands, exaggeration, insult, manipulation, control and threats are all communication killers. Avoid them" (Ontario English Catholic Teachers Association, n.d.)

Additionally, teachers should avoid engaging in ECE shoptalk with family members or peppering their conversations with ECE jargon that will be incomprehensible to many of them. Teachers should also avoid using phrases like "Why don't you . . .?", "If I were you I would . . .", "I don't think you understand . . .", "You should . . .", or any sentence that contains a "but," since it negates everything that comes before it—"That approach is okay, but . . .".

The tone and delivery of a verbal communication carry as much expressive weight as the actual, spoken words. Teachers need to be aware that, however carefully worded, a message expressed in a joking manner may be interpreted as sarcastic and inappropriate by some family members. Teachers also need to monitor the volume of their delivery. Being too soft-spoken can be just as frustrating to the listener as speaking to non-English-speaking parents in a very loud voice under the misguided belief that the greater the volume, the greater the understanding. The speed of delivery also affects the way messages are interpreted. Teachers should observe parents' reactions carefully and when in doubt ask for confirmation that the communication was understood. Teachers should also make an effort to learn key words and phrases in the various languages spoken by family members in the centre.

In order to communicate in a nonjudgmental manner, teachers should make use of "I" language. Consider this example. Taryn's father is late for the second evening in a row. Rather than say "You're late again," adopt a less aggressive approach by using "I" language: "When you're late I feel upset because it means that I will miss my train." A teacher who uses this example of "I" language communicates, in a non-accusatory manner, three things: the other person's behaviour, her feelings about it, and the consequences of that behaviour.

Appropriately used, humour can defuse a difficult situation.

Verbal Communication Skills

1. Do you communicate with family members in a clear, concise, and respectful manner?

2. Do you make every effort to see things from the parent's perspective?

3. Do you use inclusive language that empowers family members?

4. Do you choose your words carefully, using "I" language to demonstrate your awareness of nonjudgmental communication?

5. Do you make an effort to learn key words and phrases in the languages spoken by the families in your centre?

6. Do you encourage family members to express themselves and take care not to dominate the conversation?

7. Do you make arrangements to support family members who are not able to effectively communicate in English or use sign language?

8. Do you avoid the use of ECE jargon where appropriate?

When communicating with family members whose first language is not English, an interpreter may be required. Dotsch (1999) outlines some ideas for consideration: "[T]rained professional interpreters are not easy to find. There are many different languages and dialects spoken, interpreters may not be readily available, there may be funding issues, the family may feel embarrassed to ask for an interpreter and finally, some agencies require that families find their own interpreters." She emphasizes the importance of finding professional interpreters who are fluent in the language. They should have a certificate or letter validating their training, and centres should ask for references. It is also helpful if the interpreter has a background in working with families and young children and is familiar with concepts and terminology in early childhood education. It is critical that they be able to interpret information accurately and without distortion. Interpreters should also be cognizant of refugee or immigrant issues and be sensitive to nonverbal responses while displaying equal respect to both parties.

Some Helpful Hints

- Make sure the interpreter is oriented to the purpose of the session, their role, and the process.
- Prepare written information ahead of time for discussion with the family.
- Organize the information in a logical sequence.
- Use visuals (props, pictures, animation, gestures).
- Content should be very focused and limited.
- Keep sentences short and simple, and avoid jargon.

Many, and sometimes most, of the critical meanings generated in human encounters are elicited by touch, glance, vocal nuance, gestures, or facial expressions with or without the aid of words. From the moment of recognition until the moment of separation, people observe each other with all their senses, hearing pause and intonation, attending to dress and carriage, observing glance and facial tension, as well as noting word choice and syntax. Every harmony or disharmony of signals guides the interpretation of passing mood or enduring attribute. Out of the evaluation of kinetic, vocal and verbal cues, decisions are made to argue or agree, to laugh or blush, to relax or resist, or to continue or cut off conversation."

Source: Brislin, 1993: 211, in Samovar et al., 2007: 195.

- Convey one idea at a time and in a logical sequence, and provide opportunities for questions and discussion.
- Provide summaries instead of detailed information.
- Provide enough pauses for the interpreter to organize the information.
- Verify or clarify the information gathered from the interpreter.
- Teachers must be patient enough to let the interpreter speak uninterrupted.
- Teachers should be attentive and maintain interest when the interpreter is speaking to the family.

A more in-depth look at the role of the interpreter is available in Dotsch (1999).

NONVERBAL INTERACTION

We cannot not communicate! Our nonverbal interactions with others "speak" for us even if we are not aware of it or did not intend it. We are capable of 700,000 different physical signs, 250,000 facial expressions, 5,000 distinct hand gestures, and 1,000 different postures. Most nonverbal messages arrive before the verbal and will influence the interaction and so there are many opportunities for misunderstanding. Most facial expressions last for two or three seconds but micro expressions—which occur when people are concealing how they feel—last for

Courtesy of University of Toronto, Child Care "on Charles Street"

Nonverbal communication can send powerful messages.

only a fraction of that, just 1/25 of a second. Most of us miss these valuable nonverbal signs but they can provide valuable insight into true feelings. It is not surprising that, at times, we have difficulty interpreting the meaning of our observations. Teachers need to be conscious of their nonverbal interactions and aware of the messages they are sending. Some actions serve to block communication—arms folded across the chest, foot tapping, pen flicking, leaning back, or turning away. Facial expressions that are welcoming—a warm smile upon greeting family members and children, a gentle touch to console a troubled child—contribute to a positive and open climate for communication.

Reactions to various nonverbal behaviours vary significantly from culture to culture and from family member to family member. It is important to know that someone's cultural background doesn't necessarily predict certain behaviours. Few cultural patterns are rigid or apply to all members of a particular culture. For example, not maintaining eye contact may indicate indifference or boredom to one parent but respect to another. In North American or western cultures, a good listener is seen as paying attention if direct eye contact is made with the speaker. But eye to eye contact is not the correct custom in many Asian or Native cultures. Something as simple as angling your body away from a family member may indicate a lack of interest or concern. Similarly, touch can be perceived as an invasion of personal space in some cultures but a gesture of endearment in others. What may seem to the teacher as a simple gesture, for example, touching the top of a child's head may in fact be a gesture that to the parent means the teacher has stolen the child's spirit. Touching rules

are governed by status, power, and respect. We become more aware of our own patterns of nonverbal communication when we are exposed to those who patterns are different from ours. As teachers become more familiar with individual families, they will be able to adapt their behaviour accordingly.

Teachers who always appear too busy to talk when families arrive tend to convey the message that they are not interested in communicating with them. Family members who rush into the centre and pick-up their child with barely a word to the teachers communicate a similar lack of interest. These are all silent but powerful messages. Teachers need to expand their ability to understand silent messages in ways that they were intended.

Gestures

Gestures are both innate and learned. They are used in all cultures, tend to be tied to speech processes, and are usually automatic. Arabs have catalogued 247 separate gestures they use while speaking. In a large study of 40 cultures 20 common hand gestures were isolated that had a different meaning in each culture. You can see the importance of gestures in intercultural communication because some gestures that are positive, humorous, or harmless in some cultures can have the opposite meaning in other cultures. Because there are thousands of gestures found in every culture, the teacher will have to do his or her homework!

EFFECTIVE LISTENING

Although we're capable of understanding speech at rates up to 600 words per minute, the average person speaks between 100–140 words per minute.

INSIDE LOOK

After missing an exam, a Japanese student came to [my] office hours. During the visit, the student continually giggled, averted her eyes, and held her hand over her mouth. From a Western perspective, the student's nonverbal behaviour suggested she was not serious (laughing), deceptive (averting eyes), and very nervous (hand over mouth). . . . The student offered no reason for missing the exam and did not ask for a retake. She simply apologized for not being there. A third party, however, had already told your author that the student's absence was due to the death of her grandfather. This demonstrates the importance of not assuming that nonverbal feedback in one culture carries the same meaning in another.

Source: Samovar et al., 2007: 345.

EXHIBIT 6.1 TEST YOUR LISTENING HABITS

Respond with "often" or "seldom" to each of the following situations. The speaker is a family member and you are the teacher.

When you and I are talking together . . .

 1. Your attention is divided. You interrupt our conversation by answering the phone or addressing the needs of others who come by your door. _____

 2. You begin shaking your head or saying "no" before I finish. _____

 3. You fidget, squirm, and look at the clock as though you cannot wait to move to other, more important projects and conversations. _____

 4. You begin asking questions before I finish my message. _____

 5. You ask questions that let me know you were not really listening.

 6. You finish my sentences for me as though nothing I have to say could be new to you. _____

 7. You try to speed things up and leap ahead with ideas or conclusions as though we are in a rush. _____

 8. You change the agenda by taking over and changing the content of the conversation. _____

 9. You express interest by asking thoughtful questions and by contributing your insights. _____

10. You make jokes about things that are serious to me and thereby belittle my concerns. _____

11. You get defensive and argue before I can fully explain my point. _____

12. You make me feel as if this is the most important thing you could be doing right now and that your time is truly mine. _____

13. You follow up on what we discussed and keep me posted on what is happening. _____

14. You are sensitive to the tone of what I have to say and respond respectfully. _____

15. You give me credit for ideas and projects that grow out of our communications. _____

16. You smile at me and make me feel comfortable and valued. _____

17. You seem to assume I have something worthwhile to say. _____

18. You ask questions that demonstrate your efforts to understand what I have to say. _____

19. Whether or not you agree with me, you make me feel that my opinions and feelings are respected. _____

Source: Adapted from *Are You Listening?* (Redmond, WA: Exchange Press), p. 977. Reprinted by permission.

Therefore, we have a lot of spare time to spend while someone is talking. The trick is to use this spare time to understand the speaker's ideas better rather than let our attention wander (Adler, Rosenfeld, and Towne, 1992: 217–18).

Although effective listening is critical to relationship-building, we listen carefully only a small percentage of the time. In the playroom, the teacher is bombarded with sounds—music, laughter, blocks crashing—that interfere with the ability to listen carefully. When family members are dropping off their children and relaying messages, it can be very difficult for a teacher to give them the attention they deserve. As family members are speaking, teachers may be listening for signs that the children are restless or need help, or they may be thinking of what needs to be done in the playroom, or perhaps they are wrapped up in their own personal concerns. In difficult situations, some teachers spend their listening time preparing a rebuttal rather than concentrating on what is being said.

PERCEPTION-CHECKING

Misunderstandings frequently arise during communication. Families may misinterpret information that the child brings home, or a child may not understand a teacher's intention. Conversely, a teacher may be unclear about information the child shares about his or her family. Face-to-face interactions may also be misinterpreted. An important

Teachers need to maintain a positive approach when interacting with an angry parent.

meant; (2) two or more possible interpretations of the behaviour; and (3) a request for clarification.

The key to perception-checking is to restate the other person's comments or nonverbal communication in your own words. Thus, a teacher might say to a parent: "When you left the centre this morning you seemed upset. I'm not sure if you were worrying about getting to work on time or if there is something about the care we are giving Rashid that you are unhappy with. Is there anything you are feeling uncomfortable about that you would like to share with us?" A perception check can succeed only if the teacher's nonverbal behaviour reflects her words. It is crucial that teachers deal with ambiguous situations as they arise, seeking clarification rather than second-guessing family members or making decisions based on inaccurate information.

AVOIDING JUDGMENTS

Most teachers would agree that it is essential to understand a family member's ideas before forming an opinion, but many teachers tend to make snap judgments before hearing them out, especially when a family member's ideas or values conflict with their own. For example, a challenging parent who is critical, complaining, and overprotective may be masking feelings of inadequacy, guilt, or feelings of exclusion.

strategy teachers can use to verify what family members have communicated to them is paraphrasing or perception-checking. This strategy comprises three sequential components: (1) a restatement of what the teacher thought the parent

INSIDE LOOK

It is the end of the day. Tamara, a preschool teacher, is engaged with two children. A parent enters the playroom and Tamara nods her head in recognition. Tamara leaves the children and begins to busily organize the drying rack with her back to the parent. The parent picks up her child and leaves the room. Not a word was spoken by either party. Tamara has deliberately chosen not to engage this parent, who she finds difficult to work with. What she doesn't know is that this parent has recently lost her mother and is struggling in her own role as a parent. The parent just didn't feel close enough to Tamara to discuss her loss and how it has affected her and her family.

INSIDE LOOK

Whenever Samir's parents came to pick him up at the end of the day, he would always be anxious to discuss his artwork or projects with them. It seemed to me that they showed little interest in his work. I used to wish they would be more outwardly expressive and positive about his accomplishments. It wasn't until I was invited to their home and saw Samir's work proudly displayed in a place of honour that I realized they were as pleased with Samir's work as I was. They just celebrated in another way.

Teacher: I find it very frustrating dealing with Kelly's mother. She brings Kelly in most mornings after 10:30 a.m. We are often getting ready for our walk, and a few times we have had to wait for her. Not only that, but Kelly misses out on all of the morning activities. I don't think her mother appreciates how inconvenient it is for us. It says in our family manual that the children are all to be in the centre by 9:30 a.m. I have tried to talk to Kelly's mother about this, but she refuses to change her morning routine.

Kelly's mother: I work the night shift and arrive home about the time that Kelly wakes up in the morning. This is the only time during the day that Kelly and I have to ourselves and it is very special to me. We have breakfast together, play some of her favourite games, go to the park, and read books. The daycare teachers seem more concerned about their routine. If they were really interested in Kelly they would see that it is important that we spend time together. They also seem to forget that I pay for their service.

Our educational, religious, cultural, familial, and socioeconomic backgrounds all influence our perceptions of problems. It is critical that teachers examine their own beliefs for biases that may adversely affect their relationships with family members. Teachers may also want to consider their unconscious reactions to family members. For example, teachers who have unresolved hostilities toward their own parents may have difficulty relating to the parents in their centre. "People alienated by unconscious emotional responses," Gestwicki (1992: 126) observes, "will have great difficulty really hearing and speaking to each other clearly."

SELF-MONITORING

Perhaps one of the most effective communication tools teachers can use is monitoring their own behaviour. The ability to be self-reflective, to analyze interactions with family members, and to look for opportunities to improve on skills is the mark of a competent communicator. According to Adler and Towne (1993: 34), self-monitors "are more accurate in judging other's emotional states, better at remembering information about others, less shy and more assertive."

Many ECE students returning from their field placement experiences relate stories about inappropriate staff-room discussions where teachers would gossip about each other and about parents.

I couldn't believe what the teacher was saying about Evan's parents. In front of the whole staff room, students and teachers, she said that if they would just spend more time with Evan, he wouldn't be having these problems at the centre. She went on to describe how Evan's mum dressed for work, that her skirt was too short and she then said that Evan's dad was out of town on business way too often. I didn't know where to look, I was embarrassed and I felt that this teacher had no idea how hurtful her comments were. I wondered if this teacher ever engaged in self-reflection!

According to Fox (2003), the subject of gossip is increasingly attracting the attention of researchers across a wide range of disciplines. Although the word "gossip" was originally a positive, or at least neutral term (deriving from "God-sibb"—a person related to one in God, a close friend or companion), it has more recently acquired some pejorative connotations. Yet most of the current research highlights the positive social and psychological functions of gossip: facilitating relationship building, group

I tend to be an optimistic person and am upbeat most of the time. When I first graduated and started teaching, I guess I just felt that most people liked me and enjoyed being with me. But I began to realize that not all parents responded to my high energy level and that some seemed overwhelmed by me. I've tried to watch parents' nonverbal responses, and with some family members I am working to be more low-key and calm.

Amanda: Being both a teacher and a parent of two young children has given me valuable insight into the struggle many parents experience when trying to work at a full-time job and care for their family at the same time. Last Monday morning, Saorise's mother, Diane, arrived in the infant room. Just by looking at her I could tell that she hadn't had much sleep over the weekend. Saorise is Diane's first baby and she has been colicky and sometimes awake most of the night. As I walked toward Diane to take the baby from her, I asked how the weekend had gone. She looked up at me and burst into tears. I quickly put my arm around her and gave Saorise to another staff. Then I took Diane to the staff room.

Diane: When I walked into the infant room, Amanda asked how our weekend had gone with Saorise. I took one look at her and began to cry. Saorise is four months old now and we have had a very difficult time. She cries constantly and no matter what we do we can't get her to calm down. I guess she's not the "perfect" baby we had anticipated. My husband and I take turns getting up with her in the night, but we rarely get more than two or three hours' sleep at a time. Now that I'm back to work, I feel that I just can't cope. I need this job and I'm desperate for this to work out. Amanda and the other staff at the centre have been so helpful. With our parents living in other provinces, the staff at the centre have become our support system. I don't know what I would do without them.

bonding, clarification of social position and status, reinforcing shared values, conflict resolution and so on. Two-thirds of all human conversation is gossip, because this "vocal grooming" is essential to our social, psychological, and physical well-being.

Despite this, gossiping can undermine relationships between teachers, students, and families. The NAEYC Code of Ethical Conduct (1998: Principles P-2.9) states: "We shall maintain confidentiality and shall respect the family's right to privacy, refraining from disclosure of confidential information and intrusion into family life." Leitch Copeland and Bruno (2001: 23) discuss the necessity of a centre-based policy to "create a culture of safety, encouragement and respect that is consistent with the Code. . . . The director must assiduously avoid any temptation to listen to the gossip that she abhors. She must articulate the mission, confront gossip and negativity immediately and promote peer responsibility to do the same. . . . A gossip-free centre culture supports everyone in the centre community and eventually helps them focus on the mission and the work to be done on behalf of children and families."

EMPATHY

Teachers need to "put themselves in the parent's shoes" and try to identify why family members may be responding this way or why they may be challenging a particular practice in the centre.

According to some researchers, empathy is the most important communication skill.

"One feature that distinguishes effective communication in almost any context is commitment," state Adler and Towne (1993: 34). "In other words, people who seem to care about the relationship communicate better than those who don't." Many family members lead very difficult and tragic lives. Over the course of their careers, teachers may encounter family members who live in abusive relationships, whose spouse is in jail, or who have substance-abuse problems. It is the teacher's responsibility to find ways to develop positive relationships with these families, motivated always by what is in the best interest of the child. Few family members in these situations want pity; what many of them will respond to is a genuinely empathetic and caring teacher who is clearly focused on finding ways to involve and support the family with a hopeful approach. This support may also include being part of a team of social workers, probation officers, child protection officers, and so on.

Teachers also need to guard against giving advice, especially when it is not asked for. Teachers may instead want to try a more tentative approach while assuring parents that there is no one right way to do things despite what the experts say: "You may want to try . . ." or "At the centre, we've had some success with . . .".

EXHIBIT 6.2 NOTHING SUCCEEDS LIKE SUCCESS: STRATEGIES FOR IMPROVING COMMUNICATION

- Get involved. Know the family and children on a personal level. Become familiar with their interests, situations, and values.
- Make a commitment. People who care about a relationship communicate better than those who don't.
- Keep in mind the personal and economic pressures that may be affecting family members.
- The family and the child must be looked at in a cultural context. Learn about cultures and learning styles predominant in different cultures, but remember that the individual culture of each family may not reflect the traditional cultural ways.
- Demonstrate respect for the diversity of families.
- Remain calm, take a deep breath, and watch your nonverbal responses.
- Work on being non-defensive. Remember that hostility inhibits communication.
- Never get into a shouting match with a family member. It frightens the children and serves no useful purpose.
- Be aware of your feelings and identify them. Use self-monitoring techniques.
- Remember the need for privacy. Some conversations that begin on the floor as casual exchanges progress into dialogue that should be private.
- Demonstrate respect for parental concerns.
- Ask for more information and listen carefully. Often we don't understand the whole picture.
- Make sure family members have an opportunity to say everything they want to say. Allow enough time for thoughtful discussion.
- Make sure that family members understand that your role is to function as a team member working with them to solve problems.
- Be precise and keep focused on what is best for the child. Remind yourself that the vast majority of parents want the best for their child.
- Consider how vulnerable family members may feel and how they may question their own ability to be effective parents.
- Resist answering a problem with a simple solution. There are no quick and simple answers to complex problems.
- Ask family members if they have any solutions to their concerns.
- Express concerns constructively, in concrete terms, and in a tactful, sensitive manner.
- Help the family member save face when they know they have acted in an inappropriate fashion. They will thank you for it and may one day return the favour.
- A sincere and well-worded apology should be given to families if you have acted inappropriately.
- Call on more experienced people for help. Use a team approach. Some family issues may be best discussed with the whole staff—but remember that confidentiality is an important consideration.
- Take action. Respond to requests. What you do is often more important than what you say.
- Check back with family members after a few days to discuss how they are feeling.
- As your confidence grows, defending your expertise will take on less importance.
- Remember that learning is a lifelong process. Continue to look for ways (through workshops or courses, for example) in which to improve your communication skills.

FAMILY–TEACHER CONFLICTS AND STRATEGIES FOR RESOLVING THEM

If teachers can remember difficult times in their own lives when they relied on a trusted friend, family member, or perhaps a teacher—people who were patient and understanding—they can draw on this strength to give back to others.

Conflict is inevitable in any meaningful relationship. When conflict occurs, a host of feelings come to the surface: confusion, frustration, anger, disappointment, annoyance. The most common cause of conflict is a lack of information. How teachers deal with conflict is critical to how they develop positive relationships with family members.

Gonzalez-Mena states:

[D]issonance is where growth takes place. Professionals need to be able to problem solve in ways that make differences manageable. Some problems can't be solved, in which case both professional and parent need to develop conflict coping skills. Even though harmony may be a goal, it's not a final state but merely a temporary condition. Professionals have to recognize the richness that comes from an environment where there are differences and disagreements. Only when professionals acknowledge that diversity is good, necessary, and provides growth will they be able to effectively respond to children and their families. (1999: 8)

Swick (1992: 129) identifies the two main types of confrontation that occur in daycare settings: (1) the sudden, unexpected outburst of a parent or teacher, and (2) the type of emotional discharge that results from some simmering issue that has not been resolved. Lack of communication, whether verbal or written, is at the root of most parent–teacher conflicts. Even when the conflict is brought out in the open, it may be perpetuated by the failure of one or both parties to take the other person's position into consideration.

Conflict may arise over such issues as a parent's overprotectiveness, the type of curriculum being delivered, developmental questions (the time at which toilet learning should begin, for example), the setting of limits for children's behaviour, centre menus, the cleanliness of the children at the end of the day, lost clothing, the timely administration of medication, problems in the playroom (for example, one child's biting another), and the lack of family involvement. Conflict may also arise over centre policies related to ill children. Family members are often overwhelmed when a sick child requires that they stay home from work. For some it may mean the loss of a day's pay which, in some families, may mean that the rent won't be paid. In some situations, the family may send the child to the centre and thereby create great stress for teachers who are concerned about the well-being of all the children. Even mildly ill children require extra support, and this places even more pressure on teachers, most of whom are already overburdened. Differing values may also create conflict as the following Inside Look demonstrates.

Teachers become resentful of family members who are consistently late when picking-up their child. Even if an individual family member is late only occasionally, teachers may, given the total number of families in a centre, find themselves staying behind every night to accommodate tardy families. To deal with this problem, some centres have introduced late fees—a response that only adds to the tension between families and the teachers. What happens when one teacher follows the late fee rules established at the centre and another teacher excuses the lateness?

More communication does not necessarily make things better. There are times when it is appropriate to say nothing. If the family member is having a difficult time or if the teacher is upset, it may be best to postpone a discussion until everyone is better able to cope; teachers will need to trust their instincts in this regard.

Greenman and Stonehouse (1996: 264) remind us that if we take any ten or fifteen people, a few will be "difficult" and one will be "impossible"

INSIDE LOOK

Though I teach in the infant room and am a working mother myself, it is sometimes difficult for me to come to terms with my attitudes about working mothers. My parents made great sacrifices so that my mother could stay at home with my sister and me. When a child is brought to the centre ill, or when we enroll infants when they are very young, I can't help thinking that some of these children would be better off at home. I know that I have felt very guilty about going back to work myself, but staying at home wasn't financially viable for me. But I don't know that this is true of some of the parents whose children are at my centre.

and all will be difficult occasionally. It is true of staff and true of parents. The most difficult parents to form a partnership with are those who are critical of the center and staff, irresponsible, always demanding or uncooperative, or who neglect their child. Often, these are the parents who need the most help and support, and they are behaving in ways that are least likely to elicit them. It is the essence of professionalism to serve these parents well.

THE CONFLICT-RESOLUTION PROCESS

Conflicts between a family member and a teacher should be resolved in such a manner that each party feels it has won. The first step is for the family member and teacher to identify and define the problem in precise terms. The two parties should then discuss the issue, focusing particular attention on what needs are not being met and what each party wants. It is important during this phase that both parties make every effort to see the situation from the other person's point of view. Once the issue is on the table, the next step is to propose and discuss possible solutions. The final step is to implement the agreed-on solution. A further meeting should be scheduled at which the family member and teacher can evaluate the outcome of the conflict resolution and make any necessary adjustments.

Consider the following example of the conflict-resolution process:

Step One: Identify the Issue

Hanesana's mother is concerned that Hanesana is napping at the centre and is not ready for bed at home until late at night.

Step Two: Establish an Appropriate Time for Discussion

Hanesana's mother approaches the teacher with her concern. The teacher and parent agree to meet the next morning, when both parties are available and less likely to be tired at the end of a long day. The supervisor takes over the room so that the teacher can have as much time as is needed to resolve this conflict. They meet in the supervisor's office, where they can have privacy away from the children and they will not be interrupted.

Step Three: Both Parties Outline the Issues

At the meeting, Hanesana's mother explains that it is difficult for her to complete the tasks she needs to do in the evening, as well as study for her exams at school, when Hanesana is unable to settle until late at night. She does not want Hanesana to nap during the day. The teacher explains that it would be difficult to have Hanesana stay up during the naptime, since this is the time when staff have their lunches, clean up, and prepare for the afternoon activities. She also explains that Hanesana needs some quiet time, since the child-care routine is very busy and tiring.

Step Four: Brainstorm Possible Solutions

Hanesana's mother and the teacher consider each other's points of view with an open mind, and then brainstorm the following ideas:

- Hanesana could visit her younger brother in the infant room and "help out" when her lunch is over.
- Hanesana could take back the kitchen trolley and help the cook with the cleanup routine.
- Hanesana could assist the teacher when she cleans up in the room and sets up activities for the afternoon.
- Hanesana could have some special toys, available only at naptime, to play with while she lies on her bed until the teacher has completed her set-up activities.
- A special quiet space could be organized in the room for Hanesana and other non-sleepers where they are engaged but respectful of their peers who are sleeping.

Step Five: Pick the Best Solution

Hanesana's mother and the teacher agree to this solution: Hanesana will rest on her bed for approximately 20 minutes with special naptime toys while the teacher tidies the lunch area. The teacher will then set up quiet activities and invite Hanesana to participate.

Step Six: Evaluate

Hanesana's mother and the teacher agree to implement this solution for a week and then meet again to discuss how well it has worked for both parties.

Not all conflicts that arise in a child-care centre are between families and teachers. The conflict-resolution strategy outlined above can also be applied to conflicts that arise between teachers or between teachers and administrators.

WHAT TO SAY: HANDLING DIFFICULT SITUATIONS

Especially for new teachers, what to say when confronted with an angry family member can feel overwhelming. The following examples are "food for thought."

> "I can see that you are very upset right now but speaking in an angry voice in front of the children really frightens them. Let's see if the supervisor can come into the room and let's talk about this privately."

> "When your child was bit today, it was very upsetting for all of us. 'We have a lot of experience helping children get through biting. We try to observe when it happens, so we can anticipate it; we give children other things to bite or chew; we let them see that the other person is hurt; and we offer alternative ways for them to express their idea or feeling. Sometimes the biting stops after a few incidents, and other times, it persists for a while. If that happens we will make sure there is a teacher close to Ari most of the time to help keep him and his friends safe. It can also be helpful to the parent to know that you have a plan if the behaviour continues.'" (Keyser, 2006: 55–56).

> "Under no circumstances can you speak to any of the teachers at the centre in an angry way. If you have concerns, we are more than happy to speak to you about these. Please call me and we will make arrangements to meet when you are feeling calmer."

> "I know that this is very difficult but I cannot allow you to take Sarah home. You have been drinking and you should not be driving. I am very happy to call someone in your family or someone on your emergency pick-up list to come to the centre and take both of you home. Who would you like me to call?"

> "I'm so sorry that Muna's mitts that have gone missing. I know how annoying this can be. We try very hard to keep everyone's clothing in their cubbies but during the dressing and undressing routine, sometimes things go missing. We will certainly have another look for them. Let me call you at the end of the day when all of the children have been picked up and I will let you know if I have found them. It would also be really helpful for us if Muna's name was labelled on her clothing."

> "When you are late this often, it is very difficult for the teachers to leave to take care of their own families. It cannot continue to happen. Perhaps we can see if one of the other parents who live near you might be able to pick-up Serge or perhaps we can help you find another child care arrangement that works better for you, one that has longer hours to accommodate your work schedule."

CULTURES IN CONFLICT

CULTURAL INFLUENCES ON COMMUNICATION

Cultural identity is as important in shaping styles of communication as it is in shaping our value system. Every culture is different in the way it defines appropriate listening and speaking behaviours, in its use of body language and eye contact, in its use of silence and the meanings it attaches to silence, in the importance it assigns to taking turns in conversation, in its expectations for formality and informality, and in its understanding of what is appropriate in regard to who addresses whom and under what circumstances, and what is considered polite and impolite (Chud and Fahlman, 1995: 107).

Exposure to different cultural perspectives provides us with an opportunity to learn more about ourselves and others. Teachers must never forget that families will not always see things the way they do and that it is easy to misinterpret a parent's actions. Chud and Fahlman (1995: 109) cite five potential stumbling blocks to successful cross-cultural communication:

1. language and patterns of communication,

2. nonverbal signs and symbols,

3. perceptions and stereotypes,

4. the tendency to make snap evaluations, and

5. anxiety.

The way that people communicate during conflicts varies widely from one culture to another. Some cultures encourage a straightforward, self-focused approach; others consider the concerns of the group more important than those of any individual. When teachers and families from two different cultural groups enter into a conflict, neither one may be prepared to understand the conflict from another perspective. Teachers should think twice before they question and challenge family practices that are not harmful to the child and are a reflection of a parent's love and concern.

INTERCULTURAL VALUE CONFLICT AREAS

We generally find most difficulties arise from the different assumptions concerning the following eight areas, as discussed by Gonzalez-Mena (1993: 22–23).

STRATEGIES FOR RESOLVING CONFLICTS BASED ON CULTURAL DIFFERENCES

1. **Take it slow.** Don't expect to resolve each conflict immediately. Building understandings and relationships takes time. Some conflicts won't be resolved, they'll just be managed. You have to learn to cope with differences when there is no common ground or resolution.

2. **Understand yourself.** Become clear about your own values and goals. Know what you believe in. Have a bottom line, but leave space above it to be flexible.

3. **Become sensitive to your own discomfort.** Tune in on those times when something bothers you instead of just ignoring it and hoping it will go away. Work to identify what specific behaviours of others make you uncomfortable. Try to discover exactly what in yourself creates this discomfort.

4. **Learn about other cultures.** Books, classes, and workshops help, but watch out for stereotypes and biased information. Your best source of information comes from the families in your program. Check out what they believe about their cultures, and see if those beliefs fit with other information you receive. But don't ever make one person a representative of his or her culture. Listen to individuals, take in the information they give you, but don't generalize to whole cultures. Keep your mind open as you learn. Check out your point of view. There's a difference between finding and celebrating diversity and explaining deficiencies.

5. **Find out what the families in your program, individually, want for their children.** What are their goals? What are their caregiving practices? What concerns do they have about their child in your program? Encourage them to talk to you. Encourage them to ask questions. You may find out about cultures this way, or you may find out about individual or familial differences. All are important.

6. **Be a risk-taker.** If you are secure enough, you may feel you can afford to make mistakes. Mistakes are a part of cross-cultural communication. It helps to have a good support system behind you when you take risks and make mistakes.

7. **Communicate, dialogue, negotiate.** If you have a chance to build a relationship before getting into negotiations, you're more likely eventually to reach a mutually satisfying point.

8. **Share power.** Empowerment is an important factor in the dialogue-negotiation process. Although some see empowerment (allowing others to experience their own personal power) as threatening, empowerment creates, in reality, new forms of power. Some teachers and caregivers fear that empowerment means giving away their own power, but this is not true! No one can give personal power, and no one can take it away. We all have our personal power, though we can be discouraged or prevented from recognizing or using it. Sharing power, or empowerment, enhances everyone's power.

Many teachers can easily experience firsthand learning because of the cultural diversity of the parents in their program. To what extent they seize the opportunity depends on their attitudes and openness. I see a progression of attitudes toward differences from awareness, tolerance, and acceptance to respect and appreciation. Beyond that lie celebration, support, and finally using differences as resources to expand and enrich one's own life.

THE CRITICAL CONNECTION: DAY-TO-DAY INTERACTION WITH FAMILIES

HOW MUCH TIME DO WE SPEND IN DISCUSSION?

Not surprisingly, most family–staff communication occurs at transition times. Further, family–staff communication occurs two or three times or more a week for most family–staff dyads, with typical conversations lasting less than one minute (Minish, 1986). A study by Endsley and Minish (1991) reveals that approximately two-thirds of these transition-time family–staff communications involve conversations of a median length of 12 seconds. It's hard to imagine that much relationship-building can occur in less than one minute, let alone 12 seconds!

EXHIBIT 6.3 CULTURES IN CONFLICT

CONTRAST TO NORTH AMERICAN VALUES	NORTH AMERICAN VALUES
1. Individual versus family	
• Every individual is perceived in the context of his or her family.	• The individual is perceived as a separate entity
• Involvement and dependence on family are encouraged.	• Individual responsibility is most important.
• Decisions must involve the older respected members of the family.	• Decisions must involve the individual as much as possible.
2. Acceptance of others	
• Individuals from other cultures react to other people in terms of the whole person, not the role.	• North Americans relate to others in terms of their role.
• Individuals from contrast cultures tend to accept or reject others completely and have difficulty working with those who are unacceptable.	• North Americans don't need to like or agree with someone to avail themselves of his or her services (for example, student and teacher).
3. Social relations	
• Differences in status and hierarchical rank are noted and stressed.	• Differences in status are minimized to make others feel comfortable.
• Communication follows a predictable, formal series of steps that make others feel more comfortable.	• A direct, informal style of communicating is also used to achieve the same results.
4. Progress versus fate	
• Man is perceived by many cultures in a fatalistic manner, and such things as disease and suffering are accepted more easily.	• North Americans believe man is rational and can construct machines and develop techniques to solve problems.
5. Time	
• Time is perceived in terms of the right time to do something (supper is when you eat).	• Time is perceived in terms of clock time (supper is at 5:30 p.m.).
• Time moves slowly; man must integrate himself with the environment, and adapt to it rather than change it.	• Time moves quickly, from past to present to future; one must keep up with it, and use it to change and master one's environment.

Source: Reprinted from M. J. Miner and M. Kim Harker, *Honouring Diversity* (Suggested Activities and Material #3.13) (Ottawa: International Briefing Associates, n.d.). Reprinted by permission.

Even more alarming is Ghazvini and Readdick's (1994) finding of a high percentage of cases (43 percent) involving preschool caregivers and family members in which absolutely no communication, not even a greeting, occurred between the two parties. "Caregivers rated all forms of communication as more frequent and more important than parents [did]. Thus, caregivers perceived messages from program to home, back-and-forth communication exchanges, and referrals to other programs as more important and occurring more frequently than parents did" (1994: 215). What is encouraging is that research suggests that "communication attitudes between parents and caregivers become more positive as communication frequency increases" (Powell 1977).

WHEN DO THE DISCUSSIONS TAKE PLACE?

Endsley and Minish (1991) found that while parents seemed to have more time in the afternoon, caregivers were more likely to be free to talk in the morning. Thus it would appear that the ideal communication times for caregivers and parents are at odds. The situation is further complicated by the fact that at the end of the day many parents arrive at the same time to pick-up their children. The last half-hour that a centre is open is often the busiest, which makes in-depth conversation between families and teachers difficult, if not impossible.

WHAT DO WE DISCUSS?

Family–staff communication can be divided into three areas: social exchanges, sharing of information, and discussion that leads to decision-making. Of these, social exchanges are the most frequent. Endsley and Minish (1991) found that greetings, discussion of routine matters, and small talk were followed in frequency by more substantive topics such as the child's behaviour, medical and health concerns, and the child's day at the centre. Adult-focused and home- or family-focused substantive communication occurred somewhat less frequently, while child-rearing information and cognitive and social-development issues were almost never discussed.

Importantly, Endsley and Minish (1991) discerned a focus on the adults as people rather than as parents and caregivers. In fact, the adults' health and activities away from the centre were the fifth and sixth most common substantive topics discussed. This finding supports the conclusion drawn by other researchers (for example, Hughes, 1985; Pink, 1981; Powell, 1977) that, for some parents, the child-care centre can be a source of adult support and friendship. However, parents tend to be reluctant to discuss family problems with caregivers. According to Powell (1989: 61), "Studies indicate that parents generally do not share caregivers' desire for exchange of family-related information."

WHICH FAMILY MEMBERS DO WE TALK TO THE MOST?

Research suggests that family members of younger children communicate more frequently than family members of older children. Their conversations last longer and are generally more substantive than routine in nature. Whitehead (1988) suggests that parents of infants may wish to spend more time interacting with caregivers because they are a source of information on such topics as feeding and sleeping patterns, and because they generally help to ease the transition from home to daycare and vice versa. As the child grows older, families tend to

become less dependent on caregivers for practical child-care information. Families of children in after-school care may see staff members at pick-up time but feel less need to spend time conversing, since only a small portion of their child's day is spent in care.

Supervisors have observed that some teachers engage in different behaviours with different parents. For example, a teacher might unconsciously discourage one family member from entering the playroom while inviting another to do so. When considering why they respond more positively to some parents than to others, teachers need to ask themselves several questions: Are they gravitating to families whose cultural backgrounds are similar to their own? Do they favour families who appear to be more appreciative of their efforts as teachers? Are they less tolerant of less-educated parents? Do they assume that parents who are economically disadvantaged are less able parents?

Kontos and Wells (1986: 47) asked staff in four centres to identify specific parents whom they felt were doing a good, adequate, or poor job. They found that the mothers held in low esteem had less education and were more likely to be divorced: "Those mothers most in need of support or assistance from the child-care staff may be those least likely to get it." A 1990 study of parents in Atlanta, Georgia, revealed that teachers were more likely to rate mothers' parenting skills more favourably when the mothers in their group had higher incomes and were better educated. The racial factor was also important, with black staff members tending to see white parents in a more positive light (Galinsky, 1990). Furthermore, Epstein (1986) notes that

[r]esearch on teachers' practices to promote parent involvement indicates that when teachers take clear, deliberate actions to involve parents, then the socioeconomic status and education level of parents disappear as factors in the willingness of parents to be involved. However, when teachers don't actively work to involve parents, then those factors become important indicators for the level of parental involvement. Typically, mainstream parents of higher social class and level of education are more involved in their children's education. Parents with higher levels of education may have more flexible work arrangements and be more available to work in the centre and therefore over time build stronger relationships with teachers than those parents who are limited in their interactions.

EXHIBIT 6.4 FACILITATING FAMILY–TEACHER INTERACTIONS: STAFF DO'S AND DON'TS

Do:
- Schedule staffing so that teachers are available to talk.
- Prepare materials before family members arrive by coming to the centre early.
- Leave tidying up until families have left.
- Choose activities at the beginning and end of each day that children can manage on their own, thereby freeing up time for teachers to spend with families.
- Approach family members as they arrive and welcome them by name.
- Send positive messages by inviting families into the room and helping them to feel comfortable when they want to play with the children or engage in an activity. Make sure comfortable chairs are available.
- Use drop-off and pick-up opportunities to share meaningful observations about the child—something pleasant, touching, or funny.
- Compliment family members whenever possible.
- Establish a tracking system to record communications with family members in order to identify those who may require more opportunities to interact with teachers.
- Utilize written communication and telephone calls in locations where car pools or busing take place, since these factors can significantly reduce face-to-face communication time at the end of the day.

Don't:
- Avoid dealing with family members by engaging in nonessential housekeeping tasks.
- Talk over the child as if he or she were not there. Try to include the child whenever possible, or retreat to a private area if the conversation is one the child should not overhear.
- Bombard family members with problems when they enter the room. Try the "sandwich" technique instead: talk about a positive aspect of the day first, express your concern, and finish with another positive remark.

Source: E.L. Morgan, "Talking with Parents When Concerns Come Up," *Young Children*, January 1989, p. 55. Reprinted with permission from the National Association for the Education of Young Children.

BUILDING MEANINGFUL FAMILY–TEACHER INTERACTIONS

In a study by Whitehead (1988), over half of the parents and almost three-quarters of the caregivers surveyed expressed dissatisfaction with parent–teacher interactions. Obviously, a great deal of thought and effort must go into developing strategies for maximizing the amount and quality of daycare interactions with families. As a practical matter, Hendrick and Chandler (1996: 168) recommend that the beginning of the day be devoted to family time in order to "build bridges of deepened understanding between the home and centre."

In order to develop trusting relationships with families, teachers need to be on the lookout for potential barriers to communication and to listen carefully to what the families say. They also need to use their observation skills to determine the right time to share information with family members. Greeting a family member everyday with details about how his or her child acted out can damage the relationship to the point that the parent begins to deliberately avoid the teacher. If possible, the child should be included in a conversation that refers to him or her rather than talking about the child as if he or she doesn't exist. The parent–child reunion takes place in a stress-free atmosphere if teachers instead greet family members with positive news (of a memorable moment, for example, or a thoughtful gesture on the part of the child, or a special art project). If issues are serious, a more formal private meeting should be scheduled.

Teachers should also look for opportunities in their day-to-day interaction with family members to solicit their opinions on specific practices in the centre. Teachers need to be proactive and deal with issues as they arise rather than wait until a situation has deteriorated beyond the point of repair. Finally, it is helpful if the supervisor is "on the floor" at drop-off and pick-up times to allow teachers to discuss important issues with family members.

REFERENCES

Adler, R.B., L.B. Rosenfeld, and N. Towne. 1992. *Interplay: The Process of Interpersonal Communication*. Toronto: Harcourt Brace Jovanovich.

Adler, R.B., and N. Towne. 1993. *Looking Out/Looking In*, 7th ed. Fort Worth, TX: Harcourt Brace Jovanovich.

Are You Listening? Redmond, WA: Exchange Press.

Brislin, R. 1993. *Understanding Culture's Influence on Behavior*. Fort Worth, TX: Harcourt Brace Jovanovich.

Chud, G., and R. Fahlman. 1995. *Honouring Diversity within Child Care and Early Education*. Ottawa: Ministry of Skills, Training and Labour in conjunction with the Centre for Curriculum and Professional Development.

Code of Ethical Conduct and Statement of Commitment: Guidelines for Responsible Behavior in Early Childhood Education. 1998. National Association for the Education of Young Children. Washington, DC.

Dotsch, J. 1999. *Non-Biased Children's Assessments*. Toronto: Bias-Free Early Childhood Services.

Endsley, R.C., and P.A. Minish. 1991. "Parent–Staff Communication in Day Care Centers during Morning and Afternoon Transitions." *Early Childhood Research Quarterly* 6.

Epstein, J. 1986. "Parents' Reactions to Teacher Practices of Parent Involvement." *The Elementary School Journal* 86 (3): 287–94.

Fox, K. 2003. "Evolution, Alienation and Gossip." Social Issues Research Centre. Available at http://www.sirc.org/publik/gossip.shtml.

Galinsky, E. 1990. "Why Are Some Parent–Teacher Partnerships Clouded with Difficulties?" *Young Children*. July.

Gestwicki, C. 1992. *Home, School and Community Relations*, 2nd ed. Albany, NY: Delmar.

Ghazvini, A.S., and C.A. Readdick. 1994. "Parent–Caregiver Communication and Quality of Care in Diverse Child Care Settings." *Early Childhood Research Quarterly* 9.

Gonzalez-Mena, J. 1993. *Multicultural Issues in Child Care*. Mountain View, CA: Mayfield.

———. 1999. "Dialog to Understanding across Cultures." *Child Care Information Exchange* 128. July–August.

Greenman, J., and A. Stonehouse. 1996. *Prime Times: A Handbook for Excellence in Infant and Toddler Programs*. St. Paul, MN: Redleaf Press.

Hendrick, J., and K. Chandler. 1996. *Total Learning: Developmental Curriculum for the Young Child*, 6th ed. Toronto: Prentice Hall Canada.

Hughes, R. 1985. "The Informal Help-Giving of Home and Center Childcare Providers." *Family Relations* 34.

Hughson, P. 1994–95. "Learning Together: A Parent's Perspective." *Zero to Three* 15 (3). December–January.

Keyser, J. 2006. *From Parents To Partners: Building a Family-Centered Early Childhood Program*. St. Paul, MN: Redleaf Press.

Kontos, S., and W. Wells. 1986. "Attitudes of Caregivers and the Day Care Experiences of Families." *Early Childhood Research Quarterly* 1.

Leitch Copeland, M., and H.E. Bruno. 2001. "Countering Center Gossip." *Child Care Information Exchange* 3.

Miner, M.J., and M.K. Harker. N.d. "Suggested Activities and Material 3, no. 14." *Honouring Diversity*. Ottawa: International Briefing Associates.

Minish, P.A. 1986. "Creating an Instrument to Assess Parent–Caregiver Communication during Morning Drop-Off and Afternoon Pickup Times in Proprietary Day Care Centers." Unpublished manuscript, University of Georgia, Athens.

Morgan, E.L. 1989. "Talking with Parents When Concerns Come Up." *Young Children*. January.

Ontario English Catholic Teachers Association. N.d. "Positive Professional Parent Teacher Relationships."

Pink, J.E. 1981. "Social Networks among Parents and Caregivers in Day Care." M.A. thesis, University of Georgia, Athens.

Powell, D.R. 1977. *Day Care and the Family: A Study of Interactions and Congruence*. Final Technical Report. Detroit, MI: Merrill-Palmer Institute.

———. 1989. *Families and Early Childhood Programs*, vol. 3. Washington, DC: Research Monographs of the National Association for the Education of Young Children.

Samovar, L.A., R.E. Porter, and R.E. McDaniel. 2007. *Communication between Cultures*. Toronto: Thomson Wadsworth.

Swick, K. 1992. *An Early Childhood School–Home Learning Design*. Champaign, IL: Stipes Publishing.

Whitehead, L.C. 1988. "Cohesion and Communication between Families and Day Care: A Proposed Model." *Child and Youth Quarterly* 17 (4). Winter.

CHAPTER 7

Family–Teacher Conferences

"Education is not filling a bucket, but lighting a fire."

—William Yeats

LEARNING OUTCOMES

After studying this chapter, you will be able to

1. outline the benefits of conferences for both families and teachers

2. discuss teachers' and families' concerns about conferences

3. identify strategies for planning and conducting conferences

4. describe follow-up and evaluation procedures that teachers can implement after the conference

Before beginning this chapter, it is important to note that family–teacher conferences are no more important than any other means of connecting with families. But because of the more formal nature of this type of interaction, conferences sometimes create anxiety for all involved. By being well prepared, however, teachers will feel less anxious and will see conferences as opportunities for quality one-on-one time with families. It is a wonderful opportunity to celebrate the lives of the children!

REASONS FOR ORGANIZING CONFERENCES

Conferences allow families and teachers to meet in order to share information that assists both in developing their relationship and in setting appropriate goals for the children. Conferences should be held on a regular basis; some centres schedule them three times a year. Conferences may be held on fixed dates each year or organized spontaneously to address immediate issues that families and teachers wish to discuss. Either way, these meetings are of particular benefit to families and teachers of younger children, who are progressing rapidly through the developmental stages. Some of the general benefits of conferences for families and teachers are outlined below.

HOW FAMILIES AND TEACHERS BENEFIT FROM CONFERENCES

At the conference, families can

- express their feelings and discuss goals for their child,
- provide examples of their child's growth and development,
- find out how their child is getting along with other children and adults in the program,
- ask questions about their child's development,
- find out how they can contribute to their child's development at home,
- be reassured about the teacher–child relationship when the teacher's insight into their child becomes apparent,
- ask for clarification about their role in the centre,
- discuss how their family values relate to their child-rearing practices,

- talk about other family members, and
- include other family members who are interested in attending.

At the conference, teachers can

- encourage family support and involvement in the program,
- explain the developmental milestones that are being reached in the child's life,
- discuss the centre environment and how it contributes to the development of the child,
- gain insight into the family's expectations for both the centre and the child,
- find out how the child feels about the centre and about the teacher–child relationship,
- be made aware of emerging issues related to the child (for example, developing fears, health concerns, changes in sleep routines), and
- learn more about the child's home environment.

At the conference, both teachers and families can

- reduce misunderstandings,
- raise issues,
- identify future goals for the child, and
- discuss strategies for strengthening the home–centre partnership.

CONCERNS ABOUT CONFERENCES

Teachers' Concerns

1. **No experience with conferences.** I've never done a conference before. I'm not sure what to do or say and I'm not even sure how to start preparing for it.

2. **Lack of self-confidence.** I'm a really shy person. I'm fine with the children, but when I have these conferences I feel awkward and uncomfortable. I feel my face turning red and I stumble over everything I say. I know I have to work on feeling more confident about myself and my skills as a professional.

3. **Being unable to answer parents' questions.** I work hard to prepare for a conference with families because I am terrified that they will ask me a question that I can't answer. I don't want them to think that I'm not knowledgeable. What if I make a mistake? I have a hard time thinking this is just a learning

opportunity for me because I worry about what the families will think of me.

4. **Not being taken seriously if the teacher has no children of her own.** I sometimes wonder if parents think I don't have a real understanding of what it is like to be a parent because I'm not one myself. I'm still new to the field and several of the parents in the room are the same age as my own parents.

5. **Dealing with an angry parent.** In my personal life I avoid confrontation, because I almost always end up in tears. My greatest fear is that a parent will get angry with me and there will be a confrontation.

6. **Handling issues that are beyond the teacher's control.** The late-fee policy at our centre is a really big issue for one of our parents. I know that he will bring it up at the conference and I'm not sure how I will respond.

7. **Communicating effectively with ESL families.** My biggest concern is how to have a productive interview with families whose language I don't share. I have several families whose English is limited but whom I can speak to; however, I'm worried about doing or saying something that will offend them. I'm not familiar enough with their customs to be comfortable.

8. **Demanding or hard-to-please parents.** I know that I have to work harder at my relationship with Maria's family. They seem so resistant to accepting the limitations of group care, and their expectations of me seem so high. No matter what I do I can't seem to please them.

9. **Broaching serious concerns with families.** I'm dreading the interview with Joshua's family. I've been gathering information over the past few months and have serious concerns about a delay in his development. I know that I have to discuss this with his family, but I'm worried about their reaction.

10. **Not being seen as a professional.** I want to be appreciated by the families. My work with the children is more than a job for me—it is my life's work. Yet some families treat me as though I were nothing more than a baby sitter. I don't think these families have an understanding of the time and effort I put into this job.

11. **Lack of parental interest.** There is not much point in holding conferences at our centre. The families are just not interested in what we have to tell them. They rush in and out, never even asking how things have gone or if there have been any problems.

12. **Personal history.** My parents weren't involved in my school life and I wonder if I react differently to the parents who are very involved in our centre? My mother was very involved, but my father felt uncomfortable being around my teachers; does my experience growing up impact the relationships I have with the families at our centre?

Family Concerns

1. **Being confronted with some wrongdoing on the part of their child.** When I was little, I was the troublemaker in my family. My parents were called into the school several times to talk to the teacher and principal because of something I had done. When we got the letter from the toddler teachers saying they wanted to speak to my wife and me about Jason, all my old fears kicked in.

2. **Being judged by teachers.** I didn't do well at school and always felt intimidated by my teachers. I am very uncomfortable around my son's teachers. I guess I feel that they are making judgments on whether or not I am a good parent. Being a good mother is important to me, and I'm afraid of what they might say.

3. **Having their parenting skills scrutinized.** Amy is my first child, and although I am trying my best I sometimes wish I knew more about how to be a better parent. I'm worried that the teachers are going to quiz me about my parenting techniques and I won't be able to provide satisfactory answers.

4. **Having their child compared to another.** The teachers really seem to prefer Sarah and her family. They seem to ignore me when I am in the centre but they have lots to say to Sarah's parents about how her day went. I'm concerned that the teachers prefer Sarah and her parents over me and my child.

5. **Being informed that their child is not developing "normally."** Our four-year-old is going through an acting-out phase. What if the teachers tell us he is developing a serious behaviour problem?

6. **Lack of teacher commitment to the well-being of their child.** My biggest concern about the family–teacher conference is not how well Rashid is doing in the program but how much this teacher is really connected to him. Does she really like him? Is she really willing to work with us on his behalf?

7. **Cultural insensitivity on the part of teachers.** Our South Asian heritage is very important to us. We want our child to adjust to his life here in Canada, but we also want to retain the richness of our own culture. Will the centre value our religious and cultural beliefs?

8. **Differing school backgrounds.** My schooling was very different from what I see the teachers doing with the children in this centre. We had to be very quiet and respectful of the teachers at all times. We would never have spoken to the teachers in the way the children do at this centre. I think there should be more structure and a greater emphasis on reading and writing. I feel pretty confused about the right way to teach children.

9. **Jeopardizing the teacher's relationship with the child.** I have a problem with the nap routine and the length of time Ryan is sleeping, but I'm afraid to bring it up because the teachers might get defensive and take it out on Ryan.

10. **Problems with arrangements for interpreters.** My English-language skills are not good and the teacher has asked me to bring my 12-year-old daughter to interpret for me. But there are things I want to talk about that I do not want my daughter to hear. I know that we should go to the meeting, but we probably won't.

11. **Lack of privacy.** I remember being in a gym full of parents, waiting for an interview with my older daughter's school teachers. Interviews were three minutes long, with one minute allowed for parents to rush to the next teacher. At one point I was so upset with one teacher's comments that I began to cry in front of all those people. I've never attended a conference at a child-care centre before. What if the setup is the same and there is a repeat of my humiliating experience?

It is hardly surprising that all participants in a conference situation may be nervous and unsure of themselves. The information in this chapter should help to alleviate many of these fears and concerns.

STRATEGIES FOR PLANNING THE CONFERENCE

ADVANCE PLANNING

The purpose of family–teacher conferences should be explained in the centre's family handbook and discussed during orientation. For families that are new to the centre, a family–teacher conference might be arranged after they have been with the centre for a few months or at any time when the families request it. In preparing for conferences, a staff meeting is a good place to start so that all staff can problem-solve for families who may have more than one child in the centre, coordinate if a translator is needed, and organize where meetings will be held. Most importantly, the centre should take into consideration families' busy schedules. Some families may find early-morning meetings more convenient; others may prefer noon-hour, naptime, evening, or weekend appointments. Child care will also be helpful for families who have more than one child in the centre and must coordinate conferences. In some cases it may be more feasible to hold the conference at the child's home than at the centre.

Gonzalez-Mena (2008: 47) reminds us that the concept of time needs to be addressed and what it means to be late. For some people, being early is important and so when the appointed time comes, they are already there and waiting. For others, the goal is to walk in the door one minute before the scheduled time; they don't like to wait. For others, forgivably late means five or so minutes. For some people, clock time has very little meaning and appointments may have even less. In their culture, arriving several hours or even days after the appointed time is within the bounds of courtesy.

Once started, it is critical that sufficient time be allocated to the conference. Rotter and Robertson (1982: 21) note that "a little extra time taken for the conference . . . can considerably reduce the follow-up time needed to correct any misunderstanding created by rushing in the first place." Teachers should make sure that the conferences do not conflict with national holidays, religious festivals, or popular events (for example, the last game of the World Series).

Divorced or separated parents may choose to meet with teachers together or separately. Step-parents, live-in partners, and other family members

Janeway

Child Care Centre

NOTIFICATION OF CONFERENCE: SAMPLE LETTER TO FAMILIES

Dear Ms. Khan:

Now that Jamal has been with us for six weeks, we would like to get together with you to discuss his adjustment to our room. We are looking forward to having time to share information about Jamal with you. During the week of November 3–8 we will be holding our family–teacher conferences. Ms. Ahluwalia will again be available to interpret for you. Child care will also be provided while you are meeting with us. Please sign the list on the parent bulletin board for a time that will be most convenient for you or let one of us know when you are dropping Jamal off at the centre.

   The conference will be an opportunity for you to talk about your feelings about the centre and our program. The following are some of the items that you might like to discuss with us when you come to the conference, but please feel free to add any new ideas or issues:

1. What does Jamal enjoy about being in the centre?
2. What are your feeling about his adjustment to group care?
3. Does he discuss any favourite activities or learning centres in the room?
4. Whom does he like to play with?
5. Does Jamal have any issues that you would like to discuss with us?
6. Do you have any issues that you would like to discuss with us?

Sincerely,

Alexander Dougall

Alexander Dougall

---

or individuals who play an important part in the child's life may also be included in the conference. Additionally, arrangements should be made to include foster families and other support personnel who may be working with their child.

   Families should be notified in a variety of ways about the upcoming conference. A letter should be sent home well in advance of the date so that families have an opportunity to organize their schedules. ESL families should receive letters in their own language; if this is not possible, they should be notified in person. Other communication strategies may include email, fax, text message, a notice in the newsletter with a clip out portion to returned to the teacher, or a sign-up poster at the front door.

   Once all of the times have been coordinated, the teacher should send home a note to officially confirm the date, time, and location of the meeting. To help families prepare for the conference, teachers might invite them to come in beforehand and

spend some time observing in the playroom. Teachers may initiate an agenda, but families should also have an opportunity to add their own items.

TEACHER PREPARATION

Nothing is more frustrating for families than attending a conference in which the teacher speaks in generalities and appears to know little about their child. When preparing for a conference, teachers should consult with other adults who work with the child or who did in the past. As an objective observer of both the child and the teacher, the supervisor is often able to provide valuable insights. It is a good idea to have an experienced teacher or the supervisor take new teachers through the preparation process. It may also be helpful to role-play some of the potential situations during a staff meeting.

In some centres, there is a scheduled 20–30-minute time period for each family; other centres are less structured. The length of time available for the meeting should be communicated to families in advance.

Throughout the year teachers should formally record their observations of the children. Any comments they make at a conference can then be supported by documentation. Record-keeping with respect to a child's development can take many forms. One teacher might record milestones and significant events on adhesive notes kept inside her cupboard door until they can be transferred to a binder—indexed for each child—at the end of each week. Another teacher might prepare an index box with file cards organized alphabetically for each child, and then jot down observations throughout the day. Other teachers might record their observations following weekly meetings with other staff.

Ongoing record-keeping is critical to planning and assessment. According to Martin (2007: 259),

> [a]ssessment is a process of gathering information about an individual's behaviour, health indicators, growth, sensory levels, performance in specified tasks, intellectual abilities, social relationships, receptive and expressive language, personality traits, motor skills, spontaneous play activity, potential, or other predetermined criteria. The process may take many forms, including informal observation, standardized tests, teacher appraisal, developmental checklists, parental observations, the individual's own evaluation, medical diagnosis, or any combination of these or other methods.

In many centres, experienced teachers create their own assessment tools using a checklist format. ECE students are not always trained in the use of all assessment tools, but some are accessible for new teachers. Teachers should be mindful of whether the tool is inclusive and reflects the socioeconomic and cultural diversity of the children it assesses. The Nipissing District Developmental Screen (NDDS), which can be accessed at **www.ndds.ca** is one such tool.

PORTFOLIOS

Teachers should be in the habit of documenting all interactions and communications with families. Documentation in the form of portfolios is a powerful instructional tool because they offer children, teachers, parents, administrators, and policy makers an opportunity to glimpse the sweep and power of the children's growth and development. When carefully structured, portfolios display the range of a child's work. Above all, they integrate instruction and assessment (Meisels, 1993: 38). Portfolios are opportunities for teachers to find creative ways to document learning!

A portfolio is a record-keeping system consisting of significant information about a child (health data, work samples, teachers' observations, etc.). The system enables child-care professionals to keep records over time, add items as necessary, evaluate the child's performance, evolve plans to meet the child's needs, and review progress. It enables families to understand their child's progress over time and to become more familiar with what is going on in the playroom.

Martin (2007: 220) suggests a portfolio might contain

- **health records;**
- **family intake forms;**
- **notes forwarded from previous caregiving agencies;**
- **observation records;**
- **developmental checklists;**
- **parental input in a variety of forms;**
- **assessment results from standardized tests (attention should paid to ensure the tests are linguistically and culturally appropriate);**
- **information from psychologists, social workers, and so forth;**
- **photographs of special moments in the child's life, things the child has made, and so on;**
- **special items selected by the child;**
- **artwork samples;**
- **samples of the child's writing;**
- **audiotapes of the child's language, reading, or music;**
- **videotapes of the child's activities;**
- **the child's own records-of-achievement journal;**
- **a learning log of the child's lifetime experiences; and**
- **questionnaire responses.**

Genishi (1993) suggests that teachers review each portfolio to see how well it presents the story of the child's development, then add or subtract pieces as necessary to ensure the story is full and accurate. Portfolios should include less tangible

At our centre we are trying a new strategy this year. We have created a checklist that states all the important learning centres in our room as well as important social and emotional areas that we want to highlight. We always have a camera available in the room and we are using it to take photographs of the children to capture those memorable moments. The checklist with each child's name on it helps us to see what photos we need to collect. We will put the photos into an album for the family and use the album as a tool for discussing their child's development at the family–teacher conference. When it is over we will give the album to the family to take home. We think it will be a treasured keepsake.

When children advance to the next age group in the centre, the portfolio can become a valuable tool for orientating their teachers. When the child leaves the centre to go to another child-care setting or goes into the school system, the portfolio can be an effective and informative way to introduce the child and his family to the new teachers. Creating a communication book that travels with the child through his or her life at the centre may become a treasured family item. It is important to remember that all information gathered about children is confidential and should be stored in a manner that protects their privacy. Portfolios may be used as a marketing and public relations tool—but only after obtaining the families' and child's permission to use the material. In these cases teachers can organize the portfolio materials into a larger portfolio to show families who are considering enrolling their child in the centre. When families leave the centre, the child's portfolio, memory books, etc., should travel with them to their new school environment; this creates a valuable learning opportunity for a new teacher.

In programs where teachers in school-age child-care programs work alongside primary school teachers, these teachers should be invited to family–teacher conferences. They have much to offer because they see the child in a different situation. On-going communication between the child-care centre and the school is critical to providing the best possible experience for the child and his or her family.

information too: records of the child's enthusiasm, confidence, or kindness, for example. Learning stories can be included that provide real insight into a child's thoughts, feelings, and development. When adding selections of children's work to portfolios, teachers may wish to make a note on why it is significant. School-age children may be interested in contributing their own work and written comments to their portfolios; doing so will provide them with an opportunity to reflect on their own growth and development. The portfolio might also contain notes written by the families, memories, or samples of work completed at home.

Gathering information for the portfolio on a regular basis facilitates conference preparation. A table of contents, perhaps organized by development issue or subject area, with dates of entry should be part of each portfolio. Teachers can use plastic containers, large manila folders, expandable files, binders, or scrapbooks to organize the material. Another possibility is to create an elaborate box, decorating one side as each year passes, to store photographs, records of milestones, videos, artwork, audiotapes, and other relevant items. The

centre might also consider hosting a portfolio party where creative portfolios are designed by the children and their families.

PREPARING THE WAITING AND CONFERENCE AREAS

The location of the meeting should be clearly signposted, with multilingual signs provided as necessary. A waiting area should be set up, seating should be comfortable, and articles and handouts should be provided to help families pass the time. The waiting area might include a display of the children's books that are being used in the playroom, a family bulletin board, and photographs of the children. A video of the children in the playroom or during outdoor play could be shown as families wait. Posting a list of appointments and checking names off as each conference is completed gives families a sense of their waiting time. Refreshments (coffee, tea, cookies made by the children, etc.) should also be provided.

The conference area itself should be neat and tidy, private, and inviting. Even a simple touch such as fresh flowers will do much to enhance the

The implementation of portfolios provides many varied opportunities for teachers to support children's learning by capturing the whole child. One of the most beneficial aspects of the portfolio process is the rich family involvement. Through observations, work samples, photographs, and audio or video recordings, we are able to share with the family the many "missed and precious" moments on an ongoing and systematic basis. By opening the learning process to the family, we engage them in the life of the centre. This leads to increased trust and respect.

Video portfolios offer families the opportunity to hear language, observe movement, and view the overall development of their own child and of others. They're a great teaching tool! Here are a few examples of how video portfolios touched the lives of our families:

- One of our families moved to Canada from China before their child was born. Many members of their family have never met the child. The father sent the video home and the entire extended family spent many hours viewing the tape and sharing in her Canadian child-care experience.
- Another parent saved the video of her daughter to view together on Mother's Day. She told us that she cried with joy when she saw her child in action and that it was the best Mother's Day gift she had ever received.
- One mother used the video to help in her child's adjustment after leaving the centre. The child was missing her friends and teachers and they would play the tape every night and laugh as they remembered the happy days at the centre.
- Videos can also be used to alleviate parental fears. For example, some families had expressed concerns about field trips. After sending home the "trip tapes," the families were more relaxed and trusting because they saw for themselves that the children were well supervised and having fun.
- We created a mini-portfolio for one of our new families. The child was experiencing separation anxiety and the family was experiencing guilt and fear that their child would not adjust to a child-care situation. We put together a small photo album depicting the child's steady progression (from anxiously waiting at the door to onlooker play to parallel play) over a period of several weeks. This effort was greatly appreciated by the families.

Whatever method of portfolio implementation you decide to use, be assured that your parent–teacher relationships will benefit.

Source: Contributed by Jane Cawley and Darlene Meecham, Centennial College.

environment. Paper and writing utensils should be on hand so that families can take notes. To avoid creating a barrier between themselves and the family, teachers should refrain from sitting behind a desk; instead, a round table with adult-size chairs at which both family members and teachers can sit is ideal. Never ask an adult to sit on a playroom chair, particularly a very tall father! Attention should be given to lighting, ventilation, and the temperature of the room.

SHOULD CHILDREN ATTEND THE CONFERENCE?

Mathias (1967: 86–87) advises that

[y]oung children are usually excluded from parent–teacher conferences. If we believe that

teachers should seek more opportunities for furthering development, perhaps children should not only attend but actively participate in conferences where goals and objectives for their development and education are being determined. Both parents and teachers are more apt to be positive in their discussions if children are present.

According to Readdick et al. (1984: 69), "The appropriate level of child involvement in the conference [should be] determined by the child's development (general intellectual, social, and emotional competencies) and prior experience in dealing with the specific tasks of the conference."

As a rule, conferences should not be attended by children who are too young to understand the process. There are times when parents and teachers

Children often benefit when they are involved in the conference.

decide that it is in the best interest of the child not to be present. In some situations the child's presence may inhibit family members from openly discussing family issues. Decisions on children's involvement in conferences should be made on a case-by-case basis.

Teachers in both the school and care setting should be coordinating and conducting the family conference together when they share the same site. Each teacher sees the child in a different environment, and each has information from her own perspective to contribute to the discussion. The child benefits; all the adults working with him or her are apprised of the goals and strategies for achieving them. We need to work toward a united front that blends the skills of the school and the child-care environment. All children benefit from this approach, but it is especially important for exceptional children, in whose cases consistency and skill development are critical.

THE ROLE OF THE SUPERVISOR

Though the supervisor may be on hand to greet family members as they arrive, her role in the family–teacher conference is, essentially, an organizational one. Many supervisors meet with staff to review procedures for gathering information on children and presenting it to family members. They also support and problem-solve with staff as they prepare for the conference. Supervisors may, however, sit in on some conferences, contributing their expertise and observations.

GETTING STARTED

Consider how to greet the family in a culturally appropriate manner. Many families would be pleased to be greeted in their first language: "Ni Hao" in Mandarin, "Dobar Dan" in Croatian, or "Namaste" in Hindi for example. Some families would expect a very formal greeting, in other families, the father may be seen as the only acceptable individual to engage in a conversation with the teacher. It is up to the teacher to understand what greeting will make the families feel the most welcome.

www **EXHIBIT 7.1** CONFERENCE CHECKLIST

_____	Conference letter sent home
_____	Sign-up sheets prepared
_____	Convenient time arranged
_____	Confirmation letter sent home
_____	Reminder phone call or note right before the date
_____	Child-care services organized, if required
_____	Portfolio organized
_____	Interpreter arranged if needed
_____	Agenda ready
_____	Signs prepared
_____	Meeting area and waiting area prepared
_____	Refreshments organized
_____	Support material for families available

Family members will bring a variety of attitudes to the conference itself. Some are eager to begin; others appear shy or uncomfortable, and still others will want to socialize first. Some parents may be reluctant to share their concerns because of cultural beliefs related to the authority of the teacher. Many parents would also be surprised to know that the teacher, especially a new teacher, may be as nervous as they are. Therefore the first few minutes are critical for setting the tone for the conference. It is important for teachers to adjust their conference styles to accommodate individual family members.

Before beginning, teachers may decide to take families on a tour of the playroom—an especially appropriate gesture for those who are new to the centre or who missed the orientation process. The teacher can explain the child's favourite learning centre or favourite toys on this tour. Teachers may want to begin by reviewing the agenda and then giving family members an opportunity to add items they would like to discuss. For some families, a brief explanation of the purpose and goals of the conference may be helpful. Beginning the conference with some positive comments about the child is a good way to acknowledge the enormous emotional investment that families have in their children—an investment that teachers sometimes forget that families have.

Some teachers like to get the meeting off to a positive start by commenting on a successful parent–child interaction they have observed: "I've been wanting to tell you that I really admire the way you are so patient with Shanaz at the end of the day. It is such a hectic time and yet you take the time to listen to what he is saying about his day. I can see how proud you are of his accomplishments." Recounting a story that reveals a sensitive or caring moment in the child's daycare experience is another positive way to begin: "Yesterday, one of the children fell on the playground and really hurt herself. Helleca raced over and by the time I got there she had the situation in hand. She was holding the child in her lap and rocking her back and forth. Her empathy and care for others is always evident." A videotape of the child is also a wonderful way to begin the meeting and can be used as a springboard for discussion. Every parent will be pleased to see their child in action in the playroom, especially for those who are not always able to participate or do drop-off and pick-up.

The teacher should stress the importance of families and teachers regularly sharing information. The teacher may then move to a discussion of the child's portfolio. Materials in the portfolio can be used to demonstrate the child's personal development, strengths, and learning goals. Families should be reassured by this demonstration that the teacher has a keen understanding of the child. A well-organized portfolio is a particularly useful tool for inexperienced teachers in that it provides the kind of structure that allows for an effective conference. The teacher should encourage family input into the discussion of the portfolio. At the conclusion of this discussion, it should be clear what goals are being established for the child; strategies for achieving these goals should be reviewed by the teacher and family members.

EFFECTIVE COMMUNICATION

"Styles of communication are influenced by individual personality and temperament as well as the rules of talking that people learn in family and culture . . . Personal temperament affects your communication style. Whether you are an introvert or

---

INSIDE LOOK

Jonathan and Rebecca were dropped off in the morning and were told that their mother would pick them up at lunch time and take them to their grandmother's. The next day the mother told me that she in fact had taken the children to the dentist. She had been afraid to tell them ahead of time. I told her that had she let me know that she was taking them to the dentist, and if had they been worried about the visit, we could have set up the dramatic play area or I could have organized a visit to a local dentist as well as circle-time stories and discussions.

Grimalda was two days away from going to the hospital to have her tonsils out. During a dramatic-play discussion, she expressed her fears about going in for surgery. She wanted to know whether she could take her teddy bear with her. I shared this with her parents. Soon after, Grimalda was much relieved to know that her favourite stuffed animal would accompany her through the surgery.

an extrovert, slow-to-warm or quick-to-warm, flexible or structured will affect your communication strategies" (Keyser, 2006: 35). When presenting verbal messages, teachers need to observe the different ways people take in information through sensory modes. A teacher who learns to communicate using words that reflect the way the parent views and interacts with the world should have a better chance of enlisting the parent's cooperation. A visual person responds best to phrases such as "I see what you mean" and "I get the picture." An auditory person finds appealing such phrases as "Sounds good" and "I hear what you're saying." A kinesthetic person reacts favourably to statements such as "That feels right" or "I feel that . . . " (Buckner and Meara, 1987: 283–87).

As Studer (1993–94: 76) observes, "Teachers need to adjust the conference dynamics to the perceptual modes of their audience. A visual learner wants to see examples, an auditory learner wants to hear examples, and a kinesthetic learner wants to handle materials." Voice tone is a critical element in effective communication. Your tone of voice can convey a wealth of information, ranging from enthusiasm to disinterest to anger. If your tone conveys an undercurrent of anger or frustration, sounds distracted or preoccupied, or is heavy with sarcasm, it will influence how others hear what you are saying and how they interpret your message.

To be effective communicators teachers must also put their observation skills to work. Family members may be too embarrassed or afraid to say what they are really thinking or feeling. Like a good detective, teachers must look for clues. They must look beyond verbal messages to non-verbal indicators that a parent is becoming upset, restless, or confused, or doesn't understand what has been said. Reflect on the impact of culture in interactions between teachers and families; for example, the mother may defer to the father in these discussions.

Effective listening is another critical component of a teacher's communication style. If family members

Courtesy of Scotia Plaza Child Care Centre

Conferences are opportunities to exchange and share important information.

Sometimes I have used my own personal experience to help a parent feel more comfortable. I had one parent who broke down in the middle of conference. As a single mother, she was overwhelmed with the responsibilities of raising her son on her own and her financial situation was a growing concern. I shared with her my own struggles as a single mother. My ability to reveal my own challenges strengthened our relationship. We had something in common beyond our parent–teacher relationship and I was able to share with her some of the community resources that had helped me.

leave feeling that they did not received an opportunity to discuss their concerns, they may be reluctant to attend another conference. There are times when just being able to talk to a sympathetic teacher who is a good listener helps a family member to resolve his or her problems. Active listening ensures that teachers are connected to both content and emotions expressed.

As a rule, teachers should be conscious of talking only 50 percent of the time (Berger Hepworth, 2000: 223). They should refrain from changing the topic when family members are speaking, and they should be wary of overwhelming families with too much information. Teachers will have to trust their instincts and be sensitive to families' needs when determining how much information to present at a conference. Teachers should not feel that they need to fill any silences that may occur during the conference. These may in fact be opportunities for a family member to take the lead in the discussion or to reflect on what has been said. There are times when it is important to give up the prepared agenda and just listen to what families are saying.

QUESTIONING STRATEGIES

The types of questions that teachers ask and how those questions are phrased may either facilitate or undermine communication with family members. Open-ended questions allow families to contribute as much as they feel comfortable doing. The following statements and questions could be used to draw reluctant or hesitant parents into the conversation:

- I've had so much to share with you and now I would really like to get some feedback from you.
- What do you think Sari's feelings are about the preschool room?
- What activities does Sari enjoy at the centre? Are there activities that she doesn't enjoy?
- I've talked about Sari at the centre, but I would like to hear what you hope Sari will enjoy doing here with us.
- What types of responsibilities does Sari have at home?
- How do you feel about your involvement with the centre?
- How can I be more supportive of you and your family?

If a family member makes a statement that indicates concern, the teacher might paraphrase the statement and ask for clarification: "You say that you are having trouble getting Sari to sleep. Could you tell me more about how she reacts when you put her down?" Family members who seem anxious that their parenting skills will be criticized may respond to promptings such as "Many toddler parents are concerned about behaviour issues, so I wonder how you might be feeling about Sari's interactions at home or at the centre."

SOURCES OF CONFLICT

According to the Ontario English Catholic Teachers Association's publication *Positive Professional Parent Teacher Relationships* (n.d.):

[t]o handle a conflict with a parent successfully, learn to understand the sources of conflict. In general there are six main categories:

1. *Resources:* Conflicts may occur when resources are limited. A parent with a special needs child may not understand the lack of resources due to inadequate government funding. A parent may not understand the teacher's decision over the allocation of scare resources in the classroom. Conflict over the distribution of resources can take many forms—the need for power, the need for recognition, jurisdiction of authority, and assertion of self-esteem.

2. *Psychological needs:* When psychological factors such as self-esteem, feelings of belonging or happiness are threatened, people can sometimes become aggressive. A parent who thinks that he or she has been belittled by a teacher or who believes the child has been picked on, may lash out.

3. *Values:* People may feel personally attacked if they think their values are threatened. It is not usually the difference in values but the fear that one set of values is dominating. These conflicts can be difficult to resolve.

4. *Divergent goals:* Conflict may result when a teacher and a parent have completely different goals. A teacher who stresses drama, for example, may come into conflict with a parent who values math and science above all.

5. *Incongruent role expectations and behaviour norms:* A parent who encourages a child to challenge authority figures may not accept the teacher's discipline of the child for "insubordination."

6. *Incompatible personalities:* Sometimes conflicts are caused by personality differences.

DEALING WITH DIFFICULT SITUATIONS

No matter how well a person does in his or her job, there are always times when one will have to deal with a difficult situation. At times it is our lack of understand of the cultural context of a situation that may be a cause of concern. Adler, Rosenfeld, and Towne (1992: 386) state:

> Conflict is a natural and unavoidable part of any relationship. Since conflict can't be escaped, the challenge is how to deal with it effectively, so that it strengthens a relationship rather than weakens it. If we believe in partnerships with families, then partners strive to cooperate instead of compete; to focus on rather than avoid the issues in dispute; and to seek positive, long-term solutions that meet one another's needs.

Differing cultural values may also be a source of conflict. Collectivist cultures value cooperation and interdependent relationships and are, at times, in conflict with an individualist culture where independence and competition is valued. For example,

> Andrea and Neil brought their newborn, Alyssa, into their bed at night. They all slept comfortably and Andrea was able to breastfeed easily during the night. Sleeping together even made them feel closer as a family. But their friends, their pediatrician, and their family all warned them to get her into her own bed quickly or she would be spoiled. They were very torn between what felt right and what their culture told them was right. (Wittmer and Peterson, 2006)

If Alyssa is put to sleep in a sleep room far away from caregivers and other children then she may have a very difficult time during this transition. Andrea and Neil may be shocked to find the babies in a dark room, confined in a crib with no human contact. They may think it unduly harsh to expect preschool children to lie by themselves on a cot a few feet from other children and not be allowed to touch them. Co-sleeping is the norm in many cultures and bedtime and night wakings are not considered a problem.

Meredith Small writes in *Our Babies Ourselves* that human contact during sleep assists infants in regulating their body temperature, breathing, and heart rate. Mothers' and infants' sleep cycles are synchronized with each other. SIDS is almost nonexistent in cultures where co-sleeping is commonly practised and breast feeding is certainly more convenient. Children who sleep with someone are less likely to need "transitional items" such as a special blanket or stuffed animal. In families where close contact is more important than early independence, co-sleeping fits. In this situation, to understand cultural differences, teachers and families must communicate with each other. We need to avoid either/or choices and explore how two seemingly opposing views can both be right. Teachers must be open to diversity and dedicated to respecting all perspectives while still considering what is in the child's best interests. We need to be creative and finding common ground in order to working in harmony and understanding with all cultures (Gonalez-Mena and Bhavnagri, 2001: 91).

THE SANDWICH APPROACH

Many teachers know the value of beginning in a positive manner, celebrating the strengths of the child, dealing with the difficult issue, and then ending again on a positive note—the Sandwich Approach! When bringing up issues that may be difficult for families to hear, teachers must employ tact and sensitivity. Avoid language that lays blame or that labels the parent or child. Avoid words such as behind or ahead, fast or slow, normal or abnormal, and words that may trigger feelings of anxiety on the part of parents. Words that avoid labels and judgment are most helpful. Many difficult situations can be handled successfully if the teacher listens and is prepared to help. Rudney (2005: 51) states: "I have watched tension drain from the faces of parents when teachers, instead of showing detachment or criticism have said, 'This must be hard for you. What could be done here at school that would help?' The parents may not know what would help, but they will appreciate a sincere offer." It is important for the teacher to demonstrate a positive attitude toward accomplishing a goal.

Planning is a crucial factor. "It has been said that failing to plan is planning to fail," states Harris (1994: 38). "Nowhere is that more true than in a communications situation where both the person delivering the information and the person who is to receive it are reluctant, apprehensive, and emotional" (Harris, 1994: 38). Difficult issues should not be sprung unexpectedly on family members or left to the final minutes of the conference. Take care in presenting information so that the message is delivered with tact and sensitivity.

Behaviour Issues

Families are often concerned about behavioural issues. As the following vignette illustrates, being informed by a teacher that certain behaviours are normal for a particular age group can have a reassuring effect:

> Raul's mother looked very worried when she confided to his teacher that she didn't know where this two-year-old was learning to throw his tantrums. "His father has a temper too," she said anxiously. The teacher calmly cited Raul's endearing qualities. She pointed out that many two-year-olds sometimes simply short-circuit from the overload of pressures growing up puts on them so young. The child's mother smiled affectionately and in relief. (Morgan, 1989: 54)

No doubt there will be situations, for example, feelings about corporal punishment, which cannot be negotiated between the teacher and the parents. We need to help parents understand the negative impact of physical coercion and emphasize that it is not allowed under child-care regulations.

When other more serious behavioural issues need to be addressed, Pat Campbell of Caregiver Care offers the following suggestions to teachers:

> If we are to be partners with parents in the behaviour guidance of their children in our care settings, then we must know what they believe and do currently about misbehaviour and the most effective ways to guide and teach their children.

- Do you fully understand the difference between punishment and discipline?
- In what ways are you able to deal with your own anger and frustration when you are in program?
- Have you done the proper observations, consulted with team teachers, made program adjustments for this child? What and when?
- Are you genuinely open to the suggestions of others, or do you persist in your own evaluation and remedy?
- Have you mentally labelled this child as troublesome?
- Are you able to keep treating the child in a positive and affectionate manner? If not, what can you do?
- Do you know how humiliating it is for a parent to hear that their child has misbehaved? Use gentle words.

- When a parent tells you that this behaviour does not happen at home, do you believe them and show that you do?
- Do you then ask the parent what they would suggest, what works at home before you tell them what you are going to do?
- Are you willing to try what they suggest and agree to meet in the near future to compare notes?
- Are you willing to have a consultant come in and evaluate your program and the children's interactions, not just the child in question?
- What extra resources do you need?

Being Professional Under Pressure

Professional assertiveness is important when addressing a difficult situation. A parent who becomes angry may be acting out of fear of being misunderstood or not being heard. For some parents, their life situation "colours" all of their interactions; illness, divorce, change in employment, or financial issues may be causing pressure that makes family life difficult. If the parent is raising honest concerns, it is the teacher's responsibility to address the concern and it is in the teacher's best interests to respond in a professional, calm manner. Don't try to avoid the problem; if one parent is expressing a concern, the chances are that other parents also have the same issue. When confronted by an angry parent, teachers can mask their own nervousness by lowering their voices, moving closer to the parent, and looking the parent straight in the eye (Whitaker and Fiore, 2001). Gestwicki (2004: 586) advises that "[a]s a conversation proceeds, teachers must be careful that any disagreeing statements concern facts and issues, not personalities. In discussing different viewpoints, participants should use descriptive statements, not evaluative ones. It is easier to deal with descriptions, rather than labels."

At the same time, teachers should never have to tolerate rudeness, threats, or abuse. Terminate the conference if the parent continues to be intimidating in any way and make an attempt to reschedule the meeting when everyone is calmer. A teacher should never meet on his or her own with a parent who has demonstrated these behaviours in the past. The centre supervisor should attend all future meetings. Teachers should record notes on this interaction in case further follow up is needed.

At all costs, teachers must avoid discussing other children in the centre. Teachers have a professional responsibility to protect the privacy of the other children and their families. The following is an account of how one teacher handled a parent's attempt to breach that privacy:

> Katherine's mother was very angry that her daughter had been bitten several times last week in the toddler room. During the conference she insisted that we reveal the name of the child who had bitten her. She planned to have all the other parents sign a petition asking for the removal of the child from the centre and then present the petition to the supervisor. We told her that it was our policy not to reveal the names of children in biting incidents. We then discussed at length the factors that contribute to this behaviour in toddler rooms. Finally, we outlined how we intended to monitor the situation and gave her some articles on biting to take home to read.

An explosive situation can often be defused if the teacher accepts responsibility for an inappropriate action:

> As Jane's mother, Sara, arrived at our parent–teacher conference, she noticed that the tips of her daughter's ears were bright pink. I had neglected to put sunscreen on her ears when we went to the park, and her baseball cap had not fully covered her ears. Sara was furious. She approached me in an aggressive manner and shouted at me in front of the children. As I tried to manoeuvre her out of earshot of the children, her eyes filled with tears and she became even more agitated. I waited until she had an opportunity to vent all her feelings and then immediately apologized for my error.
>
> The moment I accepted responsibility for my actions, Sara calmed down. I told her I would place a sign at the exit to remind me to do one final check to make sure that all the children were wearing sunscreen. I was very tempted to tell her that I had many children to care for and that one child had been sick as we were preparing to leave that afternoon, but I made a real effort not to be defensive and to see things from her point of view. It was only after further discussion that I fully understood Sara's concern. Last summer, Jane's older brother had been hospitalized with a serious case of sun poisoning.

When teachers have done something that is inappropriate or a mistake has been made, it is best to contact the parents first. By contacting the parents as soon as possible, much of their anger can be diverted. Apologizing is the single best neutralizer. We will all make mistakes but taking ownership for our errors rather than becoming defensive and denying we did anything wrong, and apologizing and having a clear plan of action to prevent a repeat of the error, will go a long way to establishing more trusting relationships.

In the following example, the teacher responded to a parent's criticism by being informative rather than defensive:

> Manjit's mother was concerned that all we did at the centre was play. She felt that Manjit would not be properly prepared for Grade 1. I decided that the best way to explain how play is an integral part of an early childhood education program was to take her on a walking tour of the playroom. I went through each of the learning centres and explained the skills and knowledge that Manjit was acquiring. His mother came away from the conference with a whole new understanding of our program. It is important to help families understand that learning is not a race to reach milestones ahead of everyone else. Children do not benefit from being pushed or overwhelmed by experiences that are not age appropriate. This interaction with this parent made me realize that other parents may have been feeling the same way. I decided that I would create a poster for each of the centres in the room, outlining the skills that the children would be learning through a play based approach.

Teaching partners should be careful not to be drawn into a discussion that pits them against one another. It is usually best if the teacher who has the strongest relationship with the family leads the discussion:

> When we held our conference with Eugene's mother and father, I was hoping that it would give me an opportunity to strengthen my relationship with them. I felt that Eugene's mother was having a great deal of difficulty accepting me, since I was replacing a teacher in the centre with whom she had been very close. During the conference, I allowed my teaching partner, Patricia, to lead the discussion because the family seemed more comfortable with her. I tried to contribute in a positive manner where appropriate. At the end of the conference, Eugene's mother remarked that Eugene seemed to be adjusting to a new teacher much more easily than she was. I acknowledged her feelings and was pleased that

she was able to talk openly about the issue. We are now making real progress in building a more positive relationship.

Criticizing teachers in front of a child who is present during the conference is very confusing for him or her. Even very young children notice negative emotions being expressed. Children often attribute heroic characteristics to their teachers, believing that they actually live at the school! The child may be confused and uncomfortable about their loyalties to both their family members and the teacher. Criticizing the teacher in front of the child does not solve the underlying conflict and in older children, it may result in aggressive and defiant behaviour towards the teacher. As parents discuss issues with their children, they are modelling ways to express problems and frustrations in every day life. How well are both parties—parents and teachers—modelling life skills for the child? A teacher who begins to feel threatened or intimidated during a conference should involve the supervisor or another teacher right away. It may be in everyone's best interest to end the meeting and schedule another one.

A more formal, signed agreement may help parents realize that they also have a parent code of conduct that is expected: "We know how rushed your life is, and how many responsibilities you have. There will be times when you are very frustrated. When you speak to our staff, remember that other children are present. We cannot allow the children to hear any angry words from parents. This includes the way you speak to your own child in this centre. Children are hurt and frightened by an angry adult. Our responsibility is to protect all the children in our care. We know that you will understand" (Campbell, n.d.).

Family members may be concerned about administrative or policy matters. On such occasions it is advisable to have the supervisor sit in on the conference:

> Mala's father became visibly upset when he began to talk about the late-fee bill he had just received from the centre. To defuse the situation, I asked our supervisor to join us. She did a great job of outlining the need for the late fee. I honestly believe that he left the conference with a better understanding of the issue. During the conferences it was really reassuring to know that I could call on the supervisor if a situation got out of hand.

There may be times when, despite the efforts of all the participants, it becomes clear that the centre and the family are not a good match. In such situations the centre should do all it can to support the family in exploring alternative care situations.

HELPING PARENTS FIND THEIR STRENGTHS

Some families say that everything at home is "fine." This response can really shut the communication door. It may often be a reflection of a parent's overloaded life, and an acknowledgment of difficulty means one more thing to worry about. A strategy for the teacher may be to mention a few examples that demonstrate situations where the child is having difficulty and then ask, "When this happens at home, what do you do?" Often this lead-in provides an opening for real communication. We need to constantly remember that parents will respond from their heart and are most vulnerable when issues related to their child emerge. Their response may not be what the teacher might expect, they can respond with anger, frustration, withdrawal, and tears. Above all, the family must know that we have their child's best interests at heart and we are anxious to work together to resolve any issue that may arise.

Helping parents lead with their strengths may also be an effective strategy in supporting them when dealing with challenging situations. Ask parents to describe a time when they felt really successful in dealing with their child and help parents look for opportunities to apply it to a different challenge. Our goal is to enable and empower families to make informed decisions themselves.

In other situations, families may find it difficult to express what they are trying to say. If the silence becomes prolonged, teachers can reassure family members by stating that they understand that it is sometimes difficult to put their feelings into words. Simply by acknowledging this, a teacher may help family members feel more comfortable and allow them to proceed. Teachers need to be flexible and remember that what works for one family may not work with another!

As the following suggests, openly admitting one's lack of knowledge of a subject is not only honest—it can also bring positive results.

> During the conference one of the parents expressed an interest in Kwanza [an African-American cultural festival celebrated annually in late December]. In our most recent newsletter we announced that we would be celebrating Kwanza in our playroom. This was a new area for me,

however, and the parent asked me for more details than I was able to provide. I told her that I was in the midst of my research and would get back to her with the information she had requested. I also invited her to an upcoming circle time at which a family that celebrates Kwanza was going to speak to the children.

BOOKS FOR CHILDREN

The Anti-Bullying and Teasing Books for Preschool Classrooms, by B. Sprung, B. Hinitz, and M. Froschl

The Ant Bully, by J. Nickle

Andrew's Angry Words, by D. Lachner

Don't Rant and Rave on Wednesdays: The Children's Anger Control Book, by A. Moser and D. Pilkey

From Mad to Worse: Anger Control Activity Book, by J. Boulden

Hands Are Not For Hitting, by M. Agassi

Hot Stuff to Help Kids Chill Out: The Anger Management Book, by J. Wilde

How to Take the GRRRR Out of Anger, by E. Verdick and M. Lisovskis

I Was So Mad!, by N. Simon

I'm Mad, by E. Crary and J. Whitney

Mad: How to Deal with Your Anger and Get Respect, by J. Crist

Mad Isn't Bad: A Child's Book about Anger, by M. Mundy

Mad Me: Anger Control Activity Book, by J. Boulden

The Penguin Who Lost Her Cool: A Story about Controlling Your Anger, by M. Sobel

The Very Angry Day That Amy Didn't Have, by L. Shapiro

What to Do When Your Temper Flares: A Kid's Guide to Overcoming Problems with Anger, by D. Huebner

When I Feel Angry, by C. Maude Spelman

When Sophie Gets Angry—Really, Really Angry, by M. Bang

When You're Mad and You Know It, by E. Crary and S. Steelsmith

BOOKS FOR ADULTS

Raise Your Kids without Raising Your Voice: Over 50 Solutions to Everyday Parenting Challenges, by S. Chana

Time-In Parenting, by O. Weininger

What Am I Feeling?, by J. Gottman and the Talaris Research

Positive Discipline A–Z: 1001 Solutions to Everyday Parenting Problems, by J. Nelsen, L. Lott and H. Stephen

Positive Discipline: The First Three Years, by J. Nelsen, C. Erwin and R.A. Duffy

The Everything Parent's Guide to Tantrums, by J. Levine

Please Don't Sit On the Kids: Alternatives to Punitive Discipline, 2nd ed., by C. Cherry

The ABCs of Bullying Prevention: A Comprehensive School-wide Approach, by K. Shore

The Bully, The Bullied, and The Bystander: From Preschool To High School, 2nd ed., by B. Coloroso

Cyberbullying and Cyberthreats: Responding to the Challenge of Online Social Aggression, Threats, and Distress, by N. Willard

Sidestepping the Power Struggle: A Manual for Effective Parenting, by A. Miller and A. Rees

Kids Are Worth It!: Giving Your Child The Gift Of Inner Discipline, by B. Coloroso

The No Cry Discipline Solution: Gentle Ways to Encourage Good Behaviour without Whining, Tantrums and Tears, by E. Pantley

CHILDREN WITH SPECIAL NEEDS

Every teacher is at some point faced with telling a family that she has concerns about their child's development. Early identification of children with special needs is often critical and child-care teachers—as individuals who observe children across time and in a variety of situations—can play an important role in initiating this procedure. "Unfortunately, we sometimes do not refer young children because of the fear of 'labelling' or 'mislabelling' or because we hope the child will 'outgrow' the problem. In too many cases, we do the child and the family no good by not recognizing and acting on a problem" (Abbott and Gold, 1991: 13).

When [Jonah] was four years old, in his second preschool year, other parents started hinting around . . . and recommending books and so on. I started getting kind of panicky about what I was doing wrong as a parent, and started to read and find out everything I could about parenting things. Then, out of the blue, one of the preschool teachers said, "I'm giving up on Jonah. I've tried everything I know how to do and nothing works." She had said nothing to me up to that point to indicate she was at her wit's end or needed help with him. So I just burst into tears at this interview. I didn't know how seriously to take what she was saying about Jonah.

On the other hand, I sort of did think [subconsciously] there was something probably wrong with him. . . . I wish that they [had said] something like "Here's what you can expect of a typical three-year-old or a typical four-year-old. Here are the kinds of behaviours that they all show sometimes, and this is how they should be progressing by the time they've been in preschool for a year or so. Now, there's variation, sure, but that's just a yardstick of normal sorts of behaviour." And I also wish that at parent–teacher conferences or informal chats somebody had said, because obviously they're experienced, "I've been in the business for 15 years. I've seen 326 kids come my way and your child is on an extreme end of these sorts of behaviours. I'm not someone who could put a diagnosis on it, but I think this is something that you might want to consider looking at." I felt that there [was] too much of this tiptoeing around, instead of saying what they [saw as] the real difference between my son and other kids.

Source: *Special Link* 5, no. 1 (October 1994), p. 4. Reprinted by permission.

However difficult it may be to break the news to families, teachers have a professional responsibility to share with them the information they will need to be able to support their child. The child's best interest must always be paramount.

When informing families, teachers need to "recognize that during the conference, family members may panic or show signs of anxiety, grief, or depression. These are all common and understandable reactions for parents with children who demonstrate developmental delays" (Strauss and Munton, 1985: 371). Parents may also respond with anger or denial; they may even blame the teacher or the centre for the child's situation. Abbott and Gold's (1991: 13) advice to the teacher is to "be an active listener and allow them to express their feelings. Be prepared to listen to expressions of anger and sadness. Family members may also blame each other. Try to focus them on the problem." Our role as teachers is to help parents problem-solve by sharing our knowledge and experience but we need to have reasonable expectations regarding how and when issues may be resolved.

BOOKS FOR ADULTS

Conducting Effective Conferences with Parents of Children with Disabilities: A Guide for Teachers, by Milton Seligman

WRAPPING UP THE CONFERENCE

Before thanking the family for attending the conference, the teacher can spend a few minutes summarizing the main points to have emerged from the conference. Parents should be given an opportunity to ask further questions. Families should also know how and when they can contact the teacher in order to maintain contact. Are there specific times when this is more convenient or is communication more open-ended? This is also a good time for the teacher to pass along resources (articles, books, support agency information, and so on) that pertain to issues discussed during the conference and to schedule another conference, if required. Above all, the conference should end on a positive note. This is also a good opportunity to

The teacher took the final moments of the conference to say that she was impressed with the way in which I was supporting my child. She acknowledged the difficulties and challenges confronting our family, given my son's autism. For the first time in my experience with child care, someone whose opinion I trusted and respected said that I was doing a good job. She understood how complicated my life was and I was overwhelmed with gratitude for her reaffirming words.

thank families for any contributions they have made to the centre. It is important to personally acknowledge these efforts. Presenting families with a folder of items featuring the child's accomplishments is a wonderful way to conclude the conference. Before the family leaves, the teacher might ask them to leave a note for the child, who will see it the next day.

FOLLOW-UP AND EVALUATION

As soon as the conference is over, the teacher should quickly make notes before the next family arrives. Later, when there is more time to reflect, the teacher can organize this information more for-mally. It is important that the teacher not take notes during the conference itself, since doing so may be intimidating to some family members. Families might be provided with a written summary of conference highlights; this would be particularly helpful if only one parent was able to attend. A sample format for a conference summary is provided in Exhibit 7.2.

If the teacher promises during the conference to gather information for families, it is imperative that this be done as soon as possible. When evaluating the conference, teachers should focus particular attention on their own role and how their performance might be improved at future conferences. A sample teacher self-evaluation is provided in Exhibit 7.3.

w(w)w **EXHIBIT 7.2** FAMILY—TEACHER CONFERENCE SUMMARY

Child's name:_____ Age group: _____

Teacher(s) conducting the conference:_____

Parent's/Parents' name(s):_____

Date of conference:_____

Topics discussed	Action to be taken	Time line

General comments: _____

_____

_____

EXHIBIT 7.3 FAMILY–TEACHER CONFERENCE: TEACHER SELF-REVIEW

YES	NO	SOMEWHAT	
___	___	___	Did I check to make sure I knew all of the family members first and last names?
___	___	___	Did I review my files before the interview began?
___	___	___	Did I help the family feel comfortable when they arrived?
___	___	___	Was my portfolio complete and reflective of the child?
___	___	___	Did I have the necessary documentation and was I able to validate my comments with specific examples and materials?
___	___	___	Was I able to adapt to the individual family members' level of language use?
___	___	___	Did I demonstrate that I was genuinely interested in what the family had to say by listening attentively, using respectful language, and being open-minded?
___	___	___	Was I aware of my own body language throughout the conference?
___	___	___	Was I open to learning about the child and his or her family?
___	___	___	Did I demonstrate that I valued what the family had to offer and not consider myself the expert on their child?
___	___	___	Did I learn anything that will allow me to better support the child?
___	___	___	Was I able to balance my need to have information about the child with respect for the family's privacy?
___	___	___	Did I use open-ended questions that allowed family members to voice their concerns?
___	___	___	Did I give family members an opportunity to talk freely without interruption?
___	___	___	Did I listen as much as I talked?
___	___	___	Did I allow the family to express their dissatisfaction with the centre or with my own performance?
___	___	___	Were we able to problem-solve together and set positive, measurable goals for the child?
___	___	___	Was a time line established, if required?
___	___	___	Did I avoid discussing other families or children?
___	___	___	Did I summarize the conference effectively in the last five minutes?
___	___	___	Did I use this conference as an opportunity to explain to the family how they could become more involved in the centre?
___	___	___	Did I acknowledge that not all families may be able to participate in "traditional" ways?
___	___	___	Did I begin and end the conference on positive notes, and was I free with praise?
___	___	___	Was I aware of the timing and pace, and did I begin and end on time?
___	___	___	Did I remember not to use ECE jargon?
___	___	___	Is a partnership developing with this family?
___	___	___	If I promised further feedback or resources, did I follow through in a timely fashion?
___	___	___	Overall, do I think the family felt the conference was productive?
___	___	___	Overall, do I think the meeting was productive?

REFERENCES

Abbott, C.F., and S. Gold. 1991. "Conferring with Parents When You're Concerned That Their Child Needs Special Services." *Young Children.* May.

Adler, R.B., L.B. Rosenfeld, and N. Towne. 1992. *Interplay: The Process of Interpersonal Communication,* 5th ed. Fort Worth, TX: Harcourt Brace Jovanovich.

Berger Hepworth, E. 2000. *Parents as Partners in Education,* 5th ed. Upper Saddle River, NJ: Prentice Hall.

Buckner, M., and N.M. Meara. 1987. "Eye Movement as an Indicator of Sensory Components in Thought." *Journal of Counseling Psychology* 34.

Campbell, P. N.d. Personal communication.

Genishi, C. 1993. "Art, Portfolios, and Assessment." *Scholastic Early Childhood Today.* October.

Gestwicki, C. 2004. *Home, School, and Community Relations,* 5th ed. New York: Thomson Delmar Learning.

Gonzalez-Mena, J. 2008. *50 Early Childhood Strategies for Working and Communicating with Diverse Families.* Upper Saddle River, NJ: Pearson Prentice Hall.

Gonzalez-Mena, J., and N.P. Bhavnagri. 2001. "Helping ECE Professionals Understand Cultural Differences in Sleeping Practices." *Child Care Information Exchange* 138 (March/April): 91–93.

Harris, J. 1994. "The Bad News Blues: When Messages Aren't Easy to Deliver." *Child Care Information Exchange* 99. September–October.

Keyser, J. 2006. *From Parents to Partners: Building a Family-Centered Early Childhood Program.* St. Paul, MN: Redleaf Press.

Martin, S. 2007. *Take a Look: Observation and Portfolio Assessment in Early Childhood,* 4th ed. Don Mills, ON: Addison-Wesley.

Mathias, D. 1967. "Parent–Teacher Conferences: There Is a Better Way." *Grade Teacher* 85. October.

Meisels, S.J. 1993. "Remaking Classroom Assessment with the Work Sampling System." *Young Children.* July.

Morgan, E.L. 1989. "Talking with Parents When Concerns Come Up." *Young Children.* January.

Ontario English Catholic Teachers Association. n.d. *Positive Professional Parent Teacher Relationships.* Toronto: OECTA.

Readdick, C.A., S.L. Golbeck, E.L. Klein, and C.A. Cartwright. 1984. "The Child–Parent Teacher Conference: A Setting for Child Development." *Young Children.* July.

Rotter, J., and E. Robertson. 1982. *Parent–Teacher Conferencing.* Washington, DC: National Education Association.

Special Link. 1994. 5 (1). October.

Strauss, S.S., and M. Munton. 1985. "Common Concerns of Parents with Disabled Children." *Pediatric Nursing* 11.

Studer, J.R. 1993–94. "Listen So That Parents Will Speak." *Childhood Education.* Winter.

Whitaker, T., and D.J. Fiore. 2001. *Dealing with Difficult Parents and with Parents in Difficult Situations.* Larchmont, NY: Eye on Education.

Courtesy of Lynn Wilson

CHAPTER 8

Staying Connected

Courtesy of Lynn Wilson

"I never see what has been done; I only see what remains to be done."

—*Buddha*

LEARNING OUTCOMES

After studying this chapter, you will be able to

1. outline the benefits of effective written communication and its role in developing positive relationships with families

2. describe the kinds of written communication used at the outset of the family–centre partnership

3. discuss the purpose, design, and thematic components of the family handbook

4. discuss the playroom handbook as an extension of the family handbook

5. outline the primary forms of ongoing written communication, from menus to bulletin boards

6. describe how a family resource area might be organized and what items it might contain

7. identify some of the implications of new technologies for the field of early childhood education

THE BENEFITS OF WRITTEN COMMUNICATION

For families who are on tight schedules that don't allow for discussion at either end of the day, or for those who have not as yet built trusting relationships with teachers, written material may be the best way for the centre to communicate. In some two-parent families, only one parent is responsible for pick-up and drop-off duties; it is important to send home information for the rarely-seen parent. When families first come to the centre, they find out much about the history, organization, and objectives of the program through such written materials as the family handbook and newsletters; written material is an effective way to continue to keep families informed about the centre, upcoming events, and curriculum issues. This chapter outlines various types of communication, along with strategies for making all forms of communication as effective as possible.

INSIDE LOOK

I met a family from El Salvador in my placement. The parents spoke very little English and their son spoke no English. Neither the parents nor the centre could afford an interpreter so I decided to create pictures to help the young boy communicate. I also compiled a list of frequently used words in preschool vocabulary and translated them into Spanish. Upon discovering the positive effect of this strategy, I began using an Internet website to translate letters to the family. By the end of my placement the child was using many English words and the family was able to understand what the child was learning in the centre. Our relationship was one of friendship.

Source: Holly Starkes, ECE graduate

EXHIBIT 8.1 GUIDELINES FOR WRITTEN COMMUNICATION

- Ensure that written communication reflects the needs and interests of the families in the centre.
- Carefully consider the style of writing to be used; whether informal or formal, it must be appropriate for the intended audience.
- Keep in mind the length of the material. Conciseness is generally preferable. If it takes more than five minutes to read, it is too long. Additional material can be made available to families on request.
- Consider the tone, cold, authoritarian, and condescending communications undermine a sense of partnership. Stay positive and respectful.
- When writing about controversial issues, maintain a positive attitude.
- Carefully proofread all written communication prior to distribution.
- Computer programs now enable written communication to be presented in an attractive and accessible format. When appropriate, support the written material with photographs and drawings by children in the centre.
- Remember that a handwritten note is a more personal form of communication and in some situations more appropriate than photocopies of the same note.
- When photocopying is done, the material should be legible and correctly collated.
- Respect copyright laws.
- Remember that any written communication from a centre is a form of publicity. As such, it should reflect a high degree of professionalism.
- Communications should be directed to all those who play a significant role in the child's life.

- Share appropriate communications with the community, it is a form of advocacy.
- Make every effort to have written communications translated into the first languages of all families in the centre. Translated materials should be accompanied with visuals placed in the text where appropriate. Several software translation programs are now available, but they should be used carefully to ensure that the essence of the translated content is captured. The final translated version should be proofread to ensure correctness.

INITIAL WRITTEN COMMUNICATION

LETTER OF CONFIRMATION

Any centre that has a reputation for delivering quality care to children will attract the attention of many families in its community. Families who wish to enroll their child in the centre have their names placed on a waiting list. The centre should send families a letter briefly outlining waiting-list procedures.

ORIENTATION FORM

On their first visit to the centre families may be overwhelmed by the amount of information they are given. A self-contained orientation package with clear instructions on how to complete the required forms can be of great assistance. In some centres, supervisors help families who are not proficient in English complete the forms. Depending on the circumstances, a family member, a translator, or another staff member may be called on to assist.

A typical orientation package includes the following forms: an Intake Form, an Emergency Contact Form, a Health and Immunization Form, an Emergency Treatment Release Form, an Authorization for Pick-up Form, a Permission-to-Video-and-Photograph Form, and an Excursion Permission Form. Most families want to share as

Janeway

Child Care Centre

Dear Mr. Potter and Ms. Chu:

Thank you for your interest in our centre. You have now been officially placed on our waiting list, and we will contact you as soon as a space becomes available. Although spaces are generally allotted on a first-come, first-served basis, priority is given to the siblings of children already enrolled. In addition, since this is a workplace centre, employees working at Janeway Plastics receive priority. The centre's board of directors has the final approval on admissions. Because we have many families on our waiting list at this time, we advise you to contact other centres while you wait to hear from us again. Please find enclosed a checklist that will assist you in choosing a quality child-care setting for you and your family.

Sincerely,

Theresa Sanchez

Theresa Sanchez
Supervisor

much information about their child with the teacher as possible. One teacher asked her parents to write her a letter in which they could share anything they wanted her to know about their children. She said that some letters were long and some quite short, but from all of them she gleaned more information than she ever thought she would, and more than she would have learned through the standard forms and paperwork. Parents were anxious to write about their children (Rudney, 2005: 43).

Intake forms, such as the one presented here, record background information about the child and the family. Centres may wish to design separate intake forms for different age groups or choose questions from the following form that best suit their needs. It is important to remember that privacy and confidentiality are very important to families, so information gathered on these forms should be treated with respect.

Janeway

Child Care Centre

Intake Form for Infants, Toddlers, and Junior Preschoolers

A. Personal Data on the Child

Date enrolled in centre: _____ Health card number: _____

1. Child's name: _____

2. Child's age: _____ Birth date: _____

3. Country of birth: _____ Child's birth weight: _____

4. Was he/she full term? Yes _____ No _____

   If not, how premature? _____

5. Were there any complications or unusual circumstances surrounding the pregnancy and/or delivery? Yes _____ No _____

   If yes, please give details: _____

6. Physician's name: _____ Address: _____

   Phone number: _____

7. Has your child had a serious illness or hospitalization? Yes _____ No _____

   If yes, please give details that may affect our care of your child: _____

   _____

8. Does your child receive medication on a daily basis? Yes ___ No _____

   If yes, please give details: _____

9. Does your child have asthma? Yes ___ No ___

   If yes, please describe treatment: _____

10. Does your child have any other allergies or sensitivities? _____

    _____

11. Does your child wear eyeglasses? Yes ___ No ___

(continued)

12. If your child was adopted and you wish to share this information with us, do you have any specific instructions for the centre? _____

13. Does your child have any brothers or sisters? Yes ____ No ____

    If yes, please complete the following:

    Name: _____ Age: ____ Sex: _____

    Name: _____ Age: ____ Sex: _____

    Name: _____ Age: ____ Sex: _____

14. Do these siblings live with you and your child? Yes ____ No ____

15. Are there other family members or friends who also live with the child?

    Yes ____ No ____ If yes, please identify: _____

16. Are there any significant adults in your child's life that we should be aware of?

    _____

17. What languages are spoken at home? _____

18. Does your child have any pets? Yes ____ No ____

    If yes, what type of pet and what is its name? _____

B. Data on Household Members

Name: _____

1. Relationship to the child: _____

2. Address: _____

3. Telephone numbers: Residence: _____ Work: _____

4. Cell phone/pager/e-mail address: _____

5. Occupation: _____

6. Place of employment/school: _____

7. Is your place of employment a possible site for a field trip? ____ Yes ____ No

8. Do you have any special interests or hobbies that you would be willing to share with the children? _____

9. Visiting rights of parents, if separated or divorced: _____

Please note: In situations where parents are separated or divorced, the daycare does not have the authority to deny a parent access to his or her children without a court order. If a legal agreement is in place, the centre should have a copy on file.

C. Toileting

1. Does your child have regular bowel movements? Yes _____ No _____

   Colour: _____ Consistency: _____

(continued)

2. Is your child prone to diaper rash? Yes _____ No _____

   If yes, do you use a special ointment? _____

3. What type of diaper do you use at home?

   Disposable ___ Cloth ___ Combination ___

4. Do you use plastic pants? Yes ___ No ___

5. On average, how many times a day would you change your child's diapers? _____

6. Does your child signal or use particular words when having a bowel movement or urinating? Yes ___ No ___ Please describe: _____

7. Has your child learned to use the toilet? Yes ___ No ___

8. Is your child comfortable using adult-size toilets? Yes ___ No ___

9. Does your child require assistance in the bathroom routine? Yes ___ No ___

10. Is your child generally dry through the night? Yes ___ No ___

11. Does your child nap with a diaper? Yes ___ No ___

D. Sleeping

1. Does your child experience any sleeping problems? Yes ___ No ___

   If yes, please give details: _____

2. How long does your child typically sleep at night? _____

3. What are your child's sleeping patterns for the day? a.m.: _____ p.m.: _____

4. Does your child have a special bedtime routine? Yes ___ No ___

   If yes, please describe: _____

5. Does your child sleep with a particular item? Yes ___ No ___

   If yes, please identify (toy, pacifier, bottle, special blanket, etc.): _____

6. What kinds of signals does your child give when sleepy? _____

7. How long would your child usually nap during the day? _____

8. If your child has a preferred sleeping position, please describe: _____

9. If you have any special way of helping your child get to sleep, please describe:

   _____

10. Does your child usually sleep in a room by him/herself? Yes ___ No ___

11. Is your child bothered by noise when sleeping? Yes ___ No ___

12. Does your child usually cry when he/she wakes up? Yes ___ No ___

13. Does your child experience nightmares? Yes ___ No ___

    If yes, please give details: _____

14. Does your child have any fears that we should be aware of? Yes ___ No ___

    If yes, please give details: _____

(continued)

E. Feeding

1. Do you have any concerns about your child's eating habits? Yes ＿＿＿ No ＿＿＿

   If yes, please give details: ＿＿＿＿＿＿＿＿＿＿＿＿＿＿＿＿＿＿＿＿＿＿＿＿＿＿＿＿＿＿＿＿

2. Is your child breast-fed? Yes ＿＿＿ No ＿＿＿

   If yes, is there any way we can support you at the centre so that you can continue to breast-feed? ＿＿＿＿＿＿＿＿＿＿＿＿＿＿＿＿＿＿＿＿＿＿＿＿＿＿＿＿＿＿＿＿＿＿＿＿

3. What type of food does your child eat?

   a) Formula ＿＿＿＿＿＿＿＿＿ Amount: ＿＿＿＿＿ Frequency: ＿＿＿＿＿

   b) Cereal ＿＿＿＿＿＿＿＿＿＿ Amount: ＿＿＿＿＿ Frequency: ＿＿＿＿＿

   c) Strained foods ＿＿＿＿＿＿ Amount: ＿＿＿＿＿ Frequency: ＿＿＿＿＿

   d) Others: ＿＿＿＿＿

4. Check:

   Your child needs to be fed ＿＿＿＿＿＿＿＿＿

   Eats slowly ＿＿＿＿＿＿＿＿＿＿＿＿＿＿

   Feeds self with assistance ＿＿＿＿＿＿＿＿＿

   Eats quickly ＿＿＿＿＿＿＿＿＿＿＿＿＿

   Feeds self independently ＿＿＿＿＿＿＿＿＿

5. If your child drinks from a bottle, please describe his/her preferred drinking position (for example, being held, lying down, sitting up, etc.): ＿＿＿＿＿＿＿＿＿

6. Check one: Your child drinks from a cup with a lid ＿＿＿ without a lid ＿＿＿

7. Does your child have any allergies or sensitivities to particular foods? Yes ＿＿＿ No ＿＿＿

   If yes, please list the foods: ＿＿＿＿＿＿＿＿＿＿＿＿＿＿＿＿＿＿＿＿＿＿＿＿＿＿＿＿＿＿

8. Are there any food restrictions that we should be aware of? Yes ＿＿＿ No ＿＿＿

   If yes, please describe: ＿＿＿＿＿＿＿＿＿＿＿＿＿＿＿＿＿＿＿＿＿＿＿＿＿＿＿＿＿＿＿

9. Is your child on a special diet? Yes ＿＿＿ No ＿＿＿

   If yes, please give details: ＿＿＿＿＿＿＿＿＿＿＿＿＿＿＿＿＿＿＿＿＿＿＿＿＿＿＿＿＿＿

10. List your child's favourite foods:

    a) ＿＿＿＿＿＿＿＿＿＿＿＿＿＿ c) ＿＿＿＿＿＿＿＿＿＿＿＿＿＿＿＿

    b) ＿＿＿＿＿＿＿＿＿＿＿＿＿＿ d) ＿＿＿＿＿＿＿＿＿＿＿＿＿＿＿＿

11. List any foods your child especially dislikes:

    a) ＿＿＿＿＿＿＿＿＿＿＿＿＿＿ c) ＿＿＿＿＿＿＿＿＿＿＿＿＿＿＿＿

    b) ＿＿＿＿＿＿＿＿＿＿＿＿＿＿ d) ＿＿＿＿＿＿＿＿＿＿＿＿＿＿＿＿

12. What would you consider a normal portion for your child? ＿＿＿＿＿＿＿＿＿＿＿＿

13. Are there family food preferences that you would like us to honor? ＿＿＿＿＿＿＿＿

(continued)

F. Other Information

1. What is your child's usual reaction to being bathed or changed by someone other than yourself? _____

2. We would like to know how your child reacts to different situations and people in order to facilitate his/her comfort level:

   a) What does he/she do when you leave him/her alone to go to another room?

   _____

   b) What does he/she do when you leave him/her at home:

   with relatives: _____

   with siblings: _____

   with a baby sitter: _____

3. Are there other adults who also take care of your child? Yes ____ No ____

4. Has your child ever been in a group-care setting before? Yes ____ No ____

5. How does your child generally relate to other children? _____

6. How does your child react to situations that make him/her angry or frustrated?

   _____

7. Describe any strategies for guiding your child's behaviour that you think would be helpful for staff to know: _____

8. What strategies do you use to comfort your child when he/she is distressed?

   _____

9. What does your child enjoy doing during the day? What are his/her interests?

   _____

10. Please describe your child's language skills: _____

11. Please describe any dressing habits that staff should be aware of:

    _____

12. Please provide any other information about your child that you think the teachers should be aware of: _____

13. What celebrations are important to your family? _____

14. Please describe any traditions, customs, foods, or symbols associated with this celebration that you would like staff to be aware of: _____

15. Please describe any family values of particular importance to you that you would like the teachers to know about: _____

The completed intake form—plus a home visit—provides teachers with the tools they need to provide a warm, supportive environment that enhances the growth of the whole child—physically, socially, emotionally, cognitively, and creatively.

INCIDENT REPORT/INJURY FORM

In order to keep families informed about serious injuries, some centres complete and have families sign an injury report. This form provides families with detailed information about incidents as they occur. A minor fall may result in a bruise that the parent may question a day later; the injury form provides a record of the incident. The centre may give a copy of the report to parents and keep the original in the child's file. The reports also provide centres with information regarding common injuries and opportunities to change practices or the environment.

Janeway

Child Care Centre

Health and Immunization Form

Each medical officer of health (MOH) in Canada is responsible for the health of children in centres within his or her geographic area. As a requirement for admission to the centre, families need to complete health and immunization forms.

Janeway

Child Care Centre

Emergency Contact Form

Please list below the names of people we should contact, in the event of an emergency, if we are unable to reach you.

Name: _____ Home phone: _____

Address: _____ Business phone: _____

Relationship to child: _____

Name: _____ Home phone: _____

Address: _____ Business phone: _____

Relationship to child: _____

Janeway
Child Care Centre

Emergency Treatment Release Form

I authorize the Janeway Child Care Centre to act on my behalf to ensure immediate medical treatment should the staff deem it necessary. I give permission for my child, _____, in the event of an emergency, to receive full medical attention deemed necessary by a physician at the _____ hospital. I understand that my child will be accompanied to the hospital by a child-care staff and that every effort will be made to reach me and/or my emergency contact person. I agree to accept any financial responsibility for any emergency medical care necessary.

Signature of family member: _____

Date: _____   Witness: _____

Janeway
Child Care Centre

Permission to Video and Photograph Form

For educational and/or child-care-related purposes, photographs, videotapes, and/or audio tape recordings of the children participating in our program may occasionally be taken. I hereby give permission for _____ to be taped, videotaped, and photographed while in attendance at the _____ centre.

Signature of family member: _____

Date: _____

Janeway
Child Care Centre

Excursion Permission Form

I, _____, give the staff of the Janeway Child Care Centre permission to include my child, _____, in child-care excursions. I understand that I will be notified of time, date, destination, and type of transportation prior to the excursion.

Signature of family member: _____

Date: _____

THE FAMILY HANDBOOK

A well-organized, effectively written, attractively designed family handbook helps families decide if a particular centre meets their needs. The handbook outlines the obligations and responsibilities of the families and staff and provides information on the day-to-day running of the centre. A valuable marketing tool, the handbook can be distributed throughout the community; doctors' offices, local hospitals, community information centres, and schools are all possible distribution points. The diversity and inclusiveness of the centre should be documented in design, photos, and content. If cost is a problem, a smaller brochure outlining the strengths of the program can be distributed instead. Besides being a useful orientation tool for families who are new to the centre, the handbook serves as a valuable reference for currently enrolled families.

Care should be taken not to include more information than is necessary. Material must be chosen carefully and expressed in a clear and concise fashion. In order to reflect the communities they serve, some centres have their handbook translated into a number of different languages. (One centre has translated its handbook into 18 languages.) The handbook should be carefully proofread for grammatical and spelling errors. If possible, a professional copy editor and/or proofreader should be consulted.

Once families have been with the centre for some time, ask them for feedback on the handbook. How effective was it in meeting their needs? They might also be invited to write a testimonial for a revised edition of the handbook:

> I was so excited when we were notified that our baby daughter would have a space at the Janeway Child Care Centre. It has a wonderful reputation in our community and after talking to the supervisor of the centre it seemed like the perfect place for us. I spent a week in the infant room with my daughter and the teachers, helping her make a gradual transition to her new surroundings. Then came the day that I actually had to leave her to return to work!
>
> Nothing could have prepared me for the overwhelming sense of loss I felt as I left the centre that first morning. Our daughter giggled and laughed with one of the staff as I waved goodbye (after about five hugs and kisses). I cried all the way to work. For several weeks I got a lump in my throat whenever I left. It is only because of the support and empathy of the staff that I survived those first few weeks. They called me at work several hours into the first day to reassure me that things were going well and they greeted me at the end of the day with a Polaroid picture of our daughter happily playing with a toy. She is now in the senior preschool room and we continue to feel we are a part of a larger sense of family in this centre.

Government officials, doctors, educators, and other community members who have been involved with the centre might also be invited to submit testimonials. They go a long way toward reassuring new families.

DESIGN AND LAYOUT

A handbook's layout and design are critical to its effectiveness, and there are many software programs available to assist in producing a handbook. Photographs and drawings by the children add a personal touch and will encourage families to read the content. A logo for the cover might be designed by staff, parents, children, or a local artist. Some centres differentiate the sections of their handbooks by having them printed on paper of different colours. (When choosing coloured paper check that the text is readable, that the photographs reproduce clearly, and that the colour is not too bold to tire the reader in long documents.) Other handbooks use tabs to separate sections. Consideration should also be given to such factors as paper quality and binding. Using standard-size paper helps to reduce costs. If the handbook is to retain its professional appearance, it should be reprinted on a regular basis rather than revised by hand. The handbook may also be made available on disk or CD-ROM, or emailed to families as an electronic document.

CONTENTS

The handbook may be divided into the comprehensive subject areas outlined in the following sections.

I. Welcome to the Centre

The introduction to the handbook should welcome interested families and set the tone for the remainder of the handbook. It should reflect the spirit of the centre and the critical role that families can play. Particularly significant information should be provided here; for example, in a co-operative child-care centre families are expected to contribute their time.

II. History of the Centre

Many centres have interesting beginnings and parents feel a greater connection to the centre when they understand the often perilous road that centres have travelled. The following excerpt, from the Campus Community Co-Op Day Care Centre in downtown Toronto, reflects the tumultuous history of this particular centre:

> About 350 supporters of the Campus Community Co-Op Day Care Centre carried out the first occupation of Simcoe Hall in U of T history today. . . . Lorenne Smith, assistant philosophy professor and a member of the daycare co-operative, [gave] the crowd a [brief] history of the daycare centre's struggles with the university. "As a woman," Mrs. Smith said, "I find it insulting. It's unthinkable that a woman must give up her career or not be able to work when she needs to support a family because she has children." (*The Varsity*, 26 March 1970)
>
> When Lorenne Smith spoke to a crowd of parents and babies at a rally that winter afternoon in 1970, Campus Co-Op had already been in existence for a year, founded by a core of feminists negotiating with university administration to support their Sussex Street daycare centre, staffed entirely by parents and volunteers. Frustrated by the lack of administration interest in supporting mothers who worked for the university—and, by inference, women everywhere—the parents simply [took] over the Sussex Street building and began warming bottles and setting up cots.

III. Practical Information

This section of the handbook includes the centre's name, mailing address, main telephone number, and information about telephone extensions; an e-mail address or website address should also be noted. Some centres also provide the telephone numbers of subsidy offices, government ministries related to child care, support groups, and children's help lines. Transportation information might also be included (for example, the nearest subway stop or the number of the connecting bus). Centres located within a larger complex or a school might provide a map. Finally, this section should include hours of operation, days when the centre is closed (statutory holidays, for example), any special days such as religious holidays observed by families in the centre, and information about weather closings. School-age programs should outline their program for winter, spring, and summer breaks, along with the centre's policy on professional development days.

IV. Philosophy

This section of the handbook helps families decide whether the centre will meet the particular needs of their family. While some centres take a holistic approach to the child, others focus on a particular aspect of child development. Families may, for example, choose a centre that emphasizes creative development in music and the arts. The philosophy statement should reflect not only the centre's beliefs but also the interests and needs of the parents and children in the centre. Some centres use this section to articulate their support for cultural diversity and inclusiveness. Exhibit 8.2 is adapted from a philosophy statement developed in the lab schools at George Brown College in Toronto.

It is not enough for a centre simply to make grand statements about its philosophy. Families must be able to *see* how this philosophy translates into action; this is effectively accomplished by including a list of the centre's goals. These goals summarize the ways in which the families and teachers work together to provide the best possible environment for the children. Each philosophical statement should be accompanied by specific and measurable actions, as illustrated by the following:

Philosophy Statement	Action
An environment that reflects cultural sensitivity and incorporates each child's cultural heritage into the centre's day-to-day activities.	1. Foods are nutritious and reflect cultural diversity. 2. Playrooms contain a wide array of props and materials from a range of cultures (e.g., musical instruments, music, dolls, dress-up clothes, art materials, books, puppets, science materials, manipulatives, pictures, bulletin boards, furniture). 3. Families are asked to share their ideas for providing a culturally sensitive environment.

EXHIBIT 8.2 PHILOSOPHY STATEMENT

What I hear, I forget
What I see, I remember
What I do, I understand

Children deserve the best start in life! As early childhood educators, we believe that we must not only strive for excellence in the provision of physical and nurturing care but also excel at providing an enriched learning environment. We are aware of the vast differences that exist among children even at the earliest ages. The teacher's role is to determine the developmental level of each child and to plan for curriculum that encourages growth in the areas of his or her social, emotional, physical, creative, and cognitive development in a play-based environment. We are constantly evaluating and refining our program to meet the needs of the children. We believe that each aspect of development is interrelated, and therefore we endeavour to provide a program that meets each child's needs in a consistent and progressive manner. We establish this in cooperation and consultation with families.

We offer:

- family input and involvement as an extension of the family environment
- a program that emphasizes individual and small-group learning experiences and that utilizes the child's natural means of learning through play
- a commitment to a play-based environment because we believe that play helps the child to explore and understand the real world
- an opportunity for the child to explore, experiment, problem-solve, discuss, discover, ask questions, create, and master the real world of things, people, and events in a warm and relaxed environment
- experiences that develop communication and language
- an environment that reflects the developmental needs and interests of the children
- a wide range of equipment and materials that encourage and stimulate the child's learning potential
- a connection to the community through scheduled trips and walks
- an opportunity for the child to develop his or her feelings of self-worth through positive reinforcement, the recognition of personal choice, and respect for the child's feelings and opinions
- a spirit of trust, respect, and cooperation in which relationships with children and adults have an opportunity to develop
- relationships that display an unconditional positive regard for the child and a sincere interest in each child's uniqueness
- an opportunity for children to demonstrate appropriate prosocial behaviours such as cooperation, sharing, turn-taking, and problem-solving
- encouragement for appropriate behaviours through role modelling and positive reinforcement based on social responsibility and respect for others
- an environment that reflects cultural sensitivity and incorporates each child's cultural heritage into the centre's day-to-day activities
- for children whose first language is not English, opportunities to use their primary language
- a curriculum that values equality and promotes a bias-free perspective
- a safe and healthy environment in which the emphasis is on nutrition and the development of self-care
- a program that encourages respect for the environment
- a program that encourages enjoyment and satisfaction as ends in themselves and as a motivation for further learning

V. Administration of the Centre

The centre can use a simple chart to illustrate its organization by age group. A simplified flow-chart gives families an overview of the centre's basic organizational structure. (The cook, the caretaker, and other part-time staff who work at the centre on a regular basis should be included in the chart.)

In the case of school-age programs, the administrative connections between the school setting and the daycare should be delineated.

VI. Qualifications of Staff

Families should receive relevant information on staff training, education, and work experience. The qualifications of all centre personnel, from cook to bookkeeper to supervisor, should be included here. This section should also include information on specialized training by staff (for example, supporting children with special needs), centre support of staff through ongoing professional development and skills upgrading, and languages spoken by the staff. If ECE students or high school students complete field placements in the centre, this is also relevant information for families.

VII. Admission Procedures

Besides clearly explaining admission procedures, this section of the handbook provides information on the admission of children who have received subsidies as well as children with special needs. Health requirements (immunization, doctor's examination, and so on) are clearly outlined. Families who are on a waiting list will want to know the criteria used by the centre in granting spaces.

No. of Children	Group	Age	No. of Staff
10	Infants	6 weeks–18 months	4
10	Toddlers	18 months–2.5 years	2
16	Preschoolers	2.5 years–6 years	2
30	School age	6 years–12 years	3

President, Janeway Corporation

Linda Le

Board of Directors, Janeway Corporation

| Charlie McCloskey | Nadine Visalli | Cathy Bellevue |
| Melinda Samuels | Ned Thompson | Helleca Sanderson |

Supervisor of Child Care

Theresa Sanchez

Infant Staff	Toddler Staff	Preschool Staff	School-Age Staff
Kelly Antram	Olga Tamar	Kate Dougall	Drew Easton
Michael Bailey	Alexandra Brown	Alex Swartz	Farzaneh Gupta
Jennifer Cho			
Sonia Chavez			

VIII. Fee Structure

One of the most important pieces of information for any new family entering a centre is the cost of the service. Some centres require families to sign a statement that outlines the fee schedule and method of payment; this statement becomes the contract between the centre and the parent.

The fee-structure section should include information on

- registration fees and procedures for payment (cheque or credit card, weekly, biweekly, or monthly payments);
- procedures in the event that families are late with their fees or are unable to pay;
- the way sick days and holidays are accounted for in the fee structure;
- the administration of income-tax statements;
- extra charges above the normal monthly fee for special trips, supplies, breakfast and lunch programs, and so forth;
- special arrangements made in the case of parents who are divorced or separated (some centres collect fees only from the custodial parent, because he or she may be the only parent with whom the centre has regular contact);
- special funding or enhancement grants made available to the centre by government or business sources;
- withdrawing a child from the centre (financial repercussions should be addressed here);
- review of fees and when families might expect fee increases;
- information for families in communities where subsidy may be available;

- a contract stating that the family understands the centre's late-fee policy (not all centres with such a policy ask families to sign).

IX. Prosocial Behaviour and Child-Abuse Policy

The handbook should clearly outline the centre's strategies for encouraging prosocial behaviour on the part of children. Approaches not condoned or used at the centre might also be mentioned, so that families clearly understand the centre's approach.

Families also need to be aware of the centre's policy on child abuse. For example, staff, family members, and children will not use the following actions in the centre:

- corporal punishment (hitting, shaking, spanking, kicking, pushing, shoving, grabbing, squeezing, pinching);
- deliberate harsh or degrading treatment that would humiliate or undermine a child's self-respect; and
- abusive or humiliating language, yelling, and screaming.

Families should be advised that the staff are required by law to report suspected abuse to local authorities.

The board of directors may, on rare occasions, request that a child be suspended or withdrawn from the centre. It is important for families to understand that while every effort is made to accommodate all children in the centre, there are times when the safety and needs of the group outweigh the needs of one child. In some school-age settings, children under suspension from the school are not allowed in the child-care centre.

INSIDE LOOK

Our philosophy at the Janeway Child Care Centre is that positive reinforcement and encouragement are the most effective means of helping children learn prosocial behaviours. By recognizing personal choice and by allowing the child control over his or her environment, we encourage the child to express feelings and opinions. We provide opportunities for the child to see the validity of different perspectives and to respect the limits created by mutual consent. As teachers, we attempt to model appropriate behaviour by being courteous and by developing warm and trusting relationships with the children.

X. Health and Exclusion Policy

Families want to have a clear understanding of the centre's policy on sick children. A centre might require a child to be excluded when

1. an illness prevents the child from participating in routine activities

2. the child requires more individual care than the staff are able to provide without compromising the needs of the other children

3. the child risks infecting other children or caregivers as defined in the exclusion guidelines (Pimento and Kernested, 2000: 172).

For some families, a child's illness can be a challenge. Family responsibility leave has yet to be legislated and many families lack the job flexibility, extended family, or close friends that enable them to care for their ill child. Though it is important to consider the needs of all the children in a group-care situation, supervisors and teachers may occasionally decide that it is in the best interests of the parents and the child to make alternative arrangements. For example, a preschooler with a sprained ankle might easily be accommodated in the toddler room during outdoor time until her injury heals.

This section of the handbook should include the names of agencies that provide emergency care in the community (those agencies that provide translation services should be noted for ESL parents); information about the parents' role with respect to health-related matters; information on the storage and administration of medications at the centre; information on sun block and appropriate summer and winter clothing; and dental information. Families are reassured to know that the centre is a nonsmoking environment and that toys are disinfected on a regular basis. Finally, this section should address how children with allergies or other special health-care needs are accommodated in the centre. For example, some children have such serious nut allergies that centres are responding by turning the centre into peanut-free zones.

XI. Safety Issues

Information on how the centre meets local licensing requirements, which vary from province to province, is imperative. Besides reassuring families that every attempt has been made to ensure that their children are playing in a safe indoor and outdoor environment, this section should provide information on centre procedures for notifying families in the event of a serious injury; information on first-aid training undertaken by staff; and information on fire, theft, and liability insurance. Where applicable, procedures for using security codes or security cards should be given. Families in school-age programs, for example, may need to be aware that certain doors are locked at certain times and that access is gained only through designated doors. Finally, this section should explain fire-drill and evacuation procedures and name the location of temporary premises in the event of an emergency.

XII. Food and Nutrition Policy

This section should communicate that good nutrition is an important, intrinsic part of the program. It should include discussion on how the centre adheres to Canada's Guide to Healthy Eating and information on related issues such as food storage and handling guidelines, the location of menus, and the procedure for notifying families if changes are made to menus. This is an opportunity for the centre to show that the menus reflect the cultural diversity of the children and to invite families to become involved in menu planning.

Procedures for accommodating children with special dietary requirements or restrictions (whether for medical or religious reasons) should be outlined here. Ingredients and methods of preparation are of particular importance to families of children with allergies. Menus should emphasize seasonal fruits and vegetables and unprocessed food that is low in sugar content.

Families of babies need to know if the centre provides bottles or solid food. Families of older children will need to know the following:

- Will the centre provide a breakfast program?
- Will snacks be served?
- How will the lunch program be run?
- Will hot lunches or supplements be served?
- Will children be expected to bring their own lunch?
- Will junk food (pop, chips, chocolate, and so on) in the children's lunches be restricted?
- Will children be able to heat their lunches in a microwave?
- Will garbage-less lunches be promoted?

Children should be encouraged to have tasting amounts of all foods offered, with teachers

Courtesy of Lynn Wilson

Including photographs in the manual helps to break up the text and, as you can see, a picture is worth a thousand words.

modelling a positive attitude by eating with the children and encouraging a relaxed, comfortable experience.

This section should also explain the centre's policy on celebrations such as birthdays. Does the centre encourage elaborate celebrations involving magicians and loot bags or are more modest events the norm? A centre generally decides on a policy that reflects the wishes of the majority of families.

XIII. Drop-Off and Pick-Up Procedures

This section outlines procedures for checking in with a staff person in the morning and, in most centres, repeating the procedure in the evening. It should be stressed that drop-offs and pick-ups are easier for everyone involved if a regular routine is followed. If parents know that they will be later than usual, they should notify the centre so that staff can reassure the child. Procedures relating to school-age children must also be explained.

It should be made clear to families that they are responsible for bringing their child to the centre. Some centres will not assume responsibility for a child until he or she is signed in. Other centres will accept older children without a parent being present if a release letter from their parents is on file. Families should be assured in this section that children will be released only to those people they have designated in writing. Parents who are separated or divorced should be advised that the centre does not have the authority to deny a parent access to his or her children without a court order.

XIV. Field Trips

This section should reassure families that they will be provided with complete information about any trip that takes the children out of the centre, including the purpose of the event, the itinerary, method of travel, teacher–child ratios, and safety procedures.

XV. What to Bring on the First Day

This section should list the items families are required to bring to the centre on the first day. Items that are not appropriate (umbrellas, for example) might also be listed. For the convenience of families, this section could take the form of a checklist, as illustrated in the box on the next page.

The checklist can be adapted to accommodate different age groups. Some centres do not allow toys, money, or candy to be brought from home; such restrictions should be discussed in advance with families. Families should be advised to label all articles with the child's name.

XVI. Involving Families

This section should provide information on the mechanisms for home–centre communication, orientation to the centre, home visits, resources available to families (newsletters, books, videos, parent bulletin boards, and so forth) as well as ways in which they can become actively involved with the centre (for example, by participating in fundraising events, by volunteering, by sending in "beautiful junk," or by serving on the board of directors).

XVII. Special Features

Any special features of the program, such as involvement with an intergenerational program, should be discussed in this section of the family handbook. Sometimes centres that are located close to universities or hospitals are asked to participate in studies or surveys; families should be advised that they may decline if they do not wish their child

First Day List

1. Paperwork
    a) Intake Form ____
    b) Health and Immunization Form ____
    c) Permission to Video and Photograph Form ____
    d) Excursion Permission Form ____
    e) Emergency Treatment Release Form ____
    f) Authorization for Pickup Form ____
2. Blanket ____
3. Soft cuddle toy ____
4. Seasonal change of clothing ____
5. Extra socks and underwear ____
6. Diapers ____
7. Toothbrush and toothpaste ____
8. Bathing suit and towel ____
9. Picture of the family to place in cubby ____

to participate in special projects. Agencies whose services are available to the centre (developmental assessments and referral services, public health departments, dental and visual screenings, and so on) should be outlined; in the case of school-age programs, information on after-four programs, language classes, and community events could be provided.

THE PLAYROOM HANDBOOK

The playroom handbook provides information about the centre's individual rooms. This benefits both families who are new to the centre and families of children who are moving to new age groups within the centre. Like the "Qualifications of Staff" section in the family handbook, the playroom handbook might include professional information about the teacher (educational background, length of employment at the centre, and work experience). More personal information (family life, hobbies, etc.) may be included at the teacher's discretion.

The playroom handbook can expand on the centre's philosophical statement by addressing the specific age group. Many parental concerns are alleviated when the ways in which appropriate practice is applied in the playroom are clearly outlined. For example, procedures for dealing with biting in the toddler room might be provided.

The daily schedule should also be discussed, with particular reference to ways in which the philosophy of the centre translates into action in the playroom. The lunch routine, for example, might be described as follows: "In the senior preschool room, the children participate in a family service format. They help themselves and do their own pouring. We feel it is important that the teachers eat with the children, because this offers the children role models for appropriate behaviour and attitudes. The atmosphere is relaxed and social." This statement reinforces the philosophical goal of encouraging self-help skills and a sense of cooperation and sharing. Teachers should point out that the schedule is not written in stone but changes with the needs and interests of the group.

The playroom handbook should outline the organization of the room. Because families may be unfamiliar with the learning centre approach, descriptions of each of the learning centres in the room—from the art centre to the science and exploration centre—might be provided. These descriptions could also be posted in the room near the appropriate learning centres as a source of information for families and visitors to the centre.

The handbook should discuss the development of curriculum and provide examples of the way teachers plan and program for the children's individual needs. This section of the handbook will emphasize developmentally appropriate programming. Monthly planning calendars used in the past provide families with an overview. Ongoing activities (swimming lessons, trips to the local library, and so on) and yearly events (such as a pancake breakfast, a summer barbecue, intergenerational picnics) can be mentioned in this section of the playroom handbook.

CENTRE DOCUMENTATION

Documentation is the process of gathering information about children's ideas, words, and their work, as well as documenting the teacher's work with the children over time. It is the process of recording and reporting on children's learning through multiple mediums. Documentation expands the role of the teacher and provides a tool that enables teachers to be more effective in their work with the children. It helps teachers understand children's thinking processes and fosters teachers' facilitation skills. It requires them to become critical thinkers, strong observers of the children, and researchers in the playroom. Documentation is a visual representation that makes children's learning visible. Teachers must observe, collect data, analyze the information, and then determine the next steps.

The type of documentation that teachers do is not so far removed from our own past. Burrington and Sortino (2004) reflect on how our mothers raised us:

> They saved anything—newspaper clippings, school photos, report cards, Sunday school diplomas, obituaries, and even teeth were tucked away. The images and artifacts are by-products of the meaning that we made in our lives. They are like words in the language of our families,

fragments of memories. They represent and evoke the time, place, thoughts, and feelings of those particular moments, and we revisit these documents and artifacts of our childhood again and again, with our parents, our siblings, our friends, and our own children. . . . Yet their artifacts tell a story that is incomplete, for without words, without a narrative, there is only a shadow of an anecdote with no particular shape, without substance. . . . The documentation on our walls and in our archives is a visual and literary account of events, ideas, projects, learning, people, and community. It represents our history. Our documentation marks the passing of time, honors relationships, celebrates moments, and conveys the inner thoughts and feelings of children and their teachers. We are more present in our daily encounters because we have an identity that is part of something larger. The images of strong, competent, thoughtful children remind us that we have an immense responsibility to the future. (2004: 225, 237)

The concept of documentation originated at the preschools of Reggio Emilia in northern Italy. It informs viewers of the processes children went through in their play and the meaning it had for them. It is a tool that teachers use to record and communicate information to the children themselves, to families, and to colleagues. Like all good stories, the documentation process includes a beginning rooted in observations of the children, a middle, and an ending that summarizes what the children have learned over time. This process of documentation involves collaboration with children, colleagues, families, and sometimes community members.

Courtesy of Lynn Wilson

Mary Bianci and the children selecting their seeds and tools for their gardening project.

Throughout the year, children in the Kindergarten room at Esther Exton participate in a variety of projects. Project ideas are based on children's interests and fostered according to children's developmental levels. The process of exploring, experimenting, investigating, and problem-solving is where the learning takes place as demonstrated in our Gardening Project. Teachers helped to facilitate and enrich children's interests and learning by researching for information and materials from different sources. Field trips were an integral part of our gardening project. We took a trip to the gardening store, the market, and the farm. We purchased seeds and gardening tools with the children and they planted the seeds in our own child-care garden. Families were encouraged to participate by bringing in materials, filling in research cards, and sharing person expertise with us. This allowed families to feel that they were an integral part of their child's learning. Families felt more connected and involved with what the children learn during the day. It is our belief, as reflected in the child-care centre philosophy that "partnership between the family/home, community and the child-care centre is a major factor in fostering seamless learning for children and that learning is a smooth continuum."

Source: Contributed by Mary Bianci, Kindergarten teacher and Joyce Gee, Manager, Esther Exton Child Care Centre

Displaying documentation in the playrooms and entranceways allows the families as well as the outside community to see what the teachers are doing and gives them more credibility. As families and visitors to the centre read the information and see the work the children are doing in the program, they can understand how much serious consideration teachers give to all aspects of the children's learning (Fraser, 2000).

Harris Helm, Beneke, and Steinheimer (1997) state that documenting children's learning may be one of the most valuable skills a teacher can learn. Regular and consistent documentation of children's work can benefit teachers in five ways:

1. Teachers who can document children's learning in a variety of ways are able to respond to demands for accountability.

2. Teachers who document are more often able to teach children through direct, firsthand, interactive experiences that enhance brain development.

3. Teachers are more effective when they document.

4. Teachers who can document children's work are better able to meet special needs.

5. Children perceive learning to be important and worthwhile when teachers document their learning.

During field placement experiences, ECE students who have an opportunity to complete a form of documentation benefit by

1. practising and improving observation and recording skills.

2. increasing their understanding of children's play, thinking, and problem-solving.

3. deepening their understanding of how children make sense of their world and the meaning that they construct.

4. providing an opportunity for the children to demonstrate the sequence of learning. By telling the story of children's learning, investigations, skill acquisition, and discoveries, students demonstrate their understanding of how learning progresses and defines the beginning, middle, and end of documentation. When children learn, the content of learning moves from

- concrete to abstract,
- simple to complex,
- present to future and past,
- facts to concepts, and
- known to unknown.

5. providing a permanent form of communication that can be viewed with children, families, and staff and allows the student to interact in a meaningful way with families.

6. providing a permanent record from which further program decisions can be made.

7. demonstrating respect for the children and their efforts. The children will feel their efforts are valued by the student teacher and other adults in the room.

Bertrand (2008: 83) relates how teachers in New Zealand have introduced learning stories from early

FIGURE 8.1 STUDENT DOCUMENTATION PANELS

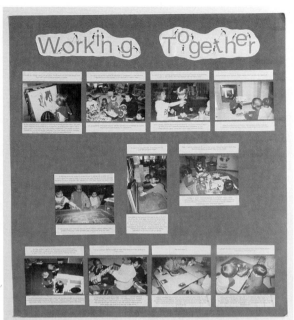

INSIDE **LOOK**

The Reggio Emilia's Project Approach and the resulting documentation have proved to be an effective means of communicating with families. One parent comments:

I knew that lots of interesting things were happening at the centre as the children and teachers worked on a project about whales. Shakil came home every day with new information and insights to share with us. Since we live near the ocean, whale sightings were not uncommon, but I was struck by the intensity of the learning taking place for these four- and five-year-olds. Photos of the children at work, and on their trip to see the whales, and samples of their drawings and stories were placed on bulletin boards at the entrance to the centre for parents and children to view. As the work progressed, new documentation was posted on a regular basis, so we were able to monitor the children's headway. One day we were even greeted by whale sounds playing on a tape recorder at the door.

I was impressed by the children's concern for the whales, and through this process they all became media stars. The supervisor contacted a local television station and the children were interviewed and their documentation recorded. What the project documentation demonstrated to me was the children's ability to problem-solve and to think in divergent ways well beyond what I thought they were capable of.

These projects, completed by the children, are documented as a permanent record in the book centre to which families and children can refer.

childhood programs to offer snapshots of children's learning and development in action by describing actual, unique experiences: "Teachers document children's activities and early childhood educators assess what learning and development are taking place and plan for the next steps. The observation, documentation, and analysis of learning stories create a sample of children's learning that is rich in context, articulate, and complete in terms of the situation, the actions and the conclusion. Learning stories are narrations that document children's engagement in learning experiences, including the analysis or assessment of that learning and the child's emerging developmental skills. The stories and assessments can be presented in children's portfolios for children, families, and practitioners to read and re-read."

ONGOING WRITTEN COMMUNICATION

Effective written communication has the potential to help teachers build positive relationships with families. Research underscores parents' readiness to learn more about parenting and more about the ways in which their children learn. Centres are always looking for effective ways to ensure that families receive written information. Many notices sent with the children never make it home—or, they arrive home covered in yesterday's lunch. In centres where families pick up information themselves, the information should be placed in an accessible location. A clothesline arranged by the centre entrance, with pockets for each family, provides an efficient pickup system and an easy way for staff to check which families still need to pick up their messages. We must also be aware of the tone of our messages: warnings and messages on the door may well keep parents out.

CENTRE MENUS

Menus that are posted in the centre should reflect an understanding of the importance of good nutrition and its positive effects on the health and well-being of the children. Menu selections should reflect the diversity of the families that the centre serves. Children should have an opportunity to eat food that is familiar to them as well as to try new foods in a positive and encouraging environment. Families should be encouraged to share recipes with the cook at the centre and with other families as well. Some centres produce and sell at fundraisers

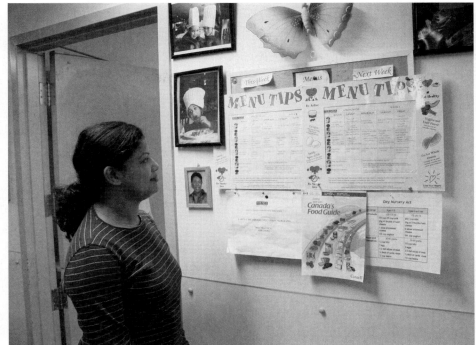

Courtesy of Scotia Plaza Child Care Centre

Menus should be posted in an accessible location.

cookbooks that feature a favourite recipe from each family.

PLANNING FORMS

In order to keep families informed about programming that is happening in the room, a planning form should be posted in an accessible location. The form explains to families what is happening in the centre on a weekly basis. Planning forms provide an opportunity for teachers to share information about emergent curriculum and appropriate practice.

Courtesy of Scotia Plaza Child Care Centre

Posting planning forms allows families to see how they might be able to contribute to the curriculum.

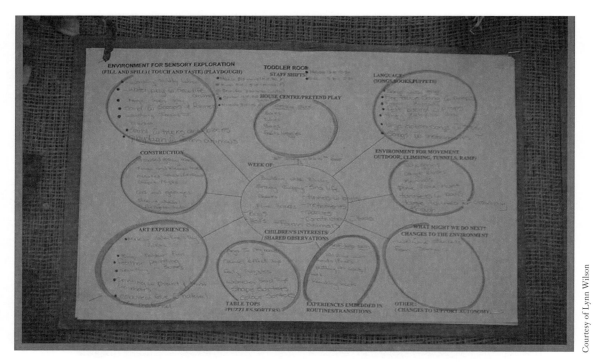

A detailed planning form reassures families that their child's day is well organized and positive learning experiences will take place.

DAILY CHARTS

A daily chart is a chart on which both families and staff record information about the child. By providing a way to share pertinent information the daily chart helps to smooth the transition between centre and home. Such charts are particularly useful when they are maintained for infants; knowing when the last feeding has taken place or how well the infant has slept during the night will help a teacher determine how best to support the child. Families can use the chart to record such information as changes to their daily work routine (different phone numbers at which they can be reached, for example). Teachers can use daily charts to record interesting or significant happenings. Ideally, translated versions of charts should be provided to ESL parents; pictorial charts are another possibility (see Figure 8.2).

At the Esther Exton Child Care Centre, the senior preschoolers contribute to their charts by illustrating some of the highlights of their day. Teachers discuss the chart with the child and record any information the child wishes to add. Rather than use clipboards, some centres use a small binder in which to record daily information about the child. This form of information-gathering is often referred to as a communication book. This concept can be expanded to include a booklet that travels between child care and home and in which families and teachers record their observations on a regular basis.

BROCHURES AND FLIERS

It is a good idea for the supervisor to keep a record of where and how families first learned about the centre. With this information the centre may be better able to market its services to the community. Brochures about the centre can be distributed to local community centres, clinics, health-care professionals, hospitals, and local businesses. The centre can generate further publicity for itself by participating in such community events as fundraising, fairs, parades, and festivals.

In order to emphasize the importance it attaches to family involvement, the centre can design a brochure outlining various strategies for achieving effective communication and summarizing the ways in which families can participate in the day-to-day life of the centre. The brochure is a good place to outline parents' rights and responsibilities and to encourage the active

FIGURE 8.2 INFANT CHART

Infant Chart

Name _____   Date _____

Last night I went to sleep at _____ p.m.

I awoke at _____ a.m. today.

For breakfast I had _____ .

Last B.M. _____

Information about medication _____

Special notes from my family _____

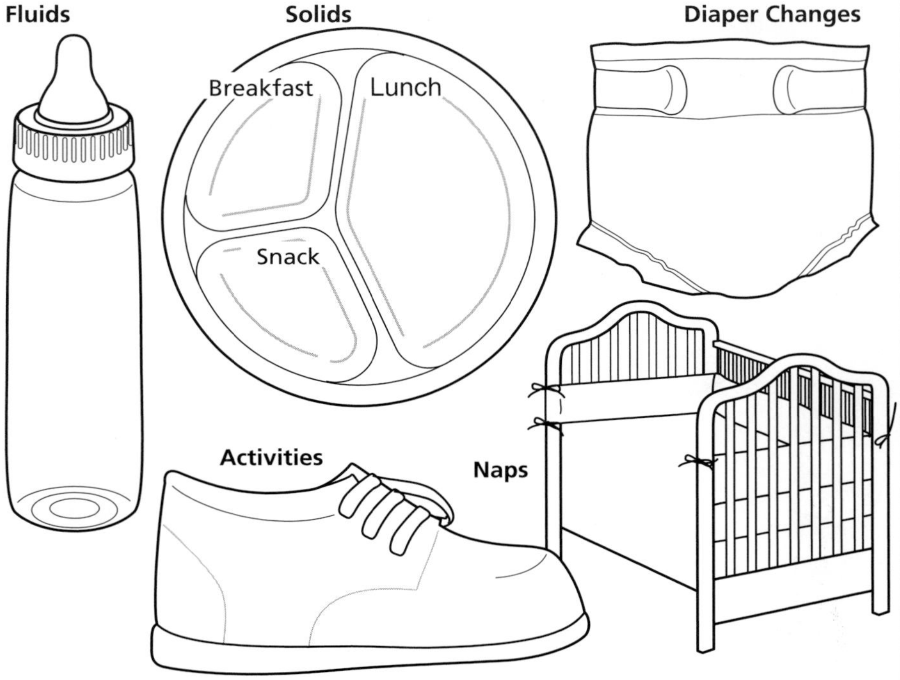

_____

_____

Fluids   **Solids**   **Diaper Changes**

Breakfast   Lunch

Snack

Activities   **Naps**

Special notes from staff: _____

_____

_____

Source: Artwork by Lisa Chiarello, YTV Centre.

involvement of men in the centre (the brochure could feature photographs of fathers, male teachers, and other men who play a significant role). The centre could also include in its brochure basic information about community resources and support agencies. Some centre brochures are in effect condensed versions of the family handbook. Like family handbooks, brochures can be distributed to appropriate settings throughout the community.

FIGURE 8.3   BROCHURES AND FLIERS PREPARED BY ECE STUDENTS

Fliers can also serve as an effective information tool. Written material should be concise and translated into languages that reflect the community. Fliers should be colourful, well designed, and attention-getting. School-age children might be encouraged to assist with the production of fliers.

JOURNALS

In some situations, ongoing journals may be a useful communication tool. Teachers use the journal to record their observations of the child during the day and invite families to respond in the evening with written comments or observations of their own; the child may also contribute. Some teachers have the children record their thoughts about centre events or important moments in their child care life throughout the year. When the child leaves the centre, the journal becomes a wonderful memory of the time spent at the centre.

Brochures or fliers can provide parents with important ways in which they can enhance their learning in the home. The following, from Invest in Kids (**www.investinkids.ca**), is an example of material that might be sent home.

Ten Ways to Enjoy Different Learning Experiences at Home

1. Improve your child in creating his own presents, greeting cards and gift wrap. This is a lovely chance for him to explore different art techniques like paper maché, collage, painting, sculpting with play dough, and to discover the enjoyment that comes from making something for another person.

2. Create a special storage box for dramatic play materials. Include things like hats, gloves, aprons, cooking tools like a plastic bowl and wooden spoons, dolls, and stuffed animals. Your child can then role-model things she sees you doing and practise many important self-help skills as well.

3. Provide board books for your child to read to her teddy bears and dolls. She will model reading behaviours she has observed, and practise emerging literacy skills like turning pages, telling stories about what is in the pictures, and recognizing letters and words.

4. Demonstrate different uses of numbers for your child. Do simple household arithmetic using a calculator. Measure a window space for new curtains. Weigh ingredients on a kitchen scale. Cross off days on a calendar. Use a timer when cooking. He will see the different ways people use numbers.

5. Listen to different styles of music at home (e.g., classical, rock, choral, baroque, jazz, opera, folk, and music from different cultures). Your child can dance, pat the beat on his lap, play along using instruments made from beautiful junk, or try to sing the words. This will build an appreciation of music.

6. Walk in the neighbourhood with your child or bring a ball to the park and play soccer or catch. Encourage your child to explore the climbing equipment, climb the ladder, or slide down the pole. These are great ways to get some fresh air, to burn off a little bit of energy, and to just enjoy each other's company.

7. Plant a garden or provide indoor planting experiences like creating a terrarium or sprouting seeds. Gardening invites children into the world of fruits, vegetables, herbs, flowers, and even weeds! Gardening lets children learn with their senses—touching soil, smelling flowers, seeing colours, or tasting scarlet runner beans.

8. Look at magazines and catalogues with your child. Ask her to cut out pictures of words that begin with different letters of the alphabet and glue these onto paper to create her own alphabet book. This will give her the opportunity to recognize the sound that each letter in the alphabet makes and to build her vocabulary.

9. Teach familiar songs and nursery rhymes to your child which include numbers. "One Two Buckle My Shoe," "The Ants Go Marching One by One," and "This Old Man" are fun songs that will help him learn to count to ten. He will want to sing these familiar songs again and again.

10. Cook with your child. Bake bread, brew tea, freeze popsicles, and shake cream into butter; all are ways to help your child to learn about the different foods people eat and how they are prepared, as well as concepts like change of state, hot and cold, and liquid and solid. When children cook, they observe, compare, and problem solve.

PHOTO ALBUMS

Some teachers create photo albums that record special events or the day-to-day interactions within the playroom and store them in the book centre. They may encourage photo albums to be signed out and taken home by families. If budgets permit, individual photo albums can also be created. In some centres, finances would prohibit picture taking but families could be asked to send in their own photos to create the albums. Other centres produce yearbooks featuring photographs of special events and comments from staff, parents,

Journals provide opportunities for children to record their thoughts and ideas.

and children. A parent who is adept at photography might volunteer to visually chronicle events at the centre.

Photo albums can also be a wonderful way for students to introduce themselves to a new centre at the beginning of their field placement. One student from Korea created a powerful album of her home in Korea, her parents, siblings, and photos of her as a child the same age as the children in her care. This simple tool allowed her to share her own culture in a meaningful way and paved the way for an impressive beginning.

THE DAILY FLASH

A large dry erasable board or chalkboard located at the entrance to the playroom provides a space for instant communication to families. The following list suggests some messages that could make up the daily "flash":

- the day's most important events
- the birth of a sibling
- an adoption
- a birthday announcement
- the arrival of a new child to the room
- children who are moving to an older group

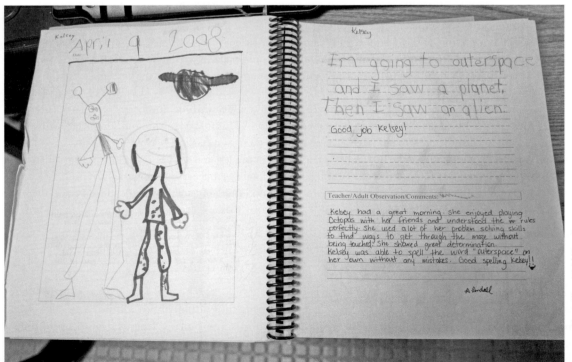

This journal provides two-way communication between the centre and home and will be a wonderful memory of the child's time in the program.

Mary Bianchi, teacher in the Kindergarten program at the Esther Exton Child Care Centres shares an innovative strategy:

In the morning circle, we would often sing "Hello My Friends" in the languages in the room. Children started to talk about the languages they spoke at home, where their family members come from, and other countries they had visited. Children want to learn how to say hello in other languages and learn more about each other. And so, the Family Heritage Book was born. Each child was assigned a page in the book which they took home. Families could add recipes, pictures, photographs—anything that represented their life at home or their heritage. Words were added to the book in different languages, flags, stamps, pictures of cultural festivities, ornaments or decorations that represent a special holiday. When the book was returned to the centre, the child and sometimes family members shared their page with the rest of the group. The book circulated until everyone had a chance to add something to it. This activity became one of the most popular projects in the room and evolved into other activities. Some expansions included word cards and labels in other languages, simple cooking activities, families brought in figurines and special decorations used during special holidays (dreidels, menorahs, books, ornaments, food boxes, post cards, fabrics, etc.). Families became very involved in this activity.

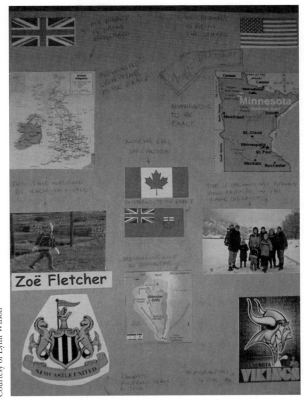

Courtesy of Lynn Wilson

Zoë Fletcher

This is an example of one of the pages from the Heritage Book.

- the words to a new song
- quote of the day (a famous quote or a wise or funny comment made by a child)

- menu items that the children particularly enjoyed
- the names of special visitors to the centre
- the name of a new student teacher to the room
- the name of the supply teacher, if a staff member is absent
- a warning about the onset of illness in the room and possible symptoms
- reminders about upcoming events
- items families should bring to the centre the following day
- information about where the children are if they are out of the room ("We are at the park until 4 p.m.")

LISTS

Sometimes the simplest gesture can provide the greatest support. Having a list posted on a bulletin board or beside the telephone of all the families (with their permission), their address, email address, and telephone number allows families to arrange play dates, create car pools, support each other with babysitting, and just the ability to stay in touch with each other. With family permission, this could also be sent home in a newsletter.

The newsletter provides an opportunity for teachers to communicate information about happenings in the centre. An informative newsletter should reduce the need for individual fliers and reminders to go home to families. A monthly newsletter could be distributed on the same day of each month (the last Friday of the month, for

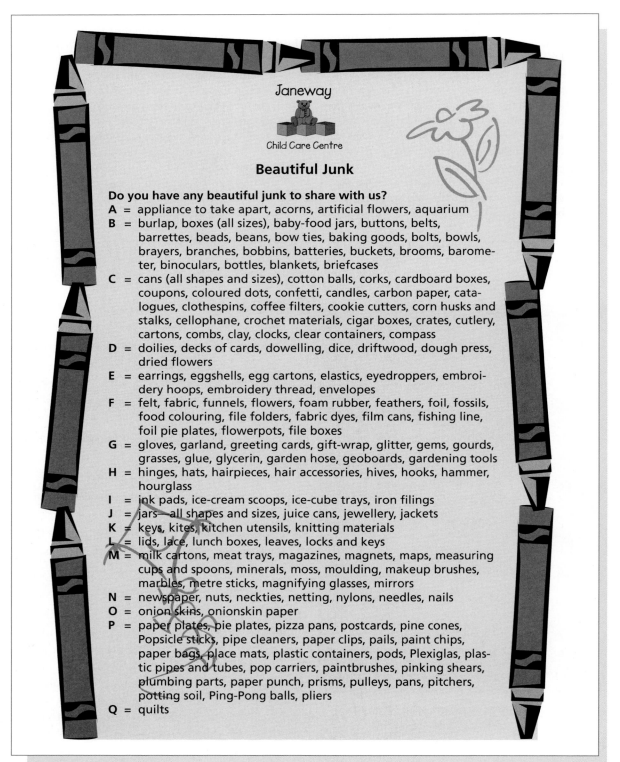

Janeway

Child Care Centre

Beautiful Junk

Do you have any beautiful junk to share with us?

A = appliance to take apart, acorns, artificial flowers, aquarium

B = burlap, boxes (all sizes), baby-food jars, buttons, belts, barrettes, beads, beans, bow ties, baking goods, bolts, bowls, brayers, branches, bobbins, batteries, buckets, brooms, barometer, binoculars, bottles, blankets, briefcases

C = cans (all shapes and sizes), cotton balls, corks, cardboard boxes, coupons, coloured dots, confetti, candles, carbon paper, catalogues, clothespins, coffee filters, cookie cutters, corn husks and stalks, cellophane, crochet materials, cigar boxes, crates, cutlery, cartons, combs, clay, clocks, clear containers, compass

D = doilies, decks of cards, dowelling, dice, driftwood, dough press, dried flowers

E = earrings, eggshells, egg cartons, elastics, eyedroppers, embroidery hoops, embroidery thread, envelopes

F = felt, fabric, funnels, flowers, foam rubber, feathers, foil, fossils, food colouring, file folders, fabric dyes, film cans, fishing line, foil pie plates, flowerpots, file boxes

G = gloves, garland, greeting cards, gift-wrap, glitter, gems, gourds, grasses, glue, glycerin, garden hose, geoboards, gardening tools

H = hinges, hats, hairpieces, hair accessories, hives, hooks, hammer, hourglass

I = ink pads, ice-cream scoops, ice-cube trays, iron filings

J = jars—all shapes and sizes, juice cans, jewellery, jackets

K = keys, kites, kitchen utensils, knitting materials

L = lids, lace, lunch boxes, leaves, locks and keys

M = milk cartons, meat trays, magazines, magnets, maps, measuring cups and spoons, minerals, moss, moulding, makeup brushes, marbles, metre sticks, magnifying glasses, mirrors

N = newspaper, nuts, neckties, netting, nylons, needles, nails

O = onion skins, onionskin paper

P = paper plates, pie plates, pizza pans, postcards, pine cones, Popsicle sticks, pipe cleaners, paper clips, pails, paint chips, paper bags, place mats, plastic containers, pods, Plexiglas, plastic pipes and tubes, pop carriers, paintbrushes, pinking shears, plumbing parts, paper punch, prisms, pulleys, pans, pitchers, potting soil, Ping-Pong balls, pliers

Q = quilts

(continued)

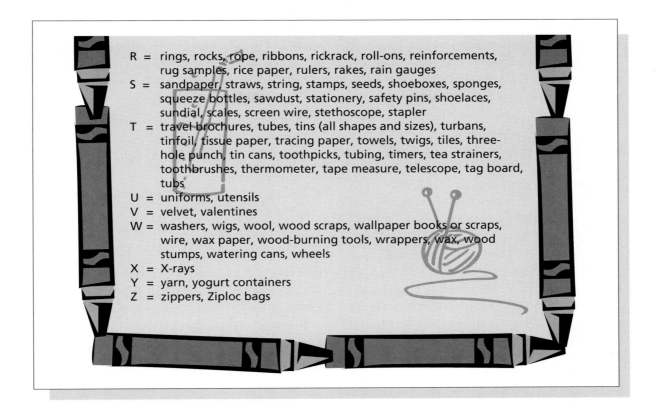

R = rings, rocks, rope, ribbons, rickrack, roll-ons, reinforcements, rug samples, rice paper, rulers, rakes, rain gauges

S = sandpaper, straws, string, stamps, seeds, shoeboxes, sponges, squeeze bottles, sawdust, stationery, safety pins, shoelaces, sundial, scales, screen wire, stethoscope, stapler

T = travel brochures, tubes, tins (all shapes and sizes), turbans, tinfoil, tissue paper, tracing paper, towels, twigs, tiles, three-hole punch, tin cans, toothpicks, tubing, timers, tea strainers, toothbrushes, thermometer, tape measure, telescope, tag board, tubs

U = uniforms, utensils

V = velvet, valentines

W = washers, wigs, wool, wood scraps, wallpaper books or scraps, wire, wax paper, wood-burning tools, wrappers, wax, wood stumps, watering cans, wheels

X = X-rays

Y = yarn, yogurt containers

Z = zippers, Ziploc bags

example) so that families come to expect it. If it appears on the same coloured paper each time, parents will know what is at the bottom of the knapsack! If translations are needed to accommodate ESL families, financial constraints may require less frequent publication of newsletters; producing fewer newsletters is preferable to excluding ESL parents. Centres should draw on the expertise of families when producing the newsletter. The newsletter provides an opportunity for families to contribute and reinforces the need for two-way communication. The newsletter should reflect cultural sensitivity and a high degree of professionalism. Back issues of newsletters should be kept on hand to assist with the orientation of families who are new to the centre.

Teachers should keep notes on "meaningful moments" in the playroom; these notes can provide the basis of a newsletter anecdote:

> As we were preparing to watch *The Wizard of Oz* with the school-age children, Barrett told his friend Megan that he was worried about watching the video. A staff person reassured Barrett that he could leave the area and play somewhere else if he felt too uncomfortable. Megan turned to Barrett, put her arm around his shoulder, and said, "Don't worry, Barrett, I will hug you during the scary parts."

Ideas, photographs, artwork, and other potential newsletter material should be stored in a central file that can be accessed by families or teachers who are working on the newsletter. In school-age programs, children may enjoy producing their own newsletters. A number of computer software programs are available to enable teachers, parents, and children to prepare their newsletter.

Though the content of a newsletter differs from month to month, the inclusion of regular features provides a sense of continuity. Following are suggestions for regular features:

1. **Message from the Supervisor.** In this column the supervisor might deal with centre-specific issues or ECE issues in general. This space could also be used to make announcements about staff and program changes, to acknowledge special contributions by parents or children, or to welcome new staff and student teachers.

2. **Teacher of the Month.** Each teacher in the centre could at some point be profiled in the newsletter. Information about teachers' backgrounds, work experiences, philosophies, interests, and hobbies may be included at their own discretion.

3. **Family of the Month.** Families who have contributed their time and energy should be

acknowledged in the newsletter. A positive profile may encourage other families to become active participants in the centre.

4. **Staff News.** Teachers may take turns writing on a specific issue, discussing a professional development workshop they attended, or reviewing a relevant book.

5. **Family to Family.** Families could use this space to address parenting issues contributing letters, book reviews etc. A variation of this feature would be a "Families Ask" column, in which teachers respond to questions often asked by families over the years.

6. **News from the Cook.** The centre cook could write about nutrition issues, share favourite recipes with families, recommend good children's cookbooks, and ask families to submit a favourite recipe to share with everyone in the centre. The recipe might also be posted on the bulletin board when the dish is being served, along with a photo of the family.

7. **Doctor's Report.** A physician affiliated with the centre could use this space to write about child-related health issues and concerns.

8. **Homemade Toy of the Month.** A teacher or a parent could give easy-to-follow instructions for toy-making that both children and parents could participate in.

9. **Activity of the Month.** This column would describe the children's favourite activity over the past month.

10. **Book of the Month.** A teacher or parent could review a good children's book.

11. **Committee Reports.** This column would give parent committees an opportunity to update families on their activities.

12. **Report from the Board of Directors.** The column is an opportunity for the board of directors to share relevant information.

13. **Resource Area News.** The supervisor could use his space to announce new additions (books, videos, and so on) to the family resource area.

14. **Surveys.** The newsletter is expected on a regular basis and attaching surveys will most likely ensure that families will read it.

Other possible newsletter items include:

- words of popular finger plays and songs;
- quizzes designed for families;

- seasonal suggestions for activities that family members and children can engage in together;
- reviews of toys, family television programs, local children's theatre, videos, and parenting magazines;
- information on exchanges (babysitting, skates, videos);
- columns on where to get items for children at reasonable prices;
- accounts of field trips taken by the children (photos included);
- tips on organizing birthday parties;
- highlights of family meetings;
- results of family surveys;
- information on national and local celebrations (Week of the Child, Children's Book Week, Freedom to Read Week);
- a space for community people to share helpful and informative information for families;
- announcements of upcoming community workshops, lectures, or seminars on parenting issues;
- safety tips (childproofing the home, bicycle safety);
- recipes for modelling clay, silly putty, playdough, etc.;
- ideas for keeping children engaged on long car trips;
- recipes for tasty and nutritious snacks and ideas for school-age lunch bags;
- ideas for healthy and safe outdoor activities;
- interviews with children, family members, and teachers; and
- inspirational poetry.

INDIVIDUAL ROOM NEWSLETTERS

In addition to whole-centre newsletters, some centres produce individual room newsletters that reflect the uniqueness of each room and focus on the developmental issues of children in each room's age group. An individual room newsletter might feature upcoming events, developmental milestones, ideas for parental participation, issues and concerns (for example, biting in the toddler room, sibling rivalry in the preschool room, street proofing for school-age children), curriculum issues, how families can extend curriculum into the home environment, information about pets in the room, and announcements of the addition of new

FIGURE 8.4 NEWSLETTER

NEWSLETTER

Preschooler Thank-yous

Thanks go out to Christopher's mom, Talin, for the special gift of a colour package. Our playdough, water table, and paints are very vibrant and effective with all the lovely new colours to play around with.

Report

The preschoolers are all having fun being involved in many different winter activities. With our mild winter so far we have been able to get outside more than usual for the season. Here is an update on what to expect in the Preschool Room over the coming weeks.

Birthdays

Happy 4th birthday to the following preschoolers:

- Emma Bambrick, Jan. 17
- Colombe Nadeau-O'shea, Jan. 31
- Cassidie Baril, Feb. 25
- Hailey Huels, Mar. 27
- Tali Sato, Mar. 28
- Alexina Clements, Apr. 5

Recipes

A few of the preschool parents have expressed an interest in our playdough recipe so here it is:

2 cups flour
1 cup salt
2 tbsp. oil
2 cups water
X amount of food colouring

Cook over medium heat until a solid ball forms.

Clothing

On rainy days, please provide your child with an extra set of clothing for their cubbies and make sure they have snowpants and boots with them every day.

Cold weather can be harsh on a child's delicate skin. If redness or chafing occurs, apply a light covering of Vaseline over the affected area. This serves as a good preventative measure before taking your child outdoors.

---

items (software, toys, books, and so on) to the room. Some rooms have found it helpful to enclose in the newsletter a monthly calendar that outlines upcoming events.

Newsletters that originate in the room are generally of high interest to families, especially if their children have played a part in producing them. School-agers can play a particularly active role in preparing the newsletter. As families leave a particular room and their child graduates to an older age group, the individual room newsletter provides a perfect forum for acknowledging the contributions these families have made to the centre and to the room.

CALENDARS

Effective communication of daily and upcoming events is critical to the smooth running of the centre. Some centres post a large wipe-off calendar that is clearly visible to families as they arrive. This calendar should closely resemble the one sent home to families in the individual room newsletter.

The older children could make personalized magnets to hold up their own calendar on the fridge. Out-of-date calendars could be placed in a photo album and become a record of the child's time in the room. Staff might also prepare a calendar of community events that would be of interest to families; this calendar could be posted near the centre entrance or on the parent bulletin board. An organization, Curriculum Associates, has produced a calendar called "A Calendar of Home Activities," which suggests a different activity for each day of the week and for different age groups. These are available for different age groups and are a fun way to incorporate learning with a play-based focus.

HAPPY LETTERS

A happy letter is a communication from a teacher to a family that celebrates something positive about that family's child, whether a memorable moment in his or her life or a kind deed. For families who have been conditioned to believe that any communication from teachers means trouble, the receipt of a happy letter comes as a welcome relief. At the end of a busy day, families appreciate the sight of a happy letter on the child's cubby or locker (see Figure 8.5).

When creating a happy letter, teachers are limited only by their imagination. Paper in shapes ranging from animals to birthday cakes can be purchased commercially, but teachers can develop their own letters. For example, a teacher might cut out a hand shape, write a note in the palm area, and attach it to the child's back for an appropriate "pat on the back." Some teachers buy stickers to create a border around the sheet of paper, and write the message inside. This idea may be replicated with a piece of acetate, so that the children can take off the stickers and reuse them at home. Some suggestions for happy letter starters include:

Wow! You won't believe what happened today!

_____ is a superstar! She . . .

_____ is a hero today! He . . .

You're terrific because . . .

Tips for Parents

Smiles Made Easy are note cards and envelopes in a tin that start the writer off with a positive thoughts such as: "I love when . . . " or "I have fun when . . ." or "I am proud when. . . ." A child or parent can fill out these cards to encourage expressions of gratitude or just an opportunity to share a kind thought. These are fun to include in lunch boxes or under pillows or even mailed home—everyone enjoys receiving a happy letter. Smiles Made Easy note cards are available at **www.smilesmadeeasy.com**.

Happy Letters from the Child to the Family

Some days, children have exciting events that they would like to share with their families. In this situation the teacher can provide fancy paper, interesting blank cards, etc., along with a variety of writing instruments. Sentence starters, such as "Today at the centre I . . ." can help children get started. The children will look forward to giving these Happy Letters to their families at the end of the day.

Happy Letters from a Parent to a New Teacher

One teacher invites families who are transitioning to her room to write a letter to her sharing what they want her to know about their child. These letters help the teacher to understand the child on a more intimate basis, more so than the formal intake form. As well, parents often share their hopes and dreams for their family and for their child.

Happy Letters from a Child to a Student

"In my fourth placement I worked with a family who had recently arrived from Poland and the mother was worried about her son's language skills. She told me that he would come home saying that he was the worst student in the room. I worked with the mother on ways to increase his self-esteem. He became a special helper in the room and we talked about bullying and ways to be empathetic with each other. After my placement I got a letter in the mail from the boy. It was a hand made card that said 'Thank you for everything. I will miss you.' It made me really happy to think that I had made a difference with this family. I will always treasure this card" (Nancy Bettencourt, ECE graduate).

CARDS AND LETTERS

Nothing is quite so special for a child as receiving a card or letter in the mail from his or her teacher. A birthday card or get-well card is appreciated by child and parent alike. Children who attend centres that close over the summer and re-open in the fall will appreciate a letter from the teacher welcoming them back and telling them what they can look forward to when they return. As with all written communication that goes to the home, every effort should be made to create an attractive and eye-catching design (see Figure 8.6). A quick

FIGURE 8.5   IDEAS FOR HAPPY LETTERS

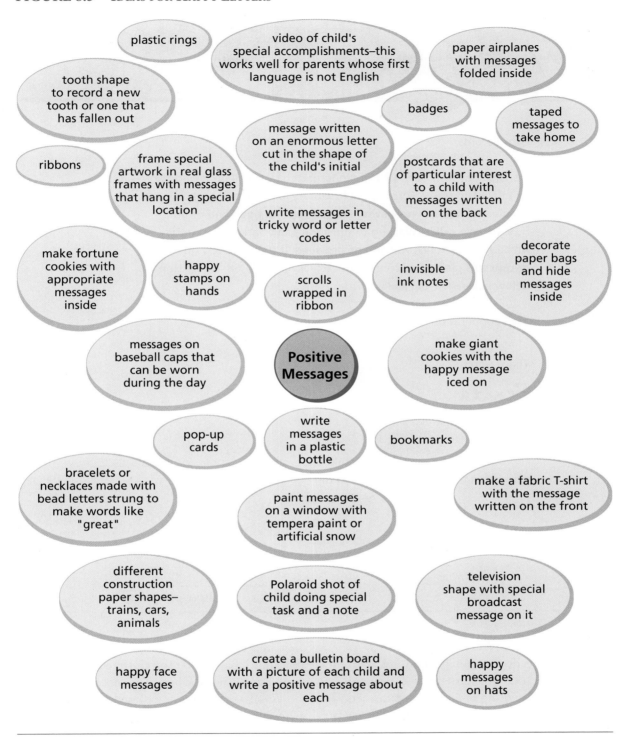

letter attached to a child's work going home such as "We are so proud of Hyun Ju's effort on her animal drawing. She worked all afternoon on it!" can reinforce the child's efforts and it is sure to bring a smile to the parent's face! Simple but effective!

BOOKS FOR TEACHERS

Family-Friendly Communication for Early Childhood Programs, by D. Diffily and K. Morrison

Powerful Parent Letter for K–3, by M. Duggan

FIGURE 8.6   FIELD TRIP LETTER

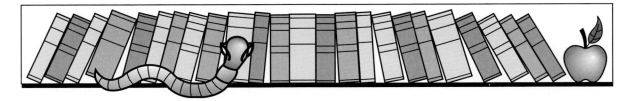

Dear Parents,

On Thursday, February 15, the Kindergarten class will be taking part
in a field trip to the Toronto Public Library located at Bloor and
Spadina Rd. We will be leaving the centre at 12 noon and return
by 2 pm. We will be walking to the library and back to the centre.
An early picnic lunch will also be provided. If there are any questions
or concerns please feel free to contact Olivia or myself. Please sign
below before leaving today.

Your cooperation is greatly appreciated.

Thank you.

Renata

Student Teacher

I do/do not (circle one) give my child _____
permission to attend the outing to the Public Library.

I can participate: YES _____

                            NO _____

                            _____
                            Signature of Parent

BULLETIN BOARDS

Bulletin boards do more than communicate information about the teachers and the program. A well-designed, inviting bulletin board can serve as an effective public relations tool for the centre. Besides being visually appealing, bulletin boards should be clearly labelled and located in well-travelled areas. They should also provide a space for families to post messages and respond to teachers or to other families.

When designing effective bulletin boards, organization is critical. One strategy is to simply pin everything up on the board with thumbtacks, then step back and see if it works! Is it visually appealing? Balanced? Too cluttered? All material should stay inside the board and not spill out. Once the visual appearance is deemed satisfactory, the material can be stapled in place. Teachers should use colour combinations on the board that enhance the overall design of the room. Avoid visual clutter. A *few* complementary colours on all of the boards in the room are preferable to the clash of boards each with its own colour combination. A three-dimensional look is often eye-catching. Pictures of children are a terrific way to attract families to the board.

FIGURE 8.7 BORDERS AND BACKGROUNDS

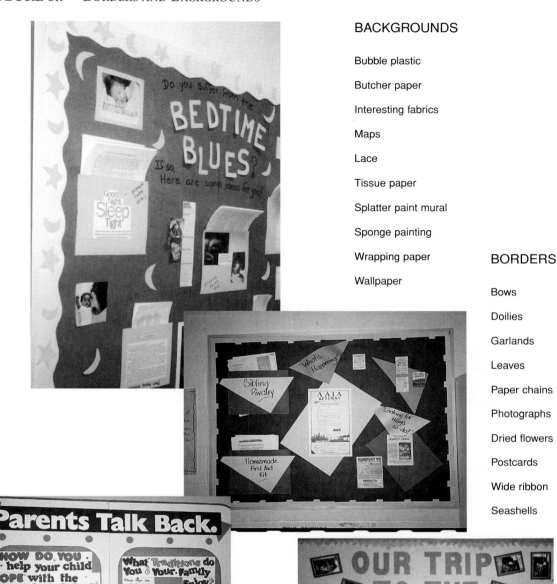

BACKGROUNDS

Bubble plastic

Butcher paper

Interesting fabrics

Maps

Lace

Tissue paper

Splatter paint mural

Sponge painting

Wrapping paper

Wallpaper

BORDERS

Bows

Doilies

Garlands

Leaves

Paper chains

Photographs

Dried flowers

Postcards

Wide ribbon

Seashells

The content of bulletin boards should be changed regularly. New information should be added when appropriate. Contributions from families should be especially welcomed. Possible bulletin board items include the following:

- newspaper or magazine articles on subjects of particular interest to families

- general information on the centre (philosophy statement, menus, schedules, licensing documents, and so on)

- photographs of staff accompanied by biographical sketches

- a copy of the most recent newsletter

- a list of people interested in car pools

- movie, video, or book recommendations for specific age groups
- cartoons that express the challenges of parenting
- photo records of field trips or special events in the centre
- congratulations corner to acknowledge new babies, parent donations, special fundraising efforts, and parent volunteers
- a list of volunteers needed, with task descriptions
- a coupon-exchange board or buy-and-sell board
- a list of upcoming community events of interest to families
- information on educational opportunities for families
- recipes for play dough, goop, etc.
- guidelines for purchasing appropriate toys and play materials

One centre used Valentine's Day to create a surprise bulletin board for teachers. In the morning (before teachers arrived), the supervisor made heart-shaped pouches and hung them on the bulletin board, one for each teacher. Families, who had been told about the surprise ahead of time, brought in valentines for teachers with messages that expressed appreciation for their work. The surprise bulletin board proved to be an extremely successful morale booster for all concerned.

Another idea is to give families the responsibility for the design and upkeep of one of the bulletin boards in the centre. The board or a parent wall

This bulletin board was created based on requests from families for more information about how to support early literacy.

may focus on documenting the children and parent involvement in the centre, similar to an approach used in Reggio Emilia. Bulletin boards that are interactive and require family input are an effective way to connect families with one another. A question posed at the top of the board such as "What Is Your Favourite Family Meal?" asks families to write out a recipe for their favourite foods. Photos of each family can be placed beside their recipe. Other questions might include "What Is Your Favourite Place to Take Children in the City?", "Best Tips for Travelling with Children," "Suggestions for Staying Sane over the Holidays," "Words of Wisdom/Proverbs You Grew Up With," "Does Anyone Know Where To Buy Children's Shoes At Wholesale Prices," "Would Anyone Like To Set Up A Child Care Exchange On Night A Week?", and so on.

THE FAMILY RESOURCE AREA

While not every centre has space enough to allocate a separate room for a family resource area, it is important that some space, no matter how small, be designated for the purpose of providing materials and resources for families. Regardless of its size or location, the designated family resource area should reflect both the families served and the centre's philosophy. It should also communicate the belief that learning is valued and that sharing resources makes all our lives richer and more meaningful. Teachers can help parents take responsibility for their children's learning outcomes by providing materials and ideas for activities that families can do at home and in the community with their children.

The physical environment should be as inviting as possible—a comfort zone with couches, a coffee table, tables and chairs, carpets, and comfortable chairs. Bookcases, filing cabinets, bulletin boards, and magazine racks help organize the resources available to parents; plants serve to soften the space. Access to a telephone may provide parents with privacy when making important calls. Access to a computer may be the only opportunity some families have to technology. The space should be adequately lighted. Coffee, tea, fruit juice, and occasional baked goods are always appreciated. A bulletin board can be used to display items parents might like to share with one another; for example, books or articles they have read, items they may want to trade, awards given to family volunteers,

Courtesy of Lynn Wilson

children's artwork, lists of food banks, and so forth.

Once the space is established, it must be maintained and organized on a regular basis. A family committee could be established to take over the organization and running of the resource area. Parents will be reluctant to use a space that is cluttered and in disarray. An inventory should be kept of the resource room holdings.

Centres that have yet to establish a family resource area might begin by surveying parents to find out what resources they would like included there. Families may also serve as resources for other parents. They may, for example, be self-employed and offer services that would benefit others. Possible resource items include:

- phone and address list of all families (with permission)
- yearly calendar of centre-based events
- photo albums of centre history or events
- books (in the languages spoken in the centre) on child development, parent–child relationships, social issues facing families, behaviour guidance, etc.

- simple phrase books in many languages created by families for other parents and teachers
- ECE journals and parenting or child-development magazines
- children's health pamphlets and brochures
- articles organized in binders on child-care issues such as safety, nutrition, children's fears, street-proofing, provincial regulations on child care, and so forth
- ECE catalogues that include equipment and play materials
- teacher resource books
- lists of community organizations with accompanying map and phone numbers
- bus schedules, taxi phone numbers
- list of translation services in the community
- copies of old centre newsletters
- posters
- announcements about upcoming community events that might be of interest to families
- trip ideas for families, with vacation tips on, for example, travelling long distances with children

This family resource area provides a meeting place for families and teachers.

- a list of items for sale or exchange
- brochures designed by the teachers with helpful hints or strategies (tips on reading aloud to children, monitoring television viewing, toileting, and so on)
- videos/DVDs about the centre, on parenting, and for children (parents might want to set up a video exchange)
- community newspapers reflecting the centre's ethnic mix
- CDs and audiotapes
- a recipe book prepared by the cook of the children's favourite recipes, or a recipe exchange board for families
- parent-initiated babysitting exchange list
- a "borrowing area"—extra umbrellas, hats, mittens, etc.
- clothing-, toy-, or shoe-exchange area
- junk or craft bin, craft bags
- group photos with the names of the children and teachers accompanying
- stationery, calculator, photocopier
- computer and printer to allow parents to research topics on the Internet, write up résumés for jobs, complete centre-based projects, etc.

New additions to the family resource area might be noted in the centre newsletter. Families who are leaving the centre might be encouraged to donate items to the resource area. A dedication nameplate representing the family can be included as a way to remember their gift. In one centre each family is invited, on its child's birthday, to add a book to the resource centre in its child's name. A sign-out book should be clearly visible and "how-to" instructions made available to parents in order to keep track of materials.

As a way of sharing the responsibilities of the child-care centre, one centre used a large shelving unit in the resource area, on which staff placed a large bin for each teacher, labelled with his or her name. When teachers found themselves out of time but needing work done that was important to the classroom operations, they placed the materials and instructions for completing these tasks inside their bin. Family members who were interested could complete the required task (Whitaker and Fiore, 2001: 175–176). This bin approach may also be an opportunity to involve families who cannot spend time at school but want to participate in a meaningful way by taking the bin home and completing the task there.

RESOURCE-AREA EXTRAS

Borrow-a-Book Program

In an effort to encourage an ongoing interest in books, some centres establish borrow-a-book programs. Books can be stored in Ziploc bags, which are then punched and hung on hooks on a pegboard. Another strategy is for each child to have his or her own hand-sewn borrow-a-book cloth bag to bring to the resource area. School-age children could sew up their own bags and decorate them with fabric paint or embroidery. Under the program, children are invited to choose a book from the collection to take home in their bag. Extra bags should be sewn so that children who leave theirs at home will not be disappointed. Centres that are unable to afford new books for this project may invite parents to donate books as their children outgrow them. A booklet may be included for chil-

This is an example of a Borrow-a-Book bag.

dren and their families to write their thoughts about the book, draw a picture, and so on.

Story Boxes

Story boxes, which can be created by parents or teachers, contain materials and props that are related to a specific story or series of books enjoyed by the children. Each container is identified on the outside to reflect the story inside. Using the *Clifford, the Big Red Dog* series as an example, story box materials might include a Clifford puzzle or audiotape, a pencil with Clifford designs on it accompanied by red paper, Clifford stickers, story-related finger puppets, photocopies of the pages of the book for the children to put in order, and so on. An inventory should be included in the story box to ensure that all materials are returned. The story box might also include a response sheet asking parents what their child enjoyed most about the story box and what improvements might be made to it (what new materials might be added, for example).

Share-a-Tape

Botrie and Wenger (1992: 82) share an interesting classroom strategy that could easily be adapted to school-age programs:

> While studying a unit on our country, we invited parents and/or grandparents, through our newsletters, to share their experiences. Robin's grandparents, both age 78, live in a small town outside of the city and were unable to respond in person. They had both experienced interesting childhoods and were keen to share their memories with the children in our class. Robin, with tape recorder in hand, visited his grandparents. With their assistance, he formulated a set of ten questions he wanted to pose to these venerable citizens and became an interviewer. Robin, who is a quiet boy in class, blossomed in his role and used strong interviewing skills. His grandparents responded superbly and shared childhood memories that fascinated the students in our class. The program has great potential for strengthening effective language skills.

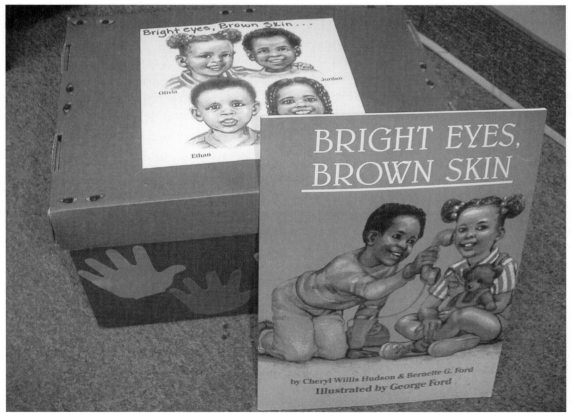

Courtesy of Lynn Wilson

The Story Box is filled with activities related to the book, Bright Eyes, Brown Skin *and was developed by an ECE student during her field placement.*

This child is playing a learning game that her family has donated to the centre.

Courtesy of Scotia Plaza Child Care Centre

Families might also enjoy taping their favourite music or singing their favourite songs, nursery rhymes, or lullabies. Teachers may also record the children singing playroom favourites so parents can learn the words and sing along at home.

Travelling Suitcases

Travelling suitcases are small, inexpensive cases used to store interesting materials that children can take home. In communities where resources for parents are limited, items in the suitcases may be kept by the child; for example, a suitcase might contain Play-Doh, a recipe, and a variety of implements. The recipe and Play-Doh would remain at home and only the implements returned. Some centres allow the children to choose items in the playroom that they would like to take home in a suitcase overnight or for the weekend. Most children are taught that this is a special privilege are very responsible about the care and maintenance of the suitcases; however, teachers must expect a certain degree of damage and loss and be prepared to add materials to the suitcases as necessary. Wherever possible, include books that related to the contents of the suitcases. Teachers can encourage parents to assist in the development of these travelling kits, which might include the following:

- writing kits (fancy pens, Chinese brushes, notepaper and envelopes, calligraphy pens, erasers, rulers, stamps, and stamp pads)

- games and puzzles

- recipes for favourite daycare food

- instructions and materials for science experiments family members and children can do together

- projects (friendship bracelets, for example) with instructions and materials

- favourite songbooks and tapes/CDs

- instructions and materials for outdoor games (for instance, clue cards for a community treasure hunt)

- musical instruments and tapes

- infant activity boards

- sewing cards, needlework, and other craft projects

- dramatic play (jewellery collections, dress-up clothes, puppets, purses)

- manipulatives (such as Lego, Duplo, and Tinkertoys)
- file folder games with a bag of dice or "men" attached
- art supplies for creative projects such as scissors, smelly markers, oil pastels, glue, fancy paper, and stickers

A special suitcase—prepared by the teachers and children for a sick child—containing get well notes, a video message, and favourite play room toys might also be kept on hand. If suitcases are in short supply, a backpack is an easy-to-carry substitute.

Porta Paks

Developed by Kathy Hartely, a teacher at Orde Street Child Care Centre in Toronto, Porta Paks are simplified versions of travelling suitcases. Consisting of small, unusual play items stored in Ziploc bags, they can be taken home by children or used by the centre and taken on bus trips. Porta Paks for younger children can include such items as sensory "feely bags" and cause-and-effect toys. By using materials that are available in most homes, families can be encouraged to use the Porta Paks as models for creating their own learning materials. For example, by using juice lids and

adding stickers to them, families can make a simple matching game.

Toy Lending

Toy lending, according to Brock and Dodd (1994: 18),

> affords teachers an opportunity to share quality toys with families and to demonstrate their effectiveness in fostering early literacy development. While parents play with their children, experimenting with different types of toys and modeling ways to use them, they gain a better understanding of the ways children grow and learn. As a result, parents often become more adept at selecting toys to buy their children because they have had access to quality toys.

Families may contribute their own ideas based on the existing resources in the area. In some centres, families encourage other members of the centre to bring in their craft items for sale. In another, one parent created travelling kits. These included tips for travelling with young children as well as a number of travelling games that she invented. The possibilities are endless!

Travelling Teddy Bear

"One kindergarten had a traveling teddy bear that was accompanied by a journal intended to record

Each of these bags contains instructions and all materials necessary to carry out a science experiment. The bags can be carried home in travelling suitcases.

his adventures in the homes he visited. The bear and the journal came in a backpack and went home with a different child each weekend. The idea was for a family member to read parts of the journal to the child and help him or her write additional journal entries, which could be dictated by the child and written by the parent" (Gonzalez Mena, 2008: 36).

EVALUATING THE FAMILY RESOURCE AREA

Adapted from Brock and Dodd (1994: 20), teachers can pose the following are questions to family members and children—either verbally or in writing—in order to evaluate the success of the family resource centre.

Parents

1. How often do you use the Family Resource Area?

2. Which family member(s) usually shares with your child the books or materials you check out?

3. Tell me about the ways you and your child share books or materials.

4. Have you purchased any of the books or materials that you have checked out from the Family Resource Area? If so, which ones?

5. What new information have you learned about your child as a result of sharing the books or materials from the Family Resource Area?

6. What new information have you learned about parenting as a result of the books or materials you have checked out?

Children

1. What are your favourite books to check out?

2. What are your favourite objects, materials, and toys to check out?

3. Tell me how you and your family share the books and materials you check out.

TECHNOLOGY AND COMMUNICATION OPPORTUNITIES

"Electronic communication will never be a substitute for the face of someone who with their soul encourages another person to be brave and true."

—Charles Dickens

There is no question that the development of new, advanced communication systems over the last twenty years has made our world seem smaller. Communication satellites, sophisticated television transmission equipment, and fiber-optic or wireless connection systems permit people throughout the world to share information and ideas instantaneously. With the simple click of a mouse, you can now "talk" to anyone almost anywhere in the world (Samovar et al., 2007: 4).

According to Internet World Stats, 28,000,000 people or 84.3% of the Canadian population are internet users (2008). Technology—faxes, electronic mail, and the Internet—are opening up additional communication opportunities for families and teachers. E-mail allows still photos or full-motion videos to be easily distributed to family members, as well as providing a way to communicate with families who have access to a computer but who are unable to attend events at the centre. E-mail reminders may also be sent before upcoming events and happenings.

There are any number of ways that computers can enhance communication between families and the centre. In one centre, for example, a computer program monitors parent fees. A key pad near the child's cubby allows parents to access the status of their current fees. In another centre children are able to send and receive messages from the parents or other relatives through a touch screen program. Some families will not have access to technology; even if access is available in local libraries, parents may not have the resources to use them. A computer in the family resource area of the centre may be the only access some families will have this type of technology.

THE TELEPHONE AS A COMMUNICATION TOOL

Technology is changing the ways in which telephones are used and will continue to provide alternative ways in which families and teachers can keep in touch. Before phoning parents at their workplace, teachers should check that such calls are acceptable to the employer. Teachers might also phone family members at home to ask about a child who has been absent due to illness or another event; they can also use this time to pass along information that the family might have missed during the child's absence. It is exciting for

It Keeps Getting Faster: Changing Patterns of Time in Families

"Computers and technology have contributed to the acceleration of activity in all domains including work, leisure and private life with the result that speed and efficiency have become heralded cultural values. Technology creates a new kind of impatience. . . . Technology gives rise to an intolerance for waiting and a desire for immediate results and gratification. High speed networks, beepers and cellular phones give rise to the expectation of an immediate response thereby putting a finer edge on the meaning of punctuality."

The Vanier Institute of the Family

Kerry Daly, University of Guelph, 2000

Source: www.vifamily.ca/library/cft/faster.html

the child to speak to the teacher, if they are able. Teachers should consider the timing of a call to the home; no one wants to be disturbed during their dinner hour. There should be an effort to make the conversation short, informative and to the point. Teaches should stay focused on the reason for the call and avoid chit-chat. When a family member calls the teacher it is important to return the call as soon as possible. If the topic becomes sensitive, it would be important to arrange for a personal meeting. Some teachers keep track of which family members they have communicated with by phone by creating their own telephone log.

The telephone can also be used to give family members advance warning about any incidents that staff considers serious. For example, if the child has had a fall, a phone call will help parents prepare for a nasty scrape or bump before they arrive. If the teacher involved in a particular incident will be leaving before the family member arrives, it is always a good idea for that teacher to call and explain the situation beforehand rather than have the family member receive the news secondhand from another staff member.

In order to encourage on-going communication, some teachers give family members their own home phone numbers, along with times they are available to talk with them. "The 'on-call' attitude of professional teachers separates them from nine-

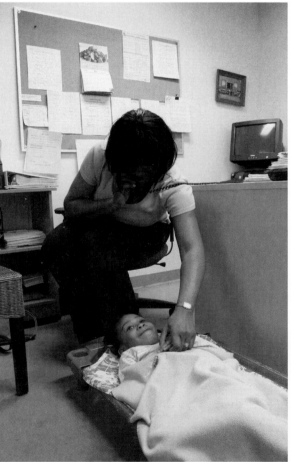

Courtesy of Scotia Plaza Child Care Centre

This supervisor is caring for a sick child in her office and is calling to inform the parent.

Janeway
Child Care Centre

Sample Telephone Log

Date: _____   Time: _____

Child's Name: _____   Parent Name: _____

Telephone: Home _____   Work _____

Record of Call:

_____ Busy   _____ Left Message   _____ No Answer   _____ Call-backs

_____

_____

_____

to-five workers," Hildebrand (1991) observes. "Teachers know that children sometimes go home confused or with real or imagined slights. The child may have left a dearest treasure at school. A call to the teacher can straighten things out so that the family's evening goes smoother. Parents should feel it is all right to call the teacher at home" (1991: 508). Texting is also a quick and easy way to communicate.

Centres might also put in place an information line that enables family members to access a designated extension number for information about their child's playroom. The prerecorded message might give pertinent details about an upcoming field trip or a family–centre social event. The messages can also be recorded in a variety of languages spoken by the families. Other telephone systems can be established to automatically dial all the numbers designated by the teacher to deliver messages or reminders.

While telephones in the playrooms allow for a convenient exchange of information, the fact remains that lunch hour, a favourite time for families to call, is often one of the busiest times for staff, as they feed, change, and put the children down for their nap. In school-age lunchrooms there are often large groups of children moving about, involved in getting their lunches microwaved, or heading outdoors, so locating a child may place additional demands on an already busy teacher. A specific time for incoming calls might be arranged so that families and teachers can organize themselves accordingly. At the same time, families should be reassured that all their communications with the centre are welcome.

The advent of text messaging and, more recently, camera phones provides a unique and immediate way to capture unexpected moments that can be shared with families. What a wonderful way to celebrate a child's accomplishment!

Videos/DVDs

Videos provide a wonderful opportunity to share the children's day to day activities with families

---

INSIDE   LOOK

When Jan's teacher called to see how he was feeling, we were all surprised to hear from her. In all the years that my older children had been involved in child care, the only time I ever heard from any of the teachers was when something was wrong. It was such a lovely gesture, and Jan was thrilled to hear from her.

who find it hard to spend time on the playroom floor. Many family members can share in the video at the family's leisure. This is a great opportunity to involve siblings, grandparents, aunts and uncles.

CENTRE WEBSITES

Many centres have created websites to post information, special events, photographs, or video segments. It will be important to obtain parental permission to post photos or video clips of the children online and to ensure the security of the site.

EMAIL

Teachers are using email to communicate with families more frequently. Email is a helpful tool in distributing important information about the centre or upcoming events. Notes, messages, newsletters, centre events can now be sent to many families by email. The advantage is that it is immediate and for those in work place child care centres, this may be a real advantage. Email is not the best way to communicate sensitive information since this information can be saved, printed or forwarded to others and so appropriate discretion should be used.

BLOGGING AND WEBSITES FOR PARENTS AND TEACHERS

Blogs for parents are gaining popularity. Blogs may give parents an opportunity to say things they might not in more formal settings. They also allow parents to connect with each other when they might be unable to sleep at night after a night feeding. Websites such as **www.weewelcome.ca** and **www.urbanmoms.ca** are operated for those who want to connect with other mothers. Many controversial topics are raised and there is a forum for women to discuss the issues facing motherhood. Forums allow women with different viewpoints and parenting styles to exchange information and to learn from a variety of different viewpoints. Online communities are available night and day, 24/7, and mothers may find that by participating in a forum or by reading a blog they are in contact with mothers outside of their own culture or social group and find that they are exposed to different ways of doing things helping them rethink and reframe their own ideas of mothering.

The Invest in Kids website, "Comfort, Play and Teach: A Positive Approach to Parenting" (**http://www.investinkids.ca/ContentPage.aspx?name=Parents_AboutCPT**), provides practical information and resources for families in their day-to-day interactions with their children. Families and teachers can subscribe to the site and receive regular emails. Invest in Kids—a national, charitable organization—supports the healthy social, emotional, and intellectual development of children by strengthening parental knowledge, skills and confidence. The three core messages are Comfort, Play, and Teach: When you comfort your child, she learns to feel secure, loved and valued; when you play with your child, he learns to explore and discover the world and his role in it; when you teach your child, she learns how to relate to others, solve problems and communicate (Invest in Kids, 2007). In addition to the parenting focused resources, the professional section of their website offers many practical tools and resources for teachers in their work with families and young children that are well worth exploring.

CAMERAS IN THE PLAYROOM

A growing number of centres in Canada and the United States are installing systems that link video cameras in the playroom to websites that families can access from work. Most of these systems ensure that security is tight, and encrypted passwords and secure connections make the system hacker-proof. This system allows parents or relatives to log in at any time during the day to observe the child. Some systems enable photos to be printed out.

TECHNOLOGY AT WORK

Computer programs developed for child care are becoming more sophisticated. Some alert administrators to upcoming due dates for immunizations for children in the centre, monitor family fees, and so on. Despite the benefits of these technologies, teachers need to recognize that they are no substitute for face-to-face communication.

From recipes for Play-Doh, strategies for getting your child to sleep at night, finding the best price for a new stroller to connecting with other parents with child-rearing challenges, the Internet has dramatically changed how we access and share information. For parents who travel away from home, it is possible to set up web-cams to participate in bedtime stories or watch a family event that might have otherwise been missed. When children live far away from a parent, a web cam can encourage family participation. Handheld personal organizers such as Palm Pilots and Blackberrys help us

During a child care centre visit in Suzhou, China, I was very impressed with how effectively they used a computer and photographs of the children to communicate with families. In the main lobby of the centre, a lap top was set up. Parents access their individual child's group, then a specific file for their own child. Inside the folder are photos of activities that the child has engaged in during the day and they are added to on a regular basis. This has become an effective communication tool between the centre and the families.

organize our lives by consolidating our phone lists, creating a working calendar, etc.

Technology now allows teachers to take photographs of the children, download them on a centre website and email them to parents. Teachers may create a montage for each individual child and present these to families at important events or as "graduation" gifts. These montages may also reflect the "Day in the Life of . . ." and provides another opportunity to communicate about developmentally appropriate practice.

At Jessie's Centre for Teen Parents, staff at the centre video tape infants once a month. When the family leaves, the video is a developmental record of the child as well as her interactions with teachers and other children at the centre.

A PARENT TRAVELLING TIP

Many retailers, including online retailers such as iTunes, sell audiobooks on tape, CD, or in mp3 format. Families on car trips can pop a CD into the car's CD player or download a book and plug their mp3 player into the car's adaptor and listen away. This is a great and innovative way to encourage an interest in children's books! Portable DVD players also provide an opportunity to choose educational and entertaining materials for children while travelling.

ABILITY ONLINE

Ability Online is a noteworthy computer-based service in Canada. In the past, a child confined to a bed or recuperating at home often couldn't communicate readily with other kids. Recently, however, advances in computer technology have allowed children, parents, teachers, and doctors to exchange written messages with children who are in hospital or convalescing long-term at home. Now children with and without special needs, teenagers, and adults can talk to each other entirely by computer and modem.

Developed by child psychiatrist Arlette Lefebvre of Toronto's Hospital for Sick Children and computer consultant Brian Hillis, the network was initially designed to enable children hospitalized for a long time to keep in touch with their friends and their schools. But since its inception in 1990, Ability Online has grown far beyond anything its designers had ever imagined. As Ability Online has shown, chatting in cyberspace is extremely popular with kids who might otherwise feel shy about talking to other people—perhaps because of hair loss due to chemotherapy, or because of facial or other deformities. Ultimately, Ability Online is a terrific way to boost kids' self-esteem, to disseminate health information to children and their families, and to learn communications and computer skills. (Rosenkrantz, 1995: 102)

REFERENCES

Bertrand, J. 2008. *Understanding, Managing, and Leading Early Childhood Programs in Canada*. Toronto: Thomson Nelson.

Botrie, M., and P. Wenger. 1992. *Teachers and Parents Together*. Markham, ON: Pembroke Publishers, Ltd.

Brock, D., and E. Dodd. 1994. "A Family Lending Library: Promoting Early Literacy Development." *Young Children* 49 (3): 16–21. March.

Burrington, B., and S. Sortino. 2004. "In Our Real World: An Anatomy of Documentation." In Joanne Hendrick, ed., *Next Steps toward Teaching the Reggio Way: Accepting the Challenge to Change*. Columbus, OH: Pearson, Merrill Prentice Hall.

Fraser, S. 2000. *Authentic Childhood: Experiencing Reggio Emilia in the Classroom*. Toronto: Nelson Thomson Learning.

Gonzalez-Mena, J. 2008. *50 Early Childhood Strategies for Working and Communicating With Diverse Families*. Columbus, OH: Pearson, Merrill Prentice Hall.

Harris Helm, J., S. Beneke, and K. Steinheimer. 1997. "Documenting Children's Learning." *Childhood Education*. Summer: 200–5.

Hildebrand, J. 1991. *Introduction to Early Childhood Education*. Reston, VA: NAEYC.

Pimento, B., and D. Kernested. 2000. *Healthy Foundations in Child Care*, 2nd ed. Toronto: Nelson Thomson Learning.

Rosenkrantz, O. 1995. "Special Families, Special Needs." *Today's Parent.* November.

Rudney, G.L. 2005. *Every Teacher's Guide to Working with Parents.* Thousand Oaks, CA: Corwin Press.

Samovar, L.A., R.E. Porter, and E.R. McDaniel. 2007. *Communication Between Cultures*, 6th ed. Florence, KY: Thomson Wadsworth.

Statistics Canada. 2006. "Canadian Internet Usage Survey." *The Daily.* August 15. Available at http://www.statcan .ca/Daily/English/060815/d060815b.htm.

Courtesy of Lynn Wilson

CHAPTER 9

Families We May Meet

Geoff Manasse / Photodisc Green / Getty Images

"Let us put our heads together and see what life we will make for our children".

—*Sitting Bull, Lakota*

LEARNING OUTCOMES

After studying this chapter, you will be able to

1. identify the diverse families found in Canada today

2. evaluate the role of the teacher in supporting families with diverse situations, challenges, strengths, and needs

There is always a danger of organizing information in a way that leads to the assumption that families can be grouped together on the basis of similar characteristics and issues. In fact, nothing could be further from the truth! Regardless of common elements that exist in some families, each is unique. **It is the teacher's responsibility to hear each family's story and to focus on each family's strengths.** To help teachers understand and work with the families they serve and the situations that face them, books for both adults and children are useful resources. ECE students are encouraged to make contact with the Canadian Children's Book Centre, which has an office in Toronto and regional offices in Alberta, British Columbia, Manitoba, and Nova Scotia. Students can visit their website for more information at **www.book-centre.ca**. Another helpful resource is Parent Books, whose website is **www.parentbooks.com**.

ABORIGINAL FAMILIES

Mary is a teacher in an Aboriginal Head Start program. This is an early intervention program for young Aboriginal children and their families. Mary's sister Sarah teaches in the same program on their reserve. Mary and Sarah have worked with elders in their communities to design and implement curriculum that includes culture and language, education, health promotion, nutrition, social support programs, and family involvement. Both Mary and Sarah have young daughters who attend this program, and they are pleased that they are all learning Ojibway from an elder.

According to Statistics Canada, Aboriginal identity refers to those persons who reported identifying with at least one Aboriginal group, North American Indian, Métis, Inuit, and/or those who reported being a Treaty Indian or a Registered Indian as defined by the Indian Act of Canada, and/or those who reported they were members of an Indian Band or First Nation. "The terms Indigenous and Aboriginal are used almost synonymously in Canada to refer to the population of peoples who identify themselves as descendents of original habitants. . . . Some prefer the term Indigenous because it connects to a global advocacy movement of Indigenous peoples who use this term, most notably the Maori in Aotearoa/New Zealand. The term 'Aboriginal' was coined in the 1800s by the colonial government in Canada as a catch-all label, and some people refrain from using this term because of its colonial derivation" (Ball et al., 2007).

Native peoples want the right to choose and define the kinds of child-care services that meet their needs.

According to the 2006 census, the Canadian Aboriginal population is 1,172,785; 3.8 percent of Canadians claim Aboriginal roots. This is an increase of 45 percent in 10 years, six times faster than the non-Aboriginal population. Forty-eight percent of the Aboriginal population is under 25 years of age. The birth rate is about 1.5 times the overall Canadian rate (Statistics Canada, 2007a).

It is important when discussing Aboriginal families that we understand the differences among these groups living in Canada. The experiences of an Inuit family living in the Northwest Territories will be vastly different from a Métis family living in Alberta.

FACTS ABOUT ABORIGINAL FAMILIES AND THEIR CHILDREN

When we examine the lives of Aboriginal children and their families in Canada, we cannot help but be shocked by the following statistics:

- Infant mortality is 1.5 percent higher than the national average.
- Fetal Alcohol Syndrome Disorder (FASD) may affect 1 in 5 Inuit and First Nation children.
- Fifty percent of children who live on reserves are overweight or obese.
- Ninety-one percent are affected by dental decay, and 7.8 percent are affected by six years.
- Tuberculosis (TB) rates in northern Aboriginal communities are four times the national

average; the rates of respiratory diseases in Inuit children is the highest in the world.

- Hearing loss and speech and language delays are far greater in Aboriginal communities.
- There are concerns about early school-leaving, juvenile detention, incarceration, and juvenile suicide.
- Life expectancy is 5–7 times lower than that of other Canadians. (Ball, 2008)

Sheila Fraser, Canada's Auditor General states in her report on the status of Aboriginals in Canada that while the Indian and Northern Affairs Department did some studies and began a few new programs, it made little progress on a range of problems cited in 2000, including a large gap in the number of native versus non-native high school graduates. Ms. Fraser criticized Ottawa for failing native children who live on reserves. She said school funding is so inadequate compared to provincial public schools that it will take 28 years for them to catch up to the high school graduation rates of their non-native peers. Most native schools are in communities with fewer than 500 residents, making it difficult to offer a range of services (Fraser, 2008).

Phil Fontaine, Assembly of First Nation National chief addresses the concerns of housing: "There are 4.5 people in every First Nations home, compared to 2.6 in every non-aboriginal home in Canada. This may mean that people may need to

INSIDE LOOK

Former Prime Minister Paul Martin states in an editorial to *The Globe and Mail* that "Aboriginals—our fellow Canadians—desperately need our help. And we've got the resources to do it. They don't want us to dictate solutions. They want us to work with them. How, years from now, will we answer the question of why we turned our backs on their need?

"In my travels to aboriginal reserves and urban communities . . . I have found two constants: the heartwarming welcome evident in the smiling faces of the children; and the heart-rending discovery of the conditions in which these children and all members of the community live, the challenges they face, the burdens they carry.

"A recent study found that Aboriginals who do have a high-school diploma tend to find jobs and live lives that not only equal but can exceed the success ratio of other Canadians. In other words, access to education is a practical way to fix what has gone so wrong.

"For too long, the infectious optimism of aboriginal youth has succumbed to hard realities. It doesn't have to. We hold within our power the ability to make today's children the generation that is given the tools and opportunity to succeed. With the help of Canadians, this can be the Aboriginal generation that breaks the cycle of despair" (Martin, 2008)

TABLE 9.1 An Overview

Inuit	Métis	First Nations

About The Inuit

For many centuries, outsiders called Inuit "Eskimos," but the Inuit no longer find this term acceptable. They prefer the name by which they have always known themselves—Inuit—which means "the people" in their own language, Inuktitut. In 2006, 4 percent of the Aboriginal population identified they were Inuit, an 8 percent increase from 2001. About 55,700 Inuit live in 53 communities across the North.

Where They Live

- 78 percent of the population live in Inuit Nunaat, the Inuktitut expression for "Inuit Homeland" an area of 4 regions in the Arctic
  - 49 percent live in Nunavut
  - 19 percent live in Nunavik in northern Quebec
  - 6 percent in the Inuvialuit region of the North West Territories
  - 4 percent in Nunatsiavut in northern Labrador

Households

In 2006, 18 percent of Inuit lived in a household that was home to more than one family. Inuit have traditionally lived in family groupings but the serious shortage of housing in most communities has forced many families to live in cramped conditions.

About The Métis

Métis are descendants of marriages of Cree, Ojibway, Saulteaux, and Menominee peoples to French Canadians, Scots, and English. In 2006, an estimated 389,785 people reported that they were Métis. This population has almost doubled (increasing by 91 percent) since 1996. The Métis represented just 1 percent of the total population of Canada. In 2006, 9 percent of all people in the Northwest Territories reported they were Métis, followed by 6 percent in Manitoba, 5 percent in Saskatchewan and 3 percent in Alberta and Yukon Territory.

Where They Live

- 87 percent of all Métis live in the West and in Ontario in 2006
- 7% lived in Quebec
- 5% in Atlantic Canada
- The remaining 1 percent live in one of the three territories
- 7 out of 10 lived in an urban area, 40,980 Métis live in Winnipeg the largest Métis population in one location

Households

Overall there was a decrease in the share of Métis living in crowded homes or in homes needing repairs since 1996. Rural Métis living in rural locations in the Prairie provinces still suffer these conditions.

About First Nations

First Nations people accounted for 60 percent of Aboriginal people in 2006. 698,025 identified themselves as First Nations. The First Nations population increased 29 percent between 1996 and 2006. There are more than 600 bands across Canada.

Where They Live

- 40 percent live on reserve
- 60 percent off reserve
- 3 out of 4 people living off reserve live in urban areas. The Prairie provinces are home to young First Nations populations.

Households

First Nations people are five times more likely than non-Aboriginal people to live in crowded homes, especially on reserves with 26 percent living in these conditions and four times more likely than non-Aboriginals to live in dwellings requiring major repairs.

Family Structure

In 2006, nearly 70 percent of Inuit children aged 14 and under lived in a family with two parents. Twenty-five percent lived in lone-parent families: about 30 percent live with a female lone-parent and 6 percent with a male lone-parent. Four percent lived solely with a grandparent, with no parent or other relatives present.

Language

The word Inuktitut is routinely used to refer to all Canadian variants of the Inuit traditional language, and it is recognized as one of the official languages of Nunavut and the Northwest Territories. It is spoken in all areas north of the tree line, including parts of the provinces of Newfoundland and Labrador, Quebec, to some extent in northeastern Manitoba as well as the territories of Nunavut, the Northwest Territories, and traditionally on the Arctic Ocean coast of Yukon. The traditional language is a system of closely interrelated dialects that are not readily comprehensible from one end of the Inuit world to the other.

Family Structure

A total of 54,735 Métis children, or 65 percent of the total, lived in a two-parent family, while 27,955 youngsters, or 33 percent, lived with a lone parent. The percentage of Métis children living with a lone parent in urban centres is 42 percent, almost double the proportion of 22 percent in rural areas.

Language

Michif was a trade language that developed originally in the 1700s between the French/English fur traders and the Cree/Algonkian/Sioux speakers from Ontario and Manitoba. The most common language is Cree an Algonquian language. In 2006, 9,380 Métis could carry on a conversation in Cree. Older Métis were more likely to speak an Aboriginal language—12 percent aged 75 and older. Less than 3 percent of Métis aged 44 and under spoke an Aboriginal language.

Family Structure

Just over one-half (54 percent) of First Nations children lived with two parents. Just under one-third (31 percent) of First Nations children aged 14 and under lived with a lone mother. Six percent of First Nations children lived with a lone father.

Language

Over 60 different languages are spoken by First Nations grouped into distinct language families: Algonquin, Athapascan, Siouan, Salish, Tsimshian, Wakashan, Iroquoian, Haida, Kutenai and Tlingit. In 2006, 29 percent said they could speak well enough to carry on a conversation. The figure is higher for those living on reserve (51 percent) than off reserve (12 percent).

The language spoken by the largest number of First Nations people is Cree, followed by Ojibway.

Source: Statistics Canada 2008. Aboriginal Identity Population by Age Groups, Median Age and Sex, 2006 counts for Canada, Provinces and Territories, Released January 15, 2008; http://www12.statcan.ca/english/census06/data/highlights/aboriginal/pages/Page.cfm?Lang=E&Geo=PR&Code=PR&Code=01&Table=1&Data=Count&Sex=1&Age=1&StartRec=1&Sort=2&Display=Page

TABLE 9.2 — WHERE DO ABORIGINAL PEOPLE LIVE?

PROVINCE	POPULATION
Newfoundland and Labrador	23,455
Prince Edward Island	1,730
Nova Scotia	24,175
New Brunswick	17,650
Quebec	108,425
Ontario	242,495
Manitoba	175,395
Saskatchewan:	141,890
Alberta	188,365
British Columbia	196,075
Yukon Territory	7,580
Northwest Territories	20,635
Nunavut	24,915

Source: Table 20, Statistics Canada; http://www12.statcan.ca/english/census06/analysis/aboriginal/tables/table20.htm

sleep in shifts to give children the rest they need to learn effectively. Those dwellings are generally smaller and in greater need of repair. 87,000 new housing units are needed to address overcrowding. An additional concern is that in 2007 there are more than 100 communities under boil water advisories" (Fontaine, 2007).

Ontario's former Lieutenant-Governor, James Bartleman, whose mother is Ojibwa, was so concerned about the reserves he called "Ontario's Third World" that he sent more than a million books to fill the empty class shelves and began summer literacy camps. He also twinned 100 northern native schools with schools in the south which have pledged to send books.

RESIDENTIAL SCHOOLS

One of the most significant events affecting First Nation communities was the creation of residential schools by the Canadian federal government; these schools were largely operated by the Anglican, Roman Catholic, Methodist, and Presbyterian churches. The Aboriginal Healing Foundation

INSIDE LOOK

Prime Minister Harper Offers Full Apology On Behalf Of Canadians for the Indian Residential Schools System

On behalf of the Government of Canada and all Canadians, Prime Minister Stephen Harper offered an historic formal apology today to former students of Indian Residential Schools and sought forgiveness for the students' suffering and for the damaging impact the schools had on Aboriginal culture, heritage and language. "The treatment of children in Indian Residential Schools is a sad chapter in our history," Prime Minister Harper said. "Today, we recognize this policy of assimilation was wrong, has caused great harm, and has no place in our country. The Government of Canada sincerely apologizes and asks the forgiveness of the Aboriginal peoples of this country for failing them so profoundly." Today's apology reinforces numerous other government initiatives designed to address the tragic legacy of Indian Residential Schools, including the ongoing implementation of the historic Indian Residential Schools Settlement Agreement which includes: a Common Experience Payment; an Independent Assessment Process; Commemoration Activities; measures to support healing; and the Indian Residential Schools Truth and Reconciliation Commission. "The Government recognizes that the absence of an apology has been an impediment to healing and reconciliation," said Prime Minister Harper. "Years of work by survivors, communities and Aboriginal organizations culminated in an Indian Residential Schools Settlement Agreement and the Truth and Reconciliation Commission. These are the foundations of a new relationship between Aboriginal people and other Canadians, a relationship based on knowledge of our shared history, a respect for each other and a desire to move forward together with a renewed understanding that strong families, strong communities and vibrant cultures and traditions will contribute to a stronger Canada for all of us."

Source: http://pm.gc.ca/eng/media.asp?id=2149.

As an aboriginal ECE, I think it is important to see positive Aboriginal role models who are proud of who they are. Not stereotypical pictures of an "Indian" dressed up in war tribe gear—feathers and a painted face. We need to see Aboriginals as doctors, police officers, teachers, etc.

Source: Reta Hamlin, ECE graduate

I travelled north to Canada's Arctic to work as an instructor in a program called Educators in Native and Inuit Child Care Services. I lived in a remote Inuit community in Nunavut (population 750) where traditional knowledge continues to be part of everyday life. I did my best to prepare before I travelled. I read books and talked to people about the language, culture, land, and history but no amount of reading can prepare for your first trip to the arctic. My class consisted of 14 women ranging in age from 18–55 and English was a second language for all of them. The course was competency-based and delivered with an interactive hands-on approach. I modelled all aspects of working in a child-care program (effective interactions with children and adults, guidance strategies, songs, circle time, activities, setting up of learning centres, etc.) for the students in the classroom and then we practiced these aspects with the children and families in the child-care centre.

The main goals of the program were for the women to build confidence in their existing skills and to develop new ones, to be introduced to new ideas and tools, and to have opportunities to put it all into practice. Emphasis was always placed on using the Inuktitut language and integrating Inuit culture into program content and values. I recognized that the success of the program and its sustainability rested on my acceptance within the community. I worked to develop partnerships with the Aboriginal Head Start program, the Arctic College Satellite, the local school and other community organizations and also to build relationships with Elders. I made every attempt to connect with people by involving myself in community gatherings and demonstrating a genuine interest in the language and culture. I consistently reminded myself that I was a guest and focused on displaying respect and openness to all that was unfamiliar to me. I travelled north to teach Early Childhood Education and returned south with more awareness and knowledge that could only be gained through my experience.

Source: Rachel Brophy, faculty

(2002) reported that the residential school system operated across Canada between 1800 and 1990, peaking in 1930 when 80 schools were in operation. More than 150,000 Native children aged six years and older were placed in the national network of residential schools, which were built far away from reserves to ensure that the children would be educated in European ways without parental or cultural influences. While not all children had negative experiences in these schools, incidents of abuse have been cited by many former students. The system has contributed to the loss of language and culture among Aboriginal people; a key objective of the residential school system was the assimilation of Aboriginal children. The negative effects of these schools have, in many cases, been passed from one generation to the next. As a result, only one-quarter of the Aboriginal population reported that they had an Aboriginal language as mother tongue. Cree was the Aboriginal mother tongue most often spoken, followed by Inuktitut and Ojibway. The majority of Aboriginal people—about 68 percent—reported English as their mother tongue, while 6 percent reported French.

Leroy Joe, a member of the Lil'wat Nation and the father of five girls, says:

> I grew up on the rez and life is different here. I grew up with a lot of social, economic, and spiritual chaos, and I suffered a lot of spiritual, emotional, and mental pain because of it. We all did. The growth of spirit, mind, and body that is needed for recovery is not for the faint of heart. My healing process was very taxing. I either had to learn or die. It took a long hard time to mature into becoming a father, long after my kids were born. With 39 years of life behind me, and with the help of my wife, I feel like I am finally becoming a man. At last I'm growing strong, spiritually, socially, emotionally, and as a father.

Source: Ball et al., 2007.

According to *The Toronto Star* (2007a), a 1996 UN report classed Aboriginal languages in Canada as among the most endangered in the world. Statistics Canada (2007a) concluded that only three languages out of 50—Cree, Ojibway, and Inuktitut—had large enough populations to be considered secure from extinction in the long run.

The first study of Aboriginal fathers in Canada was completed by Dr. Jessica Ball at the University of Victoria, a team of Aboriginal fathers from each of five First Nations, and a number of partnered urban Aboriginal organizations. Questionnaires and interviews were gathered from 73 First Nations and seven Métis fathers who all had at least one child under the age of five. These Aboriginal fathers emphasized the socio-historical conditions associated with colonialism that have shaped Indigenous fathers' self-reported challenges in "learning to be a father" and "becoming a man."

Qualitative analyses guided by grounded theory methodology suggested three patterns of response to becoming a father: an avoidance pattern termed "fathers-in-waiting"; learning fathering through play; and stepping up/settling down to fathering responsibilities. Fathers described a gradual process of accepting and learning fatherhood, often years after the birth of their first child. Widespread shifts in gender roles and constructions of masculinity were identified as reciprocally influential conditions that have enabled some Indigenous men to become more involved in care-giving roles with their children. Fathers pointed to a lack of supports, especially in rural and remote settlements, and especially for men who were raising their children alone. All fathers described incidents where they felt that programs, policies, and society as a whole are biased in favour of mothers (Ball, in press for 2009).

Findings from this study and planned future research will extend community practice beyond a prevailing focus on mothers, and extend fathering theory beyond a prevailing European-heritage perspective. Supporting Indigenous fathers' involvement requires sustained, macro-system, policy-driven efforts to reduce barriers to initiating and sustaining positive engagement with children. Steps include increasing information about declaring paternity on birth records, accessing birth records, and engaging Indigenous fathers with adolescents (e.g., in schools) to promote awareness of how fathers' can be important in children's lives (Ball, 2008). ECE practitioners need to acknowledge fathers in children's programs and decision-making about children, and work towards implementation of "kith and kin" policies in child protection programs to keep children closer to home (Ball and George, 2006). This project produced a resource kit that includes a documentary DVD that features interviews with First Nations fathers of young children, a booklet for Aboriginal fathers, and a booklet for community-based practitioners. Visit **www.ecdip.org/fathers** for more information.

TRADITIONAL EDUCATION

"The traditional way of education was by example, experience, and storytelling. The first principle involved was total respect and acceptance of the one to be taught, and that learning was a continuous process from birth to death. It was

ABORIGINAL FAMILIES IN CHILD-CARE SETTINGS

© Sergei Bachlakov / Shutterstock

Many Aboriginal families want their children to be involved in rituals and ceremonies that recall their traditional past.

> Look into the eyes of your child once a moon and see there . . . the miracle of the Great Spirit.
>
> —Tribal Laws of the Eastern Algonquin

In traditional Aboriginal approaches to child care, Thomas and Learoyd (1990) observe, the child is perceived as a "child of the community. All those people with whom the child comes into regular contact often become part of the 'extended family' and as such assume responsibility for the care of the child. . . . The child in a Native community is raised on values which emphasize autonomy, belonging, mastery and generosity" (1990: i). Grandparents play a significant role in raising children as they pass on Aboriginal traditions and values.

"Native people firmly believe that children represent the primary means through which a culture can preserve its tradition, heritage, and language. Children are considered the trust of the past and the hope of the future" (Federation of Saskatchewan Indian Nations, 1983). Eva Cardinal, a Cree educator based in Edmonton, states: "My people believe children are a gift from the Creator. Our children are only loaned to us. Children are our future leaders. Children are highly valued. I will not pretend all Native parents act on these beliefs. We have our share of neglect and abuse. But we consider this to be every bit as dysfunctional as the dominant culture does. Our children are precious to us, even when we cannot act on this belief" (1994: 23).

> If it be necessary to punish a child, do it in such a way as to improve his strength or his mind, but lay not your hand upon him for you may damage the possession of your god, his gift to you. (Tribal Laws of the Eastern Algonquin)

total continuity without interruption. Its nature was like a fountain that gives many colours and flavours of water and that whoever chose could drink as much or as little as they wanted to whenever they wished. The teaching strictly adhered to the sacredness of life whether of humans, animals or plants."

—Art Solomon, Ojibwe elder, residential school survivor, (**www.shannonthunderbird.com/residential_schools.htm**)

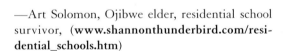

"Aboriginal family life, like that of other families in Canada, has undergone enormous changes in recent decades. The Aboriginal family in traditional, land-based societies was, until recently, the principal institution mediating the participation of individuals in social, economic, and political life. The extended family distributed responsibilities for the care and nurturing of its members over a large network of grandparents, aunts, uncles and cousins. While many Aboriginal people have moved to the city, and many others residing on reserves and in rural towns and villages engage in wage labour rather than traditional harvesting, the notion of the caring, effective, extended family continues to be a powerful ideal etched deep in the psyche of Aboriginal people."

Source: Castellano, 2002.

ROLE OF THE TEACHER

- Many teachers in non-Native child-care centres have little knowledge of values and practices toward children in the Native community. Child-care staff must ask themselves what stereotypes and assumptions they bring to their teaching of Native children. Failure to do so can lead to misunderstandings in the playroom. For example, Native children who are quiet and shy in a non-Native child-care setting may be interpreted as being resistant, withdrawn, or noncompliant.

- Native children's education must ensure two basic principles: (1) family and community involvement and (2) local control and participation in decision-making and delivering of curriculum.

- Recognize that many people may "parent" the child and they should be included in the centre.

- Understand the cultural differences in behaviour. For example, Native children are often uncomfortable speaking in front of groups and are more at ease in small-group settings, where they can work in cooperation with others. Also, eye contact is often difficult for them to maintain, since avoiding it is a sign of respect.

- Some children are less verbal and more autonomous at an earlier age. Teachers much recognize that traditional Native culture places a high value on individual freedom, and elders give guidance. Strategies best used with young children are modelling, influences from the larger group, and the expectation of positive behaviour.

- Provide parenting information as well as information about workshops, seminars that will help to strengthen parenting skills.

- Teachers should be knowledgeable about health conditions that Native families may be facing. Given the high incidence of Diabetes Type 2 in the Native population, families may be interested in workshops related to preparing nutritious meals based on the Native Food Guide. It is important to remember that workshops are always more successful and best received when the ideas come from the families themselves.

ROLE OF THE TEACHER IN THE PLAYROOM

- The oral language is the Native way of preserving and understanding their culture. Encourage families and elders to share their oral culture with the children. Invite an elder into the centre to explain the cultural relevance of materials that might be placed in the dramatic play centre so that children learn to treat these resources in a respectful manner.

- Materials in the centre should be concrete, real, and relevant to the children and their families, and should reflect an understanding of their history.

- A diversity of opinion exists on ceremonies such as smudging, naming, and praying; therefore, teachers should consult the families in their program. Traditional opening and closing ceremonies should be observed if relevant to the families in the centre.

- Connect older children to Native history. Many towns and cities, as well as places within them, have Native names. Discuss these with the children.

- Learn words in the families' language and use them in the playroom and in interactions with families whenever possible.

- Use written language to label items around the room in the first language of the children in the centre. Provide books written and illustrated by Native people.

- Give examples of Native heroes and present them as role models for children.

- Invite families to the centre to share a tradition, for example, to cook traditional foods.

- Avoid segregating children by placing them into cultural groups when doing activities in the room.

- Teachers should spend as much time creating a positive learning environment in the outdoors because a fundamental Native principle is living in harmony with nature. Richardson (1994) believes that schools for Native children should be designed with large, open spaces. They should take into account aspects of the medicine wheel and spirituality; be alive with plants, water, and animals; and encourage the Native spirit by including skylights and bare ground where sweat lodge ceremonies can be

TABLE 9.3　　HOW TO INCLUDE ABORIGINAL CULTURAL CONTENT

DO	DON'T
Do include activities and materials that reflect the specific Aboriginal groups represented in your program, community, and/or geographic region. Whenever possible, involve Aboriginal elders and families in all aspects of programming. This will help ensure relevance and authenticity for both Aboriginal and non-Aboriginal children.	Don't assume that all Inuit, Métis, Dene, and/or First Nations cultures are alike. While there are many commonalities, there are also major differences between groups and individuals, in terms of history, values, traditions, customs, language, current interests, and concerns. Use materials that accurately reflect both similarities and differences among Aboriginal peoples (e.g., all First Nations people celebrate special events but, depending on their particular band or nation, their celebrations may be quite different).
Do use books, posters, and other resource materials that accurately portray Aboriginal peoples in a wide variety of both traditional and contemporary roles and settings—work, sports, the arts, family activities, and special celebrations. Look for and use books and materials written and illustrated by Aboriginal people.	Don't use stories or pictures that include "I is for Indian" or "E is for Eskimo" as part of the alphabet, or that portray "playing Indian" with feather head-dresses and tomahawks. Such materials stereotype and trivialize Aboriginal people and traditions. Don't make up Aboriginal legends or ceremonies.
Do include Aboriginal traditions, legends, and related materials in a meaningful context and in age-appropriate ways. When focusing on the past, do so for both Aboriginal and other cultures, in order to avoid stereotyping or romanticizing the "olden days" only for Aboriginal peoples (e.g., "I wonder what each of our grandmothers wore [ate, played with, etc.] when they were little girls").	Don't use materials that show Aboriginal people in a stereotypical or exclusively historical context—wearing buckskins, living in igloos or teepees, or living off the land with bows and arrows.
Do include lots of opportunities for outdoor play and contact with plants and animals, as part of strengthening children's appreciation of the natural world.	Don't assume that all Aboriginal children, especially those living in urban areas, are "connected to the land" and familiar with their traditional, land-based heritage.
Do represent Aboriginal families as living in both urban and rural environments and as having a range of perspectives and views on ecological issues.	Don't represent Aboriginal peoples as living only in the wilderness, on reserves, or in small communities. Don't portray them as the "first ecologists."
Do acknowledge and accommodate different learning styles, experiences, and goals. Examples of some Aboriginal children's preferred learning styles include: • more learning through watching and imitating, self-directed experiences and trial-and-error, rather than through following verbal instructions; • more emphasis on cooperation and group learning activities, rather than on competition or individual performance and achievement; • more focus on a holistic or global approach to learning, rather than emphasis on learning about an abstract subject (e.g., numbers and letters) out of context from daily living.	Don't assume that all children learn the same way or that one child-care program fits all when dealing with children and families from Aboriginal and/or minority culture backgrounds. A child- and family-centred approach means introducing new learning opportunities while also reflecting and reinforcing for children what's familiar and comfortable from home.

Source: Canadian Child Care Federation, "Aboriginal Cultural Content in Early Childhood Care and Education," Interaction 12, No. 2. Reprinted with permission from the Canadian Child Care Federation.

performed. Once schools show that being Native is an act of being, Native children feel good about themselves and the school they attend (1994: 27).

ABORIGINAL PROGRAMS

In recent years, early childhood development programs designed specifically for Aboriginal children have been introduced in many communities. The development of Native teacher training programs and the involvement of Native people are both crucial to the promotion of successful educational experiences for Native children. Native teachers will have an intimate understanding of Native ways of life and are most able to bring Native linguistics and cultural resources to the classroom (Mallea and Young, 1990). According to Thomas and Learoyd (1990: ii), an Aboriginal-run urban child care "would incorporate culture in both its structure and program content, employ Native staff, and would involve grandparents and extended family in transmitting Native culture, values and traditions to Native children." According to Friendly, Beach, and Turiano (2003) there are seven federal government programs for Aboriginal ECEC targeted to specific populations and, in some cases, specific provinces. The evaluation survey results for 2001 tell us that Aboriginal people occupy 90 percent of full-time positions and 87 percent of part-time positions in Aboriginal Head Start (AHS) projects across the country.

Aboriginal Head Start (AHS)

The AHS Program was established in 1995 in urban and northern communities, and in 1998 on reserves. AHS is a Health Canada-funded early childhood development program for First Nations, Inuit, and Métis children up to six years old. The primary goal of the initiative is to demonstrate that locally controlled and designed early intervention strategies can provide Aboriginal children with a positive sense of themselves, a desire for learning, and opportunities to develop fully as successful young people. There are 129 AHS off reserve sites in urban and northern communities across Canada—in eight provinces and three territories. There are 332 on reserve programs across the country serving 9,400 children (2009). Projects typically provide half-day preschool experiences that prepare young Aboriginal children for their school years by meeting their spiritual, emotional, intellectual, and physical needs. All projects provide programming in six core areas:

- **Education and school readiness:** To foster a desire for lifelong learning, focus on early childhood development and provide children with opportunities to develop school readiness skills.

- **Aboriginal culture and language:** To offer an understanding of, respect for and participation in and responsiveness to the culture and language of children, families and communities.

- **Parental and family involvement:** To acknowledge parents and guardians as the primary teachers and caregivers of the children, ensuring that they play a key role in the planning, development, operation and evaluation of the program. The Building Strong Spirits program supports extended families in teaching and caring for children, particularly elders and traditional people.

- **Health promotion:** To support the family in assuring that the child receives regular preventative health care and professional attention to health problems.

- **Nutrition:** To use a balanced approach to meet the nutritional requirement of the children/meet children's nutritional needs by using Aboriginal Food Guides comparable to Canada's Food Guide and is respectful of local traditions and customs; and encourage parents' healthy eating habits.

- **Social support:** To provide opportunities for the child to develop social and emotional skills with are consistent with Aboriginal core values.

AHS directly involves parents and the community in the management and operation of projects. Parents are supported in their role as the child's first and most influential teachers, and the wisdom of elders is valued. There is no charge to parents for participating in an AHS program.

National Aboriginal Day

In 1982 the National Indian Brotherhood (now the Assembly of First Nations) launched a national campaign to have June 21 recognized as National Aboriginal Solidarity Day. In cooperation with national Aboriginal organizations, the government of Canada chose June 21 because it is also the summer solstice, the longest day of the year. For generations, many Aboriginal peoples have celebrated their culture and heritage on or

The program at Misipawistik Cree Nation Head Start Program, in Grand Rapids, Manitoba, is in some respects a typical Head Start Program. However, this program is unique because of its increased collaboration, enhanced training opportunities, child-centred curriculum, and increased opportunities for families and their children to attend a program.

- **Increased collaboration**. The staff works as a collaborative unit. Planning occurs at all levels—coordinator, early childhood educators, cook, and custodian. Additionally, whenever possible all staff, including the cook and the custodian, have the opportunity to attend workshops together. This fosters an enhanced understanding of the child, the family, and the program.
- **Development of training workshops**. The coordinator and staff, in partnership with the University College of the North, have developed and continue to develop area workshops to meet the specific training needs of their program. These opportunities are extended to other programs in the Northern community and are offered as credit toward diploma completion. Participants attend the workshop, complete assignments via distance learning, and receive credit upon successful completion of the assignments. In a past workshop, 32 individuals attended the workshop from five different communities.
- **Child-centred curriculum**. The program embraces a "play-to-learn" philosophy and is continually striving to improve the active play experiences of the children through further education, individual research, and increased resources.
- **Expansion of opportunities**. An additional half-day program is offered for two-year-olds in the community. There is a dual purpose to this activity. First, it provides an opportunity to families who have no access to a program to attend. Second, it provides a bridging to children and families who potentially will participate in the program when the children are three years old.

Source: Contributed by Dr. Ingrid Crowther

These children at this Head Start Program in Manitoba have opportunities to explore with a variety of media.

Courtesy of Ingrid Crowther

Vancouver Aboriginal Supported Child Development Program (VASCDP)

The VASCDP receives funding from the Ministry of Children and Family Development to support Aboriginal children from birth to age 12 who have a developmental delay or disability (no diagnosis required) who require extra support to attend child care or preschool; services for children aged 13–19 may be provided on an individual basis. Through VASCDP these children can fully participate in inclusive neighbourhood child-care programs in Vancouver. Families can include birth, adopted, and foster families. The program is open: Aboriginal families can be on or off reserve, and can be Status, Non-Status, Métis, or Inuit; band affiliation is not necessary.

Guiding Principles

- Recognize and build on the strengths and needs of the families.
- Encourage parent decision-making in partnership with team members.
- Support the families with flexible services and respect whatever level of participation they choose.
- Provide services and supports free of charge. Parents are responsible for child-care fees. This is a voluntary program and parental consent is required.

Both the Vancouver Native Health Society and Douglas College are currently involved in an educational partnership and are piloting a course titled "Strengthening the Family Spirit: Working from an Aboriginal Perspective with Elder's Teachings."

Source: Contributed by Flo Lewis, Team Leader Vancouver Aboriginal SCD Program, Jan Kubli Carrie, Dean Faculty of Child Family and Community Studies, Douglas College

---

EXHIBIT 9.1 NATIVE CHILD-CARE PHILOSOPHY

Brokenleg and Brendtro (1989) describe four distinct aspects of Native child-care philosophy:

1. Significance is nurtured in a cultural milieu that celebrates the ethos of belonging. Within Native society, a sense of belonging fashions young people to be more responsive to advice from other clan/band members. . . . Native youth listen and reflect upon advice given to them by respectful and caring adults. A sense of belonging extends beyond the family, encompassing nature as well.

2. Competency is enhanced by extensive opportunities for mastery. Success and mastery produce social recognition as well as inner satisfaction. Native children are taught to generously acknowledge the achievements of others, but a person who receives honour must always accept this without arrogance. Someone more skilled than oneself is seen as a model, not a competitor.

3. Power is fostered by encouraging the expression of autonomy. As opposed to contemporary white culture's pressure on children to become independent, assertive, and competitive at an early age, the children must first have opportunities to be dependent, learn to respect and value elders, and be taught to obey through explanation for desired behaviour.

4. Virtue is reflected in the preeminent value of generosity. Native children are taught to be generous, unselfish, and to give without expectations. As the Native community is based upon reciprocity, personal wealth and possessions do not elevate one's social status. . . . Altruism is considered the highest of virtues.

Source: M. Brokenleg and L. Brendtro, "The Circle of Caring: Native American Perspectives on Children and Youth," p. 10. Paper presented to Child Welfare of American International Conference, Washington, DC, 1989.

near this day. This day is a chance for Canadians to celebrate the rich contributions Aboriginal peoples have made to Canada. Educators should consult the website **www.ainc-inac.gc.ca/nad/index_e.html** at the Department of Indian Affairs and Northern Development for more information that they can use to honour this day in the classroom. An article in the journal *Interaction* (1998) outlines additional strategies for Aboriginal cultural content in early childhood care and education (see Table 9.3).

The Prime Minister's Awards for Excellence in Early Childhood Education

The Prime Minister's Awards for Excellence in Early Childhood Education are designed to honour the overall accomplishments of a single educator or a team of up to three educators. The awards recognize the efforts of outstanding early childhood educators who excel at fostering the early development and socialization of the children in their care, and at helping build the foundation children need to meet life's challenges. Certificates of Excellence are awarded to the 10 top-ranked nominees (individuals or teams), with at least one award designated for each of the following regions: British Columbia; Prairies; Yukon, Northwest Territories and Nunavut; Ontario; Quebec; and Atlantic Canada. In addition, one of the Certificates of Excellence is designated for the top-ranked Aboriginal early childhood educator. A financial award of $5000 is provided directly to the recipient to fund professional development, equipment, resource materials or other tools to improve developmental programming and children's experiences related to the educator's work.

In 2007, Gail King-Seegers, a graduate of George Brown College's ECE program and teacher at Toronto Aboriginal Head Start Program was awarded the Aboriginal Award of Excellence. Native Child Care and Family Services of Toronto state that Gail "is a fine example of the best NCFST has to offer. Caring, positive and absolutely focused on the good and welfare of kids, Gail embodies all of what we try to stand for and is an incredible role model for us all." In 2008, Sister Celeste of the Child Development Centre in Tulita, Northwest Territories won this award (see page 71).

First Nations Partnership Programs

Contributed by Jessica Ball, Coordinator, First Nations Partnership Programs

Ten partnership programs between the University of Victoria and First Nations communities have explored the value of bringing community elders and other community resource people alongside mainstream teaching and learning in postsecondary training in order to ensure bicultural, community-relevant, community-involving processes and outcomes. First Nations community partners engage with a curriculum team from the mainstream institution to develop and deliver community-based, culturally sensitive course work leading to a diploma in Child and Youth Care. The program was first offered in 1988 when Saskatchewan's Meadow Lake Tribal Council approached Dr. Alan Pence, a noted early childhood educator, to cooperatively develop a bicultural curriculum that prepared First Nations students to deliver quality child-care programs both on and off the reserve. The partnership resulted in the Generative Curriculum Model for creating curriculum, in which cultural knowledge about child development, child-rearing practices, and community life are considered alongside Euro-Western theory, research, and practice. These partnerships have shown the tremendous positive potential of involving the community in every step of program development and delivery, and grounding the development of human service practitioners in intergenerational relationships, community collaboration, and cultural revitalization.

BOOKS FOR ADULTS

Supporting Indigenous Children's Development, by Jessica Ball and Alan Pence

The Visiting Schools Program

This program is a partnership between the Native Canadian Centre of Toronto and Indian and Northern Affairs Canada. It is an interactive project that has been set up to help promote and foster a greater understanding of Aboriginal people in Canada and their distinct culture. Children are exposed to the teachings and traditions of First Nations, Inuit, and Métis people. A standard presentation revolves around the pow-wow format, which includes the drum and various styles of dancing. Some of the topics covered are the contributions of Native people throughout history, traditional stories and oral teachings, the six styles of dancing, the significance of the drum, and the different nations of people within the Native community. Also offered are specialized workshops such as traditional bread making and lessons in dream catcher assembly.

Books for Children

Sky Sisters, by J. Bourdeau Waboose and B. Deines

The Polar Bear Son: An Inuit Tale, by L. Dabcovich

Solomon's Tree, by A. Spalding and J. Wilson

Secret of the Dance, by A. Spalding and D. Gait

The Elders are Watching, by R. Henry Vickers

Books for Adults

Rethinking Columbus: The Next 500 Years, by B. Bigelow and B. Peterson

Iroquois: The Six Nations Confederacy, by J. Duden

Canada's First Nations: A History of the Founding Peoples From Earliest Times, by O. Dickason

A Concise History of Canada's First Nations, by O. Dickason

A People's Dream: Aboriginal Self-Government in Canada, by D. Russell

Multiracial Families

Since my son started daycare, I've heard a lot of comments about how beautiful or exotic biracial children look, and a lot of discussion about how to deal with the hair—that's a hot topic. As my child gets older, though, I expect the issues will get tougher. Which group will he identify more with? Will he have to choose? Which group will he hang out with in school? Will there be a mixed group? Somehow I doubt it, but if there is, will they be cool or uncool? Then I ask myself how I can best prepare my son for this uncharted course he must take. And of course the answer is he must have a strong sense of self.

He must be confident in his knowledge of who he is when people ask him to declare "what" he is—black or white. So what can his daycare teachers do now for my son? They can make sure there are biracial families and children in the books he reads and the pictures he sees. They can make sure he feels he belongs, that his family is accepted, and they can support his developing personality to build all the self-esteem he's going to need to be confident in whatever group he finds himself (Lucy Patterson, Queen Street Child Care Centre).

Mixed-race people have a long history in North America, starting with the Métis, unions between French traders and native women in the 1700s. There were 289,420 mixed race couples, married and common-law, in 2006—one third more than recorded in the 2001 census. As the population grows, more and more mixed-race people appear in the media. Golfer Tiger Woods has famously referred to his mixed-race identity as "Cablinasian" a word derived from Caucasian, Black, American-Indian, and Asian (Khoo, 2007). Actress Jennifer Beals has an Irish mother and African American father; supermodel Naomi Campbell has a Jamaican mother and a Jamaican Canadian father. All routinely placed on "most beautiful people" lists by entertainment magazines, Johnny Depp claims Irish, German, and Cherokee ancestry; Angelina Jolie's parents were French Canadian and Iroquois (mother) and Czechoslovakian (father); and Keanu Reeves' parents were English (mother) and Hawaiian Chinese (father). Canada's Governor General, Michaelle Jean, and her husband Jean-Daniel Lafond are a prominent interracial couple. Wendy Roth, a sociologist at the University of British Columbia, reasons that intermarriage and mixed unions prove so interesting because they serve as a litmus test of social relations between different groups. Mixed unions have experienced a steady, though not huge, increase; the fact that it continues to be steady in different censuses suggests that barriers between cultural groups are diminishing. The vast majority of interracial couples in the last census (85 percent) involve a white person and a visible minority, and 15 percent are marriages among couples from two different visible minority groups (La Rose, 2008).

Multi-racial people are helping us rethink what it means to be Canadian because, in addition to exploring their own identities, mixed-race people are challenging our notions of race, ethnicity, and national identity. This has implications for public policy and for society as a whole. Murphy Kilbride et al. (1998: 20–21) state:

> To this point, Canadian experience has shown that across generations, people are increasingly inclined to marry across ethnoracial boundaries. . . . The latest data show that almost 2% of Canadians who identify themselves as visible minorities have multiple visible minority racial origins. Children with multiple ethnoracial origins (for example, white European and black Caribbean, Asian and African, South Asian and Latin American) have reported in recent Canadian research that their experience of racial exclusion by other groups of children is minimal in early childhood, but increases as other children become aware of racial differences in new and hostile ways. Biracial children, for example, can find themselves rejected by others who come from both parents' racial groups: white peers may shun them as black, for instance, and black peers may have doubts about their "blackness" and presume that their experiences are so different that a biracial individual cannot understand a black individual's situation. . . . Biracial and multiracial children can assist educators in developing new sensitivities, as we move from a presumption that all children in a group we consider to be visible minorities have similar challenges in our society to the more careful distinction among the actual experiences that children have.

Murphy Kilbride (1998: 203) states further that "[s]ince studies of various types of interracial marriages, both legal and common-law, indicate that the most common involve a white mother and a father from another race, rather than the reverse, it is not surprising that the inability of the mother to understand or identify with the experience of the children is a repeated refrain."

For some mixed-race people, the priority is to move beyond race completely, or to refuse to be defined by classic notions of race. Some say that gender, class, religion, language, location, occupation, age are all more important than race (Khoo, 2007).

Today, the groups least likely to marry another religion, according to a 2006 Statistics Canada study, are Sikhs, Muslims, and Hindus. For many parents,

Teachers must ensure their child-care setting reflects multiracial families.

"I have three children and our cultural background is Chinese/Portuguese/Jamaican/Scottish. They all look very different. One has blond hair and blue eyes and we get asked every day if she is adopted. I am always ready with a quick comeback for the curious on lookers, but I wonder about what this is doing to this child. Will she grow up wondering why she is so different? Will she question her own cultural makeup? We do a lot of talking and she is very aware of her diverse cultural makeup, but I am not sure that's enough."

Source: *The Toronto Star*, 2007c.

EXHIBIT 9.2 A MODEL FOR BIRACIAL IDENTITY DEVELOPMENT

W.S. Carlos Poston (1990) has conducted research on American biracial children that has looked at two main issues for them: their personal identity, including their self-esteem, self-worth, and interpersonal competence; and the reference group orientation, including racial identity, racial esteem, and racial ideology. Poston then developed a model for biracial identity development that includes five stages individuals may pass through toward a healthy biracial identity:

1. **Personal identity.** Very young children are not always aware of membership in a particular ethnic or racial group; identity is primarily based on personal factors developed within the family context.

2. **Choice of group categorization.** This can be a time of crisis and alienation, as children feel pushed to choose a racial identity in order to belong to peer, family, or social groups. Hall (as cited by Poston, 1990) identified several key factors influencing this choice: status of the groups at issue, social support from parents and other family members, and personal factors like language, appearance, age, political involvement, cultural knowledge, and so on.

3. **Enmeshment and denial.** Choosing, as a result of external pressures, one identity that isn't fully expressive of one's family background can produce confusion, guilt, and a sense of disloyalty to the parent whose background is omitted in a monoracial identity.

4. **Appreciation.** At this stage, individuals begin to appreciate their various sources of identity and broaden their reference group orientation and may begin to learn about their heritages, but still tend to identify with one group, influenced by factors prevalent in their choice phase.

5. **Integration.** Individuals now recognize and value all their sources of identity and develop a secure, integrated identity.

Source: Reprinted from W.S. Carlos Poston, "The Biracial Identity Development Model: A Needed Addition," *Journal of Counselling and Development* 69, no. 2 (1990), pp. 152–55. © ACA. Reprinted with permission. No further reproduction authorized without written permission of the American Counseling Association.

---

religious differences are the hardest to overcome. Japanese immigrants are the most likely minority group to enter into a mixed union (74.7 percent), with Latin Americans (47 percent) and Blacks (40.6 percent) following. In contrast, Chinese and South Asians are among the least likely to form a union outside their group (La Rose, 2008). One hypothesis, put forth by Siad, Kassam, and Bhattacharya (2007) for this breakdown of likelihoods is that the Japanese have been in Canada longer and the idea of intermarriage does not seem strange to the third generations (La Rose, 2008).

ROLE OF THE TEACHER

- Teachers need to examine their own feelings about interracial marriage and ask whether a bias may interfere with their ability to support multiracial families.

- Find out what terminology parents are using and use this to support their choice.

One father shares his story: "Once at daycare, I remember the look of horror on a new worker's face as I walked through the door at the end of the day. I was the last parent to arrive and there was one child left. The worker looked at me and then at Kevin and then back at me, and you could read her expression as on a billboard: 'Oh, my Gawd! I've given the wrong kid away." As I stood in supermarket checkout lines or bank queues holding Mr. Pitt the Younger on my hip, I was asked more than once, 'So where's he from then?' assuming that Kevin was adopted from some faraway land."

One of Pitt's most negative experiences happened at his son's daycare centre. He arrived at daycare to see his son Kevin, a toddler, using a wide brimmed straw hat to play peek-a-boo with several younger children. With each peek-a-boo, the chorus of baby belly laughs grew louder until everyone was dissolved in tears of hilarity. "As I stood there, a fellow dad joined me. For five seconds, we both stood there in silence, two proud papas. And then my companion nudged my arm, pointed at Kevin and said, 'Check out the little Paki with the hat.' It was like being kicked by a horse. For a few seconds, I couldn't see Kevin the way I was used to (simply as my son) but saw him instead as he looked to this stranger. For the first time I realized that no matter what Kevin becomes or accomplishes in his life ahead of him, to some he will always be a 'Paki' first, and Kevin second. I wish I could tell you that I set that guy straight, but I was simply too stunned. All I could do was walk away in silence to retrieve my son in full view of the other dad. He never spoke to me again or even looked at me. I returned the favour."

Source: Pitt, 2004: 28.

- Be sensitive to every family. Each family is unique and should be treated as such; no one should be stereotyped.

ROLE OF THE TEACHER IN THE PLAYROOM

- Teachers should provide experiences and opportunities that allow for the child's positive identification of both parents.
- When families share their ethnoracial heritage, teachers should ask how families would like to see it celebrated in the playroom. What will important issues for them be? Would they be willing to share with the children?
- Show multiracial families as only one of many types of families in discussions and family related activities.
- Provide a safe place for children to discuss racial issues, similarities and differences in physical appearance, feelings, and reactions to unkind comments.
- Help older children by role playing how they might handle bullying.
- Look for resources, dolls, books, photos, posters, puzzles, videos, etc., that support positive images of multiracial families.

- Incorporate a wide range of music, dance, and food for all cultures.
- Celebrate people in the both the local and larger community who are multiracial.

BOOKS FOR CHILDREN

Hot, Sour, Salty, Sweet, by S. Smith

Black Is Brown Is Tan, by E. Arnold McCully

Black, White, Just Right, by I. Trivas

The Colour of Us, by K. Katz

All the Colours of the Race, by A. Adoff

BOOKS FOR ADULTS

Does Anyone Else Look Like Me? A Parent's Guide to Raising Multiracial Children, by Donna Jackson Nakazawa

Of Many Colours: Portraits of Multiracial Families, by G. Kaeser, P. Gillespie, and G. Valentine

Tomorrow's Children: Meeting the Needs of Multiracial and Multiethnic Children at Home, in Early Childhood Programs, and at School, by F. Wardle

White Chocolate, by E. Atkins Bowman

Everyday Acts against Racism: Raising Children in a Multiracial World, by M. Reddy

OLDER FAMILIES

Sylvie, 36, and Carlos, 42, have lived together for 12 years. Sylvie is an editor at a large publishing firm. Carlos is a successful lawyer. The couple lives in a condominium in downtown Vancouver. Sylvie is three months pregnant. Both she and Carlos are looking forward to being parents. They made the decision to have this child after much discussion about how their lifestyle and relationship would be affected. Sylvie hopes that she will be able to work from home for the first few years of the baby's life.

Canadians today are having fewer children. They are also often delaying first childbirth until their late 20s and early 30s. In 2003, women were, on average, 28.0 years of age when they had their first child; this is up from the average age of 23.6 from the 1960s. In 2001, 7.8 percent of children aged 4 and under had mothers who were between the ages of 40 and 49; this had increased to 9.4 percent by 2006.

As a report on this data states, "[t]his aging trend among mothers of young children, which translates into a larger age gap between mothers and children, can be observed for married, common-law and lone mothers. The distribution, however, is slightly older for married mothers of children aged 4 and under. The most common age group for married mothers of young children was 30–34 years, while it was 25–29 years for lone mothers and mothers living common-law (Statistics Canada, 2007a).

Factors such as greater economic opportunities for women and the growing popularity of common-law unions have contributed to the postponement of first marriage. For many young men and women, as Lochhead (2000) found, there are powerful and economic incentives to delay childbirth:

Marrying and having children later allows young people opportunity to pursue post-secondary education, and additional time to gain employment experience and security in a highly competitive labour market. In addition, many women are able to pursue the goal of financial independence through education and employment prior to marriage and family. Today's first time mothers and fathers are not only older, but on average, have more formal education are more likely to be part of a dual earner family, and as a result, have considerably higher family incomes. The percentage of first time mothers with a university degree increased from 4–18% between 1971 and 1996 and from 11–20% among first time fathers. As a result of the increased employment of mothers, the majority of today's couples having their first child are dual earners—72% in 1996, compared to 44% in 1971. The average total family income before taxes of first time parents increased by $14,400

TABLE 9.4	DISTRIBUTION BY AGE GROUPS AND CENSUS FAMILY STATUS OF MOTHERS OF CHILDREN AGED 4 YEARS AND UNDER, CANADA 2006			
	ALL MOTHERS	MARRIED MOTHERS	COMMON-LAW MOTHERS	LONE MOTHERS
AGE GROUPS OF MOTHERS	PERCENTAGE			
Total	100.0	100.0	100.0	100.0
15 to 19 year	1.1	0.1	1.7	5.0
20 to 24 years	8.8	3.8	16.4	23.3
25 to 29 years	23.2	20.2	31.0	27.2
30 to 34 years	33.7	37.6	28.4	21.3
35 to 39 years	23.8	27.8	15.9	14.8
40 to 44 years	8.2	9.2	5.7	6.9
45 to 49 years	1.2	1.3	0.8	1.5

Source: Statistics Canada, Census of Population, 2006: http://www12.statcan.ca/english/census06/analysis/famhouse/tables/table3.htm

between 1970 and 1995, from $36,600 to $51,000 (lone-parent families are excluded from this analysis).

Decisions to postpone having children result in decreased fertility rates, smaller families, and more one-child families. Ward (2002: 144) reports, "More women are now having their first children after they are 30 years old. Twenty-seven is the age at which a woman's chance of getting pregnant begins to decline. At 20, the risk of miscarriage is about 9%; it doubles by 35 then doubles again by the time a woman reaches her early 40s." As Gibbs (2004) found: "[a]t 42, 90% of a woman's eggs are abnormal; she has only a 7.8% chance of having a baby without using donor eggs." Because older women are less fertile than younger ones, they "are more likely to turn to reproductive technologies. As a result, they are at risk for multiple births.... Others have 'caboose' or 'afterthought' children through middle-aged carelessness or as a child of a second marriage" (Ward, 2002: 144).

Adoption by single women in the 30–45 age-bracket are also becoming more common. Maurin (2007) reports on research at McGill University's Reproductive Centre where the idea of young women freezing their eggs for future use—"it's the age of the eggs, not the age of the woman, that makes all the difference"—will continue to spark debate. There is no question that this technology, though only in its infancy, has the potential to allow women the choice to have children when its right for them, without the fear that time will pass them by.

As older parents, parents may be more established in their careers, lifestyle, and routines. As a couple they may have known each other longer. Some people experience difficulty with the adjustment of having a baby in their lives and the disruption of their relationship as a result of the day-to-day realities of parenting. Women currently in their forties are often working, caring for both young children and elderly parents, and beginning to experience ill health themselves (de Wolff, 1994: 13).

When couples decide to start a family later in life the decision is often at odds with their careers. Some older parents find that their career commitments flourish at the peak of parental responsibilities. Older parents also report that they long for an empty nest again, so they can once again enjoy the privacy and freedom of living without children. Children who are born to older parents usually benefit from the financial and emotional stability that their parents have developed over the years, as well as the attention given by parents who have waited a long time to have children. But children of older parents also face specific challenges as parents often become frail when their children are still young. Older parents need to plan for the guardianship of their children, and children can become burdened with the anxiety about their parents' health and mortality. Children with older parents may have to care for their parents before their own adult lives are established (Riedman, Lamanna, and Nelson, 2003: 334–45).

Because their family may no longer live in the same vicinity, many new parents are looking to books, magazines, and the Internet for advice. Arnup (2003) asks, "So what is the situation now that parenting books and magazines have become a multimillion dollar industry? Things are probably even more confusing. There are so many experts dispensing advice using many different methods and approaches. It can be overwhelming for new mothers, especially at a time when they may be vulnerable." Arnup points out that today's older parents are used to being competent and successful at what they do. Being new parents, "while wonderful and thrilling, can make them feel nervous, inexperienced, and terrified of making mistakes." New and inexperienced teachers may encounter parents who are the same age as their own parents. This situation may create a sense of unease. A form of accommodation will need to be established between the two parties—one that takes into account the age difference while allowing the teacher to feel confident about her skills and training. Like all parents, older parents who see the teacher celebrating the accomplishments of their child will also see the benefits of the family–teacher partnership.

ROLE OF THE TEACHER

- When dealing with older families, the recent graduate must remember that she brings with her a certain expertise that allows her to be a meaningful partner in contributing to the child's total well-being.

- Adopting a professional approach, exhibiting a strong understanding of child development, and expressing genuine interest in the children are some of the ways in which inexperienced teachers can begin to build significant relationships with older parents.

- Older parents may have well-established careers in areas that may be complementary to the business of running the child-care centre. Teachers can encourage them to become more involved in the centre.

- Linking older parents with other parents in a similar situation at the centre may develop into a support network.

ROLE OF THE TEACHER IN THE PLAYROOM

- Some school-age children may be fearful that their parents will die as they learn more about the life cycle. Teachers can reassure children by helping them focus on the present.

- Some children may find it difficult, particularly if they are the youngest in a larger family, being "parented" by older siblings as well as their parents. Stories about younger children as "heroes," managing independently, may be helpful.

- Books, posters, and photographs in the centre should reflect parents of all ages.

GRANDPARENTS RAISING THEIR GRANDCHILDREN: SKIP-GENERATION FAMILIES

"When Grandmothers speak, the earth will be healed."

—Hopi Prophecy

Ed and Kerri are in their late fifties. Their 18-year-old daughter, Leslee, is the mother of a two-and-a-half-year-old, Erin. Leslee lives on social assistance in a small basement apartment. She continues to go to school, and it is there that Erin attends a daycare centre recently built for teen parents. Leslee is trying to complete her high school education, but her attendance is erratic and her grades are falling. Although she curtailed her drug use while she was pregnant with Erin, she is using drugs again. Ed and Kerri are very concerned about the well-being of both Leslee and Erin. Several months ago they found Leslee unconscious from a drug overdose in her apartment and Erin crying hysterically. Since then, Erin has been living with Ed and Kerri. A reluctant Leslee has entered a drug-rehabilitation program in a nearby city. Erin is still attending the daycare at Leslee's school.

Skip-generation families are a growing phenomenon that crosses all ethnic groups in urban and rural communities across the country and all socioeconomic groups; it affects grandparents in their 40s as well as those in their 70s. A skip-generation family is one in which a child lives with one or both grandparents without the presences of a parent or middle generation. Statistics Canada (2007a) found that in 2006, about 28,000 children aged 14 and under lived in this type of family. Furthermore, 62,500 grandparents—12.1 percent of the grandparenting population—report raising their grandchildren on their own (Statistics Canada, 2007a). These grandparents were disproportionately female (59%), of First Nations heritage (17%), and out of the labour force (57%) (Fuller Thomson, 2005).

As of 1996, one in three households of grandparent caregivers included a grandparent with a disability, one in six of the grandparents was an immigrant, and one in five households contained two or more grandchildren (Fuller-Thomson, 2005).

Two racial groups are substantially over-represented among Canadian grandparent caregivers: black Canadians and First Nation Canadians. Many Caribbean Canadian grandparents cited economic necessity and high levels of migration from the Islands as reasons that promoted such patterns of shared caregiving. The willingness of First Nation grandparents to provide care may be influenced by traditional involvement of extended kin in child care in Aboriginal communities (Fuller-Thomson, 2005).

Grandchildren move into this situation either through a legal process or a family agreement. There are various reasons for this; for example, a parent's drug or alcohol abuse may result in a court-ordered removal of the child or children. Some grandparents become guardians to avoid seeing the children placed in foster homes. Children may come to live with their grandparents when a parent dies, when child abuse and neglect are present, when a parent has a serious or terminal illness, when a parent has been incarcerated, when a parent is experiencing mental illness, or when divorce or desertion has broken up the family.

KINSHIP CARE

The Child Welfare League of America (CWLA) defines kinship care as the "full time nurturing and protection of children who must be separated from their parents by relatives, members of their tribe or clans, godparents, stepparents or other adults who

Many grandparents are raising their grandchildren.

have a kinship bond with a child" (CWLA, 2005). The group Grand Parenting Again Canada, which strives to provide support and information for skip-generation families, believes that the involvement of kin as alternative caregivers could prevent the need for children to come into foster care. Preliminary research outcomes indicate that kinship care homes reduce the number of moves experienced by children, are less traumatic, and permit continuity of care within or close to the family.

Throughout Canada there are a number of kinship care programs run through CAS organizations. One such program is the Calgary Rock View Program in Alberta, which seeks kin rights from the moment of the child's intake. In the programs, "[f]amilies receive a per diem and social work support similar to foster families. Alberta reports that the cost of children in kinship care is not lowered, but outcomes for children are improved and foster care resources are less strained. Rocky View has moved at least 60 children from foster care into kinship care since 1998" (Grand Parenting Again Canada, n.d.).

Unfortunately, the "traditional" concept of the nuclear family affects government policies and professional practices, which as a result do not reflect the growing diversity in family structures. Many of these policies make it difficult for grandparents to access adequate support for their family. For example, if grandparents decide to become foster parents in order to access funding, they give up their rights to decisions affecting the child. When undertaking research on grandmothers raising their grandchildren, Callahan, Brown, McKenzie, and Whittington (in press) gained "some insight into why grandmothers 'just did it'. Some feared that if they did not, the government safety net, child welfare, would take them into foster care. They considered this a far worse option than providing that care themselves. Some were worried that if government got involved in the situation, then they may lose custody of their grandchildren because social workers would think that they were too old to be parents again or that they had done a bad job with their own children and thus should not be parents again." Fuller-Thomson (2005) found that "Grandmother caregivers were poorer, less likely to be married, more likely to be out of the labour force and more than twice as likely to provide 60 or more hours per week of unpaid child care than were grandfathers."

There are many emotional issues for both grandparents and their grandchildren. Miles (n.d.: 1) states: "Many grandparents who are parenting their grandchildren are deprived of a positive relationship with their own child. In fact, many start their role grieving an actual or emotional death of their child. 'That's not my daughter,' one woman said. 'Drugs have taken over. That's not the girl I raised, love, and nurtured.' Thus, grandparents are often dealing with feelings of failure, guilt and embarrassment." Grandparents may also be faced with a situation in which they have physical custody of the child but not legal custody. Gaining legal custody or guardianship can be a costly process and at the same time requires the termination of the rights of the child's parent. If the grandparent hopes that their own child may at one point be ready to assume their parental role again, they may be unwilling to proceed with legal guardianship.

According to CANGRANDS, a grandparents' advocacy and support organization in Canada founded by Betty Cornelius in 1996, many of the grandchildren in these families are angry with their parents, confused by their absence, and divided in their loyalties. They may be afraid of showing affection to their grandparents in front of their parents or vice versa. Because children who have been separated from their parents have already experienced much emotional turmoil, grandparents are often confused about what parenting approach to take. Some grandparents decide that discipline will only make a child feel lonelier and more punished, so they become very permissive; these grandparents may become overprotective of their grandchildren. On the other hand, some grandparents worry that their grandchildren will repeat the virulent behaviour of their parents, and so decide to impose rigid rules and penalties (CANGRANDS, 2003: 1). Grandparents may also have concerns about raising an older child who may have been traumatized or neglected in early infancy and the implications for brain and attachment development.

The lives of grandparents change dramatically when young children come to live with them. In a study by Jendrek Platt (1993: 620), "almost half of all custodial grandparents reported problems with family and friends, the first line of defence for most people in times of stress." However, this same study also found that "almost two-thirds of the custodial grandparents reported having more of a purpose for living because of providing care to their grandchild; the grandchild keeps them young, active, and 'in shape'" (1993: 620). According to Miles (n.d.: 1), "In the best of circumstances, the renewal can be both biological and emotional, adding new social networks and experiencing emotional self-fulfillment in being able to support the positive development of a generation that carries a family forward." Another study found that "for Grandma, it's a distinct feeling of déjà vu. For Grandpa, who may have seen little of his own children while they were growing up, having kids around for 24 hours a day can be quite a shock. For a single grandparent, it's twice as hard" (Toledo and Brown, 1995: 25–26).

ROCKS (Raising Our Children's Kids Safely), a nonprofit organization of grandparents headed by Roger LeChaîne, provides advice and support to grandparents in Ontario. In LeChaîne's experience, over 80 percent of the grandparents seek custody of their grandchildren because of the drug and alcohol dependency of their own children. Many grandparents have incurred enormous legal costs in trying to gain custody of their grandchildren. For some, this has meant the loss of their life savings, their homes, even their jobs. The cost of child care is a major deterrent for many grandparents, some of whom are living on small pensions. Increasing structural and financial supports to grandparents, LeChaîne suggests, would enable them to provide safer environments for their grandchildren. He favours a formalized negotiation process involving parents and children over the adversarial conditions that attend settlement in a court of law.

Many grandparents report that raising their grandchildren keeps them young, active, and in shape.

Jan is a 29-year-old college student and the mother of a two-year-old daughter. She comes from St. Lucia, which she left at the age of eight. Jan's mother moved from St. Lucia to Toronto in 1968 with the hope of getting settled in Canada and then sending for her two daughters they could have a better life and education in their new home. From the age of seven until the age of eight, Jan lived with her grandmother and sister in St. Lucia. "My grandmother was very strict. We were brought up with the expectation of proper behaviour at all times, and especially that we would show respect to our elders. Because my sister was four years older than me, I was expected to respect her as well and do what she said. My older sister, as in many West Indian families, was expected to look after me when Gramma was busy. And I was expected to do as my sister said. Gramma was from the old school, a devout Catholic, who stressed the importance of self-discipline and study. I don't remember my grandmother expressing affection readily. She seemed more concerned about raising us as proper young ladies. When I was eight, we moved to Canada to join my mother. The pattern of interaction between me and my sister stayed the same throughout my childhood. My mother was a single working mother who relied on my sister's help in raising me and maintaining the household. Even today, all these years later, when I talk about my parents I really am referring to my sister and my mother.

Source: Baxter, 2008: 41.

I am a nontraditional mum—a grandmum. Extended family care, in particular by the grandparents, is becoming more and more common. When we started raising our grandson eight years ago, strangers frequently regarded me as an "older mum." Now I get fewer surprised looks and more remarks like "Lucky boy to have such a caring grandma." Few realize that the care extends beyond the park, the movie theatre, or the sidewalk on which he careens on his Rollerblades. We are his parents in all but name and we are happy about it. However, we . . . are not a textbook example of what a family should be. It is unlikely he will ever have a brother or sister, certainly not one who lives with him; and we find it harder and harder to socialize with parents of his friends, who are probably as uncomfortable with us as we are with them. We are not old, not even particularly old-fashioned, but we do seem to talk a different language and I dread the day when our grandson says to us, "You are so old compared to the other parents." But he is sensitive and kind, so maybe he won't.

Source: Freeman, 1994: 9.

Grandparents who had raised their grandchildren often reported later in life that, once grown, the adult grandchildren gave them extensive assistance (Weibel-Orlando, 1997).

If financial impediments to grandparents were removed, many children who are presently in foster care could be returned to their extended family members. The continued lack of government initiatives to provide adequate financial resources to those grandparents who need it, is a challenge for all concerned. Because they are older, grandparents may be concerned that they will not be able to care for their grandchildren for as long as is necessary. A trust or custody arrangement may need to be put in place. For some retired grandparents, financial necessity may mean that they will have to re-enter the workforce.

ROLE OF THE TEACHER

- Many grandparents will not have had experience in child-care settings and teachers will need to spend time with them to explain the program, policies, procedures, etc.

- Grandparents may need up-to-date information about child development and parenting strategies and teachers should be prepared to supply information or resources whenever possible.

- For those raising children with special needs, children who have been victimized, or children who have suffered neglect in their previous environment, accurate information can help grandparents better understand their grandchild's particular needs and how they can best support them.

- In situations where the mother or father plays a continuing role, the ground rules for communication among all the parties need to be clearly established. Legal restrictions may impose barriers for access to information so teachers need to be informed.

- Children may feel a sense of abandonment even if they are happy living with their grandparents. The teacher's close link with the family is critical in supporting both the child and the grandparents.

- Teachers can put grandparents in touch with other families who might be able to help them with the drop-off, pickup, or other reciprocal arrangements.

- It is important for teachers to realize and be understanding of the fact that even those grandparents who enjoy raising their grandchildren may at times feel angry and resentful and concerned about their financial situation and dramatic change in lifestyle.

- Linking grandparents with relevant community resources or support agencies is another service teachers can provide. For example, Robyn's Nest, at **www.robynsnest.com**, is a comprehensive interactive community website for parents, grandparents, teachers, and families, featuring expert parenting advice, a chat room, and bulletin boards.

- Accessing other programs in the community may give grandparents some respite time. Some grandparents may not even be aware that these resources exist in their community or think that only parents are eligible for this type of support.

- Grandparent involvement in the centre is something teachers and grandparents need to determine on a case-by-case basis.

ROLE OF THE TEACHER IN THE PLAYROOM

- A family in which a child lives with his or her grandparents is just another type of family that is respected in the playroom. A growing collection of children's books that feature seniors as main characters and specific books about grandparents raising their grandchildren can be used in the playroom. Selecting a variety of books that present diversity in behaviours, appearance, and roles helps to raise awareness and sensitivity on the part of all the children. Posters, photographs, and other visual materials posted in the room should also reflect this family type.

- Having the child keep a journal where appropriate and creating a comprehensive portfolio of the child's accomplishments may be an important reminder of the time spent in the centre and may become an important communication tool if the child is reunited with his or her biological parents.

- Active grandparents can dispel many myths about physical, intellectual, and emotional loss with aging and, if possible, should be invited into the playroom to share their expertise, skills, etc.

- In 1994, the Canadian parliament set aside a special day—the second Sunday in September—for grandparents. Teachers can celebrate this important date with the children and their families.

- Though many grandparents will be able to keep up with their energetic grandchildren, others may be struggling with failing health. Teachers can support these grandparents by helping their grandchildren with boots and snow pants and other potentially difficult tasks.

An Innovative Program—GrandFamilies House

GrandFamilies House, a 26-unit "mini-village" with a gabled roof and a broad, inviting front porch, is the $4-million (US) co-venture of three Boston nonprofit groups. The once-abandoned nursing home has been reborn with a playground, daycare centre, and multi-age enrichment program. The result is an acknowledgment of the special needs of the burgeoning population of grandparents raising grandchildren. Substance abuse, incarceration, AIDS, and immaturity are only some of the causes of a missing generation of parents who cannot care for their children (Mehren, 1999).

BOOKS FOR CHILDREN

Chelsea's Tree, by M. McCarn

Robert Lives With His Grandparents, by M. Whitmore Hickman

BOOKS FOR ADULTS

Living with Your Grandchildren: A Guide for Grandparents, by J. Lee and L. Cowan

Grandparents as Parents: A Survival Guide for Raising a Second Family, by S. deToledo and D. Edler Brown

Raising Our Children's Children, by D. Doucette-Dudman

Ticklebelly Hill: Grandparents Raising Grandchildren, by H. Osborne

At Grandma's House We. . . .Stay, S. Houtman

Second Time Around: Help For Grandparents Who Raise Their Children's Kids, by J. Callander

FOSTER FAMILIES

Binh and Lee have been foster parents for more than 20 children in the past 16 years. They have cared for newborn infants, young children, and teenagers. They have two biological children, ages 12 and 10. While some of their foster children stay for only two or three weeks, others have been with them for many years. Recently, they adopted eight-year-old Riley, who has lived with them for six years.

Foster care is a temporary arrangement, usually made between a family in distress and a child-welfare agency, whereby a child is placed in the care of a foster family until such time as he or she can be returned to the family of origin or else placed for adoption. Advances in medical science mean that children are less likely to be orphaned today, and improvements in benefits available to lone parents mean that children are less likely to enter care because of a parent's death or because of extreme poverty. Instead, they are more likely to have behavioural problems or to be victims of abuse.

The Canadian Foster Family Association estimates that 20,000 families in Canada care for 41,000 foster children annually; the number of children in foster care has increased significantly in the past three years (Manning and Zandstra, 2003).

Aboriginal children are three times more likely to be in foster care than non-Aboriginal children, according to the Assembly of First Nations. Many are taken from their communities and put into non-Aboriginal homes. On March 5, 2007, the Assembly of First Nations launched a human rights complaint against the government for failing to stop the increase of Aboriginal children in care. The Assembly argues that there are too many Aboriginal children in foster care—up to 27,000—and the First Nations need more money to deal with the situation. The number of kids in apprehension has increased by 65 percent, a statistic that reflects the circumstances in communities, but which also includes children suffering from difficulties, such as fetal alcohol syndrome, and suffering from poverty (Manning and Zandstra, 2003).

Philp (2007) found that psychotropic drugs are being prescribed to almost half—47 percent—of the Crown wards (children in permanent CAS care) in a random sample of five Ontario children's aid societies. The prescriptions were to treat depression, ADD, anxiety, and other mental health problems. With histories of abuse, neglect, and loss, children in foster care often bear psychological scars unknown to most of their peers. The high percentage of prescriptions, however, kindles fears that the agencies are overusing medication with the province's most vulnerable children.

Children entering foster care tend to be older and to have more emotional and physical challenges. By the time they arrive at a child-care centre, older foster children may have lived with several foster families, each with its own set of expectations and standards. Some children are moved from home to home, as foster families are unable to deal with their behaviour. Entering a new environment can be an anxious experience for foster children, many of whom have spent their lives in a state of uncertainty. Given the problems foster children can bring into the family, and given that mothers are increasingly likely to be employed outside the home, foster families are in short supply. Since foster care is seen as a temporary phase for the child, contact between the child and his or her birth parents is encouraged so that the move home will be smoother.

I have had the opportunity to work with Aboriginal foster children by being a foster sister. I have come to love and accept them as wonderful, beautiful, and intelligent children. Most have come to my home with FAS and I have made a commitment to make their early year's experiences as positive, warm, and nurturing as possible. What puts a smile on my face is seeing the smiles on their faces when they are with me and my family.

Source: Guadalupe Figieroa, ECE graduate

Guidelines published by the Canadian Foster Family Association are intended to ensure that all children in Canada receive good care while living in foster families. Foster parents come from all walks of life. They may be experienced parents, young couples who are raising their own children, or single people. Foster parents are commonly mature, flexible, child-focused, patient, and understanding. They enjoy family life, can cope with stress, respect and accept other cultures, work as part of a team, are financially stable, and are willing to learn.

Each province and territory has its own system for organizing foster parent programs. For example, in Saskatchewan, families are organized into practitioner, specialist, and therapeutic homes. About 80 percent of the foster homes are practitioner-level homes; specialist foster care is for children who cannot be managed in a practitioner home or a group home or for whom an institutional placement is inappropriate; and therapeutic foster care homes provide services to children who require intensive one-to-one support and counselling as an alternative to residential treatment.

Prior to the granting of foster parent status, a social worker usually does a home visit in order to assess the family's suitability. Other requirements include a police check and a medical examination. This procedure varies from province to province, but the intent in every jurisdiction is to ensure stable environments for foster children.

From the ages of 15–19, I lived in a Residential Group Home. It was a house that had up to nine children living in it and anywhere from ages 11 to 19 years of age. Everyone in the house received "treatment" for their various issues. Some residents came from foster care, some were wards of CAS, and some lived with their parents beforehand. There were staff working there (at least two on at a time) and one slept overnight. Living in this environment really opened my eyes to the various family-types, issues that others faced and made me realize how lucky I was to have some of the luxuries I take for granted. It also helped open my eyes to the various struggles that others face. I understood the underlying issues that families have to deal with on a day-to-day basis and its effects on children. This experience has taught me that family isn't always biological and you can have more than one place that you call home. I think this experience will help me identify with families that I will be working with when I graduate and be better able to support them because I have learned so much from my experience. I will be able to empathize with families that are separated from each other and for children who live in more than one house. I will also feel more comfortable talking about harder issues and building a better understanding of where they come from.

Source: Brenda, ECE graduate.

Foster families need to be sensitive to the needs of their own children as well. These children have to share their parents and adjust their position within the family (for example, the status of the oldest may change when a foster child arrives). At times the rules may be different for the foster child, depending on his or her needs. The other children in the family may resent this and will need extra support.

ROLE OF THE TEACHER

- Gather appropriate background information. For example, will the child be with the centre on a temporary or long-term basis?

- Teachers need to display sensitivity when gathering information and respect confidentiality.

- Know the court arrangements. Is the biological parent permitted to visit the child at the program or pick the child up? If so, under what circumstances?

- It is crucial that all parties—social workers, foster families, teachers, and other significant adults—meet and plan ways to create a warm and nurturing environment for the child.

- It is important to support the foster family. Share information on the child's strengths, strategies that work successfully, and activities the child enjoys.

- If the child is to be moved to a new foster home, teachers may offer to meet with the new family to discuss the child, sharing their expertise and knowledge. This may be reassuring to the child.

ROLE OF THE TEACHER IN THE PLAYROOM

- Discuss foster families as just one of many types of families to be respected in the playroom.

- Be respectful of the child's personal boundaries when trying to engage him or her in activities. This also applies to situations where the teacher may attempt to provide warmth and affection.

- Foster children may test the limits in a new centre by challenging teachers to "give up on them." Catch the child doing things right and celebrate accomplishments. Consistency and perseverance are key. Realistic expectations are important.

- Empower children to make their own decisions and choices and accept responsibility for their outcomes.

- Be mindful of other children and their response to the foster child. Foster children are often vulnerable to teasing or bullying.

- Encourage foster families to participate in the centre as you would any new family.

- When older foster children leave the centre to move in with an adoptive family, it's a time for celebration, but teachers should listen to and acknowledge any fears or concerns.

- A child's moving to a new foster family presents its own problems. Teachers can express their connection to the child and let her know that they will miss her. Teachers and children can continue to correspond.

- Photographs, special projects, and artwork can be important keepsakes for departing foster children. Teachers may consider having the children create a special booklet in which each child records a special event or meaningful moment they shared with the foster child. This is important, because children often are moved to new locations and leave behind treasured possessions.

INSIDE LOOK

When Amy, age seven, goes to sleep at night, she doesn't dream about games and parties, or even about monsters. She dreams of social workers and wakes up screaming. In her nightmares social workers snatch her from home. In real life, Amy, a ward of the foster care system, lived with six families before she was six, shuttled back and forth between foster homes and the home of her mother, who was unable to care for the girl's sickle cell anemia.

Source: Azar, 1999.

BOOKS FOR CHILDREN

Maybe Days: A Book for Children in Foster Care, J. Wilgocki

Finding the Right Spot: When Kids Can't Live With Their Parents, by J. Levy

Kids Are Important: A Book for Young Children in Foster Care, by J. Nelson

Families Change: A Book for Children Experiencing Termination of Parental Rights, by J. Nelson and M. Gallagher

Zachary's New Home: A Story for Foster and Adopted Children, by G. Blomquist, B. Blomquist, and M. Lemieux

The Star: A Story to Help Young Children Understand Foster Care, by C. Miller Lovell

BOOKS FOR ADULTS

On Their Own: What Happens to Kids When They Age Out of the Foster Care System, by M. Shirk and G. Strangler

Building a Home Within: Meeting the Emotional Needs of Children and Youth in Foster Care, by T. Heineman

A Guidebook for Raising Foster Children, by S. McNair Blatt

ADOPTIVE FAMILIES

Ever since she was a young girl, Elaine knew that she wanted to adopt a child. Her best friend was adopted and she felt that adoption would be a wonderful way to have a family. Elaine and her husband Linton started the process through their local Children's Aid Society. They attended parent training seminars, met with parent support groups, and met with a social worker who would complete their home study. On October 8, 2008, Elaine and Linton met with their children for the first time: Tara (age 5) and her brother Mark (age 7). Like any transition, the placement was not without its obstacles; however, Tara, Mark, Elaine, and Linton are all doing very well in a home filled with love and support.

Adoption is the legal transfer of parental rights and obligations from birth parent(s) to adoptive parent(s): the *adoptive parent*s become the legal parents of the child or teenager. Adoption is a permanent, legally-binding arrangement. It is estimated that one in five persons will be touched by adoption in his or her lifetime.

In Canada, adoption is a provincially mandated issue and each province and territory has its own rules and regulations on all aspects of adoption. As such, the prospective adoption process must comply with the policies and procedures that exist in the family's province or territory of residence.

© Rob Marmion / Shutterstock

Adopting a child can be an exciting and anxious time for the family.

DOMESTIC ADOPTION (ADOPTIONS WITHIN CANADA)

In Canada, there are two types of domestic adoption: public adoption and private adoption.

Public Adoption

Public adoption is an adoption arranged through a provincial ministry or an agency funded by government. Since public agencies are government-funded they provide services at no cost. An example of a public agency is a Children's Aid Society.

Private Adoption

In Canada, private adoption is an adoption arranged by a privately-funded, **licensed adoption agency**. Private agencies are non-government bodies licensed by the province in which the agency operates. Private agencies charge fees for their services and usually involve the adoption of infants.

Given the provincial mandates surrounding adoption in Canada, reliable and up-to-date national numbers on adoption, foster children, and children in care simply don't exist. "We keep better track of used cars than we do of children, and that's a disgrace," says Judy Grove, former Executive Director of the Adoption Council of Canada [ACC]. The ACC estimates that 85,000 children are in foster care throughout Canada, and about 22,000 of those children are permanent wards of governments—meaning the courts have ruled they probably won't be returned to their birth families.

Fortunately, the Adoption Council of Canada continues to work on educating Canadians about children available for adoption across the country. A major part of the ACC's Adoption Awareness Initiatives is in its program, Canada's Waiting Children (CWC). The focus of the CWC program is to raise awareness of Canadian children in need of permanent families. Since the program first launched in 1997, 894 children have been referred to Canada's Waiting Children and over 85 percent of them have found their *forever families*. The Canada's Waiting Children (CWC) program is intended to be an additional resource to prospective adoptive parents who are going through the adoption process. Their website, **www.canadaswaitingkids.ca**, contains photos and background information about Canadian children waiting for permanent adoptive families and provides information about domestic adoption of children currently in the care of provincial, territorial, and First Nations child welfare agencies. This program was made possible by grants from the Dave Thomas Foundation for Adoption and support from Wendy's Restaurants of Canada.

One of the biggest myths about adoption in Canada is that there are no Canadian children available for adoption. According to Grove, there are more than 76,000 children in the care of child welfare organizations across Canada and more than 22,000 of these children have parents whose parental rights have been terminated by the courts, supporting claims by the ACC. Typically, these children have no permanent family and will live in foster care or small institutional placements until they are legally of age. Most children referred to this program range from three years of age to the age of majority, but even newborns have been referred to the program. The children referred to the program tend to be more challenging than most of the Canadian children in need of permanent families; they are referred to the CWC program when no other resources can be found for them in their home region.

INSIDE LOOK

When Michael was four, he asked, "Mommy, was I the most beautiful of all my brothers?" Confused, his mother asked him to explain. "Did you and Daddy pick me because I was the most beautiful of all my brothers at the hospital?" Finally, his mother understood. Michael seemed to have the notion that his adoptive parents came to the hospital and chose him from his "brothers." His mother reassured him that even though he was quite beautiful, he had no brothers remaining at the hospital from whom he was chosen. Michael's question is one indication that, even as young as four-years-old, he had begun the complicated psychological search for self.

Source: Springate and Stegelin, 1999: 205.

Openness in Adoption

Birth parents and adoptive parents often agree to have an open adoption, with ongoing contact between their families. Their open adoption agreement may be verbal or written, but it is not legally binding. The agreement spells out how much contact will exist, and it might specify the frequency and manner of contact between adoptive and birth families, or between siblings placed separately. The families might exchange letters and photos, either directly or through an agency, or schedule phone calls and visits.

According to the Adoption Council of Canada's website at **www.adoption.ca**, there are two types of open adoptions: open and semi-open. In an open adoption, the families exchange names and addresses, and have a full and ongoing relationship. In a semi-open adoption, the families exchange non-identifying information, such as messages and photos, through an intermediary. They do not, however, know each other's last names or addresses. These are, clearly, very different from a closed adoption, in which confidentiality is the rule. The families do not share identifying information and have no contact (Adoption Council of Canada, 2008).

INTERNATIONAL ADOPTION

International adoption is an adoption of a child living in a different country from the adoptive parent(s). Canada has recently seen a decline in international adoptions, partially because of new requirements made by the adoption authorities in other countries, such as China. Although China is still the most popular country for international adoptions, the numbers have significantly declined since 2004; the more stringent regulations put in place by the Chinese government have resulted in far longer wait times, and some families are now choosing to adopt from other countries.

The statistics in Table 9.5 are from the Adoption Council of Canada's website and reflect the recent trends in international adoptions by Canadians.

Transracial and Inter-Country Adoption

Over the past 30 years, many families from developed countries have adopted children from other countries. Historically, a lack of regulation and the potential for financial gain contributed to the development of services in which profit took priority over the best interests of children. Resulting abuses include the sale and abduction of children, the coercion of parents, bribery, and trafficking.

TABLE 9.5	INTERNATIONAL ADOPTIONS IN CANADA, TOP 15 COUNTRIES		
	2006	**2005**	**2004**
People's Republic of China	608	973	1,001
Haiti	123	115	159
Republic of Korea	102	97	97
United States	96	102	81
Russia	95	88	106
Ethiopia	61	31	34
Philippines	53	70	62
India	36	41	37
Socialist Republic of Vietnam	34	X	6
Colombia	31	18	38
Ukraine	23	39	16
Thailand	21	21	40
Jamaica	19	22	23
Pakistan	19	17	7
Liberia	16	10	X
x - From 0 to 4			

Note: Due to privacy considerations, some cells in this table have been suppressed and replaced with the notation "x".

Many countries around the world, including Canada, have recognized these risks and have ratified the Hague Convention on Inter-Country Adoption, which is designed to put into action the principles of the UN convention on the Rights of the Child. These rights include ensuring that adoption is authorized only by competent authorities, that inter-country adoption enjoys the same safeguards and standards which apply in national adoptions, and that inter-country adoption does not result in improper financial gain.

Children who are adopted out of the country face unique challenges. Not only have these children lost their homeland but many of them will never be able to connect with family members and friends. It may be difficult for these children to develop a sense of identity in the absence of others from their culture. As a racially diverse family, it must be recognized that although race may not be an issue within the parent's home, it remains a societal issue. In turn, transracial adoptions may occur within Canada, as families may adopt a child that is of a different race or ethnicity than their own.

Sad . . . Sad

When our son turned two years old, I made a book for him about his arrival (at three and a half months) and about our family. He is now almost three and has asked to hear "Eric's story" many times. Once he told a friend, "I'm 'dopted—it's in my book." A few days ago we were reading the book again, and he had a reaction that touched me deeply. When we turned to the page with his foster mother's picture and read, "The nice lady loved him and was sad to see him go, but she knew that he was his mommy and daddy's special baby. . . . She was happy he would be with them," Eric's eyes filled with tears. He seemed to be experiencing such a deep emotion that I felt he needed to just sit for a moment. These tears seemed to come from the depth of his soul. I asked why he was so sad. He only said, "Sad . . . sad," and pointed to the picture. We simply sat together for a while, then we talked about it a little. For about an hour he continued to be subdued and inward. Although I cannot know the meaning of this for Eric, I felt I had received a gift in seeing briefly into the depth of my child's being. It brought to mind how sad leaving and loss really is and how valuable a shared moment of deep feeling can be.

Source: Bonnie Malouf, quoted in N. Sheehan and L. Wood, *Adoption and the Schools Project: A Guide for Educators* (Washington, DC: Department of Health and Human Services, 1993), p. 41.

Many people are under the impression that race "doesn't matter," but they soon come to find that it is one of the most challenging and complicated issues faced in transracial adoption. When preparing a child for intrusive questions or difficult situations it is important to discuss race and racism with the child, and to establish a trusting atmosphere for open communication. By being empathetic and acknowledging the importance of this issue to the child, and by making the child privy to your thoughts and understanding, the child's trust will be strengthened. By talking about racism, discrimination, and prejudice you are helping the child—and all children in your care—understand the issues of equality for all.

Children may also come to Canada with health problems that may be unknown to the new parents. It is critical that these children receive testing that reflects the challenges of those who come from specific countries outside of Canada. A child may be a carrier of Hepatitis B or have Hepatitis C and show no symptoms for many years but Maslen (2004) states that having these tests conducted on any child adopted from Asia is of critical importance. Children adopted domestically may also have a range of needs; therefore, it is important to learn as much about the child as possible. Information sharing varies and each family situation is unique: some families may have only limited information about the birth mother and father; others have photographs, medical records, and even letters or videos from the birth parents; still others may have face-to-face contact. A range of openness exists in adoption and the child's best interests are always kept at the forefront.

FAMILY ADJUSTMENT

All members of the family undergo a major transition and adjustment period when a new child enters their care. In some situations, the news of the adoption comes quickly, giving family members little time to prepare for their new role. It is important for teachers to also focus on the siblings of the newly adopted child. If other children are being negatively affected by the new family member, parents may feel guilty and responsible for destroying the equilibrium of the family they once knew. Parents may even resent the new child for causing distress in the other children. New children may struggle with understanding the new family rules and expectations, they may want to fit it and yet don't know how. Teachers can play a supportive role in these situations by understanding that other children in the family will need extra support (Wheeler, 2004).

Preschoolers comprehend the complexities of adoption only insofar as it is something that makes everyone happy and that makes them the focus of this happiness. As children reach school age, however, the familiar warm story of being chosen by

EXHIBIT 9.3 TALKING WITH YOUR CHILD ABOUT ADOPTION: GUIDELINES FOR ADOPTIVE PARENTS

1. **Start Early:** Even though your child may not understand, it's practice for you. Your child, even as an infant or toddler, gets to hear the word "adopted" in a positive context.

2. **Be Honest:** If you don't know the answer, say so. Show that you share your child's curiosity and that you would like to know too.

3. **Use Positive Adoption Language:** Use positive language for example, "biological parent" as opposed to "real parent."

4. **Answer the Questions Your Child Asks:** If you are not sure what the question really is, ask your child what they mean.

5. **Include Information About Your Child's Actual Birth If You Have This:** Many adoptees report that they have grown up thinking that they weren't born like other people are because nobody talks about their birth.

6. **Don't Wait For Your Child To Raise The Subject:** Keep the communication lines open. Raise the subject every once in a while by saying for example, "I was remembering when we adopted you and we made the trip to . . ." or "I was just thinking of your birth mother and wondering if you ever think about her . . ."

7. **Once Is Not Enough:** Your child's understanding is developing and growing all the time. Don't assume that your child got all the details that you told them the last time.

8. **Paint A Positive Picture Of The Birth Parents:** Refer to them by name if known. Your positive attitude is very important to building your child's self esteem.

9. **Acknowledge And Accept Your Child's Feelings:** Listen for the feelings behind your child's comments and questions. Curiosity and sadness are natural responses to being adopted. Don't take your child's expressions about wanting to see their birth family as a reflection on you or your parenting. We don't like to see our children experiencing sadness or pain, but adoption is a mixture of joy and pain, loss and gain for all of us. Acknowledge this and help to make your child feel comfortable about talking about it.

10. **Prepare A Lifebook Of Photos And The Adoption Story:** Be sure to include birth family information, foster family, orphanage, etc., as applicable. Include photos of birth family if available.

11. **Check Out Your Child's Understanding From Time To Time:** Tell her "Mary was asking about . . . (something to do with adoption). What would you say to her?" Read about child development and children's understanding of adoption.

12. **Reach Out To Others:** Join a support group. Talk to other adoptive parents, share and learn from them. Consult an adoption professional, if you feel the need. If you are troubled by some of the issues you face as an adoptive parent, reach out. Others can help you work through these issues so that you can be comfortable in talking with your child about adoption. Make sure your child gets to know other adopted children.

Source: From Fenton, Pat, "Talking With Your Child about Adoption – Guidelines for Adoptive Parents" Adoption Roundup. *Journal of the Adoption Council of Ontario,* Winter, 2004. Reprinted with permission.

families who very much wanted a daughter is now complicated by the child's awareness of a mother, or parents, who no longer have the baby born to them: "If I was adopted by these parents, some other parents had to give me away." This kind of reciprocal thinking is simply not possible before the level of maturation reached by the young school-age child (Sheehan and Wood, 1993: 38). Older children have a greater understanding of adoption and may begin to grieve the loss of their biological family. The grief reactions can be overt or hidden. They may stop asking questions or go silent on the topic. They also realize that not everyone else is adopted and they wonder "Why didn't they keep

Siblings of a newly adopted child will also have a period of adjustment as a new member is added to the family.

biological families. "Even worse," Edwards and Sodhi (1992: 6) observe, "[children] are often expected to feel grateful for being adopted. Expecting gratitude denies the fact that adoption means a child's life was marked by loss."

POST-ADOPTION SUPPORT

According to AdoptOntario (2008):

> It is not uncommon for families formed by adoption to require support. Adoptive parenting is a special role and adopted children often find that adoption adds unique dimensions to their lives. Birth parents find that placing a child for adoption, whether voluntarily or not, can create challenges that may need support. In short, all parties to adoption, birth parents, adoptive parents and adopted persons, can benefit from support services. Post placement support and services can take a variety of forms. Informal supports are available through support groups, some of which form around a type of adoption, or stage of adoptive development. Other supports may take the form of special events, seminars and workshops, printed resources, videos, audiotapes, and Internet sites. More formal support services include experienced adoption professionals and other professionals who provide specialized services for adoptive families. There is a need for more adoption-friendly professionals who can provide these kinds of services.

The AdoptOntario website, at **https://www.adopt-ontario.ca/howtoadopt.post_adoption_support.aspx**, offers additional support and information for families going through the adoption and post-adoption process and teachers will find it a valuable tool to increase their understanding of the situation.

ROLE OF THE TEACHER

Pat Fenton (2004), former Executive Director of the Adoption Council of Ontario shares her insights with teachers:

> Like all families, adoptive families are unique, and each adoption story is in turn unique. Rather than a one-time legal event, adoption is now understood as an on-going developmental process that is a blend of joy and pain, loss and gain. Some adoptive families have concerns that professionals don't really understand adoption and its dynamics, and consequently they are reluctant to share adoption information. They would like to have confidence that their child's teacher can be an ally and play a supportive role in promoting understanding of adoption as a fully accepted means of family formation.

me? Where is my birth mum, is she sad because she lost me, do I have birth brothers and sisters, are they looking for me, what if they find me, does my birth mum want me back, does she think about me?" (Sheehan and Wood, 1993: 38). Furthermore, "a child who remembers abuse may be fearful that the abuser will find him" (1993: 39). When little information is available about the birth parents, these children may create their own fantasy. As well, older children generally have a more difficult time adjusting to adoption. Many older children have well-developed defense mechanisms that have enabled them to survive the hard times of their lives. They are not likely to drop these defenses and become open, loving, and grateful children quickly (Wheeler, 2004).

Children who are adopted may carry with them an emotional connection to their biological family even though they are no longer living with them. They will have unanswered questions about their background and about why they were "put up for adoption." Some children may feel that they were adopted because they were unworthy of their

Teachers can begin by becoming familiar with, and using, the accepted positive language of adoption.

Including adoptive families as examples in discussions of kinds of families can help to normalize the adoption experience. If a child has a baby born into his family, mention that some children join their family by adoption. Do you have books or do you tell stories that include adoptive families and adopted children? Be sensitive to the challenges an adopted child may face when asked to do assignments or class activities such as bringing in baby photos or doing a family tree. Check with local adoptive parent groups—they welcome the opportunity to offer resources, workshops, book suggestions, and speakers.

- Teachers need to respect families' wishes as to how much information is to be shared with the children and other staff members. Teachers should never share the information they do have about an adoptive situation without obtaining the approval of the family and/or the child. Some families may choose not to disclose the adoption (even on the intake form), and teachers may never know the details of the child's situation.

- Whether adopted children are in the group or not, teachers should bring adoptive families into playroom discussions.

- "The overall emphasis can be placed on the 'belongingness' definition of a family, rather than on the circumstances surrounding a particular child's birth" (Stroud, Stroud, and Staley, 1999).

- While some children are adopted into two-parent families, a single parent adopting a child will need a strong support network.

- Adoptive parents are faced with a whole new set of challenges particularly if the child has special needs. We know that early intervention in these situations is critical.

- According to Ross, adoptive families don't seek help early enough—often not until the child is a teenager. Professionals who deal with adoptive families in child care and early childhood in general could help parents by finding out what support services are available in their community and referring families to adoption support groups or play groups for adoptive families (an easy way to meet others and make lifelong friends) and to websites where many people go for support.

- Teachers should be willing to meet with social workers or foster families if the adoptive parents feel an exchange of information would be helpful in the support of the child.

- Teachers need to be aware of the reaction of siblings who may also be in the centre. A number of children's books view the adoption process from the point of view of the child already in the family.

ROLE OF THE TEACHER IN THE PLAYROOM

- Teachers may want to include in their program information about a child's country if he or she has been adopted from overseas; many families welcome the opportunity for children to share in their dual heritage.

- Older adopted children who have had a difficult and perhaps traumatic beginning need to be linked with teachers who are warm and nurturing and able to clearly articulate realistic expectations and limits.

- Consistent routines and procedures provide the child with a sense of stability. Teachers should be aware that some children find changes in staff—or abrupt departures from the normal routine—highly unsettling. Others have difficulty building relationships with adults. Teachers will need to be patient.

- Some children may act in a way that appears to the teacher to have no bearing on the particular event or moment. The behaviour may be the result of something that triggers an unpleasant memory, an act of abuse, or other traumatic situation for the child. Families may be able to help teachers identify some of the stressful situations that trigger these unpleasant memories.

- Teacher observations of the child in his or her day-to-day interaction with adults and children are especially important to the families, who are bound to have concerns about the development of the child, particularly if little background information is available.

- Each November, the North American Council on Adoptable Children and the Adoption Council of Canada sponsors National Adoption Awareness Month. This may be a good time to display books on adoption (both children's and adult) and to ask parents who have been adopted to share their stories with the children.

- Many adoptive families celebrate the anniversary of their child's adoption. Teachers can discuss with families whether they would like this day to be celebrated in the centre as well.

- Teachers who themselves come from adopted families may choose to share the positive experiences that they have had. When assigning family-related projects to older children, teachers should give adopted children wide latitude in deciding what to share. When describing the project to the children, the teacher may use an adopted family as an example.

- Today there are many children's books available, but these do not reflect all the ways in which children are adopted; therefore, they should be chosen with care. Families may have already created their own more personalized family books and might be willing to share these with the children.

- Teachers should be sensitive about asking for such materials as baby photos, since these may not be available to the adopted child. However, creating family booklets with photos of their present-day lives is a great way to share the diversity that exists in families.

- Teachers should avoid showing movies or videos that depict adopted children as "out of control" or "bad."

- Teachers should guard against the negative impact of adopt-a-theme programs. As Johnston (1993: 119) points out, "these programs range from the adopt-an-animal program of zoos across the country, to silly not-for-profit fundraising ideas, such as adopt-a-rubber-duck river races, sponsored by a local radio station to benefit a food bank, city adopt-a-park and adopt-a-pothole programs, commercial adopt-a-product promotions, to Humane Society animal placement programs. Those of us who are parents by adoption and adoption activists, however, believe that such programs trivialize a very serious topic and that they further myths and misconceptions about this family planning method to yet another generation of children. Unfortunately, they turn upon a kind of 'save the rejects' image that may seem cute and harmless to grownups but which confuses concrete-thinking children—be they adopted or not."

- Teachers need to be consistent in their use of positive adoption language. As Edwards and Sodhi (1992: 21) observe: "Positive adoption language can stop the spread of misconceptions such as these. By using positive adoption language, we educate others about adoption. We choose emotionally 'correct' words over emotionally-laden words. We speak and write in positive adoption language with the hope of impacting others so that this language will someday become the norm."

EXHIBIT 9.4 POSITIVE AND NEGATIVE ADOPTION LANGUAGE

Positive Language	Negative Language
Birth parent	Real parent
Biological parent	Natural parent
Birth child	Own child
My child	Adopted child
Born to unmarried parents	Illegitimate
Terminate parental right	Give up
Make an adoption plan	Give away
To parent	To keep
Waiting child	Adoptable child, available
Biological father	Begetter
Parent	Adoptive parent
International adoption	Foreign adoption
Adoption triad	Adoption triangle
Permission to sign a release	Disclosure
Search	Track down parents
Child placed for adoption	Unwanted child
Court termination	Child taken away
Child with special needs	Handicapped child
Child from abroad	Foreign child

I usually "forget" that I didn't birth Tanya until I am "reminded" by strangers or new acquaintances whose curiosity results in unintentional insensitivity. "Is Tanya your grandchild?" or "Who is Tanya's mother?" are common questions when it is obvious that Tanya is biracial and I am not. I guess it's human nature to try and connect the dots. However, I wish the person would think first about how my child will feel about the question. We have two daughters, one by birth and one by adoption. There is never any question that we are "real" parents to both of them. But we are aware that we can't know what Tanya's experience of being biracial is like, and we respond to her need to be connected to her racial and ethnocultural backgrounds. This enriches our lives as we benefit from involvement in Afro-Caribbean culture. Like all parents, we hope that both our children won't have too many closed doors through their childhood and adolescence, but we also know that challenging life experiences build strength of character. Supportive teachers along the way for Tanya continue to validate her as an individual whose blueprint includes her racial background and adopted family, realities that contribute to who she is.

BOOKS FOR CHILDREN

What is Adoption?, by S. Stergianis.

Adoptive Families Are Families for Keeps: Activity Book, by L. Cowan

Bringing Asha Home, by U. Krishnaswami

Finding Joy, by M. Coste

Journey Home, by L. McKay, Jr.

My Family Is Forever, by N. Carlson

My Mei Mei, by E. Young

A Sister for Matthew, by P. Kennedy

The Starlight Baby, by G. Shields

We Are Adopted, by J. Moore Mallinos

I Love You Like Crazy Cakes, by R. Lewis and J. Dyer

Over The Moon: An Adoption Tale, by K. Katz

I Don't Have Your Eyes, by C.A. Kitze

BOOKS FOR ADULTS

What Is Adoption? Helping Non-Adopted Children Understand Adoption, by S. Stergianis and R. McDowall

Born In Our Hearts: Stories of Adoption, by F. Casey and M.C. Casey

The Post Adoption Blues: Overcoming the Unforeseen Challenges of Adoption, by K. Foli and J. Thompson

Becoming a Family: Promoting Healthy Attachments with Your Adopted Child, by L. Eshleman

From China with Love: A Long Road to Motherhood, by E. Buchanan

LESBIAN, GAY, BISEXUAL, TRANSSEXUAL, TRANSGENDERED, AND QUEER FAMILIES (LGBTQ)

Sarah and Pam have been living together for five years. Sarah is a teacher and Pam owns her own catering business. They live in a small house with Sarah's seven-year-old daughter, Megan, from her first marriage. Pam is six months pregnant with a baby conceived through insemination. Sarah, Pam, and Megan are all looking forward to the birth of this child.

Individuals and parents who identify as lesbian, gay, bisexual, transsexual (people who want their bodies to match the gender they feel they truly are), transgendered (anyone whose gender identity falls outside of the stereotypical expected behaviours of men and women), and queer (historically a derogatory term but it has been reclaimed and a movement is underway to use it in a positive way) may also include individuals who are Questioning (a person who is questioning his or her sexual orientation or gender identity), Intersex (a person who may be born with external female genitalia but internal male reproductive anatomy) and Two-Spirited (First Nations people who believe in the existence of three genders: male, female, and male-female).

FACTS ABOUT LGBTQ FAMILIES

- Canada became the third country in the world to legalize same-sex marriage in 2005, after the Netherlands (2000) and Belgium (2003). Spain (2005) and South Africa (2006) followed shortly thereafter.

- The 2006 census counted same-sex married couples for the first time, reflecting the legalization of same-sex marriages for all of Canada as of July 2005. In total, 45,345 same-sex couples were enumerated, of which 7,465 (16.5 percent) were married couples. Over half (53.7 percent) of same-sex married spouses were men in 2006, compared with 46.3 percent who were women.

- Same-sex couples represented 0.6 percent of all couples in Canada; this number is comparable to statistical data from New Zealand (0.7 percent) and Australia (0.6 percent).

- Same sex married spouses were more likely to have children present in the home (16.2%) compared to same sex common-law partners (7.5%) (Statistics Canada 2007a).

- Furthermore, about 9.0 percent of persons in same-sex couples had children aged 24 years

and under living in the home in 2006. This living situation was more common for females (16.3 percent) than for males (2.9 percent) in same-sex couples (Statistics Canada 2007b).

- Half of all same-sex couples in Canada lived in Montréal (18.4 percent), Toronto (21.2 percent), and Vancouver (10.3 percent) in 2006.

"HOW DO I FEEL ABOUT LGBTQ PEOPLE?"

Clarifying our attitudes helps us to become more conscious of how we feel. The purpose in responding to the following statements is not to try to change your attitudes, but to bring them forward for examination. There are no right or wrong answers. The important thing is to understand what you actually feel; not how you think you should feel. These questions are meant to provoke discussion and thoughtful reflection.

Read each statement below and indicate the number that best represents your opinion, using the following value scale: 1 = strongly agree up to 5 = strongly disagree.

1. I would feel comfortable if an LGBTQ person with a young child participated in a family resource program/daycare where I work. ____

2. I am comfortable around LGBTQ people unless they flaunt their lifestyle. ____

| TABLE 9.6 | DISTRIBUTION OF SAME SEX COUPLES BY CONJUGAL STATUS CANADA PROVINCES AND TERRITORIES, 2006 |

| REGIONS | SAME-SEX COUPLES | | | PERCENTAGE OF |
	TOTAL	MARRIED	COMMON-LAW	ALL COUPLES
	45,345	7,465	37,885	0.6
Newfoundland and Labrador	310	50	255	0.2
Prince Edward Island	140	15	125	0.4
Nova Scotia	1,255	140	1,115	0.6
New Brunswick	770	125	650	0.4
Quebec	13,685	1,260	12,425	0.8
Ontario	17,510	3,765	13,745	0.6
Manitoba	935	100	835	0.4
Saskatchewan	565	100	465	0.3
Alberta	3,055	510	2,540	0.4
British Columbia	7,035	1,370	5,665	0.7
Yukon	30	10	20	0.5
Northwest Territories	40	15	25	0.5
Nunavut	15	10	15	0.3

Source: Statistics Canada, Census of Population, 2006; http://www12.statcan.ca/english/census06/analysis/famhouse/tables/table9.htm

3. I am comfortable around transsexual or trans-gendered people as long as they pass as either male or female. ____

4. I can accept gays or lesbians, but bisexuals just can't make their minds up. I can't understand that. ____

5. LGBTQ folks are freaks and will probably go to hell. ____

6. I would feel uncomfortable if my boss were LGBTQ. ____

7. I would feel comfortable if I learned that my child's teacher was LGBTQ. ____

8. I would feel uncomfortable if LGBTQ issues were being taught to my child as part of the school curriculum. ____

9. LGBTQ people who have "come out" should not be teachers. ____

10. If my child were LGBTQ, I would feel I had failed as a parent. ____

11. I'm uncomfortable around people who don't conform to stereotypical masculine/feminine gender roles (in dress, appearance, etc.). ____

12. All LGBTQ people are white, of European background, and are from the middle or upper socio-economic class. ____ (Gower, 2005)

Corbett (1993: 31) asks how many early childhood teachers have considered "that in our care are children who will grow up to be lesbian and gay adults and that while a handful may show early indications of seeming 'different' in some way, the vast majority will offer no clue to even the most observant eye." Teachers must challenge the issues of heterosexism, that is, the belief that all people are or should be heterosexual and that heterosexuality is inherently superior to and preferable to homosexuality or bisexuality. In a society that tells homosexuals constantly through our laws, our acted-out prejudices, and our ignorant and uncaring behaviour that they are unacceptable human beings, how do we attempt to rear a generation that accepts homosexuality as a fact of life? Greenspoon (1998: 18) states that "there is a perception that issues related to people's sexual orientation is a moral question, often with religious prohibitions, rather than a question of diversity and equal rights." Gonzalez-Mena (2008: 119) argues that we must unlearn biases around sexual orientation and gender identity:

> Oppression is oppression and you don't want to have any part of it—either supporting oppressive systems, practicing discrimination yourself or harboring internal oppression. Recognize that taking on challenges make you stronger. Struggling with your own religious beliefs and honouring all families at the same time may seem overwhelming. If the struggle isn't within you, you may find it among colleagues, or among families themselves. It may be hard to facilitate relationships with these struggles going on, but you have to do your best. As teachers, we have been challenged to plan and implement a bias-free curriculum that focuses on all types of family units.

INSIDE LOOK

For gay, male teachers, Janmohamed (2006) quotes Campbell and Forrester who state:

I am painfully aware of the assumptions that are often made about a male who demonstrates an interest in working with young children. Those who hold such stereotypes to be true may ultimately dismiss this passion as dangerously pathological. This fear may be further compounded by the fact that gay men, in particular, are falsely regarded by some to be frequent abusers of young children. Although these sweeping generalizations remain unsubstantiated by reputable research they continue to pervade mainstream public consciousness and serve as a potential barrier to my relationships with parents in particular. As a gay teacher, I have made a concerted effort to include homosexuality as an integral component to anti-bias education within the classroom . . . it is important for children to learn and know about the many differences in their world. The fact that someone may have two moms or two dads, or that their friend's parent might not have always been a woman or man, is fact, not fiction. In fact, early childhood educators need to be aware that the children may also be experiencing gender identity issues and need to be cared for in an environment that is accepting of all people. Early Childhood Educators have the responsibility to create environments that are safe for all children and families.

What LGBTQ community would ask is that we expand our celebrations of families to include children with gay or lesbian parents.

Corbett (1993: 31) says: "I have often seen parents and teachers tell children of same-sex families (especially boys) that physical affection is inappropriate. The homophobia at the root of this behaviour is sending a harmful message to all children—those who will be homosexual adults and those who will not."

Gay men are also making inroads but for some, challenges still exist. Strader (1993) studied the issues facing gay fathers who are noncustodial and he discusses the difficulty of working through the grief about the loss of contact and quality time with his children. Gay fathers must work to maintain a healthy parent–child relationship while establishing, developing, and feeling proud of their gay identity. Homosexuality's stigma still affects gay fathers and their children. Male partners who wish to adopt a child still face a number of obstacles in some provinces; however, barriers are slowly being eliminated.

LGBTQ FAMILIES AND THEIR CHILDREN

Imagine the following scenarios. According to Epstein (2003: 77), each one is commonly faced by LGBTQ parents.

- You have to explain over and over again how your child was conceived.

- You are repeatedly asked in public settings whether you are a "real" parent.

- Your child cannot play with his/her friend from school because the friend's parents are disgusted by your relationship with your partner.

- You are visited by a worker from the Children's Aid Society who has been called by your neighbour complaining that you are an unfit mother.

- Your child is in a medical emergency and you are not allowed to make decisions about the care she/he is to receive.

- Your child's teacher will not speak to you about your child's progress at school.

- Your in-laws will not recognize you as a legitimate parent of their grandchild.

- You are forced to constantly defend your right and your ability to be a parent.

LGBTQ families engage in their lifestyles at great personal risk and cost. Their commitment to parenting demands our respect. Gay and lesbian families are obviously concerned about protecting their children from homophobia. Older children, in particular, may be reluctant to disclose their family situation to teachers and other children for fear of inviting a negative reaction. While some gay and lesbian parents feel comfortable discussing their family situation with supervisors and teachers, others fear that disclosure will stigmatize their child and invite censure or criticism. Wickens (1993) relates the comments of two fathers who did not disclose their family situation until the last few months of their child's time in preschool but who offered full disclosure when the child entered public school.

It was a learning thing. The learning was that there is no choice but to bring it up. There's no way to hide it. Not that we were doing it so much on the conscious level. But it's much more wise to be open about it because you don't have a choice anyway. The child is going to tell everyone. Then it's much harder to explain it all after the fact. It's much easier to be out right at the start. It's also giving a very negative message that what you're doing is wrong. So how can a child have a clear, positive concept and understanding about what this relationship is about if someone's telling him not to tell anybody? (Wickens, 1993: 26–27)

Janmohamed (2006) states that "although LGBTQ parents have fought hard to win the right to be recognized as parents legally through the birth and adoption process, LGBTQ families continue to face isolation and homophobia in their day to day experiences or parenting and social interaction."

Foulks Boyd (1999: 40) comments that "parents' beliefs on these topics may conflict with the teacher's, and teachers may feel torn between their personal beliefs and their responsibilities as educators." Greenspoon (1998:2) comments that "teachers have a fear of the conflict and negative repercussions which might arise if content about gay and lesbian parents is introduced." She also reports that some homosexual early childhood teachers live in fear of being discovered and labelled as pedophiles: "On my office bulletin board I have many buttons that express some of my fondest beliefs, and there is a black button with a pink triangle. It is the Nazi designation for a homosexual person and the symbol today for gay

Stephen and I publicly adopted our first child, a nine-month-old boy in 1998. While both Stephen and I were fully included in the adoption process, I was the only one who could legally be Ronan's adoptive parent. Ronan was subsequently adopted by Stephen in a separate court application the following year, thereby giving both of us equal and legal guardianship of our son. Conversely, in 2002, when Stephen and I adopted our second boy, Josh, who was one-year-old at the time, we were able to adopt together in one application to the courts. Within three short years, the Canadian laws went from not recognizing Stephen and me as common-law, to including [same sex common-law] in the government's definition of a family. Not only are we accepted as a family in the eyes of the government but closer to home our friends, family, and the children's educators have opened their arms and minds to our lifestyle. We are so thankful to have had an opportunity to be involved with two different daycare centres. Both centres have not only accepted us, but asked all the right questions to make Stephen, myself, and our children feel welcomed, loved, and important. When special days roll around like Mother's Day or Father's Day, the kids are welcomed to make cards and gifts for their dad and papa, and the daycare staff are consistently aware and supportive of our family differences.

Source: Byron Silver

Several years ago, when my daughter was about three, her daycare teacher approached me at the end of the day. The preschool room was doing a family unit, and the teacher had asked each child to say something about their mother and father. "Jesse got really angry," the teacher told me, "and insisted that she didn't have a father. I told her that every child has a father somewhere. Then she got really mad, and started yelling, 'I don't have a father.'" The teacher looked at me, waiting for my sympathetic response to her story. Instead, I responded in shock and outrage. "She was right," I said. "She doesn't have a father." When she looked puzzled, I continued: "Obviously every child has a biological father somewhere, but Jesse does not have a social father. So from her point of view, she was right. I hope you never contradict her explanation of her family again."

Ten years later I still feel upset when I think of that incident. If I had one message to convey to teachers it would be this: "Listen to the children. They will tell you what you need to know." Lesbian and gay families have many ways of defining themselves. Some families may have two mothers. Others may refer to themselves as Mommy and Bonnie or Suey or Mary. In some cases where the original lesbian parents have split up, there may be even more than two mothers. Children born into a heterosexual marriage may have a father; children whose conception is the result of alternative insemination generally do not have a father. Attempting to define what a lesbian or gay family looks like, and trying to impose that definition on children, will do far more harm than good. Teachers must also realize that some lesbian and gay families may choose not to disclose their sexual orientation, because of employment or family concerns. In such cases, pushing children to provide details of their family life may put considerable stress on both the child and the family.

Source: Contributed by Katherine Arnup, School of Canadian Studies, Carleton University.

pride. Quietly and simply it sits on my board, not only as a declaration of my own values but also to say to gay parents, gay staff members, or gay job applicants that they are safe here" (1993: 30). Many same-sex parents feel that there is a need for them to constantly defend their family structure while constantly being compared to heterosexual family models.

"Lesbian parents talk about feeling that they are being viewed through a lens that foregrounds their lesbianism, and that attributes any problems their children experience at school, or any non-conforming behaviours on the part of their children, as stemming from the sexual orientation of the parents. Some, conscious of the tendency for their behaviour to be viewed as 'lesbian behaviour,' are reluctant to make waves, fearing that it will have negative repercussions for their children. While many have had positive experiences with individual teachers, they also describe their parenting status as being tolerated but not acknowledged in the classroom" (Epstein, 2003: 91–92).

What can we learn about gender roles and assignments of tasks and household responsibilities that may differ from heterosexual family structures? Stacey and Biblarz in Epstein (2003: 175) surveyed 21 studies of the children of lesbians, conducted between 1981 and 1998. From this research they concluded that the children of lesbians differ in "modest but interesting ways" from children with straight parents. They attribute some of these differences to the ways that gender and sexual orientation interact to create new kinds of family structures and processes. Some differences they highlight are discussed below:

- Children with lesbian moms exhibit an increased awareness and empathy toward social difference and tend to describe themselves in ways that indicate higher self-esteem and better mental health than do the children of other moms.

- Children of lesbians appear less traditionally gender-typed. For example, lesbians' daughters may be more than twice as likely to aspire to nontraditional jobs, and lesbians' sons are less aggressive than those raised by heterosexual mothers.

- Two women co-parenting may create a synergistic energy pattern that brings more egalitarian, compatible, shared parenting and time spent with children, greater understanding of children, and closeness and communication between parents and children.

Flaks (1995) compared 15 lesbian couples and the children born to them through donor insemination with 15 heterosexual-parent families. Assessment measures evaluated the children's cognitive functioning and behavioural adjustment and the parents' relationship quality and parenting skills. Flaks found no significant differences between the two groups of children, but he did find that lesbian couples exhibited more parenting awareness skills than heterosexual parents (1995: 105–14). Hare and Koepke (1990: 21) similarly note that "while it is true that growing up in a lesbian family presents unique challenges to children, the evidence is that lesbian families are strong and healthy ones. More important, lesbian families are increasing in number and are, by and large, raising their children with very little social support."

According to Clay (1990), one of the most commonly asked questions among teachers is whether having a gay parent has any effect on the sexual identity of the child. In fact, "studies show that the

INSIDE LOOK

Audre Lorde writes about what it means to be the child of a lesbian of colour:

There are certain basic requirements of any child—food, clothing, shelter, love. So what makes our children different: We do. Gays and Lesbians of Color are different because we are embattled by reason of our sexuality and our Color, and if there is any lesson we must teach our children, it is that difference is a creative force for change, that survival and struggle for the future is not a theoretical issue. It is the very texture of our lives.

Source: Lorde, in Pollack and Vaughn 1987: 313.

incidence of being gay among children of gay and lesbian parents is approximately the same as in the rest of the population. There is no apparent relationship between a parent's sexual orientation and the sexual identity of the child" (1990: 33). Ullyott (1990) cites research by Martha Kirkpatrick, "a Los Angeles psychiatrist who compared 5- to 12-year-old children of lesbian mothers with the children of straight mothers. Her findings: no significant psychological differences" (1990: 107).

Teachers and administrators often lack knowledge of the resources to support them in addressing gay and lesbian issues, but more and more helpful material has become available. One resource that can be invaluable is a document from the Toronto District School Board and Elementary Teachers of Toronto, published in 2002. Entitled *Rainbows and Triangles: A Curriculum Document for Challenging Homophobia and Heterosexism in the K–6 Classroom*, it is filled with practical teaching ideas on this topic. It also includes practical responses to questions children might ask, such as "Is homosexuality against religion?" "What if you find out you're gay and your religion thinks it's wrong?" The book suggests that teachers respond with something like the following: "Sometimes even within the same religion people disagree. Some consider homosexuality a sin, others consider it a personal choice, while others consider it a gift from God. There are gays, lesbians, and bisexuals in every religious group around the globe."

ROLE OF THE TEACHER

- When dealing with gay and lesbian families, it is critical that teachers examine their own values and attitudes for possible biases. Children are very astute and pick up on a teacher's confirming or disconfirming attitude.

- The supervisor of the centre must "lead the way" in creating centre safety for staff and for families and ensure that anti-oppression policies are in place. The centre's written philosophy and practice should reflect the Human Rights Code Section 4 which "provides that every person has a right to freedom from discrimination…"

- Be proactive. Advertise that your program is LGBTQ friendly to attract both staff and families.

- Create a positive atmosphere by learning the differences between tolerance, acceptance, celebration, and advocacy for same-sex families.

- Teachers should view a parents as a child's mother or father, not as the child's gay father or lesbian mother. Parents should be made to feel welcome and included right from the beginning of their association with the centre.

- Ask families how they would like to be referred to since some labels or terminology may be offensive to some—some options are same-sex family or gay or lesbian family. Always use the same language used by the parents and their children.

- Teachers need to use appropriate non-discriminatory language. Avoid the use of common colloquial phrases that denigrate same-sex individuals, for example, referring to strange or unusual objects or occurrences as "gay." Encourage inclusive language with older children to avoid the assumption that everyone is heterosexual. Use terms such as "partner" or "significant other" in place of "boyfriend," "girlfriend," "husband," or "wife."

- Don't assume that all LGBTQ families will have the same needs or lead the same lifestyle. Each family must be celebrated for its uniqueness. Families cross all socio-economic, racial and cultural backgrounds and may be at various stages of being "out."

- Protecting confidentiality is an important teacher responsibility. Do not disclose or "out" an individual. Teachers need to respect and honour the rights of parents to maintain silence about their homosexuality.

- Registration forms and all centre-generated written communication should include "parent and/or co-parent," replacing the traditional "mother and father."

- Home visits may be particularly important for these families for privacy can be ensured and a fuller discussion can take place.

- Gay and lesbian parents may feel constant pressure to exceed societal expectations of parenting—to prove that the benefits of raising children in a gay or lesbian family parallels those offered by their heterosexual counterparts. In fact, these families are different and should be celebrated for what they can teach us. Teachers should be sensitive to these issues for all families.

- Teachers need to be prepared to challenge insensitive jokes, anti-gay or lesbian comments by adults in the centre in the same way that they would challenge any racist slur. Don't be a silent witness to hate speech. The centre needs to reflect this fundamental principle in the working environment and in all its interactions. Teachers must take personal responsibility and be prepared to intervene when necessary.

- If teachers are uncomfortable with the way in which their colleagues are handling same-sex families in their centre, professional development workshops would be a positive strategy for challenging negative attitudes. Resource people are available in the community to carry out these workshops in a positive and sensitive manner.

- Teachers should consider that a colleague may be gay/lesbian and afraid to disclose their identity for fear of harassment and discrimination. How can you contribute to a safe and inclusive work environment?

- Teachers should also be mindful that members of the LGBTQ community have suffered death and grieving continues to play a role in many of their lives. Compassion and empathy is the role of the teacher.

ROLE OF THE TEACHER IN THE PLAYROOM

- When gay and lesbian families visit the centre it is important that they see representations of themselves. "How must the scores of children living with gay parents feel," Corbett asks, "never to see any representation of their lives in any book, any song, or any television program?" (1993: 31). Books, photos of families in the room, posters, and artwork should reflect all families.

- Recognizable symbols in the classroom such as rainbow flags, safety zone stickers, or LGBT (lesbian, gay, bisexual, and transgender) posters raise awareness and identify the teacher as a supportive one.

- When children use names such as "fag", "dyke", "queer," etc., teach the children what the words mean and how they might be hurtful and let them know that this language will not be tolerated.

- With older children, open discussion about discrimination and its consequences can be held. Guests from the community might be invited to share appropriate information with the children.

- When teachers are unsure of how to handle a situation that might arise, they are encouraged to discuss strategies with the gay or lesbian family. The family is the best resource to use and may have many helpful suggestions. It has probably had to deal with these issues in the past.

- When dealing with younger children, it is sufficient for teachers to explore the concept that all families are different and that each is acceptable. For school-age children, a more detailed explanation may be in order. It may be helpful to discuss with older children the many talented politicians, writers, athletes, actors, and musicians who are gay or lesbian.

- Hoy Crawford (1996) says, "There is general societal homophobia which results in parents' and teachers' concern about children's play where they are acting out non-stereotypical gender roles. 'Tomboy' or 'sissy' play looks like stereotypical 'gay behaviour,' and any child who exhibits this behaviour may be shamed and marginalized. All children suffer because of these narrow limits of what is deemed to be acceptable. . . . Gender and racial stereotypes hamper the growth of individuals by limiting their expectations for themselves" (1996:7). Teachers need to support all types of play for boys and girls in the program.

- Display posters for community activities, resources, agencies, etc., for all families in the child-care centre. Learn about what is available in the community for LGBT families. Teachers should also be aware of resources that are available to support them in their teaching.

- Activities need to be inclusive—for example, create two Mother's or Father's Day cards (calling it Family Day would include all family structures). In child care we celebrate everything in order to include everyone! Celebrate Pride Day!

Family Pride Canada

The Family Pride Canada website is a project of the University of Western Ontario Research Facility for Gay and Lesbian Studies in cooperation with the LGBT Parenting Network at the David Kelley Lesbian and Gay Community Counselling Program, Family Service Association of Toronto. The project is made possible through a generous grant from the Counselling Foundation of Canada. Their focus is to provide Canadians from all walks of life with reliable information on LGBT family issues in a variety of scholarly and popular forms—academic books, specialist periodicals, magazine articles, documentary videos, parenting manuals and children's books. Their website is **http://www.uwo.ca/pridelib/family**.

PFLAG

PFLAG is a nonprofit organization made up of families and friends of lesbians and gays and is a support group for parents whose child has just "come out." One family comments: "we are very proud of our gay son, our first born. He did not choose to be gay any more than we chose to be straight. He lives his life with courage, dignity, and good humour, in a positive relationship. . . . He is loved and respected by his four younger siblings and a large extended family. If you met him you would say, 'What a fine young man.' And you would be right. We wouldn't have had the courage to have chosen to parent a gay person, but we have come to feel that it is a privilege" (PFLAG, n.d.). More information about the group can be found on

their website at **www.pflag.ca**.

The LGBTQ Parenting Network

The LGBTQ Parenting Network provides resources, information, and support to LGBTQ parents and their families. They publish a newsletter, *Pride and Joy*, organize discussion forums on relevant topics important to LGBT parents and parents-to-be, and are planning a handbook for LGBTQ parents on dealing with schools. They also work with a community centre to present a course for gay men, Daddies and Papas 2B, considering parenthood and offer training to professionals and community agencies interested in making their services more accessible to LGBTQ families. Dykes Planning Tykes is a course for Lesbian, Bisexual and Queer Women considering parenting. Daddy, Papa and Me is a monthly queer positive gathering for dads and their kids and Mum's The World is a gathering for lesbian, bisexual and transsexual/transgendered mothers and their children.

The organization has collaborated with the Pride Library at the University of Western Ontario who have developed a national website on LGBT family

and parenting issues, **www.uwo.ca/pridelib/family**. E-mail Rachel Epstein at the LGBT Parenting Network at rachelep@fsatoronto.com for more information.

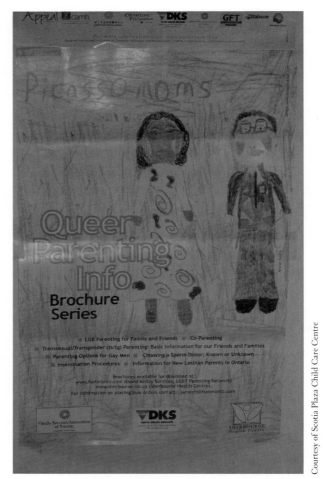

Supervisors can help connect families with supportive community resources.

BOOKS FOR CHILDREN

123: A Family Counting Book, by B. Combs

ABC: A Family Alphabet Book, by B. Combs

Asha's Mom, R. Elwin, by M. Paulse

Daddy's Roommate, by M. Willhoite

The Family Book, by T. Parr

Heather Has Two Mommies, by L. Newman

Molly's Family, by N. Garden

Mom and Mum are Getting Married, by K. Selterington

BOOKS FOR ADULTS

For Lesbian Parents: Your Guide to Helping Your Family Grow Up Happy, Healthy and Proud, by S. Johnson and E. O'Connor

TEEN FAMILIES

Kristy, 18, lives with her mother, a younger brother and sister, and her stepfather. Kristy's mother has just given birth to Dana, her first child with Kristy's stepfather. Kristy is two months pregnant. She is in her last year of high school and has been involved with her boyfriend, Emilio, for two years. Kristy and Emilio have decided that they want to parent the baby. Because they both want to finish high school, they will continue to live with their families once the baby is born. Kristy is aware that having two infants in the house will be a challenge, but her parents have been very supportive. Kristy and Emilio plan to move in together once they graduate.

In Canada, the teen birth rate has been declining, and recent statistics show that it has leveled off; there were 14.9 births per 1,000 in 2002; 13.6 in 2004; and 13.4 in 2005. The rate of second or subsequent births to Canadian teenagers fell from 18.5 percent in 1993 to 15.2 percent in 2003. This drop partly reflects a downturn in the overall teen fertility rate; nonetheless, during that period nearly 25,000 Canadian teenagers gave birth to their second or subsequent child. For the 2001–2003 period the average annual rate of second or subsequent births was strikingly high in Nunavut—31.9 per 1,000 girls aged 15 to 19—and was well above the national average of 2.6. Also above the national average for second or subsequent births are Manitoba (6.8), Saskatchewan (6.3), and Alberta (3.1); rates were below the national average in Nova Scotia, Quebec, and British Columbia. Teenagers delivering their second or subsequent child were highly concentrated in low-income neighbourhoods (Dryburgh, 2003).

Provinces and territories with high rates of second or subsequent births to teens tended to have relatively large numbers of Aboriginal residents. Unlike the overall Canadian population, Aboriginal peoples have not experienced the trend toward delayed first births. In 1999, more than one in five First Nations babies were born to mothers aged 15 to 19 years; the comparable figure for Canada as a whole was one in twenty.

The age of first sexual experience is 16.5 years in Canada. The federal government has put guidelines in place for sex education but programs differ by school board, school and classroom. The programs are not uniform enough across the country to make a consistent contribution to the health of Canadian youth. The use of condoms and hormonal birth control has increased with 87 percent of teens having safe sex. Access to the morning after pill, while readily available, requires a consultation with a pharmacist which costs up to $45 plus the drug fee; the medication must be taken within 72 hours of sex. Less than one in six hospitals provided abortions in 2006 and many provinces do not have full health insurance coverage for terminations done in clinics (Gulli, 2008).

It is important to remember that the above statistics reflect teen births, which is not the same thing as teen pregnancies, which include births and abortions and which is a truer picture of teens dealing with pregnancy.

When we consider adolescent development we know that they are developing their self identity, they are seeking peer acceptance, they may have concerns about their body image, and they are striving for independence. They are experiencing mood changes and experimenting with adult behaviours and formulating their sex roles. How will these developmental tasks impact on a teenager who finds out that she is pregnant or that he will be a father?

According to Dryburgh (2003), in the last 25 years there has been an overall decline in the teenage pregnancy rate in Canada (possibly due to the growing availability of contraceptives and the increased awareness of risks of unsafe sex). Older teens have a higher pregnancy rate than younger teens, and are more likely to have a live birth; women aged 15–17 are most likely to have an abortion. The days of shame and stigmatization have

FIGURE 9.1   TEEN BIRTHS IN OTHER COUNTRIES

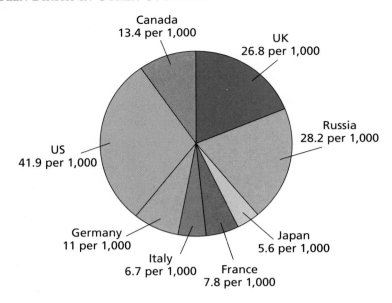

Canada
13.4 per 1,000

UK
26.8 per 1,000

Russia
28.2 per 1,000

US
41.9 per 1,000

Germany
11 per 1,000

Italy
6.7 per 1,000

France
7.8 per 1,000

Japan
5.6 per 1,000

Source: C. Gulli, "Suddenly Teen Pregnancy Is Cool?" *Maclean's* January 28, 2008: 41.

lessened in some cultures and although it may be now more socially acceptable to have a child out of wedlock, there are still serious health risks for the babies of teen mothers, including low birth weights and associated health problems. Dryburgh points out that the mothers themselves are at risk of various health problems, including "anemia, hypertension, renal disease, eclampsia and depressive disorders. As well, teenagers who engage in unprotected sex are putting their own health at risk of sexually transmitted infections" (2003: 1). Children of teen mothers are more likely to suffer from health risks associated with low birth weight and/or prematurity, mainly due to the high rate of cigarette smoking among teenage mothers: over 45 percent of teenage mothers smoke (Health Canada, 2006, in Shimoni and Baxter, 2008: 41). Someone marrying for the first time in their teens faces a risk of a marital breakdown that is almost two times higher than that of a person who married between the ages of 25–29 (Statistics Canada, 2006b).

Compared to their childless peers, teen mothers face a greater chance of living in poverty with low career and educational prospects. This is even more likely if they have more than one child (Zabin et al., 1992; Nock, 1998; Solomon and Liefeld, 1998). Teen mothers are also more likely to marry early and have a higher rate of divorce (Manning, 1993). This situation tends to be repeated in children of teen

parents, who are more likely to have lower academic achievements and early, unmarried pregnancies (Haye, 1987; Alexander and Guyer, 1993). Geronimus (1991) is careful to point out that it is not certain how much of this results from other background characteristics (such as living in poverty), rather than specifically from teen pregnancy. Teens also run the risk of violence which is more likely to start during pregnancy. Unfortunately, teen parents often become stereotyped as "losers," though this negative societal image overlooks their diversity, experiences, and educational and career aspirations (Camarena et al., 1998).

Ambert (2006) gathers research that points to the fact that for some young women, having a baby may be a form of social status: the young woman has someone to love, gets a lot of attention from her family, and, for a period of time, receives a great deal of peer interest. Ambert (2006) also provides evidence that the rates of teen pregnancy increase in families where there are sexually active siblings. In families where the mothers are openly sexually active with a variety of men and where there is little parental supervision, the incidence is also likely to increase. A smaller but significant number of teenagers become pregnant through coerced sex: at least 20 percent of teen mothers have experienced involuntary intercourse (Shimoni and Baxter, 2008: 120).

According to one analysis of national data, teen parents are more responsible than other teenagers. Furthermore, teen mothers are less likely than their childless female peers to drink alcohol or socialize with friends who do; teen fathers who acknowledge their child tend to be employed or engage in other "socially productive work," such as volunteering, more than their male peers (Kowaleski-Jones and Mott, 1998; Riedman, Lamanna, and Nelson, 2003: 342).

Balancing motherhood with selfhood, particularly adolescent selfhood, calls for maturity, psychological strength, and a full complement of family and external supports. To be a student (and often a worker), a daughter, a friend, a girlfriend, and a mother is demanding for anyone. To assume these roles at 16, within a milieu in which there is virtually no margin for error, requires extraordinary talent and fortitude (Musick, 1990: 24). We must celebrate that many teen parents do manage with great courage and sacrifice to love and care for their child. With support from the community, much can be accomplished.

Many compelling issues and concerns face teen families. Will they receive adequate prenatal and postnatal medical and nutritional care for themselves and their child? How will they support themselves and the child? What impact will the child have on their education? Are they prepared for the realities of parenthood? What kind of input can they expect from their own families? Will they be able to handle the expenses associated with raising a child (babysitters, transportation, childcare services, dentists, and so on)? Have they come to terms with the new restrictions on their independence and their consequences (for example, diminished social life)? Where will they live?

This will be an unsettled time for teen families—a time of redefining themselves and discovering how the child affects their personal as well as professional lives. Some young parents feel resentful at times and trapped in their new lifestyle. Some receive a great deal of support from their extended families. Sixty percent of Canadians 20–24 years of age still live with their parents and pregnant teens may feel they will have more support in raising their child if they stay at home. In fact, 30–50 percent of teen mothers continue to reside in their family of origin up to two years post partum (Ambert, 2006). Others teens must cope with their new circumstances entirely on their own. One trend observed by Pauline Paterson, director of the YWCA's girls and family programs, is a phenomenon called "multi-daddying." Teen moms are having more than one baby with various fathers as a way of forming bonds with new men in their lives, another way that adolescents are putting their stamp on parenthood and establishing new family models (Gulli, 2008).

Teenage males are often pleased when their girlfriends get pregnancy. They sometimes want a baby just as much as the teenage mother does and usually for the same reasons. The baby may be their first real possession and caring for a baby may represent a real accomplishment for both teens (Shimoni and Baxter, 2008: 125). Many social workers and policy makers point to the need for including the teen father in programs and services.

INSIDE LOOK

In June, Lindsay Kretschmer, 25, will graduate from Centennial College's three-year creative advertising program. In the audience will be her seven-year-old daughter Emilee. Getting by with two part-time jobs and student loans, Kretschmer has won awards and accolades for her volunteerism and leadership, including being honoured as a YWCA Young Woman of Distinction in 2002. She left home at 13, bunking first with friends and then living on her own, and she found out at 17 that she was pregnant. For some young women, becoming a mother is a turning point in their lives, giving them direction and purpose. They draw on inner strength and community resources to cope with the challenges of teen parenting. Clearly this was the case for Lindsay. She was inspired by the many people who helped her dream big and not to "limit yourself," including the unique Literature For Life Program which brings groups discussions on books to young mothers. She not only attended the program when she was a new mother but has also worked for it in a variety of positions including group leader. A success story!

Source: Crawford, 2008.

Some young, unmarried fathers do offer support, but they are often hampered by unemployment and their involvement with their child tends to decline as the baby gets older and their relationship with the mother grows increasingly distant or strained (Rangarajan and Gleason, 1998; Riedman, Lamanna, and Nelson, 2003: 342). These fathers tend to be more often unemployed, or employed in low-paid jobs, and are less educated than fathers who have a child after marriage (Hardy et al., 1998). Many teen fathers have a history of child-hood aggressiveness and other behavioural difficulties (Capaldi et al., 1996). The keynote address at the Toronto Father Involvement Forum (www.toronto.ca/health/moh/fif_index.htm) held April 19, 2002, stated that teen fathers are at high risk for low involvement and/or dysfunctional parenting behaviours, and their children are at risk for low birth-weight and other forms of illness. Following targeted parenting group education, teen dads dramatically increased their participation in prenatal activities and their babies tended to have higher birth-weights than a comparable group where fathers were not so involved. We must encourage teen fathers to participate in programs that empower them rather than making them feel that they need "help"; we must avoid terminology that may be offensive for example, "support group"; and we must make gatherings accessible in regards to time and place. It may also be beneficial for these sessions to be run by men and other teen fathers.

ROLE OF THE TEACHER

- It is important to remember that adolescent parents will vary greatly and many are competent parents. Teachers who come in contact with teen families must be available to provide support with a focus on the best interests of the child.

- When working with teen families, teachers need to establish an atmosphere of trust and respect. Teen families are more open about their experiences and problems if they feel that the teacher is willing to listen in a nonjudgmental manner.

- Maintaining confidentiality is critical.

- Teens should see strategies for dealing with infants modelled by the staff.

- Be involved, celebrate and praise their efforts with their child.

- Teen parents, like all parents should be consulted and encouraged to contribute to the program as they are able.

- In a quality program, teen families receive practical advice on such matters as housing and financial options.

- As a source of additional support, teens should be encouraged to build relationships with other teen families or other families in the centre.

- Teachers need to remember that young fathers need support and encouragement; they are struggling with role expectations that they may not be able to live up to and societal attitudes that are often hostile and rejecting.

- Programs could be offered at the child-care centre that focuses on strengthening parenting skills, father's groups, or cooking programs that help parents prepare inexpensive yet nutritionally sound meals, first aid courses, etc.

- Kids Help Phone 1-800-668-6868 and Parent Help Line 1-888-603-9100 are also resources for teen families. The Parent Help Line maintains a national database that provides referrals to other organizations, counselling, health centres, etc. Counsellors are also available to handle crisis situations.

- Programs should be flexible enough to support teen parents who are trying to balance school and their personal life. Teachers should be alert to times when parents could use respite care and help to connect them to appropriate community resources.

- The evidence is very clear in regards to education: a teen parent who completes their education has a better chance of economic stability and a personal sense of achievement. Teachers can provide information about full-time and part-time programs at their local high school, alternative school, college or university.

Community Support: Jessie's Centre for Teenagers

Contributed by Cathie Leard, Parent Child Counsellor, Community Education Co-ordinator

Jessie's is a nonprofit, charitable organization funded by the Ministry of Community and Social Services, the City of Toronto, Health and Welfare Canada, the United Way corporations, foundations, and private donors; it provides programs in collaboration with the Toronto Board of Education and the Toronto Board of Health. It was established in 1982 in recognition of the large number of teenage parents who were struggling to raise their children, sometimes without adequate financial resources, family support, affordable housing, child-care facilities, and access to parenting information and health services. Each year, Jessie's serves more than 500 young families. Programs include pregnancy counselling, individual support and counselling, health services, nursery drop-in and parent relief, housing assistance, 24-hour respite care, prenatal and parenting groups, high school credit courses, and a variety of discussion and support groups.

Jessie's has many regular volunteers who work in child-care tutoring, labour support, and administration as well as a 15-member board of directors from a broad spectrum of backgrounds that includes graduates of the agency. In 1998, Jessie's was chosen by the United Way to receive Success By 6 funding. This grant has allowed Jessie's to

expand many of its parenting services and create the Community Education Project, through which the staff and parents act as educators and ambassadors to schools and organizations throughout Toronto. In 2002, Jessie's initiated the Intensive Parenting program. A staff member is now dedicated to working with a small number of families who display symptoms of being at risk. Because changes to Ontario's child welfare legislation have also increased the number of children placed in foster care, the agency offers support for families whose children are in care or are newly reunited.

Jessie's mission is supported by a feminist, anti-oppression framework. The agency attempts to empower young families through both the direct services available at the agency and individual and systemic advocacy to assist their access to community support and entitlements.

SEPARATED, DIVORCED, JOINT-CUSTODY, AND LONE-PARENT FAMILIES

Monique, 25, has been living alone with her two children, ages two and four, since her husband left her when she became pregnant with her youngest child. Monique has divorced her husband, who has since disappeared from their lives. In defiance of a court order, he has not paid any child support in two years. Monique lives on welfare in an inner-city housing project in Halifax. She is about to enter a government-sponsored training project that allows her to go back to school while her children attend a local child-care centre. Monique put aside her ambition to become an occupational therapist when she became pregnant with her first child. Now she is excited at the prospect of a new, independent life for herself and her children.

Junlin and her former partner, John, have two children ages six and eight years. The court has awarded joint custody to both parents. Financially able to do so, they have purchased two semi-detached homes that are side by side. They have a formalized routine, with each parent having the children live with them one week at a time but the children move freely back and forth. Junlin and John both feel that this arrangement is the in the best interests of all concerned.

Tani is a 37-year-old financially independent teacher. For some time she has been thinking about having a child. Tani is not in a serious relationship, but she realizes that her biological clock is ticking and she is considering asking a man she has been intimate with in the past to be the biological father of her child. She wants

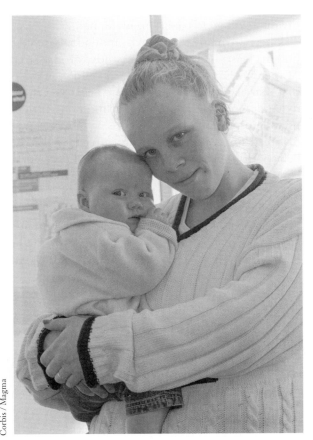

This teen mother decided to raise her child with the support of the father.

to raise her child without the help or involvement of this man. She has a strong support network of family and friends.

SEPARATED AND LONE PARENTS

Lone parents represented 15.9 percent of all census families in 2006, higher than any other recorded census figure in the last 75 years. However, the proportion was up only slightly from 15.7 percent in 2001, which could indicate that the upward trend may have recently stabilized. The majority (80.1 percent) of the 1,414,100 lone-parent families in 2006 was comprised of women and children; the remaining 19.9 percent consisted of lone-parent families headed by men. Between 2001 and 2006, lone-father families rose 14.6 percent, more than twice the pace of 6.3 percent for lone-mother families. A significant change that could account for these statistics is that increasingly court rulings are favouring joint custody arrangements and fewer mothers are granted sole custody following a divorce; 43.8 percent of dependents were awarded to both father and mother in 2003, continuing an upward trend of joint custody arrangements (Statistics Canada, 2007a).

DIVORCE

A recent article in *The Toronto Star* (2007b) cited a number of important statistics about divorce in Canada. More than two million Canadians ended a relationship between 2001 and 2006, either from a separation or divorce. Just less than 50 percent of these dissolutions were common-law relationships. Canadian common-law relationships last, on average, 4.3 years whereas the average length of a Canadian marriage is 14.3 years.

Seventy-six percent of those seeking a divorce used formal legal services such as lawyers, family law information services, and mediation. The percentage of Canadians who sought some form of social service support varied depending on age: 30 percent of Canadians under 30 years of age who were involved in a relationship breakup sought some form of social service support; 70 percent of Canadians over 30 years of age involved in a relationship breakup sought some form of social service support (*The Toronto Star*, 2007b).

With the passing of the Divorce Act in 1968, grounds for divorce were extended to include "no-fault" divorce based on separation for at least three years; the separation period was revised to one year in 1986. The easing of Canada's divorce laws,

combined with other social changes, marked a significant shift in the way Canadians perceived marriage and divorce. According to Statistics Canada (2003), in 1998, 36 percent of married couples in Canada had dissolved their marriages before celebrating their 30th anniversary.

Despite the divorce rate's dramatic increase over the past 30 years, Canadians' marital stability measures well internationally. The Canadian divorce rate is lower than that of most industrialized nations; the American rate is almost double. Gary Direnfield discusses the state of Canadian divorces on his website **www.yoursocialworker.com**. He estimates that 80 percent of divorces are low conflict (the parents able to manage between themselves, co-operate, and inform the daycare of their situation to support the child). In the other 20 percent of divorces, 5–10 percent can be classified as medium conflict (the parents require outside resources and operate separately from the daycare) and 5–10 percent are high conflict (the parents involved in the court system in the divorce and may draw the daycare into conflict as a source of data to support their position or to restrict access to information and/or the child). Only 2–3 percent of divorces will go to trial (Direnfeld, n.d.).

There are many reasons why individuals divorce but at least one American study of divorced women, by Kurz (1995, in Fox, 2001: 166), suggests that marriages end because of the negative gender dynamics in the relationships. "Almost one-fifth of them (especially middle-class women) had divorced for reasons involving conventional male behaviour—the man's failure to share housework, child care, and even emotional work, and/or his need to be in control." Other reasons suggested were their partner's violence, "another woman," drug or alcohol abuse, and his absence from home. Age at marriage is probably the strongest predictor of divorce in the first five years of marriage. Second marriages are more likely than first marriages to end in divorce; the divorce rate for second marriages is about 10% higher than in first marriages. Along with co-habitation, more research is needed in this area.

Abraham (1999), in an interview with Robert Glossop of the Vanier Institute of the Family, quotes Glossop as saying: "the major problem with divorce is the depleted economic circumstances that most children fall into afterward. Sixty percent of single female parents live below the poverty line in Canada. That means the majority of children whose parents

TABLE 9.7	DIVORCES BY PROVINCE, 2003
NUMBER OF DIVORCES	
Canada	70,828
Newfoundland/Labrador	662
Prince Edward Island	281
Nova Scotia	1,907
New Brunswick	1,450
Quebec	16,738
Ontario	27,513
Manitoba	2,352
Saskatchewan	1,992
Alberta	7,960
British Columbia	9,820
Yukon	87
Northwest Territories including Nunavut	..
Northwest Territories	62
Nunavut	4
.. not available for a specific period of time.	

Source: Statistics Canada CANSIM table 053-0002; http://www40.statcan.ca/l01/cst01/famil02.htm

are separated or divorced will experience poverty." Statistics Canada (2003) reports that a study of married people who became separated between 1987 and 1993 showed that women who were lone parents remained 21 percent below their pre-separation family incomes five years after separation. By contrast, men who were lone parents reported a five percent gain in income after five years.

Economic disparity between male and female lone parents exists for many reasons. On average, women earn less than men. In addition, lone fathers tend to be older and better educated, have more labour force experience, and have older children. For many, their careers are established before they become lone parents and their children are already school-aged. The low levels of child support awarded by the courts and the high number of men who do not comply with the court orders are significant causes of the financial hardship experienced by many lone mothers and their children (Vanier Institute, 1994: 83–84).

CHILD SUPPORT

On May 1, 1997, reforms to Canada's child support system came into effect. The main features of the reform are:

• the introduction of child support guidelines,

• changes to the tax treatment of child support,

• additional enforcement measures, and

• increased tax credits to low-income families. (Department of Justice Canada, 1997)

Though eight in ten children live with their mother, the number of fathers seeking custody is increasing, as are joint-custody agreements. Concerns regarding child support, however, continue to grow. In Ontario, for example, "the number of people considered 'non-compliant' with court orders (those who paid less than 85 percent) rose from 33.3 percent to 34.8 percent. Those who paid their entire child support bills decreased from 32.4 percent to 31 percent. Some 105,436 people— 69 percent of those on the office's Ontario rolls— were behind in their payments, up from 67.6 per cent five years ago" (Dale, 2008).

After a separation or divorce, parents undergo a grieving process of their own, during which time "they often find it difficult to provide the support their children need as they watch their security shatter. In a sense, children lose both parents when one parent dies or leaves—the one who remains will never be the same again" (Newman, 1993: 113–14). Despite divorce having become common, and no matter how much public attitudes have changed over the years, no study of divorce and

Joan McBurney of Ottawa has lived apart from her three boys (11, 12, and 15) for six years, and she laments missing the everyday events that help parents to feel grounded in their children's lives. "By the time I hear about them, it's old hat to the kids, and telling me these everyday things that I want so much to hear about doesn't seem to count for much to them. It really used to get me down", admits McBurney, who sees her boys every other weekend but phones every second day or so to help keep up that connection. "Sometimes they'll say, 'I can't talk now, I'm busy.' And I ask, 'Oh yeah, what are you doing?' 'Playing video games,' they'll say." Any parent of a Nintendo addict will know that this is fairly typical behaviour, but for a non-custodial parent striving to maintain a link with her kids it might feel like a stab in the heart. "Oh yes, I've had to learn to roll with the punches and not take it seriously."

Source: Hoffman, 1997.

marriage breakdown has ever shown it to be normative and routine for those involved. Separation and divorce usually mean that individuals involved have to redefine themselves as people. The roles they have filled within the marriage are now lost, and to lose a role is to lose part of oneself. One of the difficulties with divorce is that our society has no readily defined role for the formerly married. They must work out new ones for themselves as unmarried people, but also often as people with children. There is also little social guidance for how one should behave in a "normal" divorce (Ahrons, 1999).

Furstenberg and Cherlin (2001: 493) quote psychologists Chase-Lansdale and Hetherington, who have labelled the first two years following a separation as a "crisis period" for adults and children. The crisis begins for children with shock, anxiety, and anger upon learning of the breakup (the harmful effects on children of marital conflict may begin well before the breakup). For children, divorce strikes at the very core of their world, but we need to be cautious about the conclusions we reach about the socioemotional consequences of divorce for children and their parents. For adults the immediate aftermath is a dismaying and difficult time. It is especially trying for mothers who retain custody of the children. During the crisis period, it is important address the following two needs of children: "additional emotional support as they struggle to adapt to the breakup; and the structure provided by a reasonably predictable daily routine" (Furstenberg and Cherlin, 2001: 493). However, it is difficult for many single parents to constantly and consistently meet these needs. Single parents, depressed and worried themselves, are often unable

to comfort their children and, as a result, their children lose some of the support they need. Many single parents feel anxious and overburdened and let daily schedules slip. There is also evidence, from a number of psychological studies, to suggest that the fallout of the crisis period is worse for boys than for girls (though boys and girls react to stress differently and this may be a factor).

Most parents and their children recover from the trauma of the separation "crisis period" within two or three years. In some situations, the child may be separated from their biological parent as well as their siblings, have less contact with aunts, uncles, and grandparents compounding the stress of the separation. Wounds from the breakup heal and both parents and children are able to stabilize their lives. Furstenberg and Cherlin (2001: 493) note, "With the exception of some difficulties between single mothers and their sons, parent–child relationships generally improve. And the majority of children, it seems, return to normal development with time." Many people enter into another relationship at some point in their lives and this bring with it new joys and challenges. In a study released in 1999, Statistics Canada found that Canadian children most affected by the divorce era have more conservative family values than either their parents or grandparents. The finding indicates a clear repudiation of the choices made by the liberal baby-boom generation (Abraham, 1999: D6).

SUPERVISED ACCESS

"When parents separate, access visits with children may be a problem. Sometimes, difficulties arise at the time of the exchange of the child between the

FIGURE 9.2   THE DIVORCE ONION

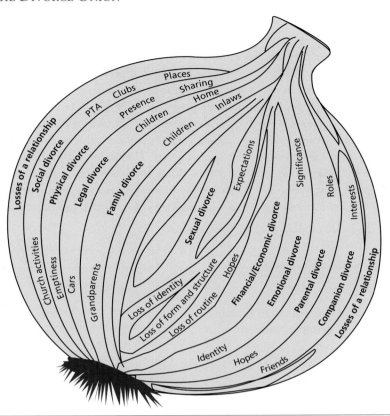

Source: From GESTWICKI. Home, School, & Community Relations, 5E. © 2004 Wadsworth, a part of Cengage Learning, Inc. Reproduced by permission. www.cengage.com/permissions

parents, or between the parent and a relative, such as a grandparent. Other times, there may be concerns about the visits themselves. The Supervised Access Program offers separated families a way to deal with some of these problems. Supervised access centres provide a safe and secure setting where visits and exchanges can take place under the supervision of trained staff and volunteers. The program is funded by the Ministry of the Attorney General and is delivered through partnerships with community-based organizations such as: children's mental health centres, neighbourhood support centres, YMCAs, and local children's aid societies (Ministry of the Attorney General, 2007). As outlined on the website of the Ministry of the Attorney General, at **http://www.attorneygeneral.jus.gov .on.ca/english/family/supaccess.asp**, these sites "provide a safe, neutral, and child-focused setting for visits between a child and non-custodial family member; ensure the safety of all participants, including staff; provide trained staff and volunteers who are sensitive to the needs of the child; and provide the court and/or lawyers with factual

observations about the participants' use of the service." Most centres charge a fee based on guidelines set by the ministry, but the fees must be adjusted to accommodate those who cannot pay the full amount.

Freeman (1994: 46) identifies a number of factors that may adversely affect a child's ability to deal with divorce:

- negative economic consequences (especially in the child's primary residence);
- erratic contact or no contact with the nonresidential parent;
- custodial parent less emotionally available to the child because of his or her own need to adjust to the new situation;
- ongoing parental conflict;
- parental dating or remarriage;
- residential parent less available (i.e., because of the obligation to work full-time);
- continued exposure to psychologically disturbed parent (or parents);

For Pat Hinds the hardest thing about separating from her husband seven years ago was abandoning the family home and moving her three children to the only place she could afford: a rundown, low-income housing complex in northwest Calgary. Garbage was strewn everywhere, the fences and playground equipment were crumbling, and the grass was long and untended because none of the tenants owned a lawn mower. "The first thing I did was sit down and cry," recalls Hinds. "Then I thought, I can crawl in a hole and die—or I can change it." Hinds chose the latter. In addition to working full-time and raising her kids, she spearheaded a major cleanup campaign. Hinds and her neighbours held bottle drives and sold old toys to raise enough money to buy two lawn mowers. They successfully lobbied the city and their landlords to replace the playground gear and fences. They even convinced Calgary retailers to donate flowers they could plant. Last week, in recognition of her community service, Hinds became one of 46,000 Canadians to receive a commemorative medal marking Queen Elizabeth's golden jubilee.

Source: Wickens, 2002: 52.

- changes in residence and consequences thereof (for example, loss of peer group, change in school, living with relatives);
- reactions of family and friends; and
- more time spent in child care.

More specifically, Patten (1999) states,

very little is known about the effects of divorce on children younger than 2 years of age. . . . Children from 3 to 5 years of age who go through divorce tend to be fearful and resort to immature or aggressive behaviour. They might return to security blankets or old toys. Some may have lapses in toilet training. . . . Preschoolers may also become less imaginative and cooperative in their play. Children may spend more time playing by themselves than with friends. They also may show more anxiety, depression, anger, and apathy in their play and in their interactions with both children and adults. Socially, preschoolers tend to spend more time seeking attention and the nearness of adults. At the same time, they may resist adult suggestions and commands. Some children become much more aggressive. On the positive side, preschool children also try to understand the situation. They attempt to bring some order to their world by trying to explain to themselves what is happening and by trying to be well behaved. . . . Children 6 to 8 years old have some understanding of what the divorce means. With their better sense of what is taking place, these children are able to deal with what is happening. Many young school-age children experience deep grief over the breakup of the family. Some children are fearful and yearn for the absent parent. If

the mother has custody, boys tend to behave aggressively toward her. Many children feel conflicts in loyalty to one parent or the other, even if the parents made no effort to make the child take sides.

When custody is awarded to women, Ward (1994: 186) observes, "men are sometimes at a loss as to how to manage the father–child relationship on their own. Often visits are seen as play time, with very little discipline involved. Sometimes the father will spend increased time with his parents, since their home provides a convenient place for visits to occur." Eichler (1997) indicates that the fathers who were most involved with their children before the divorce were more likely to lose contact with their children. These fathers "experience the greatest role loss, suffer more from their children's absence, and experience the constraints of a visiting relationship more acutely than fathers who were minimally involved in child care while married" (1997: 74).

JOINT CUSTODY

Both the Children's Law Reform Act and the Divorce Act enable a Canadian court to award custody to both parents. Joint custody, which includes several options, is an agreement in which legal and physical custody of the children is shared between the two parents. In one option, the parents together make all decisions regarding the children and the children live part-time with each parent; in another form of joint custody, there is joint legal custody but the children physically reside with one parent.

As Bogoroch-Ditkofsky (1991) describes it, "the joint-custody order allows the parents to continue sharing in the upbringing of the children without either feeling like a victor or a loser. There are different joint-custody arrangements. In one arrangement, the child lives most of the week with one parent and lives at the other parent's house on weekends. Other arrangements have the child splitting his or her time evenly between the two households or living full-time with one parent but with the other parent having extremely liberal access. Regardless of the arrangement, both parents are involved in all important decisions affecting the child" (1991: 10). Parents often try to create living arrangements that support the children. In some situations the parents try to locate close to each other; in others the children stay in the home and the parents come and go, creating a greater sense of continuity. These arrangements may be more challenging when an infant is involved, especially is the mother is breast feeding.

In some cases, the parent granted access but not custody has suffered from a mental disorder or alcohol or drug problems. The court will work hard not to sever the parent–child relationship in these cases. If the court feels that the access parent has something of value (emotional, not material) to offer the child, it will consider that the child should not be deprived of the opportunity of knowing this parent. The court will normally allow the troubled parent to visit the children under either strict or lax supervision, depending on the case. If the parents of a child are no longer living together, the centre should require as a term of the contract of enrollment a copy of the separation agreement or court order (Bogoroch-Ditkofsky, 1991: 7–8, 12).

An interesting shift in how divorced parents care for their children is highlighted in a book *Reconcilable Differences* by Cate Cochran. Many parents, though not able to continue in a marital relationship, are looking for innovative living arrangements that allow their children close proximity to both parents and with little interruption to their routine. In some cases, parents live in different floors of the house, live side-by-side, or live in close proximity to each other.

ATTACHED BUT APART
It is also interesting to note that families, such as those who work in the military, may spend a great deal of time away from each other. In other situations, one of the parents may work far from home

and return only when their jobs allow. Another emerging family profile are family members who decide that they will be happiest as a family when the adults live in two separate locations but consider themselves a family.

LONE-PARENT FAMILIES BY CHOICE
It is becoming increasingly acceptable for single people to adopt children. When a single mother has a good income, her child's development is similar to that of a comparable married mother's child. The good news is that according to the NLSCY (2007), most single parents are doing a good job of raising their children, and most children of lone-parent families show no problems. Despite the emotional, social, and financial pressures involved when one adult is responsible for all child-rearing and household duties, the outcomes for most children are no different from those for children in two-parent households.

WIDOWED PARENTS
Some parents have found themselves to be lone parents through illness or sudden death. Single parents who have been widowed deal not only with the same issues as divorced or separated parents but with the grief associated with losing their life partner. Death often strikes suddenly, leaving the widowed person unprepared to cope with single parenting. There are very few supports for young widows or widowers raising children on their own and for most, it means redefining their life. A widow described her life as "walking on ice. You can walk along just like everyone else, but there are those days where you step on a crack and you don't know it until the cold slushy water washes over your head. Then you struggle out and keep walking. With time, the cracks may be spaced out a little further from each other, but they are always there." MacLean (2003: L9) states, "The thing about being a widow is being alone, being the only one responsible for everything and needing to ask for help in a way you never had to before." Teachers can be a lifeline in situations like these.

Ambert (2006) suggests the possibility that family formation via single parenting could become a far more functional alternative for children and adults in the future. This would be particularly so under the following circumstances:

1. If women earned incomes equal to those of men, then the poverty rate of families headed

Many single parents successfully raise happy well adjusted children.

by women would diminish substantially, and so would children's problems.

2. If young males were socialized to be nurturant and equally responsible for their offspring, then even children in one-parent families would have two parents invested in them and supporting them.

3. If society was willing to invest in children regardless of their parents' marital status, such a policy would prevent these children from crossing below the poverty line.

4. If social reproduction was valued by society and if what is now unpaid work was remunerated, mothers and their children would have more options.

5. If child-care centres of good quality were subsidized to meet the demand, more mothers could be employed full-time and without worrying about their children's safety. Furthermore, were such centres geared toward the education of children, the latter would benefit in terms of cognitive development.

INSIDE LOOK

I met Stephanie and her daughter, Madison, when my preschooler and I joined the centre. The staff introduced us to each other and it wasn't long before we realized that, as single mothers by choice, we were struggling with many of the same issues. Both of us were renting small but expensive apartments. We served on a newsletter committee at the centre and became very good friends over the next six months. When Stephanie's lease was coming up for renewal, she started to look for a bigger and less expensive residence. One morning she showed me a newspaper listing for a wonderful house with a garden in the back yard. If we combined our two incomes, we quickly calculated, we could afford to rent this house. Three years later, we continue to share the house with our two children. What started out as a financial decision turned into one of the major supports in my life! We are a family—not in the traditional sense but certainly in terms of the emotional support we give each other.

Most daycares deal with parents who have custody and parents who have access. Centres may have an important role to play with parents who have "supervised" access. Both the Children's Law Reform Act and the Child and Family Services Act provide for supervised access—that is, one parent's access to the child when the other is present. For many parents, supervised access means visiting a child at the custodial parent's home with some other adult present. This makes the relationship between the access parent and the child difficult, because they have no freedom to communicate without the third party's monitoring. If, however, the parent and the child could enjoy their time together in the friendly and stimulating environment that a daycare centre provides, the parent–child relationship may have a better chance of blossoming. Daycare centres are equipped to instruct access parents on how to parent, on how to play with children at age-appropriate levels, and how to effectively discipline without corporal punishment or deprivation. This could be done on a user-fee basis that permits the daycare centre to earn extra revenue without imposing an undue expense on the access parent.

Source: M. Bogoroch-Ditkofsky, *Daycare and the Law: A Guide for Canadian Child Care Programs and Other Non-Profit Boards* (Toronto: Child Care Initiatives Fund, Health and Welfare Canada, and Umbrella Central Daycare Services, 1991), p. 20. Used by permission.

6. Delaying motherhood until adulthood and greater maturity would be the last necessary ingredient to making single parenting more functional for children and their parents than it currently is.

ROLE OF THE TEACHER

- Teachers may first need to examine their own feelings and emotional reactions about divorce, separation, and single parenting. We bring our own histories to our teaching practice. Divorce or separation may trigger intense feelings and teachers need to make every effort to contain these to provide the best possible support to the families and their children. A positive and hopeful approach will always be best. Look for ways to see the strengths in families!

- Teachers should work to create a climate of trust so that parents feel comfortable about approaching them when issues arise.

- The child-care centre must be seen as a safe and stable place for the child and all family members. For children whose parents are in conflict, the child-care centre may be a respite from the conflict.

- Teachers need to learn the names of all significant members of the child's family since the names may not be the same. This is a simple gesture of courtesy. When appropriate, teachers should meet with the parents to discuss strategies for supporting the child through the transition if the parents are separating or divorcing.

- Although the details of a separation or divorce agreement may seem personal and private, some details should be shared with the centre. Teachers and supervisors need to know, for example, whether both parents have the right to make inquiries and be given information about the child, new contact information for the parent who may no longer be living in the home, whether both parents want to be informed of school events, who should be contacted during emergencies, etc.

- Unless the court orders otherwise, a spouse who is granted access to a child of the marriage has the right to make inquiries and to be given information.

- Separating or divorcing parents require nonjudgmental support from teachers, who should refrain from taking sides and instead maintaining a neutral position and focus on the best interests of the child. Avoid being drawn into taking sides or placing blame. Avoid reporting on the "other" parent. Parents need to respect the boundaries that need to be in place and reflect the limitations of our training.

- Parents may be too caught up in their own grief and anger to fully appreciate their child's needs. This does not mean that they are uncaring or unconcerned, only that their circumstances have left them feeling paralyzed and depressed.

- Ongoing communication between families and teachers is important. During this difficult time, teachers can advise parents of support groups or agencies that may be of assistance. Teachers must remember the limitations of their training and redirect family members to community counselling. Teachers can provide print resources about divorce, etc., for parents and these should be accessible in the Family Resource Area.

- If parents are interested in common issues, such a budgeting or preparing a will because of their changed circumstances, the centre could facilitate such workshops at the families' request or link families to community resources.

- In some situations and with permission of the parents, teachers may offer to share their insights about the child with social workers or psychologists who are working with him or her or attend counselling sessions with a child who may have lost a parent through divorce or death.

- One of the greatest challenges facing some newly separated or newly divorced parents is living on a reduced income. Some parents benefit from an extended fee-payment schedule. It is also important to recognize that some lone parents are not in any financial difficulty. Never make assumptions. If a parent is struggling financially be cautious about asking for extra money for field trips or special lessons offered in the centre.

- Depending on the circumstances, teachers may decide not to ask parents to contribute time and effort to centre activities. Additional responsibility or pressure may be the last thing these parents need. For others, involvement in the centre is a welcome relief from their day-to-day life.

- Parents who enter into joint-custody family living are generally anxious for the process to succeed, and clearly both parties are focused on providing a stable situation for their child. It takes a great deal of cooperation and coordination in order to experience success, and the teacher should look for opportunities to support all parties.

- Workshops may be provided to help families, especially blended families to create new family traditions. Having family members share their most significant traditions will be a memorable opportunity for sharing.

- Some lone parents may be lonely. They find themselves gradually excluded from contact with couples and at a loss to know how to handle holidays without a spouse. Notices about community activities such as meetings of Parents Without Partners (see below) or We Care (for those whose spouse has died) should be routinely posted. Organizations such as Big Brothers and Big Sisters may also provide much needed support to children, who may also be lonely.

ROLE OF THE TEACHER IN THE PLAYROOM

- Teachers can assist children by providing a stable environment and predictable routines.

- Teachers need to guard against feeling so sorry for the child that they become less insistent in maintaining expectations for routines and behaviour. Predictability and the security that can be found in routines is critical for the child.

- Teachers should be prepared for uncharacteristic or regressive behaviours on the part of the child (sucking thumb, wetting pants, and so on) and help families understand that these changes are not uncommon when children are dealing with stress.

- The book centre should have reading material for children that reflects all families, including books about children living in one-parent, divorced, separated, or joint-custody families. Many resources in this area are now available

- Though many children welcome an opportunity to discuss what is happening in their family, others are reluctant and withdraw. Teachers should take their cue from the child. Newman (1993: 121) advises teachers to "help the child to understand that anger is part of the process of grieving, a necessary part. Help them to separate their anger at the behaviour of a parent from the love they have for the person."

- Providing a "soft" space in the room where the child can go in order to self-regulate will be beneficial. The teacher may want to stay with the child and use this one-on-one time to talk, read, or just engage the child in conversations that have nothing to do with their situation. It is an opportunity to reinforce that the child is valued and cared for.

- Though it is important to keep the child busy and engaged, reasonable limits should be maintained. Teachers may wish to consider holding off on events that may further confuse or worry the child (for example, moving the child to another age group).

- When children ask questions about separation and divorce, teachers should provide age-appropriate information that is respectful of the parent's wishes and in the best interests of the child. Children need to understand why the divorce happened, and to hear the explanation in age-appropriate language.

- Teachers should reassure children that they are not to blame for the separation or divorce. Besides looking for opportunities to engage in one-on-one interaction with the child, teachers should plan activities (dramatic play, creative movement, music, water play, woodworking, art, puppetry, felt board stories, and so on) that allow for and encourage the expression of feelings.

- Having a bulletin board with photographs of all the families at the centre will help children see that their family is similar to others and may provide some comfort to them.

- Most children want to know what changes will take place in their lives. If the teacher is unsure of how to respond, she may relay the child's concerns to the parent (or parents).

Additionally, many children fear that they will not see the parent who leaves. Teachers can share this concern with the family if the child expresses it.

- In a joint-custody situation, effective communication is especially important. As children move back and forth between parental residences, it is easy to see how communication may break down. Creating a journal that stays in the child's cubby with important information may facilitate drop-off and pickup when both parents are involved and on different schedules.

- Having extra clothing or school supplies handy may support a family in transition; knowing the supplies are available at the centre can reduce the child's anxiety about not being prepared (e.g., on Pyjama Day having a few sets of "extras" may help any parent who has forgotten this special event).

- "A teacher can guide children to work through feelings by opening up an area for discussion and understanding and accepting a child's reactions: 'It can be pretty scary not to have both your daddy and your mommy living in your house together anymore.' 'Sometimes children get pretty mad at their mommy and daddy when they change a lot of things in their family.' 'You're going to your Dad's for Thanksgiving? Sometimes it is hard to do new things, but I'll bet you'll have fun'" (Gestwicki, 2004).

INSIDE LOOK

www.ourfamilywizard.com

Paul Volker, a parent in a blended family, has created an online calendar and message board where parents can make requests and leave information for each other, a data bank on each child, a log for recording expenses that are supposed to be shared, and a journal to record important events. The website costs $99US per year per parent, with free access to limited areas for children. It's also $99 per year for professionals such as mediators or lawyers. Grandparents and other interested third parties who just want to view information can register for $25 per year. All information is kept private. "It's a new and innovative use of technology in the family law area," says Jim Williams, a judge in the family division of the Supreme Court of Nova Scotia. The website gives people a practical tool to reduce conflict, and in many areas in the United States, judges order its use.

Source: Frey, 2002: K4.

Children themselves are often more aware and thoughtful than adults may realize. Teachers can learn from their wisdom. Here's what 12-year-old Reuven Scott had to say about his family in an article in *Canadian Living Magazine*: "I have two wonderful sisters, one older than me and one younger. My dad and mum are separated, but we all get along. I always think of my family as a circle, because when someone falls out of the circle there is always someone there to help them back in."

Parents Without Partners

"Parents Without Partners provides single parents and their children with an opportunity for enhancing personal growth, self-confidence, and sensitivity towards others by offering an environment for support, friendship, and the exchange of parenting techniques. . . . [It] is now the largest international, nonprofit membership organization devoted to the welfare and interests of single parents and their children" (Parents Without Partners, n.d.). Single parents may join one of approximately 400 chapters, whether they are male or female, custodial or noncustodial, separated, divorced, widowed, or never-married. There are 50,000 members in the United States and Canada, of which 55 percent are female and 45 percent are male. Ages range from 18–80 years and most participants have teenage children. All chapters, to comply with their PWP charters, run programs balanced among three areas: educational activities, family activities, and adult social and recreational activities. More information is available at **www.parentswithoutpartners.org**.

BLENDED FAMILIES

Julie and George have recently married. Both have been married before. Julie has two children, ages three and five, and George has a son, Brent, age nine. Brent lives with his mother but visits George and Julie every other weekend, one night every week, and for longer periods of time during the summer. Julie and George are considering having a child together.

In 2006, according to Statistics Canada, there were 261,000 married step families, 243,000 common law step families and 231,000 blended families (Statistics Canada, 2006c). Stepfamilies in North America still lack recognition and legitimacy, despite their huge presence in today's society (Church 2003: 56). Even though the traditional nuclear family (where children live with their two married parents) now represents only a minority of Canadian families, it still is seen as the "ideal" family. This bias even permeates professional literature on families. Researchers often focus on only the problematic aspects of stepfamilies, and Church (2003: 70) points out that most research has omitted cultural, sociological, and economic aspects: "it has focused primarily on white, middle-class, heterosexual, married families with a residential mother and stepfather." There have been studies that show couples with lower socioeconomic status are more likely to divorce than those with higher socioeconomic status (Ganong and Coleman 1994; Stone 1990), but corresponding studies have not been done in relation to stepfamilies even though these factors are likely to be as significant. The family's financial situation may also improve when two households come together but there may also be a lack of resources when child support payments or alimony are paid to the "first" relationship. Although second marriages are usually about as happy as first marriages, they tend to be slightly less stable. Riedman, Lamanna, and Nelson (2003: 512) show how the lack of a "cultural script" may play into this: "Relationships in immediate remarried families and with kin are often complex, yet there are virtually no social prescriptions and few consistent legal rules to clarify roles and relationships. The lack of cultural guidelines is clearest in the stepparent role." In addition to their role ambiguity, stepparents are often burdened by financial strains and rejection by their stepchildren.

Despite this, Ward (2002: 249) states, "One of the main difficulties in remarriage families is that there are too many candidates for the available roles. This fact affects the stepparent in particular. The children already have two biological parents and are not usually interested in replacing them. If the new spouse tries to take over the role of the parent of the same sex, he or she will meet resistance and resentment from the children. Loyalty issues are involved." Conflict can break out over many issues,

A blended family brought together these two boys of the same age.

from meals that are too different from what the children are used to eating, to behaviour guidance. A key time for discomfort is any special event involving the child. Guilt frequently plays a role in blended relationships. A divorced father who lives with his new wife's children and sees his biological children only intermittently may be especially prone to feelings of guilt.

One of the biggest challenges facing blended families is reconciling and harmonizing long-entrenched attitudes, values, and routines that may be at considerable variance. The newfound need to share power and decision-making can place further strain on relationships. Shifting roles among blended family members can be a source of apprehension and confusion. Children may compete with children of the stepparent over the sharing of space, toys, and, most important, their biological parent. Parents in blended situations may fantasize that everyone will be accepting and life will be harmonious—a fantasy in direct competition with that of their children who fantasize that their biological parents will get back together again. "Children in blended families experience higher levels of parental conflict than do other children. This is because they encounter more "intrahousehold" conflict than children in original families as well "interhousehold" conflict, thus having two sources of possible family conflict. This is likely to increase their stress level and lead to concern about the negative outcomes regarding child well-being" (Couchenour and Chrisman, 2000: 97).

Jennifer Jenkins, a professor of human development and applied psychology at the University of Toronto, collaborated with researchers in Rochester and Britain to study 296 children from

127 families in England. Studying the families over a period of time allowed researchers to see the extent to which children and adult partners influence each other. Children who saw their parents arguing about them showed increasing behaviour problems at school including defiance, impulsiveness, shouting, and aggression. In turn, those problems led to more marital conflict at home. The results were even more pronounced in families with step-children. What's new about this research is the finding that it is a two way street, with challenging children often provoking arguments between their parents. She states: "kids who are a bit more difficult create more stresses in a family and more stresses in a family contribute to kids being more difficult. It's absolutely not about blame or people feeling responsible. It's about complicated interactions" (Gordon, 2005: D5).

ROLE OF THE TEACHER

- Keep the lines of communication open with all of the members of this extended family.

- Learn parents' names. Always check the names of the children and the parents, because they may not be the same.

- Depending on the conditions of custody, biological parents should not be excluded. Teachers may communicate with biological parents by phone, by letter, or by inviting them to visit the child at the centre. Some blended families may all want to come to the centre together. Teachers will know that maintaining a healthy relationship with the ex-spouse will help to make the transition as smooth as possible for everyone involved.

- Link families with others in the same situation, if appropriate and desired

- Make sure that notices about relevant local agencies or resources are posted for families to see.

- Help parents find time for themselves, one centre has a *Date Night* where the children sleep over at the centre and the parents have time for themselves.

ROLE OF THE TEACHER IN THE PLAYROOM

- Teachers shouldn't automatically expect problems from a blended-family situation. Many children make a successful transition. A child with involved parents and stepparents is twice blessed!

- Teachers should observe the children closely and be active listeners, helping them to articulate their feelings. Help children understand that it takes time for a new blended family to get to know one another. A common issue for children is the embarrassment over the divorce and remarriage. It is important to acknowledge the child's feelings.

- Eliminate the use of terms like broken home that may offend remarried or single families. Ask the parents to determine whether reconstituted, step, or blended are preferred terms. Children can devalue themselves if they hear terms that appear to be derogatory. Other children might conclude that some students are different and inferior (Hepworth Berger, 2004: 118).

- Confusion is the order of the day for some children who have to learn to become members of two households and transitions to one of these homes at the end of the week often happen in child-care centres. Teachers can help the child to organize and prepare for this adjustment.

- Teachers should be sensitive to the fact that the child's order in the family has likely changed. It's a big transition to go from being the "baby" of the family to being a middle child, or to go from having only sisters to having a brother as well. These adjustments to new siblings often are brought on abruptly in contrast to the gradual adjustment of a newborn sibling.

- In the playroom, teachers should encourage discussion and provide books, tapes, and other materials that send positive messages about blended families. Teachers should avoid material that depicts stepparents in a negative way.

- Provide opportunities through sensory experiences, art, drama, etc., for children to express their emotions.

- The stepmother or stepfather might be invited to the playroom to share a talent or interest, or just to visit. Let the child be the tour guide.

- Be aware of when transitions are taking place in the child's life (visitation, changes in their schedule) and be sensitive to their needs.

BOOKS FOR CHILDREN

Two Homes, by C. Masurel

When My Parents Forgot How to Be Friends, by J. Moore-Mallinos

The Not So Wicked Stepmother, by L. Boyd

Amber Waiting, by N. Gregory

A Day with Dad, by B. Homberg

Do I Have A Daddy? A Story about a Single Parent Child, by J. Warren Lindsay

Daddy's Getting Married, by J. Moore-Mallinos

BOOKS FOR ADULTS

Creative Interventions for Children of Divorce, by L. Lowensiten

The Practical Guide to Weekend Parenting, by D. Hewitt

Remarried With Children: 10 Secrets for Successfully Blending and Extending Your Family, by B. LeBey

Single Parenting That Works: 6 Keys to Raising Happy Healthy Children in a Single Parent Home, by K. Leman

Single By Chance, Mothers by Choice, by R. Hertz

Stay Close: 40 Clever Ways To Connect With Kids When You're Apart, by T. Gemelke

My Father Married Your Mother: Writers Talk About Stepparents, Stepchildren, and Everyone In Between, by A. Burt

NEWCOMER FAMILIES

IMMIGRANT FAMILIES

Miguel came to Canada from Portugal. He was sponsored by his brother, who had come several years earlier, and he left behind his wife and three children. More than two years passed before Miguel was able to afford to bring his family to Canada and to complete all the government requirements. The separation was difficult for the entire family. Adjusting to a new environment has been particularly challenging for his wife, Maria. Though there is a large Portuguese community where they live, she misses her parents and siblings.

Why do people move? What makes them uproot and leave everything they've known for a great unknown beyond the horizon? Why enter a jungle of foreignness when everything is new, strange, and difficult? The answer is the same the world over: people move in the hope of a better life.

—Yann Martel, *Life of Pi*

MULTICULTURALISM IN CANADA

There are significant dates in government policies that have impacted immigration to Canada. In 1967, immigration policy was changed so that preferential entry based on the place of origin replaced the points system. In 1971, Canada was the first country to adopt multiculturalism as an official policy. All Canadians are guaranteed equality before the law and equality of opportunity regardless of their place of origin. Canada affirmed the value and dignity of all citizens regardless of their racial or ethnic origins, their language, or their religious affiliation. In 1977, Parliament passed the Canadian Human Rights Act barring discrimination on the basis of race, sex, age, national or ethnic origin, colour, and religion. In 1982 The Charter of Rights and Freedom was adopted and, in 1985, The Multicultural Act was passed. The Multicultural Act recognized the existence of communities and the use of languages other than English and French; it also acknowledged the freedom of those who want to preserve and enhance their cultural heritage.

Moving to a new country is never easy. Differences between customs from the "old" country and life in Canada may be a source of conflict in immigrant families. Ward (2002: 40) says,

The fact of immigration affects families and their relationships. First, traditional values are challenged by Canadian ways. Second, immigration may mean separation from family members. Female domestic workers may leave children and extended family members behind when they come to Canada on temporary visas. Some form family-like relationships with others in their situation. The immigrant woman who comes to Canada with her husband's family and leaves her own relatives behind in the old country may be especially isolated and have few sources of support if she has conflicts with his parents or brothers. It is even more difficult for her if she does not know English or French because she cannot access services outside her ethnic community. . . . Third, many immigrants have seen Canada as a 'promised land.' Once they arrive, however, they may face economic hardship. Professionals may not have credentials or experience that is recognized in Canada and . . . those without much education often face poverty.

It is also relevant to note that when we talk about problems being associated with being

TABLE 9.8	IMMIGRANT POPULATION BY PLACE OF BIRTH, 2006 CENSUS, CANADA
PLACE OF BIRTH	**POPULATION**
United States	250,535
Central and South America	381,165
Caribbean and Bermuda	317,765
Europe	2,278,345
United Kingdom	579,625
Other Northern and Western Europe	489,540
Eastern Europe	511,095
Southern Europe	698,080
Africa	374,565
Asia and the Middle East	2,525,160
West-Central Asia and the Middle East	370,515
Eastern Asia	874,370
Southeast Asia	560,995
Southern Asia	719,275
Oceania and Other	59,410
Total	6,186,950

Source: Statistics Canada 2006 Census of Population, Canada; http://www40.statcan.ca/l01/cst01/demo34a.htm

My husband has been unemployed for over a year now. He had a very good position as an administrator with lots of benefits when he was in Hong Kong. The first year we were here, he found a job as a clerk. He was getting less than half of what he was making before. . . . But then the company went bankrupt, and he was unemployed. He's so depressed now that he is making me down too. He also kept blaming me for making him come here. We've had a lot of fights, and I'm not sure what will happen next. We talked about separating. I'm just living day-to-day at the moment.

Source: Man, 2001: 427.

I am an ECE student in a program in Vancouver, British Columbia. I was born in Iraq and my family moved to Canada when I was six. I have fallen in love with a man who is Hindu from India. We are becoming more serious with each other although my family does not know anything about him. I have recently asked my mother what would happen if I just happened to meet a Hindu and wanted to marry him. She became very upset and when my boyfriend spoke to his family about him marrying a Muslim the reaction was the same. We are both really torn between wanting to be respectful of our families and their values and our love for each other. For now, we continue to see each other in secret but we want to marry and have children. Will our decision tear our families apart?

Source: An ECE Student

exposed to a new language, we are talking about two ideas: language acquisition and the ways of speaking unique to the new culture. Both of these can delay the adaptation process. Harper (in Samovar et al., 2007: 352) summarizes this view when she notes, "lack of language skills is a strong barrier to effective cultural adjustment and communication whereas lack of knowledge concerning the ways of speaking of a particular group will reduce the level of understanding that we can achieve with our counterparts."

Recent immigrants are more likely to live in three-generation households than people born in Canada. Such households are most common in British Columbia and Ontario where there are areas with high concentrations of newcomers. Those coming from developing regions, especially South Asia, prefer to live with relatives, even in crowded quarters, than to live with non-relatives. Also, many older individuals have come to join their younger relatives. They are not eligible for welfare or government pensions for a considerable length of time after arrival. If they do not have financial resources, they may have no choice where to live. There is also a growing concern about the access to services for new Canadians. The inability to communicate in English or French and a lack of knowledge about the services and where they can be accessed is a problem. For example, new immigrants also feel intimidated in situations where their lack of English makes it difficult to communicate, such as in an emergency room of a hospital when interpreters may not be available and staff do not understand their cultural practices.

Paul Anisef and Kenise Murphy Kilbride of the Joint Centre of Excellence for Research on Immigration and Settlement and Joanna Ochocka and Rich Janzen of the Centre for Research and Education in Human Services completed "Parenting Issues of Newcomer Families in Ontario," a study which explored the issues faced by immigrant parents within diverse ethnic backgrounds in

As a South Asian ECE student, I have had the opportunity of learning in a variety of environments. As a student in India, I was able to gain insight into the ethnocultural differences that students bring into the classroom. My experiences in both a developing country and in the Canadian education system have given me the advantage of being able to appreciate the best of both worlds as well as broadening my mind to various new methods of learning and teaching. The ECE program gave me the opportunity to integrate theory and the practical application of working with young children and their families in a manner that is child-focused and not teacher-directed. I understand the importance of understanding and appreciating the individual child within the context of family, culture, and society and treating each family with due respect.

Source: Kanika Mehta, ECE graduate

Toronto, Ottawa, and Waterloo. The study focused on families in 12 language groups who had arrived in the past three years.

Their findings showed that most participants were optimistic of their children's future in Canada. Participants often said that they were hoping their children would have a better life than they themselves had. These high expectations were held despite the fact that many parents were struggling, even making person sacrifices in order to provide for their families here in Canada. Study participants put major emphasis on education and school. They often found a second job or borrowed money to help children concentrate on education. A significant number of parents, however, also expressed fear of their sons' involvement in drugs and violence and their daughters' in pre-marital sexual relationships.

Newcomer parents, especially fathers, believed their job-related difficulties since their arrival had negatively influenced their roles as parents. Their decreased job-related status and financial constraints had decreased their self confidence and lowered their esteem as parents. On the other hand, a large number of fathers also indicated that their families had become closer and benefited because they were at home more (if unemployed) or that their diminished capacity to earn money had led to more mutual support within the family. Parents whose culture was very different from Canadian culture expressed greater concern about the risk of their children's rejection of their inherited culture and assimilation into the Canadian culture. Some parents believed their cultures would be better preserved by limiting contact with other groups and promoting their distinctive identity as a cultural

group. Others believed their children should learn to function successfully in both cultures by interacting with people from both.

Recommendations emerged in 12 areas where families felt the need for additional support to enhance fulfilling their responsibilities as parents: education, language support (English learning and translation), culture, first language and religion, extracurricular activities for children, family housing, employment-related supports, specific parenting support, holistic family support, mental health, collaboration among service providers and funders, and further research and information. Some recommendations are in areas where most parents articulate the need for assistance, such as finding child care and housing that is both good and affordable or successfully guiding teenagers.

REFUGEE FAMILIES

Anayanci has been in Canada for three years. She, her husband, and their two sons fled El Salvador when she found out that she was about to be apprehended by the local militia for her antigovernment activities. Her brother was shot in front of her parents just hours before they fled the country. With no relatives in Canada, the family came to Toronto and found housing. Anayanci's husband had trouble adjusting to a new society. Unable to find work, he returned to El Salvador, leaving Anayanci with the two boys.

The United Nations defines a refugee as "any person who, by reason of a well-founded fear of persecution for reasons of race, religion, nationality, membership in a particular social group or political opinion, (a) is outside the country of his

In my first placement, we had a new child come into the kindergarten room at the same time that I arrived. He was new to Canada and new to child-care centres. He had some problems with language, not necessarily understanding but more so expressing himself in positive ways. I took it upon myself to help Daniel adjust. I had cut and laminated different emotion cards (a picture and a written word) and action cards so that at any point of the day, he could point to the card that best represented what he was feeling. By the end of my seven-week placement, he had improved so much! Instead of lashing out and throwing toys, he started to tell me his feelings instead. It was a great feeling of accomplishment for me but Daniel benefited most. He was able to integrate more successfully into the room and with his peers.

Source: Anik van Draanen, ECE graduate

These cards provide a visual cue for children who are English learners. These cards are also used with children with other special needs such as those with autism.

Courtesy of Lynn Wilson

(her) nationality and is unable, or by reason of such fear, is unwilling to avail himself (herself) of the protection of that country, or (b) not having a country of nationality, is outside the country of his (her) former habitual residence and is unable, or by reason of such fear, is unwilling to return to that country" (in James, 1989: 38). There are 18 million refugees around the world, most of whom have found refuge in a neighbouring country. Only a minority seek asylum in Western countries.

Many refugee families that arrive in Canada will have witnessed atrocities, lost family members, or lived in camps for long periods of time. As Fantino (1993: 5) observes:

It is only natural that [refugee] children, along with their families, will go through a process of mourning [their] losses; however, the grieving

Sagher Chatta's children are just preschoolers, but the Pakistani immigrant is bracing himself for "big time" culture clash down the road. Once his daughter, 4, and son, 18 months are in full time school, they may balk at speaking Urdu at home. They may pull away from some of the Muslim traditions they are being raised with. In a decade, they'll be forging their own identities, merging their Pakistani roots with Canadian teen culture. He's prepared to negotiate and give the kids freedom to make their own choices. But he realizes it might not be easy. That's one reason that about 40 other men have assembled at the Ahmadiyya Muslim Community Canada Mosque in Maple, Ontario. Inside, fathers, grandfathers, and young men hoping one day to become dads gather in the men's prayer hall to participate in a six week program on fatherhood run by dads and for men only. During the 90 minute evening sessions, the men discuss such topics as reading and playing with young children, discipline without physical force, postpartum depression, and the cultural and spiritual aspects of child rearing. Five of the six sessions are in Urdu and the accompanying workbook *What A Difference A Dad Makes* is also in Urdu. It is also available in nine other languages. For the first time the program is being delivered in a place of worship, in hopes of reaching more dads who need support. It will soon be launched in a synagogue and in Sikh and Hindu temples. Adjusting can be particularly jolting for fathers raised in cultures where extended families were the main source of support and advice, and where fathers' roles were primarily as authoritarians and breadwinners. In Canada, they are expected to be nurturers and equal partners in child rearing while also trying to find work and settle the family. Often, they have lost their economic and social status. They may face discrimination. It is not uncommon for their wives to find employment more quickly, and establish a social circle faster. They watch their kids soak up the new language and culture and quickly become translators for their parents.

Source: A. Gordon, "Immigrant Men Learn How to Broaden Paternal Role." *The Toronto Star*. May 17, 2008. L1.

process in refugee children is seldom recognized as such, in part because of the myth of the resilient and adaptable child, and in part because children in general do not express their sadness, their homesickness, in words; [instead] they act, they behave or misbehave, they draw, they dream or have nightmares.

The Canadian Centre for Victims of Torture outlines the issue of children and torture. It is shocking to associate children with torture. It is, however, a reality that children suffer from oppression, war, and torture directly or indirectly. In the twentieth century, children have increasingly become the target of oppressive regimes. It is alarming to comprehend the magnitude of the phenomenon; children make up half the world's refugee population. Organized violence can affect children in numerous ways. Direct forms of torture used on adults have also been carried out on children: kidnapping; rape; forced labour and executions; and witnessing scenes of extreme violence such as murder, rape, beatings, or torture of others, including one's parents. A situation of war, fre-

quently experienced by refugees, has a disorganizing and traumatizing effect on the entire family. Trauma of this sort, occurring before or after a child's birth, can limit or damage the parenting skills of the parents. Parents may be preoccupied, depressed, anxious, in mourning, or otherwise rendered incapable of properly caring for their child or children as a result of the trauma.

Few early childhood educators are prepared for the impact of dealing with families who have been confined to camps, separated from their loved ones, or subjected to the threat of military or civilian violence. "It is estimated that 50 percent of the people living in refugee camps are children, many of whom have spent their entire lives there" (Fantino, 1993: 2). Children and youths who have lived through a war may have been traumatized directly or indirectly and may exhibit a wide range of symptoms. This variation of symptoms depends on the nature of the trauma, the child's developmental stage, the child's gender, the dynamics of the child's family and available supports, and the child's personality. These children may demonstrate

In the multicultural city of Toronto, many children come from different cultural and ethnic backgrounds. Because of the different perspectives regarding respect for teachers in class and the concept of teachers' authority, Chinese children are usually very quiet. They may listen to teachers without actively responding to the teacher's questions. I found that both in my college classrooms and in early childhood environments this was very noticeable. In an interactive teaching environment like here in Canada, passive students may make teachers who don't know this cultural difference feel disrespected or even frustrated. They may label these children or students as unresponsive, shy, quiet, or unable to talk. I grew up with the belief "Modesty helps one to go forward, whereas conceit makes one lag behind." Like many others, my parents and teachers reminded me not to be proud of myself, there was always someone better than me. Because of this influence, I grew up into a person without high self-esteem like many other Chinese children. So, teachers, please balance the power you have over children according to their cultural differences and their parents' expectations.

Source: Hua, ECE student

numerous symptoms such as recurring nightmares and they may have trouble distinguishing between reality and fantasy. For children, exposure to traumatic experiences can create anxieties and insecurities that cause them to perceive every aspect of the world as being unsafe and frightening. It is important for healing to take place in a supportive environment such as within the realm of the family. Healing is dependent on the family's remaining structure and its protective and nurturing qualities. Healing for the child is also dependent on the degree to which the family adapts to the new culture and,

FIGURE 9.3 REFUGEE CHILD'S DRAWING

A study from the NLSCY from 1994 to 1998 found that overall, children of immigrant parents started school with less-developed skills in reading, writing, and mathematics than did their classmates with Canadian-born parents. However, with each passing year, they made gains in overcoming this disadvantage. In fact, their performance generally reached, or even exceeded, the performance of children of Canadian-born parents before they completed elementary school. Children from immigrant families in which the mother tongue was one of the official languages were in a better position when starting school and were able to catch up to children with Canadian-born parents by age nine. Children of parents with high levels of education had above-average performance in school according to the study. Generally, teachers rated girls' performance better than boys' during elementary school. On average, girls were 11 percent more likely to be considered near the top of the class or above the middle in reading, 17 percent more likely in writing, and as likely as boys in mathematics.

Source: Statistics Canada, 2001b.

in turn, the degree to which the child adjusts to a new life—at school, with peers, and with a new culture and language.

The Vancouver Association for Survivors of Torture says, "Talking about these traumatic experiences is not a threat to their psychological well-being, nor a challenge to their ability to 'grow out' of those experiences. On the contrary, children may need validation of those experiences, support and help to learn how to cope with the memories of traumatic experiences" (DeAndrade, 1992: 10).

Despite their often high educational qualifications, many immigrant parents are able to find employment only in the low-paying service sector. This has an enormous impact on the family unit as skilled professionals find it necessary to take work in low-paying, menial positions.

The lack of accessible, affordable, high-quality child care is a major problem facing immigrant families. Parents who are able to obtain a subsidized space may have difficulty coordinating their schedules with that of the child-care centre, especially if they are involved in shift work. Teachers can support parents by supplying them with "basic facts about sources of information on employment, the evaluation of foreign credentials, training in job-seeking skills, upgrading and so forth" (Murphy Kilbride, 1994: 11).

The NLSCY shows that immigrant children have fewer emotional and behavioural problems than children born in Canada—despite the fact that almost 30 percent of immigrant children live in poverty, an environment which is almost always associated with poor mental health. Furthermore, immigrant children come from families that are less dysfunctional and whose parents are in better mental health (National Research Conference, 1998: 103).

ROLE OF THE TEACHER

- Teachers need to know the steps involved with culture shock and be sensitive to the symptoms that children may be experiencing. Teachers should also be aware of their own reactions to each family's story, particularly those who have come from war torn countries. You may well be overwhelmed by the trauma the family has suffered and may need to seek support for yourself.

- Some families may want to maintain traditional ways while others may want their children to quickly assimilate into the "dominant" culture, it is important for the teacher to understand how she can best support each of these families.

- Listen to what the families have to say about their dreams for themselves and their children. This insight will provide you with opportunities to provide meaningful support.

- A family who lived in a rural community may be dealing with the additional stresses and confusion of adjusting to urban life for the first time.

- Find out which families and children have never experienced a cold climate and help prepare them for winter by setting up a winter clothing exchange program.

EXHIBIT 9.5 SUPPORTING IMMIGRANT OR REFUGEE FAMILIES: AN INFORMATION CHECKLIST

Meyers (2007) provides a checklist of questions for teachers who are working with young immigrant or refugee children.

- **Are the parents alive and are they together with the children?** I have had students from Hong Kong with an absent parent, as well as children from war-torn countries, whose parent have been killed, imprisoned, or are missing.
- **Have the siblings been separated? How long and where?** Often, one child is given over to a trusted relative who is ready to immigrate. In other cases, an older sibling has come ahead and paved the way for the rest of the family. Sometimes, it takes years before the whole family can be reunited.
- **Have all the siblings had schooling? In which languages?** Many older students have had some training in English in their homeland but usually the lessons were grammar-based. Students may read and write basic English but they do not understand the rapid pace of our speech and they have lack experience speaking in English. Younger siblings may not even know our alphabet system. Moreover, students who have resided in several countries often have learned to read and write in a language that is different from the language(s) spoken in their homes.
- **Has the family joined friends or relatives in the new country?** A family is fortunate if they have relatives or associates who can assist with translations and explain our customs. Such assistance helps to reduce the initial impact of culture shock that all immigrants experience. (Many of us have heard the story about the Vietnamese family who had just got settled in their new home only to be terrorized on their first night by masked hooligans who kept up a steady barrage of screaming and knocking on the door. It was Halloween.
- **What is the family's immigration status?** A refugee is initially not allowed to work in this country and that may give you some indication of the family's financial status. It is especially important to know this information if there are several children within that family who may be asked for trip monies.
- **Is there someone in the home who can speak any English?** If a student is highly motivated and if there is someone in the home who can assist with homework, then language acquisition can be speeded up. It is also important to know if school notices will be understood in the home.
- **Is anyone in the household employed?** The D. family from Egypt had seven children. The older two went to work to support their mum and siblings. They spoke little English and did not get a chance to learn English on the job. The younger children, however, acquired English rapidly and became the family translators. During the first winter the children did not have appropriate clothes so the teacher introduced the family to the local Red Cross.
- **Does the family have knowledge of its ethnic associations in our city?** Knowing where to turn for assistance and advice is essential for all of us, and is even more so for a new immigrant family with few cultural connections to this new country.
- **Has the child witnessed or been the victim of any trauma before or during the move to our country?** Information from parents can indicate if a student(s) has either witnessed or been a victim of trauma. It is better to ascertain such information and be forewarned, than to observe signs of post trauma stress syndrome PTSS in a child during class. Symptoms may include a lack of affect, extreme behaviors (passivity or aggression), incontinence, or poor social skills.
- **Is the family here for business, for example, a three-year term?** The motivation to learn to communicate in a new language may not be as great if children think they will be 'going home' soon.
- **Does a family member have previous experience with North American culture and/or education?** A family member with knowledge of North American norms will be a great asset to his/her family in every way.

Source: From MEYERS. Teaching to Diversity: Teaching and Learning in the Multi-Ethnic Classroom © 2007, Irwin, a part of Cengage Learning, Inc. Reproduced by permission. www.cengage.com/permissions

Role of the Teacher in the Playroom

- Green (1998: 31) cautions early childhood educators to realize that "agreeable" refugee children may be needier than teachers believe. Statistics show that 78 percent of immigrant and refugee children have short- or long-term problems in psycho-emotional or academic functioning.

- Some children will benefit from an extended orientation to the program with a family member staying with them for a longer period of time. Each child will respond differently to the new setting.

- Parents and children might be unfamiliar with the English language. Teachers can reassure a child and at the same time demonstrate respect for his/her identity by learning a few key words in the child's first language, or by using student translators informally for minor things: to reassure, give directions or state procedures. Do not use student interpreters when there is access to staff interpreters or ethnic agencies. There may be information that is shared that the parent may not want a student or a sibling who has greater English fluency to know.

- Foster an atmosphere of acceptance in class, in which children feel comfortable expressing themselves in their home languages. Teachers can also get parent support to include books and materials that reflect students' heritages. Children benefit enormously when they are invited to participate in an ambience of respect and friendliness.

- Help the children find ways to contribute to the program in significant and meaningful ways and focus on the child's strengths.

- Naptime may frighten children, and teachers should be prepared for this. Don't belittle children's behaviours, listen patiently to what the children say (or ask parent(s)) and take the fears seriously.

- Learn breathing and relaxation techniques. Yoga For Children before naptime would be a great opportunity for the child to collect himself.

- Teachers should be prepared to adapt to family expectations for toileting (for example, washing rather than wiping, using only one hand) and feeding routines and dietary requirements.

- Many children act out their feelings during their play situations and teachers can use the observed behaviours to deal with issues at a more appropriate time. The dramatic play area should reflect the many ways in which food is prepared.

- Understand that many families may have remedies for illnesses with which you may not be familiar. This is a great opportunity to learn more about health practices in other cultures.

- Ethnic associations can contribute flyers and notices in the students' home languages regarding city agencies, food banks, and employment centers and adult English classes. These should be displayed prominently for all families. Create a "What's In Our Community" booklet for families new to the centre to help them access the resources they need. Translate it if possible.

Blackburn (1999) states:

Meaningful community events based on the cultural norms can also help to maintain hope and stability in an ever-changing environment. Even in the midst of war and poverty, traditional cultural rituals, celebrations, and gatherings can be adjusted to the conditions to enable individuals and families to either maintain or reestablish a sense of community and a sense of self. The development of a sense of purpose and meaning for the suffering is an important ingredient in healing and reinforcing suffering. Children and families often need guidance, support, and a format to initiate or enhance this healing process. This is the final stage of recovery. To move beyond the pain and devastation, individuals must be able to generate reasons to endure their losses and painful history and a hope for the future.

Dotsch (1994: 25–26) suggests a number of strategies that teachers can adopt during this difficult time. With the first separation from the parent, symptoms of extreme anxiety may occur, such as screaming, vomiting, and shaking. In some cases it may be necessary to recall the parent. Anger, too, may be displayed, as well as crying, or great despondency. When a child exhibits this behaviour, the teacher must approach the child slowly and gradually, offering gestures of comfort only when the child is ready to allow them. Sometimes it may be another child who will fulfill this role; but if effective strategies are implemented, as confidence comes, the child will begin to play with toys, allow a teacher to help, and accept food.

Materials translated into a variety of languages helps families stay connected.

The following recommendations, made by Bernhard and Freire (1994), will give teachers a better understanding of how to facilitate the adjustment and recovery process of refugee families.

1. Child-care registration forms should be modified to include pertinent questions about family background and status in Canada.

2. Educators need professional development time to upgrade their education and better equip themselves to respond to the needs of the refugee population.

3. ECE outcomes and competencies should stress preparation to enable caregivers to work with populations of different ethnolinguistic back-

INSIDE LOOK

Three-year-old Ly Ly can hear the noise as she nears the room. She doesn't know what to expect, but her mother has told her that she is now old enough to go to "school." A strange-looking woman has come close to her and is saying something she doesn't understand. She hides her head in her mother's skirt because the noise and confusion are overwhelming. Some bigger boys race by and she begins to cry. Her mother looks very uncomfortable and embarrassed. The teacher has told her that it will be easier for Ly Ly if she leaves quickly. The mother hesitates because she has never left her daughter before. She departs with tears in her eyes as Ly Ly screams, cries, and kicks the door. When the mother tries to go back, she is told through a crack in the door that she really should leave because she is making her daughter more upset. Ly Ly can see and hear her mother through the crack in the door. Maybe her mother will never come back and she will be trapped with these strange people forever. Suddenly, another adult pulls her away from the door. Ly Ly frantically tries to escape but is no match for the much stronger teacher.

So many things have changed in Ly Ly's life—her home, her toys, the place where she sleeps, even the people with whom she lives. If only the parent had been encouraged to stay; if only one of the teachers had been able to speak some Vietnamese so that Ly Ly could feel more secure; if only the teacher had had some training in the experience of separation and how the trauma of immigration affects children.

Source: From "Supporting the New Immigrant/Refugee Family in Child Care," by J. Dotsch, *Interaction* 8, no. 2, Summer 1994. Reprinted by permission of the Canadian Chld Care Federation.

grounds. In the case of the refugee population, training and education need to address post-traumatic stress disorder and other problems associated with the refugee experience.

4. In their practicum, students should have appropriate supervision while working with children of refugees. Caregivers need to be made aware of the particular needs of refugee families and children. They need to be aware too of their own important position as potential family stabilizers.

5. ECE programs should include education on cross-cultural and bilingual child-rearing practices; on the value of first-language maintenance and second-language learning; and on the stages of post traumatic stress disorder.

In conclusion, Nirdosh (1998: 5) summarizes the situation succinctly: "The refugee children and parents we encounter are survivors of extreme situations. It is important to acknowledge the strengths and resilience they possess—Perhaps in our lifetime, the limits of our strength may never be so challenged. . . . A system or organization which neglects to sensitize its staff to become aware of the possible challenges and implications of working with refugee children and their families is likely to re-victimize this group. You can make a difference!"

The Mosaic Centre, Calgary, AB

The Mosaic Centre is a family resource centre, hosted by the Calgary Immigrant Aid Society (CIAS), for immigrant and refugee families with children age six and under. Developed with input from community agencies, community members, staff, and consultants, the centre provides multitiered preventive and intervention services. The partners in this project share the belief that the health and well-being of young children need to be addressed within the framework of the family and the community. The Mosaic Centre is designed to ensure easy access to direct services that are culturally sensitive and adapted to specific needs of the population. A wide range of programs is provided to support the family as a unit as well as the individual health, educational, and psychosocial needs of parents and children. The use of first language is extensive in all program aspects. There is a well-equipped multi-age playroom, as well as an open space for large motor activities, comfortable spaces for adults to sit and talk, and a kitchen for preparation of snacks. The Saturday Morning Playgroup has worked well in attracting immigrant fathers and their children. Fathers have appreciated the choice and the range of activities, and the opportunity to socialize with other fathers.

BOOKS FOR CHILDREN

Our New Home: Immigrant Children Speak, by E. Hearn and M. Milne

Being Muslim: A Groundwood Guide, by H. Siddiqui

The Best Eid Ever, by A. Mobin-Uddin

INSIDE LOOK

Teresa Ingles makes her living caring for young children in her southeast Vancouver home. She learned the skills needed for family home day care through Vancouver Community College. But because she comes from El Salvador and didn't speak English well at the time, the college taught her in Spanish. The VCC program—also delivered in such languages as Vietnamese, Cantonese, and Punjabi—is just one example of the innovative work being done at BC's 28 public post-secondary institutions. VCC's Gyda Chud and Christine Blackmore of the Westcoast Child Care Resource Centre state that 150 immigrant women have been taught to care for preschoolers in their homes. "We used a mentor model," said Chud, the college's senior coordinator of early childhood care and education programs. "We found somebody within the language community who preferably had a child-care background but, if not, had a related kind of background. We partnered that person with an experienced family child-care instructor and they worked together to prepare the materials." The program—seemingly the only one of its kind in Canada—is in its fifth year.

Source: Wigod, 2000.

In The Small, Small Night, by J. Kurtz

Our Global Community Series, by L. Easterling

Our New Home: Immigrant Children Speak, by E. Hearn and M. Milne

Making It Home: Real Life Stories from Children Forced To Flee, by B. Naidoo

From Far Away, by Robert Munsch

Hannah Is My Name: A Young Immigrant Story, by B. Yang

BOOKS FOR ADULTS

English Language Learners: The Essential Guide, by D. Freeman and Y. Freeman

Empowering Children through Art and Expression, by B. St. Thomas and P. Johnson

Let's Celebrate Canada's Special Days, by C. Parry

Refugees in a Global Era, by P. Marflett

REFERENCES

Aboriginal Healing Foundation. 2002. Available at http://www.ahf.ca/english/residential_resources.shtml.

Abraham, C. 1999. "The Kids (of Divorce) Are All Right." *Globe and Mail*. 11 September.

Adopt Ontario. 2008. "Post Adoption Support." Available at https://www.adoptontario.ca/howtoadopt.post_adoption_support.aspx.

Alexander, C.S., and B. Guyer. 1993. "Adolescent Pregnancy: Occurrence and Consequences." *Pediatric Annals* 22: 85–88.

Ambert, A. 2006. *One-Parent Families: Characteristics, Causes, Consequences, and Issues*. Ottawa: The Vanier Institute of the Family.

Archibald, L. 1993. Oral Traditions: A Multi-Disciplinary Conference. Saskatoon, 28–30 October.

Arnup, K. 1995. *Lesbian Parenting: Living with Pride and Prejudice*. Charlottetown: Gynergy.

———. 2003. "Parenting in the 21st Century." Available at http://www.carleton.ca/cu/research/spring2001/article4.html.

Azar, B. 1999. "Foster Children Get a Taste of Stability." *American Psychological Association*. Available at http://www.apa.org/monitor/nov95/orphana.html.

Ball, J. 2008. "Policies and Practice Reforms to Promote Positive Transitions to Fatherhood among Aboriginal Young Men." *Horizons: Government of Canada Policy Research Initiative* 10 (1): 52–59.

———. In press for 2009. "Indigenous Fathers' Involvement in Reconstituting 'circles of care'." *American Journal of Community Psychology*.

Ball, J., and R.T. George. 2006. "Policies and Practices Affecting Aboriginal Fathers' Involvement with their Children." In J.P. White, S.K. Wingert, P. Maxim, and D. Beavon, eds., *Aboriginal Policy Research: Moving Forward, Making a Difference*. Toronto: Thompson Educational Press.

Ball, J., C. Roberge, L. Joe, and R. George. 2007. "Fatherhood: Indigenous Men's Journeys." Available at http://ecdip.org/docs/pdf/IF%204%20pg%20summary.pdf.

Belanger, A. 1999. *Report on the Demographic Situation in Canada, 1998–1999: Current Demographic Analysis*. Catalogue No. 91-209-XPE. Ottawa: Statistics Canada.

Bernhard, J., and M. Freire. 1994. "Latino Refugee Children: Families of War and Persecution in the ECE System." *Interaction* 8 (2). Summer.

Bernhard, J.K., L. Lefebvre, G. Chud, and R. Lange. 1995. *Paths to Equity: Cultural, Linguistic and Racial Diversity in Canadian Early Childhood Education*. North York, ON: York Lanes Press.

Blackburn, C.A. 1999. "Resilient Children and Families." Available at http://www.ecdgroup.com/cn/claudia.html.

Bogoroch-Ditkofsky, M. 1991. *Daycare and the Law: A Guide for Canadian Child Care Programs and Other Non-Profit Boards*. Toronto: Child Care Initiatives Fund, Health and Welfare Canada, and Umbrella Central Daycare Services.

Brokenleg, M., and L. Brendtro. 1989. "The Circle of Caring: Native American Perspectives on Children and Youth." Paper presented to Child Welfare of American International Conference, Washington, DC.

Callahan, M., L. Brown, P. McKenzie, and B. Whittington. In press. *Knitting Up The Raveled Sleeve of Care: Grandmothers Making Families with Their Grandchildren*.

Camarena, P.M., K. Minor, T. Melmer, and C. Ferrie. 1998. "The Nature and Support of Adolescent Mothers' Life Aspirations." *Family Relations* 47 (2): 129–37.

Campaign for Equal Families. n.d. Fact sheet.

Canadian Child Care Federation. 1998. "Aboriginal Cultural Content in Early Childhood Care and Education." *Interaction* 12 (2). Summer.

Canadian Council on Social Development. 2003. "Census Shows Increasing Diversity of Canadian Society." Available at http://www.ccsd.ca/pr/2003/diversity.htm.

CANGRANDS. 2003. "Tips for Grandparents Raising Grandchildren and Other Family Members." Available at http://www.cangrands.com/grgtips.htm.

Capaldi, D.M., L. Crosby, and M. Stoolmiller. 1996. "Predicting the Timing of the First Sexual Intercourse for At-Risk Adolescent Males." *Child Development* 67: 344–359.

Cardinal, E. 1994. "Effective Programming: A Native Perspective." *Early Childhood Education* 27 (1). Spring–Summer.

Castellano, M.B. 2002. "Aboriginal Family Trends: Extended Families, Nuclear Families, Families of the Heart." Ottawa: Vanier Institute of the Family.

Child Welfare League of America. 2005. "Kinship Care: Fact Sheet." Available at http://www.cwla.org/programs/kinship/factsheet.htm.

Church, E. 2003. *Kinship and Stepfamilies*. In M. Lynn, ed., *Voices: Essays on Canadian Families*, 2nd ed. Toronto: Thomson Nelson Learning.

Clay, J.W. 1990. "Working with Lesbian and Gay Parents and Their Children." *Young Children*. March.

Corbett, S. 1993. "A Complicated Bias." *Young Children*. March.

Couchenour, D., and K. Chrisman. 2000. *Families, Schools and Communities: Together For Young Children*. New York: Delmar Thomson Learning.

Crawford, T. 2008. "Teen Moms Beat Odds To Succeed." *The Toronto Star*. March 11: Section L.

Dale, D. 2008. "Deadbeat Dads On Upswing." *The Toronto Star*. September 6.

DeAndrade, Y. 1992. *VAST Project: Children and PTSD*. Vancouver: Vancouver Association for Survivors of Torture.

de Wolff, A. 1994. *Strategies for Working Families*. Toronto: Ontario Coalition for Better Child Care.

Department of Justice Canada. 1997. "Child Support." Available at http://canada.justice.gc.ca/eng/pi/sup-pen/index.html.

Direnfeld, Gary. n.d. Workshop material. Available at http://www.yoursocialworker.com.

Dotsch, J. 1994. "Supporting the New Immigrant/Refugee Family in Child Care." *Interaction* 8 (2). Summer.

Dryburgh, H. 2003. *Teenage Pregnancy* 12 (1). Catalogue 82-003. Ottawa: Statistics Canada.

Edwards, L., and S. Sodhi. 1992. *Me and My Families: A Handbook on Adoption and Foster Care for School Professionals*. Washington, DC: Department of Health and Human Services.

Eichler, M. 1997. *Family Shifts: Families, Policies, and Gender Equality*. Toronto: Oxford University Press.

Epstein, R. 2003. "Lesbian Families." In M. Lynn, ed., *Voices: Essays on Canadian Families*. Toronto: Thomson Nelson Learning.

Fanjoy, S. 1994. "Meadown Lake Tribal Council Indian Child Care Program." *Focus*. January.

Fantino, A. 1993. "Refugee Children in Canada: Reshaping Identity." Speech given to the Canadian Council for Refugees, Calgary. 11–13 November.

Farris Manning, C., and M. Zandstra. 2003. "Children in Care in Canada." *Child Welfare League of Canada*. March. Available at http://www.nationalchildrensalliance.com/nca/pubs/2003/Children_in_Care_March_2003.pdf

Federation of Saskatchewan Indian Nations. 1993. Available at http://www.FSIN.com.

Fenton, P. 2004. "Talking With Your Child about Adoption: Guidelines For Adoptive Parents." *Adoption Roundup: Journal of the Adoption Council of Ontario*. Winter.

Flaks, D.K. 1995. "Lesbians Choosing Motherhood: A Comparative Study of Lesbian and Heterosexual Parents and Their Children." *Developmental Psychology* 31 (1).

Fontaine, P. 2007. "Improving Quality of Life for First Nations People." *The Toronto Star*. February 5. A15.

Foulks Boyd, B. 1999. "Should Gay and Lesbian Issues Be Discussed in Elementary School?" *Childhood Education*. Fall.

Fox, B. 2001. "As Times Change: A Review of Trends in Personal and Family Life." In B. Fox, ed., *Family Patterns Gender Relations*, 2nd ed. New York: Oxford University Press.

Fraser, S. 2008. "Auditor General Has Point on First Nations." June 10. Available at http://www.fcpp.org/main/publication_detail.php?PubID=2203.

Freeman, R. 1994. "Outcomes of Divorce for Children." *Profiling Canada's Families*. Ottawa: Vanier Institute of the Family.

Frey, J. 2003. "Putting the Byte on Custody Disputes." *The Toronto Star*. 9 August.

Fuller-Thomson, E. 2005. "A Program for Research on Social and Economic Dimensions of an Aging Population." *Grandparents Raising Grandchildren in Canada: A Profile of Skipped Generation Families*. SEDAP Research Paper No. 132.

Furstenberg, F., and A.J. Cherlin. 2001. "Children's Adjustment to Divorce." In B. Fox, ed., *Family Patterns Gender Relations*, 2nd ed. New York: Oxford University Press.

Ganong, L., and M. Coleman. 1994. *Remarried Family Relationships*. Thousand Oaks, CA: Sage.

Geronimus, A.T. 1991. "Teenage Childbearing and Social and Reproductive Disadvantage: The Evolution of Complex Questions and the Demise of Simple Answers." *Family Relations* 40 (4) (October): 463–71.

Gestwicki, C. 2004. *Home School and Community Relations*, 5th ed. New York: Thomson Delmar Learning.

Gibbs, N. 2004. "Making Time For A Baby." *Annual Editions: Child Growth and Development*. New York: McGraw-Hill/Dushkin.

Gonzalez-Mena, J. 2008. *50 Early Childhood Strategies for Working And Communicating with Diverse Families*. Columbus, OH: Pearson/Merrill Prentice Hall.

Gordon, A. 2005. "Family Feuding A Two-Way Street." *The Toronto Star*. February 11: D5.

———. 2008. "Immigrant Men Learn How To Broaden Paternal Role." *The Toronto Star*. May 17: L1.

Gower, R. 2005. "Opening Doors to Understanding and Acceptance". In Z. Janmohamed, ed., *Building Bridges, Lesbian, Gay, Bisexual, Transsexual, Transgender and Queer Families in Early Childhood Education*. Toronto: Ontario Coalition for Better Child Care.

Grand Parenting Again Canada. n.d. "Kinship Care." Available at http://www.grandparentingagaincanada.com/kinshipcare.htm

Green, C. 1998. "Working with Refugee Children in Our Schools." *Interaction* 11 (4).

Greenspoon, B. 1998. "Addressing Gay and Lesbian Issues." *Interaction* 12 (2).

Gulli, C. 2008. "Suddenly Teen Pregnancy Is Cool?" *Maclean's*. January 28.

Hardy, J.B., et al. 1998. "Like Mother, Like Child: Intergenerational Patterns of Age at First Birth and Associations with Childhood and Adolescent Characteristics and Adult Outcomes in the Second Generation." *Developmental Psychology* 34: 1220–1232.

Hare, J., and L. Koepke. 1990. "Susanne and Her Two Mothers." *Day Care and Early Education* 18 (2). Winter.

Harper, A.M. 1997. Cultural Adaptation and Intercultural Communication: Some Barriers and Bridges. Paper presented at the Annual Convention of the Western Speech Communication Association. Monterey, California. 13 February.

Hayes, C.D. 1987. *Risking the Future: Adolescent Sexuality, Pregnancy and Childbearing*. Vol. 1. Washington, DC: National Academy Press.

Hepworth Berger, E. 2004. *Parents as Partners in Education: Families and Schools Working Together*, 6th ed. Toronto: Prentice Hall.

Hoffman, J. 1997. "See You On The Weekend." *Today's Parent*. May.

Hoy Crawford, S. 1996. *Beyond Dolls and Guns: 101 Ways to Help Children Avoid Gender Bias*. Portsmouth, NH: Heinemann.

Indian and Northern Affairs Canada. 2004. "Inuit, March 2000." Available at http://www.ainc-inac.gc.ca/pr/info/info114_e.html.

James, C.E. 1989. *Seeing Ourselves: Exploring Race, Ethnicity and Culture*. Oakville, ON: Sheridan College.

Janmohamed, Z. 2006. *Building Bridges: Lesbian, Gay, Bisexual, Transgender, Transsexual and Queer Families in Early Childhood Education*. Toronto: Ontario Coalition for Better Child Care.

Jendrek Platt, J. 1993. "Grandparents Who Parent Their Grandchildren: Effects on Lifestyle." *Journal of Marriage and the Family* 55 (August).

Johnston, P. 1993. *Adoption and the Schools Project: A Guide for Educators*. Washington, DC: Department of Health and Human Services.

Jones, D. 1998. "Canada's Real Adoption Crisis." *Chatelaine*. May.

Kemuksigak, P., and S. Tuglavina. 1998. Inuit Creating a Foundation for Child Care Services. Linking Research to Practice. A Canadian Forum. Banff, Alberta, 25–27 October.

Khoo, L. 2007. "Mixed Blessings. Mixed-race Identity." *CBC Radio's The Current*. September 7.

Kowaleski-Jones, L., and F.L. Mott. 1998. "Sex, Contraception and Childbearing among High-Risk Youth: Do Different Factors Influence Males and Females?" *Family Planning Perspectives* 30 (4): 163–69.

Kurz, D. 1995. *For Richer, For Poorer: Mothers Confront Divorce*. New York: Routledge.

La Rose, L. 2008. "Mixed Race Marriages on the Rise." *The Toronto Star*. April 2.

Lightfoot, L. 1995. *New York Sunday Times*. June 18. 9.

Lipman, M. 1984. "Adoption in Canada: Two Decades in Review." In P. Sachdev, ed., *Adoption: Current Issues and Trends*. Toronto: Butterworths.

Lochhead, C. 2000. "The Trend toward Delayed First Childbirth: Health and Social Implications." *A Profile of Mothers and Fathers in Canada: 1971–1996*. Ottawa, ON: Policy Division of Health Canada.

Lorde, A. 1987. "Turning the Beat Around: Lesbian Parenting 1986." In S. Pollack and J. Vaughn, eds., *Politics of the Heart*. New York: Firebrand.

MacLean, J. 2003. "No How-To Guide for Catastrophe. Widowhood Not Meant for the Young." *The Toronto Star*. 6 September. L9.

Mallea, J.R., and J.C. Young. 1990. *Cultural Diversity and Canadian Education*. Ottawa: Carleton University Press.

Man, G. 2001. "From Hong Kong to Canada: Immigration and the Changing Family Lives of Middle-Class Women from Hong Kong." In B. Fox, ed., *Family Patterns: Gender Relations*, 2nd ed. New York: Oxford University Press.

Manning, W.D. 1993. "Marriage and Cohabitation Following Premarital Conception." *Journal of Marriage and the Family* 55 (3): 839–50.

Martin, P. 2008. "There's Only One Way to Break the Aboriginal Cycle of Despair: Education." *The Globe and Mail*, February 5. A17.

Maslen, M. 2004. "Important Medical Information For Your Child." *Adoption Roundup: Journal of the Adoption Council of Ontario*. April.

Maurin, R. 2007. "Special Delivery." *Fashion*. November: 161.

Mehren, E. 1999. "Grandparents Raising Their Children's Children." *The Toronto Star*. January 30: L9.

Meyers, M. 1993. *Teaching to Diversity: Teaching and Learning in the Multi-Ethnic Classroom*. Toronto: Irwin.

Miles, S.C. (n.d.) "Grandparents Raising Grandchildren." Available at http://www.wvu.edu/~exten/inforest/pubs/fypubs/240.wl.pdg.

Ministry of the Attorney General. 2007. "Supervised Access." Available at http://www.attorneygeneral.jus.gov.on.ca/english/family/supaccess.asp.

Mitchell, A. 1992. "Newborns Go with Dollar Flow." *The Globe and Mail*. November 30.

Murphy Kilbride, K. 1994. "Working with Immigrant Families: Good Partnerships Need Good Information." *IMPrint* 10. Fall.

Murphy Kilbride, K., J. Pollard, M. Friendly, and J. Dotsch. 1998. *Early Differences Experienced by Visible Minority Children*. Metropolis–Toronto Centre of Excellence. Research and Policy.

Musick, J.S. 1990. "Adolescents as Mothers: The Being and the Doing." *Zero to Three*. December.

National Research Conference. 1998. *Linking Research to Policy*. Banff, AB: National Research Conference.

Newman, F. 1993. *Children in Crisis: Support for Teachers and Parents*. Toronto: Scholastic Canada.

Nirdosh, S. 1998. "Refugee Families: Reactions to Stress and Trauma." *Early Childhood Diversity Network Canada Newsletter*. Fall.

Nock, S.L. 1998. "A Comparison of Marriages and Cohabiting Relationships." *Journal of Family Issues* 16 (1): 53–76.

Office of the Prime Minister. 2008. "Prime Minister Harper Offers Full Apology on Behalf of Canadians for the Indian Residential Schools System." June 11.

Parents without Partners. N.d. "Mission Statement." Available at http://www.parentswithoutpartners.org/about.htm.

Patten, P. 1999. "Divorce and Children, Part 1: An Interview with Robert Hughes, Jr., Ph.D." Available at http://npin.org/pnews/1999/pnew999/int999e.html.

PFLAG. N.d. Available at http://www.pflag.ca.

Philp, M. 2007. "Nearly Half of Children in Crown Care are Medicated." *The Globe and Mail*. June 9. A1.

Pitt, S. 2004. "Kinda Brown." *Tree House Canadian Family*. March: 28.

Poston, Carlos W.S. 1990. "The Biracial Identity Development Model: A Needed Edition." *Journal of Counselling and Development* 69, 152–55.

Rangarajan, A., and P. Gleason. 1998. "Young Unwed Fathers of AFDC Children: Do They Provide Support?" *Demography* 35 (2): 175–86.

Report Card on Child Poverty in Canada 1989–1999. 1999. Toronto: Campaign 2000.

Richardson, B. 1994. "Improving Native Education." *Early Childhood Education* 27 (1). Spring–Summer.

Riedman, A., M.A. Lamanna, and A. Nelson. 2003. *Marriages and Families*. Toronto: Thomson Nelson.

Ross, E. 2008. Interview. March.

Ryerse, C. 1994. "School-Based Infant Care Program." *Focus*. October.

Saskatchewan Learning. 2004. "Michif and Metis Cultural Site." Available at http://www.saskschools.ca/curr_content/creelang/.

Sheehan, N., and L. Wood. 1993. *Adoption and the Schools Project: A Guide for Educators*. Washington, DC: Department of Health and Human Services.

Shimoni, R., and J. Baxter. 2008. *Working with Families*, 4th ed. Toronto: Pearson Addison Wesley.

Siad, S., A. Kassam, and S. Bhattacharya. 2007. "Mixing and Matching, To Mom's Chagrin." *The Toronto Star*. July 1: A1.

Soloman, R., and C.P. Liefeld. 1998. "Effectiveness of a Family Support Center Approach to Adolescent Mothers: Repeat Pregnancy and School Drop-Out Rates." *Family Relations* 47 (2): 139–44.

Springate, K.W., and D.A. Stegelin. 1999. *Building School and Community Partnerships through Parent Involvement*. Columbus, OH: Merrill Prentice Hall.

Statistics Canada. 2001. "Age Groups (12B), Number of Grandparents (3A) and Sex (3) for Grandchildren Living with Grandparents With No Parent Present, for Canada, Provinces and Territories, 1991 to 2001 Censuses—20% Sample Data." Available at http://www.statcan.ca/english/census01/products/standard/themes/RetrieveProduct Table.

———. 2001b. "School Performance of Children from Immigrant Families." *The Daily*. November 14. Available at http://www.statcan.ca/Daily/English/011114/d011114a.htm.

———. 2003. "The People: Break Up." *Canada eBook*. Available at http://www.43.statcan.ca/r000_e.htm.

———. 2005. "Canada's Aboriginal population in 2017." *The Daily*. June 28. Available at http://www.statcan.ca/Daily/English/050628/d050628d.htm.

———. 2006. "Aboriginal Peoples in Canada in 2006: Inuit, Métis and First Nations, 2006 Census." Table 20. Available at http://www.12.statcan.ca/english/census06/analysis/aboriginal/children.cfm.

———. 2006b. "The risk of first and second marriage dissolution." *The Daily*. June 28. Available at http://www.statcan.ca/Daily/English/060628/d060628b.htm

———. 2006c. General Social Survey, 2006. Table 1. Available at http://www.statcan.ca/english/research/89-625-XIE/2007001/tables/tab1-en.htm.

———. 2007a. *Census 2006 Analysis Series*. Available at http://www.12.statcan.ca/english/census06/analysis/index.cfm.

———. 2007b. "2006 Census: Families, Marital Status, Households and Dwelling Characteristics." *The Daily*. Available at http://www.statcan.ca/Daily/English/070912/d070912a.htm.

———. 2008a. "Census 2006, Release no. 5, Aboriginal Peoples." January 15. Available at http://www.12.statcan.ca/english/census06/release/aboriginal.cfm.

———. 2008b. "Aboriginal Peoples in Canada in 2006." *The Daily*. January 15. Available at http://www.statcan.ca/Daily/English/080115/d080115a.htm.

Steinhart Holland, J. 1993. *Adoption and the Schools Project: A Guide for Educators*. Washington, DC: Department of Health and Human Services.

Stone, L. 1990. *Road to Divorce: England 1530–1987*. Oxford: Oxford University Press.

Strader, S.C. 1993. Non-Custodial Gay Fathers: Considering the Issues. Paper presented at the Annual Convention of the American Psychological Association, Toronto, August 20–24.

Stroud, J.E., J.C. Stroud, and L.M. Staley. 1999. "Adopted Children in the Early Childhood Classroom." *Parent News*. Available at http://npin.org/pnews/1999/pnew999/int999d.html.

The Toronto Star. 2007a. "Aboriginal Languages." *The Toronto Star*. February 18. 1A.

———. 2007b. "Divorce Canadian Style." *The Toronto Star*. June 23. L12.

———. 2007c. "Parents of Multiracial Children, Grownups Say The Darnedest Things." *The Toronto Star*. April 7. L5.

Thomas, L., and S. Learoyd. 1990. "Native Child Care: In the Spirit of Caring." Speech delivered to the Native Council of Canada, Ottawa. January.

Toldeo, S. de, and D.E. Brown. 1995. *Grandparents as Parents: A Survival Guide for Raising a Second Family*. New York: Guilford Press.

Ullyott, K. 1990. "My Folks Are Gay." *Chatelaine*. November.

Vanier Institute of the Family. 1994. "Profiling Canada's Families." Pamphlet. Ottawa: Vanier Institute of the Family.

Ward, M. 2002. *The Family Dynamic: A Canadian Perspective*, 2nd ed. Toronto: Nelson Canada.

Wheeler, L. 2004. "Adopting An Older Child: How To Help Yourself and Your Child." *Adoption Roundup: Journal of the Adoption Council of Ontario*. April.

Wickens, B. 2002. "How We Live." *Maclean's*. November 4.

Wickens, E. 1993. "I Will Have a Child in My Class with Two Moms." *Young Children*. March.

Wigod, R. 2000. "Conference Celebrates Unique Education: There Are Hundreds of Innovative College Programs That Often Go Unnoticed by Many Who Benefit." *Vancouver Sun*. May 1.

Zabin, L.S., R. Wong, R.M. Weinick, and M.R. Emerson. 1992. "Dependency in Urban Black Families Following the Birth of an Adolescent's Child." *Journal of Marriage and the Family* 54 (3) (August): 496–507.

CHAPTER 10

Families in Transition: Issues Facing Many Families

© Monkey Business Images / Shutterstock

"While all children are born equal, they don't all have the same opportunities to flourish. . . nothing in today's society is more disgraceful than the marginalization of some young people who are driven to isolation and despair. We must not tolerate such disparities."

—Michaelle Jean, Governor General of Canada, September 27, 2005

LEARNING OUTCOMES

After studying this chapter, you will be able to

1. analyze the impact of becoming a parent, the stages of parenthood, and the ways parenting styles influence children

2. discuss the impact of siblings on the family unit

3. assess the needs of families with children with special needs and develop strategies for supporting them

4. discuss the impact on families when an adult member has a chronic illness, disability, or a death occurs

5. explore the issues of substance abuse and the impact on families

6. identify the challenges facing families living with violence

7. examine the needs of families when one member is incarcerated

---

In this chapter we will explore the role of parenting and a number of issues that may affect any of the families that you have been reading about in this text.

STAGES AND STYLES OF PARENTING

Despite the many pressures on modern-day families and the shifting roles of men and women, the birth of a child remains perhaps the most joyous event a family can experience. With the arrival of a baby, parents embark on an exciting journey that will last for the rest of their lives.

STAGES OF PARENTING

Galinsky (1987: 86) summarizes her views on how parenthood changes adults:

> Taking care of a small, dependent, growing person is transforming, because it brings us in touch with our baser side, it exposes our vulnerabilities as well as our nobility. We lose our sense of self, only to find it and have it change again and again. We learn to nurture and care. We struggle through defining our own rules and our own brand of being an authority. We figure out how we want to interpret the wider world, and we learn to interact with all those who affect our children. When our children are teenagers, we redefine our relationships, and then we launch them into life. Often our fantasies are laid bare, our dreams are in a constant tug of war with

realities. And perhaps we grow. In the end, we have learned more about ourselves, about the cycles of life, and humanity itself. Most parents describe themselves as more responsible, more accepting, more generous than before they had children.

Galinsky (1987) also outlines the six stages of parenthood:

- **Image-making:** Parents prepare for pregnancy and for changes in themselves and in their relationships with others.

- **Nurturing:** From the birth of the child until and lasting 18 to 24 months, parents balance their own needs with the child's and set priorities.

- **Authority:** From the child's second birthday and lasting two to three years, parents become rule givers and enforcers as they attempt to set structure and order in place.

- **Interpretive:** From the child's preschool period and extending to adolescence, parents interpret the world for their children, teaching morals and values.

- **Interdependent:** Parents share their power with the children.

- **Departure:** Parents evaluate themselves as the children prepare to leave home.

PARENTING STYLES

Parenting style is a concept initially identified by Baumrind (1967) to describe patterns of parenting behaviour and how they relate to patterns of child

---

INSIDE LOOK

My children are adults now, young women just entering the workforce, compassionate, strong, funny, vulnerable—ready to take on the world! Over the years, I know that I have learned more from them than they have ever learned from me. They enrich my life in ways that are inexplicable. We are woven together in a tapestry of love and a multitude of experiences. While I might have chosen a different path for myself, in the end I wouldn't have missed this for the world!

behaviour. A survey of 23,000 children and their parents asked 23 questions about their parenting styles in 1994 and 1996 and found that one-third of parents are what American psychologist Barbara Coloroso has termed "backbones"—the most positive parents who provide a loving, caring environment; encourage independence; are consistent; and provide one-on-one interaction. One-quarter are "brick walls"—inflexible, authoritarian, and demanding—and another one-quarter are considered irresponsible parents.

Parents display a variety of parenting styles, some of which may be very different from the ones by which they themselves were raised. They bring their own history and social skills to the process of parenting. "In addition, parents' behaviour is related to their satisfactions in other areas of their lives, such as their marriages and their work" (Brooks, 1998: 13). The shift in parental roles and

© 273472546 / Shutterstock

Parenting style has a bigger impact on a child's behaviour than any other factor.

responsibilities has created new stressors as families attempt to find a balance in their new lifestyle. Additionally, the age of the parents has an impact on family relationships. Boys may be raised differently from girls, in accordance with cultural and social ideas on gender roles. Or, two parents in the same family may have different styles of parenting, each based on his or her own family history or lifestyle.

Carey (1998), reporting on a recent study, states: "Parenting style has a bigger impact on a child's behaviour than any other factor, including living in poverty or with a single parent." Bandura (1997) asserts that family socioeconomic status has only an indirect effect on children's academic achievement, promoting the aspirations of parents and prosocial behaviour in children. Parents who have high efficacy beliefs about influencing their children's cognitive development have high aspirations for their children, and raise their children's beliefs that they are capable of regulating their own learning and academic achievement.

According to the Canadian Council on Social Development (2006: 14), parents are more likely to adopt a positive parenting style with younger children than with older ones. Using a scale which measures positive parenting such as giving praise, talking, playing, and laughing together, 92 percent of children under age two lived with parents who had a positive parenting style in 2002. Rates of positive parenting styles were the same, regardless of the gender of the child or the family income.

Fully 62 percent of parents with children living at home say one of the biggest worries in their lives

INSIDE LOOK

Thomas Wolfe wrote *You Can't Go Home Again,* but James Agee said you do go home again in the lives of your children. It is a sort of re-experiencing what you experienced when you grew up—they're reading the same books you read, the conflicts they have are the ones you remember having with your parents, and issues that mattered to you as a child are issues for them. When you have time to reflect on them, they bring you back over and over again to issues in your own childhood that I guess you have a second opportunity to resolve. You have a different perspective on them than you did before.

Source: Excerpt from *Parenting,* Second Edition, by Jane Brooks. Copyright © 1998 by Mayfield Publishing Company. Reprinted by permission of the publisher.

is whether they are raising their children properly. Of the key childbearing group, aged 18 to 34, the figure is 70 percent. Money is not driving this anxiety: 80 percent of the parents say they can afford a good lifestyle for their children. In fact, the angst is present no matter what the family's income level is, no matter how old their children are, and whether both parents work or if someone stays home with the children. The sticking point is Canadians' inability to reconcile between what they think is best for women in society with what they think is best for children.

> Bombarded with new information about the importance of proper neural development in the first few years of a child's life, yet committed to the ideal of economic independence for women, Canadians are floundering. The confusion is compounded by the fact that there is no common belief system about the right way to raise children. There's no single set of rules to be measured against. But what really leads to the night sweats is the fact that emerging research is concluding that parenting style, more so than education or income, is the key to a child's success. (*Globe and Mail,* 1999: A7)

Being a parent is a multifaceted and challenging opportunity to support and contribute to the growth and development of a child. Parental competence involves behavioural, affective, and cognitive components; parental self-efficacy is an important competency component. For example, the following findings have been reported about parents with high self-efficacy:

- They believe that they have the ability to effectively and positively influence the development and behaviour of their children and engage in positive parenting behaviours (Coleman and Karraker, 1998).
- They are more responsive to the needs of their children and they engage in direct interactions with their children (Mash and Johnson, 1983).
- They exhibit active coping strategies (Wells-Parker, Miller, and Topping, 1990).
- They perceive fewer behavioural problems in their children (Johnston and Mash, 1989).

The opposite is true for parents with low self-efficacy:

- They have higher rates of depression (Teti and Gelfand, 1991).

- They demonstrate greater defensive and controlling behaviour (Donovan, Leavitt, and Walsh, 1990).
- They have greater perceptions of child difficulties (Halpern, Anders, Coll, and Hua, 1994).
- They report higher stress levels (Wells-Parker et al., 1990).
- They have a passive parental coping style, focus more on problems in relationships, demonstrate more negative affect, experience elevated autonomic arousal, feel helpless in the role of parent, and use of punitive disciplinary strategies (Bugental and Cortez, 1988; Bugental and Shennum, 1984).

Successful parents value learning, become involved in the child's school, and encourage their child to participate in community programs, to develop appropriate leisure time activities, and to cultivate beneficial peer relationships. The social networks that develop as a result of community involvement provide positive role models, constructive activities, and support for values and social norms (Elder, 1995; Furstenberg et al., 1999). Yet for every parent who feels successful in their role, there are parents who are addicted, dysfunctional, or suffering from a mental illness, or who have limited skills or resources to support them in their role. Research shows a significant connection between family dysfunction and mental health problems among children. The National Longitudinal Survey of Children and Youth (NLSCY) measures family functioning by looking at how well a family works together. "Dysfunctional" families experience a great deal of stress in their daily lives. They often live in poverty and have few social supports. Children in families with incomes under $30,000 were twice as likely to live in dysfunctional family circumstances as children in families with incomes over $60,000 (Canadian Council on Social Development, 2006: 14).

Invest in Kids Foundation

Invest in Kids Foundation is a Canadian organization, established in 1992, which has been founded with the sole purpose of promoting the healthy development of children from birth to the age of

This study is part of a two-year longitudinal investigation that examined the development and implementation of 14 Parenting and Readiness pilot centres. Approximately half of the centre participants were from recently immigrated families. Many early intervention programs have been shaped by the notion that children's development should be studied in the contexts of family and community. Reciprocal parent–child interaction is a key feature of child development in those contexts. Parent involvement, parental self-efficacy, and parenting style are factors that influence parent–child interactions and contribute to early development, the transition to school, and future child outcomes. This study examined parent factors and teacher strategies to foster parent involvement and efficacy. Overall findings suggest that parents who perceive themselves as more effective are more involved in their children's education at the pre-school level. Teacher strategies are described as a key feature in facilitating parent involvement and parental self-efficacy. Each component of the partnership model affects the others in a positive, interrelated manner, contributing to the healthy development of the child. Parents provide emotional and social support to the child within the school environment while gaining valuable skills to extend learning into the home. Teachers can better attend to the influence of cultural diversity (parenting style, for example) when they are able to observe the child within the context of the parent–child relationship. Children who have the opportunity to acclimate to a school environment combined with home support may have a better chance of being ready for kindergarten and future academic success.

Source: Pelletier and Brent, 2002: 45.

---

five. Research shows that the "miracle years" between birth and five years of age are the period of greatest human development—and the period during which adults have the most profound influence on a child's future. Yet most parents feel uncertain about their own parenting behaviour, as we've seen. Furthermore, the Foundation's 1999 poll (see Exhibit 1.4) suggests parents aren't getting the support they need.

Invest in Kids is working on four critical fronts to provide all of us with the skills we need to make a difference:

1. **Supporting discovery:** Identify what works by searching out and supporting best practices and model approaches; identify what's important by pinpointing gaps between knowledge and practice; work to develop a better understanding of the attitudes, behaviours, and needs of Canadians when it comes to caring for our youngest children.

2. **Changing the climate:** Work to create a social environment that enhances understanding of the critical importance of our children's ear-

liest years and the crucial role that all of us play in determining a child's future; sponsor the Invest in Kids mass-media public education campaigns, which reach millions every year with new messages and new skills for change.

3. **Providing the tools:** Develop educational resources such as videos, booklets, magazine supplements, and posters that equip parents, caregivers, and other Canadians with the knowledge and skills they need to nurture children best.

4. **Turning theory into practice:** Support training through workshops, conferences, and curricula to help professionals develop more proactive and effective healthy-child development practices.

Invest in Kids has an online Professional Newsletter that provides information for parents and teachers as well as information about upcoming workshops across the country. You can sign up for their newsletter, as well as read about their initiatives and resources, at **www.investinkids.ca**.

EXHIBIT 10.1 INVEST IN KIDS NATIONAL SURVEY OF PARENTS OF YOUNG CHILDREN

In January 1999, Invest in Kids polled 1,645 Canadian parents on their knowledge about raising kids under the age of six:

- 92 percent believe being a parent is the most important thing they can do
- 85 percent are certain babies learn from birth
- 51 percent are certain emotional closeness with a baby can influence intellectual development
- 47 percent are certain a child needs stimulation, such as being read to, comforted, and held, for peak brain development
- 34 percent are certain that a child's experiences before the age of three greatly influence his or her ability to do well in school
- 8 percent are certain a baby less than six months old can get depressed
- 29 percent are confident they know what signs to watch for that would indicate that a child is developing physically about right for his or her age
- 13 percent are confident they know what signs to watch for that would indicate that a child is developing emotionally about right for his or her age
- 17 percent are confident they know what signs to watch for that would indicate that a child is developing intellectually about right for his or her age
- 13 percent are confident they know what signs to watch for that would indicate that a child is developing socially about right for his or her age
- 43 percent have confidence in their parenting skills
- 33 percent don't understand their kids' feelings and needs
- 34 percent don't know how to handle difficult situations with their kids
- less than 50 percent realized the brains of babies who don't receive appropriate stimulation, such as reading, playing with, and touching and holding, will not develop as well as the brain of a baby who does receive these kinds of stimulation
- about 50 percent hadn't learned that "emotional closeness" with their babies can strongly influence their intellectual development
- only 40 percent fully agree that Canada values its young children

According to the poll, only about half of parents felt they received enough emotional and practical support from others before their first baby was born.

Freda Martin, a psychiatrist for more than a quarter-century and a foundation advisor, said parents shouldn't take the poll personally, because it takes a community to raise a child. According to the poll, only half of parents received enough emotional and practical support to elevate them to supernurturing status. Senator Landon Pearson, a children's advocate, said the most disturbing finding is that parents feel abandoned. The poll, she said, reflects cutbacks in services that help parents with small kids. Parents are not sure what signs to look for to tell them their child is healthy or about right for his or her age. Their knowledge of physical development is low and of social and emotional development even lower.

Source: A National Survey of Parents of Young Children, Lynn Oldershaw, PhD, © Psych, Invest in Kids 2002.

SIBLINGS

Almost 80 percent of Canadians have at least one sibling. It is an important type of family relationship and one that outlasts the parent–child relationship (Ambert, 2006). Recent research suggests that sibling relationships may have as much, or more influence on the development of children than the parent–child relationship (Kluger, 2006). During childhood, it is likely that siblings spend more time together than with their parents or with friends. Although conflicts are inevitable among siblings, sometimes the relationship is

EXHIBIT 10.2 GROWING TOGETHER

Growing Together: An Early Intervention and Prevention Model is an example of an Invest in Kids project. "Growing Together" is a demonstration model of effective prevention and early intervention services designed to improve the social and emotional development and readiness to learn of young children in impoverished neighbourhoods. Partnering with the Hincks-Dellcrest Centre and the Toronto Public Health Department to support the Growing Together model in St. Jamestown, Toronto, it was the winner of the 1995 Peter F. Drucker Award for Canadian Nonprofit Innovation.

Similar initiatives are under way in Dartmouth and Cape Breton, in partnership with the I.W.K. Grace Hospital and the Nova Scotia government, and in Montreal, where, in partnership with Sainte-Justine Hospital and the Centre Local de Services Communautaires (CLCS), Côte-des-Neiges, the foundation has worked to replicate the Growing Together model—as Grandir Ensemble—in the city's high-risk district of Plamondon in Côte-des-Neiges.

© Andresr / Shutterstock

Ninety-two percent of parents believe that parenting is the most important thing they will ever do.

family. It can be exiting and unsettling at the same time for a young child. Changes in the child's routine should not coincide, if possible, with the arrival of the new baby. Some hospitals run sibling workshops in which the upcoming event is explained in age appropriate terms. The infant room staff might invite the child to practise helping out with the babies. The child-care centre might also support the child by setting up the dramatic play centre as a nursery with a variety of dolls and materials borrowed from the infant room. The family could also be invited to the centre with their preschooler(s) taking the lead to introduce the baby to his or her friends. In support of this transition, Mary Bianci at Esther Exton Child Care Centre created a project book that chronicled the pregnancy, delivery, and celebration of one of her kindergarten children's new sister.

Sibling rivalry is inescapable in most families. Some children initially make a wonderful connection with the new baby, only to have issues of territory or jealousy surface later in the baby's life as they become more mobile. Anderson and Rice (1992) found that girls demonstrated more positive behaviours, such as empathy and support, toward brothers and sister than did boys, but they showed equal amounts of aggression and hostility as boys. Negative sibling relationships were more common in stepfamilies and divorced families than in non-divorced families. These researchers emphasize that despite the conflicts among siblings, children in all types of families demonstrated a great deal of positive behaviours toward their siblings (Couchenour and Chrisman, 2000: 55).

characterized by warmth, affection, and mutual support, while in other family's jealousy and rivalry extend into the adult years (Shimoni and Baxter, 2008).

As families grow, the news of an approaching child will have an impact on all members of the

Courtesy of Lynn Wilson

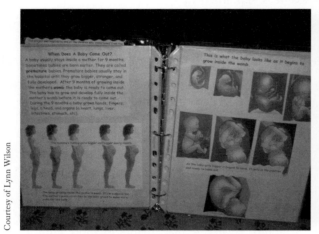

Courtesy of Lynn Wilson

Courtesy of Lynn Wilson

This "Becoming a Big Sister" book helped to ease the transition of a new sister in this family.

BOOKS FOR CHILDREN

Waiting for the Sun, by A. Lohans

Welcome Precious, by N. Grimes

Hello Baby, by L. Rockwell

How to Drive Your Sister Crazy, by D. Shore and L. Rankin

The New Baby, by M. Mayer

Baby on the Way and What Baby Needs, by W. Sears, M. Sears, C. Watts Kelly, and R. Andriani

BOOKS FOR ADULTS

Siblings without Rivalry, by A. Faber and E. Mazlish

Making Brothers and Sisters Best Friends: How to Fight the Good Fight at Home, by S. Mally, S. Mally, and G. Mally

Loving Each One Best: A Caring and Practical Approach to Raising Siblings, by N. Samalin and C. Whitney

Families with Children Who Have Special Needs

Five large Canadian studies have reported that 25–30 percent of five-year olds in the general population are developmentally delayed at school entry in one or more of crucial school-readiness skills (Doherty, 2007: 30). Medical advances have made it possible for children with serious medical issues to survive and, as a result, we are seeing more and more of these children in child-care settings.

The past few decades have brought enormous changes to the ways in which families, teachers, and governments define the place of children with special needs in child-care environments. Initially, some teachers worried about how they would accommodate children with special needs, given their limited experience in dealing with these children. Although the concept of inclusiveness has become increasingly entrenched in ECE practice and philosophy, barriers to the successful integration of children with special needs in traditional settings persist to this day. The presence of a child with special needs can place enormous demands on a family and we must be committed to providing comprehensive, coordinated, and family-focused services that will provide the support that this family will need.

A national study, *Working Towards Inclusive Child Care,* was launched in April 1996. Researchers Sharon Hope Irwin, Donna Lero, and Kathleen Brophy collected information in 1996–97 from over 300 child-care professionals across Canada. Together, the 136 centres in the sample provided care to over 8,000 children. About 40 percent of the centres had five or more children with special needs in their program at the time of the survey. In addition, 68 percent of these centres were providing care to children with undesignated special needs, behavioural challenges, or other high-risk factors. Frontline child-care professionals in this survey were actively involved in increasing their knowledge. Half had taken a college or university course related to inclusion since 1990, and 84 percent had attended at least one conference or workshop on a topic related to children with special needs. Since 1990, child-care professionals have reported both positive and negative changes that affect their capacity to be inclusive. While ECEs generally reported positive changes, 85 percent of centre directors indicated that changes in provincial policies and funding support negatively affect their programs.

Cheryl Shuman, director of genetic counselling at The Hospital for Sick Children in Toronto, Ontario, states that every couple has a 2–3 percent chance of having a child with a birth defect (White, 2004). The response of parents to their child's disability and the feelings associated with it can significantly affect the parent–teacher partnership. "Although the involvement of parents in child care of children with special needs is known to be important," Krajicek and Moore (1993: 13) observe, "it does not occur until parents have adapted to the children's disabilities. Not all parents adjust. Those who do become committed to all facets of the care of their infants and toddlers with special needs. These parents realize the benefits that they and their children alike derive from quality child care."

A growing concern also exists for children suffering from mental illnesses, that is, children who are depressed, or who suffer from anxiety, schizophrenia, bi-polar, or conduct disorders; roughly one in five Canadian children suffer from these illnesses and a lack of services and funds is a huge crisis. With only an average of ten child psychiatrists graduating each year, and with cuts to education and social service funding, there are fewer social workers and psychologists available in schools and in communities to intervene early and refer children at risk for help (Gordon, 2005: D5).

All members of the family are affected when a child has special needs. "For some families, there are increased tensions that may magnify any marital discord and feelings of inadequacy. Spouses and siblings alike may feel rejected or abandoned. Some statistics indicate that the divorce rate is higher when there is a child with a disability within the family" (Alper, Schloss, and Schloss, cited in Rockwell, Andre, and Hawley, 1996: 78). Not surprisingly, the more severe the child's disability, the greater the impact on the family situation. Some families may benefit from counselling that will help the family face continuing periods of grief and assistance in handling the special problems and environmental adjustments that having a child with a disability entails. Counselling may help parents understand the diagnosis, educational planning and future prognosis. Sessions also provide a forum in which parents can openly express and work through any feelings of anger, fear and anxiety, fear and anxiety. They offer coping self-help skills, group relaxation, self-praise, and self-instruction. As siblings are an important aspect of family-centred practice, in many cases the counselling sessions will actively involve them (Winzer, 2008).

What might have been considered alternative therapies at one time have now become mainstream strategies for supporting children and their families. One such example is chiropractic services. Deirdre Edwards is a chiropractor and public health nurse who has been in the health care sector since 1971, primarily focusing on children within the family unit, and she contributes the following information:

There is much investment in maternal and fetal health during pregnancy to ensure a healthy mother and baby. Electronic screening helps monitor progress, preventing and limiting problems: however some labours are more difficult than others. Long labours can create pressure on the baby's head (born bruised) or with cone shaped heads, or a short labour, which can result in a "whiplash" effect on the newborn. Some require assistance by hand (due to resistance, like a cord round neck) or Ventouse (suction) or Forceps, and sometimes both, or Caesarean section (surgical assistance). From births like these, there are no statutory cranial or skeletal checks to ensure the integrity of the cranial bones or skeletal alignment. Later children cry and often present with behavioural problems which are currently labelled as "developmental delay," processing disorder, attention deficit, ADHD, or Autistic Spectrum disorder. However, how much could be attributed to *pain*? Pediatric pain is measured by behavioural changes, yet often we disregard these signs. These problems can accumulate to become:

- Children with poor eating and sleeping patterns
- Children that "fidget," or are "clumsy"
- Children with excessive temper tantrums

Some children could accumulate all the above acquiring a myriad of labels, and ultimately their development is delayed.

The body is made up of a network of nerve fibres, much like a network of roads. These nerve fibres carry the messages from the brain, down the brain stem and spinal column, dividing equally to relay impulses to every aspect of the body—down to the fingertips and back up again. In order for the body to function healthily and at its optimum, this network must be free-flowing. However, nerve interference—over-firing or under-firing—can lead to reduction of tissue oxygenation, adversely affecting vascular flow to the cells, tissues, and organ systems. Some children are more affected or compromised than others with multiple stressors. These are referred to as the three Ts:

1. **Trauma:** difficult birth, accident, abuse
2. **Toxins:** chemical abuse during pregnancy, condition-related treatment, food additives
3. **Thoughts:** emotional trauma, labelled syndromes—ADHD (Attention Deficit Disorder with Hyperactivity), autism, loss, divorce

As professionals, teachers must have a "briefcase" containing the most accurate and helpful tools of reference. A chiropractor specializing in children can help with an early assessment. These practitioners are skilled at detecting areas of interference and with minimal, non-invasive intervention can ensure the neural network is functioning at its best. A patient and mother of three children between the ages of one and twelve years states:

When I gave birth to Alistair and he screamed just like the other two had, it nearly broke the family up. However with the recommendation of chiropractic services I felt that I had nothing to lose. Within weeks, Alistair was happy, feeding well, and we all sighed with relief. Now one year later, Alistair has been a delight. He is the happiest little boy imaginable. Both Megan (seven years, was willful, angry and overactive) and Josh (twelve years, was difficult to get to bed and sleep, lacked in concentration) have been assessed and treated chiropractically for different problems, both of whom are now totally different. They are happier, more balanced, and not only can their father and I see the differences but so can they. Their teachers are really surprised with the progress. I wish that I had known about chiropractic services before. I wouldn't have had to leave parties so early, or been so tired myself. I could have enjoyed the children more and sooner.

Many families may also want to form groups of parents who have children with similar disabilities. McMaster University researchers conducted a study of nine parent-run support groups in Ontario to explore the group's perceived effect in providing parents with support, reducing stress and improving parents' ability to deal with disability issues. Results indicated substantial benefits for those belonging to the groups. Parents were seen to gain increased skills, a greater sense of power, and a sense of belonging. Participants were able to connect with each other and provide support and skills to deal with the day-to-day issues of raising a child with special needs (Winzer, 2008).

Monsebraaten (1998a) states that working parents of children with disabilities and health problems pay a high price financially and emotionally because of inadequate child care and a lack of workplace support. A two-year study, commissioned by the Canadian Union of Postal Workers, co-authored by Sharon Hope Irwin and University of Guelph family studies professor Donna Lero, is the first Canadian research on the employment barriers that parents of children with special needs experience when they want to participate fully in the workforce and attempt to find child care. For the 6–10 percent of

working parents of children with special needs, the financial penalties include extra expenses and forgone employment income. According to the study

- 39 percent worked reduced hours,
- 26 percent changed jobs,
- 46 percent altered their work schedule,
- 68 percent turned down overtime,
- 27 percent passed up a promotion,
- 64 percent of two-parent families with one parent unemployed reported their child's special needs as the major factor in losing their job,
- 88 percent said they felt tired and overloaded, and
- 90 percent said they were stressed as they tried to balance work and family obligations.

A more recent Statistics Canada study of 155,000 children between the ages of 5 and 14 who have activity limitations supports Irwin and Lero's research. Seventy percent of mothers surveyed had been negatively affected and had their pay cheques slashed because of a child's disability. Among children with mild to moderate disabilities, about 40 percent had family members whose jobs were affected. Among

INSIDE LOOK

We have been through sleepless nights, toilet training, temper tantrums, food allergies, first day of school, discipline, behaviour challenges, medications, tube feeding, specialized equipment needs, government programs, graduation, planning for the future—these are some of the challenges parents face when raising children with special needs. Most parents look to others for guidance, advice, and comfort and found it in other parents. When our children have disabilities, we especially need one another. We want to talk to another parent who has 'been there.' When parents are raising children with disabilities, they are usually in uncharted territory, even the people who are closest to us—our families and friends—may have difficulty knowing how to support us best and may distance themselves. This can leave families isolated and on their own.

The Hamilton Family Network brings families together by connecting parents to one another for information and emotional support. Resource Parents are trained and experienced so they can offer support to other parents. Families are carefully matched based on disability and/or a specific challenge that arises from the child's disability. The support Resource Parents offer to other parents is the foundation upon which rests all the other work of the Network. *The KIT: Keeping It Together* (**www.hamiltonfamilynetwork.com**) is an organizational tool for parents with children with disabilities, developed by the CanChild Centre for Childhood Disability Research and the Hamilton Family Network. It is organized information for when parents are interacting with different services systems, for example, health, education and recreation.

Source: Family Alliance Ontario, 2007: 4.

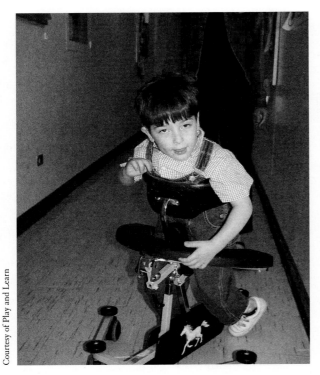

Courtesy of Play and Learn

Teachers may need support from families learning how to use specialized equipment.

children with severe to very severe disabilities, this proportion almost doubled to 73 percent. Of the 155,000 children with disabilities, about 52,000 had parents who said they needed help with housework, family responsibilities, and time off for personal activities because of their child's condition (Orwen, 2003: A16).

Parents may also face isolation, particularly if the child has a disability that draws attention to them in public. They may prefer to remain within the "safety" of their own home. Consideration must also be given to different cultural responses to disability. Some cultures view disability as fate and as something that must be endured. Other cultures see disability as the result of something the mother did wrong in pregnancy or as punishment for a sin, thus as the family's fault and the family's responsibility. Such families find it difficult to accept, let alone seek, assistance from nonfamily members (Doherty-Derkowski, 1994). In working with families from a variety of cultural backgrounds, teachers must consider that families language differences may be one major barrier to participation or engaging support for their family.

INSIDE LOOK

Innovative Program at Canada Post

In 1996, a special-needs pilot project became one of 12 programs funded by the CUPW Child Care Fund. As stipulated in the most recent union contract, Canada Post puts $250,000 into the Child Care Fund every three months. Bankrolled by the corporation and developed and coordinated by the Canadian Union of Postal Workers, the special needs project helps parents pay for extra costs related to children's disabilities. It also offers families support and advice by phone, points them in the direction of community resources, improves their advocacy skills, and keeps them in touch with each other through a regular newsletter. Eight years into the project

- 93 percent of parents say it has reduced over-all family stress levels
- 99 percent say it has reduced financial stress
- 81 percent feel it has improved their morale and effectiveness at work

Child care coordinator Jamie Kass states that among participants, 80 percent say the additional support they've been able to afford has helped their child's language, academic, and recreational skills. Ninety percent say their child is happier and has more self-esteem. Kass hopes the program can be expanded to include adult children with special needs who are cut off from many programs after age 19 and to aid employees who are caring for an ill parent or spouse. A book the union has published on the project, *Moving Mountains: Work, Family and Children With Special Needs*, is available through its website.

For more information about this program, contact CUPW at **www.cupw-sttp.org** and click on child care.

Source: Henderson, 2003: K11.

FIGURE 10.1   PARENTAL REACTIONS TO THEIR CHILD'S DISABILITY

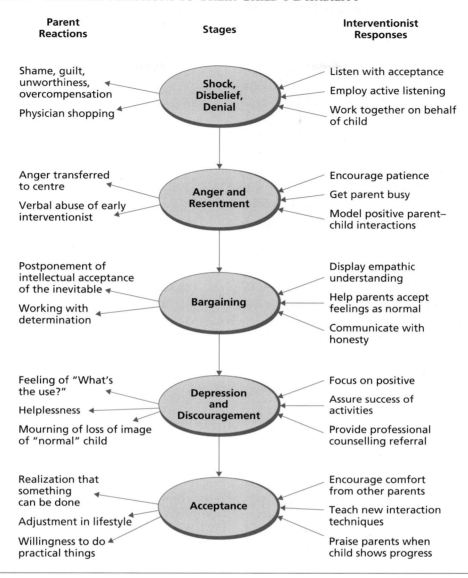

Source: ADAPTING EARLY CHILDHOOD CURRICULUM FOR CHILDREN IN INCLUSIVE SETTINGS, 5/E by Cook/Tessier/Klein. ©1996. Reprinted by permission of Prentice Hall Inc., Upper Saddle River, N.J.

Teachers need to be aware of religious beliefs and family traditions that might impact on the family dynamic.

According to Greey (1995: 19–20), many cultures "intertwine health beliefs and attitudes towards disability with Christian, Muslim, Jewish, Hindu, or Buddhist religious or spiritual beliefs. Consequently, if a family believes that ghosts, demons, or evil spirits inhabit the body of a child with special needs, rituals of expiation will be much more highly valued than the support services of an infant development worker."

WAYS IN WHICH FAMILIES CAN SUPPORT TEACHERS

- Collect and submit medical records.

- Provide background information for staff on the child's condition.

- Monitor and assist in individualizing the training so that procedures are geared specifically to the child.

- Keep staff up to date on developments, health, and so on.

- Assist staff in advocating for necessary supports.

It was difficult for us to accept the fact that Matthew wasn't just a high-energy child who needed teachers who would be accepting of his needs and just plain liked being with him. We felt he needed someone who could see that he was bright and had many strengths. We spent a lot of time blaming the teachers in the program for being too harsh and for having Matthew sit on a time-out chair many times during the day. We were worried about his self-image. He was quickly becoming the "bad kid" in the room, and whenever something went wrong he was assumed responsible. Virtually every night we were greeted at the door with another list of inappropriate things Matthew had done. Finally we met with the supervisor to discuss our concerns.

She said the teachers in the room were at a loss as to what to do with Matthew. None of the strategies they had tried seemed to work. She suggested that we have Matthew undergo an assessment at our local children's hospital. We reluctantly agreed. Over a period of several months Matthew was given a battery of tests. They revealed that he had attention deficit disorder with hyperactivity. He is now on medication and is calmer, happier, and able to concentrate. He is also building positive relationships with the children and teachers.

In retrospect I realize that we didn't want to believe there was something different about Matthew. It was easier to blame the teachers than to accept the truth. The teachers have since shared with us that although they had known something was not quite right with Matthew, they had not the expertise to identify a child with attention deficit disorder. Instead they had attributed much of what was happening with Matthew to what they saw as our neglect of him. Recently, the teachers met with us and with Matthew's doctors to find out how best to support Matthew. Once adversaries, we are now partners. It's too bad that so much valuable time was lost while we adults were busy blaming each other for Matthew's behaviour—because in the end it was Matthew who suffered.

HOW PARENTS CAN SUPPORT TEACHERS

It is vital for parents of children with special needs to have a sense of control over what happens with their children. When other people make important decisions about a child without the parent's input, the parent feels powerless and dependent. It takes a long time to gain a balance between feeling entitled to services and feeling humbly grateful for everything received.

ROLE OF THE TEACHER

- Teachers need to help families see that the disability or the label is just one small piece of who the child is. We need to stress that these are ordinary children with somewhat extraordinary needs for support. Not surprisingly, it is often the family that teaches this to the teacher.

- Teachers need to know that the stages parents with a child with a disability will go through

I had dreams for my child that were too often challenged by individuals who stimulated panic, fear, depression, and pain. But we set goals, became visionary, and exerted a significant influence to compensate for the weaknesses. I did not "buy into" the overwhelming prognosis that because of her developmental lags, weak motor skills, and language deficits, her future would, unquestionably, be limited. On the contrary, knowing and taking the time to understand her learning dysfunctions, I found professionals who could give me guidance. I had nothing to lose by remaining positive and challenging and, most of all, supportive of her every effort. She is now seventeen and a half and preparing to embark on the next stage in her life—college.

Source: I.F. Wax, "Don't Give Up the Dream," *Learning Disabilities Association of Toronto* 1, no. 4 (May–June 1996), p. 12. Reprinted by permission.

are not necessarily linear. Each family is unique, some will cope effectively and others may struggle feeling helpless and lost. A wise teacher will know the difference and adjust and accommodate to the best of their ability.

- Teachers need to appreciate that every member of the family will be impacted by a child with special needs. Thoughtful and sensitive attention should be paid to the siblings of these children.

- Teachers must understand that parents need to have hope; lack of hope paralyzes families.

- Strong communication skills—verbal and written—and an appreciation of cultural responses to children with special needs are important.

- Teachers need to have a strong child development background, and the ability to seek answers and to use resources to learn how best to support families.

- Teachers should share teaching strategies and new research information with the family on a regular basis through informal meetings and telephone calls.

- When exceptional children join the centre, it may be the first opportunity parents have had to see their child in a setting with children his or her own age. Teachers should encourage parents to look for ways in which the children are similar rather than different.

- As exceptional children grow older, the gap between them and the other children may become more apparent. Teachers need to continue to stress the gains they make.

- Parents—some of whom are coping without the assistance of family and friends—require teachers' support. ESL families in particular may have trouble communicating with doctors and other medical professionals. Teachers can help by assisting parents with medical terminology, liaising, and so on. Teachers should be prepared to work with other professionals in the support of this family.

- Like all families, parents of children with special needs are looking for teachers who will accept their children and not resent the extra time and effort they might require.

- Teachers must be flexible enough to adapt activities, the environment, and out-of-centre experiences so all children can participate. In the case of wheelchairs, teachers need to check the accessibility of outside locations when arranging field trips or outings for the children.

- Teachers who work with exceptional children need to be sensitive to the financial, medical, and emotional challenges parents may be facing.

- Other family members and children (if age appropriate) in the centre should be given a simple, matter-of-fact explanation of the child's disability. The parents of the child could be part of this discussion, providing information about medication, special equipment, toileting procedures, and so forth. It is important that everyone who works with the child has an understanding of how special equipment works.

INSIDE LOOK

Our son, Jeffrey, has spina bifida. As I think back over the teachers he has had, one in particular always comes to mind. He was constantly asking me how he could support Jeffrey, and the effort he put into trying to put those ideas into place made him different from any other teacher that we had encountered. Nothing was impossible in this school-age program. The teacher would research and visit trip sites in advance to find the best possible routes for Jeffrey. There was never any question that Jeffrey wouldn't be included in any outing. This teacher was constantly focusing on Jeffrey's self-esteem.

One of his most successful ideas came when he located a wheelchair and held wheelchair races in the hallways. Jeffrey raced the teachers and the other children—and he always won! We have encountered many wonderful teachers, but what made this one different was that he saw Jeffrey as a whole person. He also recognized that we were the experts on Jeffrey's condition, and he worked with us to provide the best possible environment for him. He will never really know how much we appreciated his total acceptance of Jeffrey and the energy and enthusiasm he demonstrated!

Source: Julie Cowie, Parent

- In cases where the exceptional child has siblings who are also enrolled in the centre, teachers should do everything they can to support these children, who may resent the fact that their brother or sister receives more attention than they do, who may have to deal with negative reactions to the disability from their peers, and who may be pressured by their parents to excel in order to "make up" for the child with special needs. They may also be given additional household responsibilities as well as caring for their sibling's needs.

- Above all, teachers should demonstrate respect, concern, empathy, and a sincere desire to work cooperatively with parents.

"It's up to us to plant positive visions until the rest of mainstreamed society catches up. Until one mother's dream is realized that the birth of every child be celebrated. . . . I'm beginning to see the potential of early intervention to reverse the negative, tragic, deficit-fixing mindset that parents may fall into when they find out their kid is different. If we could start right there convincing parents that different is OK—that we truly value diversity and do not just tolerate it—then we could restore a sense of normalcy to families" (Rocco, 1994: 15).

The integration of children with special needs reinforces the principle that every child should have equal access to child care.

The Roeher Institute: An International Information Centre on Disability

The Roeher Institute is Canada's leading institute for the study of public policy affecting people with intellectual impairments and other disabilities.

INSIDE LOOK

At a meeting for parents of Special Needs Children, we were asked, "What is your dream for your child?" I never had a dream for my son Daniel, who has special needs, nor for my two other special children. I always felt that they should have the dream and I should give them the opportunities for it to come true. But after thinking about it, I realized I do have a dream for Daniel—a very simple dream. I dream of Daniel taking an apple to his teacher, of packing his lunch for school, of seeing him in a school play, and of him bringing home his report card. These are very ordinary things for most parents, but to the family of a medically fragile child, these are dreams that will bring unexplained joy.

And I have another very special dream for Daniel that is coming true right now. While at Play Group, Daniel's friend Evan sits with him (in case Daniel should fall over or hurt himself) while the attendant is helping to prepare the snack. You should know that Evan is three-years-old. I hope that this dream will continue—that when my son is in high school, his friends will say, "Daniel doesn't need an attendant all day. We'll help him with his lunch. We'll make sure he gets to classes. We'll help him to get on and off the bus. We'll take him to the school dances and basketball games. Simply because he is our friend and we care about him."

Source: Parent quoted in L. Carson, *Integration Means All Our Children Belong* (Fredericton: Department of Education, Student Services Branch, 1987), p. 13. Reprinted by permission.

The institute has an extensive network, nationally and internationally, and acts as a clearinghouse for information on disability issues around the world. It houses an unparalleled collection of books, reports, and journals, as well as material in alternative formats—all dealing with disability from the perspective of inclusion and human rights. Visit the Roeher website at **www.roeher.ca/english/about/about.htm.**

SpeciaLink

SpeciaLink, the National Centre for Child Care Inclusion at the University of Winnipeg, is housed in the UW's Helen Betty Osborne Building in inner city Winnipeg. Within the same community hub, SpeciaLink shares space with the University's innovative Wii Chiiwaakanak Learning Centre and other Aboriginal education initiatives such as Community-based Aboriginal Teacher Education Program (CATEP), and Winnipeg Education Centre (WEC) ACCESS Program, as well as the World Council for Gifted and Talented Education. SpeciaLink's goal is to expand the quality and quantity of opportunities for inclusion in child care, recreation, education, and other community settings, to young children with special needs and their families. SpeciaLink is a helpline, clearinghouse and virtual resource and research centre, SpeciaLink provides personalized responses to specific questions, referrals and links to other organizations, and sources of help, information, and technical assistance including curriculum development and program evaluation. We share SpeciaLink fact sheets, books and videos, as well as training in your community in partnership with community organizations. We maintain an alert network of key inclusive child-care advocates across the country, who can quickly identify and respond to opportunities and threats to inclusion quality and funding. SpeciaLink is committed to action research that is informed and shaped by practice, building from the experiences of real-world child care with its limitations and its strengths. It connects researchers and policymakers with inclusive practices on the frontline. By identifying innovative practices, testing them, and presenting them to the wider field and to policymakers, SpeciaLink helps improve practice and inform policy. More information about SpeciaLink is available online at **http://www.specialinkcanada.org.**

BOOKS FOR CHILDREN

Oliver Onion: The Onion Who Learns To Accept and Be Himself, by D. Murrell (Autism)

The Sibling Slam Book: What It's Really Like to Have a Brother or Sister with Special Needs, by D. Meyer

What to Do When Your Brain Gets Stuck: A Kids Guide to Overcoming OCD, by D. Huebner

BOOKS FOR ADULTS

Cup of Comfort for Parents of Children with Autism: Stories of Hope and Everyday Success, by D. Flutie, L. Flutie, and C. Sell

More Than a Mom: Living a Full and Balanced Life When Your Child Has Special Needs, by H. Fawcett and A. Baskin

Driven To Distraction Recognizing and Coping with Attention Deficit Disorder from Childhood through Adulthood, by E. Hallowell and J. Ratey

Breakthrough: Parenting For Children with Special Needs, by J. Winter

Parenting a Child with Sensory Processing Disorder: A Family Guide to Understanding and Supporting You Sensory Sensitive Child, by C. Auer and S.L. Blumberg

Parenting Your Complex Child: Become A Powerful Advocate for the Autistic, Down Syndrome, PDD, Bipolar Or Other Special Needs Child, by P.L. Morgan

Reflections from a Different Journey: What Adults with Disabilities Want All Parents to Know, by S. Klein and J. Kemp

The Secret Life of the Dyslexic Child, by R. Frank and K. Livingston

Autism Heroes: Portraits of Families Meeting the Challenge, by B. Firestone

Kids in the Syndrome Mix of ADHD, LD, Asperger's Tourette's Bipolar and More, by M. Kutscher

Living With FASD: A Guide for Parents, by S. Graefe

MENTAL HEALTH, CHRONIC ILLNESS, OR DISABILITY IN FAMILIES

Teachers may also encounter families where a parent has a mental health issues, chronic illness, or a disability that may affect their parenting and their ability to provide for their family. The majority of children live with parents who report that they are in very good or excellent health. But that rate has been declining. In 1994, 77 percent of parents stated they were in very good or excellent health; in 2002, 72 percent made the same statement (Canadian Council on Social Development, 2006: 14). One in three individuals will experience a mental health problem at some point in their lives. In Canada, that translates into more than 10 million people. It's been estimated that mental illness costs the Canadian economy $33 billion each year in disability and lost productivity. Another $6–8 billion is spent annually to treat mental disorders. More hospital days are consumed by people with a mental illness than by cancer and heart disease patients combined. At the same time, research shows that two-thirds of adults who experience mental illness never seek help; for adolescents, the figure is 75 percent (Andrews, 2008). In a 2008 survey, more than half of the workers surveyed (55 percent) said that at least one of their colleagues has been away from work for a period of time because of a mental health problem; 68 percent said it made them more sensitive to their own mental health; 81 percent claimed to be more sensitive to the mental health of the people around them; and 82 percent were more careful about acting in a way that promotes good mental health in the workplace (Desjardin Financial Survey, 2008).

On May 8, 2002 the Honourable Michael Kirby, Chair of the Mental Health Commission of Canada, made a speech at The Empire Club of Canada. He stated that children's mental health issues in this country are reaching crisis proportions. Only one in six children is adequately diagnosed, often long after the original concerns were raised. This means that five out of every six children will not get the support they need. Early diagnosis is critical but the lack of doctors trained in diagnosing and in treating mental health issues exacerbates the problem. In a recent survey, 38 percent of parents are embarrassed to say that their child has a mental health issue. This reinforces the notion that the stigma attached to a mental health issues continues to plague effective treatment and we must bring these issues out of the "shadows."

FACTS ABOUT DEPRESSION AND ANXIETY

While only a small minority of children live with depressed parents, the impact on the child's well-being can be significant. Parent who are depressed are often withdrawn, tired, and despondent about the future; this creates a very stressful family environment. In 2000, less than 10 percent of children under the age of 12 lived with parents who were experiencing symptoms of depression, down slightly from 1994 (11 percent). Unfortunately, children in low-income families are more likely to live with a parent who is depressed. In 2000, 20 percent of children in low-income families (under $30,000 per year) had a parent who was depressed, compared to 6 percent of children in families with incomes over $60,000 (Canadian Council on Social Development, 2006: 14).

The Bayridge Anxiety & Depression Treatment Center lists the following statistics on its website **(www.bayridgetreatmentcenter.com/index.html)**:

- In any given year, about seven percent (between 13–14 million people) will experience a depressive disorder.

- Depression/anxiety continues to be Canada's fastest-rising diagnosis. From 1994 to 2004, visits for depression/anxiety made to office-based doctors almost doubled. In 2003, that meant 11.6 million visits to doctors across Canada about depression/anxiety. Of those who develop depression/anxiety, only about 20 percent will receive adequate treatment.

- About 97 percent of those reporting depression/anxiety also reported that their work, home life, and relationships suffered as a result.

- According to Health Canada and Statistics Canada, approximately eight percent of adult Canadians will experience a major depression/anxiety at some point in their lives, and around five percent will in a given year.

- Twice as many women as men are diagnosed with depression/anxiety. However, this may simply indicate that men are less comfortable seeking help or do not get an accurate diagnosis since depression/anxiety in men often manifests itself as a substance use problem.
- Children with depression are more likely to have a family history of depression/anxiety.
- A nationwide survey of Canadian youth by Statistics Canada found that 6.5 percent—more than a quarter million youth and young adults between 15 and 24—met the criteria for major depression in the past year. (Bayridge Anxiety & Depression Treatment Centre, n.d.)

For teachers working with depressed mothers it is important that they understand that the research indicates the mothers "look at their infants less often, touch them less often, have fewer positive facial expressions, and vocalize with infants less often than do non-depressed mothers . . . babies of depressed mothers are fussier, more irritable, and less active than are babies of non-depressed mothers. Depression in babies is observed at birth. They have higher sensory thresholds and therefore need more stimulation to respond. They already show flat affect and low activity levels. Babies of mothers who are successfully treated for depression show no long-term adverse effects of their infant experience. Because of the effects of mothers' depression on infants' behaviour are reversible, intervention to help depressed mothers and their infants are essential" (Brooks, 2008: 268).

Serious Illness

For families where a serious illness is diagnosed there will be a period in which the family will need time to adjust and adapt to the situation. Ward (2002: 288) says, "During the initial phase of illness, the needs of other family members are often ignored. Meals may become 'catch as catch can.' Laundry may pile up. Children may receive very little attention and supervision. . . . One or more family members may get burned out. They no longer have the energy to respond to the physical and emotional demands placed on them. As a result, they become irritable and tend to withdraw from others. They may in turn become ill themselves. The family system itself starts to break down as family resources can no longer meet the demands of illness. The family goes into crisis."

Hamilton (2003: 8) provides some strategies for helping parents explain serious illness to children:

- Tell your children what is happening as soon as possible. They will sense that something is wrong. It is far better for them to hear it from you than find out another way.
- Tell all your children at the same time, even if there is an age gap. The younger ones may not understand at the level of the older ones, but they will feel included. When the children know there are no secrets, they will be better able to support each other.
- Be open and honest. Children need your trust more than ever right now. Don't risk losing it.
- Children tend to cope best when they are well informed and there are not surprises about what is happening. Keep children up to date.
- You may want to practise or write down what and how to say things. This may not be your usual way to talk with your children, but explain that what you have to say is really important and that you want to make sure you explain it correctly.
- Let other people caring for the children know how you have explained things and give them some direction on how to respond to children's questions, fears and behaviours. Some parents write down explanations or answers to questions so that others will know how to respond to the children.
- Sometimes, different generations have different ideas of how or when to include children when something like this happens. Some believe you shouldn't tell or involve children because you don't want to upset them. Some believe children should be protected from the pain. Experts now believe we should not protect children from what is happening in their own family and that children will have a smoother adjustment to change if they feel included and if they know, to their level of understanding, what is going on. Children then have the opportunity to work at, and to work through their feelings at the same time as everyone else. It is important for parents to take the lead and instruct others on how to respond and what to say to the children.
- A check to gauge that you are open and honest with children is if you can talk freely with other adults on the phone or face to face, and not have

to be too careful about what you are saying because the kids are around. For example, use the word cancer. Let them hear it first from you.

- Explain the treatments planned for the near future or as much as you know. Will the parent be in hospital/at home? Will their appearance change? What will be the likely side effects of the disease or treatment?

- Explain how things will change for the children, and who will be looking after them. Will they be staying in their own home? Will they still be going to their usual activities? If plans are still uncertain/unknown, tell them you will let them know as soon as you know. Try to give your children even a rough idea of the length of time the treatment and recovery may take: months; by the season ("maybe after the end of the summer"); by a certain holiday or celebration; or "We just don't know how long Mommy is going to be sick," "I am going to be sick for a long time before I can get better."

- It is amazing what children can hear in the neighbourhood, at school, or at a friend's house. Explain how information can get mixed up and what they should do if they hear something that conflicts with what you've told them.

- For many parents, the hardest thing about explaining serious illness to their children is talking about the dying issue. As uncomfortable as it may be, this issue needs to be addressed in one of your early conversations. If you don't address it, children will think it is off limits to discuss and it becomes a barrier to completely open communication. "Right now the doctors feel I am going to do fine and that I will get better, but if anything changes I will let you know."

WHEN A CHILD IS HOSPITALIZED

In many situations, children are taken to hospitals for routine procedures but there are times when an illness may mean a longer stay and, in some situations, children are rushed to emergency wards due to injuries.

At some point in their career, teachers may also be faced with a child who is chronically or terminally ill. Children are highly compassionate and ask many questions about children with skin rashes, hair loss (due to chemotherapy), and so on. Staff should use this opportunity to teach the children about the illness and to encourage their

sense of concern and caring. One teacher recounts his story:

> In our 10-plus school-age program we were all devastated when we learned that Jason had a brain tumour that would require surgery and chemotherapy. We waited anxiously for several months for the results of the tests. Fortunately the prognosis was positive. While we awaited Jason's return to our group, the children knew that he had lost most of his hair, since many of us had visited him during his recovery at the hospital and at home. A group of the boys approached me about shaving their heads, so that when Jason came back he wouldn't feel so awkward. I was moved by their compassion for Jason and their ability to look for a way to make his return a happy one. With their parents' permission we all visited the local barber, and the next morning when Jason arrived with his family, he was greeted by a roomful of bald heads including mine!

Hospital-based programs have been shown to be effective in reducing the anxieties of children who are facing a period of hospitalization. Teachers can invite people involved in these programs to visit the playroom for a demonstration and discussion of the hospital stay. Children can touch and play with the medical equipment they will see on the day of their procedure. They will also be given age appropriate information about how the equipment is used.

Teachers can encourage children to act out their concerns by setting up the dramatic play centre to reflect a hospital theme. Drawing and other art activities also allow for meaningful self-expression. The following information can be gathered so that the child can be prepared and reassured:

- How long will the child be hospitalized?
- Will there be other children in the room?
- Will there be X-rays, anesthetic, blood tests, urine tests, etc.?
- Can the child bring a comfort toy into the operating room?
- Will it be alright to bring other familiar objects—toys, books, clothes from home?
- How will the child feel after the surgery or treatment?
- What are the rules about visiting, parental involvement, sleeping over, etc.?
- What will the meals be like?
- Will television be available?
- What play facilities are available in the hospital?

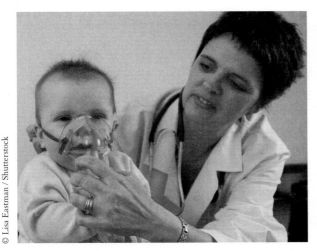
A hospital stay can be a difficult and challenging time for children and their families.

Children are most concerned about interacting with new people and if pain is going to be a factor. One of the hardest things for children to understand is that something that hurts or feels strange is actually helping them. Anticipation and not knowing can make it worse. Family members should encourage their child to express their feelings and listen carefully for the questions the child might ask and the ones they don't. For parents, a loss of control and a sense of helplessness only create more anxiety and fear. Hospitalization will affect the whole family so it is important that accurate and age appropriate information is given to siblings.

DISABILITY AND THE WORK FORCE

According to Johnson, Lero, and Rooney (2001: 13), only 38 percent of working-age women with disabilities (aged 15–64) were in the labour force, compared to a figure of 76 percent for women without disabilities. The participation rate for men with disabilities was 49 percent, compared to 91 percent among men without disabilities. Labour force participation rates for persons with disabilities decline dramatically with age. Census data indicated that in the 15- to 34-year age range, 63 percent of men with disabilities were labour force participants. The rate declined to 29 percent for men aged 55 to 64.

DISABILITY AND SUCCESSFUL PARENTING

Blackford and Israelite (2003: 135) believe that "the disability of a parent must be understood not merely as a problem for the family that must be 'fixed' through a medicalized therapeutic approach. Instead, it is important to acknowledge problems that rest outside the individual and to question the extent to which barriers to successful parenting are societally imposed. . . . A narrow view of families with a parent with a disability that focuses only on what happens inside the family fails to sufficiently take into account stigma and ableism in the larger society. Such a view results in what has been called 'blaming the victim'" (Ryan 1972). Society frequently views parents with disabilities, especially mothers, as totally dependent individuals who have somehow committed an immoral act by becoming

INSIDE LOOK

When Yun's parents informed us that she was taken to the hospital, it was a difficult time for all of us at the centre and particularly for her kindergarten friends. Initially we did not know what the diagnosis was but when we learned that she had childhood leukemia we understood why she had appeared so tired, short of breath, and had frequent nose bleeds. We were encouraged when her parents shared that 90 percent of this type of leukemia goes into remission but we knew that Yun and her family had difficult days ahead. She responded to the chemotherapy but was nauseated and she was losing her hair. As a group we decided that we must do what we could to support this family. Teachers in the kindergarten took turns visiting Yun at the hospital bringing letters and drawings from her peers which she happily posted in her room. The supervisor brought some interesting puzzles and books on her favourite topic— dinosaurs! On another visit we took a video that we had made with all of the children singing get well songs. We played the video in the hospital playroom and this drew a great crowd. Other teachers took food to the home and since the parents were spending so much time at the hospital, they appreciated a home cooked meal. We are happy to say that Yun is now back in the centre with us in full remission!

parents (Fine and Asch 1988; Finger 1991). Mothers with disabilities, in particular, 'shoulder the burden of society's perception of them as incompetents who have irresponsibly become mothers who will, along with their offspring, unquestionably become a burden on society' (Baskin and Riggs 1988: 240).

Dr. Blackford's (1990) findings in a study conducted in conjunction with Persons United for Self Help in north eastern Ontario show children and their parents with various disabilities creating flexible family systems that are not always bound by traditional expectations of the division of labour with regard to age, gender, and physical condition. Many family members were more accepting of difference in their relationships outside the family. Children and parents lived in and for the moment, rather than constantly anticipating the future. These results suggest that consideration of families with parents with disabilities can enlarge our view of what family life could or should be.

 The Centre for Independent Living in Toronto initiated the Parenting with a Disability Network (PDN) at **www.cilt.ca/Parenting/PDN.htm**.

BOOKS FOR CHILDREN

Wishing Wellness: A Workbook for Children of Parents with Mental Illness, by L.A. Clarke

Living Well With Serious Illness, by M.E. Heegaard

Mom and the Polka Dot Boo Boo: A Gentle Story Explaining Breast Cancer To A Young Child, by E. Sutherland

Hair for Mama, by K. Tinkham

Imagine a Rainbow: A Child's Guide for Soothing Pain, by B.S. Miles

Sammy's Mommy Has Cancer, by S. Kohlenberg

Can I Catch It Like A Cold? A Story to Help Children Understand a Parent's Depression, by The Centre for Addiction and Mental Health

BOOKS FOR ADULTS

The Ghost in the House: Real Mothers Talk about Maternal Depression, Raising Children and How They Cope, by T. Thompson

The Mother To Mother Postpartum Depression Book: Real Stories From Women Who Lived Throught It and Recovered, by S. Poulin

We Carry Each Other: Getting through Life's Toughest Times, by E. Langshur and S. Langshur

Every Day Counts: Lessons in Love, Faith and Resilience From Children Facing Illness, by M. Sirois

Helping Your Child Cope with Your Cancer: A Guide for Parents and Family, by P. Van Drenoot

Can I Still Kiss You? Answering Your Child's Questions about Cancer, by N. Russell

How to Help Children through a Parent's Serious Illness: Supportive, Practical Advice from a Leading Child Life Specialist, by K. McCue

Preparing the Children: Information and Ideas for Families Facing Terminal Illness and Death, by K. Nussbaum

DEATH IN THE FAMILY

In 2003 in Canada, 3,561 children under the age of 19 years died, many of them after long terminal illnesses (Statistics Canada, 2006). In addition, 16,053 adults between the ages of 20 and 49 years died in that year. It is likely that many of these adults were parents, leaving children under the age of 21. These numbers mean that a very large number of children are affected by death and dying every year in Canada (Hadad, 2008). There is no question that a death in the family will alter the family make up, often creating new roles for family members.

Kubler-Ross (1974) identifies five stages in the grieving process: **shock and denial, anger and protest, bargaining, depression and despair, and finally adjustment and acceptance** (Shimoni and Baxter, 2008: 172). Hadad (2008) states that children's attitudes toward death are very much coloured by whether their parents have discussed death with them, how their parents handle death within the family, and whether the end of life has remained a hidden subject. If the child witnesses a grieving parent behaving stoically and showing little emotion when a loved one dies, the message communicated is that emotions should not be displayed, no matter what pain is felt. The child may then retain into adulthood the idea that public displays of grief are not acceptable and that the difficulty a grieving person may have in dealing with daily life is a sign of weakness or psychological disorder. However, if the child sees family members showing their grief, the message received is that grief is acceptable and expected. If a child has been inculcated into a religious belief, it plays a large part in determining attitudes toward death. Depending on the beliefs, they may form an attitude of calm acceptance of death or a fear of final judgment. Cultural background also influences a family's attitudes and its practices. "Children often feel they have caused and are responsible for everything" (Ginsberg and Opper: 1987).

For instance, five-year-old Sam screamed at his older brother, 'I hate you, and I wish you were dead!' He was haunted with the idea that his words created his brother's murder the following day. Due to Sam's age-appropriate egocentrism and magical

TABLE 10.1 OVERVIEW OF CHILDREN'S UNDERSTANDING OF AND REACTIONS TO DEATH

AGE	CONCEPTS	NORMAL BEHAVIOUR
Less than 3 years	little understanding of death sense of separation or abandonment	increased crying fussiness clinginess regression change in sleep, eating and elimination behaviours resistance to change
3–6 years	death is seen as temporary or reversible magical thinking	sadness aggression magical thinking regression nightmares bladder/bowel problems non-compliance
6–9 years	gradual comprehension that death is final some magical thinking personification of death	guilt compulsive caregiving phobias possessiveness aggression regression difficulty expressing grief difficulty concentrating psychosomatic symptoms
9–12 years	cognitive awareness of death and its finality difficulty conceiving of their own death or that of a loved one concrete reasoning about how and why death occurs	defiance phobias possessiveness aggression psychosomatic symptoms
12+ years	death is irreversible, universal and inevitable abstract and philosophical reasoning understand all people and self must die, but believe death is in distant future	anger defiance risk taking increased sexual activity substance abuse aggression possessiveness psychosomatic symptoms suicidal ideation

When I was three, my father passed away leaving my mother to raise my sister who was six at the time and myself. What I remember as most painful was doing crafts for Father's Day. All of the teachers knew that I didn't have a father, but they still had the whole class do the craft. I write this because I want us as ECEs to know that even young children may have to face losing a parent, teachers should know about the history of the families in the centre and be sensitive to this issue. Years later this memory still stays with me.

Source: Justina Dorrington, ECE graduate

perception, he saw himself as the centre of the universe, capable of creating and destroying at will the world around him. Reversibility also characterizes children's grieving. For example, Jack, a five-year-old first-grader was very sad after his dad died in a plane crash. Age-appropriately, he perceived death as reversible and told his friends and family that his dad was coming back. Jack even wrote his date a letter and waited and waited for the mailman to bring back a response (Goldman, 2006).

The media will also colour a child's interpretation of death. One estimate indicates that by the time children graduate from elementary school, they will have witnessed at least 8,000 murders on television alone. When death occurs, it is important to ask children what they want to know and then work towards finding the answers.

When a child, sibling, parent, or extended family member dies, or when a death occurs through miscarriage or stillbirth, it is a difficult time for everyone involved. It is important for the teacher to know the cultural and religious practices of the family. In some instances, teachers may be active participants in the grieving process (e.g., attending the funeral) and in other situations; the family will prefer a more private arrangement. Sending food to the home or doing drop-off and pick-up if the child is attending the centre may be another way of supporting the family. For the teacher, it is important that they find out how mourning is conducted in cultures that may be different from his/her own.

Parents may also ask if the teacher thinks the child should attend the funeral and how to support the child during this difficult process. Much of this will depend on the age of the child, religious teachings, and cultural influences. For some children, this may be a way of bringing closure to a difficult family time; for others it may create more anxiety. Each child's reaction will be unique and so there is

no right or wrong answer here. In some situations, finding a way to honour the person who has passed, for example by creating a photo album, finding a special picture of the loved one to put into a frame, drawing pictures of happy time together and framing those, may be a way of helping the child deal with their loss. There are also many wonderful books that have been written to explain this process. Many of these strategies will also be important if a child has died at the centre. Classmates will need support and an opportunity to celebrate the life of their friend.

ROLE OF THE TEACHER

The symptoms of grief are wide and varied. The Dougy Center for Grieving Children has worked with thousands of grieving children and teens since their program began in 1982. They hear nearly every day from caring parents, teachers, and adult caregivers who want to support grieving children but aren't sure how to go about it. What they have learned from children is that everyone grieves differently. Cultural traditions, religious beliefs, family experiences, and personality differences all influence the way we choose to express our grief. Their advice to teachers? When in doubt, ask a child or teenager what helps and they will tell you. It is also important that teachers be alert to behaviours that may require interventions by mental health counsellors.

The center has created a booklet, *35 Ways to Help a Grieving Child*. The suggestions included in the pamphlet are invaluable and all teachers are recommended to explore this publication and to visit **www.dougy.org** to discover additional resources. The following fifteen suggestions are particularly key in a child-care centre:

1. Listen.
2. Be honest. Never lie to a child.

3. Don't force kids to talk but answer the questions they ask—even the hard ones.

4. Talk about and remember the person who died.

5. Expect and allow all kinds of emotions.

6. Encourage consistency and routines. Set limits and rules and enforce them.

7. Understand that grief looks different at different ages and respect differences in grieving styles.

8. Get out the crayons, pens, pencils, paint, and chalk.

9. Run! Jump! Play! (Or find other ways to release energy and emotions).

10. Help the child at naptimes. Sleep may come hard for grieving children.

11. Resist being overprotective.

12. Remember: "Playing" is "grieving."

13. Remember special days that impact the child.

14. Be available for children when they need you and hug with permission

15. Take care of yourself and do your own grieving and ask for help if you need it.

Rainbows: Guiding Kids Through Life's Storms

"Rainbows is an international not-for-profit organization that fosters emotional healing among children grieving a loss from a life-altering crisis. These losses, among others, include separation, divorce, death, incarceration and foster care. Often youth are expected to accept the changes in their family or sort out their feelings alone. They can become 'silent mourners,' and often confused and angry, they reveal their pain by acting out with negative behaviour and withdrawing in unhealthy ways. Rainbows provides a safe and supportive environment for participants to process their feelings, build self esteem and learn positive coping tools to last a lifetime—because 'it doesn't need to hurt forever.' This is accomplished through our unique 12-week peer support programs available from preschool through to adult. Rainbows partners with the community to make the program available free of charge to children and youth in 1,620 trained sites located in more than 496 Canadian communities. These sites include schools, social service organizations, community centres, and places of worship. The National Office of Rainbows Canada is located in Barrie, Ontario. Rainbows Canada is a National Chapter of Rainbows International." (Rainbows Canada, n.d.) For more information on this program, visit **http://www.rainbows.ca/**.

BOOKS FOR CHILDREN

Lifetimes, by B. Mellonie

I'll Always Love You, by H. Wilhelm

When Dinosaurs Die: A Guide to Understanding Death, by L. Krasny Brown and M. Brown

---

INSIDE LOOK

My ECE field placement experience took place at the Hospital for Sick Children in Toronto in the Pediatric Medicine, Respiratory Medicine, and Infectious Diseases Units. During my placement, I developed close relationships with many of the children and their families. It was amazing to see the dedication of those parents who spent their days at the hospital and a little heartbreaking to see those that couldn't. I understand how important it is for the children and their families to continue as normal a routine as possible while in the hospital. I found that spending time with the children on a one-to-one basis, listening to parents' concerns, and doing whatever I could was a rewarding experience. During my stay, one of the children I worked with died. The day before her death, the child had asked for me and wanted to take me home with her so that we could continue to do crafts. I'm glad that she and I had an opportunity to spend time together because maybe it made a difference to her and her parents. Working at the hospital has given me a new appreciation for children and their families in a new setting. This was my first opportunity to work with children with special needs and it has opened me to other career options I previously had not considered.

Source: Bridget, ECE student

I Miss You! A First Look at Death, by
P. Thomas and L. Harker

When Your Grandparent Dies: A Child's Guide
to Good Grief, by V. Ryan and R.W. Alley

BOOKS FOR ADULTS

Why Did You Die? Activities to Help Children
Cope With Grief and Loss, by E.
Leeuwenburgh and E. Goldring

Creative Interventions for Bereaved Children,
by L. Lowensiten

Kids Grieve Too! A Handbook for Parents, by
T. Easthope

When Children Grieve: For Adults to Help
Children Deal with Death, Divorce, Pet
Loss, Moving and Other Losses, by J.W.
James, R. Friedman and L. Matthews

Help Me Say Goodbye: Activities for Helping
Kids Cope When a Special Person Dies, by
J. Silverman

FAMILIES IN WHICH THERE IS SUBSTANCE ABUSE

According to the Canadian Centre on Substance
Abuse (1999), the most recent statistics available state,

the declining trend in alcohol sales observed
throughout the 1980s and 1990s did not continue
in 1996–97. Sales expressed in terms of absolute
alcohol increased from 7.4 litres per person in
1995–96 to 7.6 litres per person in 1996–97, the
first increase to occur since the early 1980s.
According to the 1993 General Social Survey

(GSS), nearly one in 10 adult Canadians (9.2%)
reported having problems with their drinking.
The most common problems affect physical
health (5.1%) and financial position (4.7%). Also,
43.9% say they have had problems from other
people's drinking, such as being disturbed by loud
parties (23.8%), being insulted or humiliated
(20.9%) and having serious arguments (15.6%). It
is estimated that 6,503 Canadians (4,681 men and
1,823 women) lost their lives as a result of alcohol
consumption in 1995, and 80,946 were hospitalized (51,765 men and 29,181 women) due to
alcohol in 1995–96. In 1995, there were 804 arrests
(695 men and 108 women) in Canada attributable
to illicit drugs. In 1995–96 there were 6,947 hospi-
talizations attributable to illicit drugs. Annual
productivity losses in Canada due to substance
abuse have been estimated at $4.1 billion for
alcohol, $6.8 billion for tobacco and $823.1 million
for illicit drugs.

Alcoholism is a disease that has physical, psychological, and social repercussions. Although there is
no conclusive evidence of a genetic predisposition
to the disease studies show that 50–80 percent of
alcoholics have had a close alcoholic relative. Ward
(2002: 291) refers to an "alcoholic family system"
rather than to "a family with an alcoholic member"
because so much of family life focuses on the
alcohol abuse that it becomes the main organizer;
that is, the entire family system is involved with
alcoholism.

The Addiction Research Foundation (1996)
states: "The same amount of alcohol affects a
woman more than a man. This is because women
have less water in their bodies than men. So
alcohol is less watered down in women's bodies.

INSIDE LOOK

Steve, age 35, has been an alcoholic for 20 years. He has three young daughters. Until a year ago, his
children and wife had existed only in the peripheral haze beyond his bottle. "I wanted to do what I
wanted to do. I drank whatever money there was. I stayed out for days and nights. When I was home, I
beat my children. I wasn't able to function." After attending a fathers' support group, Steve has not had
a drink for a year. He continues to have marital strife but the father's support group helped him cope with
these problems separately, and to pursue a relationship with his children he has never had. "What I
learned the most is a personal identity as a father. I've learned to look at my children as individuals, and
to spend time with them. I'm dealing with the stress and I take time for myself. I have a little more
patience and a little more tolerance. I don't let the kids get control of me. I know my limitations."

Source: De La Barrera and Masterson, 1988: 10–13.

Numerous barriers stand between women, especially mothers, and drug treatment. For example, women often resist entering treatment programs because they must release their children to someone else's care and fear never seeing them again. Despite this reality, only a handful of residential drug treatment programs accept women with their children. Treatment programs need to be developed that treat parents, especially mothers, in the context of their families.

Source: Zuckerman and Brazelton, 1994: 82.

Alcohol also does more physical damage to women more quickly than it does to men." The long term effects for newborns born to addicted women can have life-long consequences. Weston et al. (1989: 3) state that "child-care providers may have drug-exposed infants who are irritable and hypersensitive to external stimulation; exhibit feeding and sleeping problems; have tone, reflex and movement abnormalities; and produce decreased vocalizations." Many parents who are addicted are not able to provide the nurturing that children need and the economic well being of the family may well be jeopardized when adults lose jobs due to their addiction. All substances alter, in varying degrees, an individual's state of consciousness, memory, affect regulation, and impulse control.

Robinson (1990: 69) observes that children of alcoholics "are at higher than average risk of becoming alcoholics, workaholics, compulsive gamblers, compulsive spenders, or sex and drug addicts. Eating disorders are also common. The bedrock of these problems is laid in the preschool years. Early identification can lead to primary intervention that can interrupt the disease cycle before it is implanted and before it takes its toll on the child physically, cognitively, emotionally, and socially."

According to Stark (1987: 59), children who live with an alcoholic parent are very fearful of accidents. Will a parent pass out while smoking a cigarette and set the house on fire? Will she injure herself during a fall? Children are also terrified of the arguments that usually go on between their parents. The atmosphere of argument and tension in an alcoholic household is frequently more upsetting to children than the parents' actual drinking. And children often have reason to fear for their own safety. Victims of incest and child abuse often come from alcoholic families. Often the threat of embarrassment causes children to isolate themselves from their peers at a time when they should be forming and building relationships, and enhancing their social skills. Children may also take on the role of the adult in the family.

Children of alcoholics, according to Robinson (1990: 71), are "children of fear":

They are afraid of what is happening at home and terrified that something awful is going to happen to them. Many of them cope by building walls around themselves. Intervening in their creative activities and talking about their painting or the roles they play in dramatic play can help them remove a few stones from the walls. Helping

It's awful in the long run. . . . When you grow up you have to deal with a lot more problems, 'cause when you're little you don't realize everything that's happening, and you try to understand and you don't. And then when you get older, it's so hard to think that your mom would do that to you. I mean she'll tell you that she loves you and that she'll help you any way she can—she just doesn't. She tries, but she can't; the drugs just take over. And, I don't know, it's just hard. It's really hard.

Source: *Brandy, age 16* (quoted in Howland Thompson, 1998: 34).

these children establish friendships with other children and their families may provide a haven for them, a place where they are accepted and life is calm.

ROLE OF THE TEACHER

Robinson (1990: 70–71) makes the following suggestions of ways in which the teacher can help:

- Play therapy—the use of creative materials such as clay, water, sand, and paint—may help the children express their feelings and provide soothing, calming experiences. Teachers need to help children recognize and label their emotions.

- Many homes are in a constant state of upheaval. A sense of order and consistency in the daily routines in the child-care centre is critical.

- Teachers need to educate themselves about the adverse consequences for children who live with an alcoholic or drug-addicted parent. Insecurity and loss of control are two of the psychological consequences.

- Teachers can help children to "gain a sense of mastery over their environment by giving them choices to make and challenges that are developmentally sound and that ensure their ability to manage and control their lives. Teaching autonomy through simple decision-making processes in the classroom can help break children's fear and dependency" (70).

- Teachers can further restore children's sense of security by establishing positive, loving relationships with them and by setting clear and consistent limits. Some of these children will test the limits, since they are used to making decisions for themselves without adult supervision or intervention.

- Finding one-on-one time for these children is crucial.

- Teachers must follow through on promises made to the children.

- Many of these children become adept at hiding their feelings. Observe them carefully and look for opportunities to build bridges.

- Older children may be provided with information on alcoholism; a number of children's books are available to assist teachers in this endeavour.

- While teachers must make every effort to support children of alcoholics, they also need to understand that they "cannot replace the alcoholic parent and should not try to do so. Allowing the child to become too dependent on you would be a disservice, because this child must continue to deal with the alcoholism long after leaving your classroom" (70).

- A teacher who feels that a parent is under the influence of alcohol or drugs and in no condition to pick up his or her child after school (especially in a car) might suggest that the parent take a cab home or even offer to drive the family herself. It is no easy thing to challenge parents who may respond angrily to what they perceive as interference. Under such circumstances, however, the child's well-being is the most important consideration. Diane Buhler, Executive Director, of the organization Parents Against Drugs, has this advice for child-care teachers:

> The most typical concern of child-care centres in the area of substance abuse is primary prevention. For young children, this means discussing situations involving those drugs—medicine, caffeine, and tobacco—that are part of daily living. For example, when daycare providers dispense medication, they can communicate respect for the powerful effects of the drug. Possible messages include:
>
> – Even a little too much medicine can hurt you.
> – Some medicines look like candy and that is why medicine must be kept in a safe place.
> – We use medicine only if we really need it.
> – Only trusted adults can give you medicine.

- Other teachable opportunities are present in the daycare schedule; for example, when kindergarten children are accompanied to their school program, they often encounter teenagers who are smoking. A daycare worker could discuss the addictive nature of tobacco with the children and assure them that the best choice is not to start smoking in the first place.

- Other issues regarding substance abuse that may arise concern the well-being of a child if the daycare has reason to believe that the primary caregivers are abusing alcohol or other drugs. Children in these circumstances have the potential of suffering neglect or even abuse—the usual reporting procedures need to be followed.

- Children who grow up in families where an immediate family member or frequent visitor abuses alcohol or other drugs can begin to develop anxieties and other behaviour patterns that are characteristic of "children of alcoholics." These characteristics can range from being overly responsible or "parentified" to being overly suspicious and withdrawn. A day-care provider cannot necessarily ascertain that familial substance abuse is the cause of these behaviours, but should be aware that the possibility exists. An excellent resource is a booklet for parents with very young children titled "An Early Start: Drug Education Begins at Home" (1999), published by the Addiction Research Foundation (now a division of the Centre for Addiction and Mental Health). E-mail the CAMH at mktg@arf.org.

Breaking the Cycle: A Success Story

Research shows that drug abuse among pregnant women is rising. It is estimated that between 4,000–6,000 babies are born drug-exposed in Toronto each year, more than 10 percent of all newborns. Before now, services addressing these problems were fragmented and sometimes difficult to get access to. This meant addicted women who were pregnant or had young children were unlikely to stick to a regular round of separate programs designed to tackle different aspects of their problems. This situation contributes to the relapses into addiction, child maltreatment, and parenting breakdown.

Breaking the Cycle is an agency that offers help to women who are addicts and are pregnant or the parents of young children. The agency also offers support to small children who are affected by their mothers' use of drugs or alcohol. Breaking the Cycle offers a friendly, nonjudgmental atmosphere where several services are available, including addiction counselling, personal counselling, medical help, and social connections with other mothers in similar circumstances. The agency also provides meals for the mothers as well as a clothing exchange for mothers and children. With funding from Health Canada, the agency is operated by five organizations: the Canadian Mothercraft Society, the Jean Tweed Treatment Centre, the MotheRisk program at the Hospital for Sick Children, the Metro Children's Aid Society, and the City of Toronto's public health department.

One mother, Venus Carter, says: "I was worried about the baby and how I could stop using [the drug] and stay clean when all I had known for years was how to survive on the street. I really wanted Jamai but I was terrified he'd be taken from me. You want this baby but you want this drug, too. If you're an addict, it's a tough choice." Venus says her baby son Jamai is alive and well today only because of her own willpower, bolstered by Breaking the Cycle (Dineen, 1995: B3).

BOOK FOR CHILDREN

Wishes and Worries: A Story to Help Children Understand a Parent Who Drinks Too Much, by the Centre for Addiction and Mental Health

BOOKS FOR ADULTS

In The Realm of Hungry Ghosts: Close Encounters With Addiction, by G. Mate

Addiction Proof Your Child: A Realistic Approach to Preventing Drug, Alcohol and Other Dependencies, by S. Peele

Trouble Don't Last Always: When a Child Becomes a 4-Year-Old Parent, by S. Lenard Rico Salter

Working with Children and Families Affected by Substance Abuse: A Guide for Early Childhood Education and Human Service Staff, by K. Pullan Watkins and L. Durant

Addiction: Why They Just Can't Stop, by R. Books

HOMELESS FAMILIES

Canada is one of the few countries without a national housing policy. The federal Liberals downloaded housing costs and responsibilities to the provinces in the early 1990s. Using Ontario as an example, just 3,575 affordable housing units have been built in Ontario since 2003. More than 250,000 households (400,000 people) live in subsidized housing in Ontario and more than 120,000 families are on a waiting list for subsidized housing, including about 75,000 in Toronto. The average two-bedroom apartment in Toronto rents for $1,100.00 per month; average rent for a two-bedroom apartment in public housing is $350.00 per month. About half of Toronto's 58,000 public housing units are more than 35-years-old and in desperate need of repair. The

Toronto Community Housing Corporation is facing a $300 million capital repair deficit (*The Toronto Star*, 2007).

The very nature of homeless families makes counting them nearly impossible. Regardless of how a homeless family is defined, no current, accurate, or comprehensive statistics are available regarding the number of such families in Canada. Pollack (2001) lists the following statistics about Canadian homelessness:

- In almost every urban centre across Canada, conservative estimates indicate that there are 200,000 Canadians—men and women—who are homeless. This conservative number does not include thousands of people who live outside, are seasonally homeless, or are homeless for brief periods of time.

- The fastest growing segments among the homeless are young people under age 18 and families with children.

- Fewer and fewer low-cost rental units, the withdrawal of federal and provincial support for social housing, and the rise in poverty among single-parent families headed by women have contributed to the rising statistics.

- A study has shown that one-third of the homeless people are living with mental illness (75 percent of homeless single women suffer from a mental disorder).

- Many of the homeless have been discharged from hospitals or jails without proper community resources.

- In Toronto each night some 50,000 homeless people seek shelter but only 4,500 will find a space for the night.

- Increasing numbers of people with HIV/AIDS, tuberculosis, hepatitis, sexually transmitted diseases, and communicable infections are being recorded in the homeless population.

Of pressing concern is the growing number of homeless women and children. Life as a homeless woman or child can mean life on the streets, life in substandard housing, life in a series of motel rooms, or a life of enforced dependency on the welfare system.

While shelters provide a welcome relief from the street, families who use them often live in very cramped conditions and members are sometimes separated. The following are some characteristics of homeless children:

- sleep disturbances
- nighttime anxieties about possessions, even wearing their shoes to prevent theft
- lethargy and inattention at school
- children may hoard food at school
- nutritional deficiencies
- delays in immunizations

INSIDE LOOK

Homeless women in Toronto are dying at 10 times the rate of other women between 18–44 according to a new study released in the *Canadian Medical Association Journal*. A commentary accompanying the study calls the "stunning" death rate among homeless women "a clarion call to our society and our health care community. This smoldering public health crisis can no longer be ignored." HIV/AIDS and drug overdose are the most common causes of death among younger homeless women. Depression leading to suicide was also a high risk, according to the study, co-authored by Dr. Stephen Hwang of St. Michael's Hospital and Dr. Angela Cheung of the University Health Network. Yet homeless women get little attention and few treatment programs, said Dwang, who is part of St. Michael's inner city health research unit. Toronto's 15 shelters for single women have a total of 565 beds but they housed a record high of 5,683 different women during 2002. "We're certainly seeing more women who have complex problems, serious mental health issues and addiction issues," said Fiona Murray, manager of planning and development for Toronto's hostel services. If a homeless woman does decide to go to a hostel, "there's a good chance there won't be a bed to go to," said Lynn Hemlow, a registered nurse who struggles to provide health care and preventative programs at the 416 Drop-In. "For men, it's different. There is a huge, huge organization."

Source: Carey, 2004: A1.

- insecurity
- trouble playing with other children and making friends
- aggression
- anxiety
- language and other developmental delays. (Couchenour and Chrisman, 2004)

As Ward (1998: 363) points out, these characteristics are not the only negative effects of shelter life:

> Like other poor children, those living in shelters suffer in both their health and education, but the effects are more extreme. Usually by the time families reach shelters, they have already moved several times, staying with friends and relatives, perhaps even sleeping in a car. As a result, children often have a high number of respiratory infections and other illnesses. They also suffer psychologically. Two-thirds of homeless parents report an increase in their children's acting-out behaviour.

The child-care centre or school may be the only stable environment for the family during its period of homelessness. Given these circumstances, the teacher plays a vital role in supporting parents and children who are living in shelters. Families may need assistance in settling into their new environment. Children may require individualized attention and extra reassurance, not only when they are in a shelter but during their reintegration into the community. The loss of a home robs a child of the familiarity and sense of place most of us take for granted. Teachers need to be vigilant in their efforts to protect these children from ridicule or censure from their peers. Many of these children live in crisis much of the time, and the child-care setting should be low-key and perceived threat in the classroom at a low level. Giving the child breakfast upon arriving at the centre, lunch, and a hearty snack at the end of the day will ensure adequate nutritional needs are met. The extra effort on the part of teachers can make a great difference in building positive and healthy relationships between staff and these families.

FAMILIES LIVING IN SHELTERS

The following excerpt from a recent news article in *The Toronto Star* offers illuminating details about life in a homeless shelter:

> Every year about 3,000 school children in Toronto live in homeless shelters. Yet despite this long-standing problem—the number of affected children has remained steady for the last five years—there are no government or school board policies to ensure the educational and emotional needs of these vulnerable children are being met, says *Lost in the Shuffle*, the first Canadian study on the issue. "As long as governments allow family homelessness to continue, it is necessary to understand the educational experiences of homeless children and to put in place the supports they need for educational success," says the report by Toronto's community social planning council and Aisling Discoveries Child and Family Centre. The $65,000 study funded by the United Way was conducted between June 2006 and March 2007, and was based on interviews with 198 parents, children, educators, and staff in Toronto-run family shelters and Violence Against Women shelters. Even though school enrolment from a shelter happened within a day or two, educational assessments and enrolment in special needs programs were "subject to delays and a serious impediment to education," the study says. A majority of these children have experienced or witnessed violence that can cause behaviour that interferes with learning, the study found, and yet access to support and training for teachers is uneven. Parents reported difficulty finding a quiet space in shelters for their children to do homework and said a lack of access to computers was a problem for kids in higher grades.
>
> Some parents go to great lengths to shield their children from the dislocation that comes with homelessness. Estelle, a 40-year-old mother of four who spent 11 months in a women's shelter in 2004 and 2005, travelled by bus three hours a day with her daughters, then four- and five-years-old, so that they could continue attending school in their old neighbourhood. "I didn't want to upset their education," says the woman who was escaping a violent spouse. "But I know they suffered academically. They were always so tired. We had to leave the house at 7 a.m. to get there on time." Her two teenaged sons chose to live with relatives so they, too, could stay in their old schools, she said. "It was extremely hard on everyone." (Monsebraaten, L., 2007)

BOOKS FOR CHILDREN

Fly Away Home, by E. Bunting and R. Himler

December, by E. Bunting

Lily and the Paper Many, by R. Upjohn

The Family Under the Bridge, by N. Savage Carlson

The Lady in the Box, by A. Mcgovern

Trish Horrigan, a child advocate with a family residence program, provides the following glimpse into the lives of homeless families. She suggests ways in which teachers can support these families:

A number of Canadian families have no place to call home. These are the men, women, and children who find themselves seeking refuge in shelters and hostels. Some have been evicted, forced to leave unsafe living conditions; some are fleeing domestic violence; others are new immigrants to Canada. No matter the circumstances, all of these families are facing crisis. They have left behind their homes, friends, and belongings. This is a stressful time for parents and their children. The relations between families and other members of the community are strongly affected by this stress, including relations between parent and teacher. Factors that might affect parent–teacher interaction include the following:

- Living in a shelter environment that is crowded, unstable, and without privacy can lead to high levels of stress.
- A transient lifestyle may prevent parents from developing an affiliation with a particular child-care centre or school. Members of the family may see themselves as temporary members of the community and therefore make no effort to forge a lasting relationship.
- Newly arrived immigrant families may have limited or no English skills. Also, the cultural background of the family will often dictate the level of interaction with teachers and caregivers. For example, parents from some countries may view teachers as authority figures and feel it inappropriate to question them.
- Mothers fleeing an abusive relationship may be hesitant to enroll their children in a school or child-care setting because of concerns for their physical or emotional safety. Trust is a critical issue for these families.

Source: Contributed by Trish Horrigan

BOOKS FOR ADULTS

Homelessness, by J. Layton

Dying For a Home, by C. Crowe

Street Stories: 100 Years of Homelessness in Vancouver, by M. Barnholden and N. Newman

Can't Get There From Here, by T. Strasser

FAMILIES LIVING WITH ABUSE AND VIOLENCE

FAMILY VIOLENCE

This information in this section is based on excerpts from two publications developed by Boost Child Abuse Prevention & Intervention: Making A Difference: The Community Responds To Child Abuse, Fifth Edition, by Pearl Rimer (2007); and Looking For Angelina: A Learning Guide On Family Violence by Giselle Rishchynski, Pearl Rimer, and Jonah Rimer (in press). We gratefully acknowledge Pearl Rimer's contribution and participation.

Home is supposed to be the safest place of all. However, family violence remains a pervasive and persistent issue in Canada and around the world. At least one in three women globally has been beaten, coerced into sex, or abused in some other way, most often by someone she knows, including by her husband or another male family member (UNICEF, 2006). Family violence can be found across all ethnic, cultural, racial and class backgrounds (Menjivar and Salcido, 2002). "Violence and abuse toward an intimate partner is arguably the most common form of violence in society" (Wolfe and Feiring, 2000: 360).

The reality of family violence in Canada is staggering. Recent research has revealed that 29 percent of women in Canada are affected by men's violence (UNFPA, 2000). Between 70–85 percent of women who are sexually assaulted are assaulted by men they know. As outlined by Johnson (1996), of all incidents of sexual assault, 24 percent took place in the victim's home, 20 percent in the perpetrator's home, 10 percent in someone else's home, 25 percent in a car, and 21 percent in a public place

FIGURE 10.2   "I HIDE IN THE CLOSET"

I hide in the closet when my dad hits my mom.

(1996: 127). Spousal violence against Aboriginal women is three times higher than for non-Aboriginal women. Aboriginal woman were also significantly more likely than non-Aboriginal women to report the most severe and life-threatening forms of violence, including being beaten or choked, having had a gun or knife used against them, or being sexually assaulted (Statistics Canada, 2006b: 65). Amnesty International (2004) reported that Aboriginal women aged 25–44 are five times more likely than other Canadian women of the same age to die of violence (2004: 14). Each year in Canada, between 1996 and 2006, 56–65 women were murdered by their intimate partner (Juristat, 2006).

This is only part of the picture. Statistics Canada does not include boyfriend/girlfriend or extramarital relationships in their intimate partner assault or homicide total. In addition, as with most illegal and hidden behaviours, the prevalence of family violence is unknown. Underreporting occurs for many reasons, including victims who do not recognize that the behaviour is abusive and illegal, shame, self-blame, fear of retaliation by the offender, loss of financial security, uncertainty if immigration status will be affected, fear that the children will be taken away, and hope that the violence will stop.

Underreporting is also the result of family, friends, and neighbours who feel that what goes on in other people's homes is a private matter and nobody else's business.

Family violence has psychological, physical, social, and economic impacts for victims, families, and society. The Canadian Federal Government estimates that the annual direct medical costs related to violence against women is $1.1 billion (World Health Organization, 2004); a figure that rises to $4 billion a year when social services, lost productivity, lost earnings, and police, courts, and prison costs are taken into account (Greaves, Hankivsky, and Kingston-Riechers,1995; Ontario Women's Directorate, 1997).

Family violence is based on an imbalance of power. The aim of family violence is to frighten, intimidate, and control. Family violence is defined as "the systemic use of tactics to establish and maintain power and control over the thoughts, feelings and conduct of an intimate partner" (Duffy and Momirov, 1997: 137). Klein (2005) further explains:

Domestic violence is not about relationships, good or bad . . . It is about abusers and their use of violence. Domestic violence is . . . not accidental violence . . . Abusers do not strike their partners because they are out of control. They strike their partners to maintain control over them, humiliate and debase them, isolate them, or punish them for asserting their independence.

Family violence is also referred to as woman abuse, intimate partner violence, domestic violence, spousal violence, spousal assault, and violence against women. The use of the term "family violence" throughout this information does not indicate gender neutrality, but rather is an attempt to convey that the intimate partner, along with the children and youth exposed to the violence, are impacted by violence in the home.

Family violence can erupt in all families, and does not exist solely in male–female relationships. Family violence is also found in same-sex relationships and in homes where extended families live together. In heterosexual relationships, men are not the only perpetrators of family violence. However, statistically, women are most likely to be victimized by family violence and the perpetrator is likely to be her male partner. Therefore, the partner being abused is referred to using feminine terms and the abuser using masculine terms.

Overall, the violence experienced by women tends to be more severe and more often repeated than the violence directed at men. Women are more likely than men to be the victims of family violence such as physical assault, sexual assault, criminal harassment/stalking, and homicide. Female victims of family violence are more likely than males to report being injured, requiring medical attention, experiencing multiple assaults, and fear for their lives and the lives of their children. About 60 percent of female homicides in Canada are committed by current partners or estranged partners with a history of family violence (Statistics Canada, 2006b). In some cases, men kill spouses and children together; women do not (Wilson and Daly, 1992: 206).

Forms of Family Violence

Family violence can take the form of physical, sexual, emotional, spiritual, or financial harm. While these categories are helpful in understanding family violence, it is important to realize that many individuals experience more than one form of violence.

- **Physical abuse** includes all acts that result in physical harm, as well as threats to harm the partner and/or children. Examples of physical abuse include pushing, kicking, slapping, choking, restraint, and use of a weapon/object. Physical intimidation (e.g., eye contact, destroying property) and threats of violence (e.g., "you know what's coming next," the making of a fist, the displaying of a weapon) are psychological elements of physical abuse. Psychological/emotional abuse tactics are often effectively used to control and intimidate partners, particularly the isolation of the victim (especially if there are disability, economic dependence and language barriers).

- **Sexual abuse** includes but is not limited to forced sexual acts, sexual accusations, use of sexually degrading language, and sexual assault accompanied by threats of or actual violence.

- **Emotional abuse** is the most common type of abusive behaviour, and also the most varied and complex. The three most common forms of emotional abuse are: name calling or put downs; jealousy and not wanting the victim to talk to other people; and demanding to know who she is with and where she is at all times (General Social Survey, 2004). Emotional/psychological abuse also includes: blaming the victim for the abusive behaviour; harassment (e.g., stalking); controlling and/or monitoring friendships, the use of the car and telephone; spiritual abuse (e.g., interfering with her ability to practice her chosen religion); and keeping the victim in a state of fear, leaving her feeling like she is constantly "walking on eggshells." The presence of emotional abuse is the largest risk factor and greatest predictor of physical violence (Johnson, 1996) and sexual violence (Statistics Canada, 2006b).

- **Financial/economic abuse** includes, but is not limited to: the abuser controlling all of the financial matters and decisions; keeping the victim from obtaining employment, or alternatively taking away her paycheques, making the victim dependent on him for money; enforcing a strict allowance that does not allow the victim to pay for basic necessities; and making her account for every penny.

Risk of Family Violence

Young women between the ages of 15–24 are most at risk for interpersonal violence. Other individuals at high risk for family violence are women who have just separated from a partner or at the time when the decision to separate is made; pregnant women (40 percent of woman abuse incidents begin during pregnancy [Noel and Yam, 1992; Rodgers, 1994]); Aboriginal women; women in common law relationships; and women with disabilities. The fact is that for some women and their children it may be safer to stay in the relationship than leave; violence often escalates when abusers sense that their victims are trying to leave or are using outside intervention. In 79 percent of the domestic homicide cases in Ontario (from 2002–2005), women were murdered during a pending or actual separation (DVDRC, 2005). The risk of homicide is higher in the first two months after separation (Daly and Wilson, 1993). Vallée (2007), in his book entitled *The War on Women*, addresses the question of "why does she stay"; it comes down to fear:

> Unless you have personally experienced that fear, it can be almost impossible to comprehend. But anyone who does understand it would never proclaim, "I don't know why she stayed. I wouldn't put up with it for a minute." (2007: 36)

Child Abuse

Generally, child abuse is categorized into four major conditions: neglect, physical abuse, sexual abuse, and emotional abuse. Although these divisions may be useful in principle, it is common for a child to suffer more than one form of abuse. For example, children who have been physically abused may also have been told that they are bad or stupid and that they deserve what they are getting, resulting in emotional consequences to the children.

- **Neglect** occurs when a parent or caregiver does not provide for the basic emotional and physical needs of the child on an ongoing basis. Neglect includes not providing the proper food, clothing, housing, supervision, safe surroundings, personal health care, medical and emotional care, and education. Children who are neglected physically and emotionally may not develop normally. The consequences of neglect can be very serious, particularly for young children, with some children suffering permanent damage.

- **Physical abuse** includes all acts by a caregiver that result in physical harm to a child. Physical abuse may happen if a child is punished harshly, even though the parent or caregiver may not have meant to hurt the child. Examples of physical abuse include bruises; marks in the shape of objects or handprints; shaking; burns; human bite marks; fractures of the skull, arms, legs, or ribs; and female genital mutilation. Physical abuse may result in a minor injury (such as a bruise), to a more serious injury which could cause lasting damage or death (for example, from shaking a child). Inappropriate punishment includes, but is not limited to, anything that leaves a mark on the child, or the use of an object to strike a child. Although cultural factors play a role in caring for and/or disciplining children, injuring a child is unacceptable.

- **Sexual abuse** occurs when a person uses power over a child to involve the child in any sexual act. The power of the abuser can lie in his or her age, intellectual or physical development, relationship of authority over the child, and/or the child's degree of dependency. The sexual act is intended to gratify the needs of the abuser. "Touching" is not the only criteria in defining sexual abuse. It includes acts such as fondling; genital stimulation; oral sex; inserting fingers, penis, or objects in the vagina or anus; exposing oneself; sexual exploitation over the Internet; as well as exposing a child to, or involving a child in pornography or prostitution. The offender may engage the child in the sexual activity through threats, bribes, force, lies, and by taking advantage of the child's trust. Most of the time, the offender is someone known to the child and trusted by the child or family.

- **Emotional abuse** is the continual use of any of the following by a parent or caregiver when interacting or disciplining a child: rejecting (e.g., "I wish you were never born"); criticizing (e.g., "Why can't you do anything right?"); insulting (e.g., "I can't believe you would be so stupid"); humiliating (e.g., embarrassing a child in front of other people); isolating (e.g., not allowing a child to play with friends; terrorizing (e.g., "The police will come and take you away"); corrupting (e.g., frequently swearing in front of the child or getting the child to participate in things against the law); not responding to a child's emotional needs; or punishing a child for exploring the environment. Children who are exposed to violence in their homes may suffer emotional harm.

The four types of child abuse can occur at the hands of individual caregivers, or on a larger scale. Abusive and damaging acts can occur in institutional settings with responsibility for children if caregivers do not supervise children adequately; use harmful methods of controlling children; use drugs inappropriately to manage children's behaviour; use harsh disciplinary measures such as corporal punishment, isolation, or withholding food; use excessive force when trying to deal with a child who is "out of control"; or do not report the knowledge of any abusive behaviour toward children in the setting. Societal abuse refers to acts of commission or omission on the part of society as a whole that result in children suffering, for example society's knowledge and acceptance of children living in poverty.

Prevalence of Child Abuse

The following statistics are the findings of the *Canadian Incidence Study of Reported Child Abuse and Neglect*, the first nation-wide study to examine the incidence of reported child abuse in Canada (Trocmé et al., 2001):

- There were an estimated 21.52 investigations of child abuse per 1,000 children.

- Neglect was the most common reason for investigation (40 percent of all investigations), followed by physical abuse (31 percent), emotional abuse (19 percent), and sexual abuse (10 percent).

- 69 percent of substantiated physical abuse cases involved inappropriate punishment.

- Failure to supervise leading to physical harm accounted for 48 percent of substantiated neglect cases.

- In all four categories of substantiated abuse, the majority of alleged perpetrators (93 percent) were family members or other persons related to the child.

Internet Sexual Exploitation

Sexual exploitation of children on the Internet encompasses three major forms of maltreatment against children:

- child pornography (more appropriately termed "child sexual abuse images");

- child luring/unwanted sexual solicitation; and

- child prostitution/child sex tourism.

Canadian police estimate that there are more than 100,000 websites that contain thousands of child abuse images (Alcoba, 2008). According to Cooper (2006), 50 percent of collected images between 2000–2001 were of children aged five or younger and 50 percent of all child pornography is made by family members (Cooper, 2007). Internet use knows no borders, and identifying children is very difficult and time consuming. Although there are over one million child sexual abuse images in circulation over the Internet, with approximately 100,000 different child victims, only about 800 children worldwide have been identified (Chapman and McGarry, 2007). There are more than five million children worldwide drawn into child prostitution and child sex tourism, including more than 200,000 in Canada (Flowers, 2001: 149–150).

Child Homicides

According to Statistics Canada (2001), about 100 child homicides, on average, are documented by the police every year across Canada. Data consistently has shown that the majority of family-related homicides against children and youth are committed by parents; between 1975 and 2004, 86 percent of victims under the age of 18 were killed by a parent (Statistics Canada, 2007).

As with family violence, it is difficult to determine the extent of child abuse, since so many cases go unreported, and infant homicides may be underreported since some cases of accidental deaths (e.g., falls) could actually be due to child abuse.

THE OVERLAP BETWEEN FAMILY VIOLENCE AND CHILD ABUSE

Exposure to family violence goes beyond actually witnessing (i.e., seeing) violent episodes. It refers to the multiple ways in which children are exposed to family violence:

- directly seeing and/or hearing the violence (e.g., the children are hiding under the covers, but can hear what is going on);

- being used as a pawn by the perpetrator (e.g., the perpetrator threatens to hurt the children if their mother does not "cooperate"; the perpetrator uses the children as "spies" and interrogates them about their mother's activities);

- injury during the violence (e.g., a child is injured while trying to protect another family member); and/or

- experiencing the physical, emotional and psychological repercussions of violence (e.g., a family member is physically injured; living in a tense environment dominated by fear; child protection and/or police intervention).

As expressed by Newton (2001):

Domestic violence can severely impair a parent's ability to nurture the development of their children. Mothers who are abused may be depressed or preoccupied with the violence. They may be emotionally withdrawn or numb, irritable or have feelings of hopelessness. The result can be a parent who is less emotionally available to their children or unable to care for their children's basic needs. Battering fathers are less affectionate, less available, and less rational in dealing with their children.

It is impossible to accurately determine how many children are exposed to abuse and violence in their own families, but the statistics below clearly indicate that it is a pervasive and troubling problem.

- 11–23 percent of all Canadian children witness some violence against their mother in the home. It is estimated that two to six children in each classroom have witnessed some form of woman abuse in the home over the past year (Sudermann and Jaffe, 1999).

- Studies estimate that 60–80 percent of children in families where woman abuse occurs either see or overhear it (Jaffe, Wolfe, and Wilson, 1990). Almost 40 percent of women assaulted by their spouses said their children witnessed the violence against them (Statistics Canada, 2006b).

- *The Canadian Incidence Study of Reported Child Abuse and Neglect* reported that exposure to family violence was the most common form of emotional abuse cases, making up 58 percent of all substantiated cases (Trocmé, 2001).

- Studies that have explored the prevalence of child abuse in homes where domestic violence occurs indicate that in 26–78 percent of cases, the children are also being abused (Bowen, 2000; Bowker et al., 1988; Edleson, 1999; Straus and Gelles, 1990; Suh and Abel, 1990).

- In studies of child abuse, about 50 percent of the cases also involve the abuse of the child's mother (Sudermann and Jaffe, 1999).

- In Canada, between April 1, 2005 and March 31, 2006, approximately 106,000 women and children were admitted to shelters, most often to escape abuse (Vaillancourt and Taylor-Butts, 2007).

- Between 1995 and 2004, in 4.4 percent of the spousal homicides in Canada, children of the perpetrators were also killed (Statistics Canada, 2006a).

"If domestic violence calls are dangerous, emotionally charged, and volatile for police officers, the accused and the victim, they are equally as distressing and frightening—if not more so—for children at the scene" (Benoit and Gibson, 2006: 7).

THE POSSIBLE IMPACT OF ABUSE ON CHILDREN

Where there is family violence, the home environment in which these children live is often described as "toxic"; in many cases, their well-being and development are severely compromised. There is often an atmosphere of fear, anxiety, anger and tension that permeates the home, even when incidents of physical abuse are not happening (Sudermann and Jaffe, 1999). Silence and quietness in children is often misunderstood as adequate coping and resilience but is not (Hass, 2008).

Children who have witnessed the abuse of their mothers often experience the same types of emotional and behavioural problems experienced by children who have been abused themselves (Sudermann and Jaffe, 1999). These may include symptoms of post-traumatic stress disorder, lower self-esteem and social competence, aggressive behaviour, conduct problems, anxiety and depression (The Packard Foundation, 1999).

Like all other forms of abuse against children, the extent of sexual exploitation of children over the Internet is unknown, and the effects of Internet sexual exploitation are not fully understood (Rimer, J., 2007). Generally, the trauma suffered by victims of child pornography is longer lasting and harder to alleviate (Palmer, 2004). There is also the added dimension that there is a permanent record of the abuse that will be on the Internet forever, totally out of the victim's control (Palmer, 2005; Cooper, 2006).

How the impact of child abuse, violence and exploitation may manifest in children is outlined on next page.

Self-Blame

- Some children feel they are responsible for what happens to them and around them. When they are abused, they often blame themselves. They may think they deserved the physical abuse because they were bad, or the sexual abuse because they wanted love or accepted presents from the offender. Many children feel responsible for their mother's suffering and their father's anger.

- Some children feel guilty because they did not try to stop the abuser, especially if a family member was hurt. Many children tried to protect themselves, but failed. As a result they do not try anymore. This is a type of learned helplessness.

- Children may experience a deep sense of shame, feel "different or damaged" and alone. The sense of shame and secrecy can affect their ability to express feelings openly (Jaffe, Wolfe, and Wilson, 1990).

Fear

- Children who have been abused or have been exposed to family violence are often left in fear of those they know and trust—the world is no longer a safe place.

- Children may be afraid of rejection, upset or other negative reactions, either by family, friends, or in some cases, by the offender.

- Some of the things they may also be afraid of include: that the threats the abuser has used will come true (e.g., the disclosure will result in the break up of the family); the fear that they themselves or someone they love will be hurt or killed; and that they will be abandoned if someone finds out about the abuse.

Powerless and Vulnerable

- Children feel powerless to protect themselves—nothing they did stopped the abuse of themselves or others, or they had no way to stop it.

- Some children are isolated, with no one to help or support them. Some children may think that no one has the ability to stop the abuser.

- Children may lose faith in themselves, others, and their future. Having experienced the world as unsafe and unloving, they fall into despair and give up hope that their needs will be met.

- Exposure to family violence teaches children that being male equals being powerful and abusive, and being female equals being punished and victimized. They learn that power and violence are ways to deal with decision-making, conflict resolution, and stress release. Boys particularly may be aggressive in their relationships with their mothers, girlfriends, or partners, while girls are more likely to be victims of domestic and sexual violence (Moore et al., 1990; Hagemann-White, 2006). It has also been suggested that "because of their own familiarity with violence and abuse during their earlier development, some vulnerable youth may have particular difficulty recognizing their own abusive behavior in romantic relationships or their options to terminate an abusive romantic relationship" (Wolfe and Feiring, 2000: 362).

Betrayal

- Children learn that a trusted person has hurt them or someone they care about, causing them to feel angry, betrayed, confused, and depressed.

- Children often feel confused because they love the abuser. Should they be loyal to the abuser or tell what happened?

- Children who have been betrayed often have trouble trusting others and forming healthy relationships.

Loss

Children who have been abused may suffer many losses:

- The innocence and trust of childhood.

- Any sense of control over their environments.

- Normal patterns of growth and development, including problems with: eating; sleeping; developing healthy relationships; normal sexuality; and school.

- Normal emotional attachments to primary caregivers—the most important protective factor for children exposed to violence is a secure relationship with an adult, most often a parent. Research by Zeanah et al. (1999) revealed that mothers who experienced more serious partner violence were more likely to have infants with disorganized attachments to their mothers.

- Research has revealed that brain development is negatively affected when children are exposed to trauma; this has implications for behaviours including impulsivity, aggression, the hyper-arousal and stress responses, and for cognitive and social processing (Mohr and Fantuzzo, 2000; Perry, 1995, 2004; Rossman and Ho, 2000).

- In some cases, the abuser isolates the children or the children choose not to bring friends home for fear that the violence may be uncovered. As a result, these children may not develop positive peer relationships or learn important social skills. Peer friendships are also negatively affected for those children who respond to family violence with withdrawn or aggressive behaviour. Bullying and victimization in school are associated with exposure to interparental violence (Baldry, 2003).

- On disclosure, there may be removal from homes and families, the community, and other caregivers; children may worry about who will take care of them.

Destructiveness

- Children who grow up in violent environments may engage in self-destructive behaviour, including self-mutilation, frightening displays of rage, eating disorders, substance abuse, prostitution, suicidal or homicidal tendencies, and involvement in criminal activity.

- A study by Jaffe, Wolfe, and Wilson (1990) reported that 70 percent of young offenders charged with crimes against people have witnessed violence in their families. Longitudinal studies on delinquency have shown that children who develop a "deviant career" are more likely to have parents who are abusive toward their partners, compared to those not exposed to interparental violence (Steinberg, 2000).

Effects of exposure to family violence in childhood may persist into adulthood, including: difficulty establishing and maintaining relationships; misuse of power and control; substance abuse; self-destructive behaviour (e.g., suicidal tendencies, eating disorders); post-traumatic stress disorder; anxiety; depression; and poor self-esteem.

REPORTING SUSPICIONS OF CHILD ABUSE AND FAMILY VIOLENCE

Each province and territory in Canada has its own legislation with respect to child abuse and "a child in need of protection" or "child whose security or development is in danger," although they all address neglect, physical, sexual and emotional abuse, and the death of a parent. Each province and territory addresses the age of a child who is entitled to protection under the law, the duty to report, confidentiality, and failing to report. It is imperative that all individuals who provide services to children and families be familiar with their current provincial/territorial legislation with respect to their protection; this means keeping up-to-date on any relevant legislative changes.

When one form of abuse is suspected or identified, it is important to be tuned into the possible indicators of other types of abuse occurring within the same family. In situations where there are concerns or doubts as to whether or not the indicators support suspicions of child abuse or family violence and reporting requirements, it is best *not* to ask anyone else to help you decide if the call should be made, but rather consult with a worker from the local child protection agency. It is best to avoid speaking with anyone else about the details of the suspicions until speaking with a child protection worker. It is also advisable to consult with a child protection worker before informing a parent/caregiver that you are consulting/reporting to a child protection agency, or that you have already done so. To do so could jeopardize the child and/or the investigation and court proceedings.

The *Criminal Code of Canada* sets out offences relating to neglect and physical abuse of children (e.g., abandonment, assault), sexual abuse (e.g., invitation to sexual touching, sexual exploitation), and the age of consent regarding sexual acts. The *Criminal Code* does *not* include a specific charge for "woman abuse" or "partner abuse"; however, an alleged abuser may be charged with any number of relevant criminal offences (e.g., forcible confinement, criminal harassment, attempted murder).

HELPING PARENTS WHEN THEIR CHILD HAS BEEN ABUSED

Coping with the crisis of a child's abuse and disclosure can be distressing and exhausting for parents/caregivers. It is the parent's response to the child's disclosure that is so important to the child's recovery. Parents need help staying calm for their children, providing stability and reassurance while everyone is coping with what happens after suspicions of child abuse are disclosed. Parents may ask staff/caregivers for information and advice.

The following information will assist in helping those who are in need of support.

- A child's experience of abuse may cause tremendous stress and disruption in the family. A difficult period for children and families is to be expected. Try to maintain consistent routines and limits, avoiding other new and challenging experiences, and unnecessary separations from primary caregivers.

- The child's brothers and sisters may be afraid of what is going to happen, or feel guilty for not protecting the child. It is possible that other children in the family may have been abused.

- Children communicate in their own way. Encourage children to talk by being a good listener and trying to stay calm, no matter what the child says. Let the child talk about what happened using his/her own words, without adding words or asking leading questions. This may confuse the child and affect the investigation.

- Accept any temporary regression in the child's behaviour (e.g., bed-wetting). It may be advisable for parents/caregivers to supervise the child more closely, setting clear limits on aggressive and hurtful behaviours. Children need to be reassured that their feelings, fears, and behaviours that seem babyish or out of control are normal after this type of experience. With time they will feel more like themselves.

- Some children may need nighttime comforts and strategies to cope with bedtime fears. If asked, a child may be able to tell parents what she or he needs (e.g., a night light, leaving the bedroom door open at night). It is helpful to try to protect children from re-exposure to frightening situations and reminders of the abuse.

- This is a time when parents may question their beliefs about themselves as parents and protectors, their ability to judge people, feelings about the world as a safe place, and justice. It is important to get help or advice, not only for their children, but for themselves. Staff may direct parents to the appropriate community resources to help with emotional, economic, legal and/or safety issues.

- Encourage parents to talk about their own feelings with someone they trust. It is normal for parents to feel helpless and guilty especially if they feel that they did not protect their child. Many parents think about things over and over trying to understand what has happened, being fearful that the abuse will happen again.

- Although parents' feelings need to be acknowledged, remind them that expressing intense feelings to the child and minimizing or exaggerating the child's trauma may result in overwhelming and frightening a child. Children should not have to worry about whether or not his/her parents are coping; it is the job of grown-ups to look after the children.

- Recommend to parents that they tell the child's doctor about the allegation of abuse. Parents may want the doctor to check the child for health reasons and/or to discuss getting help. The child may also need reassurance if s/he is worried about anything.

- Advise parents to contact a child protection agency with their suspicions, concerns, or questions. Parents can help the investigation by cooperating.

- Suggest to parents that they keep notes on further developments or disclosures, and their observations of their children's behaviour. This information may be helpful to the investigation and to the support people working with the child and the family.

- Reinforce to parents that even if legal proceedings do not result in charges or a conviction, the child is to be believed, and to be commended for his/her efforts. The child should never be blamed for whatever happens.

- Parents must decide whether or not, and when, to tell others about the abuse. Suggest to parents that they listen to the child's feelings as to who should be told. Ask them to respect the child's rights to privacy and confidentiality.

- Suggesting family outings and fun activities will help to reduce the stress for everyone.

- Remind everyone that "time helps the healing."

HELPING CHILDREN WHO HAVE EXPERIENCED ABUSE

Staff plan and implement many of the strategies below for *all* children enrolled in a program. However, the goals and strategies are especially critical for children who have been victims of abuse and/or family violence. Remember that many children express their pain, fear, anger, despair, and other feelings through play and "misbehaviour." Seek the advice of appropriate professionals if needed; knowledge of atypical development and therapies is a specialized area. Children are resilient, and with supports for themselves and their families, they can heal and thrive (adapted from Rimer and Prager, 1998).

"Children in a state of fear retrieve information from the world differently than children who feel calm. In a state of calm, we use the higher, more complex parts of our brain to process and act on information. In a state of fear, we use the lower, more primitive parts of our brain. As the perceived threat level goes up, the less thoughtful and the more reactive our responses become. Actions in this state may be governed by emotional and reactive things styles. . . . The traumatized child lives in an aroused state, ill-prepared to learn from social, emotional, and other life experiences. She is living in the minute and may not fully appreciate the consequences of her actions" (Perry, 2004).

- Help the child develop positive self-esteem.
  - Plan activities where success is built in, based on the child's age, development, and realistic expectations.
  - Give positive reinforcement for accomplishments and desired behaviour.
  - Display the child's accomplishments.
  - Reinforce through discussion and activities that women and men are both valued, respected, and should never be controlled through violence.
- Help the child to trust.
  - Establish limits and routines and be consistent.
  - Be loving and affectionate, and respect those children who may need more time before they feel comfortable with being touched.
  - Allow children to safely express anger without the fear of punishment.
  - Spending one-on-one time so the child feels cared for and listened to.
- Help the child to identify and express emotions.
  - Name emotions.
  - Plan sensory and dramatic play activities.
  - Provide books and other materials that help children learn about feelings.
  - Show children healthy ways to express anger and solve problems without hurting themselves or others.
  - Accept a child's need to talk about fears, sadness, and losses experienced because of abuse.

- Help the child to learn to communicate
  - Speak to children calmly.
  - Use a firm but kind tone when asking children to do things or when expressing disapproval.
  - Give children the message that it is okay to ask questions and say how they feel.
  - Spend time talking and listening.
  - Plan activities that encourage language and listening skills.
- Help the child to identify and solve problem situations.
  - Teach children that they have choices and how to make the best choice.
  - Use positive methods to guide children's behaviour.
  - Plan activities that require problem-solving.
  - Solve any conflicts that happen with nonviolent methods, and role-model calm, non-aggressive ways of dealing with anger.
- Help the child to resume developmental progress.
  - Plan activities that help practice motor and language skills.
  - Support positive relationships with friends.
  - Help children with schoolwork.
- Help the child to develop a safety plan.
  - Teach children how to dial 911 (i.e., practise memorizing the phone number; teach them to leave the phone off the hook until police arrive).
  - Help children to choose a neighbour they can go to for help.
  - Plan how to keep safe during a violent scene (e.g., identify a safe spot to hide; do not try to stop the fight).

VIOLENCE PREVENTION

Early childhood educators have an important role to play in preventing child abuse and family violence by: maintaining an environment for children and families that is physically and psychologically safe, and modelling healthy relationships; developing policies and practices to prevent abuse and violence; identifying and responding effectively to children believed to be at risk; participating in advocacy; and being responsive to the needs of their communities. Prevention materials have changed considerably, so be sure that you are using materials that are up-to-date and developmentally appropriate. For example, the reality is that most children are harmed by someone they know and trust, so the focus should *not* be on "stranger danger."

Although there has been considerable progress in Canada in the understanding and response to child abuse and family violence, the prevalence of violence, the extension of victimization into the virtual world, and lack of universal services and supports necessitate that we continue to address these issues. Participation in preventing abuse and violence in Canadian homes and communities can be accomplished on individual, collective, and societal levels.

- Examine and challenge personal values and relationships with family members, children, colleagues, and others.

- Participate in personal and professional development to update knowledge and skills, keeping current with relevant legislation and research. Subscribe to related journals, mailing lists, and websites.

- Learn about the dynamics of abuse and violence, indicators, how to respond to disclosure, and reporting responsibilities. Follow through on your legal and moral responsibility to report.

- Develop a philosophy, goals, and programs for children's learning about relationships and sexuality that build self-esteem and potential, regardless of gender and ability; peaceful problem-solving and conflict-resolution; making good choices; respect; understanding of individual rights and responsibilities; and how and where to get help. All of these help to lessen children's vulnerability to abuse and promote healthy relationships.

- Model equality in relationships and the positive use of power.

- Choose language carefully, refraining from racist and sexist words and derogatory labels, and challenge sexist jokes and discriminatory practices.

- Be open to discussion with parents about parenting, discipline, early intervention, and other related topics, and provide opportunities for parents to meet together. Examine barriers that might prevent working with parents as partners.

- Maintain an up-to-date list of community resources and agencies. Include resources specific to the cultural and language mix represented in the agency. (See the template for community supports and referrals below.)

- Advocate on behalf of children and families, encouraging those in positions of responsibility to recognize the issues surrounding child abuse and family violence.

- Become an active member of organizations that have as their mandate to battle the acceptance of violence in our society, including child pornography, children/youth in the sex trade, and the negative influence of the media.

- Be an active participant in building bridges with other services and resources in the community, including child protection and police services.

Children should *never* be given the message that they are responsible for protecting themselves, nor should staff and parents expect a child to protect him/herself. This is the responsibility of those who care for children, and the community at large. Steinhauer (1998: 12) states that

children need to be confronted by their parents and caregivers because absolute, unconditional acceptance of a child, regardless of how he or she behaves, is a recipe for an isolated, miserable, dependent, socially unacceptable child. It is through confrontation that parents and caregivers pass on their values and those of society to children.

INSIDE LOOK

To reduce fever, fatigue, headaches, asthma, muscle/tendon injuries, digestive disorders, urinary tract infections, and coughs, many cultures have a variety of treatments that may be interpreted by the uneducated as some as a form of abuse. These treatments may include cupping, in which a heated glass is placed upside down on the chest or back and it is taken off when it has cooled; this creates a vacuum which results in red, ring-shaped marks. Spooning is a treatment where a spoon is rubbed vigorously back and forth across the person's body often on the back or neck. A similar treatment—coining—involves using a coin to rub the back, neck, stomach, chest, upper arms, forehead, and temples after applying oil along the acupuncture meridians. For many, these treatments "rub out" evil winds or spirits restoring good health.

http://www.neighboursfriendsandfamilies.ca/eng/main.php

This valuable and resourceful website—Neighbours, Friends and Families—supports a public education campaign to raise awareness of the signs of woman abuse so that those close to an at-risk woman or an abusive man can help. Dr. Peter Jaffe Academic Director, Centre for Education and Research on Violence Against Women and Children states on the website "In the majority of cases there were several risk factors that family, friends or co-workers could have identified. Had they understood the significance of what they were seeing, they might have been able to inform the person who became the victim of the risk or they may have been able to intervene with the abusive man. We want to change public attitudes so that everybody, whether a friend, neighbour or a family doctor, will look at this issue differently and respond." Brochures such as "How You Can Identify And Help Women at Risk of Abuse," "How To Talk To Men Who Are Abusive," and "Safety Planning For Women Who Are Abused"; a Community Action Kit to organize in your community; and a video from neighbours, friends, and families are available and can be ordered on their website.

However, the way children are confronted makes an enormous difference. If they are confronted in ways that are violent or shameful, they will be so demoralized by the feelings that are conjured up that they will not learn from the experience. But if confrontation is done in a firm, matter-of-fact but loving way, children are likely to learn to change their behaviour to protect their relationship with their parents. Children learn nothing from a violent approach. The more violence a child is exposed to under the guise of discipline, the more violent he or she will be as an adolescent.

BOOKS FOR CHILDREN

A Safe Place to Live: A Story for Children Who Have Experienced Domestic Violence, by M. Harrison

A Family that Fights, by S. Chesler Bernstein and K. Ritz.

Do You Have A Secret?, by J. Moore-Mallinos and M. Febrega

A Place for Starr: A Story of Hope for Children Experiencing Family Violence, by H. Schor

A Terrible Thing Happened: A Story for Children Who Have Witnessed Violence or Trauma, by M.M. Holmes

Be Careful and Stay Safe, by C. Meiners

On Those Runaway Days, by A. Feigh

Your Body Belongs To You, by C. Spelman

BOOKS FOR ADULTS

When Someone Dies: An Accessible Guide to Bereavement for People with Learning Disabilities, by M. Mansfield

Breaking Free, Starting Over: Parenting in the Aftermath of Family Violence, by C. Dalpiaz

Child Abuse and Neglect: Attachment, Development and Intervention, by D. Howe

Children Exposed to Violence, by M.M. Feerick and G.B. Silverman

Cruel but Not Unusual: Violence in Canadian Families, by R. Maggia and C. Vine

It's My Life Now: Starting Over after an Abusive Relationship or Domestic Violence, by M. Kennedy Dugan and R. Hock

Young Children and Trauma: Intervention and Treatment, by J. Osofsky

KIDS HAVE STRESS TOO

An education program for parents of preschoolers to children aged nine years, Kids Have Stress Too may help educators and families find effective ways to provide support. Claire McDerment, co-chair of Kids Have Stress Too, has information that indicates stress can affect children's physical, emotional, social, and intellectual well-being. Extreme stress can have a negative effect on brain development in very young children; they have a weakened immune system and are three times more likely to catch respiratory infections. Children report that their stress comes from many different factors such as the following:

- Change is difficult for children. Moving to a new home or school can cause stress. Starting school for the first time can be hard, too.
- Having too much to do is stressful. Kids need some quiet time.
- Feeling different from other kids is very stressful. So is being teased or bullied.
- Fighting or arguing among family members is stressful. Not getting along well with brothers or sisters causes stress.
- Having trouble with schoolwork can be another cause of stress.
- Being yelled at by family, friends, or teachers is very stressful for kids.
- If families break up, children can feel stress that lasts for a long time.
- But most of all, it is stressful when kids feel lonely and unloved.

The program Kids Have Stress Too was developed by the Psychology Foundation of Canada, Toronto Public Health, and the Toronto District School Board Stress Management Committee. It includes a facilitator resource guide and a video. Training sessions are available for those who wish to become facilitators. The kit contains practical strategies for teachers and parents in a "toolbox activity" approach. Research shows that even very young children can learn to manage their stress effectively. As educators, we need to provide what children need:

- a caring adult in whom they can trust and confide
- love and affection and approval to feel good about themselves
- help in developing competence in one or more areas of their life
- friends and a time and place to have fun with other children

Information is available from the Psychology Foundation of Canada or on their website **www.kidshavestresstoo.org**.

Yoga 4 Kids

Under the leadership of Director Sherry LeBlanc, this program is based upon the yoga practices of Kundalini Yoga and Integral Hatha Yoga (**www.yoga4kids.org**). It is specifically developed to suit the needs and abilities of children. The pro-

gram combines dynamic movements, postures, and simple breath and mantra meditations with game playing, singing, storytelling, and deep relaxation into an integrated and holistic program of physical fitness, education and social and self awareness. Family yoga is also an option that strengthens the bond between parent and child. Yoga Therapy is also available for children with special needs. These programs help children be calm, inwardly focused, and to value silence and stillness among others.

BOOKS FOR CHILDREN

My Daddy Is a Pretzel: Yoga for Parents and Children, by B. Baptiste

The Yoga Adventure for Children: Playing, Dancing, Moving, Breathing, Relaxing, by H. Purperhart

A Boy and a Bear: The Children's Relaxation Book, by L. Lite

Cool Cats, Calm Kids: Relaxation and Stress Management for Young People, by M. Williams

Don't Pop Your Cork on Mondays! The Children's Anti-Stress Book, by A. Moser and D. Pilkey

Stress Relief for Kids: Taming Your Dragons, by M. Belknap

When My Worries Get Too Big: A Relaxation Books For Children Who Live With Anxiety, by K. Dunn Buron

Be the Boss of Your Body: Kit with Stress Book and Self Care for Kids, by T. Culbert and R. Kajander

BOOKS FOR ADULTS

The Highly Sensitive Child, by E. Aron

The Hurried Child: Growing Up Too Fast and Too Soon, by D. Elkind

Ties That Stress: The New Family Imbalance, by D. Elkind

The Worried Child, by P. Foxman

RESILIENT CHILDREN

What helps children overcome difficult life experiences? What makes for resilient children, those who are able to demonstrate positive outcomes even when in high-risk situations? An important

STRESS TEST FOR CHILDREN

STRESS	POINTS	CHILD'S SCORE
Parent Dies	100	
Parents Divorce	73	
Parent Separate	65	
Separation From Parent (foster placement, termination of parental rights)	65	
Parent Travels As Part of Job	63	
Close Family Member Dies	63	
Personal Illness or Injury	53	
Parent Remarries	50	
Parent Loses Job	47	
Parents Reconcile After Separation	45	
Mother Goes To Work	45	
Change In Health Of A Family Member	44	
Mother Becomes Pregnant	40	
School Difficulties	39	
Birth Of A Sibling	39	
School Readjustment (new teacher)	39	
Change In Family's Financial Condition	38	
Injury Or Illness Of A Close Friend	37	
Starts New (or changes) Extracurricular Activity (music, Brownies, etc.)	36	
Change In Number Of Fights With Siblings	35	
Exposed To Violence At School	31	
Theft Of Personal Possessions	30	
Changes Responsibilities At Home	29	
Older Brother Or Sister Leaves Home	29	
Trouble With Grandparents	29	
Outstanding Personal Achievement	28	
Move To Another City	26	
Move To Another Part Of Town	26	
Receives Or Loses A Pet	25	
Changes In Personal Habits	24	
Trouble With A Teacher	24	
Changes In Hours With Baby Sitter or Day Care Centre	20	
Move To A New House In Same School District	20	
Changes To A New School	20	
Changes In Play Habits	19	
Vacations With Family	19	
Change In Friends	18	
Attends Summer Camp	17	
Changes Sleeping Habits	16	
Change In Number Of Family Get-Togethers	15	
Changes Eating Habits	15	
Changes Amount Of TV Viewing	13	
Birthday Party	12	
Punished For Not "Telling The Truth"	11	

CHILD'S TOTAL SCORE

Add child's total score: score below 150 = average stress load, score between 150–300 = higher than average chance of stress symptoms, score above 300 = high likelihood of serious change in health and/or behaviour.

Source: From P. Foxman, *The Worried Child* (Alamdeda, CA: Hunter House, 2003).

element is the child's temperament. They are easy children: active, affectionate, and good-natured. These children seem to bring forth positive responses in the adults who care for them and they learn early to cope through both self-sufficiency and asking for help when they need it (Werner, 1995). In addition to the child's temperament, family and community components also offer protection for at-risk children. A child who lives with a great deal of family discord but somehow builds a relationship with at least one family member who is emotionally competent, stable, and willing to nurture that child is more likely to become resilient. Further, community members, especially teachers, are often seen as a source of support when at-risk children are facing crises. Characteristics of these teachers are that they listened to the children, challenged them, and rooted for them (Werner, 1995: 83, in Couchenour and Chrisman 2000: 78).

FAMILIES WHERE A PARENT IS INCARCERATED

In Canada, a federal agency known as the Correctional Service of Canada (CSC) oversees about 52 federal correctional facilities and 15 community correctional centers. The provinces and territories operate another 150 correctional facilities. Whereas Canadian federal facilities generally hold criminals sentenced to terms of two or more years, provincial and territorial prisons house inmates serving terms of less than two years. In 1998 Canada operated seven federal prisons exclusively for women, five of which had been constructed since 1995. The oldest federal facility, built in 1934, is the Prison for Women in Kingston, Ontario. Provincial and territorial facilities for women include Burnaby Correctional Centre for Women in Vancouver, British Columbia, and Portage Correctional Institute for Women in Portage, Manitoba.

- More than half of all female inmates in federal facilities in Canada are between the ages of 20 and 34. Women between the ages of 30 and 34 make up roughly one-fourth of all provincial and territorial inmates.

- Just under 60 percent of female inmates are Caucasian. Although aboriginal people make up less than two percent of the adult population of Canada, officials classify nearly one-fifth of female inmates as aboriginal. Slightly more than half of all female inmates are single.

- In Canada, women are less likely than men to be incarcerated for violent crimes. However, the proportion of female violent offenders imprisoned for homicide (roughly 40 percent) is greater than the proportion of male violent offenders convicted of homicide.

- Drug offenders comprise more than one-fourth of all female federal inmates in Canada.

- Women convicted of various property offenses make up the majority of female inmates in provincial and territorial prisons.

- In Canada, nearly half of all male prisoners in federal prisons are between the ages of 25 and 34. Younger men make up a higher proportion of the provincial and territorial prison population—about one-fourth of male inmates in such facilities are between the ages of 20 and 24.

- Nearly three-quarters of male federal inmates are Caucasian, while the government classifies one-sixth as aboriginal (indigenous Canadian peoples). The majority of all male inmates are single.

- Roughly half of all male inmates in Canada are imprisoned for violent crimes, such as homicide, assault, and robbery. Approximately one-fourth of all male federal inmates are imprisoned for homicide, while less than one-tenth are incarcerated for drug offenses.

- Male inmates in provincial and territorial prisons are most frequently incarcerated for property crimes, such as theft and fraud.

- In Canada, two-thirds of those imprisoned in provincial and territorial facilities serve sentences of less than one year. About one-quarter serve one to two years, and five percent of provincial and territorial inmates serve sentences of two years or more.

- In Canadian federal facilities, nearly one-fifth of all inmates are sentenced to life imprisonment. Roughly half of Canada's federal inmates have sentences between two and six years.

- About 40 percent of Canada's released inmates were subsequently convicted of new crimes, while 20 percent were later convicted of a violent crime.

- Anyone sentenced to more than two years in prison can be granted a private family visits which can include spouses, children, common law partners, siblings, grandparents, friends, etc., for up to 72 hours; these visits may occur every two months. Some prisoners are barred from the program either because there is a risk of family or conjugal violence or because they have access to other programs for maintaining family ties, particularly unsupervised leaves. (Vacheret, 2007)

Based on 2006 per capita crime rates from the Canadian Centre for Justice Statistics, the top 10 high crime cities are led by Regina, Saskatoon, and Winnipeg, followed by Prince George, Edmonton, New Westminster, Chilliwack, Victoria, Vancouver, and Halifax. Halifax is the only eastern city in the top 10; Montreal ranks 19th and Toronto 26th. While there are many reasons why some cities are more likely to experience crime, the type of crime varies from city to city. For example, Winnipeg leads in auto theft and robberies, aggravated assault plagued Regina, and Saskatoon led in sexual assault. The worst of the crime is often visited upon the most vulnerable, those in the poorer postal codes who are marginalized by both by race and neighbourhood. These are gathering places for the addicted, the psychiatrically disabled, and those who prey upon them.

Contenta and Rankin (2008) report that more than 70 percent of those who enter prisons have not completed high school and have unstable job histories; four of every five arrive with serious substance abuse problems. Twelve percent of men and 26 percent of women in prisons suffer serious mental health problems. Attacking the root causes of these problems seems a better alternative than criminalizing our most vulnerable citizens.

According to MacQueen (2008: 37), "the overrepresentation of Aboriginals in custody is both an indicator of one of the problems. Aboriginal youth represent 75 to 90 percent of all youth in open and closed custody, estimates a 2003 report by the Federation of Saskatchewan Indian Nations (FSIN). Often, they are both victimizer and victim. Nationally, Aboriginal people are three times more likely than non-Aboriginal people to be assaulted, sexually assaulted or robbed. They are seven times more likely to be victims of homicide and 10 times more likely to be charged with homicide. . . . having said that, Canada's overall national crime rate hit its lowest point in over 25 years in 2006, led by a drop in property crimes in all provinces."

The Aboriginal Justice Strategy (AJS) is composed of community-based justice programs that are cost-shared with provincial and territorial governments, and capacity building activities to support Aboriginal communities' involvement in the local administration of justice. The AJS supports four types of alternative justice activities and programs at the community and regional level, cost-shared with the provincial and territorial governments: diversion or alternative measures; community sentencing circles and peacemaking; mediation and arbitration in family and civil cases; and court/community Justice Program. AJS programs supported to date have been managed by First Nations and Tribal Councils, community groups, urban Aboriginal coalitions, Inuit hamlets, Métis Organizations, and other nonprofit organizations.

When a parent is sent to jail, the consequences can be devastating for the parents, the children, and other family members. Separation from a parent is likely to be traumatic for a child. Behavioural problems also tend to emerge with some children. The parent on the outside may face not only stigmatization and financial hardship but also the possibility that the child or children will be taken from them and placed in foster care. Figures are difficult to gather regarding the number of parents incarcerated but Christina Guest of Correctional Services Canada has shared the following information on these issues. On any given day in Canada,

---

INSIDE LOOK

"It is difficult, if not impossible, to ensure equality before the law for Native people in our criminal courts when so many Native people do not understand the nature of the charges against them, the implications of a plea, the basic court procedures and legal terminology, or their right to speak on their own behalf or to request legal counsel."

Source: Department of Justice Canada, Aboriginal Courtwork Program, n.d.

Spotlight on Ontario: Women in Ontario Jails

30	Average age of female inmates
70	Percentage who are mothers. Four out of five are primary caregivers
9	Average grade reached in school
7	Percentage of total jail population that is female
596	Women are in jail each day, compared to 7,414 men
161	More women are in jail each day than five years ago
20	Average remand stay in days
39.8	Average sentence, in days
52.9	Percentage who are charged with nonviolent crimes
33	Percentage charged with assault
57	Percentage increase in number of women remanded in the past five years (33.9% for men)

Source: Elizabeth Fry Society (cited in Crawford, 2007).

approximately 33,000 persons are incarcerated in federal, provincial, or territorial correctional facilities. Because of the short provincial sentences, however, approximately 150,000 persons over the course of a year are in and out quickly or stay only overnight in a correction facility of some kind. According to Guest, 59.1 percent of male offenders are parents or stepparents. If 59.1 percent of federal offenders have one or more children, this represents, at a minimum, over 11,500 children. Applying this same statistic (59.1 percent) to federal and provincial numbers, there may be 86,650 children per year in Canada affected by parental incarceration for some or all of the year. Some research suggests that 80 percent of women sentenced for federal offences are single parents. Guest states that caution must be used when reviewing these numbers since definitive statistics are not available.

Alison Cunningham, director of research and planning for the Centre for Children and Families in the Justice System in London, Ontario, co-authored a study called "Waiting for Mommy." The study examined the impact of parental incarceration on children. It found that when a mother is jailed, her children are hurt on many levels. They may be less ready for school, fail to attach to their mothers, and disrespect the justice system. This sets the child on a trajectory toward youth crime in a much greater way than if a father were in jail, because moms are usually full-time caregivers.

Maternal incarceration may place even greater burden on children if the children lose their primary caregivers. The children of incarcerated fathers typically continue to be cared for by their mother but the children of incarcerated mothers are rarely cared for by their father (Glick and Neto, 1977). While this reference is dated, one might assume that it continues to be true.

Families and Corrections Network (FCN), an American organization for and about families of prisoners, is an outstanding resource for students and teachers. One important resource for fathers is the Incarcerated Fathers Library. This is a special collection of pamphlets and readings for incarcerated fathers, their families, their children, and those who work with their children. The library is open around the clock to millions of computer users via the Internet at **www.fcnetwork.org/cpl/cplindex.html**.

Their work has found there are four main questions that children ask or want to ask their incarcerated parents:

Where are you?

Why are you there?

When are you coming home?

Are you okay?

There are also two questions in the hearts and minds of prisoners' children that they rarely ask. These questions are often "behind the scenes" in their conversations:

Do you blame me?

Do you love me?

These questions can come in many forms. Some children ask them directly with straightforward language. Other children beat around the bush. Some act out their questions by getting into trouble or by confronting adults with challenging or aggressive behaviours.

Some parents will find discussing this information very painful and avoid telling the child or make up stories about the absent parent being in the hospital, in the military, away at school, working in another province, etc. Lying to the children is often intended to minimize feelings of shame and stigma but it in fact may increase these feelings by creating a family secret that is a big burden for a small child. Parents need to weigh three choices: tell the truth and let it be out in the open, tell the truth and ask the children to keep it quiet, or make up a story. Parents, and teachers if they are included, then have to judge the dangers of each option to the child's emotional health.

Correctional Services of Canada states that many women feel tremendous concern over the loss of custody of one or more of their children and report that contact with their children, regardless of their age, is essential to personal well-being. Parenting programs are closely linked to relational theory. By encouraging women to establish positive attachments to their children, parenting programs produce benefits: more stable mothers who, after resolving their conflict with the criminal justice system, can then aid their children in acquiring pro social values and to become productive members of society.

Christina Guest, Project Officer, Chaplaincy, Correctional Services of Canada, suggests the following resources:

- **The Canadian Families and Corrections Network** is a voluntary-sector agency that specializes in developing resources for families living with incarceration and reintegration issues. They can be contacted at **www.csc-scc.gc.ca/**. The network is made up of community-oriented citizens, volunteer groups, private agencies, inmate committees, and penitentiary administrators—all committed to improving the well-being of offender families. Alone, these groups have unequal resources and are seldom in contact. Together, they have the opportunity to make a real and long-lasting difference. For example,

INSIDE LOOK

Marjorie Mayfield, professor at University of Victoria, BC, discusses prison programs established to support the family unit:

"One of the most unique locations for a family support program I have ever visited was the Preschool in Prison Project at the Fort Saskatchewan Correctional Centre in Alberta. . . . Parents who are in prison still want to see their children and families; however, these visits can be very traumatic for children. Prisons are not child- or family-friendly places by definition. In addition, young children may be tired and hungry after a lengthy trip to the prison which, combined with the security concerns that often prohibit them from bringing along their favourite toys, can make the experience even more stressful for them. Also, visiting areas have traditionally been designed for security concerns, not children's or families' needs (e.g., there are no changing areas or available water). Once at a prison families are responsible for constantly monitoring and supervising children while visiting with the incarcerated family member. The dilemma for families then becomes leave the children home or don't come as frequently or at all. This, in turn, further stresses family ties that the visiting programs are intended to sustain. Many incarcerated parents had difficult childhoods and lacked positive parenting models. The original Preschool in Prison program included not only a children's program during visiting hours, but also a six-week parenting course (Living with Children) for inmates, and an early childhood educator to coordinate this program. The children's program provided inmates in the parenting course with opportunities to observe children's play and behaviour as well as the early childhood educator as a model for them. (2001: 447)

Without programs, services, and support, a child who has a parent in prison faces many risks. While it is not a predictor of future difficulty, research shows that one of the risks related to future criminal involvement is the incarceration of a parent. Provision of services to children is crime prevention.

the Women in the Shadows program in Fredericton, New Brunswick, allows the wives of inmates to meet weekly for fellowship and support. The meetings vary from "game nights" and picnics to focusing on specific common struggles to spiritual centring. Confidential emergency help (such as money, food, and clothes) is also available through local religious organizations.

- **Children Visiting Prisons** in Kingston, Ontario, runs a variety of programs and supports for families. These supports include a children's activity area normalizing the visiting experience for children without normalizing crime, prison, or incarceration, and parenting workshops strengthening the parent–child bond.

- **The House of Hope** in Ottawa offers family support services, such as support groups for women with a partner in prison, for children, and for youths; a drop-in centre; short-term counselling, and information and referrals. Contact them at **houseofhope@on.aibn.com**.

Correctional Services of Canada (2007) is not insensitive to the needs of children and families who find themselves dealing with a parent who is incarcerated. The following material, which can be found on their website at **http://www.csc-scc.gc.ca/text/fami/archive/milhavenfs-eng.shtml**, describes a recent research initiative in Ontario:

> In 2003 the Canadian Families and Corrections Network (CFCN) received a contribution from the Correctional Service of Canada for a two-year demonstration project at Millhaven Assessment Unit (MAU) in the Ontario Region. The project used a restorative justice approach in which a Coordinator of Family Support provided information and referral service to families of offenders from the point at which the offender enters "the system."

The project had several components:

> As part of the orientation process all new offenders participated in a session on families, corrections and restorative justice. This presentation included a discussion of how criminal behaviour harms families and how that harm can be reduced now and in the future. Information was presented on the cost of telephone calls and visiting, intergenerational criminal behaviour, and the consequences of pressuring family members to relocate or to introduce contraband into the institution. Two videos were used as a part of the orientation process. *Making Links to the Community* describes

the role of the voluntary sector with offenders and their families and *Prisoner Families: Facing the Challenge* focuses specifically on the unique needs of families affected by incarceration.

> The offenders attending the orientation session were given the opportunity to request that material be sent to their families. CFCN then sent Time Together: A Survival Guide for Families and Friends Visiting in Canadian Federal Prisons to partners and intimates, while One Day at a Time: Writings on Facing the Incarceration of a Friend or Family Member was sent to parents and other family members. Additional resource material was also sent to the family upon request.

> Families had access to a toll-free telephone information service (1-866-315-8280) for referral to institutional (CSC) and community (CSC, voluntary sector and faith-based) resources and services. The Coordinator referred families to the organizations that could best meet the needs they presented. Support for voluntary sector agencies was given through these referrals so that families were aware how and where to access services.

> Here is what one family member had to say about access to this model of service delivery: "Your book was a wonderful read, and how great it was to find out that I am not alone in how I see or feel about his situation. I am not alone in my frustrations and it helped me so much to find this out."

> One of the most innovative aspects of the project was making a "virtual tour" of a CSC institution available to families on the internet. It was developed along the lines of a format used by the real estate industry. The objective was to decrease the family's anxiety, particularly before a first institutional visit, by showing what a typical front entrance, visiting room and Private Family Visit unit look like. The tour also assists a caregiver who wishes to discuss parental incarceration with a child. In addition, an online self-study course on effective service provision to families offers professional development for correctional staff, voluntary sector staff and volunteers.

> A research component was built into the project. The data was gathered through the voluntary completion of a questionnaire by offenders at Intake. They were asked about their marital status, the number and ages of their children, addictions, employment and housing issues at the time they committed their offence, and involvement of family members in the criminal justice system. The data will help inform the development of further services that are needed by families affected by incarceration and reintegration and the potential for a coordinated approach to families across the country.

A project evaluation involving feedback from the families who received the services describes the effectiveness of the approach. Kevin MacInnis, Assistant Warden of Correctional Programs at the Millhaven Assessment Unit, cannot contain his enthusiasm for this project: "I have called the CFS project a 'best kept secret.' It has been a secret in the sense that a lot of what happens is not seen. While there is a presentation to the newcomers, the focus of the project is the families in the community. On a day-to-day basis, we don't see the families or the impact that the project is having on them. What we may see in the institution is that the offenders may be calmer knowing that they can do something to assist their families, such as having the family orientation material sent to their families. They also have a designated and trusted person that their family can call for further information or support. (Correctional Service of Canada, 2007a)

 Another program offered by Correctional Service of Canada is the Mother–Child Program, which is described online at **http://www.csc-scc.gc.ca/text/ prgrm/fsw/pro02-5-eng.shtml**:

> The Mother–Child Program is unique to the women's institutions is the Mother–Child Program. Commissioner Directive 768 on Institutional Mother–Child Program aims "to provide a supportive environment that fosters and promotes stability and continuity for the mother–child relationship." It also states that the pre-eminent consideration is the best interests of the child which shall be the pre-eminent consideration in all decisions relating to participation in the Mother–Child Program. The best interests of the child include ensuring the safety and security as well as the physical, emotional, and spiritual well being of the child.
>
> Two-thirds of incarcerated women are mothers of children under five years of age, are often single parents, and for which living apart is an ordeal for both the mothers and their children. However, the development of parenting skills and the establishment of the mother–child relationship are both social characteristics and social expectations in regard to all mothers, including those who are in conflict with the law. Understanding this social fact and its implications, has led to the development of a strategy better suited to the culture and specific needs of mothers serving a federal sentence and their children.
>
> Availability of the Mother-Child Program at the women's institutions is contingent on space availability. (Correctional Service of Canada, 2007b)

ROLE OF THE TEACHER

- Be a consistent, caring teacher who understands that children love their parents even when they have committed a crime.
- Do not speak negatively about the incarcerated parent.
- Be sensitive and responsive to the needs of the child who may feel angry, sad, confused, and worried. Provide ample opportunities for children to express their feelings in all forms—dramatic play, art, written work, etc.
- Research the books that are available on this topic to help children understand the prison system.
- Provide consistent, predictable routines in the centre with reasonable boundaries.
- Answer the children's questions. Teachers should do this only after discussions with the family.
- Tell children the truth, which is often easier for the child to accept than what they might imagine. Children understand the idea of being punished for breaking the rules but they need simple descriptions of the offence—"Dad hurt someone," "Mum stole something." Older children will have more questions and may need more detail.
- Reassure the child. Often when one parent is incarcerated, the child can become very attached and worried that the remaining parent will be taken away.
- With family approval, collect examples of the child's work or photos of the child in the playroom for him or her to share with their parent by mail. Children might begin a picture or a story that the parent adds to and it is mailed back and forth.
- Give the child concrete examples of how long the parent will be away. The concept of time is difficult for a young child to understand so they will need specifics—three summers, four birthdays, etc.
- The stigma of incarceration is challenging for some children but the level of difficulty experienced may reflect the family's view of incarceration. If the family feels that the incarceration is more the result of social prejudice and less about the individual, children in these families may feel less stigma.
- Reassure older children that the incarcerated parent is safe, secure, and able to manage.

Describing what the parent has access to is sometimes helpful—"Your mother has a bed and books to read," for example.

- Reassure children that they are not to blame for their parent's mistakes.
- Support and encourage the remaining parent. Help by finding agencies or organizations that will support families in their situation; other parents may need practical community support on issues such as budgeting and legal concerns.

BOOKS FOR CHILDREN

Visiting Day, by J. Woodson

Amber Was Brave, Essie Was Smart, by V. Williams

BOOKS FOR ADULTS

All Alone In the World: Children of the Incarcerated, by N. Bernstein

My Daddy Is In Jail: Story, Discussion Guide and Small Group Activities for Grades K to 5, by J. Bender

Loving Through Bars: Children with Parents in Prison, by C. Martone

War on the Family: Mothers in Prison and Families They Leave Behind, by R. Golden

REFERENCES

Addiction Research Foundation. 1996. *Women and Alcohol*. Resource booklet.

Alcoba, N. 2008. "Child-porn Fighter to Head Cybercrime Research Centre." *National Post*. March 21.

Alper, S., P. Schloss, and C. Schloss. 1994. *Families of Students with Disabilities: Consultation and Advocacy*. Boston: Allyn & Bacon.

Ambert, A. 2006. *One-Parent Families: Characteristics, Causes, Consequences, and Issues*. Ottawa: The Vanier Institute of the Family.

Amnesty International. 2004. *Stolen Sisters: A Human Rights Response to Discrimination and Violence Against Indigenous Women in Canada*. Available at http://www.amnesty.org/en/library/asset/AMR20/003/2004/en/dom-AMR 200032004en.pdf.

Anderson, E.R., and A.M. Rice. 1992. "Sibling Relationships during Remarriage." *Monographs of the Society for Research in Child Development* 57 (2–3, Serial No. 227): 149–177.

Andrews, G. 2008. "Primed To Heal: Delivering Effective Mental Health Care." *Maclean's*. March 17.

Baldry, A.C. 2003. "Bullying in Schools and Exposure to Domestic Violence." *Child Abuse & Neglect* 27: 713–732.

Baskin, B.H., and E.P. Riggs. 1988. "Mothers Who Are Disabled." In B. Birns and D.F. Day, eds., *Different Faces of Motherhood*. New York: Plenum Press.

Baumrind, D. 1967. "Child Care Practices Anteceding Three Patterns Of Preschool Patterns." *Genetic Psychology Monographs* 75, 43–88.

Bayridge Anxiety & Depression Treatment Centre. N.d. "Depression/Anxiety—Get the Facts." Available at http://www.bayridgetreatmentcenter.com/index.html.

Benoit, D., and A. Gibson. 2006. "Impact of Violence on Children." *IMPrint: The Newsletter of Infant Mental Health Promotion (IMP)* 46: 6–10.

Blackford, K.A., and N.K. Israelite. 2003. "Families and Parents with Disabilities." In Marion Lynn, ed., *Voices: Essays on Canadian Families*, 2nd ed. Toronto: Nelson Thomson Learning.

Bowen, K. 2000. "Child Abuse and Domestic Violence in Families of Children Seen for Suspected Child Abuse." *Clinical Pediatrics* 39(1): 33–40.

Bowker, L.G., M. Arbitell, and J.R. McFerron. 1988. "On The Relationship between Wife Beating and Child Abuse." In K. Yilo and M. Borad, eds., *Perspectives on Wife Abuse*. Newbury, CA: Sage Publications.

Brooks, J. 2008. The *Process of Parenting*. Toronto: McGraw-Hill.

Bugental, D.B., and V.L. Cortez. 1988. "Physiological Reactivity and Responsive and Unresponsive Children as Moderated by Perceived Control." *Child Development* 59: 686–693.

Bugental, D.B., and W.A. Shennum. 1984. "Difficult" Children as Elicitors and Targets of Adult Communication Patterns." *Monographs of the Society for Research in Child Development* 49 (1, Serial #205).

Busch, T., and C.S. Kimble. 2001. "Grieving Children: Are We Meeting the Children's Needs?" *Pediatric Nursing* 27 (4): 414–418.

Canadian Centre on Substance Abuse. 1999. "Canadian Profile 1999: Alcohol: Highlights." Available at http://www.ccsa.ca/cp99work.htm.

Canadian Council on Social Development. 1999. *The Progress of Canada's Children into the Millennium*. Ottawa: Health Canada.

———. 2006. "The Progress of Canada's Children and Youth." *Family Life*. Ottawa: Health Canada.

Carey, E. 2004. "Homeless Women Crisis." *The Toronto Star*. April 13. A1.

Carey, W.B. 1998. *Understanding Your Child's Temperament*. New York: Simon and Schuster.

Carson, L. 1987. *Integration Means All Our Children Belong*. Fredericton: Department of Education, Student Services Branch.

Chapman, R., and B. McGarry. 2007. Victim Identification/Background Analysis. Presentation at the *Provincial Strategy To Protect Children From Sexual Abuse And Exploitation On The Internet, Multi Disciplinary Training Conference*, Gravenhurst, Ontario, March 5–7.

Coleman, P.K., and K.H. Karraker. 1998. "Self Efficacy and Parenting Quality: Findings and Future Applications." *Developmental Review* 18: 47–85.

Contenta, S., and J. Rankin. 2008. "Solving Crime? Tackle The Root Causes First." *The Toronto Star*. July 26.

Cooper, S.W. 2006. *Congressional Opening Statement of Sharon W. Copper, MD*. Available at http://energycommerce.house.gov/reparchives/108/Hearings/04042006hearing18 20/Cooper.pdf.

———. 2007. Age Determination. Presentation at the *Provincial Strategy To Protect Children From Sexual*

Abuse And Exploitation On The Internet, Multi Disciplinary Training Conference, Gravenhurst, Ontario, March 5–7.

Correctional Service of Canada. 2007a. "Support for Families from Day One." Available at http://www .csc-scc.gc.ca/text/fami/archive/milhavenfs-eng.shtml.

———. 2007b. "Mother–Child Program." Available at http://www.csc-scc.gc.ca/text/prgrm/fsw/pro02-5 -eng.shtml.

Couchenour, D., and K. Chrisman. 2000. *Families, Schools and Communities. Together For Young Children*. Florence, KY: Delmar Learning.

———. 2004. *Families, Schools and Communities. Together For Young Children*. Florence, KY: Delmar Learning.

Crawford, T. 2007. "Jailed But Not Yet Found Guilty." *The Toronto Star*. August 11. L12.110

Daly, M., and M. Wilson. 1993. "Spousal Homicide Risk and Estrangement." *Violence and Victims* 8(11): 3–16.

Domestic Violence Death Review Committee Annual Report (DVDRC). 2005. Office of the Chief Coroner of Ontario. Ministry of Community Safety and Correctional Services. Submitted by Al J.C. O'Mara B.A., M.A., LL.B., LL.M. (DVDRC Chair) on behalf of the Ontario Domestic Violence Death Review Committee.

De La Barrera, J., and D. Masterson. 1988. "Support Group Helps Troubled Fathers Learn Parenting Skills." *Children Today*. March–April.

Department of Justice Canada, Aboriginal Courtwork Program. N.d. Available at http://www.justice.gc.ca/ eng/pi/eval/rep-rap/07/acw-papa/p2.html.

Desjardin Financial Security. 2008. "Desjardin Financial Security Survey on Canadian Attitudes Towards Physical and Mental Health." *Macleans*. May 26 (Insert).

Dineen, J.M. 1995. "For Jamai's Sake." *The Toronto Star*, 22 September. B3.

Doherty, G. 2008. "Ensuring The Best Start In Life." *Institute For Research On Public Policy* 30.

Doherty-Derkowski, G. 1994. *Quality Matters: Excellence in Early Childhood Programs*. Don Mills, ON: Addison-Wesley.

Donovan, W.W., L.A. Leavitt, and R.O. Walsh. 1990. "Maternal Self-efficacy: Illusory Control and Its Effect on Susceptibility to Learned Helplessness." *Child Development* 61: 1638–1647.

Duffy, A., and J. Momirov. 1997. *Family Violence: A Canadian Introduction*. Toronto: James Lorimer & Company.

Edleson, J.L. 1999. "The Overlap between Child Maltreatment and Woman Battery." *Violence Against Women* 5(2): 134–154.

Education Wife Assault. 1985. "Fact Sheet on Wife Assault in Canada." Toronto: Education Wife Assault.

Elder, G.H. 1995. "Life Trajectories in Changing Societies." In A. Bandura, ed., *Self Efficacy In Changing Societies*. New York: Cambridge University Press.

Family Alliance Ontario. 2007. "Is Your World Touched by Disability? So Is Ours!" *The Compass*. 12 (1): 4.

Fine, M., and A. Asch, eds. 1988. *Women with Disabilities: Essays in Psychology, Culture and Politics*. Philadelphia: Temple University Press.

Finger, A. 1991. *Past Due: A Story of Disability, Pregnancy and Birth*. London: The Woman's Press.

Flowers, R.B. 2001. "The Sex Trade Industry's Worldwide Exploitation of Children [Electronic version]." *Annals of the American Academy of Political and Social Science* 575: 147–157.

Foxman, P. 2003. *The Worried Child*. Alamdeda, CA: Hunter House.

Furstenberg, F.F., J. Eccles, G.H. Elder, T. Cook, and A. Sameroff. 1999. *Urban Families and Adolescent Success*. Chicago, IL: University of Chicago Press.

Galinsky, E. 1987. *The Six Stages of Parenthood*. Boston, MA: Addison Wesley.

General Social Survey (GSS) on Victimization. 2004. Catalogue no. 85-565-XIE, Cycle 18. Statistics Canada: Minister of Industry.

Ginsberg, H., and S. Opper. 1987. *Piaget's Theory of Intellectual Development*, 3rd ed. Englewood Cliffs, NJ: Prentice Hall.

Glick, R.M., and V.V. Neto. 1977. *National Study of Women's Correctional Programs*. Washington, DC: Department of Justice.

Goldman, A., R. Hain, and S. Liben. 2006. *Oxford Textbook of Palliative Care for Children*. New York: Oxford University Press.

Gordon, A. 2005. "Crisis in Children's Mental Health." *The Toronto Star*. February 11. D5.

Greaves, L., O. Hankivsky, and J. Kingston-Riechers. 1995. Selected Estimates of the Costs of Violence Against Women. London, ON: Centre for Research on Violence against Women and Children.

Greey, M. 1995. *Honouring Diversity: A Cross-Cultural Approach to Infant Development for Babies with Special Needs*. Toronto: Centennial Infant and Child Centre.

Haas, G.A. 2008. The Impact of Intimate Partner Violence on the Children. Presentation for ACT Against Violence Leadership Seminar, Washington, DC, March 27.

Hadad, M. 2008. *The Ultimate Challenge: Coping with Death, Dying and Bereavement*. Toronto: Thomson Nelson.

Hagemann-White, C. 2006. Combating Violence against Women. Stocktaking Study on the Measures and Actions taken in Council of Europe Member States, Directorate General of Human Rights, Council of Europe.

Halpern, L.F., T.F. Anders, C.T. Garcia Coll, and J. Hua. 1994. "Infant Temperament: Is There a Relationship to Sleep-Wake States, Maternal Night Time Behaviour and Psychological Characteristics." *Infant Behaviour and Development* 17: 255–263.

Hamilton, J. 2003. *When a Parent is Sick: Helping Parents Explain Serious Illness to Children*. Lawrencetown Beach, NS: Pottersfield Press.

Henderson, A. 1990. "Children of Abused Wives: Their Influence on Their Mothers' Decisions." *Canada's Mental Health* 38 (June/September).

Henderson, H. 2003. "Project Invests in Workers and Kids With Special Needs." *The Toronto Star*. January 25.

Howland Thompson, S. 1998. "Working with Children of Substance-Abusing Parents." *Young Children*. January.

Inantry, A. 1999. "On Being a Dad with a Special Kid." *The Toronto Star*. 26 December.

Irwin, S. 1993. "SpeciaLink: The Road to Mainstream Child Care." *Focus*. October.

Jaffe, P. 1986. "Similarities in Behavioural and Social Maladjustment among Children Victims and Witnesses to Family Violence." *American Journal of Orthopsychiatry* 50.

Jaffe, P.G., D. Wolfe, and S. Wilson. 1990. *Children of Battered Women: Issues in Child Development and Intervention Planning*. Newbury Park, CA: Sage Publications.

Johnson, H. 1996. *Dangerous Domains: Violence against Women in Canada*. Toronto: Nelson Canada.

Johnson, K.L., D.S. Lero, and J.A. Rooney. 2001. *Work–Life Compendium 2001*. Centre for Families, Work and WellBeing. University of Guelph: Human Resources Development Canada.

Johnston, C., and E.J. Mash. 1989. "A Measure of Parenting Satisfaction and Efficacy." *Journal of Child Psychology* 18: 167–175.

Juristat. 2006. Homicide in Canada, 2006. Catalogue No. 85-002-XIE. 27 (8). Statistics Canada: Minister of Industry.

Keung, N. 2004. "Women Face Dilemma: Abuse or Deportation?" *The Toronto Star*. August 3.

Kirby, M. 2002. Speech at The Empire Club of Canada, May 8.

Kirwin, K.M., and V. Hamrin. 2005. "Decreasing the Risk of Complicated Bereavement and Future Psychiatric Disorders in Children." *Journal of Child and Adolescent Psychiatric Nursing* 18 (2): 62–78.

Klein, A. 2005. *A Report to the U.S. House of Representatives House Ways and Means Committee*, February 10, 2005. Available at http://waysandmeans.house.gov/hearings.asp?formmode=view&id=2960.

Kluger, J. 2006. "The New Science of Siblings." *Time Magazine*. July 2.

Krajicek, M.J., and C.A. Moore. 1993. "Child Care for Infants and Toddlers with Disabilities and Chronic Illness." *Focus on Exceptional Children* 25 (8). April.

Kubler-Ross, E. 1973. *On Death and Dying*. New York: MacMillan Publishing Company.

MacQueen, K. 2008. "Maclean's Exclusive Rankings of the Country's Most Crime Ridden and Safest, Cities." *Maclean's*. March 24.

Mash, E.J., and C. Johnson. 1983. "Parental Perception of Child Behaviour Problems, Parenting Self Esteem and Mothers Reported Stress in Younger and Older Hyperactive and Normal Children." *Journal of Consulting and Clinical Psychology* 51: 86–99.

Mayfield, M.I. 2001. *Early Childhood Education and Care in Canada: Contexts, Dimensions, and Issues*. Toronto: Prentice Hall.

Menjivar, C., and O. Salcido. 2002. "Immigrant Women and Domestic Violence: Common Experiences in Different Countries." *Gender & Society* 16 (6): 898–920.

Mohr, W.K., and J.W. Fantuzzo. 2000. "The Neglected Variable of Physiology in Domestic Violence." In R. Geffner, P. Jaffe, and M. Sudermann, eds., *Children Exposed To Domestic Violence: Current Issues in Research, Intervention, Prevention, and Policy Development*. New York: The Haworth Maltreatment & Trauma Press.

Monsebraaten, L. 1998. "Working Parents of Disabled Severely Stressed, Report Says." *The Toronto Star*, November 2: A3.

———. 2007. "Homeless Kids Neglected. Report Says Education, Emotional Support Lacking For Students Living In Shelters." *The Toronto Star*. October 1. Available at http://www.thestar.com/GTA/Education/article/262153.

Moore, T., D. Peplar, B. Weisberg, L. Hammond, J. Waddell, and L. Weiser. 1990. "Research on Children from Violent Families." *Canada's Mental Health* 38 (June/September).

Newton, C.J. 2001. "Domestic Violence: An Overview." *TherapistFinder.net Mental Health Journal*. Available at http://www.aaets.org/article145.htm.

Noel, N., and M. Yam. 1992. "Domestic Violence: The Pregnant Battered Woman." *Women's Health* 27 (4).

Ontario Women's Directorate. 1991. *Wife Assault: The Impact on Children*. Brochure.

Ontario Women's Directorate. 1997. *Prevention of Violence against Women: It's Everyone's Responsibility*.

Orwen, P. 2003. "Parents of Disabled Face Onerous Burden." *The Toronto Star*. 30 July.

Palmer, T. 2004. "Just One Click from abuse." *The Guardian*. February 10. Available at http://society.guardian.co.uk/children/comment/0,,1144430,00.html.

———. 2005. "Behind the Screen—Children Who are the Subjects of Abusive Images." In E. Quayle and M. Taylor, eds., *Viewing Child Pornography on the Internet: Understanding the Offence, Managing the Offender, Helping the Victims*. Dorset, England: Russell House Publishing.

Pelletier, J., and J.M. Brent. 2002. "Parent Participation in Children's School Readiness: The Effects of Parental Self-Efficacy, Cultural Diversity and Teacher Strategies." *International Journal of Early Childhood* 34 (1).

Perry, B.D. 1995. "Incubated in Terror: Neurodevelopmental Factors in the Cycle of Violence." In J. Osofsky, ed., *Children, Youth and Violence: Searching for Solutions*. New York: The Guilford Press.

———. 2004. *Maltreatment and the Developing Child: How Early Childhood Experience Shapes Child and Culture*. Inaugural Lecture, The Margaret McCain Lecture Series, Centre for Children and Families in the Justice System, London, ON, September 23. Available at http://www.lfcc.on.ca/mccain/perry1.html.

Pimento, B., and D. Kernested. 2000. *Healthy Foundations in Child Care*. Toronto: Nelson Thomson Learning.

Pollack, G. 2001. "Who Are Canada's Homeless?" *Reader's Digest Canada*. Available at http://www.readersdigest.ca/mag/2001/01/homeless.html.

Richters, J., and P. Martinez. 1993. "The NIMH Community Violence Project: Children as Victims of and Witness to Violence." *Psychiatry* 56.

Rimer, J. 2007. *Literature Review—Responding to Child & Youth Victims of Sexual Exploitation on the Internet*. Toronto, ON: Boost Child Abuse Prevention & Intervention. Available at http://www.boostforkids.org/pdf/RCE-Literature-Review.pdf.

Rimer, P. 2007. *Making A Difference: The Community Responds To Child Abuse*, 5th ed. Toronto: Boost Child Abuse Prevention & Intervention.

Rimer, P., and B. Prager. 1998. *Reaching Out: Working Together to Identify and Respond to Child Victims of Abuse*. Toronto: ITP Nelson.

Rishchynski, G., P. Rimer, and J. Rimer. In press. *Looking For Angelina: A Learning Guide On Family Violence*. Toronto: Second Story Press.

Roberson Jackson, B. 1995. "Early Childhood Professionals: Partners with Parents Helping Young Children Exposed to Violence." *Child Care Information Exchange* 102. March–April.

Robinson, B.E. 1990. "The Teacher's Role in Working with Children of Alcoholic Parents." *Young Children*. May.

Rocco, S. 1994. "New Visions for the Developmental Assessment of Infants and Young Children: A Parent's Perspective." *Zero to Three* 14 (6). June–July.

Rockwell, R.E., L.C. Andre, and M.K. Hawley. 1996. *Parents and Teachers as Partners: Issues and Challenges*. Toronto: Harcourt Brace & Company.

Rodgers, K. 1994. "Wife Assault: The Findings of a National Survey." *Juristat* 14 (9). Catalogue no. 85-002-XPE. Ottawa: Statistics Canada.

Rossman, B., and J. Ho. 2000. "Posttraumatic Response and Children Exposed to Parental Violence." In R. Geffner, P. Jaffe, and M. Sudermann, eds., *Children Exposed to Domestic Violence: Current Issues in Research, Intervention, Prevention, and Policy Development*. New York: The Haworth Maltreatment & Trauma Press.

Ryan, W. 1972. *Blaming the Victim*. New York: Vintage Books.

Schoen, A.A., M. Burgoyne, and S.F. Schoen. 2004. "Are the Developmental Needs of Children in America Adequately Addressed During the Grief Process." *Journal of Instructional Psychology* 31 (2): 143–150.

Shimoni, R., and J. Baxter. 2008. *Working with Families*, 4th ed. Toronto: Pearson, Addison Wesley.

Stark, E. 1987. "Forgotten Victims: Children of Alcoholics." *Psychology Today*. January.

Statistics Canada. 2001. *Family Violence in Canada: A Statistical Profile 2001*. Catalogue no. 85-224-XIE. Statistics Canada: Minister of Industry.

———. 2006a. *Family Violence in Canada: A Statistical Profile 2006*. Catalogue no. 85-224-XIE. Statistics Canada, Canadian Centre for Justice Statistics: Minister of Industry.

———. 2006b. *Measuring Violence against Women: Statistical Trends 2006*. Catalogue no. 85-570-XWE. Statistics Canada: Minister of Industry.

———. 2007. *Family Violence in Canada: A Statistical Profile 2007*. Catalogue no. 85-224-XIE. Statistics Canada, Canadian Centre for Justice Statistics: Minister of Industry.

Steinberg, L. 2000. "Youth Violence: Do Parents and Families Make a Difference?" *National Institute of Justice Journal* 2: 30–38.

Steinhauer, P. 1998. "How a Child's Early Experiences Affect Development." Paper presented at Linking Research to Practice: A Canadian Forum, Banff, Alta., October 25–27.

Straus, M.A., and R.J. Gelles. 1990. "Societal Change and Change in Family Violence from 1975 to 1985 as Revealed by Two National Surveys." In M.A. Strauss and R.J. Gelles, eds., *Physical Violence in American Families: Risk Factors and Adaptations to Violence in 8,145 Families*. New Brunswick: Transaction Publishers.

Sudermann, M., and P. Jaffe. 1999. *A Handbook for Health and Social Service Providers and Educators on Children Exposed to Woman Abuse/Family Violence*. The Family Violence Prevention Unit, Health Canada. Ottawa: Minister of Public Works and Government Services Canada.

Suh, E., and E.M. Abel. 1990. "The Impact of Spousal Violence on the Children of the Abused." *Journal of Independent Social Work* 4 (4): 27–34.

Swift, D. 1999. "Re-educating Ricky." *Tree House Canadian Family*. September.

Teti, D.M., and D.M. Gelfand. 1991. "Behavioural Competence among Mothers of Infants in the First Year: The Mediational Role of Maternal Self-Efficacy." *Child Development* 62: 918–929.

The Packard Foundation. 1999. "Executive summary." *The Future of Children* 9: 1–3.

The Toronto Star. 2007. October 6. ID4.

Trocmé, N., et al. 2001. *Canadian Incidence Study of Reported Child Abuse and Neglect: Final Report*. Ottawa: Minister of Public Works and Government Services Canada.

UNICEF. 2006. "Some of the Biggest Victims of Domestic Violence are the Smallest." Available at http://www.unicef.org/evaldatabase/index_35151.html.

Vacheret, M. 2007. "Private Family Visits In Canada, Between Rehabilitation and Stricter Control: Portrait of A System." http://champpenal.revues.org/document2322.html.

Vaillancourt, R., and A. Taylor-Butts. 2007. *Transition Homes in Canada: National, Provincial and Territorial Fact Sheets 2005/2006*. Catalogue no: 85-404-XWE. Statistics Canada, Canadian Centre for Justice Statistics: Minister of Industry.

Vallée, B. 2007. *The War on Women: Elly Armour, Jane Hurshman, and Criminal Domestic Violence in Canadian Homes*. Toronto: Key Porter Books Ltd.

Vanier Institute of the Family. 1994. "Profiling Canada's Families." Pamphlet. Ottawa: Vanier Institute of the Family.

Werner, E.E. 1995. "Resilience in Development." *Current Directions In Psychological Science* June: 81–85.

Ward, M. 2002. *The Family Dynamic: A Canadian Perspective*. Toronto: Nelson Canada.

Wax, I.F. 1996. "Don't Give Up the Dream." *Learning Disabilities Association of Toronto* 1 (4). May–June.

Wells-Parker, E., D.I. Miller, and S. Topping. 1990. "Development of Control of Outcome Scales and Self-efficacy Scales for Women in Four Life Roles." *Journal of Personality Assessment* 54: 564–575.

Weston, D.R., B. Ivins, B. Zuckerman, C. Jones, and R. Lopez. 1989. "Drug-Exposed Babies." *Research and Clinical Issues, Zero to Three* 9 (5).

White, N.J. 2004. "Kissing Cousins." *The Toronto Star*. July 3. Section L.

Wilson, M., and M. Daly. 1992. "Who Kills Whom in Spouse Killings? On the Exceptional Sex Ratio of Spousal Homicides in the United States." *Criminology* 30: 189–215.

Winzer, M. 2008. *Children with Exceptionalities in Canadian Classrooms*, 8th ed. Toronto: Pearson.

Wolfe, D., and C. Feiring. 2000. "Dating Violence through the Lens of Adolescent Romantic Relationships." *Child Maltreatment* 5 (4): 360–363.

World Health Organization (WHO). 2004. *The Economic Dimensions of Interpersonal Violence*. Geneva, Switzerland: Department of Injuries and Violence Prevention, World Health Organization. Available at http://whqlibdoc.who.int/publications/2004/9241591609.pdf.

Zeanah, C.H., B. Danis, L. Hirshberg, D. Benoit, D. Miller, and S.S. Heller. 1999. "Disorganized Attachment Associated with Partner Violence: A Research Note." *Infant Mental Health Journal* 20: 77–86.

Courtesy of Lynn Wilson

CHAPTER 11

Working with Families: An International Perspective

© Sarah Nicholl / Shutterstock

"To laugh often and much, to win the respect of intelligent people and the affection of children, to earn the appreciation of honest critics and endure the betrayal of false friends, to appreciate beauty, to find the best in others, to leave the world a bit better, whether by a healthy child, a garden patch . . . to know even one life has breathed easier because you have lived. This is to have succeeded."

—*Ralph Waldo Emerson*

LEARNING OUTCOMES

After studying this chapter, you will be able to

1. evaluate the implications of the UN Convention on the Rights of the Child and the Convention on the Elimination of All Forms of Discrimination to determine how it influences the development of early childhood services at home and abroad

2. consider the impact of the Millennium Development Goals and their implication for the health and well being of children and mothers

3. discuss the implications of war and conflict on families

4. consider the impact of early childhood education worldwide

5. evaluate organizations and their role in supporting families in the global community and the role of early childhood graduates

THE CONVENTION ON THE RIGHTS OF THE CHILD

In celebration of the 20-year anniversary of the adoption of the Declaration of the Rights of the Child, the United Nations declared 1979 to be the International Year of the Child. The goal of the International Year of the Child was to focus attention on children living in poorer nations, many of whom were undernourished and receiving inadequate health care and educational services. The original 1959 declaration challenged countries and governments across the world to review the status of children and to focus attention on improving the quality of life for children everywhere. In 1989—on the 30th anniversary—the UN Convention on the Rights of the Child (CRC) was adopted. The UN Convention differed from the Declaration in that it was a comprehensive, binding treaty consisting of 54 articles, 44 of which established that children should be treated as individuals with their own rights, and 10 which required states to put mechanisms in place to facilitate these changes. The first article defines a child as a person under the age of 18 years, unless national laws recognize the age of majority to be earlier than 18 years. The Convention has been ratified by 193 national states and is the most widely supported international human rights instrument in the world. Only two nation states—Somalia and the United States—have not yet ratified the Convention.

In 1994, Richard Reid, a director with the United Nations International Children's Fund, noted in his keynote address at the International Conference on Children's Rights:

> It has been four years since the world's countries adopted, unanimously, the Convention on the Rights of the Child at the General Assembly of the United Nations. Looking back across the world over those few years—at the avalanche of stepped-up violence against children, at the burned-out villages of the scores of savage new ethnic wars, at the streets of the big cities, and at dysfunctional homes—all of this mayhem played out, somehow, side by side with wonderfully steady gains in child health and solid advances in basic education. Can anyone . . . tell where the hands of the world's crisis clock for children stand at this moment? Does the clock say dawn, with daylight ahead of us, or are we approaching midnight? In all this uncertain mix of hope and bleakness, there is one thing we can be sure of. And that is that the Convention on the Rights of the Child is here to stay, each day more steadily afoot in the world. While other national treaties languish, the Children's Convention has swept the world in four years; more countries have bound themselves to it than any other global humanitarian treaty in history. It is a rising tide that soon enough will begin to lift all boats. All of us who work for children need to capitalize on this gathering force. (Reid, 1994)

© Marcus Brown / Shutterstock

The world focuses on improving the quality of life for all children through the United Nations Convention on the Rights of the Child.

There is still much to be done to improve the quality of life for so many children.

MONITORING CHILD RIGHTS

The UN Committee on the Rights of the Child (UNCRC) is the body of independent experts that monitors the implementation of the Convention on the Rights of the Child by State parties. The UNCRC meets in Geneva, normally holding three sessions per year. All State parties are obliged to submit regular reports of the UNCRC on the implementation of child rights in their countries. Reports are first required two years after acceding to the Convention and then every five years. The UNCRC examines each report and addresses its concerns and recommendations to the State party in the form of "concluding observations" (Child Rights Information Network, 2008).

The UNCRC also organizes Days of General Discussion and publishes its interpretation of the content of human rights provisions, known as General Comments. On September 17, 2004, the Committee devoted its Day of General Discussion to the theme "Implementing Child Rights in Early Childhood." The following recommendations were adopted by the UNCRC on September 30, 2005:

1. To strengthen understanding of the human rights of all young children and to draw States parties' attention to their obligations towards young children.

2. To comment on the specific features of early childhood that impact on the realization of rights.

3. To encourage recognition of young children as social actors from the beginning of life, with particular interests, capacities and vulnerabilities, and of requirements for protection, guidance and support in the exercise of their rights.

4. To draw attention to diversities within early childhood that need to be taken into account when implementing the Convention, including diversities in young children's circumstances, in the quality of their experiences and in the influences shaping their development.

5. To point to variations in cultural expectations and treatment of children, including local customs and practices that should be respected, except where they contravene the rights of the child.

6. To emphasize the vulnerability of young children to poverty, discrimination, family breakdown and multiple other adversities that violates their rights and undermines their wellbeing.

7. To contribute to the realization of rights for all young children through formulation and promotion of comprehensive policies, laws, programmes, practices, professional training and research focused on rights in early childhood. (UNESCO, n.d.)

AMNESTY INTERNATIONAL

"Being unwanted, unloved, uncared for, forgotten by everybody, I think that is a much greater hunger, a much greater poverty than the person who has nothing to eat."

—Mother Teresa

Amnesty International is an independent organization that works towards an ultimate goal of ensuring that everyone—adults and children—is protected by the UN Declaration of Human Rights. On their website at **http://www.amnesty .ca/themes/children_overview.php** the organization outlines its work involving children:

> Amnesty International campaigns around the world to ensure that children's human rights are protected. It calls on governments, opposition groups and all other actors who exercise control over children to adhere to the principle of "best interests of the child" as the primary consideration in all actions concerning children. . . . Almost all governments pay lip service to children's rights, but most fail to live up to their words. Children suffer many of the same human rights abuses as adults, but are often targeted because they are dependent and vulnerable or because children are not seen as individuals with their own rights.
>
> Children are tortured and ill-treated by state officials, detained in appalling conditions, and sentenced to death. Countless thousands are killed and maimed in armed conflicts. Millions are forced by poverty or abuse to live on the streets where they are vulnerable to abuse. Millions more work at exploitative or hazardous jobs or are victims of child trafficking and forced prostitution. Discriminatory attitudes and practices mean girl children suffer gender-specific abuses, such as female genital mutilation, and are particularly vulnerable to other forms of abuse, including rape. (Amnesty International, 2006)

As we review the intent of the UN Convention on the Rights of the Child and its impact on Canadian children, it is clear that there is much work to be done. The fundamental ideology expressed in the convention must serve as the basis for Canadians' work with children and families.

Policies offered in Europe are more extensive and generous. Although there are important differences across France, Germany, Finland, and Sweden, family policies in each of these countries reflect a tradition of acknowledging social responsibility for children. Canadian policies, like those in the United States, often reflect the attitude that children are the private responsibility of their parents. As a result, the outcomes for European families in all cases look much better than outcomes in Canada. Finally, more generous welfare states have not led to economic disaster—our economic record is no better in Canada despite our rather cautious programs for families.

ELIMINATION OF ALL FORMS OF DISCRIMINATION AGAINST WOMEN

In 1980, Canada signed the Convention on the Elimination of All Forms of Discrimination against Women (CEDAW). Currently, 185 countries have ratified the CEDAW, over 90 percent of the members of the United Nations. The United States is the only industrialized country that has not ratified this document. This convention stipulates that State parties submit reports every four years. In 2003, the UN Committee on the Elimination of Discrimination Against Women considered the latest Canadian report. Clauses 55 and 56 of the UN's response to Canada's report are relevant to child care in Canada:

> Clause 55: The Committee is concerned that, while the report cites laudable efforts at expanding and improving child care under all governments, there is no information, except for Quebec, indicating whether the available child-care places meet the demand and are affordable.
>
> Clause 56: The Committee recommends that the State party further expand affordable child-care facilities under all governments and that it report, with nationwide figures, on demand, availability and affordability of child care in its next report. (United Nations, Division for the Advancement of Women, 2007).

Clearly this continues to underscore the need for a comprehensive, not-for-profit, high quality national child-care policy in Canada.

UNITED NATIONS MILLENNIUM DEVELOPMENT GOALS

World leaders came together in New York on September 25, 2008 for a high-level event convened by the UN Secretary-General and the President of the UN General Assembly to renew commitments to achieving the Millennium Development Goals and to set out concrete plans and practical steps for

The Millennium Development Goals form a blueprint for a global partnership to provide primary education for all children.

action. By 2015 all 189 United Nations Member States have pledged to:

1. Eradicate extreme poverty and hunger:
   - Reduce by half the proportion of people living on less than a dollar a day.
   - Reduce by half the proportion of people who suffer from hunger.

2. Achieve universal primary education:
   - Ensure that all boys and girls complete a full course of primary education.

3. Promote gender equality and empower women:
   - Eliminate gender disparity in primary and secondary education preferably by 2005, and at all levels by 2015.

4. Reduce child mortality:
   - Reduce by two-thirds the mortality rate among children under five.

5. Improve maternal health:
   - Reduce by three-quarters the maternal mortality ratio.

6. Combat HIV/AIDS, malaria and other diseases:
   - Halt and begin to reverse the spread of HIV/AIDS.
   - Halt and begin to reverse the incidence of malaria and other major diseases.

7. Ensure environmental sustainability:
   - Integrate the principles of sustainable development into country policies and programs; reverse loss of environmental resources.
   - Reduce by half the proportion of people without sustainable access to safe drinking water.
   - Achieve significant improvement in lives of at least 100 million slum dwellers, by 2020.

8. Develop a global partnership for development:
   - Develop further an open trading and financial system that is rule-based, predictable and non-discriminatory. This includes a commitment to good governance, development and poverty reduction—nationally and internationally.

© Jean-Marc Giboux / Getty

The international community must recognize the need to finance and organize the effective distribution of a broad spectrum of medical aid to the world's neediest.

- Address the least developed countries' special needs. This includes tariff- and quota-free access for their exports; enhanced debt relief for heavily indebted poor countries; cancellation of official bilateral debt; and more generous official development assistance for countries committed to poverty reduction.

- Address the special needs of landlocked and small island developing states.

- Deal comprehensively with developing countries' debt problems through national and international measures to make debt sustainable in the long term.

- In cooperation with pharmaceutical companies provide access to affordable essential drugs in developing countries.

- In cooperation with the private sector, make available the benefits of new technologies—especially information and communications technologies. (United Nations, 2008)

CHILD SURVIVAL: A GLOBAL PERSPECTIVE

On average, more than 28,000 children under the age of five die around the world every day, mostly from preventable causes. That's one child every three seconds, and more than 10 million every year. Nearly all of these children live in the developing world or, more precisely, in 60 developing countries. More than one-third of these children die during the first month of life, usually at home and without access to essential health services and basic commodities that might save their lives. Some children succumb to respiratory or diarrhoeal infections that are no longer threats in industrialized countries, or they are victims of early childhood diseases, such as measles, that are easily prevented through vaccines. An underlying cause in up to half of the under-five deaths is undernutrition, a condition which deprives a young child's body and mind of the nutrients needed for growth and development. Unsafe water, poor sanitation, and inadequate hygiene also contribute to child mortality and morbidity. Poverty is at the root of the problem. In the least developed countries, one child out of every six dies before his or her fifth birthday. In wealthy countries, this statistic is one out of every 167 (Toycen, 2007: 4). Imagine the shock in Canada if the entire population of Nunavut was wiped out in one day or the horror if every Canadian under the age of 25 died in a single year. While this seems like a doomsday scenario, the above statistics demonstrate to us that this happens every day and every year in developing countries.

UNDERLYING AND STRUCTURAL CAUSES OF MATERNAL AND CHILD MORTALITY

Maternal, newborn, and under-five deaths and under nutrition have a number of common structural and underlying causes, including:

- poorly resourced, unresponsive, and culturally inappropriate health and nutrition services;
- food insecurity;
- inadequate feeding practices;
- lack of hygiene and access to safe water or adequate sanitation;
- female illiteracy;
- early pregnancy; and

- discrimination and exclusion of mothers and children from access to essential health and nutrition services and commodities because of poverty and geographic or political marginalization. (UNICEF, 2007: 3)

These factors result in millions of unnecessary deaths each year. The latest evidence is that four million babies die each year in their first month of life; up to half of these die in their first 24 hours. A child is about 500 times more likely to die in the first day of life than at one month of age (UNICEF, 2007: 4).

Four of the five countries with the highest child mortality rates (per 1,000 live births) are in sub-Sahara Africa: Sierra Leone has a rate of 282 deaths per 1,000 live births; Afghanistan has 257; Niger has 256; Liberia has 235; and Somalia experiences 225 deaths per 1,000 live births (Costanza, 2007: 21).

Neonatal mortality accounts for almost 40 percent of all under-five deaths. A common factor in these deaths is the health of the mother. Each year more than 500,000 women die in childbirth or from complications during pregnancy, and babies whose mothers have died during childbirth have a much greater chance of dying in their first year than those whose mothers remain alive. For every newborn baby who dies, another 20 suffer birth injury, com-

plications arising from preterm birth or other neonatal conditions (UNICEF, 2007: 4).

CAUSES OF CHILD DEATHS

Severe infections are a significant factor in child deaths. A significant proportion of these infections is caused by pneumonia and sepsis (a serious blood-borne bacterial infection that is also treated with antibiotics). Around two million children—one in five deaths globally—under five die from pneumonia each year. Despite progress since the 1980s, diarrhoeal diseases account for 17 percent of under-five deaths. Malaria, measles, and AIDS, taken together, are responsible for 15 percent of child deaths (UNICEF, 2007: 8).

HIV and AIDS

Worldwide, 2.3 million children under the age of 15 are living with HIV; 530,000 children were newly infected with the virus in 2006, mostly through mother-to-child transmission. Girls, in particular, are at risk of contracting HIV, both because of their physiology and because of social and cultural power imbalances in their relationships with men and boys. Preventing new infections is the first line of defense against AIDS. It is also the best way to protect the

---

FIGURE 11.1   GLOBAL RATES OF NEONATAL MORTALITY, 2000

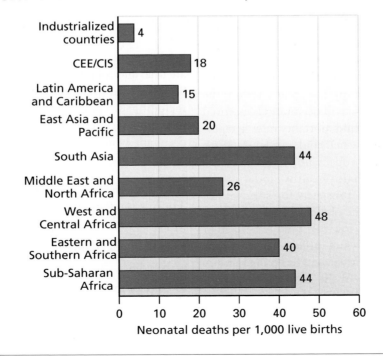

Source: From *The State of the World's Children 2008—Child Survival,* Figure 1.2, page 4. Reprinted with permission from UNICEF.

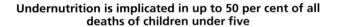

**Undernutrition is implicated in up to 50 per cent of all
deaths of children under five**

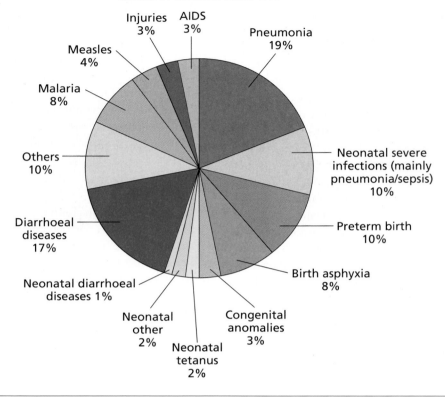

Source: From *The State of the World's Children 2008—Child Survival,* Figure 1.8, page 8. Reprinted with permission from UNICEF.

next generation. Once a pregnant woman is infected with HIV, there is a 35 percent chance that without intervention she will pass the virus on to her newborn during pregnancy, birth, or breastfeeding. Antiretroviral drug therapy can greatly reduce the chances that transmission will occur and is essential to stemming the rise in child mortality rates in countries where AIDS has reached epidemic levels. With appropriate drugs and proper care, infants who are HIV-positive can remain healthy indefinitely, though their long-term prospects for survival are unknown. Yet despite the obvious benefits of drug therapy and its relatively low cost, only 11 percent of pregnant women in low- and middle-income countries who were HIV positive were receiving services to prevent transmission of the virus to their newborns in 2005 (UNICEF, 2007: 42).

Malaria

Malaria causes more than a million deaths each year, up to 80 percent of them in children under five. Pregnant women and their unborn children are particularly vulnerable to the disease, which is a prime cause of low birth weight in newborns, anemia, and infant deaths. Preventing and treating malaria requires several basic interventions including sleeping under an insecticide treated mosquito net and providing anti-malarial drugs for pregnant women and children with evident signs of the disease (UNICEF, 2007: 13).

KEY INTERVENTIONS

The key interventions needed to address the major causes of child deaths are:

- Skilled attendants at delivery
- Newborn care
- Care of low birth-weight infants
- Hygiene promotion
- Prevention of mother-to-child transmission of HIV
- Pediatric treatment of AIDS

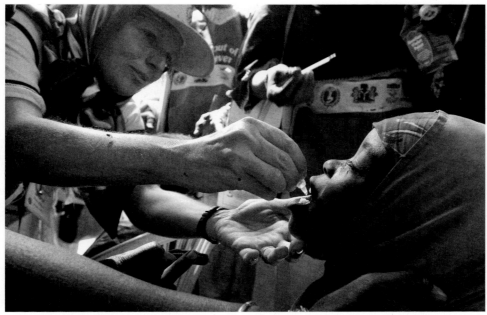

Ninety percent of mother-to-child transmissions of HIV occur in Africa.

INSIDE LOOK

Botswana: A Good News Story

AIDS is a foremost cause of maternal, newborn, and child death in southern Africa. In Botswana, almost 1 in every 4 people aged 15–49 is infected with HIV. The risk to children begins before birth; one third of pregnant women aged 15–24 in Botswana are HIV-positive. Maternal HIV-positive status leads to an increased rate of stillbirths and deaths in the neonatal period and infancy, even if HIV is not transmitted to the child. Women who contract HIV during pregnancy or while breastfeeding have a high risk of passing the infection to their newborn. Moreover, mothers are increasingly at risk of death, leaving behind babies with diminished chances of survival. AIDS is a significant cause of disability and death in babies and children beyond one month.

Interventions and Approaches: In Botswana, prevention of mother-to-child transmission of HIV (PMTCT) was initiated in 1999 with strong political commitment and high resource allocation. From the outset, the Government of Botswana planned for national coverage of interventions. Services are provided free of charge to women and children and are integrated into existing maternal and child health services. These interventions include safe obstetric practices, counselling, HIV testing, prophylaxis or treatment for HIV infection as indicated, and testing of babies for HIV infection at six weeks of age. Antiretroviral therapy is also providing to qualifying mothers and their families. Rigorous monitoring and evaluation is implemented and supply chains closely managed.

One of the central success factors in Botswana was the unified coordination mechanism around a single national scale-up plan. PMTCT was fully integrated with maternal and child health services, but ongoing adjustments were made to increase quality and service uptake. Political commitment was important, as was cohesive programme management. Community participation and male involvement were also crucial elements to support women who chose not to breastfeed and to facilitate follow-up pediatric care and support.

Results: In Botswana, the programme expanded to nationwide coverage by 2004. By 2005, 54 percent of HIV-positive mothers were receiving antiretroviral drugs during pregnancy.

Source: UNICEF, 2007: 81.

Recently, a team from the World Health Organization visited Ethiopia, Ghana, Rwanda and Zambia. These countries were the first to distribute the bed nets and medicine. The Global Fund to Fight AIDS, Tuberculosis and Malaria requested a study to see if the interventions were helping. The researchers found that the answer is yes. They looked at records of children under five. They found that malaria deaths fell by sixty-six percent in Rwanda between 2005 and 2007. Deaths fell by fifty-one percent in Ethiopia, thirty-four percent in Ghana and thirty-three percent in Zambia.

The team reported that limited supplies of bed nets could help explain the more limited effects in Zambia and Ghana. In another new study, researchers reported that vitamin A and zinc treatments might also help protect young children from malaria. Scientists in Burkina Faso found that malaria reinfection rates fell by thirty-four percent in a group of children treated with vitamin A and zinc."

Source: Voice of America, 2008.

- Adequate nutrition
- Early and exclusive breastfeeding during the first 6 months of life
- Complementary feeding combined with continued breastfeeding for at least two more years
- Micronutrient supplementation to boost immune systems
- Immunization to protect children against the six major vaccine-preventable diseases
- Oral rehydration therapy and zinc to combat diarrhoeal disease
- Antibiotics to fight pneumonia
- Insecticide treated mosquito nets
- Effective medicines to prevent and treat malaria (UNICEF, 2007).

CREATING A SUPPORTIVE ENVIRONMENT FOR CHILD SURVIVAL STRATEGIES

Infant and child mortality rates are highest in the poorest countries, among the most impoverished, isolated, uneducated, and marginalized districts and communities and in countries ravaged by civil strife, weak governance, and chronic underinvestment in public health systems and physical infrastructure. Of the 11 countries in which 20 percent or more of children die before age five—Afghanistan, Angola, Burkina Faso, Chad, the Democratic Republic of the Congo, Equatorial Guinea, Guinea-Bissau, Liberia, Mali, Niger, and Sierra Leone—more than half have suffered a major armed conflict since 1989. Similarly, fragile states, characterized by weak institutions with high levels of corruption, political instability, and a shaky rule of law, are often incapable of providing basic services to their citizens. AIDS, food insecurity, or countries that are prone to droughts are also at risk of having poorer child survival outcomes (UNICEF 2007).

EMPOWERING WOMEN TO ADVANCE MATERNAL, NEWBORN, AND CHILD HEALTH

Despite the importance of maternal health, one in four pregnant women receives no antenatal care and more than 40 percent give birth without the assistance of a skilled attendant. Empowering women, especially at the community level, is essential to both lowering the number of deaths among children under five and to reaching Millennium Development Goal 5, which aims to reduce maternal mortality by three quarters by 2015. Yet the low status of women in many societies and their limited decision-making power within the household often present serious challenges to achieving significant progress in either area. In many households, especially in South Asia and sub-Saharan Africa, women have little influence in health-related decisions in households, whether concerning their own health or that of their children. In Burkina Faso, Mali, and Nigeria, almost 75 percent of women respondents reported that husbands alone make decisions about women's health care. In South Asia, Bangladesh, and Nepal, this ratio was around 50 percent. The situation is often most severe in rural areas or in urban slums, where women are largely illiterate and suffer from sociocultural barriers to accessing health services, such as restrictions on leaving their homes or on interacting with strangers, and frequently do not have access to a health centre or a health clinic. For example, in Afghanistan, women are prohibited from receiving health care at hospitals staffed exclusively by male health personnel, while cultural norms restrict women from working and receiving advanced medical training.

A number of community health worker programs that train primarily women have successfully circumvented gender-based barriers to utilization of health services. In Bangladesh, the community health workers who have been trained are married, middle-aged women, and their "doorstep" health services allow women to circumvent *purdah* restrictions that prevent them from leaving their homes to access health facilities on their own (UNICEF, 2007: 20).

War and Terrorism

Given the uncertain times that we are living in, concerns over war and terrorism have had a direct influence on young children's lives. War Child (**www.warchild.com**) reports that 60 million people have been killed in wars during the 20th century and today more than 30 wars and conflicts rage around the world. Over 80 percent of war casualties are civilians, mainly women and children. Children are among the first casualties of any armed conflict, always the most vulnerable and

© Karel Prinsloo / Associated Press

Today as many as 300,000 children under the age of 18 serve in government forces or armed rebel groups, some as young as 8 years of age.

© Jean-Marc Giboux / Getty

The UN's Health Agency reports that a shortage of 4.3 million doctors, nurses, and other health workers is hampering the fight against AIDS and other fatal diseases.

The Other Side of the Mat: Uniting for Maternal, Newborn and Child Survival and Health by Melinda Gates

When Bill and I meet people in the developing countries we visit, it's easy to see what we have in common with them, in spite of our different circumstances. Like us, they have hopes for the future. They have parents who love them and children who need them. They have intellectual curiosity, an entrepreneurial spirit and a determination to make life better for themselves and their children.

I am especially moved by the mothers I meet. They invite me into their homes, and we sit on the floor, often on opposite sides of a small mat, talking. I have young children myself, and I try to put myself in their position. What would I do if I were on the other side of the mat? What would I want for my children?

If I were a pregnant mother in Bangladesh, I would want a skilled attendant who knew how to help me deliver my baby safely. If I were a young mother in India, I would want to know the facts: that breastfeeding instead of using formula is one of the best ways to save my newborn from cholera. If I were a mother in Malawi and my daughter got sick with diarrhea, I would hope that she could get the electrolytes she needed before it was too late.

Those would be my hopes, my dreams, my wishes. But for many, they are not the reality of their daily lives. The reality is this: in 2006, 9.7 million children died before they turned five—most from easily preventable or treatable causes.

In some countries I have visited, mothers don't give their children names for weeks or even months because they don't want to start caring about them. The chance that their children will die in those first weeks is just too high. When I hear such stories, I am jolted back to my side of the mat. How can such widespread tragedy be so common in the developing world?

On my side of the mat, when my kids are sick, they get antibiotics. On the other side of the mat, when their children get sick, they may be receiving a death sentence. Those of us in wealthy countries must try to put ourselves on the other side of the mat.

Fortunately, the story is starting to change. Governments around the world are doing more for children's health. Efforts to treat and prevent the world's most devastating diseases are improving the lives of millions of children.

To keep this momentum going, we must remember that these mothers love their children just as much as we love ours. We must see that these children have boundless potential. And we must help them realize their potential by bringing more governments, more businesses and more individuals to this work—to unite for maternal, newborn and child survival and health. When we do, all mothers will have a chance to see their children grow up happy and strong, and all children will have a chance to make their dreams come true.

Source: Gates, 2007.

innocent of victims. In the last decade alone 1.5 million children have died in wars, 4 million have been disabled, and a further 10 million traumatized (War Child, n.d.). The severe psychological wounds that war inflicts on children can scar them for life, crippling the very generations that must one day rebuild their devastated countries.

For those educators working with older school-age children, active involvement in peace and aid organizations may help these children feel positive about their contributions to others while sensitizing them to the broader world view. The National Association of School Psychologists (NASP) also has an informative website—Helping Children Cope in Unsettling Times: Tips for Parents and Teachers—at **www.nasponline.org**.

WORLD FOOD PRICES SOAR

Consumers worldwide are facing soaring food costs. Weather patterns, changes in the global economy, higher oil prices, lower food reserves, and the growing demand in China and India are all critical factors. Food costs worldwide spiked 23 percent from 2006 to 2007 according to the UN Food and Agriculture Organization. Grains went up 42 percent, oils by 50 percent, and dairy by 80 percent.

This has enormous implications for the world's poorest nations (Corcoran, 2008).

CHILD HEALTH IN COMPLEX EMERGENCIES

Meeting the health needs of children, women, and families presents considerable challenges in peacetime. These challenges are compounded many times during emergencies, both natural or human-made. Between 1989 and 2000, 110 recorded conflicts took place; 103 of them were civil wars, many of them protracted, accompanied by institutional collapse and violence directed against civilians. At present more than 40 countries, 90 percent of them low-income nations, are dealing with armed conflict (UNICEF, 2007: 18).

SUPPORTING CHILDREN IN POST-EMERGENCY SITUATIONS

In *Early Childhood Matters* (2005), Save the Children outlines seven critical types of protection that children require in disaster areas and war zones:

1. Protection from physical harm
2. Protection from exploitation and gender-based violence

Increases in global food prices threaten food security and the well-being of millions of people.

© Holger Mettes / Shutterstock

3. Protection from gender-based psychosocial distress
4. Protection from gender-based recruitment into armed groups
5. Protection from family separation
6. Protection from abuses related to forced displacement
7. Protection from denial of children's access to quality education

Sweden's Save the Children (Gustaffson, 1986) also provides a framework for Early Childhood Development in emergencies:

STOP

S = Space and Structure

T = Trust, Time, Talking

O = Opportunities to Play

P = Partnership with Parents

Space and structure: Children need a predictable routine, an anecdote to chaos, housing may not be in place so school is critical.

Trust, time, talking: Young children feel they are very powerful and feel they may have caused the chaos and feel guilty.

Opportunities to play: The healing process will begin when children have opportunities to play.

Partnerships with parents: Parents will need support and opportunities to talk. The school may provide a place of calm where they feel safe. Let them participate if they like.

COGNITIVE POTENTIAL

The Lancet (2007) outlines the conservative estimate that more than 200 million children under years of age fail to reach their potential in cognitive development because of poverty, poor health and nutrition, and deficient care. Sub-Saharan African countries have the highest percentage of disadvantaged children but the largest number live in south Asia. The children will subsequently do poorly in school and are likely to transfer poverty to the next generation. Grantham-McGregor et al. (2007) estimate that this loss of human potential is associated with more than a 20 percent deficit in adult income and will have implications for national development. The problem of poor child development will remain unless a substantial effort is made to mount appropriate integrated programs. There is increasing

Sowing Seeds of Hope

Throughout the year, World Vision mails small packets of vegetable seeds to Canadian sponsors and other donors. When a donor signs the packet and returns it with a donation, World Vision ships it to a project in Africa, Latin America, the Middle East, or Asia. In 2006, more than 60,000 Canadians sent seed packets through World Vision and raised more than $3 million. Staff members used these donations to provide vulnerable families with locally purchased farming tools and a larger supply of seeds to help them produce more bountiful harvests.

Source: World Vision, 2007: 5.

evidence that early interventions can help prevent the loss of potential in affected children and improvements can happen rapidly (Grantham-McGregor et al., 2007: 67). The most effective interventions are comprehensive programs for younger and disadvantaged children and families that are of adequate duration, intensity, quality, and are integrated with health and nutrition services. Providing services directly to children and including an active parenting and skill-building component is a more effective strategy than providing information alone (Engle et al., 2007: 239).

THEMATIC REVIEW OF EARLY CHILDHOOD EDUCATION AND CARE POLICY, OECD

Early childhood education and care has experienced a surge of policy attention in Organization for Economic Co-operation and Development (OECD) countries over the past decade. Policy makers have recognized that equitable access to quality early childhood education and care can strengthen the foundations of lifelong learning for all children and support the broad educational and social needs of families. There is a need to improve knowledge about the range of approaches adopted by different countries, along with the successes and challenges encountered. Recognizing that this cross-national information and analysis can contribute to the improvement of policy development, the OECD's Education Committee launched the Thematic Review of Early Childhood Education and Care Policy in 1998. Twelve countries volunteered to participate in the review: Australia, Belgium, the Czech Republic, Denmark, Finland,

Italy, the Netherlands, Norway, Portugal, Sweden, the UK, and the United States.

The report identifies eight key elements of policy that are likely to promote equitable access to quality ECEC:

1. A systemic and integrated approach to policy development and implementation that calls for a clear vision for children from birth to eight, underlying ECEC policy, and coordinated policy frameworks at centralized and decentralized levels.

2. A strong and equal partnership with the education system to support a lifelong learning approach from birth, encourage smooth transitions for children, and recognize ECEC as an important part of the education process.

3. A universal approach to access, with particular attention to children in need of special support.

4. Substantial public investment in services and the infrastructure.

5. A participatory approach to quality improvement and assurance. Defining, ensuring, and monitoring quality should be a participatory and democratic process that engages staff, parents, and children.

6. Appropriate training and working conditions for staff in all forms of provision. Quality ECEC depends on strong staff training and fair working conditions across the sector.

7. Systematic attention to monitoring and data collection requires coherent procedures to collect and analyze data on the status of young children, ECEC provision, and the early childhood workforce.

The children of the world had a voice at the UN Special Session on Children in 2002.

8. A stable framework and long-term agenda for research and evaluation. (Childcare Resource and Research Unit, 2001)

According to Luxton (2001: 334), "In 1995 at the United Nations fourth International NGO conference on women at Beijing, China, Canadian delegates were among the 30,000 women from over 185 countries at the NGO Forum who identified neo-liberal policies as detrimental to most women around the world. Instead, they called for a new political orientation that took account of the needs of the majority of the world's people. In the years since then, Canadian feminist and labour groups have identified a range of policies that would help families secure their standards of living and improve the conditions of women's unpaid domestic labour."

EXHIBIT 11.1 UN SPECIAL SESSION ON CHILDREN

A WORLD FIT FOR US

We are the world's children.
We are the victims of exploitation and abuse.
We are street children.
We are the children of war.
We are the victims and orphans of HIV/AIDS.
We are denied good-quality education and health care.
We are victims of political, economic, cultural, religious, and environmental discrimination.
We are children whose voices are not being heard: it is time we are taken into account.
We want a world fit for children, because a world fit for us is a world fit for everyone.

Children made history on May 8, 2002, when two child delegates from the Children's Forum addressed the opening session of the United Nations General Assembly Special Session on Children in New York. It was the first time ever that children formally addressed the General Assembly on behalf of children. The Special Session, which continued through May 10, was itself a landmark, the first such session devoted exclusively to children and the first to include them as official delegates. Four priority themes of the outcome document were these:

- Promoting Healthy Lives
- Providing Quality Education for All
- Protecting Children Against Abuse, Exploitation, and Violence
- Combatting HIV/AIDS

Source: United Nations, 2002.

THE CONSULTATIVE GROUP ON EARLY CHILDHOOD CARE AND DEVELOPMENT

Contributed by Louise Zimanyi, Director of the Consultative Group on Early Childhood Care and Development, Ryerson Polytechnic University, School of Early Childhood Education

MISSION AND STRATEGIC OBJECTIVES

Established in 1983, the Consultive Group on Early Childhood Care and Development (CG) is an international consortium of donor and UN agencies and international NGOs, national and regional organizations and networks, and academic or educational institutions that advocate and support program and policy development for young children (0–8). The CG also encourages the participation of individuals who can make a significant contribution to the field of Early Childhood.

The CG's mission is to improve early childhood policy and practice, focusing on children in disadvantaged circumstances. We do this by promoting a wider dialogue among practitioners, policy-makers, researchers and national and international agencies, through the analysis, synthesis and dissemination of knowledge, and through coordinated advocacy.

The strategic objectives include:

- contributing to the development of a diverse global knowledge base on Early Childhood, and to making such a base accessible to, and used by a wide range of actors and stakeholders;
- facilitating a broad-based global understanding of the critical importance of Early Childhood to social development and poverty reduction, and advocate for improved investments, policies and actions to support the holistic development of young children; and
- strengthening national and regional capacities to generate and disseminate knowledge, share information and advocate for the support of children's overall development.

The CG draws on the work, knowledge, and expertise of its diverse partners and other Early Childhood actors to actively:

- identify gaps, critical issues and emerging areas of need and interest related to Early Childhood;
- enhance our awareness-raising, advocacy, and dissemination efforts; and

- broaden participation in the work of the CGECCD.

FOUR CORNERSTONES TO SECURE A STRONG FOUNDATION FOR YOUNG CHILDREN

CG partners believe that early childhood programs provide a strong foundation for good health, growth, and success in education and life, and that investing in young children saves money and pays off in the long run. The following four cornerstones have been adopted as a basis for the current advocacy strategy pursued collectively by the CG partners:

Cornerstone 1: Start at the Beginning

Integrate early stimulation, child development, and parenting information into prenatal, early health, nutrition, and education services by:

- providing access to parenting programs that address holistic child development, particularly for the most vulnerable families; and
- improving services for young children and families including early stimulation, health, nutrition and child care.

Cornerstone 2: Get Ready for Success

Ensure access to at least two years of quality early childhood programs prior to formal school entry, beginning with the most vulnerable and disadvantaged children.

Cornerstone 3: Improve Primary School Quality

Increase investments and improve the transition from home or preschool to primary school and the quality of learning in Grades 1–3 by:

- providing teachers with knowledge about early childhood, learning environments and styles, and methods for teaching early literacy and numeracy during pre/in-service teacher training;
- giving children adequate learning materials; and
- ensuring smaller sized classes.

Cornerstone 4: Include Early Childhood in Policies

Address early childhood in all national policies and plans across sectors, including Poverty Reduction Strategy Papers (PRSPs), Common Country

Assessments (CCAs), UN Development Assistance Framework (UNDAF), One UN Plan documents, Education for All Plans (EFA), and Fast Track Initiative Plans (FTI). Assure adequate resources and multi-sectoral coordination by ensuring that Early Childhood is integral to development and macroeconomic planning and budgeting.

CURRENT KEY PRIORITIES AND AREAS OF FOCUS

Recognizing its strengths as a global coalition to influence knowledge dissemination, networking and advocacy processes targeting decision-makers and development partners within the Majority and Minority World contexts, the CG is using an advocacy framework based on the four Cornerstones to move work forward globally and on a regional/ national level. The framework includes:

- raising public awareness, through publications and products, campaigning, etc;

- monitoring policy, including an international progress report and national profiles;

- identifying new champions and partnerships in health, education, business, and the media; and

- supporting capacity building through regional networks.

In addition, the CG's current key areas of work include a focus on:

- young children and emergencies;
- the impact of HIV/AIDS on young children;
- developing early childhood indicators;
- climate change and implications for programming;
- costing, financing of, and investment in early childhood; and
- early childhood leadership.

Ongoing Essential Activities

- Convening of Working Groups that focus on the key areas of work

- Publishing of the *Coordinators' Notebook* annually, and related materials

- Disseminating results of research on prioritized issues

- Attending and actively being involved in key fora and international meetings

- Supporting existing regional or sub-regional Early Childhood networks and other actors

- Identifying key people, particularly from Majority World countries and regions, who can provide technical advice on programming, evaluation, and research

- Organizing at least one international consultation meeting each year

- Ongoing development and expansion of the CGECCD website (**http://www.ecdgroup.com**)

- Providing regular email news-updates and circulating of Early Childhood materials and information

For further information, and a current list of partners, see the CG website at **http://www.ecdgroup .com**.

GLOBAL EDUCATION REPORT

At the World Education Forum held in Dakar in 2000, 164 countries adopted six Education For All goals. In recognition of a growing body of research that early interventions, especially for disadvantaged young children and their caregivers, significantly contribute to preparing young children for success in life and school, the first EFA goals called for expanding and improving comprehensive early childhood care and education, especially for the most vulnerable and disadvantaged children. The 2007 Education For All (EFA) Global Monitoring Report titled "Strong Foundations," focuses on EFA Goal No. 1, Early Childhood Care and Education. The reports highlights that Early Childhood programs are vital to offset social and economic disadvantage. ECCE is an instrument to guarantee children's rights that opens the way to all the EFA goals and contributes powerfully to reducing poverty, the overarching objective of the Millennium Development Goals (UNESCO, 2005).

REPORT FINDINGS

Although some progress has been made, the findings of this report indicate that global attention to Early Childhood Care and Education programs for children from 0–8 years of age and their parents and other caregivers, remains very limited:

- Millions of children still lack access to basic immunizations, clean water, adequate food and early stimulation that they need to survive and thrive.

- Few countries have systematic programs addressing the diverse health; nutrition, care and education needs of children from 0–3 years of age.

- Access to pre-school programs has expanded worldwide, but coverage remains very low in sub-Saharan Africa and the Arab States.

- Within countries there is a global pattern that children from poorer and rural households have less access to ECCE programs than those from richer and urban ones, yet is the poor, rural and disadvantaged children who would benefit the most from ECCE programs.

- Although ECCE programs require cross-sectoral collaboration, few countries have established national policy frameworks to coordinate such programs.

- For many governments, ECCE programs still have low priority in national budgets, including those for education.

- Most donor agencies are yet to recognize ECCE as a priority for investment.

The reports states that more attention and more investment must happen now! Increased high-level policy and political commitment to ECCE in all nations is necessary for achieving children's

---

INSIDE LOOK

Sure Start was launched in 1998 with the aim of improving the well being and health of young children and their parents through centres providing integrated services. In 2003 the Government announced its intention to set up a Sure Start Children's Centre in each of 20 percent most deprived wards in England. By 2010 the aim is to have 3,500 centres open. The Government directly funded Sure Start until 2006 when Local Authorities were given funding to set up centres to meet local needs. Whilst multi-agency integrated services continue to be required to deliver the core offer, Local Authorities have discretion about how and who will manage the Children's Centres and how commissioning arrangements will work. Local Authorities throughout England are approaching their responsibilities in different ways, some taking service management in-house and others recommissioning all their current centres. Whilst the transfer of responsibility from Central to Local government is to be welcomed in terms of mainstreaming provision, there is some concern by those working in the field that as funding is not ring fenced and the number and reach of centres is expanded resources will be spread too thinly to be effective in improving life chances for the most disadvantaged young children. The other area of concern is that partnership boards involving the local community of parents and caregivers which has proved effective in ensuring local needs are identified and addressed is no longer a requirement. Of the 20 services Sure Start, was managing 4 have been taken in-house by one Local Authority whilst in another Authority the number of services Sure Start manage has increased from 4 to 9.

But what outcomes has Sure Start demonstrated to date?

In 2005 the National Evaluation of Sure Start flagged up a number of negative impacts including failure to reach those whose need is greatest. However in March 2008 the latest report on three-year-olds and their families has shown several positive outcomes such as children displaying more independence and positive behaviour and parents offering a better home learning environment. The report commented that it takes staff about three years to get up and running so children are likely to be exposed to more effective services now than in the early years of Sure Start. A strong indicator of successful Sure Start services is leadership. A National Programme of Integrated Children's Leadership (NPQICL) was introduced by the Government and has been well received by Managers in Sure Start Children's Centres.

Targets are set across health, social care and education. Primary Care Trusts need to commit to midwives and Health Visitors in every centre. There is recognition that it takes time to build up a first class workforce in Early Years and give the same value to early Years as we do to school years. Nevertheless there is an optimism from the Government, professionals, and local parents and caregivers that Sure Start Children's Centres are a positive step on the journey to narrowing the gap between children from affluent and non affluent areas. Action For Children is pressing the Government to ensure that more support is available for the hardest to reach children and families.

Source: Moira Luccocks, Executive Director, Children's Services

Baby Matters is a program with a team of professional authors offering their expertise in their field linking health, development, and education aimed at schools, teachers, parents, and students. It is based on educating parents, especially young parents on infant and child developmental stages and when and how to detect problems with source contacts and useful tips. Trials have been done in Dorset (South) England, and implemented in 11 schools in the North of England. This will support the government initiative of Every Child Matters. A website is in the final stages of development.

Source: Deidre Edwards, Chiropractor, Visiting Nurse

---

rights and Education For All. ECCE should be included in all national budgets, all sectoral plans for education, health, sanitation and social protection and in all Poverty Reduction Strategy Papers. Significantly increased public funding of ECCE at national, provincial, and local levels is essential especially targeting vulnerable, marginalized children and their parents and caregivers—including children living in poverty, rural areas, and ethnic minority groups or affected by HIV/AIDS, malaria or other diseases, malnutrition, disabilities, conflicts or domestic violence and finally stronger political and financial commitment from international donors is urgently required for expanding ECCE (UNESCO, 2005).

There is much to learn from initiatives in other countries. It is also interesting to see how similar our focus can be as the following Inside Look demonstrates.

CANADIANS MAKING A DIFFERENCE ON THE WORLD FRONT

"If you don't like the way the world is, you change it. You have an obligation to change it. You just do it one step at a time."

—Marion Wright Edelman

It is an impossible task within one textbook to list all of the incredible organizations and individuals in Canada that are making a difference. However, some examples are highlighted below.

STEPHEN LEWIS FOUNDATION

"The Foundation will never cease its work at the grassroots in Africa until the AIDS pandemic is defeated"

—Stephen Lewis

Stephen Lewis is a Canadian politician and diplomat. He is presently the Social Science Scholar in Residence at McMaster University. In his previous position Mr. Lewis served as Deputy Executive Director of the United Nations Children's Fund (UNICEF) from 1995–1999 and was the UN Secretary-General's Special Envoy for HIV/AIDS in Africa. His work in Africa has had a profound impact and the Stephen Lewis Foundation, established in 2003, is one of the outcomes. As outlined on the organization's website (**http://www.stephenlewisfoundation.org/**):

> The AIDS pandemic is ravaging the continent of Africa. The numbers of those afflicted and estimates of the spread of the disease are horrendous—almost beyond comprehension. There is no vaccine; there is only limited treatment. More than two million people die each year. The effects on every aspect of sub-Saharan life are shattering. Much good work is being done to try to tackle the long-term structural and political issues. But women and children continue to suffer and die. We believe grassroots efforts can help many who currently have no hope. We know we can't reach vast numbers of people on their own. But we can and do commit ourselves to helping those grassroots groups who try so hard, with so little, to ease the anguish of the dying mothers and to create a hopeful future for the children they leave behind. (Stephen Lewis Foundation, n.d.)

The Foundation raised more than $10 million in its first three years and funds over 100 grassroots projects in 14 sub-Saharan African countries. Ninety percent of donations go directly to support communities in Africa.

Funds are provided in four areas to

- ease the plight of women who are ill and struggling to survive so that their lives can be free from pain and indignity;

School-age children in Havana, Cuba.

INSIDE LOOK

Cuba

In the early years, Cuban children and families are supported by an inter-professional team of health care professionals, Early Childhood Educators, and Primary teachers in their local communities. Comprehensive health and educational programs are provided from the point of conception through the primary school years. Health care professionals provide prenatal/antenatal care and immunization through the "National Maternal-Child Program." Families receive an average of 12 prenatal home visits. Preschool programs for working parents are provided through the national "Infantile Circulos Program" (Infant Circles) for 2–5-year-olds. Teachers conduct home visits and developmental assessments prior to the child's enrolment in the program.

The "Educa a Tu Hijo Program (Growing Up With Your Child) for 0–6-year-olds is a community based, family-centred early childhood development service provided to families within their local community. The primary schools also provide many services to the whole family such as recreation, art, literacy, library, and computer programs which run after school and on weekends. Some schools offer "Grandparent Programs" which are run by local grandparents. These life skills programs offer training in such skills as weaving, sewing, etc. In addition, primary schools offer the "OPJM Program" (Organization of Pioneers of Jose Marti) which is a cultural program that promotes understanding of the natural environment and Cuban culture through field trips to the countryside. The benefits of these programs are clearly evident given that Cuba has the highest literacy rates in the Caribbean.

Source: Contributed by Maxine Brown, faculty

Stephen Lewis Foundation and the Umoyo Training Centre for Girls, Zambia

The Umoyo School for Girls is the best example of girl's empowerment I've seen in many a year in Africa. It has about 50 girls, ranging in age from 14–18, all of them orphans, all of them democratically chosen by their communities. They come together in this residential setting for a year, and emerge from the desperate trauma of death and loss, fully self-confident, brimming with excitement about education and life, open and informed about the danger of HIV/AIDS and ready to tackle the world. They greeted my delegation with exultant singing (heavenly voices), and answered questions on everything from family history to future job prospects to their views on adolescent sexuality. It was exhilarating, beginning to end. The additional funds will help Umoyo increase the numbers of students; I cannot imagine a better gift.

For additional details, visit the Stephen Lewis Foundation at **http://www.stephenlewisfoundation .org/what_project.cfm?project=772**.

Source: Stephen Lewis Foundation, n.d.

- assist orphans and other AIDS affected children in every possible way, from the payment of school fees to the provision of food;

- support grandmothers, the unsung heroes of Africa, who bury their own children and then care for their orphan grandchildren; and

- assist the remarkable efforts of groups of people living with HIV/AIDS, courageous men and women who have openly declared their status.

"All of the projects we fund inspire us with their resourcefulness and dedication. We visit each initiative and remain in close contact with project staff and volunteers so that their needs can be responded to immediately" (Stephen Lewis Foundation, n.d.). In 2002, Stephen Lewis was made a Companion Of The Order of Canada. His book, *Race Against Time*, (Anansi Press) should be required reading for all students no matter what their discipline!

FREE THE CHILDREN

In 1995 Craig Kielburger, along with six other school friends, all 12 years of age, began their fight against child labour. Now "Free The Children is the world's largest network of children helping children through education, with more than one million youth involved in innovative education and development programs in 45 countries . . . . The organization has received the World's

Children's Prize for the Rights of the Child (also known as the Children's Nobel Prize), the Human Rights Award from the World Association of Non-Governmental Organizations, and has formed successful partnerships with leading school boards and Oprah's Angel Network" (Free The Children, 2008).

According to the Free The Children website (**http://www.freethechildren.com**):

[t]he primary goals of the organization are to free children from poverty and exploitation and free young people from the notion that they are powerless to affect positive change in the world. Through domestic empowerment programs and leadership training, Free The Children inspires young people to develop as socially conscious global citizens and become agents of change for their peers around the world. Free The Children has built more than 500 schools around the world and has reached more than one million young people through outreach in North America. (Free The Children, 2008)

WAR CHILD

According to Kenna (2003: A22),

Canadians carry the distinctive red maple leaf all over the world and don't shy away from the worst conflict zones. Thousands are working with aid agencies: through the federal government as election monitors and administrators in post-war zones; with churches as human shields and human-rights observers; and as flag-bearers for humanitarian groups negotiating for the safety of threatened families. . . . Many Canadians make a personal commitment to work in war-torn countries and risk their lives for peace, says Dr. Samantha Nutt, 33, co-founder and executive director of War Child Canada, a Toronto-based charity that helps war-shocked children with food, medical help, therapy, education and other aid. "On a per capita basis, Canadians are almost over-represented in this line of work," suggests Nutt, who has won numerous awards for her work in such war zones as Somalia, Sierra Leone, Burundi and Iraq. "We pride ourselves on our peacekeeping and humanitarian focus. We're used to being peace brokers . . . sitting beside the largest military power in the world. We're a small power—we do it for the right reason, not because we have the might to do it." A doctor at Sunnybrook and Women's Health Science Centre at the University of Toronto, Nutt recently returned from a three-week trip to Afghanistan, helping high-risk children and single mothers. Nutt's husband, Dr. Eric Hoskins, is president of War Child Canada and is currently in Iraq to deliver equipment, medical supplies and expertise to doctors at the children's hospital in Karbala **www.warchild.ca**.

SOS VILLAGES

The charity organization SOS Children's Villages

> was founded in 1949 by a young Austrian medical student, Hermann Gmeiner, who witnessed the suffering of so many orphaned and abandoned children after WWII and felt that something had to be done to help them. Out of his unswerving conviction the SOS Children's Village idea was born.
>
> "What orphaned and abandoned children need first and foremost is a family—a family in which they can develop normally."
>
> SOS Children's Villages has since grown to become an organization whose child-care concepts and educational principles are recognized throughout the world. In 1999, they were a finalist for the Nobel Peace Prize and in 2002, they won the prestigious Conrad N. Hilton Humanitarian Prize. (SOS Children's Villages, n.d.)

The organization's main objective is to help families so that they do not have to abandon their children, and to help those children who have been abandoned. As a result, they describe they summarize their efforts as as follows:

> SOS Children's Villages is currently raising over 60,000 orphaned and abandoned children in more than 450 SOS Children's Villages in over 125 countries. These SOS Villages provide children with a home, an SOS mother, and a sense of belonging. . . . In addition, SOS Children's Villages provides education, training, and medical care for children in SOS Villages and in the surrounding regions. We operate more than 225 Kindergartens which benefit over 23,000 young children in their villages and from the surrounding communities. We run over 175 schools to help both the children in their care and in their broader community. These schools provide education for over 100,000 children worldwide. We have developed over 350 youth facilities to help prepare the SOS Children for independent life beyond the SOS Village. We run over 60 vocational training centres which provide advanced training to help older children and young adults prepare for their adjustment to independent living. Currently there are over 10,000 participants from their SOS Villages and surrounding communities enrolled in our vocational training programs. We operate social and medical centres for the children in their care and the surrounding communities. There are over 700,000 beneficiaries of these services every year. (SOS Children's Villages, n.d.)

SOS Children's Villages Canada recognized that there were many children here in Canada who require long-term stability in a nurturing family environment and designed a program specifically to serve them. Canada's first SOS Children's Village opened in Margaretville, Nova Scotia in 1983. For close to 20 years, it raised children in urgent need. In 2002 the Village was forced to close its doors when the provincial government cancelled its funding. On Canada's west coast, SOS Children's Village BC opened its doors in 2001 to children at risk in Surrey, BC.

In 2004, SOS Children's Villages Canada celebrated 35 years and in that time SOS Children's Villages Canada has grown and evolved into a national office, with staff who are responsible for supporting the international work of SOS Children's Villages. You can read more about their work and programs at **http://www.soschildrensvillages.ca**.

SAVE THE CHILDREN CANADA

As a branch of the international Save the Children organization, Save the Children Canada

> has been working for over 87 years both in Canada and overseas to bring immediate and lasting improvements to children's lives through

the realization of their rights. Save the Children Canada is a non-political, non-religious organization committed to long-term development at the grassroots level through partnerships with local communities, government bodies and international organizations.

Save the Children Canada is a member of the International Save the Children Alliance. With 28 members and operational programs in over 120 countries, the Alliance is the world's largest global movement for children. (Save the Children Canada, n.d.)

Save the Children is active in a number of different areas. Their website—**www.savethechildren.ca**—lists the organization's main goal, which are to

- develop projects, which bring about long-term sustainable improvements and development to benefit children;

- deliver immediate relief and assistance to families affected by emergency situations, such as conflict and natural disaster;

- speak out for and on behalf of children—to make others take action and to bring about significant change to the lives of children around the world; and

- include children in the development of our programs. Save the Children firmly believes that children and young people must be active participants in the design and implementation of programs and policies that impact on their lives, as they are best placed to tell the world about their needs." (Save the Children Canada, n.d.)

P.A.C.E. CANADA: PROJECT FOR ADVANCEMENT OF CHILDHOOD EDUCATION

P.A.C.E. (Canada) was founded in 1987 by Dr. Mavis Burke. Dr. Burke has served as Education Officer and Race Relations Advisor, Ontario Ministry of Education; was president of the Ontario Advisory Council on Multiculturalism and Citizenship; chaired the Social Assistance Review Board; was a member of the Immigration and Refugee Board; and advised the Ontario government on issues of human rights and equity, among other achievements. In 1999, Dr. Burke received the Order of Ontario in recognition of her many contributions.

Women for P.A.C.E. was initially focused on assisting community-based preschools in Jamaica but its work has since expanded to include the well-being of children in Canada and the wider community of nations. P.A.C.E. promotes early childhood education with a special focus on children of preschool age in situations of racial, cultural, or economic disadvantage. P.A.C.E. is currently funded entirely by membership fees and donations from members, friends, and corporations, as well as two major fundraising events each year: the Adopt-A-School Program and the Strawberry Social and Auction.

The Adopt-A-School program provides assistance to Jamaican Basic Schools (ages three to five) in areas of need identified by local community committees. For $1, sponsors can adopt a school by selecting the parish or location of their choice or by consulting with P.A.C.E. to identify one that is most needy. One of its mandates is to provide culturally appropriate toys, books, and educational materials to children in Jamaica and Canada. Consequently, each December, P.A.C.E. conducts a toy drive.

A bursary awarded by P.A.C.E.—the David Appelt Bursary—is available to a second-year ECE student studying at a Canadian college and a similar P.A.C.E. scholarship is available for a Jamaican ECE student. The organization's Helen Sissons Canadian Children's Story Award is also presented to a Canadian writer of stories for young children that reflect the diversity of the Canadian population. The late Helen Sissons, educator, conciliator, and P.A.C.E. member, was committed to human rights and equity and to enhancing the quality of life for youth and for new Canadians. One of P.A.C.E.'s exciting initiatives is the Mobile Computer Bus—Tech de Bus, which serves the parish of St. Ann, Jamaica. The bus, which contains 10 personal computers, goes from school to school in the parish to teach four- to six-year-olds computer skills. For more information consult P.A.C.E.'s website at **www.pacecanada.org**.

TEACHERS WITHOUT BORDERS

Teachers Without Borders is a non-denominational, nonprofit, international NGO designed to close the education divide—that is, the difficulties experienced in providing education in developing countries—through teacher professional development and community education. Its inspiration has

Opportunities in international early childhood environments are life-altering experiences.

always come from UNESCO's research and objectives. It works primarily, but not exclusively, in developing countries, in order to build self-reliance, health, and capacity of education. The organization is made up of teachers and volunteers supported by those who believe in education as a passport to an optimistic future. Currently, they work in 84 countries. Teachers are the largest single group of trained professionals in the world and the key to our children's future. For more information, visit the web-

site at **www.teacherswithoutborders .org**.

EARLY CHILDHOOD GRADUATES: WAYS THAT YOU CAN MAKE A DIFFERENCE

"You must be the change you most wish to see in the world."

—Ghandi

TEACHER SHORTAGE
The growing worldwide teacher shortage creates a serious challenge to ensuring access to quality public education for all, leaders of Education

International told delegates at EI's World Congress meeting in Berlin July 22–26, 2007. Speaking before more than 2,000 representatives of teacher and education sector organizations, EI general secretary Fred van Leeuwen said that 18 million more educators—5 million in the industrial economies and 13 million in low-income countries—are needed to reach the goal of universal primary education by 2015, one of eight millennium development goals set by world leaders at a United Nations summit in 2000. "A teacher shortage on this scale could not only become the most serious challenge our profession has ever faced. It could also pose a serious threat to the survival of our public school systems worldwide." There is widespread concern about teacher quality, as well as pay and working conditions for education workers (Van Leeuwen, 2007).

ARE YOU A GOOD CANDIDATE FOR WORKING ABROAD?
The world needs early childhood educators but would you be a good candidate for work in the international community? Kealy et al. (2001)

On a scale of 1–5 indicate how prepared you think you are at this time to demonstrate the competencies found on the next page. Put an 'x' in the box that best describes your skills and abilities, where:

1 = a strength   5 = not well developed

	1	2	3	4	5
Getting Around Skills:					
Ability to use unfamiliar transportation and communications systems					
Awareness of travel documents required, local policies, and laws					
Awareness of security issues and potential strategies to travel safely					
Knowing where countries fit:					
Knowledge of your own background: country (countries) history, politics, and culture(s)					
Awareness of the impact of events, culture, politics, and geography upon history					
Awareness of global issues and current events					
Awareness of how events and cultures in one country impact on other countries					
Knowledge of the socio-economic, political, and cultural aspects of specific countries					
Communication Skills:					
Ability to develop relationships with people from backgrounds different than your own by respectfully and actively clarifying that your own behaviour is congruent with the norm of cultures other than your own					
Ability to actively and respectfully listen (e.g., suspend own assumptions)					
Ability to use body language that is understood by people from backgrounds other than your own (e.g., attentive to verbal and non verbal cues)					
Ability to use the appropriate level of formality in situations different than ones your are used to					
Ability to demonstrate culturally appropriate caring and relationship-building behaviour					
Intercultural Skills					
Curiosity about differences in people and between people					
Ability to identify the differences in people versus cultural differences					
Ability to identify similarities and differences within and between world cultures					
Ability to establish a rapport matched to styles of a context different than your own					
Ability to identify and understand religious issues and how they impact social, cultural, and political realities					

Ability to maintain personal autonomy while showing respect for others				
Ability to suspend personal assumptions and understand the assumptions under which other people operate				
Problem Solving/Decision Making Skills				
Ability to obtain information about another culture/country/ environment through the use of various mediums including the internet etc.				
Positive attitude toward learning new things, toward change				
Ability to suspend personal assumptions (tolerate ambiguity) and assess information about environments other than your own				
Understanding of the assumptions under which other people operate				
Exercising of good judgment related to the most appropriate course of action that balances your values with values different than your own				
Personal strategy for understanding of and participation in local, national, and international issues				
Ability to negotiate agreement with in a win–win way especially with people from backgrounds different than your own				
Acquisition of new ways to solve problems as a result of learning about other cultures				
Professional Competence				
Subject area of knowledge, skills, and background is demonstrated with skill				
Ability to work in teams especially with people from cultures other than your own				
Ability to plan strategically, especially in situations different that your own				
Changes in the way you practice your profession as a result of learning about its practice in socio-economic, political, and cultural settings different than your own				

researched the personal characteristics shared by those most effective in the transfer of skills in an international setting in their book, *A Profile of the Interculturally Effective Person*. The following is an adaptation of a questionnaire used for ECE students travelling abroad at George Brown College. Which competencies to you think you exhibit and which ones require more work?

ORGANIZATIONS FOR VOLUNTEERING

There are many organizations that would provide positive international experiences working with children for ECE graduates. It is impossible to include all agencies but a few are listed below.

Canadian International Development Agency

International Youth Internship Program

As outlined on the Canadian International Development Agency (CIDA) website at **http:// www.acdi-cida.gc.ca/cidaweb/acdicida.nsf/En/ Home,**

[t]he International Youth Internship Program (IYIP) is an employment program for young

Canadians between the ages of 19–30. If you're a post-secondary graduate, you could be eligible for this chance of a lifetime to work in a developing country and contribute to Canada's international development goals. Not only will this experience contribute to your personal and professional growth, your sponsor organization will lend a helping hand in your search for employment once your internship ends. (CIDA, 2008)

Canada World Youth

"Canada World Youth [**http://www.cwy-jcm.org**] designs and delivers international educational programs for youth (aged 17–24) with a focus on volunteer work and community development in a cross-cultural setting. . . . Since 1971, more than 27,000 youth have participated in Canada World Youth programs. As a team, youth live and work in communities in Canada and overseas, learning about local and international development and gaining essential job skills for the future. . . . Working in partnership with local organizations, the majority of Canada World Youth programs have a phase in Canada and a phase in one of close to 30 countries in Africa, Asia, Latin America, the Caribbean, and Central and Eastern Europe. . . . Canada World Youth is about learning by doing. Its non-formal educational model involves core elements such as the team approach, the counterpart relationship, host families and communities, and partner organizations. Canada World Youth was founded by retired senator Jacques Hébert with the mission of increasing young people's ability to participate actively in the development of just, harmonious and sustainable societies." (Canada World Youth, n.d.)

EXHIBIT 11.2 STUDENTS SPEAK!

Jessica Flynn, Russell Everett and Erin Corcoran are three of 112 students from the School of Early Childhood at George Brown College who have completed a field placement in Jamaica over the past seven years as part of the college's focus on international opportunities for students. Their comments demonstrate the tremendous impact an international field experience can have on an ECE student.

JESSICA FLYNN

"As I sit here preparing for my final—yes we have final evaluations here too—I have already given this experience an A+. I came to this beautiful island wanting to work with children and teachers and to make a difference in their lives. Now, I realize that making a difference is only half of the experience. I feel that the children and teachers have changed me. The small classroom that I am in has few resources with 32 children and led by one teacher. Even with all of these obstacles to overcome, the teacher and children have caring, respectful relationships. I have learned that a relationship like this plays the largest part of a child learning in any classroom. I know that the only way that I could really know these beautiful Jamaican children was to build that relationship with them because it is the foundation for learning. Although I will miss everything and everyone here, I know that for the rest of my life and with every child I teach in the future, Jamaica will be right here in my heart."

RUSSELL EVERETT

"The most inspiring thing about our learning experience in Jamaica was that I realized there are people all over the world striving to better the lives of children because it brings them an ultimate sense of joy knowing they've changed the world just by bettering the life of one child."

ERIN CORCORAN

"Being in Jamaica has made me realize that one of the best ways to learn and understand yourself better is by being open to learning and understanding others. There really has been an exchange of cultural 'gold' that has enriched my life."

Strong relationships are built between ECE students and the children with whom they are working!

Canadian Bureau for International Education

"The Canadian Bureau for International Education (CBIE) [**http://www.cbie.ca/index_e .htm**] is a national, bilingual, not-for-profit, membership organization dedicated to the promotion of Canada's international relations through international education: the free movement of ideas and learners across national boundaries. CBIE's activities comprise scholarship management, civil society and public sector reform, research and information services, advocacy, training programs, professional development for international educators and other services for members and learners. CBIE promotes the special interests of the international learner, both the foreign national studying in Canada and the Canadian studying abroad, through educational exchanges, scholarships, training awards and internships, technical assistance in education and other related services. CBIE believes that international education is one of the best ways to create understanding among peoples and to develop enduring political, cultural and economic links among nations" (CBIE, 2007).

For specific information about how to volunteer with this organization, consult the information at **http://www.destineducation.ca/cdnstdnt/witwigo_ e.htm**. Students may also want to consider volunteer experiences closer to home.

Volunteer Canada

"Volunteer Canada [**http://volunteer.ca/en/about/ aboutVolCan**] is the national voice for volunteerism in Canada. Since 1977, Volunteer Canada has been committed to supporting volunteerism and civic participation through ongoing programs and special projects. National in scope, Volunteer Canada's board members, partners, and members represent hundreds of different communities across Canada. Membership includes over 86 volunteer centres established throughout the country in all provinces and the Yukon Territory. Managers and directors of volunteers represent a vital aspect of volunteerism in Canada and make up an important aspect of the organization's community. By developing resources and national initiatives, they actively engage in research, training, and other national initiatives designed to increase

EXHIBIT 11.3 A GRADUATE SPEAKS!

I never anticipated how much teaching and living abroad would enrich my life, both professionally and personally. Imagine culture, language, tradition, travel, and education all in one! Mexico has given me just that, not to mention three years of irreplaceable teaching experience. My preschoolers teach me something new about their beautiful country every day, and they have inspired me to continue with this work throughout my life. Ordinary people accomplish the extraordinary every day—from three-year-olds learning in an English Immersion environment to the teachers who lead them. There are children in every corner of this planet who need people to care for, teach, and cherish them. You can never imagine how much working abroad gives back to you. Get out there. Live. Laugh. Love. Learn.

Source: Marcia Hill, ECE graduate

community participation across the country. Volunteer Canada provides leadership on issues and trends in the Canadian volunteer movement (Volunteer Canada, n.d.).

THE FINAL WORD

INTERNATIONAL INSTITUTE FOR PEACE THROUGH TOURISM

"Credo of the Peaceful Traveler"

"Grateful for the opportunity to travel and to experience the world and because peace begins with the individual, I affirm my personal responsibility and commitment to:

- journey with an open mind and gentle heart;
- accept with grace and gratitude the diversity I encounter;
- revere and protect the natural environment which sustains all life;
- appreciate all cultures I discover;
- respect and thank my hosts for their welcome;
- offer my hand in friendship to everyone I meet;
- support travel services that share these views and act upon them; and
- by my spirit, words, and actions encourage others to travel the world in peace." (International Institute for Peace Through Tourism, 2003)

"There are no boundaries in the real Plant Earth. No United States, no Soviet Union, no China, no Taiwan, East Germany or West. Rivers flow unimpeded across the swaths of continents. The Persistent Tides—the pulse of the sea—do not discriminate, they push against all the varied shores on Earth.

—Jacques-Yves Cousteau, Oceanographer and Explorer

REFERENCES

Amnesty International. 2006. "The Human Rights of Children: Overview." Available at http://www.amnesty .ca/themes/children_overview.php.

Canada World Youth. N.d. "About Us." Available at http://www.cwy-jcm.org/en/aboutus.

Canadian Bureau for International Education (CBIE). 2007. Available at http://www.cbie.ca/index_e.htm.

Canadian International Development Organization (CIDO). 2008. "International Youth Internship Program— Interns." Available at http://www.acdi-cida.gc.ca/CIDAWEB/ acdicida.nsf/En/JUD-121483217-HVQ.

Childcare Resource and Research Unit. 2001. "OECD Thematic Review of Early Childhood Education and Care." Available at http://www.childcarecanada.org/res/ issues/StartingStrong2.htm.

Child Rights Information Network. 2008. Available at http://www.crin.org/FAQs/index.asp.

Corcoran, K. 2008. "A Revolution of the Hungry." *Toronto Sun*. March 25. 12.

Costanza, K. 2007. "Worst Countries." *Child View: The Magazine For Child Sponsors*. Fall: 21.

Engle, P.L., M. Black, J.R. Behrman, M. Cabral de Mello, P.J. Gertler, L. Kapiriri, R. Martorell, and M. Eming Young. 2007. "Strategies to Avoid the Loss of Developmental Potential in More Than 200 Million Children in the Developing World." *The Lancet* 369 (January 6): 239.

Free The Children. 2008. "About Us." Available at http://www.freethechildren.com/aboutus/index.php.

Gates, M. 2007. "The Other Side of the Mat: Uniting for Maternal, Newborn and Child Survival and Health." *The State of the World's Children, 2008: Child Survival*. New York: UNICEF, 2007. Available at http://www.unicef .org/sowc08/docs/sowc08_panel_5_2.pdf.

Grantham-McGregor, S., Y. Bun Cheung, S. Cueto, P. Glewwe, L. Richter, and B. Strupp. 2007. "Developmental Potential in the First Five Years for Children in Developing Countries." *The Lancet* 369 (January 6): 67.

Hildebrand, V., L. Aotaki Phenice, M. McPhail Gray, and R. Pena Hines. 2008. *Knowing and Serving Diverse Families*, 3rd ed. Columbus, OH: Pearson Merrill Prentice Hall.

International Institute for Peace through Tourism. 2003. "Credo of the Peaceful Traveler." Available at http://www.iipt.org/credo.html.

Kealy, D., T. Vulpe, D. Protheroe, and D. MacDonald. 2001. *A Profile of the Interculturally Effective Person*. Ottawa: Centre for Intercultural Learning, Canadian Foreign Service Institute/Department of Foreign Affairs and International Trade.

Kenna, K. 2003. "Canadians Taking Peace to the World." *The Toronto Star*. August 2. A22.

Luxton, M. 2001. "Feminism as a Class Act: Working-Class Feminism and the Women's Movement in Canada." *Labour/Le Travail* 48. Available at http://www.history cooperative.org/journals/llt/48/03luxton.html.

Reid, R. 1994. Keynote Address for the World Conference on Human Rights, 1994, Vienna, Austria.

Save the Children. 2005. "Responses to Young Children in Post-Emergency Situations." In *Early Childhood Matters #104*. Bernard Van Leer Foundation.

———. N.d. "What We Do." Available at http://www.savethechildren.ca/canada/what_we_do/index.html.

SOS Children's Villages. 2008. "SOS Children's Villages Canada: Overview and History." Available at http://www.soschildrensvillages.ca/About-us/Pages/Overview-and-History.aspx.

Stephen Lewis Foundation. N.d. "About Us: Why." Available at http://www.stephenlewisfoundation.org/about_why.htm.

Toycen, D. 2007. "Millions of Young Lives in Jeopardy." *Child View: The Magazine For Child Sponsors*. Fall: 4.

UNESCO. N.d. Available at http://portal.unesco.org/en/ev.php-URL_ID=29008&URL_DO=DO_TOPIC&URL_SECTION=201.html.

UNICEF. 2007. *The State of the World's Children, 2008: Child Survival*. New York: United Nations. Available at http://www.unicef.org/sowc08/report/report.php.

United Nations. 2002. "A World Fit For Us." *United Nations: Special Session on Children*. Available at http://www.unicef.org/specialsession/documentation/childrens-statement.htm.

———. 2008. "End Poverty 2015: Millenium Goals." Available at http://www.un.org/millenniumgoals.

United Nations, Division for the Advancement of Women. 2007. Available at http://www.un.org/womenwatch/daw/cedaw/states.htm.

Van Leeuwen, F. 2007. Keynote Address for the Education International 5th World Congress, Berlin, Germany. Available at http://www.ei-ie.org/worldcongress2007/ei-ie/index5e0c.html?Id=191&SkipRec=2.

Voice of America. 2008. "A Success Story for Malaria Control." February 12. Radio broadcast transcript. Available at http://www.voanews.com/specialenglish/archive/2008-02/2008-02-12-voa2.cfm?CFID=616652&CFTOKEN=81417324.

Volunteer Canada. N.d. Available at http://volunteer.ca/en/about/aboutVolCan.

War Child. N.d. Available at http://www.warchild.ca/.

World Vision. 2007. *Child View: The Magazine for Child Sponsors*. Fall: 5.

Courtesy of Lynn Wilson

Index